Building a Safer Society

Strategic Approaches to Crime Prevention

*Edited by
Michael Tonry and
David P. Farrington*

Crime and Justice
A Review of Research
Edited by Michael Tonry

VOLUME 19

The University of Chicago Press, Chicago and London

This volume was prepared under a grant awarded to the Castine Research Corporation by the Crime Prevention Unit of the Police Department of the English Home Office. Points of view or opinions expressed in this volume are those of the editors or authors and do not necessarily represent the official position or policies of the Police Research Group of the Home Office, Her Majesty's Stationery Office, or any other government department. "Evaluating Crime Prevention" by Paul Ekblom and Ken Pease and "Implementing Crime Prevention" by Gloria Laycock and Nick Tilley are Crown copyright and have been published with the permission of the Controller of Her Britannic Majesty's Stationery Office.

The University of Chicago Press, Chicago 60637
The University of Chicago Press, Ltd., London

© 1995 by The University of Chicago
All rights reserved. Published 1995
Printed in the United States of America

ISSN: 0192-3234

ISBN: 0-226-80824-6 (cloth)
99 98 97 96 95   5 4 3 2 1

ISBN: 0-226-80825-4 (paper)
99 98 97 96 95   5 4 3 2 1

LCN: 80-642217

Library of Congress Cataloging-in-Publication Data

Building a safer society: strategic approaches to crime prevention / edited by Michael
   Tonry and David P. Farrington.
         p.   cm.—(Crime and justice, ISSN 0192-3234; v. 19)
   Includes bibliographical references and index.
      1. Crime prevention—United States.   I. Tonry, Michael H. II. Farrington,
   David P.   III. Series: Crime and justice (Chicago, Ill.); v. 19.
   HV6001.C672   vol. 19
   [HV9950]
   364 s—dc20
   [364.4'0973]   95-13321
                                                                          CIP

Contents

Preface

Building a Safer Society: Strategic Approaches to Crime Prevention, supported by the Crime Prevention Unit of the English Home Office, is the seventh thematic volume in the *Crime and Justice* series. Like others on such subjects as family violence or drugs and crime, it attempts to provide a comprehensive overview of the state of the art of research and knowledge concerning an important subject of contemporary policy relevance.

Crime bedevils Western societies, and criminal sanctions are increasingly understood to have only modest effects on crime rates or patterns. Criminal sanctions, especially incarceration, are expensive to administer and cause collateral damage to offenders and their spouses and children. Prison and jail sentences in many cases increase the likelihood that offenders will reoffend and further handicap typically disadvantaged offenders from later achieving satisfying law-abiding lives. For all these reasons, preventive approaches to crime, as distinguished from law enforcement or criminal justice approaches, are receiving new and renewed emphasis in many countries.

Crime prevention presents a double challenge to efforts to look at a subject whole. The first is the balkanization of knowledge that occurs when people working within scholarly disciplines specialize on one part of a complex problem. Too often people fail to look across the walls that divide disciplines, and important insights are as a result overlooked.

Although crime prevention research also suffers from disciplinary insularity, efforts at a comprehensive overview confront a separate challenge. Important developments are occurring in many countries, and scholars are little better at looking across national than disciplinary divides.

Crime prevention strategies, program development, and research have received more sustained attention in Western Europe than in North America and within North America have received greater emphasis in Canada than in the United States or Mexico. Governmentally funded crime prevention initiatives have been implemented far more extensively in England than in the United States, possibly because of the greater American emphasis in criminal justice policy on individual responsibility and punishment, and this is one reason why it is particularly appropriate that this volume is supported by the English Home Office.

The development of this volume followed a well-charted course. A final prospectus emerged after many drafts were circulated within a planning group consisting of Dean Ronald Clarke of Rutgers Graduate School of Criminal Justice, Professor Ken Pease of the University of Manchester, Dr. Gloria Laycock, then research director of the Home Office Crime Prevention Unit, and the editors. Essays were commissioned and their contours negotiated. Initial drafts were presented and discussed at a London conference in 1993 attended by the writers and by Trevor H. Bennett, Anthony E. Bottoms, Jon Bright, John Burrows, Janet Foster, John Graham, Barry Poyner, Albert J. Reiss, Jr., Jonathan P. Shepherd, Lawrence W. Sherman, and Helene Raskin White. Written critiques of initial drafts were also solicited from anonymous referees. Fortified by all those reactions, and additional suggestions from the editors, the writers prepared final versions of their essays.

This volume is the product of that work. Readers will decide for themselves whether the effort was worthwhile. We are grateful to the dozen anonymous referees who prepared written comments on papers, to the participants in the London conference, and to the writers who with open eyes entered into and in good spirit endured so lengthy and arduous a process. We owe special and heartfelt thanks to Kate Hamilton, associate editor of *Crime and Justice*, who coordinated every phase of production of the volume.

Finally, we are grateful to Kevin Heal, then head of the Crime Prevention Unit, and Gloria Laycock for their willingness to support an unprecedented venture organized and largely carried out in another country. We are especially grateful to Gloria Laycock, now head of the Home Office Police Research Group, for her unfailing support of the overall venture and for her remarkable acceptance as a writer of the burdens, time demands, and indignities that are the lot of those who write for *Crime and Justice*.

Michael Tonry
David P. Farrington

Michael Tonry and David P. Farrington

Strategic Approaches to Crime Prevention

No one wants themselves or their loved ones to be victimized by crime or to live in fear. Most theories of the state make public safety a core responsibility of government. The problem facing modern governments, however, is that the principal tools used to advance public safety—enactment and enforcement of criminal laws and punishment of offenders—are increasingly understood to have modest effects on rates or patterns of serious crime. As a result, a number of Western governments, including those in France, England, Sweden, and the Netherlands, have established specialized agencies to develop, test, and evaluate crime preventive initiatives using other than law enforcement tools.

North American countries lag behind, but there are signs of similar policy movements. In 1993, the Standing Committee on Justice and the Solicitor General of the Canadian government issued a report urging establishment of a national crime prevention agency and a shift in primary policy emphasis from law enforcement to crime prevention (Standing Committee on Justice and Solicitor General 1993). In 1994, the American Congress enacted the Violent Crime Control and Law Enforcement Act, a $30 billion package of anticrime legislation which for the first time since the 1970s included a major prevention component (representing roughly a third of the contemplated funds).

Building a Safer Society is an effort to transcend national and disciplinary boundaries to summarize what is now known about a variety of different strategic approaches to crime prevention. We have identified

This volume was prepared under a grant awarded to the Castine Research Corporation by the Home Office Police Research Group, London. Points of view or opinions expressed in this volume are those of the editors or authors and do not necessarily represent the official position of the Home Office Police Research Group.

1

four major prevention strategies: law enforcement, and developmental, community, and situational prevention. The first of these is discussed only in this introduction and principally to explain why we do not give it greater emphasis. In addition, an essay by Mark Moore compares and contrasts the public health approach to prevention with the law enforcement approach. We do not consider the public health approach as a distinctive prevention strategy because developmental, situational, and community strategies all include elements of the public health approach.

Some explanation of the selection of those three strategies is probably warranted. Organizing this volume provided an opportunity to reconsider the schema for crime prevention that are commonly used. In terms of government, until very recently the primary initiatives launched in the name of crime prevention have consisted of changes in criminal laws, enforcement techniques, and sentencing policy; mass media advertising campaigns intended to convince offenders that crime doesn't pay or to persuade citizens to take private preventive actions; and various situational measures intended to make particular offenses more difficult to accomplish. These are all appropriate parts of a government's crime prevention effort, but they neglect many factors known to influence crime and delinquency which, if addressed, promise to have important preventive effects.

Thus our aim is to provide a preventive framework that encompasses a much fuller range of initiatives than governments typically pursue. One possibility that we considered but rejected is the public health typology of primary, secondary, and tertiary prevention (e.g., Last 1980). This has the advantage of comprehensiveness but the disadvantage of all specialized uses of words with commonly understood meanings—only specialists are likely to understand the distinctions being made. Although efforts have been made to import the public health vocabulary into criminology (e.g., Brantingham and Faust 1976; van Dijk and de Waard 1991), no widely shared understanding has emerged of what they might mean when applied to crime.

By developmental prevention, we mean interventions designed to prevent the development of criminal potential in individuals, especially those targeting risk and protective factors discovered in studies of human development. By community prevention, we mean interventions designed to change the social conditions that influence offending in residential communities. By situational prevention, we mean interventions designed to prevent the occurrence of crimes, especially by reducing opportunities and increasing risks. Essays in this volume by Richard Tremblay and Wendy Craig, Tim Hope, and Ronald Clarke provide exhaustive surveys of the state of knowledge about developmental, community, and situational prevention.

Our proposed classification system for crime prevention initiatives is by no means watertight. There is overlap at the borders of developmental and community prevention and again at the borders of community and situational prevention. Developmental and community prevention are often included under the general heading of "social" crime prevention, but we think that they are so different that they should be distinguished.

Notwithstanding overlaps and imprecision, the classification scheme used in this volume seems to us sound because it includes a much broader conceptualization of the ambit of crime prevention than is common and because it allows coverage in one book of research and program developments occurring in many disciplines and agencies of government that, if heeded, offer important guidance on how to build a safer society. In the sections that follow, we sketch findings from research on the effects and limits of law enforcement and criminal justice approaches; somewhat more fully introduce developmental, community, and situational prevention; and outline key questions for future research and key theoretical, measurement, implementation, and evaluation issues that need to be addressed.

I. Law Enforcement and Criminal Justice

Most people see crime prevention as the primary reason why criminal laws are enacted and why the criminal law is enforced. H. L. A. Hart (1968), this century's most influential writer in English on the philosophy of punishment, for example, took it as given that criminal laws exist and are enacted in order that fewer of the proscribed behaviors should take place and that general prevention is the primary justification for maintaining a system of criminal punishment.

Most lawyers and many elected officials have long believed that crime represents a moral failure on the part of the wrongdoer and that law enforcement, including the imposition of sanctions that express condemnation of the offender, is the only morally appropriate broad-based state policy for crime prevention. This is why, in the United States, policy makers including former attorneys general Edwin Meese, Richard Thornburgh, and William Barr called for increasingly harsher penalties and disparaged recommendations by others for preventive policies aimed at addressing the "root causes" of crime. This is also why, according to Jon Bright (1992), research director of the English private-sector crime prevention organization, Crime Concern, American officials have been largely unsympathetic to preventive approaches that have attained support in other countries; other preventive approaches obscure the recognition of offenders' moral culpability.

No reasonable or informed person can doubt that enactment and enforcement of criminal laws affect behavior directly and indirectly or that law enforcement must be a component of any country's effort to protect its citizens from crime. Similarly, no reasonable or informed person can doubt that some potential offenders are deterred by fear of sanctions or that some crimes are prevented by confining some offenders or otherwise controlling their movements or activities. Those things acknowledged, however, there is an emerging consensus among researchers and public officials in many countries that law enforcement's potential effects are limited and modest and that public safety policies that rely solely or primarily on law enforcement are incomplete and insufficiently protect the public.

Law enforcement or criminal justice prevention is conventionally seen as operating directly through deterrence, incapacitation, and rehabilitation and indirectly through effects on socialization. In addition, in a politically important if intellectually vacuous sense, crimes can be caused or prevented (in the sense of eliminated) by revisions of criminal codes. We discuss these phenomena in reverse order.

A. Indirect Effects of the Criminal Law

By itself, without regard to their implementation, the enactment of criminal laws is sometimes said to serve preventive purposes. Arguments about statutory policy are often premised on the assumption that behavior is affected by statutory changes. Opponents of drug use, homosexuality, and prostitution, for example, argue that decriminalizing those behaviors would widely be viewed as tacit (or express) acknowledgment of their legitimacy. Their fear is that decriminalization, by reducing the stigma associated with unwanted behaviors, would reduce social and psychological pressures against them and lead to increases in their incidence.

Changes in criminal laws can operate preventively in a number of indirect ways. Some people who might engage in activities if they were legal refrain from them because they are illegal. Probably more important, the existence and enactment of laws serve as part of the normative context within which individuals' personal values and beliefs take shape. Many people refrain from violent and property crimes because they have been socialized to believe that those actions are wrong; they are not "that kind of person."

Indirect preventive effects have long been recognized. The nineteenth century French sociologist Emile Durkheim wrote of the criminal law's dramaturgical role in socialization (Garland 1991). The Norwegian criminal lawyer Johannes Andenaes (1974) revived interest in the "moral-educative" effects of punishment as distinct from its deterrent effects. "Communicative" theories are at the heart of modern writing on the philosophy of punishment (Duff 1995). Precisely how, to what extent, in what ways, and concerning what kinds of behavior the enactment and administration of the criminal law has indirect preventive effects is a little-examined empirical question.

The criminal law no doubt has indirect effects on socialization. In what may be no more than an admission of ignorance, we know of no rigorous evaluations that attempt to document these indirect preventive effects of the criminal law. However, socialization occurs mostly through primary institutions like the family, the church, the school, and peer networks; the effects of laws and legal processes are likely to be modest.

B. Direct Effects of the Criminal Law

The implementation and enforcement of the criminal law are widely thought to serve preventive purposes. For many writers on the philosophy of punishment, including both utilitarians (Hart 1968; Morris 1974) and retributivists (von Hirsch 1976), "general prevention" or deterrence is offered as the primary purpose and justification for the maintenance of state-administered systems of criminal punishment.

Overall, few people doubt that having some penalties instead of none influences behavior or that some crimes are prevented by means of incapacitation or that some rehabilitation programs that offer regimes tailored to the particular needs and characteristics of particular categories of offenders can reduce offenders' later offending and enhance their later social functioning.

Usually discussions among lawyers and lawmakers concern the deterrent, incapacitative, and rehabilitative effects of formal sanctions imposed after a conviction, but preventive mechanisms are broader than that. Social scientists, for example, study and demonstrate preventive effects of preadjudication criminal processes. Many people have examined the deterrent effects of arrests (e.g., Sampson 1986). The largest set of linked research projects on a single subject in the United States in recent years were replications in six sites of Sherman and Berk's (1984) Minneapolis domestic violence experiment on the deterrent effects of a mandatory arrest policy (irrespective of subsequent case processing; dismissals were the normal follow-up) for alleged domestic violence misdemeanors. The title of Malcolm Feeley's book on the operation of misdemeanor courts in New Haven, Connecticut, *The Process Is the Punishment* (1979), similarly acknowledges the effects of preadjudication processes.

There is widespread agreement over time and space that alterations in sanctioning policies are unlikely substantially to influence crime rates. In the United States, this was the conclusion of the President's Commission on Law Enforcement and Administration of Justice (1967), the National Academy of Sciences Panel on Research on Deterrent and Incapacitative Effects (Blumstein, Cohen, and Nagin 1978), and the National Academy of Sciences Panel on the Understanding and Control of Violent Behavior (Reiss and Roth 1993). Although the statistical and methodological sophistication of efforts to examine the effectiveness of sanctions has increased over time, the conclusions have changed little. The most recent National Academy of Sciences Panel, for example, in a much quoted passage, asked, "What effect has increasing the prison population had on violent crime?" and answered, "Apparently very little . . . If tripling the average length of sentence of incarceration per crime [between 1975 and 1989] had a strong preventive effect, then violent crime rates should have declined" (Reiss and Roth 1993, p. 6). They had not.

In the interests of brevity, we do not carefully distinguish the separate preventive mechanisms of deterrence, incapacitation, and rehabilitation. We also do not discuss the evaluation literature concerning the deterrent effects of mandatory penalties; with no significant exception, these studies find no, modest, or transient crime-reductive effects. (These studies are examined in some detail in Tonry [1995], chap. 5.) Also, we do not discuss the preventive effects of policing strategies (see Tonry and Morris 1992).

The conclusion that the direct marginal crime-reductive effects of foreseeable changes in the criminal law or criminal justice processes are modest has been reached in most countries that have an empirical research tradition concerning criminological subjects. In England, for example, the Home Office white paper presaging the Criminal Justice

Act 1991 observed: "Deterrence is a principle with much immediate appeal . . . But much crime is committed on impulse . . . and it is committed by offenders who live from moment to moment . . . It is unrealistic to construct sentencing arrangements on the assumption that most offenders will weigh up the possibilities in advance and base their conduct on rational calculation" (Home Office 1990, para. 2.8). More concisely, but to similar effect, the Canadian Sentencing Commission (1987) concluded: "Deterrence cannot be used, with empirical justification, to guide the imposition of sentences." In Finland, Patrik Törnudd reports, government policy to reduce the prison population over two decades was premised on similar views: "Can our long prison sentences be defended on the basis of a cost/benefit assessment of their general preventive effect? The answer of the criminological expertise was no" (Törnudd 1993).

II. Developmental, Community, and Situational Prevention

The modest claims that can be made for the preventive effectiveness of sanctions are not grounds for despair. Different crimes have different causes, different offenders commit crimes for different reasons, and sensible prevention policies should take account of those differences. Many assaults and sexual crimes, for example, are impulsive and committed under the influence of intoxicants and powerful emotions. Robberies often involve planning, while shoplifting and vandalism are often spur-of-the-moment activities. Some offenses occur as anomalous acts in generally law-abiding lives, while others occur as routine events in generally antisocial lives. Effective crime prevention must be as varied and shaped to take account of important differences in crimes and criminals.

The diversity of crimes and criminals is one reason why law enforcement is a necessary but not sufficient strategy for crime prevention. Crimes of impulse, emotion, and intoxication and crimes by individuals socialized into deviance are not likely to be much affected by law enforcement threats and criminal justice processes. A comprehensive governmental crime prevention strategy, in addition to law enforcement, should include developmental, community, and situational approaches, and we now introduce these in a little more detail.

A. Situational Prevention

Dating as a self-conscious prevention strategy from the late 1970s, when it became a major policy focus in England's Home Office Research and Planning Unit, and from the later establishment of the Home Office Crime Prevention Unit in 1983, situational crime prevention has grown rapidly as a viable strategy for reducing the occurrence of crimes.

Based on the premise that much crime is contextual and opportunistic, situational initiatives typically alter the context to diminish the opportunities. Situational prevention is not conceptually new (what is?). People have presumably always responded to perceived risks by altering their behavior to reduce the risks. Doors get locked, windows shuttered, dogs purchased, and alarm systems installed in order to make the intending malefactor's work more difficult. Merchants likewise have presumably always contemplated the economic trade-offs between easier customer access to merchandise and heightened risks of theft and have reduced access when that seemed the economically rational thing to do. (In Joanna Shapland's essay, in this volume, they are described as "amoral calculators of profit and loss.")

What is different about situational crime prevention is the systematic strategic effort of the last decade to develop and test situational techniques and the increasingly widespread recognition that situational approaches can complement law enforcement approaches. Although debates have long continued about whether situational approaches prevent crimes or merely displace them to other times, places, and targets, a consensus seems to be taking shape that some situational methods are effective in some circumstances.

Numerous situational initiatives seem to have achieved net preventive effects, both directly and indirectly through "diffusion of benefits" to adjoining areas that did not experience the new initiative but were aware of it. Convincing evidence is available of net preventive effects even after displacement of various kinds is taken into account. Moreover, since Barr and Pease (1990) showed that displacement may be benign (the frustrated shoplifter playing basketball instead) or malign (the frustrated shoplifter committing an armed robbery instead), and that predictable displacement can also be thought of as redirection, analysis has moved far beyond discussion of whether displacement is partial or total. Ronald Clarke's essay in this volume concludes that concerns about displacement and worries about the "fortress society" have generally receded in recent years.

B. Community Prevention

Communities have crime rates, and sometimes these are independent of the changing composition over time of the resident population. Put the other way around, whether individuals commit crimes often is probabilistically related to where they live. This is the key insight on which community crime prevention is premised; changing the community may change the behavior of the people who live there.

In the first half of the twentieth century, Shaw and McKay's (1942) Chicago School of Criminology focused on ecological and community explanations for crime and promoted an emphasis on community organization as a crime prevention strategy. They initiated the Chicago Area Project on Chicago's South Side. Celebrated community organization initiatives followed elsewhere, including Mobilization for Youth in New York City and many others (see Tim Hope's essay, in this volume).

Over the past thirty years, considerable energy and money has been expended on prevention efforts to alter the physical and social organization of communities. Conventionally dating from the publication of Jane Jacobs's *The Life and Death of Great American Cities* (1961) and Oscar Newman's *Defensible Space* (1972), community crime prevention has included efforts to control crime by altering building and neighborhood design to increase natural surveillance and guardianship, by improving the physical appearance of areas, by organizing community residents to take preventive actions and to solicit additional political and material resources, and by organizing self-conscious community crime prevention strategies such as recreational programs for children. At their most modest, such efforts include Operation Identification and Neighborhood Watch programs. At their most strategically ambitious, they include some of the problem estate programs of the English Home Office and Department of the Environment, parts of the massive English Safer Cities initiative, and the multimillion dollar American federal Community Protection through Environmental Design programs of the 1970s.

Unfortunately, as Tim Hope's essay makes clear, evidence of the effectiveness of community prevention is less convincing than for situational or developmental prevention. This is at least partly because of the poor quality of evaluations of community prevention strategies, which makes it difficult to draw lessons for the future from perceived failures.

C. Developmental Prevention

Most recently, over the last decade attention has been given to developmental prevention. Developmentalists, typically researchers in psychology, education, psychiatry, medicine, and public health settings, have not traditionally been much interested in crime but have nonetheless documented that risk factors that are predictive of delinquency and crime are also predictive of many other forms of antisocial behavior. Consequently, reducing these risk factors or increasing protective factors could have wide-ranging and cost-effective benefits. Researchers such as David Hawkins, Marc LeBlanc, Rolf Loeber, Joan McCord, Terrie Moffitt, Lee Robins, and Richard Tremblay have combined developmental and criminological interests and have clarified the links between developmental processes and later delinquency.

The central insight is Shakespeare's, that the child is father to the man. Interventions that improve parenting skills, children's physical and mental health, and children's school performance and reduce risks of child abuse are also likely to reduce later offending. So far, at least in the United States, commitment to the notion of developmental prevention is mostly rhetorical. No doubt it is promising that Janet Reno, the U.S. attorney general, has given strong support to proponents of developmental prevention, but political support does not currently exist for sizable increases in governmental funding.

Developmental prevention is the new frontier of crime prevention efforts. Perhaps because children are more sympathetic recipients of government attention and funds than are teenage delinquents and adult criminals, the scale of social programs, spending, and research on child development greatly exceed those for situational or community prevention. Interventions aimed at improving the life chances of children at risk warrant support for reasons entirely independent of crime prevention, but even concerning crime prevention the emerging findings are promising. Evaluations of a variety of interventions directed at life stages from birth through childhood have demonstrated either delinquency-reducing effects or beneficial effects on other indicators (e.g., school performance, hyperactivity, and impulsivity) that are associated with reduced offending probabilities (Farrington 1994). Essays in this volume by Richard Tremblay and Wendy Craig, and by David Hawkins, Michael Arthur, and Richard Catalano review developmental prevention initiatives in detail.

III. Key Issues in Crime Prevention
As editors of this volume, we have, of course, had the prior benefit of reading all the essays. In addition to the essays on prevention approaches already mentioned, others concentrate on prevention of specific categories of crimes: in the retail sector (by Joanna Shapland), in

city centers (by Per-Olof Wikström), and of substance abuse (by David Hawkins and his colleagues). Three additional essays address cross-cutting issues: multiple victimization (by Graham Farrell), implementation (by Gloria Laycock and Nick Tilley), and evaluation (by Paul Ekblom and Ken Pease).

There is a great deal of convergence on a general programmatic method for preventing crime. For example, the "Crime Analysis" approach described by Ekblom (1988), writing within a situational perspective, involved obtaining detailed information about local patterns of crime, devising prevention strategies appropriate to local problems in the light of these analyses, implementing the strategies, and evaluating the effects of the prevention strategies on crime. The "Communities That Care" approach described by Hawkins, Catalano, and associates (1992), writing within a community/developmental perspective, involved mobilizing key community leaders and forming a community prevention board, identifying risk factors in the local community, choosing local prevention strategies targeting these risk factors, implementing the strategies, and evaluating the effects of the strategies. This general programmatic method also has some similarities with "problem-oriented" or "problem-solving" policing (Goldstein 1979; Moore 1992).

A. Key Theoretical Issues

Crime prevention strategies should be based on wide-ranging theories about the development of criminal potential in individuals and about the interaction between potential offenders and potential victims in situations that provide opportunities for crime. Few existing criminological theories are sufficiently detailed or wide-ranging to provide a useful basis for prevention strategies (for an exception, see Clarke's essay, in this volume). Theorists focusing on individual development need to include postulates about how individuals and environments interact to produce crimes, while theorists focusing on the opportunistic commission of crimes need to include postulates about the development of criminal potential in individuals. Both types of theorists also need to take account of the group context of offending and of the community context of individual development and criminal opportunities.

Theorists will probably have to pay more attention to individual differences between offenders. For example, LeBlanc and Frechette (1989) distinguished between "situational" and "chronic" offenders, while Moffitt (1993) differentiated "adolescence-limited" and "life-course-persistent" offenders. It has often been suggested that situational crime prevention should be more effective with opportunistic as opposed to more committed offenders. It is important to investigate to what extent different prevention strategies are differentially effective with different kinds of offenders, offenses, and victims, in different places and times.

Another important theoretical question concerns the extent to which offenders make rational decisions, as opposed to being impulsive (lacking planning and foresight) or compulsive. Some offenders may have internal inhibitions against offending (e.g., a strong conscience or a strong "bond to society") and hence may have low criminal potential and may not make rational decisions based solely on the likely consequences of offending. More research is needed on decision making in criminal opportunities.

Criminal career research may be useful in providing information about the development of offenders, about types of offenders, and about topics that have implications for prevention, such as a person's specialization or versatility in offending. Studies of the careers of both offenders and victims are needed, to specify in what circumstances they overlap and whether there is any effect of victimization on offending (or vice versa). Developmental research is needed to identify protective factors and to determine at what stage it is best to intervene to try to reduce or eliminate a risk factor. For example, it may be better to intervene early, before risk factors or antisocial behavior are too ingrained or stabilized, but not so early that risk factors are poor predictors of antisocial outcomes (in which case the identification of high-risk individuals would be too unreliable).

B. Key Measurement Issues

As Joanna Shapland's essay makes clear, a major problem in studying prevention in the retail sector is to obtain a valid measurement of crime. For example, most shops have no valid measure of shoplifting that can be used before or after prevention strategies are implemented. Retailers may be reluctant to cooperate in surveys covering all the shops in an area, because of their competitive ethos. Innovative measures may be needed; for example, research on the systematic observation of offending as it happens may have disproportionate benefits in advancing knowledge about crime.

While the need for valid measurement is particularly pressing in the retail sector, it applies in all crime prevention research. Attempts should always be made to assess the validity of official record and victimization survey data, for example. Collaboration with public health practitioners may be useful in expanding the range of measures of crime. For example, data on victims of violence can be collected from emergency departments of hospitals, with careful measurement of injury severity, and can be compared with police data on violence (Shepherd et al. 1993).

A key issue for situational prevention, especially, concerns the amount of credence that can be given to offenders' accounts of their crimes. Some situational prevention strategies have been based on these accounts. However, offenders are particularly poor at manipulating abstract concepts (Moffitt 1990), and hence they might be particularly lacking in introspective insight about the motives underlying their behavior. In addition, their memories may be faulty or biased. Just as offenders are more influenced by immediate gratification than by long-delayed future consequences, they may be more aware of immediate influences such as their need for money or excitement than long-buried past influences such as poor parenting or school failure (Agnew 1990). Research is urgently needed on how to maximize the validity of verbal accounts by offenders. In designing prevention strategies, more use might be made of self-reported delinquency surveys.

C. Implementation Issues

Situational prevention, if successful, typically has immediate benefits, whereas the benefits of developmental prevention may be long delayed. Because of this difference in time scale, it is easier to persuade governmental agencies to implement situational measures than developmental ones. Political appointees tend to have short time horizons. The challenge to developmental researchers is to persuade policy makers to plan now to reduce crime in ten to twenty years time.

Another important implementation issue concerns the transition from carefully controlled, high-quality, demonstrably effective, innovative, small-scale prevention programs to routinely administered, large-scale programs. Sometimes, the effectiveness of a program disappears in this transition. For example, providing financial aid to unemployed ex-prisoners reduced recidivism in the small-scale, well-controlled "LIFE" experiment but not in the subsequent large-scale, more routinized "TARP" experiment (Rossi, Berk, and Lenihan 1980). Unfortunately, in deciding whether to persist with large-scale prevention programs, governmental agencies sometimes ignore the results of small-scale, well-controlled experiments. For example, Tim Hope (in this volume) reports that several small-scale well-designed studies have shown that "neighborhood watch" or "block watch" is ineffective in preventing crime, but this has not in any way dampened the enthusiasm of governmental agencies for this particular program.

A key issue in implementation is whether to target the highest-risk individuals or areas or more "normal" individuals or areas. As Per-Olof Wikström points out in his essay, there are "hot times" as well as "hot spots" of crime. The potential payoff, in terms of crime prevention, is greatest with the highest-risk units. Their need is arguably greatest, but they also tend to be the most resistant and uncooperative, and there is also the problem of undesirable labeling or stigmatization of high-risk units. Tim Hope points out in his essay, for example, that most community prevention programs have not been implemented in the most disorganized areas. There are no easy solutions to this dilemma. In practice, it is easier to implement crime prevention research projects and programs targeted at high-risk areas rather than high-risk individuals.

One possible solution to the problem of acceptability would be to make a crime prevention program attractive and desirable. For example, if all parents living on a particular housing estate were offered free high-quality day-care for their preschool children, the attractiveness of this offer might overcome concerns about its ultimate goals or why this particular housing estate had been chosen. Prevention programs can also be "sold" by presenting them in a favorable light. For example, developmental and public health approaches are essentially concerned with promoting healthy development by maximizing protective factors and minimizing risk factors (individual, family, peer, school, and community). As Mark Moore points out in his essay, the goal of promoting health may be more acceptable than the more negative and potentially stigmatizing goal of preventing crime, even though these goals may be essentially two sides of the same coin.

D. Key Evaluation Issues

High-quality evaluation research designs are needed to convince leading scholars, as well as intelligent policy makers and practitioners, about the effectiveness of crime prevention techniques. The most convincing design is the randomized experiment, which can ensure that units in one condition are identical in all possible respects to units in another condition before a crime prevention strategy is implemented and hence permit the unambiguous attribution of any change in crime rates to the effects of the strategy (Farrington 1983). As the essay (in this volume) by Richard Tremblay and Wendy Craig shows, randomized experiments have often been used in evaluating developmental prevention.

Randomized experiments have rarely been used to evaluate community or situational prevention strategies, partly because the units of interest are typically areas rather than individuals. It is not usually possible to assign a large enough number of areas at random to different experimental conditions to achieve the benefits of randomization of ensuring equivalence of units in one condition to units in anther. In general, community and situational researchers should seek to carry out more randomized experiments. As an example of what is possible, in one drug prevention project in California and Oregon, thirty schools were randomly assigned to three experimental conditions (Ellickson, Bell, and McGuigan 1993). If thirty schools can be randomly assigned, then in principle thirty areas could also be randomly assigned in a community or situational prevention experiment.

It is more feasible to carry out a nonrandomized experiment with matched areas, but very few of these have been conducted to evaluate community or situational prevention strategies. Again as an example of what is possible, nine shops in matched groups were assigned to experimental conditions in a project designed to evaluate the relative effectiveness of three methods of preventing shoplifting (Farrington et al. 1993). If it is possible to carry out experiments with matched groups of shops, it should also be possible to carry out an experiment with matched areas.

Most evaluations of community and situational prevention programs are quasi-experimental, with researchers measuring crime rates in areas before and after an uncontrolled or poorly controlled prevention strategy is implemented. In such projects, it is essential to test threats to internal validity such as regression to the mean (Cook and Campbell 1979). Prospectively designed evaluations are generally more satisfactory than retrospective ones. It is also desirable to plot dose-response curves (as in evaluating the effect of a medical treatment) and to measure strength of effect in addition to statistical significance. It may be that a realistic target for a crime prevention measure is a 10 percent reduction in crime rather than a 50 percent reduction. It is important that prevention studies should be designed with sufficient statistical power to detect the likely effects.

More complex prevention programs involving several different elements (e.g., preschool education, interpersonal skills training for children, parent management training) are more difficult to evaluate but perhaps have a greater chance of being effective in reducing offending than programs based on only one type of prevention technique. In their essay, Paul Ekblom and Ken Pease describe how the enormously complex Safer Cities program of the English government is being evaluated. Peterson, Hawkins, and Catalano (1992) outlined a strategy for evaluating the Communities That Care program, based on placing communities into matched pairs and choosing one member of each pair at random for the prevention program. A major problem with a complex prevention program is in identifying the "active ingredients" of the package.

In evaluating situational prevention programs, it is essential to plan to measure possible displacement and diffusion of benefits. In addition, it would be desirable to measure possible indirect prevention, for example, where a reduction in drug abuse leads also to a reduction in burglary and robbery (because of the decreased need for money to finance the drug habit). In evaluating developmental prevention programs, it is desirable to plan long-term follow-ups. For example, evaluating the benefits of intensive home visiting during pregnancy in preventing later delinquency and crime necessarily requires a fifteen- to twenty-year follow-up. As Richard Tremblay and Wendy Craig point out in their essay, few pregnancy or infancy programs have had such long-term follow-ups. In all cases, it would be prudent to allow for the possibility that the prevention strategy might have unwanted crime-increasing side effects.

In evaluating the success of prevention strategies, it is important to investigate the boundary conditions under which they work. For example, a strategy may be effective in one place or at one time but not in other circumstances, perhaps because of societal or contextual variations (e.g., in the prevalence of single-parent families or drug abuse). It is important to assess the generalizability of prevention effects. A troubling problem in many evaluations is that a crime prevention technique may have a short-term beneficial effect that gradually wears off. It is important to design evaluations to discover why strategies are immediately effective and why effectiveness may then decrease. For example, it may be that offenders gradually work out how to "beat the system." "Booster sessions" may be required to reinforce or reactivate the prevention effect, or prevention strategies might be rotated unpredictably to keep offenders guessing (as Sherman [1990] suggested for police crackdowns).

It would be desirable to compare the wide-ranging costs and benefits of each prevention strategy. For example, in evaluating the Perry preschool program, Schweinhart, Barnes, and Weikart (1993) concluded that every $1 invested in the program resulted in a saving of over $7 in costs such as to crime victims, in welfare benefits, and of the criminal justice system. This kind of analysis can be quite convincing to policy makers.

This volume presents a wide-ranging and comprehensive summary of the results of research on developmental, community, and situational crime prevention. We hope that it will contribute to the cumulative advancement of knowledge about crime prevention and to the increased use of effective strategies for preventing crime. That would be in everyone's interests.

REFERENCES

Agnew, R. 1990. "The Origins of Delinquent Events: An Examination of Offender Accounts." *Journal of Research in Crime and Delinquency* 27: 267–94.

Andenaes, J. 1974. *Punishment and Deterrence.* Ann Arbor: University of Michigan Press.

Barr, R., and K. Pease. 1990. "Crime Placement, Displacement, and Deflection." In *Crime and Justice: A Review of Research*, vol. 12, edited by M. Tonry and N. Morris. Chicago: University of Chicago Press.

Blumstein, A., J. Cohen, and D. Nagin, eds. 1978. *Deterrence and Incapacitation: Estimating the Effects of Criminal Sanctions on Crime Rates.* Washington, D.C.: National Academy Press.

Brantingham, P. J., and F. L. Faust. 1976. "A Conceptual Model of Crime Prevention." *Crime and Delinquency* 22:284–96.

Bright, J. 1992. *Crime Prevention in America.* Chicago: University of Illinois at Chicago.

Canadian Sentencing Commission. 1987. *Sentencing Reform: A Canadian Approach.* Ottawa: Canadian Government Publishing Centre.

Clarke, R. V. In this volume. "Situational Crime Prevention."

Cook, T. D., and D. T. Campbell. 1979. *Quasi-Experimentation.* Chicago: Rand McNally.

Duff, A. 1995. "Penal Communications and the Philosophy of Punishment."

In *Crime and Justice: A Review of Research*, vol. 20, edited by M. Tonry. Chicago: University of Chicago Press (forthcoming).

Ekblom, P. 1988. *Getting the Best out of Crime Analysis*. London: Home Office.

Ekblom, P., and K. Pease. In this volume. "Evaluating Crime Prevention."

Ellickson, P. L., R. M. Bell, and K. McGuigan. 1993. "Preventing Adolescent Drug Use: Long-Term Results of a Junior High Program." *American Journal of Public Health* 83:856–61.

Farrell, G. In this volume. "Preventing Repeat Victimization."

Farrington, D. P. 1983. "Randomized Experiments on Crime and Justice." In *Crime and Justice: An Annual Review of Research*, vol. 4, edited by M. Tonry and N. Morris. Chicago: University of Chicago Press.

———. 1994. "Early Developmental Prevention of Juvenile Delinquency." *Criminal Behaviour and Mental Health* 4:209–27.

Farrington, D. P., S. Bowen, A. Buckle, T. Burns-Howell, J. Burrows, and M. Speed. 1993. "An Experiment on the Prevention of Shoplifting." In *Crime Prevention Studies*, vol. 1, edited by R. V. Clarke. Monsey, N.Y.: Criminal Justice Press.

Feeley, M. 1979. *The Process Is the Punishment*. New York: Russell Sage.

Garland, D. 1991. "Sociological Perspectives on Punishment." In *Crime and Justice: A Review of Research*, vol. 14, edited by M. Tonry. Chicago: University of Chicago Press.

Goldstein, H. 1979. "Improving Policing: A Problem-Oriented Approach." *Crime and Delinquency* 25:236–58.

Hart, H. L. A. 1968. *Punishment and Responsibility*. Oxford: Oxford University Press.

Hawkins, J. D., M. W. Arthur, and R. Catalano. In this volume. "Preventing Substance Abuse."

Hawkins, J. D., R. F. Catalano, and associates. 1992. *Communities That Care*. San Francisco, Calif.: Jossey-Bass.

Home Office. 1990. *Crime, Justice and Protecting the Public*. London: H.M. Stationery Office.

Hope, T. In this volume. "Community Crime Prevention."

Jacobs, J. 1961. *The Life and Death of Great American Cities*. New York: Vintage.

Last, John M. 1980. "Scope and Methods of Prevention." In *Public Health and Preventive Medicine*, 11 ed., edited by John M. Last. New York: Appleton-Century-Crofts.

Laycock, G., and N. Tilley. In this volume. "Implementing Crime Prevention."

LeBlanc, M., and M. Frechette. 1989. *Male Criminal Activity from Childhood through Youth*. New York: Springer-Verlag.

Moffitt, T. E. 1990. "The Neuropsychology of Juvenile Delinquency: A Critical Review." In *Crime and Justice: A Review of Research*, vol. 12, edited by M. Tonry and N. Morris. Chicago: University of Chicago Press.

———. 1993. "Adolescence-Limited and Life-Course-Persistent Antisocial Behavior: A Developmental Taxonomy." *Psychological Review* 100:674–701.

Moore, M. H. 1992. "Problem-Solving and Community Policing." In *Modern*

Policing, edited by M. Tonry and N. Morris. Vol. 16 of *Crime and Justice: A Review of Research*, edited by M. Tonry. Chicago: University of Chicago Press.

———. In this volume. "Public Health and Criminal Justice Approaches to Prevention."

Morris, N. 1974. *The Future of Imprisonment*. Chicago: University of Chicago Press.

Newman, O. 1972. *Defensible Space*. New York: Macmillan.

Peterson, P. L., J. D. Hawkins, and R. F. Catalano. 1992. "Evaluating Comprehensive Community Drug Risk Reduction Interventions." *Evaluation Review* 16:579–602.

President's Commission on Law Enforcement and Administration of Justice. 1967. *The Challenge of Crime in a Free Society*. Washington, D.C.: U.S. Government Printing Office.

Reiss, A. J., Jr., and J. A. Roth, eds. 1993. *Understanding and Controlling Violence*. Report of the National Academy of Sciences Panel on the Understanding and Control of Violence. Washington, D.C.: National Academy Press.

Rossi, P. H., R. A. Berk, and K. J. Lenihan. 1980. *Money, Work, and Crime*. New York: Academic Press.

Sampson, R. J. 1986. "Crime in Cities: The Effects of Formal and Informal Social Control." In *Communities and Crime*, edited by A. J. Reiss, Jr., and M. Tonry. Vol. 8 of *Crime and Justice: A Review of Research*, edited by M. Tonry and N. Morris. Chicago: University of Chicago Press.

Schweinhart, L. J., H. V. Barnes, and D. P. Weikart. 1993. *Significant Benefits*. Ypsilanti, Mich.: High/Scope.

Shapland, J. In this volume. "Preventing Retail-Sector Crimes."

Shaw, C. R., and H. D. McKay. 1942. *Juvenile Delinquency and Urban Areas*. Chicago: University of Chicago Press.

Shepherd, J. P., M. A. Ali, A. O. Hughes, and B. G. H. Levers. 1993. "Trends in Urban Violence: A Comparison of Accident Department and Police Records." *Journal of the Royal Society of Medicine* 86:87–89.

Sherman, L. W. 1990. "Police Crackdowns: Initial and Residual Deterrence." In *Crime and Justice: A Review of Research*, vol. 12, edited by M. Tonry and N. Morris. Chicago: University of Chicago Press.

Sherman, L. W., and R. Berk, R. 1984. "The Specific Deterrent Effects of Arrest for Domestic Assault." *American Sociological Review* 49:261–72.

Standing Committee on Justice and Solicitor General. 1993. *Crime Prevention in Canada: Toward a National Strategy*. Ottawa: Canada Communication Group.

Tonry, M. 1995. *Malign Neglect: Race, Crime, and Punishment in America*. Oxford: Oxford University Press.

Tonry, M., and N. Morris, eds. 1992. *Modern Policing*. Vol. 15 of *Crime and Justice: A Review of Research*, edited by Michael Tonry. Chicago: University of Chicago Press.

Törnudd, P. 1993. *Fifteen Years of Decreasing Prisoner Rates in Finland*. Helsinki: National Research Institute of Legal Policy.

Tremblay, R. E., and W. Craig. In this volume. "Developmental Crime Prevention."

van Dijk, J. J. M., and J. de Waard. 1991. "A Two-Dimensional Typology of Crime Prevention Projects: With a Bibliography." *Criminal Justice Abstracts* 23:483–503.

von Hirsch, A. 1976. *Doing Justice.* New York: Hill & Wang.

Wikström, Per-Olof H. In this volume. "Preventing City-Center Street Crimes."

Tim Hope

Community Crime Prevention

ABSTRACT

Community crime prevention refers to actions intended to change the
social conditions that are believed to sustain crime in residential
communities. Different approaches have evolved, which can be best
understood as a succession of policy paradigms emerging as responses to
changing urban conditions: community organizing; tenant involvement;
resource mobilization; community defense (both intentional organizing
and environmental modification); preserving order; and protecting the
vulnerable. Prevention in high-crime areas presents particular difficulties
for community approaches. Community approaches have foundered
mostly because of insufficient understanding of the nature of social
relations within residential areas and of how community crime careers
are shaped by the wider urban market.

Community crime prevention refers to actions intended to change the
social conditions that are believed to sustain crime in residential communities. It concentrates usually on the ability of local social institutions to reduce crime in residential neighborhoods. Social institutions
encompass a diverse range of groupings and organizations—including
families, friendship networks, clubs, associations, and organizations—
which bring people together within communities and, by doing so,
transmit guidance concerning conduct in the locality. Together, such
institutions make up the social structure of residential communities.
In this essay, the distinctiveness of community crime prevention is

Tim Hope is reader in criminology, Keele University, and coordinator of the Economic and Social Research Council Crime and Social Order Research Program. The
author is grateful for comments from Tony Bottoms, Dennis Rosenbaum, Michael
Tonry, and the participants at the editorial conference in London.

21

seen to lie in its purposive concern to alter the social structure of particular communities. Not included therefore in this definition are macro-level economic and social policy measures which have chiefly an indirect effect on local social structure—though, as will be seen, these may have an important influence on the ability of community institutions to affect crime—and programs delivering social or correctional services to individuals, albeit located in community settings.

How should we think about community crime prevention efforts? It is often an implicit belief of social scientists that the findings and theories of social research can be translated directly into social programs or that such programs can be construed as the precise embodiment of particular social theories (Rein 1976; Lindblom and Cohen 1979). Yet, in reality, practitioner accounts of community crime prevention often seem muddled, inconsistent, and untheorized (see Rock 1988). In these circumstances, it is tempting to want to convert practical discourse into a rational theory. Yet this may hinder rather than help us understand the *political* character of community crime prevention. In the approach adopted in this essay, various forms of community crime prevention are interpreted not only as applications of criminological theory but also as complex pieces of sociopolitical action that also have a defining ideological and ethical character.

A conceptual tool that can help in delineating the emergence of different types of community crime prevention over the years is the *policy paradigm*, "a curious admixture of psychological assumptions, scientific concepts, value commitments, social aspirations, personal beliefs and administrative constraint . . . a guiding metaphor of how the world works which implies a general direction for intervention" (Rein 1976, p. 103). A principal question that this essay addresses is why community crime prevention paradigms change. The explanation is that paradigm replacement has not been simply the result of an accumulation of program failures and successive bright ideas—that is, a "what works"-type progression—but rather that eventually it becomes apparent that the prevailing rationale underpinning a particular paradigm has failed to comprehend the changing nature of the crime problem in the urban environment. During the twentieth century, metropolitan areas have changed dramatically, as has the perception of crime problems within them. Shifts of community crime prevention paradigm reflect those changes.

An overview is offered here of crime prevention ideas and programs as they have been proposed for residential areas. Rather than unnecessarily—and probably less successfully—duplicating the detailed findings of a number of relatively recent and comprehensive reviews of research (Titus 1984; Lavrakas 1985; Rosenbaum 1986, 1988a; Taylor and Gottfredson 1986; Skogan 1988, 1990), an attempt is made here to explore the way in which the idea of community prevention has been interpreted, what problems the emergent programs of the time were trying to counter, and whether they constituted an effective or appropriate policy response to the crime and community problems that had occasioned them.

The essay revolves around a central paradox: there has been a continuous and consistent pattern of criminological research suggesting that community structure itself shapes local rates of crime—that community crime rates may be the result of something more than the mere aggregation of individual propensities for criminality or victimization (Sampson 1987a; Bursik and Grasmick 1993). Yet much of the effort to alter the structure of communities in order to reduce crime has not been noticeably successful or sustainable. Does this mean that the community approach, as a strategy of prevention, should be abandoned, despite the weight of research pointing to the importance of community life in crime causation?

Initially, it would seem that it might be possible to resolve the paradox if we could work out whether the problems of community crime prevention were due to a failure of theory—that the program rationale was wrong—or of implementation—that the aims were right but the means to achieve them were inappropriate, inadequately implemented, or underresourced (Rosenbaum 1986). Yet, in fact, it is hard to find an example among most of the programs reviewed here where implementation was so successful that a proper evaluation of theory could be made. Indeed, it would appear impossible clearly to separate means from ends in community crime prevention. This may be because, in most formulations of the community approach, the proposed solution—a community structure that controls crime—is also the antithesis of the perceived problem—a community that does not control its own crime. With such circularity, means and ends become blurred; and a failure of implementation is as much a failure of theory as of practice.

A more helpful distinction may be between two dimensions along which local social institutions—and purposive prevention programs—operate in communities (Duffee 1980; Sampson 1987a). First, there is a "horizontal" dimension of social relations among individuals and groups sharing a common residential space. This dimension refers to the often complex expressions of affection, loyalty, reciprocity, or dominance among residents, whether expressed through informal relationships or organized activities. Second, there is a "vertical" dimension of relations that connect local institutions to sources of power and resources in the wider civil society of which the locality is acknowledged to be a part. This essay suggests that the two dimensions are equally important—and related—in their effect on local crime (Bursik and Grasmick 1993) and therefore crucial for crime prevention efforts in communities.

While the principal mechanisms for maintaining local order may be expressed primarily through the horizontal dimension, the *strength* of this expression—and hence its effectiveness in controlling crime—derives, in large part, from the vertical connections that residents of localities have to extracommunal resources. Many of the approaches reviewed here have either neglected to address sufficiently the vertical dimension of community power (or powerlessness) or have met with failure or resistance when they have done so. The paradox of community crime prevention thus stems from the problem of trying to build community institutions that control crime in the face of their powerlessness to withstand the pressures toward crime in the community, whose source, or the forces that sustain them, derive from the wider social structure.

Most of the material here comes from accounts of programs and research carried out in the United States and Great Britain, describing policy paradigms of community crime prevention in terms of responses to changes in urban conditions and governance, though these may also be similar to developments in other advanced societies (see Jacobs 1992).

The discussion of each paradigm is organized under the following headings: problem definition—which includes implicit concepts about community, crime problems, and urban dynamics; strategy—by which is meant the rationale or theory justifying the focus of prevention (i.e., whether to block criminal behavior, forestall criminal motivation, or promote social control) and the way in which program inputs were intended to result in crime prevention outputs; implementation—which includes the policy processes leading to specific programs and the course they took in practice; and evaluation, including both the available research evidence on effectiveness and the broader political assessment that occasioned the paradigm's demise or the persistence of some of its elements.

The essay is divided broadly into four sections. Section I discusses the paradigms of community prevention that emerged under conditions of urban growth during this century. These include "community organizing," "tenant involvement," and "resource mobilization." Section II considers the paradigmatic response—"community defense" to the urban problems of the 1970s and 1980s, consisting of two forms, "intentional organizing" and "environmental modification." Section III seeks to discern approaches emerging during the 1980s, particularly, the preservation of community order and the reduction of victimization. Section IV, by way of conclusion, reflects on what has been learned so far and points to the likeliest or most-promising next steps in research, program development, and policy formulation.

I. Community Crime Prevention in the Growth City

Three community crime prevention paradigms arose in response to the problems of order posed by the demographic and economic expansion of cities. The first is *community organizing*, associated primarily with the diagnosis of the urban condition put forward by the Chicago School of Sociology, and with the programs of Clifford Shaw and Henry McKay. The second—*tenant involvement*—owes much to the first, though it arose in response to problems associated with the growth of public housing, especially in mid-century Britain; the third—*resource mobilization*—is a model that came to be embodied in the troubled history of the "War on Poverty" program in the United States during the 1960s (Marris and Rein 1972; Lemann 1991) and, less directly, in the travails of the Community Development Project in late-sixties Britain.

A. Community Organizing

The Chicago School's enduring legacy for community crime prevention, and for urban reform generally, is the rationale of "community action"—or in Britain "community development": "A way must be found to modify those aspects of community life that provide the appropriate setting for delinquency careers and which give those careers the sanction and approbation on which all social behavior depends" (Shaw and McKay 1969, pp. 325–26). The general model saw the city's social and physical form as determined by relatively unregulated competition for urban space between industrial or commercial and residential uses and between social groups differentiated by income and ethnic and cultural identity (Park, Burgess, and McKenzie 1925; Bursik 1989). The land and property pricing of the city reflected the outcome of unfettered competition for access to urban resources. As immigrant groups and individuals arrived, adjusted, and made economic progress, so they would move successively to the areas of the city that were appropriate for their particular stage of social mobility, succeeding other groups further along the process of assimilation to the urban way of life. Shaw and McKay's extensive areal correlation analyses tended to corroborate this ecological depiction (Shaw and McKay 1969): despite changing ethnic populations, inner zones of American cities had high rates of resident juvenile offenders and—by virtue of their position in the ecological structure of competition for urban space—were of mixed land uses, low socioeconomic status, cultural heterogeneity, and high transience (Kornhauser 1978). Because these areas contained social groups undergoing a process of transition to urban ways, they would be disorganized, creating a moral vacuum in which youth, without guidance or control, would be free and susceptible to criminal activity.

1. *Strategy.* Shaw and McKay failed to describe the particular features of social disorganization or, from the point of view of criminological theory, to provide a consistent account of how social disorganization caused individual delinquency (Wootton 1959; Kornhauser 1978). However, it is arguable whether Shaw and McKay actually needed an individual-level theory to guide preventive action. Since the areal analysis seemed to confirm that the prevalence of delinquency was consistent with the Chicago School's structural model of the distribution of resources and pathology between neighborhoods of the city, despite changes in their populations, then it followed, logically, that delinquency would be a property of *areas*, which is the level at which Shaw and McKay thought that intervention should be targeted (Shaw and McKay 1969, p. 321). Their position seems to have been, not that individualized methods of curbing delinquency—by inculcating moral values or providing standards of guidance—would be ineffective, but that the *institutional infrastructure* for implementing these methods was lacking: "Through the leadership of local residents it is possible to effect closer co-ordination of local institutions, groups, and agencies into *a unified program for the area as a whole*" (Shaw and McKay 1969, p. 322, emphasis added).

2. *Implementation.* In order to compensate poor communities for their lack of institutional infrastructure, and mindful of the "humiliations often entailed in receiving the services of philanthropy" (Shaw and McKay 1969, p. 323), Shaw initiated the Chicago Area Project (CAP) in 1932, which, in one way or another, has been the source model for community action to the present (Bursik and Grasmick 1993). Chicago Area Project programs were initiated in about six small areas of Chicago. Reportedly, they all pursued, with varying degrees, recreational programs for children, campaigns to improve conditions in the neighborhood, and outreach work ("curbstone counseling") with delinquents and gang members (Kobrin 1962). Many of the techniques pioneered by CAP have become subsequently the staple methods of the community treatment of delinquency and of community development. Yet, in an important way, the substantive content of the programs was held to matter less than the opportunities for socializing young people that the participation of community adults, as role models, provided (Kobrin 1962).

While there have been general descriptions of the Chicago Area Project (Kobrin 1962; Finestone 1976), Schlossman, Zellman, and Shavelson (1984) provide the only detailed, long-term account of its progress. They focus on the Russell Square area of South Chicago and divide events into two periods: 1931–44, and 1944–84. They characterize the first period as one of *mutual adaptation*—between CAP's ideals and what the indigenous community were actually prepared to do: "CAP entered Russell Square slowly and cautiously, and by the time-worn path of least resistance to children and parents alike: organized recreation. . . . Shaw expanded recreational contacts with juvenile gangs to include extensive curbstone counselling. Becoming fully rooted and accepted in the neighborhood, though, required more than CAP energies alone could provide. . . . Shaw carefully courted the local catholic church and influential catholic laymen . . . to local residents, the CAP may have appeared mainly as an appendage to St. Michaels. To the pragmatist in Shaw, the church connection was essential to get his own experiment off the ground" (Schlossman, Zellman, and Shavelson 1984, p. 22).

A test of Shaw and McKay's theory of community organizing is whether community institutions survive despite population change. During the second phase of CAP in South Chicago (1944–84), the population changed dramatically from a Polish working-class neighborhood to a predominantly Mexican neighborhood with a minority of blacks (Schlossman, Zellman, and Shavelson 1984). With the departure of the Poles to the suburbs, the institutions around their local church disintegrated. Yet CAP quickly transferred its support and funding to two nascent community organizations emerging in the Mexican and black communities. Nevertheless, little attempt was made to organize the separate groups to serve the neighborhood as a whole: "Once again, the CAP accepted ethnic exclusivity as a precondition for getting things done" (Schlossman, Zellman, and Shavelson 1984, p. 30).

3. *Evaluation.* Not perhaps surprisingly, Schlossman, Zellman, and Shavelson (1984, p. 20) report that, over the years, "Shaw became more and more reluctant to cite statistical data on delinquency rates to demonstrate the wisdom and effectiveness of the Area Project." Their own attempt to assess crime levels in the community in 1980 exhibits the unreliability of ex post facto, cross-sectional analysis (Lurigio and Rosenbaum 1986). Yet, the history of CAP is important, not because it demonstrates crime reduction, but because it illustrates what will turn out to be three of the common problems facing the implementation of community crime prevention (see Skogan 1988).

First, there was the need to select communities where there was already some community infrastructure. As Finestone (1976) suggests, CAP was not actually implemented—nor did it long survive—in the most disorganized neighborhoods of the day but rather took root in somewhat more stable, ethnically homogeneous neighborhoods. Although, pragmatically, some preexisting institutional infrastructure may have been necessary for survival, such selectivity tends to undermine the primary objective of building community institutions where they are lacking. Second, there is the difficulty of sustaining indigenous community involvement over the longer term. When the institutional structure supported by CAP fell apart as a result of population change, it changed support to new embryonic structures but did not create them itself. Without the external input of CAP, it seems unlikely that the indigenous institutions would have survived the cultural and population turnover of the neighborhood.

Third, there are differences between the theoretical goals of the intervention and what the community itself defines as important and desirable as a condition of acceptance. The difficulty of engaging the voluntary commitment of adults to the theoretical aims of CAP seems to have led in practice to a degree of compromise in the goals of CAP in an effort to build the institutions of socialization. For example, "It became clear that Russell Square youth wanted to go to camp . . . and that the community considered camping an essential tool of delinquency prevention. . . . Shaw became reconciled to camping as integral to the Area Project philosophy" (Schlossman, Zellman, and Shavelson 1984, p. 22).

In sum, while CAP has shown remarkable longevity (Bursik and Grasmick 1993), that may have been due less to the scope of local institutions—that is, the horizontal dimension of community relations—so much as to the persistent sponsorship of agencies external to the community—that is, the transfer of resources down through the vertical dimension of community relations. In any event, it would seem that CAP failed its own test—of building community institutions that would regenerate themselves without external intervention and despite change in membership.

B. Tenant Involvement

The legacy of community organizing bequeathed by CAP has exerted a lasting and general influence on subsequent thinking about community work across a range of policy fields. Although not explicitly acknowledged, some of the spirit of the CAP approach reemerged during the 1970s in response to the problems presented by the expansion of public housing in Britain—specifically, the desirability of involving tenants in the management of their residential environment.

The postwar period in Britain saw a massive increase of housing in public ownership—in 1945, about 12 percent of households lived in public housing, a figure that grew to 31 percent by 1971 (Bottoms and Wiles 1986). This growth was largely due to the extension of public involvement in postwar reconstruction and urban renewal. Much of this growth involved the building of often large-scale public housing estates both in the inner cities and on the periphery of urban areas. Yet by the 1970s, at the end of this period of construction, problems of vandalism and deterioration began to emerge on public housing estates, some of which had only recently been built (Ward 1973; Power 1987a).

An investigation by the Department of the Environment for England and Wales focused on the development of "problem estates" (Department of the Environment 1981). It concluded that some estates had acquired an adverse reputation that, when combined with an inability to maintain them to an adequate standard, resulted in a spiral of decline that was characterized by vandalized and poorly maintained public spaces and little sense of community among residents. As a result, there was a high turnover of tenants, with vacancies attractive only to those in desperate need. All this led to an atmosphere of neglect making it harder for housing services to cope with increased problems of maintenance, lettings, and rent arrears. In many respects, the "problem estate" in Britain by the 1970s replicated, in the public housing sector, many of the features of high-crime communities identified in a different context by Shaw and McKay—public housing had grown, and newly created estates were bringing diverse populations together, often with concentrations both of children and poverty, while the unpopular estates were seen as an environment in which residents passed through on their way to better estates, leaving behind those families with multiple difficulties.

1. *Strategy.* Two related strands of an approach emerged: first, intensive decentralization of housing management and services to the level of the estate itself, which could then be focused with a greater degree of effort, coordination, and efficiency (Power 1984); and second, consultation with tenants on all aspects of estate improvements and the creation of ways in which they would be able to become involved in the direct management of estates. It was this latter aspect that had affinity with the CAP approach—to create institutional arrangements for tenants to control their living environments. Accessible provision of housing services would reinforce these arrangements. Together, they would help empower tenants—by making estates better places to live, they would persuade current tenants to stay, thereby providing stability to estate communities (Power 1984, 1987b). Nevertheless, although it has been claimed that crime has declined as a result of this strategy (Burbidge 1984), many have seen this as an indirect consequence of the strategy's chief aim to bring about general physical improvements to the housing estates (Glennerster and Turner 1993).

2. *Implementation.* In Britain, initiatives have sought to arrest the deterioration of problem estates by decentralization and improvements in the quality of housing management, services, and maintenance, through small-scale environmental improvements and clean-up programs and by supporting greater consultation and involvement of residents in the management of their estates (Bright and Petterson 1984; Power 1987b; Rock 1988; Foster and Hope 1993; Glennerster and Turner 1993). With respect to tenant involvement, many projects drew their inspiration from a pilot scheme in Widnes in 1975 (Hedges,

Blaber, and Mostyn 1980) sponsored by the National Association for the Care and Resettlement of Offenders. Also influential has been a government-sponsored program of projects run by the Priority Estates Project (PEP) (Power 1984, 1987b) and, later, also supported by Estates Action of the Department of the Environment for England and Wales. Both programs have been seen as models of good practice for local housing authorities to follow (Power 1987b). Typically, such schemes involve a variety of measures—including security programs for dwellings, clean-up projects, localized management, caretaking, and concierge services—though the key ingredient has always been consultation and involvement of tenant representatives in management issues.

3. *Evaluation.*   While a considerable number of estate-based initiatives have been implemented in Britain, documentation from evaluative research has been somewhat lacking. In part, this may have been due to the opacity of the processes of change involved, the scale and complexity of the interventions, the reluctance to use or accept empirical evidence or detailed analysis, and the obstacles and lack of resources that implementers may have experienced in presenting accounts of their work (Rock 1988). In part, also, there remains the general evaluative problem of isolating the particular effects of multidimensional projects (Foster and Hope 1993). A report by the Safe Neighbourhoods Unit (Safe Neighbourhoods Unit 1993a) brought together evidence from a number of management-led initiatives on public housing estates in Britain (see also Burbidge 1984), concluding that "on balance . . . estate-based local management initiatives appear to have an impact on crime problems where they are part of a broad programme of physical and social improvements . . . results from assessments are encouraging but further evidence is required" (Safe Neighbourhoods Unit 1993a, p. 108).

Recently, Hope and Foster (1992) and Foster and Hope (1993) have evaluated the impact of a management/consultation approach, implemented by the Priority Estates Project, in two areas of public housing in England—one in inner London, the other in the Northern English city of Hull (see also Glennerster and Turner 1993). The study used a quasi-experimental research design to compare changes occurring in each of the areas over a three-year period with a matched control area. A range of data sources was used: pre- and postimplementation household surveys to assess levels of victimization, fear of crime, and tenants' experiences of estate conditions, housing services, and community life;

detailed ethnographic observation and interviews with tenants over twelve months on one estate and eighteen months on the other; recorded crime figures; the regular measurement of environmental standards on the estates; and the monitoring of changes in the delivery of housing management and services.

At the outset of the study, the two estates selected to become new PEPs both had high crime rates and adverse design and social characteristics. The basic elements of PEP's housing service model—a local estate office, repairs, caretaking, lettings—were implemented on both estates (Glennerster and Turner 1993). However, in the first year of operation on the London experimental estate, the estate office was run by a housing manager who appeared to have little sympathy with the PEP approach, causing friction with the tenants and the PEP consultant. While some estate services improved, the staff problems led to disputes; tenant enthusiasm and cooperation never properly recovered from this earlier disappointment.

Ethnographic research found the Hull experimental estate community to be socially fragmented. The more established tenants had managed to insulate themselves, by and large, from the remainder who were generally more vulnerable to adverse economic and personal experiences and misfortunes. Among the vulnerable tenants could be found a number of crime-prone groups: networks of adults stealing and receiving stolen goods, and unruly teenagers who caused trouble to an extent far beyond their numbers (Foster and Hope 1993). Tenant-management-dominated PEPs operated on this estate, leading to the formation of a Neighbourhood Management Committee with directly elected tenant representatives. Additionally, about £3 million was spent on environmental improvements including damp treatment for dwellings, increasing the security of tower blocks on the estate, and, following tenant consultation, creating greater "defensible space" for about half the houses (Glennerster and Turner 1993).

On the estates studied, the capacity of the PEP model to bring about community organization and reduce crime was affected by the rate of population turnover and degree of social and cultural heterogeneity within the community. On the London experimental estate, residents experienced a greater sense of security and, as found from the victimization surveys, a significant increase in the minority Bengali residents' perception of safety from racially motivated victimization. However, other residents had become poorer, more socially heterogeneous, and more disillusioned about tenant participation and the future of their estate (Foster and Hope 1993). Victimization rates declined significantly but not by nearly as much as on the control estate.[1]

On the Hull estate, both the design improvements, and the general sense of optimism generated by PEP's efforts to involve tenants, gave support to the more established tenants who began to exude a greater confidence about their estate and its future. Yet, at the same time, a greater number of vulnerable poor were coming onto the estate—including young, homeless single people, lone parents, and those discharged from social services care or institutions. Social cohesion and "empowerment" increased among many residents as a result of environmental modifications and PEP's efforts to involve them in the improvement of services and estate management. However, many of the newcomers—particularly the young poor who were concentrated in one part of the estate—became extremely vulnerable as victims. Some of the newly arrived young unemployed had considerable difficulty in sustaining themselves independently—both financially and socially—and became involved in criminal activities of various kinds on the estate. In particular, they seemed to act as a link between existing networks of teenagers and of adults involved in crime on the estate, serving to deepen and widen networks of offending (Foster and Hope 1993).

Overall, outcomes on the Hull experimental estate reflected the interplay of conflicting forces of community control and criminality (Hope and Foster 1992)—there were reductions in victimization from some offenses (i.e., burglary) and in some parts of the estate but increases in other offenses (i.e., theft from vehicles) and in other parts of the estate. There were reductions, relative to the control estate, in residents' worries about victimization; an increasing sense of care and concern for the residential environment; and a reduction in perceptions of litter, graffiti, and other physical disorders (see Skogan 1990) as problems. However, comparison between the surveys showed an increased perception of person-related disorder—including disturbances from youths, noisy neighbors, persons hanging around drinking—and

---

[1] The much greater decline in crime on the control estate may have been due to a combination of good-quality local housing managers—delivering many of the ingredients of the PEP package, increased physical security, and greater community surveillance stemming in part at least from the stabilizing influence of a substantial Bengali community on the estate (Foster and Hope 1993). Generally, the Bengali community in Britain, though economically disadvantaged, is culturally cohesive and has a low offender rate.

indications of diminished disapproval for holding noisy parties, swearing in the streets, and hanging around in groups in public (Foster and Hope 1993). Neither did the rate of resident mobility decline.

Though the pattern of outcomes was complex, this study illustrates the dilemma of the community organization model inherent in the legacy of Shaw and McKay. First, in the London experience, much seemed to hinge on the *individual quality* of those individuals involved in organizing—something that may be difficult to replicate. Second, as with the CAP experience, the outcomes described here were shaped by forces *external* to the community. In particular, the Hull experience suggests that efforts at community organizing only weakly, if at all, acknowledged those external, structural forces—particularly poverty, cultural heterogeneity, and residential mobility—which may be increasing, simultaneously, social and cultural disorganization within communities (Kornhauser 1978). In this case, the source of destabilization arose from outside the residential community—that is, the changing pattern of tenant allocation (see Bottoms and Wiles 1986) produced greater numbers of the young poor among newcomers whose arrival significantly altered the social mix on the estate. Again, outcomes were shaped by changes occurring in the vertical relationship of the estate community to the economy of the wider society (Foster and Hope 1993). Thus, as Bursik and Grasmick conclude (1993, p. 51): "A full understanding of [community] control must also consider the effects of decisions and dynamics based outside the neighbourhood on the nature of relational networks within the community."

C. Resource Mobilization

The Chicago Area Project's implementation trajectory may have been determined by the problems of building links with and between community residents; other difficulties of implementing community action have stemmed from attempts to influence the distribution of political power and resources. The contemporary view (Bursik 1988) sees social disorganization as the inability of the community to act together to realize common values (Kornhauser 1978). Yet, as seen above, residential communities may be limited in their ability to get things done for reasons beyond their control (Sampson 1987a). The resource-mobilization model embodies the idea that it may not be sufficient merely to promote social cohesion in communities if they are starved of resources to address the social and economic conditions that are undermining that cohesion. In this sense, community action be-comes concerned with the transfer of economic and political resources to empower local communities, to give youth a stake in conformity (Toby 1957), and to relieve the frustrations of blocked aspirations and relative deprivation that induce delinquency (Cloward and Ohlin 1960).

The exemplar of the resource-mobilization approach remains the Mobilization for Youth (MFY) program on New York's Lower East Side—the paradigm for the community action programs of the "War on Poverty" in 1960s America (Short 1975). Wilson (1978) comments that the intellectual justification for MFY may have been lacking in view of the absence of hard evidence from controlled experimentation; though in the nature of the political reality of crime prevention para-digms, this omission is hardly damning. Nevertheless, the paradigma-tic shift toward resource mobilization seems to have come about through a convergence of trends in at least four separate but related areas: urban structure, urban social policy making, criminological the-ory, and social work practice.

In the first place, the period between 1940 and 1960 saw an unprece-dented, large-scale migration of blacks from the South to the Northern industrial cities following a relatively stable period of population growth after the curtailment of mass European migration in the 1920s. Bursik's (1986) longitudinal study of Chicago shows that the period 1930–40 bears out Shaw and McKay's assumptions about the stability within the urban system of socially disorganized, high-delinquency areas. Yet, in subsequent decades, the ecological distribution of high-delinquency areas within the city follows a general pattern associated with nonwhite compositional change and increases in resource depriva-tion within certain communities. The Shaw and McKay model as-sumed a private-market process of competition within the city, but the differential patterns of settlement of black migrants and white residents in later years reflected nonmarket factors (Bursik 1986), particularly racial conflict over access to housing, suburban development, economic and political factors limiting the racial integration of neighborhoods, and the entry of the public sector into the large-scale provision of low-rent housing (Hirsch 1983). Thus the concentration of offenders and poverty in certain neighborhoods was seen no longer to reflect merely the deficiencies of indigenous institutions but the neighbor-hoods' powerlessness and inability to capture economic resources that the urban process was distributing inequitably.

The support of the large foundations and the federal government for delinquency prevention through community action reflected two somewhat different concerns. First, there was a new generation of optimistic, social-science-influenced policy makers, subscribing to a new form of government—that is, "experimental social administration" (Moynihan 1969; Halsey 1978); but, second, there was the pressing imperative of dealing with the crisis in urban government occasioned by the discriminatory experiences of the great black migration (Piven and Cloward 1971; Lemann 1991): "The delinquency problem seemed an especially promising issue around which to frame a Federal program. It held out the promise of new services to blacks and, simultaneously, the promise of law and order to whites. The very services that would appeal to the swelling numbers in the ghettos would also assuage the whites who feared the ghettos" (Piven 1969, p. 173). Most important, community action was seen as a way of delivering resources to poor, black urban residents who would otherwise be denied them by existing urban government (Marris and Rein 1972).

Cloward and Ohlin's (1960) analysis emphasized the frustrations of blocked access to success goals through legitimate means as a motivating force in delinquency. Yet, they concluded (pace Wilson 1975) that the traditional outlets for status attainment in slum communities—revolving around various forms of organized criminal activity—were also disappearing along with the structure of the older, ethnic slums. Without any outlet for status achievement, they predicted that delinquent adaptations would thus become more predatory and violent in poor areas. Similarly, whereas in the older slums, economic opportunities were delivered via the local political machines, these were being replaced by income maintenance, subsidized housing, and benefit programs administered bureaucratically by state welfare agencies, reflecting also a shift in social welfare thinking away from individualized treatment and counseling (see Kahn 1968). In their view, the replacement of a political process by a welfare-distributive process served to isolate residents of poor communities further from the wider society (Cloward and Ohlin 1960, p. 209). Poor communities would thus have to be mobilized to gain resources in a way that would strengthen their "vertical" linkages with the wider resources of society.

1. *Strategy.* The Mobilization for Youth approach differed markedly from what had been done before in the treatment of delinquency in community settings (Kahn 1968): it made explicit reference to social science theory; it combined a traditional emphasis on individual adjust-

ment with a concern to address the structural causes of maladjustment; it received direct funding from the federal government, bypassing local power and patronage; it proposed to engage its professional staff in community action and political campaigning; it aimed to make services relevant to the needs of client groups in their communities; it aimed to take a holistic approach to community problems; and it recognized the possibility of conflict with municipal bureaucracy (Helfgot 1981).

Yet, while its intellectual legitimacy may have derived initially from Cloward and Ohlin's "opportunity-structure" theory, the program in practice emphasized the provision of legitimate economic opportunities for conformity and did not address the control of illegitimate opportunities for crime that the theory had also stressed (Short 1975). Importantly, while opportunity-structure theory set the general objective, it did not provide any particular suggestion as to *how* opportunities were to be delivered (Short 1975; Wilson 1975; Helfgot 1981). Indeed, some have argued that the theory actually appeared attractive *because* of its vagueness about how access to success goals for slum youth might be accomplished—it could give an intellectual imprimatur to a diverse constituency that the idea of community action needed to bring together (Short 1975; Wilson 1978).

2. *Implementation.* From different vantage points, Marris and Rein (1972), Helfgot (1981), and Lemann (1991) provide vivid pictures of the political ferment of 1960s America in which MFY and the many other programs loosely associated with it were implemented. Mobilization for Youth in practice became susceptible to a diversity of approaches and the incorporation of other objectives (Helfgot 1981). In particular, the program evinced a tension between *service delivery*, the provision of social, employment, and welfare services that were available for local youth, and *resource capture*, the mobilization of residents into political action intended to bring down more resources to the inner-city community. Inasmuch as it sought to shift the balance toward empowerment and away from welfare dependency, the program became increasingly involved in political action, displacing the immediate objective of providing services for delinquent youth and moving toward a more general challenge to local sources of political power, in which the mundane aims of crime prevention became subsumed in the broader political struggle. In the end, MFY encountered a severe reaction from municipal and other interests that led to an undermining of its funding and altered the nature of its programs (Fried 1969; Helfgot 1981). Particularly, the emergent political organization of MFY and

other community action programs came into conflict with existing political structures of city government (McGahey 1986) and lost. With the failure of its effort to capture economic resources for its community, MFY eventually transformed into a less controversial manpower training organization that aimed to equip local youth with the skills required by local employers (Helfgot 1981).

Though Mobilization for Youth has been seen as an exemplar of community action against crime (Short 1975), the history of the period shows clearly how a policy paradigm can mushroom and diverge from the circumscribed experimental mode that its social scientific planners once might have had in mind, especially if it becomes part of a wider political movement. Community action programs were promoted by central government as an effective way of delivering resources directly to the poor—and resolving abiding problems of central-local governmental relations, while program activists saw them as a vehicle for an insurrectionist restructuring of urban power. In an important contrast to CAP, action focused primarily along the vertical dimension of power, with little attention paid to building community institutions in the ghetto that might have delivered resources to local youth. Yet "the war on poverty was a political failure mainly because it made enemies of local elected officials. Its main program, community action, was a conceptual failure in the sense that it raised expectations about the revival of the ghettos that couldn't be met" (Lemann 1991, p. 344).

Community groups still try to address "social problems" in impoverished, high-crime communities (Podolefsky and DuBow 1981). Skogan (1988) has dubbed these "insurgent groups." As he points out (Skogan 1988, p. 9), insurgent groups "like all organizations . . . need to articulate their members' concerns and win victories that generate benefits for their constituents." Their priorities are much more likely to focus on bringing economic, health, and social opportunities or benefits to the community than in specifically anticrime activities. Insurgent groups tend to see crime as a consequence of their community's lack of resources (Podolefsky 1983) and therefore, inasmuch as they are concerned with crime, focus on addressing its root causes in joblessness, poverty, poor housing, and discrimination (McGahey 1986). In bringing job programs, clinics, youth training, or investment to their communities, such groups strive to redistribute urban economic resources—again focusing on developing vertical linkages with wider sources of power.

Yet there is also a dilemma familiar to community groups: whether to preserve the momentum of campaigning, though remaining in a conflictual and marginalized relationship with the sources of urban power; or whether to become the recipients and administrators of much-needed resources, through changing the relationship with the community to that of service provider—and thereby becoming an adjunct of government, and possibly complicit with the dominant political interests that the groups once opposed (Skogan 1988). Even so, the scale of resources made available by such a compromise may be less than might have been anticipated or needed. Rosenbaum (1988a), for instance, points to the problem of "dosage"—that resources actually made available for community programs—especially those seeking to address social conditions—are often so meager that little might reasonably be expected from them.

Probably the only politically feasible resource-mobilization strategy in recent years has been that of encouraging community *self-help*—of attempting to leverage public and private resources to develop community-based enterprises and training programs for high-risk youth. During the 1980s, the Eisenhower Foundation supported ten nonprofit community organizations in poor urban neighborhoods to "empower local organizations to take the lead in defining anticrime strategies best suited to their own capacities and the specific problems and conditions of their communities. . . . Organizations were free to emphasize youth empowerment over opportunity reduction, or vice versa. . . . Each group was required to develop financial self-sufficiency in the sense of creating an ongoing mechanism to continue the program for at least twelve months after the initial . . . support had ended" (Eisenhower Foundation 1990, p. 19). Eight of the ten implemented work programs that had been developed during the planning process. Two organizations focused exclusively on services for individual youth referrals; the other groups selected either opportunity reduction or "causes of crime" strategies—with only three opting for a balanced approach (Lavrakas and Bennett 1989). Nevertheless, the type of strategies adopted, and the level of implementation effort, seemed to have more to do with the organizational capacity of the community groups—including the orientation of their directors—than with their host community's responses to the groups. Consequently, the evaluators conclude that "the capacity of a 'bubble-up' planning approach . . . to generate increased community participation is uncertain" (Lavrakas and Bennett 1989, p. 66). Additionally, it is unclear whether the goal of such programs was to change the social structure of their neighborhoods or to provide services for *individual* high-risk youth, albeit in a community setting (Rosenbaum 1988*a*).

3. *Evaluation.* Not surprisingly, the essentially political process of the resource-mobilizing strategy of MFY and similar programs did not occasion any assessment of its impact on delinquency, a goal that seems to have disappeared in the process of politicization. The evaluation of the Eisenhower Program concluded that "despite the many strategies that were implemented across the sites, the impact evaluations provide little evidence that the . . . Program had documentable successes in achieving its major goals of crime reduction and improved quality of life, although there was some consistent evidence . . . [of] . . . a slight reduction in residents' fear of crime in several of the sites. Many positive changes that were noted in site-specific evaluations were relatively small and patterns of positive change at the sites were not consistent enough to support stronger conclusions" (Lavrakas and Bennett 1989).

In terms of their impact on general community change, the Eisenhower projects may simply not have been of sufficient scale or magnitude to overcome the severity of the problems in the high-crime neighborhoods in which they were targeted (Lavrakas and Bennett 1989)—the problem of the necessary "dosage" of intervention (Rosenbaum 1988*a*). The dilemma of the resource-mobilization approach, therefore, may be that asking for too much may provoke a reaction, while getting too little may have negligible effect.

The long-term impact of MFY has been primarily by virtue of the reaction it provoked: it was seen as illustrating the significance of the vertical dimension of power in local communities and the inability of community institutions to alter the social structural conditions that were held to give rise to delinquency. However, and, as it turned out, of more significance for governmental crime control policy in both America and Britain, the experience was interpreted as evidence of the folly of constructing policy on the vaunted and unsubstantiated promises of social analysis (Moynihan 1969). This argument was developed by James Q. Wilson (1975) in his influential critique of liberal crime control policy and coalesced into the prevailing mood in social policy during the 1970s that Wildavsky (1980) has termed the "strategic retreat on objectives." Thus while Wilson (1975) might concede that antipoverty programs and breaking up the ghettos might be desirable in their own right, the apparent inability of the programs that were implemented to reduce the escalating crime rates of the 1960s was held to show that social programs were not an effective means of crime control and that policy should adopt alternative strategies aimed at raising the costs of engaging in crime and of reducing the opportunities for illegitimate behavior (see Clarke and Cornish 1985).

Nevertheless, whatever may have been the reality of community action programs—whether they were underresourced and destroyed by vested power interests or were the irresponsible raising of false expectations based on unsubstantiated theory (Wilson 1975)—the experience came to take on an almost mythical character during the rise to political ascendancy of conservatism in America and Britain. In the process of constructing a new paradigm, described in the next section, the fate of community action—and its inappropriateness for crime control—may have come to take on a greater significance than it may ever have had in reality: "Rhetorically, the war on poverty was made to sound more sweeping than it really was, and so set itself up [or was set up] to seem as if it had ended in defeat when it didn't vanquish all poverty" (Lemann 1991, p. 344), or crime for that matter.

II. Community Crime Prevention in the Frightened City

During the 1970s, the crime problem in urban communities was redefined significantly in public policy making. This led to a sustained focus on community crime prevention, first in the United States and later in Europe. A new paradigm emerged, that of *residential defense*. While it aspired, like the earlier paradigms, to change the conditions of residential communities, it reflected a new policy concern about crime in the urban environment, specifically the self-policing of communities. Two strategies emerged during the 1970s to promote citizens' informal self-policing: the *intentional organizing* of community surveillance, and *environmental modification* to encourage more natural surveillance.

A. Intentional Organizing of Community Surveillance

By the 1970s, public discourse—particularly in America—was seeing the city as an increasingly dangerous place to live; an image was developing of urban residents afraid of falling victim to crime and concerned about "the standards of right and seemly conduct in the public places in which one lives and moves" (Wilson 1985, p. 28). Increasing public anxiety about rising crime rates in late-sixties America prompted a redefinition of crime as a major civil and political problem. The President's Commission on Law Enforcement and Administration of Justice (1967) marked a turning point, elevating the problems of victimization, and the fearful anticipation of it, as concerns of crime policy and urging that local communities should be supported in crime prevention efforts. This general shift in policy—the "victimization perspective" (Lewis and Salem 1981)—resulted in progressively greater legislative and funding support during the 1970s in America for the active involvement of citizens in the maintenance of order in their residential environments (Lavrakas 1985).

Whereas social order in communities was preserved, in Shaw and McKay's model, through the inculcation and maintenance of norms of conduct, primarily through the socialization of the young—and in the resource-mobilization model by ameliorating youth's frustrations at the absence of economic opportunities—the victimization perspective now focused on citizens becoming anxious about safety from the threat of predatory victimization in their home environment (Conklin 1975). The fundamental imagery had been supplied by Jane Jacobs (1962): cities serve a diverse range of interests and purposes, at once liberating but also troubling for residents because their size and complexity encourages anonymity and continually brings strangers into contact who may be dangerous because they share no common bonds of culture or kinship (see also Wirth 1938).

Jacobs believed that modern urban planning, especially the differentiation and segregation of residential environments from other land uses, was undermining residents' ability to cope with and regulate urban diversity. Paradoxically, the planned correction of the ills of the slums identified by the Chicago School—the invasion of residential areas by commercial land uses, residential proximity to transport routes, the engineering of the social composition of communities—had been incorporated as basic tenets of postwar city planning and urban renewal. The considerable involvement of municipal government in managing, planning, and building cities and providing housing environments was now being seen as misguided, primarily because such planning obstructed the basic means by which order was maintained: "The first thing to understand is that the public peace—the sidewalk and street peace—of cities is not kept primarily by the police, necessary as the police are. It is kept primarily by an intricate, almost unconscious, network of voluntary controls and standards among the people themselves, and enforced by the people themselves. . . . No number of police can enforce civilization where the normal, casual enforcement of it has broken down" (Jacobs 1962, p. 41).

The key to urban safety was thus seen as residents regaining *informal social control* over behavior in the public places of their neighborhoods (Greenberg, Rohe, and Williams 1985). How this was to be achieved was mainly through *natural surveillance*—day-to-day supervision by residents of their environment "employing the full range of encounter mechanisms [e.g., questioning strangers, in-person surveillance, intervention, calling the police] to indicate their concerned observation of questionable activity and their control of the situation" (Newman 1973, p. 4). The objective, then, was to strengthen communities' informal defenses against predation by strangers which the urban environment was impeding.

The view that urban social order could be maintained by citizens' informal self-policing of their own communities had considerable political attractiveness (Skogan 1990). At the level of expediency, it provided one answer to a growing crisis in the perception of police effectiveness, stemming both from an accumulation of research evidence (Clarke and Hough 1980) and popular reaction to rising rates of crime; it offered a promise of "doing more while spending less"—a lower-cost solution to crime control than criminal justice or social program expenditure during a period of budgetary cutbacks and fiscal restraint (in American cities during the 1970s and in Britain during the 1980s); it offered a way of dealing with property crimes that surveys suggested were the most commonly experienced and that prompted the most widespread worry (Clarke and Hope 1984); and it offered modest support for communities while diverting attention from claims to address the root causes of crime. At the level of ideology, it appealed to conservative concerns about the maintenance of standards of behavior (Wilson 1975) and to growing libertarian instincts about the importance of voluntarism, self-help (Lavrakas 1985), the role of the "active citizen," and the minimal role of the state (Brake and Hale 1992).

1. *Strategy.* Intentional organizing embodied a two-fold expectation: first, that organizing communities into collective crime prevention projects would have a direct preventive effect on crime (by increasing natural surveillance) and on fear (through joint participation); and second, that participation would indirectly reduce crime and fear through increased social interaction, a stronger sense of community solidarity, and thus more effective informal social control in the neighborhood (DuBow and Emmons 1981). A wide range of collective crime prevention projects were suggested as vehicles for neighborhood self-policing (Feins 1983), though most attention focused on the "big three"—block watch, security surveys, and property marking (Titus 1984)—which

in turn have become subsumed under the general rubric of *neighborhood watch*—that is, informal organizations of residents who agree to watch over each others' property and report suspicious activities to the police. Encouragement for the idea of block or neighborhood watch had come from an evaluation of the Community Crime Prevention Program in Seattle that suggested that participants in small block watches (who were also provided with security advice and property marking) had reductions in their risk of burglary without evident displacement to nonparticipating households and areas (Cirel et al. 1977).

2. *Implementation*. Residential defense was given substantial political support during the 1970s in America and in the 1980s in Britain. In the United States, federal funding by congressional mandate supported a range of programs to encourage both intentional organizing and environmental modification—the latter often referred to as "Crime Prevention through Environmental Design" (CPTED; see, e.g., Fowler, McCalla, and Mangione 1979; Wallis and Ford 1980; Fowler and Mangione 1982). Descriptions and reviews of these programs can be found in Skogan (1988), Lavrakas (1985), and McPherson and Silloway (1981). In Britain, the approaches were disseminated through the Home Office's long-term program of research and development in crime prevention (Clarke and Mayhew 1980; Heal and Laycock 1986), within the British police (Bennett 1989*a*), and later by central government (Central Office of Information 1989), local government, and the Crime Concern organization (Bright 1991). Major difficulties of implementation have been encountered both in program design and in specific applications of the intentional organizing approach. Three key implementation problems have been encountered—differential participation, program initiation, and program maintenance. Excellent summaries of the research on these three issues are available (Rosenbaum 1987, 1988*a*; Skogan 1988, 1990), and only the main points are rehearsed here.

3. *Differential Participation*.   A variety of studies offered two major findings. First, members of community anticrime groups are more likely to be better-off, more educated, longer-term residents who are married, have children, and own their own homes. Second, anticrime groups are least likely in low-income, heterogeneous, deteriorated, renting, high-turnover, high-crime areas (Skogan 1988).

Studies of individuals participating in community crime prevention groups suggest that their profile is very similar to those who participate in any kind of voluntary activity (Rosenbaum 1988*a*; Skogan 1988).

And surveys suggest that community volunteers differ from the rest of the population, having greater identification with local concerns (e.g., among owner-occupiers and families with young children), more social confidence and competence (e.g., excluding the young, the old, and the poor), and more free time (e.g., including the middle-aged and excluding families where both parents work and single parents [Hope 1988a]). Owner-occupation seems especially salient: Lavrakas (1981) found home ownership to characterize households who were likely to take any kind of crime prevention measure. When this is extended to collective participation in crime prevention, homeowners may have a greater commitment to maintaining the standard of the neighborhood through their personal incentive to maintain house prices and have greater freedom and responsibility than renters for taking prevention measures.

Studies of the low level of community organization in poor, crime-ridden communities suggest that residents are "deeply suspicious of one another, report only a weak sense of community, have low levels of personal influence on neighborhood events . . . and feel that it is their neighbors whom they must watch carefully" (Skogan 1988, p. 45). Mutual suspicion and lack of trust in high-crime communities may therefore undermine community anticrime efforts, particularly those like neighborhood watch that require members to exchange information about themselves (Podolefsky and DuBow 1981).

Unfortunately, these two sets of findings do not indicate whether participation (and thus, by extension, effectiveness) is a function of social composition or community context. Some areas may have a low level of participation because they contain more people who are not inclined to be participants (i.e., a social composition explanation). Or, it could be that the nature of life in certain areas, or the character of communal association, is not conducive to forming or sustaining voluntary groups, despite the inclinations of individual members (i.e., a community context explanation). If it is assumed that policy makers are keen to see the approach implemented on a wide scale and believe it is possible for communities to be organized deliberately, then it is important to know whether differential participation is a compositional or contextual problem. If the former, then there is some promise that additional organizing efforts might overcome the obstacles of communal association to reach the people. If the latter, then participation will always be partial, no matter how much organizing effort, unless the social structure of such communities is altered.

TABLE 1

Participation in Neighbourhood Watch, England and Wales, 1984–88, Percentage of Households Living in Areas Classified as Belonging to Each ACORN Group

ACORN Group	Affluent Suburbs	Poorest Council Areas
1984:*		
"Supporters"†	64	58
Households burgled (including attempts)	3	12
1987:‡		
Estimated participants	10	5
1988:§		
Scheme setup in area	29	13
Members	24	7
Participation rate‖	84	57
Households burgled (including attempts)	3	13

Note.—ACORN is a small-area geodemographic classification system based on the 1981 United Kingdom Census (see Hough and Mayhew 1985, app. F).

* Source: 1984 British Crime Survey (Hough and Mayhew 1985, table 12).

† The percentage of respondents who said they thought Neighbourhood Watch would work in their area and who were personally prepared to join, after having read a description of the concept (see Hope 1988a).

‡ Source: Hussain (1988, table 3.3).

§ Source: 1988 British Crime Survey (Mayhew, Elliott, and Dowds 1989, table 15).

‖ The percentage of members among those who said a Neighbourhood Watch scheme was operating in their area (source: 1988 British Crime Survey [Mayhew, Elliott, and Dowds 1989, table 15]).

Separating the compositional (individual level) from the contextual (communal level) reasons for nonparticipation is confounded by two likely phenomena: first, the housing market tends to differentiate people according to class and income, so that like people will more likely than not live together (Bottoms and Wiles 1986); and second, participation is a function of both inclination and opportunity (Skogan 1988). Few people will be inclined to participate if there are no available opportunities or if they judge the prospects of successful community organization in their neighborhood to be poor. Likewise, people may not voluntarily organize community groups where they judge other community members to be unreceptive.

Table 1 illustrates these issues, reporting survey data tracking the development of Neighbourhood Watch (NW) in England and Wales.

Two different kinds of social area are displayed—affluent suburbia, and the poorest council estates (public housing projects)—with differing levels of crime (see, generally, Hough and Mayhew 1985; Hope and Hough 1988). In 1984, although less than 1 percent of households interviewed in the 1984 British Crime Survey (BCS) belonged to a scheme, most people polled (89 percent) thought NW would be effective against burglary; yet over a third of all BCS respondents said they would not join a scheme—and the proportion did not differ substantially between the two very different kinds of area (table 1). Table 1 shows a survey of NW coordinators that estimates that, by 1987, residents of affluent suburbia were twice as likely to be members than were residents of the poorest estates, despite still relatively low levels of participation generally (Husain 1988). By 1988, the BCS confirmed that 90 percent of all respondents had heard of the idea, and while still only 14 percent of households said they were members, two-thirds of nonmembers said they would be willing to belong (Mayhew, Elliott, and Dowds 1989). Nevertheless, table 1 shows more schemes established in affluent suburbia, covering a greater proportion of the population, than in the poorer area. Moreover, differences in the participation rate show that, even where the opportunity to participate was available, fewer residents of the poorer area were taking it up. The findings in table 1 suggest, then, that both area and individual obstacles to participation exist.

Comparisons between members and nonmembers suggest that the type of neighborhood still has an effect on participation, after controlling for individual differences; but so also do individual differences, after controlling for neighborhood type (Hope 1986a; Skogan 1988; Mayhew, Elliott, and Dowds 1989). Bennett (1989b), for instance, found that participants had different characteristics than nonparticipants within areas that had neighborhood watch schemes. As regards the argument that making opportunities available for participation will overcome individuals' reluctance to participate, differences between "supporters" and others in England and Wales before the mass introduction of neighborhood watch (Hope 1988a) closely resemble differences between actual participants and others after considerable national effort at disseminating the idea (Mayhew, Elliott, and Dowds 1989, p. 54, n. 7). It may also be hard to get agencies to invest effort in organizing poor, heterogeneous neighborhoods: the police-based Community Organizing Response Team in Houston held most of its community meetings in the part of the target area dominated by owner-occupied, single-family homes, with little effort extended to the poorer section of the area containing blacks in rental accommodation (Skogan 1990).

Perhaps the most comprehensive test of whether individual reluctance to participate disappears given the availability of opportunities comes from the "Minneapolis Experiment" where, despite substantial block-level organizing efforts, participation was still low (Rosenbaum 1988*b*), and "even though program effort was greatest in poorer, black, and higher-crime areas, attendance at meetings was highest in white and middle-to-upper-income areas where crime problems were not substantial" (Rosenbaum 1988*b*; Skogan 1990, p. 148). The obstacles to participation would not seem solely for want of opportunities available in neighborhoods but also stem from the different orientations of low-income, renting, and nonfamily social groups.

4. *Program Initiation.* Natural histories of community crime prevention groups are sparse, and relatively little is known about the specific factors affecting their origin, maintenance, and longevity. Some research suggests that, while community members may form some inclination to "do something" in response to an increasing perception of neighborhood problems, they may also become incapacitated from taking organized action if problems become too severe and, likewise, may only become prompted into action if they are, and remain, otherwise satisfied with their neighborhood; but these findings are only inferential (Hope 1988*a*). While community groups may form around a particular criminal cause célèbre in the neighborhood, they seem equally likely to emerge for other reasons, and to be concerned about other problems in the community, in addition to, or instead of, crime (Skogan 1988).

A key policy question addressed in the literature is whether anticrime groups can be engineered—either by *transplanting* crime concerns onto existing community organizations or by *implanting* anticrime groups into neighborhoods that do not have them (Rosenbaum 1988*a*). From the perspective of central government funding, if the experience of the resource-mobilization paradigm turned into a political quagmire, American federal support for community self-help turned into an administrative quagmire (Skogan 1988). Perhaps as a reaction to the loss of political and financial control experienced during the resource-mobilization paradigm, tight administrative controls in this era seem to have strangled voluntarism, imposing considerable burdens of grant administration on local organizations and deterring fledgling and unsophisticated self-help groups (McPherson and Silloway 1981). Similarly, concerns for political stability sent the bulk of the money to "noncontroversial organizations and uncontroversial proposals" (Skogan 1988).

Manipulating concern about crime as a stimulus for group involvement in crime prevention is also an uncertain strategy. While there may be little point in attending meetings about a problem that does not exist, or is seen as much less important than other issues (Hope 1986a), an overemphasis on crime may be equally aversive. A careful evaluation of an effort to get community groups to organize block watches in Chicago found that participants came away more worried about crime, presumably because the constant focus on local crime problems undermined rather than reinforced their sense of community well-being (Rosenbaum, Lewis, and Grant 1986; Lewis, Grant, and Rosenbaum 1988). Raising crime consciousness of citizens or community groups may be pointless anyway. DuBow and Podolefsky (1982) found that 87 percent of respondents to a citizen survey already agreed with the general idea that neighborhood groups could reduce crime, a view shared equally among participants and nonparticipants.

5. *Program Maintenance.* Paradoxically, successful programs of "watching" may also contain the seeds of their own destruction. Looking out for crime that does not happen may be nearly as boring as watching paint dry, while the surreptitious nature of most property crime may evade those active citizens intent on catching wrongdoers in the act. Even though the Minneapolis Experiment found greatest success with the more affluent residents, attendance at meetings rapidly tailed off, largely because there were no real problems to deal with (Skogan 1990). The longevity of neighborhood watch schemes may have most to do with their not requiring much of participants in practice. In Britain, the most common activity of neighborhood watch members appears to be putting a sticker in the window, and only about a quarter had attended any meetings following the initial launch (Mayhew, Elliott, and Dowds 1989; see also Bennett 1990).

While members seem more likely to report incidents to the police than would comparable nonmembers, similar proportions are likely to witness crime in their area (Mayhew, Elliott, and Dowds 1989). Presumably, neighborhood watch is intended to *increase* the natural surveillance of a community in addition to making it more efficient, but there are two reasons why this may prove difficult. First, although people do seem to behave in ways consistent with natural surveillance (Shapland and Vagg 1988), people may also fail to notice crime taking place, have difficulty in deciding whether a crime has been committed, be reluctant to intervene, be reluctant to call the police, and be unable to identify the suspect subsequently (Mayhew et al. 1979). Additionally, since over half of all dwellings in England and Wales are likely to be unoccupied for three or more hours a day (Hope 1984), there may simply be little scope or advantage in appreciably raising the level of natural surveillance in residential communities (Mayhew et al. 1979). Second, most members (41 percent), reporting in the British Crime Survey, feel that the greatest benefit of participation is having one's home watched—only 13 percent thought it improved neighborliness (Mayhew, Elliott, and Dowds 1989). However, since "watching" is voluntary, there will likely be no monitoring of whether people actually do watch out as they are supposed to and thus no sanction imposed—for example, withdrawal of the watching benefit—if they do not watch out at all. In other words, the voluntary nature of neighborhood watch contains a powerful incentive for "free riding" (Hope 1988b; Field and Hope 1990), which, if enough people do it, can negate the actions of those who do not (see Olsen 1965).

Summarizing, Skogan notes that, for the survival of community crime prevention initiatives, "the critical factor is the decision by multipurpose organizations to add crime prevention to their agenda. Participation levels are high in areas where organizations are successful and attract members. Most successful organizations have complex agendas; few of them were originally organized around crime concerns, and people join them for a variety of reasons revolving around their stake in the community and their citzenly instincts. It is when these groups take on crime prevention that participation in anticrime activities is high" (Skogan 1988, p. 54).

6. *Evaluation.*   In view of the theoretical and implementation problems noted above, it is perhaps not surprising that evaluation research has not demonstrated much in the way of impact on crime for the community defense paradigm. Despite many reported claims for success, relatively few reliable program evaluations have been completed (Lurigio and Rosenbaum 1986). Evaluation research on the impact of neighborhood watch, with reliable research designs, has been carried out on programs in Seattle (Lindsay and McGillis 1986), Chicago (Rosenbaum, Lewis, and Grant 1986), Minneapolis (Skogan 1990), and London (Bennett 1990). Yet none of them have demonstrated reductions in community crime rates, and the benefits to participants reported initially in the Seattle project (Cirel et al. 1977) had disappeared after eighteen months (Lindsay and McGillis 1986). Improvements in

fear levels and community cohesion in these programs were few and sporadic.

British government support for community crime prevention during the 1980s was couched often in terms of rational self-interest: "Protecting your own home is fine, but you will enjoy greater security if every one around you is working at it" (Central Office of Information 1989, p. 26). However, a purely rational-choice interpretation of the above evidence would suggest that, were individuals to make such a calculation, they would, in many circumstances, choose *not* to participate (Field and Hope 1990). This outcome is more likely under four conditions. The first is when the perceived costs or risks of voluntary participation outweigh its apparent benefits—that is, the poor residents of high-crime communities have few personal resources to donate to voluntary activity, feel they face considerable risk in contacting neighbors whom they perceive to be dangerous (Merry 1981), and may have little personal or (as renters) financial stake in the neighborhood. The second is where neighborhood commitment has opportunity costs—for example, distracting from effort that might otherwise be spent in pursuing opportunities or accumulating resources to be able to move away. The third is where marginal additions of participation are perceived not to produce commensurate reductions in risk—no matter how much effort, neighborhood crime is unlikely to disappear, and residents still have to pay for the police, in one way or another. The fourth is where "free riding" obtains the benefit of safety at little or no cost to the individual.

Though politically attractive, efforts to get individuals to give themselves voluntarily to communal activity, where the principal benefit is seen as a reduction in their own risk of crime, does not seem to be a viable crime-prevention strategy, particularly in high-crime communities. The volume of research findings suggests that at the heart of the problem lies the paradigm's reliance on *voluntarism* as the guiding principle of communal activity. The policy of using citizen self-help as an antidote to the fear of crime paradoxically gave priority "precisely to those activities made impossible by the isolation of individuals living in the communities to be assisted" (Lewis 1979, p. 176). Implementation of the intentional organizing approach appears circular, given the reliance on voluntarism implicit in the model. Differential inclinations toward participation affect the formation and maintenance of organizations, but the availability of organizations—and the resources within the community for establishing organizations—affect the likelihood that citizens will participate. "Voluntarism" is differentially distributed among the community; and voluntarism itself makes it difficult to promote and sustain membership or activity. Either way, the residents of poor, high-crime communities end up with fewer anticrime organizations than do more affluent, lower-crime neighborhoods.

B. Environmental Modification

The idea that the residential environment itself might be changed to promote informal social control stems, in large part, from Jane Jacobs's analysis of cities but captured popular attention through Oscar Newman's theory and proposals for *defensible space* (Newman 1973). For Newman, the key to improving informal social control by natural surveillance lay in the extent to which residents felt they identified with their environment (i.e., territoriality): "Improved surveillance operates most effectively when linked with the territorial subdivision of residential areas, allowing the resident to observe those public areas that he considers to be part of his realm of ownership and hence responsibility" (Newman 1973, p. 79). Neither the causes nor the behavior of residential defense were taken to be problematic by Newman: defensiveness sprang from latent territorial tendencies common to all human groups. Nevertheless, the design of some built environments—especially mass public housing projects—prevented natural surveillance and defensiveness from expressing itself. Appropriate design would remove these obstacles, and residential control would reassert itself naturally (Hope 1986a).

1. *Implementation.* Despite policy support for the environmental model, there have been few purposive attempts to implement defensible space design changes on a sufficiently large scale and evaluated with enough rigor to control for alternative hypotheses and confounding influences. In part, this may have been due to the confusing nature of the theories and research findings generated by and in the wake of Newman's (1973) original research (Hope 1986a) and the complexity of conducting reliable research to isolate the various hypothesized effects (Rubenstein et al. 1980). There were also, inevitably, implementation problems, particularly affecting the federally funded American CPTED program managed by the Westinghouse Corporation: "Each of these demonstrations required the co-ordination of several local agencies, and it was quickly learned that the local political environment often determined what, if anything, would be done as part of the demonstration . . . the research suggested that modification of the

social environment was as important, if not more important, than modifications of the physical environment" (Lavrakas 1985, p. 100). In particular, there appears to be no available published record of what actually happened to the CPTED demonstration proposed for a residential area.

Scale and timeliness also played a significant part in staying the hand of government from implementing environmental modification programs. Newman's diagnosis of the problems was essentially ex post facto. The mass public housing projects for the most part had already been planned and built, and the onset of restraint in public spending in both Britain and America from the mid-1970s limited additional main program expenditure on public housing, other than perhaps to justify the demolition of the worst examples—for example, the Pruitt-Igoe projects in St. Louis, Missouri. Likewise, the political mood has militated against the provision both of public housing and of government-mandated planning. The policy rather appears to have been one of disseminating the "design solution" among local urban planners and designers in the hope that it might be implemented as and when the opportunity arose. Alterations to the physical environment for crime prevention purposes have thus tended toward relatively low-cost options: improving the security of individual dwellings, beautification and clean-up programs, improved street lighting, and installation of access-control and surveillance technologies (Safe Neighbourhoods Unit 1993a, 1993b).

2. *Evaluation.* There is now an extensive review literature on the possible relationships between crime and the physical environment—including the concept of "defensible space" (Mayhew 1977; Rubenstein et al. 1980; Taylor, Gottfredson, and Brower 1980; Poyner 1983; Hope 1986a; Taylor and Gottfredson 1986). Following Newman's (1973) assumptions about the "naturalness" of residential defensiveness being unlocked by appropriate design, much subsequent research—including that of Newman himself (Newman 1980; Newman and Franck 1980)—has been concerned to establish the relative independent and conjoint influences of the social and physical causes of informal social control on crime (Hope 1986a). Much of the research, though, has been correlational and suffers from a variety of confounding possibilities that have not been addressed adequately (Taylor and Gottfredson 1986). Chief among these omissions are the failure to test the linkages in the model—that is, that design promotes natural surveillance and that natural surveillance deters crime; failure to differenti-

ate the "environmental effect" as it influences the perceptions and behaviors of offenders from its influence on resident "defenders"; and
failure to take into account the prior allocative processes that assign
potentially "criminogenic" populations to supposedly "criminogenic"
environments (Hope 1989).

The multicausal confusion surrounding the environmental modification model has been replicated in the multidimensional nature of
most programs, so that it has been difficult to isolate for evaluation the
dynamics of the design effect. The Hartford Experiment during the
1970s—in the Asylum Hill neighborhood of Hartford, Connecticut—
illustrates such ambiguities (Fowler, McCalla, and Mangione 1979;
Fowler and Mangione 1982, 1986; Taylor and Gottfredson 1986).
Here, a combination of street closures and modifications—intended to
reduce the accessibility of the area to outsiders—along with localized
policing and community organizing, appeared to promote community
cohesion, neighborhood satisfaction, and feelings of safety from crime,
despite no long-term change in levels of burglary and robbery. The
piecemeal introduction, removal, and likely duration of impact of each
of the three elements makes it hard to interpret these findings.

It might seem that residents' perceptions of safety and social cohesion can be altered without affecting the community crime rate. Research on the interrelationship between residents' perceptions of crime
and their perceptions of other neighborhood values and amenities (including house prices) suggests that "the critical issue is whether victimization is thought to be a low-probability random event or whether it
is seen as one element in a class of threatening events thought to occur
commonly in an area . . . the level of threat is then judged against
one's standard—the amount of inconvenience one is willing to tolerate
given the other amenities in the neighborhood" (Taub, Taylor, and
Dunham 1984, p. 180). By contrast, the results from Hartford might
merely indicate a lag between changes in crime levels and residents'
perceptions or the dilution of direct police surveillance and organized
natural surveillance that also occurred over time (Taylor and Gottfredson 1986).

In a similar vein, while recent reviews of the effectiveness of street
lighting in reducing crime have engendered controversy in Britain (see
Ramsay 1991), the weight of evidence with regard, at least, to fear
reduction in residential areas has generally been supportive of earlier
assessments (Tien et al. 1979)—that better lighting does help residents,
especially the more vulnerable groups, to feel safer in the public places

of their residential neighborhoods (Painter 1992). In the PEP experiment on the Hull estate, described in Section I, the greatest relative reduction in burglary occurred in that part of the estate where the houses benefited from environmental modifications intended to reduce public access; this was accompanied by a significant increase in residents' territorial attitudes and a marked decline in tenant turnover (Hope and Foster 1992). However, residents in another part of the estate—which had yet to receive these environmental measures—also experienced similar, though less marked, improvements. In the latter case, it is unclear whether this increase in community safety was due to better housing management and consultation or to an anticipation of the benefits yet to come of the environmental modifications (see Clarke 1992).

In general, the evaluation of the possible *independent* effect of environmental modifications has been confounded by two issues. The first are interrelationships among design, perceptions of community, control behavior, residents' social circumstances, fear of crime, and actual levels of crime, which make it extremely hard, both theoretically and in empirical research, to disentangle 'pure' environmental effects. The second is that there is rarely a practical example of a purely environmental modification that was not accompanied by, or in turn created, other changes that might also have had an impact on crime rates (see Hope and Foster 1992). As Taylor and Gottfredson (1986) conclude, "Simple effects of physical environment on crime range from small to moderate. . . . It appears that alteration of physical environment features cannot have stand-alone crime prevention effectiveness. Resident dynamics are the key mediators of the environment-crime linkage" (quoted in Bottoms and Wiles 1988, p. 86). Nevertheless, the Department of the Environment for England and Wales has sponsored recently the Design Improvement Controlled Experiment to implement some post-Newman design proposals (Coleman 1985), whose evaluation research design may be able to isolate some of the hypothesized effects of environmental design on informal community control and, hence, on crime (Riley 1992).

III. Community Crime Prevention
in the Disintegrating City

This section considers two more recent views on community prevention that seem to be succeeding the community defense paradigm. Both, in different ways, are reactions to a perceived disintegration of order in urban residential communities. Neither, however, directs attention toward the reasons for urban disintegration—though some of these are discussed in Section IV—choosing to concentrate more on controlling its manifestations.

Each approach stems from a relatively recent insight about high-crime areas. First, communities with high crime rates also have high levels of disorderly public behavior or "incivility" (Skogan 1990). This leads to the possibility that preserving order in communities might be a way of reducing their crime rates (Wilson and Kelling 1982). Second, victimization from crime is not only very unequally distributed across residential areas (Barr and Pease 1990) but also unequally distributed among residents within high-crime areas (Trickett et al. 1992). This insight leads to the possibility that the problem of high-crime communities is, in fact, a problem of a concentration of highly vulnerable individuals and households and that such rates can be reduced by targeting effort not on the community as a whole but on its most vulnerable members (Pease 1993).

A. *Preserving Order*

Areas of poverty and residential instability not only have high crime rates but are also more likely to have high levels of social and physical disorder as perceived by their residents—for example, noisy neighbors, loitering youths, drug dealing, vandalism, trash, and so forth (Skogan 1990). American and British data suggest that community levels of disorder are also related to levels of victimization, though residents' perceptions of disorder more strongly influence their fear of crime than the level of victimization itself (Hope and Hough 1988; Skogan 1990). In general, it seems, neighborhood disorder is interpreted as the outward and visible sign of community problems, including a loss of social control (Wilson and Herrnstein 1985). However, the process by which a community comes to acquire an identity or label—*neighborhood coding*—may be the crucial intervening factor in translating residents' dissatisfaction with disorderly behavior into actual neighborhood deterioration.

The significance of disorder for neighborhood change appears to rest in its negative effect on residents' satisfaction with their neighborhood (Hope and Hough 1988; Skogan 1990). Taub, Taylor, and Dunham's (1984) study in Chicago suggests that residents' dissatisfaction with their neighborhood, fueled by perceptions of disorder and crime, prompts them to compare their communities with others where they might reasonably expect to live. If house prices and amenities in their present neighborhoods are valued, residents might be prepared to stay and tolerate a higher level of crime, fear, and disorder. Otherwise, they may determine to leave if they can. Essentially, this may involve a weighing of the neighborhood's "use value"—that is, the intrinsic values of residence in a particular locale—against its "exchange value"—that is, how properties in the neighborhood are valued in the urban market (Logan and Molotch 1987). Once a number of residents start to leave a neighborhood, departure becomes contagious, for other homeowners perceive a loss in their investment should they choose to stay (Taub, Taylor, and Dunham 1984). The stigma of negative neighborhood coding reduces the relative attractiveness of the area to prospective newcomers, housing values decline, and poorer people move in. The remaining residents, whose tolerance of newcomers may be lessened (or whose fear may be heightened) through associating them with neighborhood problems, also want to leave, particularly as the neighborhood housing stock adjusts to the lower-income market, including a shift toward rental tenure, the multioccupation of dwelling units, and a reduced level of investment in the housing stock (Skogan 1986). This further fuels the spiral of socioeconomic decline, concentrating the poor even more in such areas and, as noted above, reducing further the community resources for self-regulation.

In this respect, it perhaps matters less what the original reasons for disorder might have been than that perceptions of disorder may act as a multiplier in the process of negative coding that serves as the motor for the deterioration of individual neighborhoods within the urban housing market (Skogan 1990). As noted above, a consistent, independent, correlate of participation in individual and community crime prevention measures is home ownership. On the basis of rational calculation alone, housing tenure—and the relative market value that different tenures imply—will affect the willingness of individuals to participate in crime prevention programs, as well as the type of concern and timescale they bring with them to such programs (Field and Hope 1990). Moreover, the option of community involvement has to contend with the alternative choice of "exit" (Skogan 1988), if that can be exercised. Thus, to stabilize neighborhoods where some kind of market choice of residence operates, city government—or other institutional actors with a stake in particular localities (Taub, Taylor, and Dunham

1984)—may need to intervene to preserve the exchange value of the neighborhood (Logan and Molotch 1987).[2]

While renters have little stake, other than sentiment, in their dwellings, the owners of their properties clearly do, and it might be that property owners can be encouraged to invest in neighborhood crime prevention as a way of maintaining the value of their properties. Unfortunately, it may be that the economics of low-income rental in the urban market militate against maintenance and upkeep in favor of maximizing rental income—and against investing in neighborhood improvements (Logan and Molotch 1987). However, the public owners of social housing have a nonmarket interest in the long-term value of the neighborhoods in which their housing is located and have an incentive in neighborhood improvement that might include crime prevention activity. Thus if public authorities invest in housing, their tenants gain some of the benefit and thus their own incentive to participate—a principle underlying housing interventions such as the Priority Estates Project (Glennerster and Turner 1993). However, whether public housing tenants actually choose to forgo their option of exit depends presumably on whether the improvements are sufficient to outweigh the perceived benefits of transferring to somewhere even better, including out of the public sector, especially if they are being given incentives to make such a move (see Forrest and Murie 1988).

Trends in public housing in Britain over the past three decades tend to illustrate these processes. Long-term research in Sheffield demonstrates the central importance of housing markets as the determinants of community crime careers, particularly those that allocate tenants to public housing estates (projects) (Bottoms and Wiles 1986; Bottoms, Mawby, and Xanthos 1989; Bottoms, Claytor, and Wiles 1992). Since the 1960s, housing tenure in Britain has polarized between owner-occupation and public rental (Wilmott and Murie 1988), with the virtual disappearance of the private rental sector (Bottoms and Wiles 1986). The expansion of public housing culminated in the early 1970s with the completion of the mass public housing estates; shortly thereafter, the problem of the "difficult-to-let" estate began to emerge.

----

[2] As Bottoms and Wiles (1986) suggest, most "democratic" systems of housing market operate with some degree of resident choice. Typical public housing allocation systems operate on some ranking of needs for prospective tenants that can be bargained against housing availability and some set of criteria whereby tenants can transfer to another dwelling. The modes of exchange built into such systems constitute a form of market, albeit imperfect.

1. *Strategy.*   The issue, therefore, is whether the spiral of urban deterioration—fueled by the stigma of negative neighborhood coding and residents' use of their option of exit—can be forestalled or halted by efforts to preserve or maintain community order. Two issues emerge. First, do communities require external support in maintaining order? While the expectation of the community defense paradigm was that communities would maintain their own social order, the problems of organizing defensive groups in high-crime neighborhoods lead to the question whether the citizens of high-crime communities ought to receive more support and resources for the preservation of order from the wider community. In other words, does the effective operation of the horizontal dimension of orderly communal relations need to be supported by greater resources for control distributed via the vertical dimension of power? Second, if high crime levels are the end product of a sequence of community deterioration, stimulated by low-level disorders, then would a *preventive* approach be better directed at reducing disorder rather than targeting serious crime?

2. *Implementation.*   The maintenance of public order may require the reintroduction of low-level "functional surveillance" and environmental care. In the Netherlands, the introduction of "social caretakers" onto selected public housing estates—who place more emphasis on patrolling and surveillance in addition to cleaning and maintenance—brought about a decline in nuisance, disorder, and crime in semipublic areas of estates, particularly where there was also a high density of social caretakers to residents (reducing the anonymity of local offenders), combined with measures to restrict access to buildings (Hesseling 1992). Similar effects are claimed for receptionists and "concierges" in public housing blocks in Britain (National Association for the Care and Resettlement of Offenders 1989; Safe Neighbourhoods Unit 1993*b*). Improved caretaking and maintenance services were also accompanied by reductions in environmental nuisance and disorder in the PEP experiment, described above (Foster and Hope 1993; Glennerster and Turner 1993).

Order maintenance is also seen as a central aim of community and "problem-oriented" policing initiatives (Moore 1992). Community policing measures in Houston seem to have reduced residents' perceptions of disorder and crime and to have increased their satisfaction with their residential environment (Skogan 1990). In particular, it would seem that when police officers concentrate effort on small-scale locales—for example, individual streets or apartment blocks—and adopt a preventive, collaborative approach with local residents and officials from other agencies, they may well be able to bring the level of disorder under control, even when it is associated with drug sales (Hope 1994). In these examples it appears that disorder can be controlled by restoring order at street level through the efforts of officials who have taken responsibility for small patches of urban space. In this respect, their efforts may have supplemented or restored the "natural" street order celebrated by Jacobs (1962) but that no longer seems to exist in many urban spaces.

3. *Evaluation.* Nevertheless, there is little evidence currently that the control of disorder at the micro level leads to a reduction in serious crime, despite its effect on residents' perceptions of community safety and satisfaction. Moreover, difficulties emerge with regard to the *source* of disorder itself. First, the PEP experiment found that although improved maintenance, caretaking, and localized management seemed to reduce both perceived (Foster and Hope 1993) and actual (Glennerster and Turner 1993) levels of "environmental" disorder, such as graffiti, litter, damage, broken lighting, and wrecked vehicles, residents' perceptions of the seriousness of person-related disorder, such as disturbances from youths, noisy parties and neighbors, people mending vehicles in the street, insulting behavior in public, and public drinking and drug use, increased during the experiment (Foster and Hope 1993).[3] While few might object to cleaning up the environment and removing graffiti, there are issues both of doubtful legality and morality in applying a "clean-up" model to disorderly people, who may indeed be community residents. For example, aggressive police crackdowns on street disorder in Newark, New Jersey, seem to have bordered on the infringement of civil liberties without noticeable effect on residents' levels of fear (Skogan 1990).

Such doubts surround initiatives such as Operation Clean Sweep operated by the Chicago Police Department and Chicago Housing Authority (CHA), targeted on CHA-managed public housing blocks. The operation involves "ousting trespassers, inspecting all [dwelling] units, securing lobbies, installing security guards, and giving residents photo identity cards" that must be displayed to the guards on entering the building (Webster and Connors 1992, p. 2). Although such initiatives may bring much needed relief from the terrorism of violence suffered

---

[3] It is not clear whether this collective change of perception signifies a displacement of anxiety—or shift in tolerance—toward those disorders that remain or an actual increase in such disorders as a consequence of the changed social mix.

by residents (see Kotlowitz 1991), they may also risk turning those residents who are perceived to be the cause of disorder into "something like internal outsiders—unruly kids, marginal people—and the task is to get them off the streets and out of the picture" (Currie 1988, p. 281). Finally, periodic outbreaks of residential vigilantism and public discussion of private security patrols all point to the need for both further research and political debate into the broader question of community justice, which has so far been underresearched (Broadbent 1993).

The second difficulty with the order-preservation approach lies in the possibility that, despite its potential draconian scope, such measures may still not be sufficient to withstand the wider pressures affecting the stigmatization of neighborhoods within the operation of urban housing markets (Logan and Molotch 1987). Neither the English PEP nor the Dutch social caretaker experiments cited above managed to halt the high rate of tenant turnover on the estates studied. And if, as Taub, Taylor, and Dunham's (1984) research suggests, residents' perceptions of environmental conditions are mediated by the exchange values of the housing market, then perhaps efforts should be directed as much, if not more, toward neighborhood economic investment than to the control of overt disorder.

B. Protecting the Vulnerable

Unlike the U.S. National Crime Survey, the sampling structure and geodemographic coding of the British Crime Survey (BCS) can support contextual and areal analyses of victimization (see Sampson and Groves 1989). Combined with information on multiple victimization also provided by the BCS, such facilities have encouraged a new focus on the prevention of victimization within the community. Estimates from the BCS suggested that the residents of three types of social area, common in inner cities, with high prevalence rates for victimization—who comprised only 12 percent of the population—suffered particularly disproportionately from predatory crimes. This included 37 percent of all burglaries, 33 percent of all robberies and thefts from the person, and 23 percent of all thefts from motor vehicles that occurred in England and Wales (Hope and Hough 1988). Moreover, BCS analysis also suggests that the concentration of crime in such areas is due less to the prevalence of crime (that there were proportionately more victims among their resident populations) than to the *vulnerability* of victims living there (that each victim is likely to experience a much greater number of victimizations than would a victim in a lower-crime neighborhood) (Trickett et al. 1992). In other words, high-crime areas have many more *multiple* victims—who, of course, each contribute disproportionately to their community's higher crime rate.

1. *Strategy.* A strategy for reducing harm in high-crime communities by targeting effort on the disproportionate number of repeat or multiple victims who live there has been outlined recently by Farrell and Pease (1993; see also Farrell, in this volume). From a community prevention perspective, the approach may be considered to have a number of advantages. First, it may prove to be a cost-efficient strategy of allocating scarce preventive resources among community members, since prior victimization would seem predictive of future victimization.[4] Second, since repeat victimization is highest in the most crime-ridden areas, the approach automatically targets such areas for attention and may have a significant impact on aggregate crime levels, if successful. And third, the rate of repetition in a community offers a sensitive and realistic scheduling of the "dosage" of preventive effort, "drip feeding" crime prevention into communities. By definition, then, the approach should automatically target the most vulnerable in the highest-crime areas.

2. *Implementation.* A considerable range of initiatives targeted on multiple victims was brought to bear during the Burglary Prevention Project implemented on the Kirkholt Estate in Rochdale, England— an economically disadvantaged public housing estate of some 2,280 dwellings (Forrester et al. 1990; Pease 1992). These included upgrading the security of recently victimized dwellings, property marking, and removal of prepayment utilities meters (Forrester, Chatterton, and Pease 1988). The local Probation Service organized group work and community service programs for local offenders; this was accompanied by the establishment of a credit union for residents and a school-based program for local youth (Forrester et al. 1990). A particular innovation—in the light of the discussion of the community defense paradigm—was to establish 'cocoon' watching groups—small groups consisting only of the immediate neighbors of recently victimized households. Considerable success in organizing cocoon groups was re-

---

[4] This assumption derives from the often-noted, though little understood, observation that the frequency distribution of victimization, apparently howsoever measured, does not fit the assumptions of the Poisson process and from the empirical observation of the relatively short time interval between victimization events experienced by multiple victims (see Farrell, in this volume).

ported (Forrester et al. 1990), with seventy-five groups established on the estate within a seven-month period (Forrester, Chatterton, and Pease 1988). Cocoon groups may be successful, presumably, because they capitalize on personal vulnerability—dramatized by the recent victimization of a neighbor—and because the smallness of the group reinforces preexisting neighbor relations and increases the social pressure to participate, thus obviating the free-rider problem noted above (Hope 1988*b*).

3. *Evaluation.* The Kirkholt Burglary Prevention Project appears to have brought about a 75 percent reduction in the incidence rate of burglary on the estate over a three-year period, including an immediate and sustained reduction, to negligible proportions, of the rate of repeat victimization (Forrester, Chatterton, and Pease 1988). Nevertheless, as with many community prevention projects, it remains unclear what mechanisms were involved in achieving the reduction and, particularly, what might have been the precise contribution of the specific strategy of preventing repeat victimization. For instance, a wide range of other community development approaches and estate improvements—similar to those described in Section I—were also implemented on the Kirkholt estate before and during the Burglary Prevention Project (Safe Neighbourhoods Unit 1993*b*). Given the range, mix, and contemporaneity of these initiatives, it remains unclear to what extent the specific measures to prevent repeat victimization depended both for their implementation and for their impact on more general changes in community control that these other measures might have brought about. It is possible, for instance, that burglary could have been reduced on Kirkholt through the *cumulative* effect of all or many of the improvement measures, which together may have empowered residents, and more effectively integrated them with local institutions, in which the specific victim-prevention measures may have played an important though not necessarily unique or decisive part. For example, a combination of consistently responsive estate management, improved building security, and population stabilization on the London control estate in the PEP Experiment (see n. 1) also seems to have brought about an increase in residential surveillance and comparable, dramatic reductions (79 percent) in the burglary incidence rate over a similar three-year period (Hope and Foster 1992).

Unfortunately, weaknesses in the evaluative design of the Kirkholt Experiment obscure investigation of the mechanisms or sets of causal processes by which the reduction of repeat victimization and in the aggregate crime rate might have been brought about (Tilley 1993).[5] The observed concentration of repeat victimization in high-crime communities, and the possibility that high crime rates are due less to there being more victims than to there being more victimization (Trickett et al. 1992), constitutes one of the most intriguing—and potentially most important—criminological insights of the decade. Nonetheless, our current lack of knowledge about why this should be so hinders the design of community-oriented preventive measures based on it.

The problem turns, fundamentally, on the explanation of the concentration of victimization in high-crime communities. It might be argued that community differences in crime rates are due primarily to differences in the residential concentration of repeat victims—in other words, that there may be no collective community effect as such, merely the aggregation of vulnerable victims, on whom preventive resources should be targeted for maximum effect (Pease 1993). In this sense, area differences have no intrinsic significance other than as an effective predictor of where most victimization is likely to be located. Having located such areas, preventive action should be directed to halting the revictimization of individuals—or that occurring at crime hot spots within such areas. Measures would be individualized, aimed at reducing the likelihood of repetition by, for instance, altering the situational circumstances that occurred at the previous incident (Farrell and Pease 1993; see also Clarke, in this volume).[6] Even so, it is at present unclear whether "multiple" victims can be distinguished a priori from victims generally and, particularly, whether their "excess risk" is portable. If it were possible to find unique features that characterized potential repeat victims in advance, then it might also be possible to implement ways of affecting their residential concentration, in effect equalizing differences in areal crime rates (see Barr and Pease 1990). If, conversely, it turns out that repetition cannot be predicted prior to onset—and that the risk of repetition is situation dependent—then the strategy should be to focus on preventing repetition rather than onset (Farrell and Pease 1993).

---

[5] The general problem of evaluation in crime prevention—applicable equally to community prevention efforts—is discussed more fully in Ekblom and Pease (in this volume).

[6] The situational "bias" of this line of reasoning is reinforced by the observed short time interval of revictimization (see Farrell, in this volume), calling for a "quick and transient" response to the limited heightened risk period of revictimization (Farrell and Pease 1993).

However, to the contrary, it may be that the concentration of multiple victims in high-crime areas is not a product solely of individual vulnerability. Recently, Farrell (in this volume) has outlined a simple, formal model that suggests that if, according to routine activity theory, the "probability that a violation will occur at any specific time and place might be taken as a function of the convergence of likely offenders and suitable targets *in the absence of* capable guardians" (Cohen and Felson 1979, p. 590, emphasis added), then the excessive concentration of victimization in high-crime areas could be accounted for as a *multiplicative*—though not additive—effect of an increase (or higher level) of *all three* routine activity elements, but not of an increase in only one or two of the elements. Thus a greater concentration of vulnerable individuals would not necessarily lead to a concentration of victimization unless it occurred in circumstances where there was also a concentration of motivated offenders and an absence of guardianship. Consequently, in this interpretation, altering the vulnerability of victims alone might not reduce the concentration of victimization unless measures were taken simultaneously to reduce the motivation of offenders and to increase the capability of guardianship. Arguably, it may have been the *multiplicity* of interventions on the Kirkholt Estate (Forrester et al. 1990) that achieved this effect rather than those specifically targeted at repeat victims, even if the chief beneficiaries were those who might otherwise have been multiply victimized.

Nevertheless, the insight—that high-crime areas are so because of their rate of victimization rather than their rate of victims—is a novel one and opens up a range of research questions whose resolution might produce a radical reconceptualization of the theory of community crime prevention. In particular, the possibility that multiple victims are indicative of the routinized copresence of "criminogenic others" in space and time suggests ways in which recent social theorizing might enhance the development of routine activity theory (Bottoms and Wiles 1992)—though much more theoretical and empirical work needs to be done. A particular concern is to establish what it is that marks out some residents in a community as candidates for the repeated attention of offenders—presumably many of whom are coresidents. The form that prevention takes eventually will depend on whether the answer lies in the excessive vulnerability of some victims or in the motivation of those offenders who—in the perhaps apposite language of the school playground—repeatedly pick on them.

IV. Conclusion

What has been learned from over sixty years of effort? To return to a point made in the introduction to this essay, if community crime prevention was a cumulative science, it might be possible to gauge the answer in terms of progress made toward the utopia of crime-free communities. However, it should by now be apparent that the various community prevention paradigms of the past have arisen as responses to contemporary perceptions of the problem of crime in urban areas. To the extent that the urban crime problem is perceived to have changed, so the lessons of the past become less relevant for the future. Nevertheless, two general issues seem to have persisted. The first concerns the possibility of informal social control among residents of high-crime communities—that is, the significance of the horizontal dimension of community relations. The second concerns the dependence of local social order on the pressures and structures of the wider society— that is, the importance of the vertical dimension of community integration.

A. *Social Control in High-Crime Communities*

If there has been any continuity in this field, it is the communitarianism inherent in the legacy of Shaw and McKay—the belief that the solution to neighborhood crime problems can be achieved primarily through the self-help efforts of residents. In the community-organizing approach this involved the building of indigenous local institutions to serve as agencies of socialization for local youth. The tenant involvement approach stressed the creation of representative self-management of the residential environment. The strategy of resource capture saw the political mobilization of communities as a strategy for gaining more resources. More recently, the community defense paradigm has focused on organizing collective self-defense against predators. Efforts to preserve order have been justified to preserve informal relations within communities, while the adoption of "cocoon" watch groups in the prevention of repeat victimization seeks to build on neighborly protective self-interest. The common theme in all these efforts has been that residents should organize collectively to create or support institutions for dealing with the crime problems that beset their residential space. Braithwaite (1989, p. 85) defines a "communitarian society" as combining a "dense network of individual interdependencies with strong cultural commitments to mutuality of obligation." Interdependence and mutual obligation together provide the resource for social control; not only are members of such a community likely to be subject to shame or exclusion if they individually transgress (Braithwaite 1989) but also each individual feels confident to enlist the support of others to act on deviants and maintain the norms of the community (Kornhauser 1978). Nevertheless, it has proven difficult to initiate community organization against crime in high-crime areas and difficult to sustain involvement in low-crime areas. Does this mean that "communitarianism" does not work?

Part of the problem may be that the communitarian approach sets up communal solidarity as the sole mode of social control for residential areas. Yet, social order in affluent suburban communities may be maintained by its opposite, a strategy of social avoidance, or *moral minimalism* (Baumgartner 1988). Weak ties between residents in suburban areas, and high residential mobility, can mean that conflicts between residents are transient; residents possess little information about each other and so cannot exploit such knowledge, for better or worse; residents have multiple activity groups that divert their attention away from conflict; and residents lack the support from neighbors for vengeance or intimidation (Baumgartner 1988). Moral minimalism therefore works because the sources and opportunities for conflict among residents are avoided—privacy rather than communalism would seem to preserve the order of the suburb. Is moral minimalism a better strategy for social control?

Perhaps neither undiluted communitarianism nor moral minimalism is appropriate given one of the key defining features of high-crime communities—that residents are frequently victimized by coresidents. The ecological correlation between offender and offense rates (Bottoms and Wiles 1986) suggests that, at the extremes at least, highly victimized neighborhoods are also likely to have high rates of offenders among their residents, many of whom do most of their offending in their home locality (Brantingham and Brantingham 1984). In any event, the British Crime Survey found that the majority of residents living in the poorest, most victimized council housing areas *believed* that most offenders were local people (Hope 1986b). Nevertheless, the approaches reviewed above differ in the way they have considered the relationship between putative victimized and offending groups; particularly whether each was thought to be part of the community. The approaches described in Section I—community organizing, tenant involvement, resource capture—remained silent as to the identity and location of the victim group but saw offenders—usually adolescents—as part of the community. In contrast, the approaches described in Sections II and III—community defense, preserving order, protecting the vulnerable—saw offenders implicitly as outsiders, while community members were seen as the potential victims from primarily external predation.

The avoidance strategy of the suburbs would seem to operate mostly against strangers. Suburbanites may be extremely averse to any contact with strangers; they may readily invoke police or private security to deal with "suspicious persons" (Baumgartner 1988); their environments may be difficult for strangers to penetrate, physically and symbolically (Greenberg, Rohe, and Williams 1985); and their emphasis on privacy provides outsiders with few opportunities to gain access to their persons or property (Baumgartner 1988). Yet, when potential predators live in close proximity—and "belong" to the locality—potential victims may find simple avoidance hard. Understandably, they may be wary about trusting their fellow residents, who might turn out to be predatory, and reluctant to embrace their potential victimizers in reintegrative activities, desirable though that may be for a wider social order (Braithwaite 1989).

Surprisingly, despite its intrinsic interest and significance for local social order, there has been little systematic research on the nature of intracommunal offending and on how residents adjust their lives to it. It is possible, however, that *social networks within communities* might mediate intracommunal offending (Krohn 1986). As with the communitarian ideal, internal networks may play an important role in the prevention of local youth crime. Sampson and Groves (1989), for instance, have presented some empirical evidence from the British Crime Survey—consistent with Kasarda and Janowitz's (1974) "systemic model" of community organization (see also Bursik and Grasmick 1993)—suggesting that the extent of community friendship ties is inversely related to levels of victimization. Sampson (1985) also suggests that a high proportion of divorced or working single mothers in a neighborhood reduces informal social control because the likelihood of significant adults noticing and acting on the delinquency of neighborhood youth is reduced (Sampson 1987a). Such control is not so much a matter of the supervision of individual delinquents by their own parents as of the presence of a *network of families* that collectively sustains an infrastructure of supervision and normative reinforcement. Thus, Sampson and Groves (1989) report that community rates of family disruption are positively related to the prevalence of disorderly teenage groups. A community's network of parental support may be its "social capital"—a resource available to individual families for safe-guarding their own children's conduct, and an important, informal mechanism for socialization (Sampson 1992).

An unfortunate consequence of the general failure of Shaw and McKay to define "disorganization" (Bursik 1988) has been to foster an image of high-crime neighborhoods as an atomized collection of iso-lated households. Yet, ethnographic research in slum neighborhoods has often found strong primary links between residents (see Whyte 1955; Suttles 1968; Merry 1981; Horowitz 1983) and has repeatedly failed to find evidence of widespread interpersonal isolation (Freuden-berg 1986). The reciprocity of acquaintanceship, particularly among neighbors, would seem to be a powerful incentive for all but those living the most transitory lives, even if the qualitative content of neigh-borly relations is fairly minimal (Bulmer 1986). Social networks in a neighborhood are also an important means of communicating informa-tion about crime and mediating its effects on perceptions of community safety (Skogan and Maxfield 1981). Some residents of high-crime neighborhoods may have been able to practice a hybrid form of order-maintenance—a sort of group minimalism—by creating a segmented social order in their neighborhoods (Suttles 1968).

Ethnographic research shows how residents in high-crime areas adopt interpersonal strategies and affiliations, based mostly on primary relationships, to ensure their own safety, well-being, and prospects (Suttles 1968; Kornhauser 1978; Merry 1981; Anderson 1990; Furs-tenberg 1993). Likewise, community studies on British council estates have shown a fragmentation on cultural lines, especially the self-imposed insularity of the "respectable" working class (Reynolds 1986; Bottoms, Mawby, and Xanthos 1989; Foster and Hope 1993). The essence of such group formation is that it serves to define who can be trusted and who may be dangerous (Merry 1981), acting as a buffer to insulate individuals from potential predators and malign influences, especially among those living close by. Yet, we know very little about the extent to which offending and victimization within communities is mediated by social networks among residents. For instance, the rela-tively flat gradient in victim prevalence rates between low- and high-crime areas (discussed in Sec. III) suggests, possibly, that the victim population in any community may have finite limits. Yet, it is not clear whether the offending population is coterminous with it, while other groups remain virtually insulated from local crime.

It is possible that there may coexist subpopulations, even within high-crime communities, some of whom are heavily involved with crime—as victims or offenders—while others remain relatively immune. For example, the greater likelihood of victimization from property crime of households headed by female single parents (Smith and Jarjoura 1989) may be due to their greater likelihood of being victimized by people personally associated with them (Maxfield 1987). Similarly, changes during the PEP experiment on the Hull estate (described in Sec. I above) served, simultaneously, to widen delinquent and adult offending networks, to reduce victimization in some areas of the estate while concentrating it in other areas, and on particular social groups, while residents in other parts—comprising about 21 percent of households—retained low levels of victimization throughout the experiment (Foster and Hope 1993). This fragmented pattern of responses to change is complex, particularly calling into question the image of the community as a unitary phenomenon that will change uniformly in response to specific policy inputs. Much more work is needed to explore how intracommunal networks mediate the effects of external policy changes on patterns of intracommunal offending.

Though the impulse to ensure personal safety may lead to the formation of close-knit but fragmentary social networks, this does not mean that such a solution may be particularly effective in promoting safety or reducing crime within the community as a whole. Even in situations where the mosaic of networks appears relatively stable (Suttles 1968), segmentation may render the community incapable of *self-organization*. Regardless of whether individual groups—or even individual families (see Furstenberg 1993)—are "organized," they are unlikely to expand to recruit others or to form bridges with other groups both because they are predicated on mistrust and because their introverted nature provides few opportunities to form ties with members of other groups. Without such linkages, secondary organizations are unlikely to be extended across a community (Granovetter 1973). As with cocoon watch groups (Sec. III above), physical propinquity (Suttles 1972) and the reciprocity of neighborliness (Bulmer 1986) may provide the occasion for network formation, yet external impetus would appear to be needed in order to federate such groups into a broader community organization.

Why do victims of internal offending have neither formal nor informal redress against predation from those with whom they live? Why is the repetitive victimization of residents most common in those areas that are likely to have higher proportions of internal offenders (Sec. III above)? Again, the lack of research on intracommunal offending offers little help in answering what are surely key issues in the development of social control in high-crime communities. Two directions offer themselves for research and policy development, each reflecting the distinction between communitarianism and moral minimalism. One direction would be to continue further with the communitarian ideal of creating an institutional structure that overcomes victims' desires to exclude or avoid internal offenders, and offenders' lack of scruple about victimizing their coresidents. In order to do this, however, it would be necessary to create conditions of interdependence and mutuality among community members (Braithwaite 1989). Past efforts provide little comfort as to how and whether this can be achieved.

The other direction would be to pursue the line of inquiry suggested by Black (1983, 1984) where much crime is seen as the redress of grievance, real or imagined, for which alternative means are unavailable—including lack of access to the agencies of both criminal and civil law. Since the preservation of privacy in the strategy of moral minimalism is underpinned by easy and swift access to the protection of law (Baumgartner 1988), an approach that made legal and other forms of conflict and grievance resolution available to high-crime communities might divert those interactions between community members that might otherwise lead to criminal actions. That policy thinking, as far as it can be discerned, has failed to address either possibility in respect to high-crime communities calls for considerable rethinking of the purpose and possibility of community crime prevention.

In sum, another part of the legacy of Shaw and McKay, which may no longer be helpful for community crime prevention, is the failure to recognize other modalities of social order than the polarity between communitarianism and disorganization. Nevertheless, neither have the political or moral implications of seeking to implant strategies of segmentation or moral minimalism into high-crime communities been considered. The dilemma—that neither research nor policy has yet resolved—is whether to enforce a segmented order—with the likely consequence of social exclusion of the deviant or troublesome and a reification of their deviance (Cohen 1985)—or to strive for the integration of deviants into their communities (see Braithwaite 1989)—even if, in the short run at least, this might be more to the benefit of the deviant than to those who are subject to their deviance.

B. The Political Economy of Prevention

Throughout this essay, the operation of urban markets, primarily in housing and employment, has been identified as a crucial context both for the development of community crime problems and for community-based responses. The community-organizing approach of the Chicago Area Project was framed to counter the social imperfections of the dynamic growth of the urban market (Shaw and McKay 1969), while more recent studies of Chicago (Bursik and Webb 1982; Taub, Taylor, and Dunham 1984; Bursik 1986), Los Angeles (Schuerman and Kobrin 1986), and Sheffield (Bottoms, Claytor, and Wiles 1992) have each demonstrated how community crime rates, and resident responses, are shaped by supply-and-demand factors of land use and housing in the city. A general sequence would appear to be that changes occurring in local urban markets, often stimulated by private or public corporate investment decisions (Taub, Taylor, and Dunham 1984; Logan and Molotch 1987), alter prevailing land uses (Schuerman and Kobrin 1986) or residential preferences (Taub, Taylor, and Dunham 1984), which then engender changes in population composition (Bottoms and Wiles 1986; Bursik 1986), which consequently changes the internal culture of residential areas (Bottoms, Mawby, and Xanthos 1989), perhaps often despite community-based effort (Foster and Hope 1993). Change in the dynamics of the urban market, in which individual communities are located, thus has a major impact on their levels of crime and disorder, mediated by the employment and housing opportunities available to both current and prospective residents.

Partly because of the inheritance of communitarianism, prevention strategies have focused on the promotion of the "use values" of residential areas—that is, the benefits to residents that flow from neighborly reciprocity, informal support networks, a sense of identity, and, importantly, security and trust (Logan and Molotch 1987). Such efforts are often threatened, however, by the dynamics of a neighborhood's "exchange value"—how properties (and by extension the community itself) are valued by prospective residents, landlords, and investors (Logan and Molotch 1987). One enduring part of the legacy of Shaw and McKay is the finding that the urban market affects the internal social order of communities through its impact on the rate and type of residential mobility (Kornhauser 1978; Sampson and Groves 1989; Bursik and Grasmick 1993). It is possible then that intervention and investment in the urban market to develop the exchange value of particular residential areas would bring about a reduction in crime. However, before the implementation of ways of controlling or mediating the impact of mobility, it remains necessary, among other things, to account for Taylor and Covington's (1988) seemingly anomalous finding that gentrifying *as well as* pauperizing neighborhoods suffer increasing violence during the process of change. This points again to the problem of intracommunal offending. For example, it would be necessary to ascertain whether newcomers were being victimized by current residents, current residents were increasing their victimization of one another as social controls broke down following the departure of stable community members, or whether newcomers were importing their own violence with them. Each situation would have different consequences for social control, but these alternative possibilities also illustrate the necessity of understanding how the internal dynamics of individual communities (the horizontal dimension) are related to their position in the wider market (the vertical dimension).

Research studies along the lines of those by Taub, Taylor, and Dunham (1984) and Bottoms and Wiles (1986) would help in understanding how to influence the linkage between exchange and use values so as to reduce crime rates (Hope 1986*a*). Ironically, much of the organized activity of affluent suburban communities is concerned, in one way or another, with the promotion of exchange values (Logan and Molotch 1987). "Preservationist" community groups (Skogan 1988) are likely to adopt community defense models (Sec. II above). Homeowners, those particularly sensitized to exchange values (Taub, Taylor, and Dunham 1984), have been shown to be more likely to participate in community prevention efforts. The PEP intervention is in part intended to address the problem of difficult-to-let estates. Factors affecting exchange values therefore would seem as important for community crime prevention as those that might affect use values. An emphasis on use values tends to direct attention to the intrinsic qualities of specific neighborhoods, while a concern for exchange values directs attention equally to the position that a neighborhood has within the urban system (Bursik and Grasmick 1993).

While the nature of recent transformations of the advanced economies is complex and continuing (see Harvey 1989; Lash and Urry 1994), two key ecological processes occurring within urban systems are affecting the exchange values of communities. The first is *counterurbanization*, the general movement of jobs and populations out of the older cities into more rural areas or into metropolitan regions of considerable size and disparity (Champion 1989). The second is the *concentra-*

tion of poverty in the older urban areas—the increasing tendency for the poorest segment of the population to live in communities of general poverty and isolation from wider social and economic institutions (Wilson 1991*a*, 1991*b*). Both processes have differing consequences for community crime prevention.

1. *Counterurbanization.* The conditions of modernity would appear to have "lifted out" social relations from the close proximity of the residential environment (Giddens 1990). The spatial mobility provided by automobiles—as both cause and consequence of counterurbanization—means that the activity space for counterurban residents no longer necessarily spans the area within walking distance from home but a wide and diverse region. In particular, this provides potential offenders with the capacity to evade the control of their families and neighbors and to commit crimes far afield (Felson 1994). Moreover, because location of residence is not tied necessarily to location of employment, the exchange value dynamics of the urban market may be creating a highly socially and economically segregated set of communities within a new counterurban suburbia (Logan and Molotch 1987). None of these processes would suggest that communitarian strategies would be successful in maintaining order in the new counterurban environments; though nor, it seems, are they necessary. Since temporary access to such areas is dependent on spatial mobility (Felson 1987), and permanent access dependent on earnings and income, they may be becoming less accessible to low-income offenders who lack the means of spatial and social mobility. The reconfiguration of counterurbia may be producing a sociospatial exclusion of the "dangerous poor" (Davis 1990; see Lash and Urry 1994).

Braithwaite (1993) argues that individuals are provided in modern societies with a wide range of reference groups and communities of interest, based mainly on occupation, who could as effectively provide shame and reintegration as communal villages. Thus the residential area no longer needs to provide controls based on interdependence and mutuality. If, therefore, the civic and moral space of the suburb becomes hollowed out, then such controls as may be needed may be found simply in the strategy of moral minimalism. Paradoxically, if social control in the counterurban suburb rests on the exclusion of strangers through strategies of privacy and avoidance, then the community defense model might indeed promote social control there, provided less emphasis was given to communitarianism and more to establishing effective communication between individual householders and the police (or private security), who would then—with a commensurate allocation of resources—be able to provide more efficient guardianship of the residential space. The way in which Neighbourhood Watch has often been described in British police circles as the "eyes and ears of the police" would suggest that this point is well taken intuitively (see McConville and Shepherd 1992). Finally, such efforts in the counterurban community would probably need to be underpinned by concerted action to maintain exchange values—and to attract inward investment—in order to insure against the threat of competition, declining exchange values and, therefore, of destabilizing mobility (Davis 1990). Of course, the implications for the wider public good of this evolving social order of counterurbia have as yet to be scrutinized in political debate.

2. *Poverty Concentration.*   Counterurbanization, however, may be selective, creating a spatial mismatch between the movement of employment out of the inner city and the spatial and skills immobility of inner-city residents (Wilson 1987). Analysis of the 1984 British Crime Survey suggests that three characteristics of social areas, derived from the 1981 United Kingdom Census, stand out particularly as distinguishing high crime (incidence) rate areas: the male unemployment rate; the proportion of the population who were children aged five to fifteen years; and, importantly, a composite variable including high proportions of young adults (aged sixteen to twenty-four years), single-adult households (with and without dependent children), and households not living in self-contained accommodation (Osborn, Trickett, and Elder 1992). In parallel with American research, the high-crime area is defined increasingly by *the linkage between economic conditions and community social structure.* For instance, a high rate of male joblessness appears to influence residential community crime rates primarily through its effect on the disruption of families and on family formation among residents, indexed particularly by the rate of female-headed households with children (Sampson 1985; Messner and Sampson 1991). Moreover, the British Crime Survey suggests that in England and Wales both property crime and, to a lesser extent, personal crime have become more inequitably distributed between areas between 1982 and 1988, largely due to an increasing inequality in the rate of victimization rather than in the rate of victims (Trickett, Ellingworth, and Pease 1992).

In broad terms, then, high-crime communities in both Britain and America now seem to be characterized increasingly by concentrations of jobless young men and by single-adult households, often headed by women and often with dependent children. If the dynamics of postindustrial societies are redistributing and concentrating economic inequality among residential areas—particularly affecting the spatial concentration of the young poor (see Foster and Hope 1993)—then it may be that such community resource deprivation is being accompanied (in Britain) by an increasing spatial and interpersonal inequality of victimization and (in the United States) by high rates of violence and homicide (Land, McCall, and Cohen 1990; Messner and Golden 1992). In other words, the increasing inequality of victimization between communities may be characterized in both societies by an increase in the frequency and severity of harm, arguably as an expression of an increasing intensity of intracommunal offending.

Past approaches, particularly based on voluntary communitarianism, will not be sufficient to address these problems. If violence results from youth's detachment from institutions providing socialization and economic opportunity (Kornhauser 1978), then Cloward and Ohlin's (1960) analysis of slum youth's delinquency finds some contemporary support in recent American ethnographic research—which suggests that inner-city black youth are more likely to turn to street robbery and drug dealing in their own neighborhoods as the only source of supplemental income in their middle to late teens, given a lack of access to job markets and networks and the social and physical isolation of their communities (Sullivan 1989; Anderson 1990). The experience of the federal Violent Juvenile Offender Research and Development Program (1981–86) in high-crime neighborhoods of six American cities suggested that the real problem in these neighborhoods was not so much an absence of potential for community cohesion and leadership as that they were underserved by the social service network and were economically worse-off than other areas (Fagan 1987). What implications do these findings have for the promotion of social order?

If moral minimalism is underscored by residents' access to resources of law and to employment-based communities of interest, then the intracommunal offending, underpolicing, and chronic joblessness of areas of concentrated poverty deny residents access to these resources, and of recourse to moral minimalism. Aside from material need, long-term unemployment excludes people from the wider society and limits their horizons to the local community. As witnessed during the PEP experiment, the residential concentration of the young poor fostered a "subterranean community" both victimized and victimizing (Foster and

Hope 1993). Thus the residential concentration of youth poverty seems to be creating communities with concentrations of high-risk offenders—often young, jobless men—and multiple victims—often female heads of households (Genn 1988), linked together in a powerless, victimizing-and-victimized culture of primary relationships (see Campbell 1993).

An appropriate crime prevention strategy might therefore start by addressing the subterranean nexus of youth poverty and crime emerging within areas where crime and poverty are concentrating. Nearly two decades of policy attention to community defense and the preservation of order have diverted attention from the problem of youth crime in high-crime communities (Curtis 1988), a problem that was the primary focus of earlier prevention paradigms but which has received little attention from researchers and policy analysts, even while the intensity of crime and drug problems has increased in urban neighborhoods. Research and policy development, especially in Britain, is needed urgently to recapture the aims of earlier approaches and to recast them in the context of a contemporary urban political economy.

Yet, unlike the earlier efforts, prevention needs to deal with two major features of high-crime communities. First, areas with concentrations of offenders are also those with concentrations of victims that intracommunal relations (the horizontal dimension) may be victimizing. Thus efforts to mobilize resources of support and control for youth must be accompanied by efforts to protect the fearful, vulnerable, and victimized if the destabilization of community is to be arrested. Otherwise, residents will continue to exercise their power of "exit" where they can. But nor should the protection of the vulnerable have the unintended consequence of excluding the deviant—which the counterurban strategy of moral minimalism implies—or of escalating the criminality of offenders.

Second, community crime prevention needs to address the possibility that informal resources for prevention within contemporary high-crime residential communities are being undermined by their increasing economic, social, and political isolation from the rest of society (Wilson 1987). One of the significant legacies of Shaw and McKay's work was to highlight the importance of social institutions in holding communities together and, especially, in socializing the young. Institutions are able to function in this way because they are a two-way conduit between the community and the wider sources of wealth and power (Kornhauser 1978). For Shaw and McKay, the process of urban growth had moved faster than the development of social institutions; the task of CAP was thus to intervene to ameliorate the defects of the urban market. Now, the processes of urban decline and global economic change have undermined those fragile institutions that preserved order and fostered citizenship, albeit precariously, in the mid-century working-class community (Clarke 1987). Thus the second direction for future development is to explore the possibility of a new institutional structure of order (Dahrendorf 1985) in residential areas that have seen a concentration of crime. Disintegrating urban communities may need significant social investment in their institutional infrastructure to offset the powerful tendencies of destabilization of poor communities within the urban free-market economy (Logan and Molotch 1987). Unlike in the emerging counterurban social order, the privatized option of moral minimalism will not be sufficient; the spatial horizons of the poor, and their arena of daily life, are still rooted in their residential locality, and localized, community-based solutions are still necessary.

Of course, more research and policy analysis is necessary to develop such a strategy. Whether this happens, however, depends primarily on political will. As this essay has sought to show, community prevention models have arisen as political responses to the imperatives of contemporary urban problems. It remains to be seen whether, and to what degree, governments in the advanced economies of North America and Europe choose to respond to the imperatives of counterurbanization or to those of poverty concentration.

REFERENCES

Anderson, Elijah. 1990. *Streetwise: Race, Class and Change in an Urban Community*. Chicago: University of Chicago Press.

Barr, R., and K. Pease. 1990. "Crime Placement, Displacement, and Deflection." In *Crime and Justice: A Review of Research*, vol. 12, edited by M. Tonry and N. Morris. Chicago: University of Chicago Press.

Baumgartner, M. P. 1988. *The Moral Order of a Suburb*. New York: Oxford University Press.

Bennett, T. 1989a. "The Neighbourhood Watch Experiment." In *Coming to Terms with Policing: Perspectives on Policy*, edited by R. Morgan and D. J. Smith. London: Routledge.

————. 1989*b*. "Factors Related to Participation in Neighborhood Watch Schemes." *British Journal of Criminology* 10:207–18.

————. 1990. *Evaluating Neighbourhood Watch*. Basingstoke: Gower.

Black, Donald. 1983. "Crime as Social Control." *American Sociological Review* 48:34–45.

————, ed. 1984. *Toward a General Theory of Social Control*. Vol. 2, *Selected Problems*. Orlando, Fla.: Academic Press.

Bottoms, A. E., A. Claytor, and P. Wiles. 1992. "Housing Markets and Residential Community Crime Careers." In *Crime, Policing and Place*, edited by D. J. Evans, N. R. Fyfe, and D. T. Herbert. London: Routledge.

Bottoms, A. E., R. I. Mawby, and P. Xanthos. 1989. "A Tale of Two Estates." In *Crime and the City: Essays in Memory of John Barron Mays*, edited by D. Downes. Basingstoke: Macmillan.

Bottoms, A. E., and P. Wiles. 1986. "Housing Tenure and Residential Community Crime Careers in Britain." In *Communities and Crime*, edited by A. J. Reiss, Jr., and M. Tonry. Vol. 8 of *Crime and Justice: A Review of Research*, edited by M. Tonry and N. Morris. Chicago: University of Chicago Press.

————. 1988. "Crime and Housing Policy: A Framework for Crime Prevention Analysis." In *Communities and Crime Reduction*, edited by T. Hope and M. Shaw. London: H.M. Stationery Office.

————. 1992. "Explanations of Crime and Place." In *Crime, Policing and Place*, edited by D. J. Evans, N. R. Fyfe, and D. T. Herbert. London: Routledge.

Braithwaite, J. 1989. *Crime, Shame and Reintegration*. Cambridge: Cambridge University Press.

————. 1993. "Shame and Modernity." *British Journal of Criminology* 33:1–18.

Brake, M., and C. Hale. 1992. *Public Order and Private Lives*. London: Routledge.

Brantingham, P., and P. Brantingham. 1984. *Patterns in Crime*. New York: Macmillan.

Bright, J. 1991. "Crime Prevention: The British Experience." In *The Politics of Crime Control*, edited by K. Stenson and D. Cowell. London: Sage.

Bright, J., and G. Petterson. 1984. *The Safe Neighbourhoods Unit Report*. London: National Association for the Care and Resettlement of Offenders.

Broadbent, P. 1993. "Policing—Private or Public: Conference Proceedings." Manchester: Manchester Metropolitan University Law School.

Bulmer, M. 1986. *Neighbors: The Work of Philip Abrams*. Cambridge: Cambridge University Press.

Burbidge, M. 1984. "British Public Housing and Crime: A Review." In *Coping with Burglary*, edited by R. Clarke and T. Hope. Boston: Kluwer-Nijhoff.

Bursik, R. J. 1986. "Ecological Stability and the Dynamics of Delinquency." In *Communities and Crime*, edited by A. J. Reiss, Jr., and M. Tonry. Vol. 8 of *Crime and Justice: A Review of Research*, edited by M. Tonry and N. Morris. Chicago: University of Chicago Press.

————. 1988. "Social Disorganization and Theories of Crime and Delinquency: Problems and Prospects." *Criminology* 26:519–51.

————. 1989. "Political Decision-Making and Ecological Models of Delinquency: Conflict and Consensus." In *Theoretical Integration in the Study of Deviance and Crime*, edited by S. F. Messner, M. D. Krohn, and A. E. Liska. Albany: State University of New York Press.

Bursik, R. J., and H. G. Grasmick. 1993. *Neighborhoods and Crime*. New York: Lexington.

Bursik, R. J., and J. Webb. 1982. "Community Change and Patterns of Delinquency." *American Journal of Sociology* 88:24–42.

Campbell, B. 1993. *Goliath: Britain's Dangerous Places*. London: Methuen.

Central Office of Information. 1989. *Practical Ways to Crack Crime: The Handbook*. 3d ed. London: Central Office of Information.

Champion, A. G., ed. 1989. *Counterurbanisation: The Changing Pace and Nature of Population Deconcentration*. London: Edward Arnold.

Cirel, P., P. Evans, D. McGillis, and D. Weitcomb. 1977. *An Exemplary Project: Community Crime Prevention Program, Seattle, Washington*. Washington, D.C.: National Institute of Law Enforcement and Criminal Justice.

Clarke, M. J. 1987. "Citizenship, Community and the Management of Crime." *British Journal of Criminology* 27:384–400.

Clarke, R. V., ed. 1992. *Situational Crime Prevention: Successful Case Studies*. New York: Harrow & Heston.

———. In this volume. "Situational Crime Prevention."

Clarke, R. V., and D. B. Cornish. 1985. *Crime Control in Britain: A Review of Policy Research*. Albany: State University of New York Press.

Clarke, R. V., and T. Hope, eds. 1984. *Coping with Burglary*. Boston: Kluwer-Nijhoff.

Clarke, R. V., and J. M. Hough, eds. 1980. *The Effectiveness of Policing*. Farnborough: Gower.

Clarke, R. V., and P. Mayhew, eds. 1980. *Designing out Crime*. London: H.M. Stationery Office.

Cloward, R. A., and L. E. Ohlin. 1960. *Delinquency and Opportunity*. Glencoe, Ill.: Free Press.

Cohen, L. E., and M. Felson. 1979. "Social Change and Crime Rate Trends: A Routine Activities Approach." *American Sociological Review* 44:588–608.

Cohen, S. 1985. *Visions of Social Control*. Cambridge: Polity Press.

Coleman, A. 1985. *Utopia on Trial*. London: Hilary Shipman.

Conklin, J. E. 1975. *The Impact of Crime*. New York: Basic.

Currie, E. 1988. "Two Visions of Community Crime Prevention." In *Communities and Crime Reduction*, edited by T. Hope and M. Shaw. London: H.M. Stationery Office.

Curtis, L. A. 1988. "The March of Folly: Crime and the Underclass." In *Communities and Crime Reduction*, edited by T. Hope and M. Shaw. London: H.M. Stationery Office.

Dahrendorf, R. 1985. *Law and Order: The Hamlyn Lectures*. London: Stevens.

Davis, Mike. 1990. *City of Quartz*. London: Verso.

Department of the Environment. 1981. *An Investigation of Difficult to Let Housing*. HDD Occasional Papers, March 1980. Vol. 1, *General Findings*, April

1980. Vol. 2, *Case Studies of Post War Estates*, May 1980. Vol. 3, *Case Studies of Pre War Estates*, May 1980. London: H.M. Stationery Office.

DuBow, F., and D. Emmons. 1981. "The Community Hypothesis." In *Reactions to Crime*, edited by D. A. Lewis. Beverly Hills, Calif.: Sage.

DuBow, F., and A. Podolefsky. 1982. "Citizen Participation in Community Crime Prevention." *Human Organization* 41:307–14.

Duffee, D. 1980. *Explaining Criminal Justice: Community Theory and Criminal Justice Reform*. Cambridge, Mass.: Oelgeschlager, Gunn, & Hain.

Eisenhower Foundation. 1990. *Youth Investment and Community Reconstruction: Street Lessons and Drugs and Crime for the Nineties*. Washington, D.C.: Eisenhower Foundation.

Ekblom, Paul, and Ken Pease. In this volume. "Evaluating Crime Prevention."

Fagan, J. 1987. "Neighborhood Education, Mobilization, and Organization for Juvenile Crime Prevention." *Annals of the American Acadamy of Political and Social Science* 494:54–70.

Farrell, G. In this volume. "Preventing Repeat Victimization."

Farrell, G., and K. Pease. 1993. *Once Bitten, Twice Bitten: Repeat Victimisation and Its Implications for Crime Prevention*. Crime Prevention Unit Series Paper no. 46. London: Home Office Police Department.

Feins, J. D. 1983. *Partnerships for Neighborhood Crime Prevention*. Washington, D.C.: National Institute of Justice.

Felson, M. 1987. "Routine Activities and Crime Prevention in the Developing Metropolis." *Criminology* 25:911–31.

———. 1994. *Crime and Everyday Life*. Thousand Oaks, Calif.: Pine Forge.

Field, S., and T. Hope. 1990. "Economics, the Consumer and Underprovision in Crime Prevention." In *Policing Organised Crime and Crime Prevention: British Criminology Conference 1989*, vol. 4, edited by R. Morgan. Bristol: Bristol Centre for Criminal Justice.

Finestone, H. 1976. *Victims of Change*. Westport, Conn.: Greenwood.

Forrest, R., and A. Murie. 1988. *Selling the Welfare State: The Privatisation of Public Housing*. London: Routledge.

Forrester, D., M. Chatterton, and K. Pease. 1988. *The Kirkholt Burglary Prevention Project: Rochdale*. Crime Prevention Unit Paper no. 13. London: Home Office.

Forrester, D., S. Frenz, M. O'Connell, and K. Pease. 1990. *The Kirkholt Burglary Prevention Project: Phase 2*. Crime Prevention Unit Paper no. 23. London: Home Office.

Foster, J., and T. Hope. 1993. *Housing, Community and Crime: The Impact of the Priority Estates Project*. Home Office Research Study no. 131. London: H.M. Stationery Office.

Fowler, F. J., M. E. McCalla, and T. W. Mangione. 1979. *Reducing Residential Crime and Fear: The Hartford Neighborhood Crime Prevention Program*. Washington, D.C.: National Institute of Justice.

Fowler, F. J., and T. W. Mangione. 1982. *Neighborhood Crime, Fear and Social Control: A Second Look at the Hartford Program*. Washington, D.C.: National Institute of Justice.

———. 1986. "A Three-pronged Effort to Reduce Crime and Fear of Crime:

The Hartford Experiment." In *Community Crime Prevention: Does It Work?* edited by D. P. Rosenbaum. Beverly Hills, Calif.: Sage.

Freudenberg, W. 1986. "The Density of Acquaintanceship: An Overlooked Variable in Community Research." *American Journal of Sociology* 92:27–63.

Fried, A. 1969. "The Attack on Mobilization." In *Community Development in the Mobilization for Youth Experience*, edited by H. H. Weissman. New York: Association Press.

Furstenberg, F. 1993. "How Families Manage Risk and Opportunity in Dangerous Neighborhoods." In *Sociology and the Public Agenda*, edited by W. J. Wilson. Newbury Park, Calif.: Sage.

Genn, H. 1988. "Multiple Victimisation." In *Victims of Crime: A New Deal?* edited by M. Maguire and J. Pointing. Milton Keynes: Open University Press.

Giddens, A. 1990. *The Consequences of Modernity.* Cambridge: Polity.

Glennerster, H., and T. Turner. 1993. *Estate Based Housing Management: An Evaluation.* Department of the Environment. London: H.M. Stationery Office.

Granovetter, M. S. 1973. "The Strength of Weak Ties." *American Journal of Sociology* 76:1360–80.

Greenberg, S. W., W. M. Rohe, and J. R. Williams. 1985. *Informal Citizen Action and Crime Prevention at the Neighborhood Level.* Washington, D.C.: National Institute of Justice.

Halsey, A. H. 1978. "Government against Poverty in School and Community." In *Social Policy Research*, edited by M. Bulmer. London: Macmillan.

Harvey, D. 1989. *The Condition of Postmodernity.* Cambridge, Mass.: Blackwell.

Heal, K., and G. Laycock. 1986. *Situational Crime Prevention: From Theory into Practice.* London: H.M. Stationery Office.

Hedges, A., A. Blaber, and B. Mostyn. 1980. *Community Planning Project: Cunningham Road Improvement Scheme Final Report.* London: Social and Community Planning Research.

Helfgot, J. H. 1981. *Professional Reforming: Mobilization for Youth and the Failure of Social Science.* Lexington, Mass.: D. C. Heath.

Hesseling, R. B. P. 1992. "Social Caretakers and Preventing Crime on Public Housing Estates." In *Dutch Penal Law and Policy 06, 05–1992.* The Hague: Ministry of Justice, Research and Documentation Center.

Hirsch, A. R. 1983. *Making the Second Ghetto.* Cambridge: Cambridge University Press.

Hope, T. 1984. "Building Design and Burglary." In *Coping with Burglary: Research Perspectives in Policy*, edited by R. Clarke and T. Hope. Boston: Kluwer-Nijhoff.

———. 1986a. "Crime, Community and Environment." *Journal of Environmental Psychology* 6:65–78.

———. 1986b. "Council Tenants and Crime." *Research Bulletin* 21:46–51. London: Home Office Research and Planning Unit.

———. 1988a. "Support for Neighbourhood Watch: A British Crime Survey Analysis." In *Communities and Crime Reduction*, edited by T. Hope and M. Shaw. London: H.M. Stationery Office.

————. 1988*b*. "Everybody Needs Good Neighbours: Support for Anti-Crime Community Organizations." Paper presented at the annual meeting of the American Society of Criminology, Chicago, November.

————. 1989. "Burglary and Vandalism in Schools: A Study of Theory and Practice in the Prevention of Crime." Ph.D. thesis, University of London, Faculty of Economics.

————. 1994. "Problem-oriented Policing and Drug Market Locations: Three Case Studies." In *Crime Prevention Studies*, vol. 2, edited by R. W. Clarke. Monsey, N.Y.: Criminal Justice Press.

Hope, T., and J. Foster. 1992. "Conflicting Forces: Changing the Dynamics of Crime and Community on a 'Problem' estate." *British Journal of Criminology* 32:488–504.

Hope, T., and M. Hough. 1988. "Area, Crime and Incivility: A Profile from the British Crime Survey." In *Communities and Crime Reduction*, edited by T. Hope and M. Shaw. London: H.M. Stationery Office.

Hope, T., and M. Shaw. 1988. "Community Approaches to Reducing Crime." In *Communities and Crime Reduction*, edited by T. Hope and M. Shaw. London: H.M. Stationery Office.

Horowitz, R. 1983. *Honor and the American Dream*. New Brunswick, N.J.: Rutgers University Press.

Hough, M., and P. Mayhew. 1985. *Taking Account of Crime*. Home Office Research Study no. 85. London: H.M. Stationery Office.

Husain, S. 1988. *Neighbourhood Watch in England and Wales: A Locational Analysis*. Crime Prevention Unit Paper no. 12. London: Home Office.

Jacobs, B. D. 1992. *Fractured Cities: Capitalism, Community and Empowerment in Britain and America*. London: Routledge.

Jacobs, J. 1962. *The Death and Life of Great American Cities*. Harmondsworth: Penguin.

Kahn, A. J. 1968. "From Delinquency Treatment to Community Development." In *The Uses of Sociology*, edited by P. F. Lazarsfeld, W. H. Sewell, and H. L. Wilensky. London: Weidenfeld & Nicolson.

Kasarda, J. D., and M. Janowitz. 1974. "Community Attachment in Mass Society." *American Sociological Reveiw* 39:328–39.

Kobrin, S. 1962. "The Chicago Area Project." In *The Sociology of Punishment and Correction*, edited by N. Johnston, L. Savitz, and M. Wolfgang. New York: Wiley.

Kornhauser, R. R. 1978. *Social Sources of Delinquency*. Chicago: University of Chicago Press.

Kotlowitz, A. 1991. *There Are No Children Here*. New York: Anchor.

Krohn, Marvin D. 1986. "The Web of Conformity: A Network Approach to the Explanation of Delinquent Behavior." *Social Problems* 33:S81–S93.

Land, K. C., P. L. McCall, and L. E. Cohen. 1990. "Structural Covariates of Homicide Rates." *American Journal of Sociology* 95:922–63.

Lash, S., and J. Urry. 1994. *Economies of Signs and Space*. London: Sage.

Lavrakas, P. J. 1981. "On Households." In *Reactions to Crime*, edited by D. A. Lewis. Beverly Hills, Calif.: Sage.

————. 1985. "Citizen Self-Help and Neighborhood Crime Prevention Policy." In *American Violence and Public Policy*, edited by L. A. Curtis. New Haven, Conn.: Yale University Press.

Lavrakas, P. J., and S. F. Bennett. 1989. *A Process and Impact Evaluation of the 1983–86 Neighborhood Anti-Crime Self-Help Program: Summary Report*. Evanston, Ill.: Northwestern University, Center for Urban Affairs and Policy Research.

Lavrakas, P. J., and W. J. Herz. 1982. "Citizen Participation in Neighborhood Crime Prevention." *Criminology* 20:479–98.

Lemann, N. 1991. *The Promised Land: The Great Black Migration and How It Changed America*. New York: Knopf.

Lewis, D. A. 1979. "Design Problems in Public Policy Development: The Case of the Community Anti-crime Program." *Criminology* 17:172–83.

Lewis, D. A., J. A. Grant, and D. P. Rosenbaum. 1988. *The Social Construction of Reform*. New Brunswick, N.J.: Transaction Books.

Lewis, D. A., and G. Salem. 1981. "Community Crime Prevention: An Analysis of a Developing Strategy." *Crime and Delinquency* 27:405–21.

Lindblom, C. E., and D. K. Cohen. 1979. *Usable Knowledge*. New Haven, Conn.: Yale University Press.

Lindsay, B., and D. McGillis. 1986. "Citywide Community Crime Prevention: An Assessment of the Seattle Program." In *Community Crime Prevention: Does It Work?* edited by D. P. Rosenbaum. Beverly Hills, Calif.: Sage.

Logan, J. H., and H. Molotch. 1987. *Urban Fortunes: The Political Economy of Place*. Berkeley, Calif.: University of California Press.

Lurigio, A. J., and D. P. Rosenbaum. 1986. "Evaluation Research in Community Crime Prevention: A Critical Look at the Field." In *Community Crime Prevention: Does It Work?* edited by D. P. Rosenbaum. Beverly Hills, Calif.: Sage.

McConville, M., and D. Shepherd. 1992. *Watching Police, Watching Communities*. London: Routledge.

McGahey, R. M. 1986. "Economic Conditions, Neighborhood Organization, and Urban Crime." In *Communities and Crime*, edited by A. J. Reiss, Jr., and M. Tonry. Vol. 8 of *Crime and Justice: A Review of Research*, edited by M. Tonry and N. Morris. Chicago: University of Chicago Press.

McPherson, M., and G. Silloway. 1981. "Planning to Prevent Crime." In *Reactions to Crime*, edited by D. A. Lewis. Beverly Hills, Calif.: Sage.

Marris, P., and M. Rein. 1972. *Dilemmas of Social Reform*. Harmondsworth: Penguin.

Maxfield, Michael G. 1987. "Household Composition, Routine Activity and Victimization: A Comparative Analysis." *Journal of Quantitative Criminology* 3: 301–20.

Mayhew, P. 1977. "Defensible Space: The Current Status of a Crime Prevention Theory." *Howard Journal* 18:150–59.

Mayhew, P., R. V. G. Clarke, J. N. Burrows, J. M. Hough, and S. W. C. Winchester. 1979. *Crime in Public View*. Home Office Research Study no. 49. London: H.M. Stationery Office.

Mayhew, P., D. Elliott, and L. Dowds. 1989. *The 1988 British Crime Survey*. Home Office Research Study no. 111. London: H.M. Stationery Office.

Merry, S. E. 1981. *Urban Danger: Life in a Neighborhood of Strangers.* Philadelphia: Temple University Press.

Messner, S. F., and R. M. Golden. 1992. "Racial Inequality and Racially Disaggregated Homicide Rates: An Assessment of Alternative Theoretical Explanations." *Criminology* 30:421–45.

Messner, S. F., and R. J. Sampson. 1991. "The Sex Ratio, Family Disruption, and Rates of Violent Crime: The Paradox of Demographic Structure." *Social Forces* 69:693–713.

Moore, M. H. 1992. "Problem-solving and Community Policing." In *Modern Policing,* edited by M. Tonry and N. Morris. Vol. 15 of *Crime and Justice: A Review of Research,* edited by M. Tonry. Chicago: University of Chicago Press.

Moynihan, D. P. 1969. *Maximum Feasible Misunderstanding.* New York: Free Press.

National Association for the Care and Resettlement of Offenders. 1989. *Crime Prevention and Community Safety: A Practical Guide for Local Authorities.* London: National Association for the Care and Resettlement of Offenders.

Newman, O. 1973. *Defensible Space.* London: Architectural Press.

———. 1980. *Community of Interest.* Garden City, N.Y.: Anchor/Doubleday.

Newman, O., and K. A. Franck. 1980. *Factors Influencing Crime and Instability in Urban Housing Developments.* Washington, D.C.: National Institute of Justice.

Olsen, M. 1965. *The Logic of Collective Action.* New York: Schocken.

Osborn, D. R., A. Trickett, and R. Elder. 1992. "Area Characteristics and Regional Variates as Determinants of Area Property Crime Levels." *Journal of Quantitative Criminology* 8:265–85.

Painter, K. 1992. "The Impact of Street Lighting on Crime and Fear of Crime: Summary of Methods and Key Findings From an Ongoing Research Programme in the United Kingdom." Paper presented at the annual meeting of the American Society of Criminology, New Orleans, November.

Park, R. E., E. W. Burgess, and R. D. McKenzie. 1925. *The City.* Chicago: University of Chicago Press.

Pease, K. 1992. "Preventing Burglary on a British Housing Estate." In *Situational Crime Prevention: Successful Case Studies,* edited by R. V. Clarke. New York: Harrow & Heston.

———. 1993. "Individual and Community Influences on Victimisation and Their Implications for Prevention." In *Integrating Individual and Ecological Aspects of Crime,* edited by D. P. Farrington, R. J. Sampson, and P.-O. H. Wikström. Stockholm: National Council for Crime Prevention.

Piven, F. F. 1969. "Politics and Planning: Mobilization as a Model." In *Justice and Law in the Mobilization for Youth Experience,* edited by H. H. Weissmann. New York: Association Press.

Piven, F. F., and R. A. Cloward. 1971. *Regulating the Poor.* New York: Pantheon.

Podolefsky, A. 1983. *Case Studies in Community Crime Prevention.* Springfield, Ill.: Charles C. Thomas.

Podolefsky, A., and F. DuBow. 1981. *Strategies for Community Crime Prevention.* Springfield, Ill.: Charles C. Thomas.

Power, A. 1984. *Local Housing Management*. London: Department of the Environment.

———. 1987*a*. *Property before People*. London: Allen & Unwin.

———. 1987*b*. *The PEP Guide to Local Management*. Vol. 1, *The PEP Model*. Vol. 2, *The PEP Experience*. Vol. 3, *Guidelines for Setting Up New Projects*. London: Department of the Environment.

———. 1988. "Housing, Community and Crime." In *Crime and the City: Essays in Memory of John Barron Mays*, edited by D. Downes. Basingstoke: Macmillan.

Poyner, B. 1983. *Design against Crime*. London: Butterworths.

President's Commission on Law Enforcement and Administration of Justice. 1967. *The Challenge of Crime in a Free Society*. Washington, D.C.: U.S. Government Printing Office.

Ramsay, M. 1991. *The Effect of Better Street Lighting on Crime and Fear: A Review*. Crime Prevention Unit Paper no. 29: London: Home Office.

Rein, M. 1976. *Social Science and Social Policy*. Harmondsworth: Penguin.

———. 1983. *From Policy to Practice*. London: Macmillan.

Reynolds, F. 1986. *The Problem Estate*. Aldershot: Gower.

Riley, D. 1992. Personal communication with author. London: Department of the Environment.

Rock, P. 1988. "Crime Reduction Initiatives on Problem Estates." In *Communities and Crime Reduction*, edited by T. Hope and M. Shaw. London: H.M. Stationery Office.

Roncek, Dennis W. 1981. "Dangerous Places: Crime and Residential Environment." *Social Forces* 60:74–96.

Rosenbaum, D. P., ed. 1986. *Community Crime Prevention: Does It Work?* Beverly Hills, Calif.: Sage.

———. 1987. "The Theory and Research behind Neighborhood Watch: Is It a Sound Fear and Crime Reduction Strategy?" *Crime and Delinquency* 33:103–43.

———. 1988*a*. "Community Crime Prevention: A Review and Synthesis of the Literature." *Justice Quarterly* 5:323–95.

———. 1988*b*. "A Critical Eye on Neighbourhood Watch: Does It Reduce Crime and Fear?" In *Communities and Crime Reduction*, edited by T. Hope and M. Shaw. London: H.M. Stationery Office.

Rosenbaum, D. P., D. A. Lewis, and J. A. Grant. 1986. "Neighborhood-based Crime Prevention: Assessing the Efficacy of Community Organizing in Chicago." In *Community Crime Prevention: Does It Work?* edited by D. P. Rosenbaum. Beverly Hills, Calif.: Sage.

Rubenstein, H., C. Murray, T. Motoyama, W. V. Rouse, and R. M. Titus. 1980. *The Link between Crime and the Built Environment*. Vol. 1. *The Current State of Knowledge*. Washington, D.C.: National Institute of Justice.

Safe Neighbourhoods Unit. 1993*a*. *Crime Prevention on Council Estates*. Department of the Environment. London: H.M. Stationery Office.

———. 1993*b*. *Housing and Safe Communities: An Evaluation of Recent Initiatives*. London: Safe Neighbourhoods Unit.

Sampson, R. J. 1985. "Neighborhood and Crime: The Structural Determinants of Personal Victimisation." *Journal of Research in Crime and Delinquency* 22:7–40.

———. 1987*a*. "Communities and Crime." In *Positive Criminology*, edited by M. R. Gottfredson and T. Hirschi. Newbury Park, Calif.:Sage.

———. 1987*b*. "Urban Black Violence: The Effect of Male Joblessness and Family Disruption." *American Journal of Sociology* 93:348–82.

———. 1992. "The Community Context of Violent Crime." In *Sociology and the Public Agenda*, edited by W. J. Wilson. Newbury Park, Calif.: Sage.

Sampson, R. J., and W. B. Groves. 1989. "Community Structure and Crime: Testing Social Disorganisation Theory." *American Journal of Sociology* 94: 774–802.

Schlossman, S., G. Zellman, and R. Shavelson. 1984. *Delinquency Prevention in South Chicago: A Fifty-Year Assessment of the Chicago Area Project*. Santa Monica, Calif.: RAND.

Schuerman, L., and S. Kobrin. 1986. "Community Careers in Crime." In *Communities and Crime*, edited by A. J. Reiss, Jr., and M. Tonry. Vol. 8 of *Crime and Justice: A Review of Research*, edited by M. Tonry and N. Morris. Chicago: University of Chicago Press.

Shapland, J., and J. Vagg. 1988. *Policing by the Public*. London: Routledge.

Shaw, C. R., and H. D. McKay. 1969. *Juvenile Delinquency and Urban Areas*. Chicago: University of Chicago Press.

Short, J. F. 1975. "The Natural History of an Applied Theory: Differential Opportunity and 'Mobilization for Youth.'" In *Social Policy and Sociology*, edited by N. J. Demerath, O. Larson, and K. F. Schuessler. New York: Academic Press.

Skogan, W. G. 1986. "Fear of Crime and Neighborhood Change." In *Communities and Crime*, edited by A. J. Reiss, Jr., and M. Tonry. Vol. 8 of *Crime and Justice: A Review of Research*, edited by M. Tonry and N. Morris. Chicago: University of Chicago Press.

———. 1988. "Community Organizations and Crime." In *Crime and Justice: A Review of Research*, vol. 10, edited by M. Tonry and N. Morris. Chicago: University of Chicago Press.

———. 1990. *Disorder and Decline: Crime and the Spiral of Decay in American Neighbourhoods*. New York: Free Press.

Skogan, W. G., and M. G. Maxfield. 1981. *Coping with Crime*. Beverly Hills, Calif.: Sage.

Smith, Douglas A., and R. Jarjoura. 1989. "Household Characteristics, Neighborhood Composition and Victimization Risk." *Social Forces* 68:621–40.

Sullivan, M. L. 1989. *Getting Paid: Youth Crime and Work in the Inner City*. Ithaca, N.Y.: Cornell University Press.

Suttles, Gerald D. 1968. *The Social Order of the Slum*. Chicago: University of Chicago Press.

———. 1972. *The Social Construction of Communities*. Chicago: University of Chicago Press.

Taub, R. P., D. G. Taylor, and J. D. Dunham. 1984. *Paths of Neighborhood Change*. Chicago: University of Chicago Press.

Taylor, R. B., and J. Covington. 1988. "Neighborhood Changes in Ecology and Violence." *Criminology* 26:553–89.

Taylor, R. B., and S. Gottfredson. 1986. "Environmental Design, Crime, and Prevention: An Examination of Community Dynamics." In *Communities and Crime*, edited by A. J. Reiss, Jr., and M. Tonry. Vol. 8 of *Crime and Justice: A Review of Research*, edited by M. Tonry and N. Morris. Chicago: University of Chicago Press.

Taylor, R. B., S. D. Gottfredson, and S. Brower. 1980. "The Defensibility of Defensible Space: A Critical Review and a Synthetic Framework for Future Research." In *Understanding Crime*, edited by T. Hirschi and M. Gottfredson. Beverly Hills, Calif.: Sage.

Tien, J, V. F. O'Donnell, A. Barnett, and P. B. Mirchandani. 1979. *Street Lighting Projects: National Evaluation Program, Phase 1 Report*. Washington, D.C.: National Institute of Law Enforcement and Criminal Justice.

Tilley, N. 1993. *After Kirkholt: Theory, Method, and Results of Replication Evaluations*. Crime Prevention Unit Series Paper no. 47. London: Home Office Police Department.

Titus, R. M. 1984. "Residential Burglary and the Community Response." In *Coping with Burglary: Research Perspectives in Policy*, edited by R. Clarke and T. Hope. Boston: Kluwer-Nijhoff.

Toby, J. 1957. "Social Disorganization and Stake in Conformity: Complementary Factors in the Predatory Behavior of Hoodlums." *Journal of Criminal Law, Criminology and Police Science* 48:12–17.

Trickett, A., D. Ellingworth, and K. Pease. 1992. "Changes in Area Inequality in Crime Victimisation, 1982–88: Findings from the British Crime Surveys." Unpublished manuscript. Manchester: University of Manchester, Department of Social Policy and Social Work.

Trickett, Alan, Denise R. Osborn, Julie Seymour, and Ken Pease. 1992. "What Is Different about High Crime Areas?" *British Journal of Criminology* 32:81–89.

Wallis, A., and D. Ford, eds. 1980. *Crime Prevention through Environmental Design: The Commercial Demonstration in Portland, Oregon*. Washington, D.C.: National Institute of Justice.

Ward, C., ed. 1973. *Vandalism*. London: Architectural Press.

Webster, B., and E. F. Connors. 1992. *The Police, Drugs, and Public Housing*. National Institute of Justice Research in Brief. Washington, D.C.: U.S Department of Justice.

Whyte, W. F. 1955. *Street Corner Society*. 2d ed. Chicago: University of Chicago Press.

Wildavsky, A. 1980. *The Art and Craft of Policy Analysis*. London: Macmillan.

Willmott, P., and A. Murie. 1988. *Polarisation and Social Housing*. London: Policy Studies Institute.

Wilson, J. Q. 1975. *Thinking about Crime*. New York: Basic.

———. 1978. "Social Science and Public Policy: A Personal Note." In *Knowledge and Public Policy: The Uncertain Connection*, edited by L. E. Lynn. Washington, D.C.: National Academy of Sciences.

———. 1985. *Thinking about Crime*. Rev. ed. New York: Vintage.

Wilson, J. Q., and R. J. Herrnstein. 1985. *Crime and Human Nature*. New York: Simon & Schuster.

Wilson, J. Q., and G. Kelling. 1982. "Broken Windows: The Police and Neighborhood Safety." *Atlantic Monthly* 249(3):29–38.

Wilson, W. J. 1987. *The Truly Disadvantaged*. Chicago: University of Chicago Press.

———. 1991*a*. "Studying Inner-City Social Dislocations: The Challenge of Public Agenda Research." *American Sociological Review* 56:1–14.

———. 1991*b*. "Public Policy Research and the Truly Disadvantaged." In *The Urban Underclass*, edited by C. Jencks and P. E. Peterson. Washington, D.C.: Brookings Institution.

Wirth, L. 1938. "Urbanism as a Way of Life." *American Journal of Sociology* 44:1–24.

Wootton, B. 1959. *Social Science and Social Pathology*. London: Allen & Unwin.

Ronald V. Clarke

Situational Crime Prevention

ABSTRACT

Situational prevention seeks to reduce opportunities for specific categories of crime by increasing the associated risks and difficulties and reducing the rewards. It is composed of three main elements: an articulated theoretical framework, a standard methodology for tackling specific crime problems, and a set of opportunity-reducing techniques. The theoretical framework is informed by a variety of "opportunity" theories, including the routine activity and rational choice perspectives. The standard methodology is a version of the action research paradigm in which researchers work with practitioners to analyze and define the problem, to identify and try out possible solutions, and to evaluate and disseminate the results. The opportunity-reducing techniques range from simple target hardening to more sophisticated methods of deflecting offenders and reducing inducements. Displacement of crime has not proved to be the serious problem once thought, and there is now increasing recognition that situational measures may result in some "diffusion of benefits" to crimes not directly targeted.

More than ten years ago, situational prevention was defined in a *Crime and Justice* essay as "comprising measures directed at highly specific forms of crime that involve the management, design, or manipulation of the immediate environment in as systematic and permanent a way as possible so as to reduce the opportunities for crime and increase its risks as perceived by a wide range of offenders" (Clarke 1983, p. 225). Such measures include familiar forms of "target hardening" and property marking; more sophisticated technology including intruder alarms

Ronald Clarke is dean of the School of Criminal Justice at Rutgers—The State University of New Jersey. Thanks are due to several commentators on the draft of this essay, especially to Lawrence Sherman, University of Maryland.

and electronic merchandise tags; the surveillance of specific locations provided by employees such as shop assistants and custodians and other attempts to capitalize on natural surveillance; exact fare systems, personal identification numbers for car radios, and a variety of other measures to reduce crime inducements; and some less easily categorized measures such as the use of public ordinances to control troublesome late-night entertainment spots and the separation of rival soccer fans into different enclosures at the stadium.

While the original definition requires little amendment (explicit mention would now also be made of reducing the rewards of crime), much else has changed. In particular, the theoretical basis of situational prevention has been strengthened with the development of routine activity and rational choice approaches, experience has accumulated of the successful application of the concept in a wide variety of crime contexts, a more detailed classification of situational measures has been developed, and the threat presented by displacement has receded as its limits have been clarified by research (Clarke 1992).

These achievements have helped to establish situational prevention in a number of European countries as one component in a broader array of crime control policies. Both in Holland and Great Britain, situational prevention is promoted by crime prevention units within central government. In Sweden, a semiautonomous governmental agency serves the same purpose. Given that the limitations are being increasingly recognized of alternative approaches to crime control, such as rehabilitation, deterrent sentencing, intensive policing, and incapacitation, it may be surprising that situational prevention has not been even more widely embraced by academics and policy makers. The lack of interest in the United States may be due partly to the disappointing results attending some early attempts to implement crime prevention through environmental design (CPTED), though Bright (1992) has noted the absence of any crime prevention policy in America, which he attributes to the dislike of government intervention, as well as to the strong ethos of individual responsibility that results in punishment being seen as the most appropriate response to law breaking. More generally, situational prevention conflicts with the mind-sets of criminologists and the vested interests of criminal justice practitioners. Many of the former seem unable or unwilling to make the paradigm shift involved in focusing on criminogenic situations rather than so exclusively on criminal actors, while for most of the latter there is scant appeal in a crime control strategy that depends so little on the criminal justice system. The main reason for the relative lack of interest in situational prevention, however, may be unresolved difficulties about the implementation and delivery of situational measures and deeper concerns it provokes about the directions in which society may be moving with the approach of the twenty-first century (Bottoms 1990). Addressing these social concerns and the practical problems of implementation are among the challenges facing situational prevention in the forthcoming decade.

These implementation issues are discussed in Section V, at the end of this essay. In Section I, the theoretical background to situational prevention is described, and in Section II, a model of the opportunity structure is presented. In Section III, twelve opportunity-reducing techniques are described, together with some examples of their successful application. In Section IV, issues relating to displacement are discussed.

I. Theoretical Background

While the measures listed in the opening paragraph of this essay share the purpose of reducing opportunities for highly specific forms of crime and in this sense satisfy the definition of situational prevention, few were explicitly developed within a situational prevention framework. Rather, they were developed in isolation by people hard-pressed to solve crime problems encountered in their particular areas of responsibility. One of situational prevention's most important goals, therefore, second only to the objective of encouraging applications of the concept in fresh contexts, has been to provide a more scientific framework for some practical and commonsense thinking about how to deal with crime. This framework has three components, the first of which is a standard action research methodology (Lewin 1947) consisting of five sequential stages: (1) collection of data about the nature and dimensions of a specific crime problem, (2) analysis of the situational conditions that permit or facilitate the commission of the crimes in question, (3) systematic study of possible means of blocking opportunities for these particular crimes, including analysis of costs, (4) implementation of the most promising, feasible, and economical measures, and (5) monitoring of results and dissemination of experience (Gladstone 1980).

Possibly because of its extensive pedigree, the methodological component of situational prevention has been accepted with little change, but the two other components consisting of its theoretical underpinnings and the taxonomy of preventive measures are still undergoing considerable development. The taxonomy is discussed in Section III, while this section describes the evolution of the theory supporting situational prevention. This description includes the origins of the theory in some Home Office research on institutional treatments, its relationship with work on CPTED and "defensible space" that had been developed contemporaneously in the United States, and the more recent infusion of concepts from rational choice, routine activity, and other "opportunity" theories.

A. Early Work by the Home Office Research Unit

The development of situational prevention was stimulated by the results of work on correctional treatments undertaken in the 1960s and 1970s by the Home Office Research Unit, the British government's criminological research department (Clarke and Cornish 1983). This work contributed to the demise of the rehabilitative ideal (Brody 1976) and forced researchers in the unit, charged with making a practical contribution to criminal policy, to review the scope and effectiveness of other forms of crime control. The review concluded that there was little prospect of reducing crime through the essentially marginal adjustments that were practically and ethically feasible in relation to policies of incapacitation, deterrent sentencing, preventive policing, or "social" prevention (Tilley 1993a). But it did identify reducing opportunities for crime as a worthwhile topic for further research, largely on the basis of some findings about misbehavior in institutions. It had been discovered in the course of work on rehabilitation that the probability of a youth's absconding or reoffending while resident in a probation hostel or training school seemed to depend much more on the nature of the institutional regime to which he was exposed than on his personality or background (Tizard, Sinclair, and Clarke 1975). Particularly important appeared to be the opportunities for misbehavior provided by the institutional regime—opportunities that could be "designed out."

If institutional misconduct could in theory be controlled by manipulating situational factors, it was reasoned that the same might be true of other, everyday forms of crime. Though this was not consistent with most current theory (which treated crime principally as the expression of biological inheritance, personality, or social factors), support for the Home Office position was found in criminological studies that had found immediate situational influences to be playing an important role in crime. These included Burt's (1925) studies of delinquency in London, showing that higher rates of property offending in the winter were promoted by longer hours of darkness; Hartshorne and May's (1928) experimental studies of deceit, showing that the likelihood of dishonest behavior by children was dependent on the level of supervision afforded; geographical studies showing that the distribution of particular crimes is related to the presence of particular targets and locations such as business premises, drinking clubs, and parking lots (Engstad 1975); and demonstrations that fluctuations in auto theft reflect the number of opportunities as measured by the numbers of registered vehicles (e.g., Wilkins 1964).

The Home Office position was also consistent with some psychological research on personality traits and behavior that was finding a greater-than-expected role for situational influences (Mischel 1968) and with an emerging body of work on the sociology of deviance, including studies by Matza (1964), who argued against deep motivational commitment to deviance in favor of a "drift" into misconduct; by Briar and Piliavin (1965), who stressed situational inducements and lack of commitment to conformity; and by Yablonsky (1962) and Short and Strodtbeck (1965), who demonstrated the pressures to deviance conferred by working-class gang membership.

Taken together, this body of work suggested that criminal conduct was much more susceptible to variations in opportunity and to transitory pressures and inducements than conventional "dispositional" theories allowed. It was also becoming clear from interviews with residential burglars (Scarr 1973; Reppetto 1974; Brantingham and Brantingham 1975; and Waller and Okihiro 1978) that the avoidance of risk and effort plays a large part in target selection decisions. This dynamic view of crime provided a more satisfactory basis for situational prevention and led to the formulation of a simple "choice" model (Clarke 1977, 1980). This required information not only about the offender's background and current circumstances but also about the offender's immediate motives and intentions, moods and feelings, moral judgments regarding the act in question, perception of criminal opportunities and ability to take advantage of them or create them, and assessment of the risks of being caught as well as of the likely consequences.

This model, dubbed "situational control theory" by Downes and Rock (1982), was subsequently developed into the rational choice perspective on crime (see below), but it served initially to deflect criminological criticism of the atheoretical nature of situational prevention and, more important, to guide thinking about practical ways of reducing opportunities for crime.

B. Defensible Space, CPTED, and Problem-oriented Policing

Preceding situational prevention by a few years were two related strands of policy research in the United States, "defensible space" (Newman 1972) and "crime prevention through environmental design" or CPTED (Jeffery 1971). Neither had provided the stimulus for its development, though arguments and examples that both provided were useful in its promotion. Nor did CPTED or defensible space contribute materially to the theoretical basis of situational prevention. Both were more narrowly focused on the design of buildings and places (whereas situational prevention seeks to reduce opportunities for crime in all behavioral contexts), and both embraced somewhat questionable theories of human behavior. In Jeffery's (1971) case, his "biosocial" approach included not merely environmental change but also the more controversial ingredient of treating the genetic basis of crime. In the case of Newman (1972), his "defensible space" concept was influenced not only by Jacobs's (1961) ideas about the relationship between crime and the layout of American cities, but also by some debatable ethological ideas (Mayhew 1979) about human "territoriality" developed by authors such as Ardrey (1966).

The work on "defensible space" was invaluable, however, in providing a powerful tool for analyzing problems of crime and vandalism in public housing in Britain. Newman was especially critical of huge buildings which made it impossible for residents to recognize strangers, numerous unsupervised access points that made it easy for offenders to enter projects and escape, the location of projects in high-crime areas, and the projects' stigmatizing appearance. His work included a wealth of detailed design suggestions for creating "defensible space" through reducing anonymity, increasing surveillance, and reducing escape routes for offenders. One of the first situational prevention projects undertaken by the Home Office involved testing Newman's ideas in a British context (Wilson 1978). While its results were not wholly supportive of "defensible space" concepts, it was succeeded by more comprehensive studies (Coleman 1985) and undoubtedly contributed to British government interest in designing more secure and livable public housing environments (Burbidge 1984).

If situational prevention rode on the coattails of defensible space, it has more recently been hobbled by its association in the United States with CPTED, partly because of the latter's biological components, but more importantly because of the failure of some federally sponsored CPTED projects undertaken by the Westinghouse Corporation. These were massively funded, but misconceived because they attempted to extend the defensible space concept to school and commercial sites where "territorial" behavior is much less natural than in the residential context (see Jeffery 1977). Partly as a result of these failures, both government funding agencies and criminologists have shown little recent interest in CPTED, and, with the exception of some studies undertaken by Jeffery and his associates of convenience store robbery (Hunter and Jeffery 1992) and some work in Canada by Brantingham and Brantingham (1988), little CPTED research has been published in North America in the last decade.

More recent interest has greeted conceptually related (Hope 1994) though independent work on "problem-oriented policing" by Goldstein (1979, 1990), who has argued that the route to greater operational effectiveness for the police is not through improvements in organization and management but through the devising of tailor-made solutions for the range of problems that they are called on to handle. Goldstein recognized the need for evaluation, and his formulation of problem-oriented policing appears to reflect the same action research paradigm underpinning situational prevention (see Goldstein 1990, p. 103). Nevertheless, some important differences exist between the concepts. In particular, problem-oriented policing is a management approach designed to make most efficient use of police resources (Moore 1992), while situational prevention is a crime control approach open not just to the police but to any organizational or management structure.

C. The Rational Choice Perspective

The earlier "choice" model formulated to guide situational prevention efforts has more recently been developed into a "rational choice" perspective on crime (Clarke and Cornish 1985; Cornish and Clarke 1986). This borrows concepts from economic theories of crime (e.g., Becker 1968) but seeks to avoid some of the criticisms made of these theories, in particular the following: (i) that under economic models the rewards of crime are treated mainly in material terms (how much money an offender can make), while mostly ignoring rewards that cannot easily be translated into cash equivalents; (ii) that economists have not been sensitive to the great variety of behaviors falling under the general label of crime, with their variety of costs and benefits, and instead have tended to lump them together as a single variable in their equations; (iii) that the formal mathematical modeling of criminal choices by economists often demands data that are unavailable or can only be pressed into service by making unrealistic assumptions about what they represent; and, finally, (iv) that the economist's image of the self-maximizing decision maker, carefully calculating his or her advantage, does not fit the opportunistic and reckless nature of much crime (Clarke and Felson 1993).

Under the new formulation of the rational choice perspective, relationships between concepts were expressed, not in mathematical terms as was the case in Becker's normative model, but in the form of "decision" diagrams (Clarke and Cornish 1985; Cornish and Clarke 1986). Concepts were adapted from the other disciplines involved in the analysis of criminal decision making, as well as economics, to give greater weight to noninstrumental motives for crime and the "limited" nature of the rational processes involved. It was assumed, in other words, that crime is purposive behavior designed to meet the offender's commonplace needs for such things as money, status, sex, and excitement, and that meeting these needs involves the making of (sometimes quite rudimentary) decisions and choices, constrained as these are by limits of time and ability and the availability of relevant information.

A second important new premise was that a decision-making approach to crime requires that a fundamental distinction be made between criminal involvement and criminal events. (This parallels the distinction made by Gottfredson and Hirschi [1990] between criminality and crime.) Criminal involvement refers to the processes through which individuals choose to become initially involved in particular forms of crime, to continue, and to desist. The decision processes at each of these stages are influenced by a different set of factors and need to be separately modeled. In the same way, the decision processes involved in the commission of a particular crime (i.e., the criminal event) are dependent on their own special categories of information. Involvement decisions are characteristically multistage and extend over substantial periods of time. Event decisions, by contrast, are frequently shorter processes, using more circumscribed information largely relating to immediate circumstances and situations.

Finally, and this is of special importance for situational prevention, it was assumed that the decision processes and information used will vary greatly between different offenses. To ignore these differences, and the situational contingencies associated with them, may be to reduce significantly the scope for intervention. Nor will it be enough to make the usual crude distinctions between crime categories, such as that between commercial and residential burglary. Thus Poyner and Webb (1991) have shown that residential burglaries committed for cash and jewelry show a quite different pattern in British communities than do those committed for electrical goods. The former seemed to be committed primarily by opportunistic offenders working on foot, while the latter seemed to rely on the use of a car. These differences in modus operandi have implications for prevention; Poyner and Webb suggested, in particular, that to prevent burglaries of electrical goods houses should face each other across the street and overlook access roads, while to prevent burglaries of cash and jewelry cover at the front of houses in the form of shrubs or fences should be removed.

While the new formulation of the rational choice perspective was primarily developed to assist thinking about situational prevention, it was not intended to be limited to this role. Indeed, Cornish (1993) has argued that many features of the rational choice perspective make it particularly suitable to serve as a criminological "metatheory" with a broad role in the explanation of a variety of criminological phenomena.

D. Environmental Criminology, Routine Activities, and Lifestyles

Rational choice premises have generally been supported by recent studies in which offenders have been interviewed about motives, methods, and target choices. The offenders concerned have included burglars (e.g., Walsh 1980; Maguire 1982; Bennett and Wright 1984; Nee and Taylor 1988; Biron and Ladouceur 1991; Cromwell, Olson, and Wester Avary 1991), shoplifters (Walsh 1978; Carroll and Weaver 1986), muggers (Lejeune 1977; Feeney 1986), and bank and commercial robbers (New South Wales Bureau of Crime Statistics and Research 1987; Kube 1988; Nugent et al. 1989). These studies of offender decision making constitute one of two major analytic paths followed in the past decade by "environmental criminology" (Brantingham and Brantingham 1991). The other path has involved "objective analysis of the spatial and temporal variation in crime patterns in order to discover aggregate factors influencing the patterns" (Brantingham and Brantingham 1991, p. 239). Much of this work, which has greatly expanded evidence about situational factors in crime, consists of macro analyses of climatic variations or city structure. One important component has been research on the criminal's "journey to work," an example of which is Poyner and Webb's (1991) study, mentioned above, with its implications for preventing different forms of residential burglary. Other similar studies by Brantingham and Brantingham (1975), Maguire (1982), and Rengert and Wasilchick (1985) have shown, among other things, that the risks of commercial robbery may be increased by being located close to a main road, and those of residential burglary by being located on the outskirts of an affluent area, in both cases because the offender's target search time is thereby reduced.

Research on the criminal's journey to work is conceptually related to another body of criminological work—routine activity theory—which has also contributed to the theoretical base of situational prevention. The routine activity approach stated three minimal elements for direct-contact predatory crime: a likely offender, a suitable target, and the absence of a capable guardian against crime (Cohen and Felson 1979). It avoids speculation about the source of the offender's motivation, which distinguishes it immediately from most other criminological theories. Instead, it focuses on the convergence in space and time of the three elements of crime, that is to say, on the conditions favoring the occurrence of a criminal event, rather than the development of a criminal disposition. This reflects its intellectual roots in the human ecology of Amos Hawley (1950), who recognized that the timing of different activities by hour of day and day of week was important for the understanding of human society. These points were central also to the routine activity approach. No matter at what level data were measured or analyzed, that approach kept returning to specific points in time and space and to changes from moment to moment and hour to hour in where people are, what they are doing, and what happens to them as a result (Clarke and Felson 1993). In support of their approach, Cohen and Felson (1979) sought to demonstrate that increases in residential burglary in the United States between 1960 and 1970 could largely be explained by changes in "routine activities" such as the increasing proportion of empty homes in the day (due to more single-person households and greater female participation in the labor force) and the increased portability of televisions and other electrical goods.

Cohen and Felson's analysis also illustrates the relationship between routine activity theory and some victimological work on "lifestyles," stimulated by the flood of National Crime Survey data first released in the 1970s (Hindelang, Gottfredson, and Garofalo 1978). One of the tenets of "lifestyle" theory is that the differential risks of victimization are partly a function of differential exposure to motivated offenders (Fattah 1993). This exposure varies not only with the sociodemographic characteristics of the victim (age, race, place of residence, etc.) but also with the victim's lifestyle. A person's work and leisure activities that increase exposure to potential offenders (such as alcohol consumption in public places or late-night use of public transport) increase the risks of victimization. The implication of this is that risks might be reduced by modifying patterns of activity. A further important finding of victimological research, the implications of which are being explored in a series of recent studies by Ken Pease and colleagues (see Farrell and Pease [1993] for a review), is that some people and targets are repeatedly subject to victimization and might therefore be prime candidates for preventive attention (see Farrell, in this volume). A similar point has been made by Sherman, Gartin, and Buerger (1989) in relation to the "hot spots" of crime, places that are the source of repeated calls for assistance to the police.

Lifestyle and routine activity theories have both made opportunity a respectable topic of research in criminology and helped situational prevention attract serious scholarly interest. Both approaches are still evolving, and Felson himself has made some attempts to expand the scope of routine activity theory. He has defined minimal elements for some categories of crime other than direct-contact predatory offenses (Felson 1992) and, in order to accommodate social control theory (Hirschi 1969), has proposed a fourth minimal element for predatory crimes, "the intimate handler," or someone who knows the likely offender well enough to afford a substantial brake on the latter's activities (Felson 1986). Clarke (1992) has argued that the contribution of routine activity theory to crime prevention could be enhanced by adding a fifth element which he refers to as "crime facilitators." These are such things as automobiles, credit cards, and weapons that constitute the essential tools of particular forms of crime.

II. The Opportunity Structure for Crime

Environmental criminology, the rational choice perspective, and routine activity and lifestyle theories have all helped to strengthen situational prevention in different ways, reflecting their different origins and the purposes for which they were developed. By interviews with offenders and analyses of crime patterns, environmental criminology has provided rich information about the motives and methods of offenders, which has been valuable in thinking about countermeasures. The rational choice perspective has provided a framework under which to organize such information so that individual studies produce more general benefits and has also assisted analysis of displacement. Lifestyle theory has focused attention on what victims might do to reduce their risks of crime. And routine activity theory has served to extend preventive options by directing attention to features of the three essential elements of crime and their convergence. For example, the idea of convergence has led to the suggestion that "deflecting offenders" be recognized as a distinct technique of situational prevention (Barr and Pease 1990; Clarke 1992).

Cusson (1986) and Felson (forthcoming) have argued that the differences among the various theoretical approaches may turn out to be mainly of historical interest and that a synthesis is inevitable and desirable. The model of the opportunity structure for crime discussed in this section represents one such attempt at integration.

A. The Concept in Outline

Under this model (see fig. 1), which includes the dispositional variables of traditional criminology as well as the situational ones of the newer theories, there are three components of the criminal opportunity structure. These are targets (cars, convenience stores, automated teller machines, etc.), victims (e.g., women alone, drunks, strangers), and crime facilitators. These latter include tools, such as guns and cars, as well as disinhibitors, such as alcohol or other drugs.

The supply of targets and their nature is a function of, first, the physical environment, including the layout of cities, the kinds of housing, technology and communications, transportation and retailing systems, the numbers of vehicles and the supply of drugs and alcohol, and, second, the lifestyles and routine activities of the population, including patterns of leisure, work, residence, and shopping. These patterns either hinder or facilitate guardianship. The physical environment also determines the supply of facilitators, while lifestyles and routine activities play a large part in supplying the victims of personal and sexual attacks. Physical environment and lifestyles and routine activities are themselves determined by the broader socioeconomic structure of society, including demography, geography, urbanization and industrialization, health and educational policy, and legal and political institutions. The numbers of potential offenders and their motives are also determined partly by the socioeconomic structure of society through many of the mechanisms (alienation, subcultural influence,

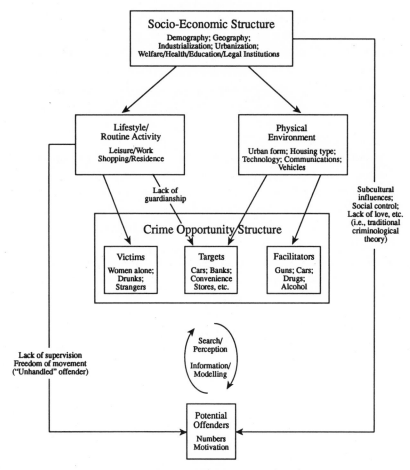

FIG. 1.—The opportunity structure for crime

neglect, and lack of love, etc.) identified by traditional criminology and partly by lifestyle and routine activities which affect the nature of social control afforded by "intimate handlers," and in other ways.

The opportunity structure is not simply a physical entity, defined at any one time by the nature of the physical environment and the routine activities of the population. Rather, a complex interplay between potential offenders and the supply of victims, targets, and facilitators determines the scale and nature of opportunities for crime. Potential offenders learn about criminal opportunities from their peers, the media, and their own observation, but they are differentially sensitized to this information, as well as being differentially motivated to seek out and create opportunities (Maguire 1980; Bennett and Wright 1984). Thus offender perceptions and judgments about risks, effort, and rewards play an important part in defining the opportunity structure.[1] These judgments also play a determining role at the subsequent stage of crime commission, where figure 1 stops short.

B. Policy Implications

Little account is taken in figure 1 of society's efforts to control and prevent crime because this might have diverted attention from the purpose of integrating the various opportunity perspectives. Some brief discussion is needed, however, of questions about the scope and reach of situational prevention which arise from consideration of the model of the opportunity structure. The first of these can be phrased as follows: if everything seems to flow from the socioeconomic structure, why not focus preventive effort at that level? Large-scale reductions in a wide range of crimes might be achieved by tackling the disposition to offend at its roots, through improved welfare and educational programs. This would appear to be more efficient than the undertaking of a vast number of small-scale efforts to address highly specific crime problems that is implied by the situational focus.

One answer to this is that "social" forms of crime prevention are already focused at the socioeconomic level and that the opportunity structure requires attention in its own right. A second, more radical reply has been provided by Morris and Hawkins (1970) and Wilson (1975), who have noted the great difficulty of bringing about some social changes (e.g., how parents can be made to love their children more), as well as that decisions about other change will only be marginally influenced by arguments about crime: most of the changes that might bring about reductions in crime, such as better welfare and education, are usually seen as desirable but as demanding resources that society cannot afford.

A second question that concerns the differential balance between dispositional and situational factors for various crimes has been raised by Trasler (1986, 1993), among others, and is as follows: even if situational measures may be appropriate in dealing with certain categories of crime (especially opportunistic property offenses), is it not the case

---

[1] Although not made explicit in fig. 1, it is recognized that these perceptions and judgments are not always individual activities, but sometimes will be collaborative with peers and co-offenders.

that more deeply motivated crimes committed by desperate or hardened offenders can only be prevented by addressing fundamental dispositional causes? This can be answered by the argument that all classes of crime, even those most deeply motivated by anger or despair, are greatly affected by situational contingencies. Whether an assault becomes a homicide may depend on the presence at the scene of a lethal weapon (Cook 1991); similarly, whether someone commits suicide is importantly determined by the availability of an acceptable method (Clarke and Lester 1989). With respect to crimes thought to be the province of "hardened" offenders, evidence is now accumulating of successes achieved by situational prevention, including the virtual elimination of aircraft hijackings by baggage screening (Wilkinson 1986) and substantial reductions in robbery achieved by target-hardening measures in post offices (Ekblom 1988), convenience stores (Hunter and Jeffery 1992), and banks (Gabor 1990; Grandjean 1990; Clarke, Field, and McGrath 1991).

Heal and Laycock (1986) and Gabor (1990) have nevertheless maintained that, because many violent crimes are less common and less likely to cluster in time or space, they are also less amenable to situational controls. However, this may be true only to the extent that the measures considered are traditional ones of target hardening and surveillance. In Section III some examples are provided of the successful control of violence through deflecting offenders (e.g., by preventing the congregation of large groups of drunken youths at pub closing time) or by controlling crime facilitators such as alcohol and guns. One instructive example is provided by the introduction of Caller-ID in New Jersey, which, by threatening the anonymity of callers, seems to have produced a substantial reduction in obscene phone calling (Clarke 1990). Without this evidence, many people might have argued that obscene phone calling, a sexual crime that seems to strike at random, is precisely the kind of offense that would be unamenable to situational controls. A similar argument might have been made about domestic violence, but encouraging evidence is beginning to emerge from an experimental program in England that providing personal alarms to repeat victims may inhibit the aggressor (Farrell and Pease 1993). The lesson is that the limits of situational prevention should be established by closely analyzing the circumstances of highly specific kinds of offense, rather than by theoretical arguments about the presumed nature of motives for broad categories of crime such as sexual or violent offenses.

A third question concerns deterrence. It relates specifically to the issue of offender choice and is as follows: rather than attempting to manipulate the opportunity structure (with the attendant costs and inconvenience of this strategy), might it not be more efficient simply to raise the stakes of offending by heavier punishments? The answer to this is that most interviews with offenders have shown that they pay much closer attention to the immediate chances of getting caught than to the nature of the punishment they might receive later. It is more efficient, therefore, to make the offender more fearful of being caught than of being subsequently punished, and one component of situational prevention does indeed consist of increasing the risks of being caught (a process referred to as "situational deterrence" by Cusson [1993]).

A final set of questions concerns the interplay between the objective reality of the opportunity structure and the way this is perceived by potential offenders. How do offenders learn about criminal opportunities, and what factors come into play when they make decisions about which ones to pursue? What proportion of crimes are the result of opportunities seized, and what proportion are the result of opportunities that are sought or created (Maguire 1980; Bennett and Wright 1984)? At issue here is the question of whether opportunities for crime really are in infinite supply, as some have argued. If so, this has serious implications for a strategy advocating their reduction. What matter the few reductions that can be achieved in criminal opportunities if these are infinite?

Consideration of the realities of crime may supply an answer to this question. While it may be true that every dwelling and automobile provides in theory not just one opportunity for crime, but if considered over time, a set of almost endless opportunities, this overlooks the substantial guardianship afforded dwellings and automobiles for much of the time (Clarke 1984). Even when unguarded, they may in actuality provide few rewards for crime. The average dwelling contains only a few portable goods that can be converted into cash, and there are limits to the number of stolen VCRs and television sets that the offender can store. It is also unclear how many such "hot" items can be unloaded onto the market without provoking a determined response from law enforcement. Clarification of these issues needs to be sought in more research of the kind recently published by Cromwell, Olson, and Wester Avary (1991) in which they undertook detailed interviews with residential burglars about their working methods.

A more basic program of research into the ways that behavior is routinely channeled by society in order to protect the privacy and security of individuals and institutions would also be of value. This could explore a variety of questions such as the following.

1. How much geographical space in a town or city has not been privatized and is readily accessible to strangers?
2. What proportion of goods for sale in retail establishments could or could not easily be stolen by shoppers?
3. What are the subtle cues in private places that progressively reduce access with the degree of intimacy between "owners" and "visitors"? (You might invite me into your living room, but not into your bedroom.)
4. What limits an offender's willingness to travel?

Answers to these questions would assist discussion about the supply of crime targets. A similar, but a possibly more restricted set of questions needs to be asked about facilitators. For example, much more needs to be learned about the reasons guns are used in committing crimes in some cultures but not in others with similar rates of crime, even when guns are equally available (Tonso 1982; Harding 1993). Some clues are provided by Harding (1993) who has found that robbers in Western Australia who had been introduced to guns by their fathers or other authority figures were much less likely to use guns in their robberies than those introduced to guns by peers (see also Wright and Rossi [1982] for similar findings in the United States). Harding also reports that, even though murder rates for Australian Aboriginals are very high, the rates of gun murder are relatively low. As one offender interviewed by Harding (1993, p. 94) explained the reason, "Guns are for shooting tucker (i.e., food) not people."

III. Opportunity-reducing Techniques

Putting situational prevention on a more rigorous footing has involved not only the development of a theoretical framework and the formulation of a standard methodology but also various efforts to classify the opportunity-reducing techniques that have been identified. None of these classifications has been widely used, however, which seems to be due to a continually expanding repertoire of measures, resulting from fresh applications of situational prevention, and improved theoretical understanding of the relationship between situational variables and crime. For example, Clarke's (1992) suggestion mentioned above that "deflecting offenders" should be a discrete category of opportunity-reducing measures arose from a consideration of routine activity theory.

This suggestion was made in the context of developing a twelve-category classification of techniques that builds on a more limited classification proposed earlier by Clarke and Mayhew (1980). The twelve categories of the new classification are described below (and presented in summary form in table 1) with some successful examples of the application of each technique.

Before launching into this description, however, some brief points should be made about the examples of "success." There are a large number of these (and more might have been cited [see Poyner 1993]) relating to a wide variety of settings and crime types. Taken as a whole, there can be little question that they provide credible evidence of significant crime reduction effects. Nevertheless, it has to be recognized that in most cases the individual evaluations were comparatively rudimentary. Follow-ups were often short, so little is known about the durability of success. True experimental designs were almost completely absent from the studies (most of which consisted of simple time-series or quasi-experimental designs), with the result that in most cases it was impossible to be sure that the identified situational measure had produced the observed reduction in crime.[2] These reductions might have been due instead to some other contemporaneous, unmeasured change or even from regression to the mean.[3] In many of the studies, several preventive measures had been deployed at the same time, and it was impossible to be sure which combination, if any, was responsible for the success. Moreover, for reasons discussed at greater

[2] Experimental designs are difficult to undertake in field settings and, even when successfully completed, can be hard to interpret. For example, Farrington et al. (1993) have recently reported an experimental study of shoplifting prevention, in which three measures (electronic tagging, store redesign, and security guards) were systematically compared for their effectiveness. They concluded that the security guards were ineffective, but with the caveat that this may have been due to the layout of the store, which prevented adequate oversight of customers, or to the inexperience, unimpressive physiques, and lack of training of the particular guards concerned. It is doubtful that the testing of rival hypotheses such as these within the confines of a rigorous experimental design would often be a practicable proposition, and, indeed, it seems preferable in the present state of knowledge to undertake as many evaluations as possible while compensating for weak designs with detailed observation of the process of implementation. (The value of this is illustrated by Farrington et al.'s observations about the caliber of the security guards in their shoplifting research.)

[3] For an illustration of this problem, see Sherman's (1992) discussion of the successes claimed in preventing robbery in convenience stores through employing two clerks.

TABLE 1
The Twelve Techniques of Situational Prevention

Increasing the Effort	Increasing the Risks	Reducing the Reward
1. Target hardening: Steering locks Bandit screens Slug rejector device	5. Entry/exit screening: Baggage screening Automatic ticket gates Merchandise tags	9. Target removal: Removable car radio Exact change fares Phonecard
2. Access control: Fenced yards Entry phones ID badges	6. Formal surveillance: Security guards Burglar alarms Speed cameras	10. Identifying property: Property marking Vehicle licensing Personal identification numbers for car radios
3. Deflecting offenders: Tavern location Street closures Graffiti board	7. Surveillance by employees: Park attendants Pay phone location Closed-circuit television systems	11. Removing inducements: Graffiti cleaning Rapid repair "Bum-proof" bench
4. Controlling facilitators: Gun controls Credit card photo Caller-ID	8. Natural surveillance: Street lighting Defensible space Neighborhood watch	12. Rule setting: Customs declaration Income tax returns Hotel registration

SOURCE.—Adapted from Clarke (1992).

length below, it was rarely possible to be sure that displacement had not negated the benefits of the observed reductions in crime, although in many cases there was little prima facie evidence of this. All of this means that, while the weight of the positive evidence cannot convincingly be denied, the successes claimed in any individual study may be open to question.

A. Target Hardening

The most obvious way of reducing criminal opportunities is to obstruct the vandal or the thief by physical barriers through the use of locks, safes, screens, or reinforced materials.

The introduction of steering locks on both new and old cars in West Germany in 1963 produced a substantial decline in the rate of car theft for the country that has persisted to this day (Webb and Laycock 1992; Webb 1994).

Decker's (1972) study showed that the use of slugs in New York parking meters was substantially reduced by changes in design, including a slug-rejector device.

The fitting of transparent screens to shield the bus driver significantly reduced assaults on one transit system (Poyner et al. 1988), and the installation of antibandit screens on post office counters in London in the early 1980s was conservatively estimated by Ekblom (1988) to have cut robberies by 40 percent.

Challinger (1991) identifies strengthened coin boxes as a significant factor in reducing incidents of deliberate damage to public telephones in two Australian states—South Australia and the Northern Territory—from a peak of nearly 6,000 in 1988 to just over 1,100 one year later.

Clarke, Field, and McGrath (1991) attributed marked reductions in armed robbery of Australian banks during the late 1980s to a program of target hardening, including the installation of fixed and "pop-up" bulletproof screens.

B. Access Control

Access control refers to measures intended to exclude potential offenders from places such as offices, factories, and apartment buildings. The portcullises, moats, and drawbridges of medieval castles suggest its preventive pedigree may be as lengthy as that of target hardening. It is also a central component of defensible space, arguably the start of scientific interest in situational prevention. A sophisticated form of access control lies in the use of electronic personal identification num-bers (PINs) that are needed to gain access to computer systems and bank accounts.

Matthews (1990) has shown that a road closure scheme to reduce access by cruising "johns" was one of the measures contributing to the rehabilitation in 1984 of a red-light district in Finsbury Park, an area of North London. Not only was prostitution very significantly reduced but also a wide range of crimes declined from a total of 475 in the twelve months prior to implementation of the scheme to 275 in the twelve months after.

Poyner and Webb (1987) found that a combination of access controls introduced on a South London public housing estate, including entry phones, fencing around apartment blocks, and electronic access to the parking garage, achieved a significant reduction in vandalism and theft. They also found that the introduction of a reception desk on the ground floor of a high-rise building achieved a marked reduction in vandalism, graffiti, and other incivilities.

C. Deflecting Offenders

The provision of public urinals, litter bins, and "graffiti boards" (the latter being supplied for people's public messages) channels people's behavior in more acceptable directions and constitutes an example of deflecting offenders. In Britain, arrival and departure of soccer fans has been scheduled to avoid long periods of waiting around that pro-mote trouble, and rival fans have been physically separated within the stadium to reduce the probability of fights (Clarke 1983). Avoiding the concentration of licensed premises in particular parts of the city has been proposed by Hope (1985) as a way of avoiding the closing-time brawls that result when large crowds of drunken people spill onto the streets late at night. Finally, Shearing and Stenning (1984) provide a fascinating glimpse into the ways in which sophisticated crowd control and management—involving the use of pavement markings, signs, physical barriers (that make it difficult to take a wrong turn), and instructions from cheerful Disney employees—greatly reduce the po-tential for crime and incivility in Disneyland.

Bell and Burke (1989) show that the leasing of a downtown parking lot in Arlington, Texas, relieved severe congestion on weekend nights in nearby streets, and associated crime problems, by providing a venue for teenage cruising.

Poyner and Webb (1987) show that thefts from shopping bags at market stalls in Birmingham, England, were reduced by over 70 percent within two years by reducing congestion, which increased the difficulty of pickpocketing and other "stealth" thefts.

D. Controlling Facilitators

Saloons in the Wild West routinely required their clienteles to surrender their weapons on entry because of the risk of drunken gun fights. In more recent times the manufacture of "less lethal weapons" in the form of guns that shoot wax bullets, electricity, or tranquilizers has been advocated (Hemenway and Weil 1990). The Scottish Council on Crime (1975) suggested that in some pubs beer should be served in plastic mugs to prevent their use as weapons, and recent studies in Britain of the injury potential of different kinds of broken glass have led to the recommendation that toughened glass be used for beer glasses (Shepherd and Brickley 1992). Controls on a range of other crime facilitators have been proposed including alcohol (which facilitates almost all crime), automobiles (which facilitate crimes such as burglary), checks and credit cards (which facilitate fraud), and telephones (which may facilitate drug dealing, frauds, and sexual harassment). Licenses and IDs restrict access to cars and alcohol for juveniles, the most crime-prone group. Access to automobiles by intoxicated drivers can be restricted by the use of Breathalyzers built into the ignition, a measure that is now being mandated for some recidivist drunk drivers (Jones and Wood 1989; Morse and Elliott 1990). To reduce drug dealing, some telephone companies have removed public telephones from places where drug dealers congregate or have altered the phones so they cannot receive incoming calls (*Law Enforcement News* 1990).

Bjor, Knutsson, and Kuhlhorn (1992) argue that "rationing" the amount of alcohol that revelers were allowed to bring into a Swedish resort town on Midsummer Eve made an important contribution to reduced levels of drunkenness and disorderly conduct.

Knutsson and Kuhlhorn (1981) have shown that the introduction of identification procedures in Sweden produced a dramatic decline in the number of reported check frauds, from a peak of 15,817 in 1970 to 10–20 percent of these figures in later years.

Clarke (1990) has provided evidence that the introduction in New Jersey of Caller-ID, a service which allows the person answering to read the number of whoever is making the call, appears to have resulted in a substantial reduction, by about 25 percent, of obscene and annoying telephone calls.

E. Entry/Exit Screening

Entry screening differs from access control in that the purpose is less to exclude potential offenders than to increase the risk of detecting those who are not in conformity with entry requirements. These requirements may relate to prohibited goods and objects or, alternatively, to possession of tickets and documents. Exit screens serve primarily to deter the illegal removal of objects. Developments in electronics have resulted in the increasing use of these situational techniques in retailing, as evidenced by the spread of merchandise tagging, bar coding, and "electronic point of sales" systems (Hope 1991).

The introduction of baggage and passenger screening at most major airports in the world during the early 1970s contributed to a precipitate reduction in the number of airline hijackings from about seventy per year (Wilkinson 1977, 1986; Landes 1978).

Scherdin (1986) reports that the installation of book detection screens, similar to those found in thousands of libraries, reduced thefts of both books and audiovisual materials at one University of Wisconsin library by more than 80 percent.

DesChamps, Brantingham, and Brantingham (1991) provide evidence that the redesign of tickets to facilitate their inspection on Vancouver ferries produced a two-thirds reduction in fare evasion.

According to Clarke (1993), the installation of automatic ticket gates on the sixty-three central zone stations of the London Underground resulted in a two-thirds reduction of fare evasion throughout the system. He also concluded that the increase in fares collected should pay for the gates within three years of installation.

F. Formal Surveillance

Formal surveillance is provided by police, security guards, and store detectives, whose main function is to furnish a deterrent threat to potential offenders. Their surveillance role may be enhanced by electronic hardware, for example, by burglar alarms and closed circuit television (CCTV). Ways of enhancing police surveillance by enlisting the help of the public are also continually being expanded. Informant hot lines and "crime stopper" programs are two recent examples. "Curfew decals" on automobiles (Clarke and Harris 1992a) that indicate to patrolling police that the vehicle is not normally in use late at night represent a program directed specifically at auto theft prevention.

Rates of vandalism, assault, and fare dodging on subways and trams in three Dutch cities were substantially reduced by hiring 1,200 unemployed young people to serve as safety, information, and control inspectors ("VICs") (van Andel 1989).

A problem-oriented policing initiative directed against auto theft in a large shipyard parking lot, featuring intensive surveillance of the yard by police officers, reduced thefts by more than one-half, or by an estimated 450 incidents in a sixteen-month period (Eck and Spelman 1988).

When CCTV was installed for the use of security personnel at a university's parking lots, Poyner (1991) found a substantial reduction in thefts, from ninety-two in the year before intervention to thirty-one in the year after. Tilley (1993*b*) has reported similar results for a number of other car parks in Britain, though in some of the cases he cites the CCTV was not monitored by security personnel.

Systematic, daily counting by security personnel of items of high-risk merchandise, such as VCRs and camcorders, resulted in declines of between 80 percent and 100 percent in the numbers of units stolen by employees at four large electronics stores and the associated distribution center in New Jersey (Masuda 1992).

Bourne and Cooke (1993) show that the widespread deployment of photo radar in Victoria, Australia, was the major factor in substantially reduced levels of speeding in 1991–92, with a consequent reduction of 25 percent in collisions, 40 percent in injuries, and 45 percent in fatalities.

Also in Australia, Homel (1993) has reported that the introduction of random breath testing (RBT) in New South Wales in 1982 was followed by an instantaneous 22 percent decline in total fatal crashes and a drop of 36 percent in alcohol-related fatal crashes relative to the previous three years. These declines have persisted as a result of a continued high level of RBT enforcement.

G. Surveillance by Employees

In addition to their primary function, some employees, particularly those dealing with the public, also perform a surveillance role. They include shop assistants, hotel doormen, park keepers, parking lot attendants, and train conductors. Canadian research has shown that apartment blocks with doormen are less vulnerable to burglary (Waller and Okihiro 1978). In Britain, less vandalism has been found on buses with conductors (Mayhew et al. 1976) and on public housing estates with resident caretakers (Department of Environment 1977). Public telephones in Britain sited where they get some surveillance by employees, such as in pubs or railway stations, also suffer fewer attacks (Markus 1984).

Hunter and Jeffery (1992) report that ten out of fourteen studies they reviewed found that having two clerks on duty, especially at night, was an effective robbery prevention measure.

Comparison of pre- and post-twelve-month figures showed that the employment of attendants to cover high-risk periods of the day was followed by a two-thirds reduction in vehicle-related offenses at a parking lot in Basingstoke, England (Laycock and Austin 1992).

The installation of CCTV for the use of station staff on four high-risk stations on the London Underground was found to have produced substantial reductions in muggings and thefts (Mayhew et al. 1979).

Vandalism of seats on a fleet of double-deck buses in the North of England was substantially reduced through the provision of CCTV for drivers. Only a few buses were fitted with CCTV, but the effect was general, so that seat repairs for the fleet declined from a peak of about eighty per month to a third of that number subsequently (Poyner 1988).

Rewarding cashiers for detection of forged or stolen credit cards helped to reduce losses resulting from fraudulent use of cards at the four large stores of an electronics retailer in New Jersey from $1.1 million in 1991 to about $0.2 million in the first eleven months of 1992 (Masuda 1993).

H. Natural Surveillance

Householders may trim bushes at the front of their homes, and banks may light the interior of their premises at night in attempts to capitalize on the "natural" surveillance provided by people going about their everyday business. Enhancing natural surveillance is a prime objective of improved street lighting (Tien et al. 1979; Ramsay 1991a), of defensible space (Mayhew 1979; Coleman 1985), and of "neighborhood watch" (Rosenbaum 1988; Bennett 1990). Despite their popularity, none of these strategies has been shown to be highly effective, and, even if some successes can be documented, the capacity of "natural surveillance" to prevent crime may have been overestimated.

Improved lighting of the exterior of stores was one component of a successful program that significantly reduced burglary on a commercial strip in Portland, Oregon (Griswold 1984).

Enhancement of lighting in four badly lit and crime-prone streets in London has been followed by substantial reductions in crime and fear of crime as well as increases in night-time pedestrian traffic (Painter, forthcoming).

Components of successful robbery prevention in convenience stores in Florida included an unobstructed view of the store's interior from outside and location of stores near evening commercial activity (Hunter and Jeffery 1992).

An "apartment watch" program combined with target hardening achieved an 82 percent reduction in reported burglaries in four apartment blocks in Ottawa (Meredith and Paquette 1992).

I. Target Removal

Some of the best examples of target removal come from attempts to deal with attacks on public telephones in Great Britain. Because the kiosk itself (especially the glass) is much more frequently vandalized than the phone, kiosks in high-risk locations have been replaced by booths. In addition, the smaller, highly vulnerable, glass panes in earlier kiosks have been replaced by larger panes in more recent designs (Markus 1984). A third example is provided by the introduction of the Phonecard, which by dispensing with the need for public telephones to store large sums of cash has removed an important target for theft.

Moore (1987) has described a highly successful theft prevention program that consisted of persuading inpatients to surrender their valuables for safekeeping or not to bring them to the hospital.

Pease (1991) has shown that a package of measures to prevent repeat victimization of houses on a public housing estate in Britain, including the removal of gas and electric coin meters that were frequent targets for theft, reduced burglaries on the estate from 526 in the year before intervention to 132 three years later.

A variety of cash reduction measures, including the use of safes with time locks, progressively introduced during the 1980s in betting shops in Victoria, Australia, substantially reduced robberies. Not only did the number of robberies decline but the average take of "successful" robberies was also substantially reduced. A cost-effectiveness calculation suggested that the measures had more than paid for themselves (Clarke and McGrath 1990).

Chaiken, Lawless, and Stevenson (1974) showed that bus robberies in New York City dropped from a high of sixty-seven per month just prior to the introduction of exact fares to seven or less per month afterward. A similar result was also reported for eighteen other cities that introduced exact fare systems for buses (Stanford Research Institute 1970).

J. Identifying Property

The most developed programs of identifying property relate to vehicles. Registration of motor vehicles was required in some U.S. states from almost the beginning of the century, and, subsequently, all vehicles sold in the United States were required to carry a unique Vehicle Identification Number. More sophisticated forms of property marking recently deployed against auto theft include PINs for car radios and LOJACK, the trade name for a system involving the concealment of a small transmitter in the body of an automobile that facilitates its recovery if stolen (Clarke and Harris 1992a).

Illinois was one of the last U.S. states to require vehicle registration (in 1934), whereupon vehicle thefts declined from 28,000 in the previous year to about 13,000 (Hall 1952).

Laycock (1991) provides evidence that property marking undertaken in three small communities in Wales, combined with extensive media publicity, nearly halved the number of reported residential burglaries, with 66 in the second year of the program compared with 128 in the year before. Theft rates of automobiles fitted with security-coded radios that cannot be operated without a PIN have recently declined in Australia (National Roads and Motorists' Association NRMA Insurance Ltd. 1990).

K. Removing Inducements

The mere presence of a weapon, such as a gun, has been found to induce aggressive responses in some people (Berkowitz and LePage 1967). This evidence suggests that, apart from reducing availability of weapons, gun controls would also remove inducements to violence. Further examples of reducing inducements can be found in Wise's (1982) suggestions for a "gentle deterrent" to vandalism, such as painting murals on the bare surfaces of walls that almost invite graffiti, and the so-called bum-proof benches at bus stops designed to prevent their use as beds by alcoholics and itinerants (Davis 1990). Arguments in favor of the rapid repair of vandalism, on the grounds that damaged objects invite further attack, also fall under the heading of removing inducements. Support for these arguments is provided by Zimbardo's (1973) finding that a car left parked in poor condition in an inner-city area rapidly attracted further depredation and Samdahl and Christiansen's (1985) finding that picnic tables that had been scratched and carved were much more likely to be damaged further than tables not so marked. The arguments have been taken a step further by Wilson and Kelling (1982) who have maintained that the failure to deal promptly with minor signs of decay in a community, such as panhandling or soliciting by prostitutes, can result in a quickly deteriorating situation as hardened offenders move into the area to exploit the breakdown in control.

Sloan-Howitt and Kelling (1990) have documented the remarkable success achieved within five years by the New York Transit Authority in ridding its 6,245 subway cars of graffiti, an important component of which was a policy of immediate cleansing. This removed the gratification for offenders of seeing their work on public display.

Substantially reduced rates of crime and vandalism on the metropolitan railways of Victoria, Australia, were reported by Carr and Spring (1993) following the introduction of Travel Safe, a program consisting of enhanced security and rapid repair of vandalism and graffiti. For example, the weekly number of train windows needing repair progressively declined from 372 in October 1990 to 105 in May 1991.

L. Rule Setting

All organizations find it necessary to have rules about conduct in their fields of jurisdiction. For example, most businesses regulate employees' telephone use, and all retail establishments require employees to follow strict cash-handling and stock control procedures. Organizations such as hospitals, schools, parks, transportation systems, and hotels and restaurants must, in addition, regulate the conduct of the clienteles they serve. Any ambiguity in these regulations will be exploited where it is to the advantage of the individual. (Most attempts to avoid income tax relate to those sections of the Internal Revenue Service tax return that are more difficult to investigate [Klepper and Nagin 1987].) One important strand of situational prevention, therefore, is the introduction of new rules or procedures (and the improvement of those in place) that are intended to remove any ambiguity concerning the acceptability of conduct. The existence of these rules means that offenders must be prepared to incur higher costs in terms of fear or conscience. Such rules would not normally require the backing of the law, but some highly specific laws and local ordinances have the character of situational measures.

In an attempt to produce consensual crowd management at the Australian Motorcycle Grand Prix, riders who were permitted to operate campsites for their fellow motorcyclists were encouraged to develop rules and procedures for use of the facilities. This was one element of a package of situational measures that produced a largely trouble-free event in 1991 at Philip Island, Victoria. In previous years, the event had been marred by brawls between the police and the crowds (Veno and Veno 1993).

Introduction of a widely supported local ordinance banning the consumption of alcohol in the streets and open public spaces of central Coventry was followed by reductions of about 40 percent in the number of complaints of insulting behavior and of more than 50 percent in the numbers of people who regarded public drinking as a common problem in Coventry (Ramsay 1991*b*).

M. "Everything Works"?

Cataloging "successes" as in this section, even while acknowledging that many are vulnerable to methodological criticism, may seem to suggest that in situational prevention "everything works," when this is patently not the case. First, impressive as are the reductions in crime (which were sometimes 50 percent or more), it is also clear that, at best, situational measures have ameliorated rather than cured the problem. Second, in some cases discussed in Section IV, the main result of situational measures was to displace not cure the problem. Third, there are numerous instances where situational measures have proved vulnerable to implementation difficulties. In some cases (examples are provided in Section V and in the essay by Laycock and Tilley [in this volume]) these difficulties have involved genuine dilemmas of ethics or costs. In others, the failures have been the result of technical or administrative ineptitude, as when anticlimb paint to deter school break-ins was too thinly applied (Hope and Murphy 1983) or when a scheme to defeat vandalism by repairing particular windows with toughened glass when they were broken proved too complicated for school maintenance staff to administer (Gladstone 1980).

Finally, there are other cases where situational measures have been implemented as planned, but which have not proved successful. This has been for a variety of reasons, as follows.

First, some measures have been too easily defeated by offenders, as in the case of the early steering locks in the United States and Britain which proved highly vulnerable to slide hammers (Clarke and Harris

1992*a*) and that of the "smart" credit cards in France which could be disabled by stamping on the chip (Levi 1992).

Second, too much vigilance has sometimes been assumed on the part of guards or ordinary citizens. Security guards rarely monitor CCTV systems as closely as expected by the designers; people pay far less attention to what is going on outside their homes than is sometimes assumed by neighborhood watch schemes and defensible space designs (Mayhew 1979); and people rarely respond to car alarms, so that the main result of their widespread deployment has been to reduce further the quality of life in cities (Clarke and Harris 1992*a*).

Third, measures have occasionally provoked offenders to unacceptable escalation as in the case of the bulletproofing of token booths on the New York subway which resulted in some attacks on booths with gasoline-fueled fires (Dwyer 1991).

Fourth, some measures have facilitated rather than frustrated crime: Ekblom (1991) cites the example of pickpockets on the London Underground who stationed themselves near signs warning of theft to see which pockets were checked by passengers on reading the signs; and one result of introducing traffic barriers in Vancouver to frustrate cruising johns was that the prostitutes could sit on the bollards and proposition clients who had been forced to slow down (Lowman 1992).

Fifth, in other cases, measures have been defeated by the carelessness or idleness of potential victims. Residents routinely frustrate entry control systems on apartment buildings by propping open the doors to save themselves from answering the door or from taking a key when leaving on a short errand. The preventive value of the early security-coded radios in the United States was reduced because car owners did not enter their private codes, thus allowing the radios to revert to a standard code known to thieves (Braga and Clarke, forthcoming).

Sixth, another reason for the initial lack of success of these radios was that some thieves did not know which radios were security-coded and continued to steal some they could not use. This flaw was remedied by the introduction of a continuously blinking light on the radio indicating that it was security-coded (Braga and Clarke, forthcoming).

Seventh, some inappropriate measures have been introduced because no proper analysis of the problem was undertaken. For example, Harris and Clarke (1991) have argued that the parts-marking provisions of the federal Motor Vehicle Theft Law Enforcement Act of 1984 are doomed to failure because parts marking was restricted only to "high risk" automobiles; leaving aside the resultant scope for displacement, most of the defined "high risk" models are taken not for chopping, but for joyriding, which will not be deterred by parts marking. Measures to disrupt prostitution in Vancouver resulted largely in displacement of the problem because, unlike the case in a London suburb where similar measures had been successful, the prostitutes involved were highly dependent on their earnings to support drug habits or for other reasons (Lowman 1992).

Eighth, other measures have proved unsuitable because insufficient thought has been given to users' needs. For example, one security innovation left senior citizens "trapped inside a fortress of heavy doors and electronic card-key devices which they found difficult to understand and to operate, while neighbours were no longer able to keep a friendly eye on them" (Sampson et al. 1988, p. 484).

As these examples make clear, situational measures do not always work in the intended ways. It is also the case that measures that work in one setting may not do so in another, and not just for the reason (as in the prostitution example above) that different groups of offenders are involved. Thus helmet-wearing laws that serendipitously but dramatically reduced motorcycle theft in Germany (see the next section) appear to have had much less effect in the United States. This is because in the United States the laws were not universally applied as in Germany but were introduced in a piecemeal and inconsistent fashion. Thus laws were introduced in some states, but not in neighboring ones; when in force, laws sometimes applied only to certain sections of the population, for example, those aged below twenty-one, and not to others; and in some states helmet laws were successively introduced, repealed, and introduced again. The result has been confusion and lack of public support. This has meant that the laws have been widely disregarded, which has destroyed their serendipitous value in reducing motorcycle theft.

None of the failures of situational prevention seriously call into question the basic validity of the concept, but they do suggest that matters are more complex than those implementing situational measures frequently appreciate. Much detailed thought has to be put into the design and implementation of measures. They have to be carefully tailored to the settings in which they are applied, with due regard to the motives and methods of the offenders involved, to the costs and acceptability of the solutions proposed, and to the possible unwanted consequences in terms of displacement or escalation. In many cases, those seeking to prevent crime will be competing with inventive and determined offenders trying to defeat the measures introduced. The task is not an impossible one, however, as shown by the many examples of success.

The challenge for research is to help practitioners avoid the pitfalls by providing a sounder base of knowledge on which to act. All we know at present is that some measures work well in certain conditions. What we need to know is which measures work best, in which combination (Tilley 1993b), deployed against what kinds of crime and under what conditions (Poyner 1993). This will require a greatly increased investment in evaluative research, making use of more complex methodology than has often been employed in the past.

IV. Displacement and Diffusion

Under the dispositional assumptions of traditional criminological theory, situational variables merely determine the time and place of offending and manipulating situations would simply cause offenders to shift their attention to some other target, time, or place; change their tactics; or even switch to some other categories of crime (Reppetto 1976). This seeming inevitability of displacement has constituted the principal theoretical criticism of situational prevention, but this has changed with the theoretical developments described in Section I. Under the rational choice assumptions that now guide thinking about situational prevention, displacement is no longer seen as inevitable but as contingent on the offender's judgments about the ease, risks, and attractiveness of alternative crimes. If these alternatives are not viable, it is entirely conceivable that the offender may settle for smaller criminal rewards or for a lower rate of crime. Very few offenders are so driven by need or desire that they have to maintain a certain level of offending whatever the cost. For many, the elimination of easy opportunities for crime may actually encourage them to explore noncriminal alternatives. However, since crime is regarded under the rational choice perspective as the product of purposive and sometimes inventive minds, displacement to apparently quite different categories of offense would not be unexpected, so long as these new crimes served the same purposes as the ones that were thwarted.

In this section, evidence about displacement is reviewed, and the implications of the rational choice perspective are more fully explored. The section closes with a discussion of the more recently recognized phenomenon of "diffusion of benefits." Like displacement, this is a consequence of situational measures, but, since it refers to unexpected reductions in crimes that have not been targeted by the measures, one that has positive implications.

A. Displacement of Crime

Numerous examples of displacement have been reported, particularly in the earlier literature (Gabor 1990). Street crimes increased in surrounding districts following a successful crackdown on these crimes in one New York City precinct (Press 1971). The reduction in robberies following the introduction of exact fare systems on New York City buses was accompanied by an increase in robbery in the subway (Chaiken, Lawless, and Stevenson 1974). In Columbus, Ohio, a police helicopter patrol (Lateef 1974) and, in Newark, New Jersey, a street-lighting program (Tyrpak 1975) appeared to shift crime to precincts not covered by the new measures. The reduced risk of auto theft for new vehicles fitted with steering column locks in Britain was found to be at the expense of an increased risk for older vehicles without the locks (Mayhew et al. 1976). Gabor (1981) found in Ottawa that a property-marking program may have displaced burglaries from the homes of participants to those of nonparticipants. Finally, Allatt (1984) found that the decrease in burglary on a British public housing estate which had undergone a program of "target hardening" was accompanied by an increase in property crimes in adjacent areas.

Apart from these and other instances in which displacement was found, it has often been claimed that researchers have failed to detect displacement that has in fact occurred. This would be especially likely where the displacement involved kinds of crimes other than the ones targeted. Thus the success achieved in reducing aircraft hijackings in the 1970s by baggage screening might possibly have led to an undetected increase in other terrorist activity, such as car bombings, assassinations, and hostage taking. The methodological difficulty encountered in detecting such displacement was explained in an earlier *Crime and Justice* discussion, as follows: "Some displaced crime will probably fall outside the areas and types of crime being studied or be so dispersed as to be masked by background variation. . . . The wider the scope of the study in terms of types of crimes and places, the thinner the patina of displaced crime could be spread across them; thus disappearing into the realm of measurement error" (Barr and Pease 1990, p. 293).

The uncritical acceptance of displacement, however, may also mean that increases in crime, which might have occurred anyway, have sometimes been wrongly attributed to displacement. It has recently been shown that the appearance of a new form of slug soon after the ticket machines of the London Underground had been modified to prevent the use of an earlier, more primitive slug was unlikely to have been due to displacement even though this was believed to be the case by the officials dealing with the problem. Clarke, Cody, and Natarajan (1994) demonstrated that the distribution of the new slugs across the stations of the London Underground was quite different from that of the earlier slugs. This suggested that different groups of offenders were responsible for the new slugs, and it was concluded that, even if action had not been taken against the original slugs, the new ones might still have appeared.

Moreover, in none of the instances of observed displacement did it seem to be 100 percent (Gabor 1990), and, with the development of rational choice analyses, evidence has begun to accumulate of the successful application of situational measures with apparently few displacement costs. Much of this evidence relates to the examples of success cited in Section III. For instance, Knutsson and Kuhlhorn (1981) could find no evidence of an increase in a range of "conceivable" alternative crimes following the implementation of new identification procedures in Sweden that greatly reduced check frauds. Following the rearrangement of market stalls and improved lighting which reduced thefts at covered markets in Birmingham, Poyner and Webb (1987) found no evidence of displacement of thefts to other nearby markets. There was little evidence that reductions in obscene phone calling in areas of New Jersey where Caller-ID became available had led to an increase of such calls in other areas (Clarke 1990). Finally, Clarke, Field, and McGrath (1991) showed that reductions in bank robbery in Australia brought about by target hardening were not followed by increases in armed robberies of alternative targets such as credit unions, betting shops, convenience stores, and service stations.

In other cases cited in Section III, the nature of the targeted offenses would have meant there was little point in looking for displacement. For example, it is unlikely that those deterred by random breath tests from drunken driving in New South Wales (Homel 1993) or those deterred by speed cameras from speeding in Victoria (Bourne and Cooke 1993) would have displaced these behaviors to some other time or place. People do not usually set out to commit these offenses but will do so when circumstances dictate (Homel 1993). One important circumstance is the perceived chance of arrest and, were the ubiquitous speed cameras or random-breath-testing patrols to be withdrawn, people would no doubt once again revert to their old ways.

Once the contingent nature of displacement is recognized, it is not usually difficult to explain why it may not have occurred in particular instances. For example, Clarke, Field, and McGrath (1991) explained the lack of displacement of armed robberies from target-hardened banks to convenience stores and petrol (gas) service stations on the grounds that these latter targets would not generally yield such large "takes" and might be beneath the dignity of the more organized criminal gangs. In explaining the apparent lack of displacement of obscene phone calls to other areas following the introduction of Caller-ID in parts of New Jersey, Clarke (1990) points out that by no means all obscene phone callers are persistent random dialers hoping to hit on a susceptible woman. Many appear to victimize only particular women of their acquaintance, and it is unlikely that, with the introduction of Caller-ID in their local telephone areas, these individuals would have begun to call to more distant parts of New Jersey where they would be less likely to know anyone. (Incidentally, as drinking and masturbation seem to be quite frequent accompaniments of obscene phone calling, it is unlikely that calling from a public phone box to avoid the risk of identification would often be a practicable alternative to calling from one's home or place of business.) Finally, in explaining why prostitutes did not simply move to other locations following successful action to close down the red-light district in Finsbury Park, Matthews (1990) cites the low commitment to prostitution of many of the women involved, who appeared to be drawn to Finsbury Park by its reputation as a good place to solicit. Interviews with some of these women revealed that many saw prostitution as a relatively easy way to make a living but on occasion were employed in other unskilled occupations, working also as waitresses or shop assistants. As the environment in Finsbury Park became less hospitable, "It would seem that over a period of about one year, most of the girls gave up prostitution or moved back home or elsewhere. For many, their normal period of involvement in prostitution may have been three or four years and, therefore, the effect of intensive policing was to shorten that period for a year or two in most cases" (Matthews 1990, p. 186).

Deeper understanding of the motives and modus operandi of target groups of offenders, as obtained in Matthews's study, provides a way of dealing with the limitations of the statistical search for displacement discussed by Barr and Pease (1990). It may not always be possible to interview offenders, but in some cases insights into motivation and methods can be provided by closer analysis of patterns of offending. For example, Clarke and Harris (1992b) have shown important differences among automobiles in their risks for different forms of theft, which reflect the motives of offenders. Thus new cars most at risk of "stripping" in the United States during the mid-1980s were predominantly European models with good audio equipment, those most at risk of "joyriding" were American-made "muscle" cars, and those at risk of theft for resale were mostly higher-priced luxury automobiles. These "choice structuring properties" (Cornish and Clarke 1987) of the target vehicles are not difficult to understand in terms of the motives of offenders and would also help to direct the search for displacement if the security were improved for any subset of vehicles. Thus if some "muscle" cars were made more difficult to take for joyriding, it would make sense to confine the search for displacement only to others of the same group.

Similar logic was followed by Mayhew, Clarke, and Elliott (1989) in their study of displacement following the reduction of motorcycle thefts in West Germany between 1980 and 1986, brought about by the progressive enforcement of helmet legislation. During this period motorcycle thefts declined by more than 100,000 because the helmet requirement substantially increased the risks of opportunistic thefts for those offenders who were unable at the same time to steal a helmet. Mayhew and her colleagues reasoned that since many opportunistic thefts would have been for purposes of joyriding or temporary use (e.g., to get home late at night), the most likely result of the reduced opportunities for stealing motorcycles would be an increase in thefts of cars and bicycles. In fact, as shown by the data in table 2, there was little evidence of displacement to either category of target. Car thefts did rise over the same period, but only by a few thousand, while bicycle thefts declined (after an initial rise) to below their previous level. Bicycles may not usually provide a realistic or attractive alternative means of transportation, whereas cars may not provide the same joyriding thrills, may require more knowledge to operate, and may be more difficult to steal.

A final illustration of the value of considering "choice structuring properties" is provided by the British gas suicide story (Clarke and Mayhew 1988). The elimination of gas suicides in Britain in the 1960s

TABLE 2

Thefts of Motorcycles, Cars, and Bicycles: Federal Republic of Germany, 1980–86

Year	Motorcycles	Cars	Bicycles
1980	153,153	64,131	358,865
1981	143,317	71,916	410,223
1982	134,735	78,543	453,850
1983	118,550	82,211	415,398
1984	90,008	72,170	376,946
1985	73,442	69,659	337,337
1986	54,208	70,245	301,890

SOURCE.—Mayhew, Clarke, and Elliott (1989).

and 1970s resulting from the introduction of natural gas (which contains no toxins) was not followed by substantial displacement to other forms of suicide. Consequently, the overall suicide rate for the country declined by about 40 percent. The lack of displacement was explained by Clarke and Mayhew in terms of the particular advantages of the use of domestic gas as a form of suicide. It was readily available in every home, it was simple to use, and it was highly lethal. It was also painless, left no marks or blood, and required little courage. No other alternative possessed all these advantages and would therefore have provided an acceptable alternative for many people. Sleeping pills and other poisons were much less lethal. Easy access to car exhaust gas was limited to a minority of the population. Guns and knives were perceived as violent and painful. In Britain, hanging is perceived to be a death reserved for traitors and murderers. Finally, most older people would find it difficult to clamber up steep cliffs or down to railway tracks.

It has been argued that it will only be a matter of time before the suicidally inclined displace to other methods and the suicide rate reverts to its former level; indeed, this is now true of the suicide rate for males. However, there is substantial evidence that for many people the urge to kill themselves is in response to situational stress (such as a bereavement) and may dissipate as depression is alleviated. It is therefore unlikely that the suicide rate has been substantially swelled in recent years by individuals who were prevented from killing themselves in earlier years by the detoxification of gas but who eventually succeeded with another method. The gradual increase in the male suicide rate may reflect, not delayed displacement, but underlying motivational trends. Even if there has been an increase in the use of other methods (including exhaust gases [Clarke and Lester 1987]), any such changes might have occurred anyway, even if poisoning by domestic gas were still available as a method.

This argument about the consequences of gas detoxification should not be taken to mean that longer-term adaptations do not occur in response to situational measures. Indeed, it is highly probable that such changes do occur. For example, it has frequently been claimed that car thieves have found ways around steering column locks, and, indeed, there is some support for this in that rates of car theft in some countries where these locks have been fitted for many years have not declined as much as expected (Clarke and Harris 1992a). However, it is too easy to assume that offenders will eventually always find a way around preventive measures. Even in the case of steering column locks, the experience has not always been consistent with this view. It has recently been shown that the reduction in the rate of car thefts in West Germany, brought about by the introduction of steering column locks in the 1960s, has persisted to this day (Webb and Laycock 1992; Webb 1994). In contrast, the rate of theft from vehicles (which steering column locks have little impact on) has increased steadily over the past thirty years (see fig. 2).

Clarke and Harris (1992a) have argued that a possible reason for the enduring success of the steering locks in West Germany (apart from the possibly higher quality of the German equipment) is that, because the locks were made compulsory for all cars on the road, theft was greatly reduced almost overnight. The long-term consequence of this was that neophytes were frequently deprived of the example and tutelage of experienced car thieves, which may have helped to destroy local "car theft cultures" in many parts of the country. This affords a marked contrast with the situation in most other countries (including the United States and Britain) where the locks were introduced only for new cars at manufacture. Consequently, car thieves could continue to operate so long as they concentrated their efforts on older vehicles. They could also gradually learn ways of defeating the steering locks and could continue to pass on the tricks of the trade to novices. This may help to explain why rates of car theft in these other countries, even though most cars on the road now have the steering column locks, are higher than in Germany (Webb 1994).

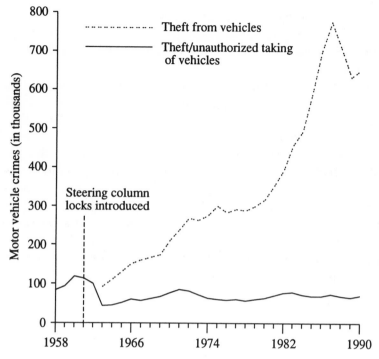

Fig. 2.—Motor vehicle crime in the Federal Republic of Germany, 1958–90. Source: Webb and Laycock (1992).

B. Diffusion of Benefits

It has been argued above that the rational choice perspective results in a more complex, and ultimately more optimistic, view of displacement. While the possibility of displacement should never be overlooked, and while it may often be difficult to detect, it is clearly not as inevitable as some of the earlier dispositional thinking assumed. Moreover, as argued by Barr and Pease (1990), even when it occurs it may sometimes be "benign" as in the case, for example, of preventive measures which bring relief to repeatedly victimized groups although at the cost of an increased risk for others. This observation provided the rationale for decisions about the allocation of scarce preventive resources in an experiment to reduce burglary in Kirkholt, a public housing estate in the North of England (Pease 1991). Target-hardening priority was given to houses that had recently experienced a burglary, with the result that, despite their higher risks, very few of these houses experienced a further burglary in the follow-up period. Pease also noted that these preventive benefits permeated, through what he called a process of "drip-feed," to other households that were not target-hardened so that the burglary rate for the whole of the Kirkholt estate declined dramatically.

The "drip-feed" effect is, of course, the reverse of displacement in that preventive action led, not to an increase, but to a reduction in crimes not directly addressed by the measures. As Clarke and Weisburd (1994) observe, similar effects have been noted under a variety of other names. For example, Miethe (1991) has referred to the "free rider" effect when residents benefit from the crime prevention measures taken by their neighbors, and Sherman (1990) to the "bonus" effect sometimes observed in police crackdowns when there is a carryover of the preventive effect beyond the period when the crackdown is in force. Scherdin (1986) used the term "halo effect" when reporting that book detection systems prevented thefts, not just of the electronically protected materials, but also of other materials as well. In some cases, the phenomenon has been reported without giving it a name. Poyner and Webb (1987) found that measures to reduce thefts from shopping bags in particular city center markets seemed also to reduce thefts in other markets as well. In his evaluation of a CCTV system installed to reduce auto theft at a university, Poyner (1991) found an equal reduction of crime in the parking lot not covered by cameras as in the ones covered. In his study of CCTV on buses, he found that damage and other misbehavior was reduced, not only on five buses fitted with cameras, but throughout the whole fleet of eighty buses (Poyner 1988).

Despite the variety of terminology, in all these cases the same phenomenon has been observed. That is to say, reductions in crime have occurred which are difficult to attribute to the direct action of situational measures. Clarke and Weisburd (1994) have argued that the generality of the phenomenon demands a standard term and have proposed "diffusion of benefits," since the geographical and temporal connotations of this term parallel those of "displacement of crime." They have defined diffusion as "the spread of the beneficial influence of an intervention beyond the places which are directly targeted, the individuals who are the subject of control, the crimes which are the focus of intervention or the time periods in which an intervention is brought" (Clarke and Weisburd 1994, p. 169). They have also distinguished between two forms of diffusion which they call "deterrence" and "discouragement." Deterrence was invoked by Scherdin (1986), for example, in explaining why the book detection system she studied also prevented thefts of items that were not electronically tagged and by Poyner in identifying reasons for the general decline in damage to the fleet when only some of the buses were fitted with CCTV cameras: "The children have learned . . . that the cameras will enable misbehaving individuals to be picked out and that action will be taken. . . . They appear to believe that most buses have cameras, or at least they are uncertain about which buses have cameras" (Poyner 1988, p. 50).

Deterrence affects offenders' assessments of risk, but, for diffusion by "discouragement," the key is not the judgment of risk, but the assessment of effort and reward. For example, one component of the successful action against burglary in Kirkholt was the removal of prepayment meters from many houses on the estate (Pease 1991). This seems to have been enough to discourage potential burglars, who could no longer be sure of finding a meter containing cash without expending much additional effort. Similarly, the drop in thefts at all Birmingham city center markets following the situational measures taken at only some of them may have been due to the fact that "the general attractiveness of this area for thieves has reduced" (Poyner and Webb 1987). Ekblom (1988) accounted for the finding that antibandit screens in London post offices had produced a reduction, not just in over-the-counter robberies, but also in other robberies of staff and customers when he speculated that would-be robbers may have received "the very general message that something had been done to improve security at the sub-post offices" (Ekblom 1988, p. 39). Finally, Clarke, Field, and McGrath (1991) have suggested that an intensive target-hardening program in Australian banks brought about a general reduction in robberies of all commercial targets (including convenience stores, gas stations, and betting shops) because robbers began to believe that this form of crime was no longer worth pursuing.

It would be difficult to overestimate the importance of diffusion of benefits if the phenomenon is as common as these various examples suggest. At the very least, the possibility of diffusion will have a profound effect on the design of evaluations, particularly those that make use of "control" areas not directly targeted by situational measures and supposedly unaffected by them. Indeed, there may already have been evaluations in which the benefits of situational action have been underestimated because falls in crime were also observed in "control" areas, with the conclusion that both "experimental" and "control" areas had been subject to a general but extraneous decline in crime. Whatever the case previously, it is clear that in the future, evaluators must pay attention not only to the problems of displacement but also to the benefits of diffusion.

It is also clear that much more needs to be discovered about ways of enhancing diffusion. Sherman (1990) has suggested that the "free bonus" of crackdowns might be increased by randomly rotating crackdowns and back offs across times and places so as to lead offenders to overestimate the actual levels of risk in force on any particular occasion. He also advocated the deliberate use of publicity about imminent crackdowns to promote this uncertainty in offenders' minds. Clarke and Weisburd (1994) argue that these strategies might be employed to diffuse the benefits of forms of "situational deterrence" (Cusson 1993) other than crackdowns, and they also identify other possible means of enhancing diffusion, such as concentrating preventive action on highly visible or attractive targets (i.e., Pease's [1991] "drip feeding" of crime prevention), so as to lead offenders to think that preventive measures may have been more generally applied.

Since these various strategies depend on influencing judgments made by offenders, we need to learn more about ways that offenders obtain and process information about preventive initiatives and what role is played in this process by their own direct observation, their relationships with other offenders, and information obtained through the media. Such research would be of broader theoretical interest if it were to be conducted within a larger program of work on how offenders perceive and evaluate the opportunity structure for crime and how they learn about ways in which this expands as well as contracts. Whatever the practical payoff from such studies and other related research on offender perceptions, it is likely that, in the 1990s, diffusion of benefits may come to supplant displacement as the principal focus for theoretical debate about the value of situational measures.

V. Ideology and Implementation

Given the numerous policy advantages of situational prevention, it might have been expected to achieve broad acceptance across the political spectrum. The Left might have welcomed its focus on local problems and local decision making; liberals might have been attracted to its essentially nonpunitive philosophy; and conservatives might have been attuned to its message concerning the need for agencies and communities to take the initiative in dealing with their crime problems. Instead, it has often been met with indifference and even hostility. The Right, and this includes most varieties of political opinion in the United States, sees it as a fundamentally irrelevant response to crime because it eschews questions of moral culpability and punishment (see Bright 1992). The Left criticizes it for neglecting issues of social justice and for being too accepting of establishment definitions of crime (Young 1988). Liberals fear that its avoidance of the "root causes" of crime, such as poverty, deprivation, and unemployment, may divert attention from these problems.

Much of this hostility has been fueled by the more unattractive, target-hardening forms of situational prevention which have been seen as harbingers of a "fortress society," in which people fearful of crime barricade themselves in their homes and places of work (Davis 1990). Increased experience with situational prevention may dispel some of these fears since many of the measures (such as steering column locks and parts marking of automobiles) are unobtrusive or may actually reduce fear of crime (e.g., through improved street lighting or defensible space architecture). Other measures which enhance security, such as bar coding of merchandise and central locking of automobiles, have considerable advantages of convenience.

It is ironic, as previously noted (Clarke 1992), that this unobtrusiveness and convenience feeds another fear: it may not be the fortress society that is imminent, but Aldous Huxley's "brave new world." The Orwellian specter of "Big Brother" state control, stimulated by the already widespread use of CCTV and intruder alarms, has been provoked by reports of rapidly approaching new forms of technology that will greatly expand the potential for totalitarian control, not of the iron fist but of the velvet glove (Marx 1986).

Little matter that these fears of the State's blanket adoption of situational controls are inconsistent with the piecemeal and analytic nature of the approach. Little matter also that such controls can often be applied only by particular private or business organizations. Rather, it seems likely that concerns about the erosion of privacy and civil liberties will increasingly be raised in opposition to situational measures. These concerns are discussed below. Also addressed separately below is another barrier to implementation: the difficulty of persuading managers not used to dealing with crime (particularly those in the private sector) to accept responsibility for preventive action. Discussion of a wider range of implementation issues can be found in the essay by Laycock and Tilley (in this volume).

A. *Privacy and Civil Liberties*

Concerns about the erosion of privacy and civil liberties have already led to difficulties for a variety of preventive measures. The best-known example relates to gun controls which are vehemently opposed by a section of the U.S. population on grounds of their supposed infringements of constitutional liberties. This has made it difficult for many states to enact mild and sensible laws, endorsed by a majority of the population, prohibiting private ownership of so-called assault weapons or requiring background checks and waiting periods at the time of purchase.

A taste of things to come may also be provided by controversies surrounding the attempted implementation of two new forms of technology, Caller-ID and speed cameras (or "photo radar," which is the name in the United States). Caller-ID (which is a device that reveals the caller's telephone number to the person answering) has a number of crime prevention advantages, apart from providing a deterrent to obscene and harassing calls (Clarke 1990). It deters fraudulent sales, bomb hoaxes, and false fire alarms. It also increases the risks for burglars in using the phone to check for occupancy and for robbers in luring delivery drivers to a convenient location for attack.

Despite these crime prevention advantages and other benefits for subscribers (such as the maintenance of a record of all numbers calling while the phone is unattended), the introduction of Caller-ID has been subject to court battles in many parts of the United States. In a number of these suits, civil libertarians have successfully opposed introduction of the service on grounds that it constitutes an unwarranted intrusion on the privacy of telephone callers, particularly those with unlisted numbers (Temple and Regan 1991). In making the case against Caller-ID, recourse has been made to various arguments: it violates some state wiretap laws; it can reveal the telephone numbers of people such as secret service agents or battered women in refuges who have good reason to keep their whereabouts secret; it inhibits the use of informant hot lines and confidential telephone counseling by the Samaritans and others; and it may facilitate the development of unwelcome forms of telemarketing.

Solutions exist for most of these problems. For example, blocking mechanisms that prevent display of the number can selectively be provided. Most telephone subscribers, even those with unlisted numbers, approve of Caller-ID. Nevertheless, the legal arguments about callers' privacy have generally prevailed, and in a number of states Caller-ID has been prohibited or introduced only with a blocking option available to all subscribers. This latter effectively undermines many of the crime prevention benefits of Caller-ID. That this should be the general outcome of the court hearings is ironic because not so long ago anyone wishing to make a telephone call had to place it through an operator who might know the caller's identity as well as telephone number. This imposed a significant control on the telephone as a facilitator of crime—a control that was removed only by subsequent developments in technology.

The recent fate of attempts in New Jersey to implement a federally sponsored experiment in photo radar constitutes a similarly sorry tale. Despite its documented successes in substantially reducing speeding and fatal accidents (e.g., Bourne and Cooke 1993), the New Jersey State Assembly voted to ban the use of the device. The assemblyman who sponsored the legislation was quoted as fearing "the depersonalization of law enforcement," possible reductions in police manpower, and higher insurance rates for convicted speeders that might result from widespread use of the devices (*Law Enforcement News* 1992, p. 7; see also Marisco 1992).

This bodes ill for other possible applications of technology in preventing crime and controlling traffic infringements, such as the equipment that has reportedly been tested in Hong Kong permitting automatic monitoring of vehicle speeds through transmissions received from small radios located in individual cars (Marx 1986). Perhaps all these devices offend people's sense of fair play. People have to be given a sporting chance of getting away with crime, especially the ordinary everyday offenses that all of us might commit. Whatever the reason, these will surely not be isolated examples, and they suggest that, far from being willing dupes in accepting "the new surveillance" (Marx 1986), people will resist its deployment in the routine situations giving rise to most crime as soon as they suspect that they might fall victim to its impersonal (and one might say unbiased) law enforcement efficiency.

B. Costs and Responsibility

Most situational prevention to date has been undertaken in the public sector, and discussion of implementation difficulties has been focused largely on ways of achieving the necessary coordination among local government agencies (e.g., Gladstone 1980; Hope 1985; Ekblom 1987). But it is now being increasingly recognized that much preventive action can be undertaken only by the private sector (e.g., by credit card companies, bus operators, offices, and shopping malls). Encouraging this action will involve government in developing a dialogue with a whole new set of actors (including the security industry, which may not welcome the potential threat to its role), most of whom can be expected to take a hard-nosed view in dealing with crime. They will see this as largely a police matter and will rarely be willing to "acknowledge that their property or operations are generating a substantial strain on police resources, accept that they have a duty, up to their level of competence, for the control of specific crimes, and take appropriate action" (Engstad and Evans 1980, p. 151). Acknowledging this responsibility would not only complicate the management task but could involve the expenditure of significant resources. Analyses of these costs are therefore likely to play an increasingly important role in crime prevention, and it is no accident that one of the first publications of the Home Office Crime Prevention Unit aimed at the private sector presents information (under the revealing title of *Making Crime Prevention Pay*) about initiatives taken by businesses that prevented crime and saved money (Burrows 1991).

The implementation issues involved are illustrated by the familiar example of shoplifting. This is promoted by many current retailing practices, such as self-service and displays that encourage impulse buying. The risks of the ensuing "shrinkage" are accepted by most stores, which rely on deterrence to contain the problem through the occasional arrest and prosecution of shoplifters. This results in significant costs being passed on to the criminal justice system, which of course are not borne by the retailers except in an indirect way through taxation.

These attitudes and practices are unlikely to change simply as a result of government exhortation (which runs the risk of being dismissed as "blaming the victim" [Karmen 1984]). Nor is it likely in the present climate that Pease's (1979) ideas about charging for police service when stores have failed to adopt preventive measures would provide a realistic alternative. However, declining retail profits, resulting from the combined pressure of a faltering economy and increased competition, might force a change. Thus it has recently been found, in the fierce competitive environment of discount electronics and appliance sales, that sustained attention to the prevention of theft and fraud can significantly improve profit margins (Masuda 1992, 1993).

Greater attention to retail security is also likely to result from improved technology which permits instant credit checks (Levi, Bissell, and Richardson 1991) and tighter stock control (Hope 1991), but in every case of its application, the technology will need to pass cost-benefit scrutiny by the retailer. This scrutiny is unlikely to take account of the criminal justice costs of the failure to take preventive action, and there will be an increasing role here for studies by economists. Field's (1993) analysis of the costs of auto theft in the United States illustrates the potential value of such work. In a study that attempted to take account of a wide range of costs (including those falling on society as a whole, on motorists as a group, on the victims, and on the criminal justice system), he found that about two-thirds of the total cost of $35 per automobile in 1985 was accounted for by insurance premiums. Only a very small proportion of the total costs fell directly on victims as a whole (though some individual victims may suffer large losses). Under these conditions, Field argues, potential victims as a group have little incentive to invest in preventive devices. Nor is there much incentive for insurance companies to demand greater built-in security for automobiles because most of their profits come from investing premium income; the greater the risks of auto theft, the larger the premiums and the higher the profits.

Though Field dismisses arguments that motor manufacturers also have a vested interest in auto theft through the demand produced for replacement vehicles (Karmen 1981; Brill 1982), he argues that they too have little incentive to produce cars with any greater levels of security than the public demands. He doubts that even the argument that if motorists were to pay less for insurance, they would be prepared to pay more for new cars, would carry much weight in an industry that has traditionally been so concerned with reducing unit costs. He concludes that in the conditions of this "imperfect market," improved vehicle security will only come about as a result of government action to mandate vehicle security standards. Assuming that these prevented only about half of the current number of auto thefts, and assuming that the average life of a car is somewhat less than ten years, this should still produce savings in insurance costs of a couple of hundred dollars per car at current prices. Given the economies of scale resulting from the universal introduction of improved security, this amount should be more than sufficient to pay for the improved security as well as to yield a net reduction in the overall costs of auto theft.

Even if details of Field's analysis can be criticized, it is still important for the fresh perspective it brings to bear on the discussion of auto theft prevention. There is little doubt that further economic analysis of the costs and benefits of crime prevention could be of great value in assisting government to find the best ways—whether involving tax incentives, publicity and persuasion, or mandated security standards—to promote preventive action in the private sector.

VI. Concluding Remarks

Although slow to gain acceptance in some academic and government circles, situational prevention is in a better position than when last reviewed for *Crime and Justice* in 1983. In particular, its theoretical and empirical base has been strengthened by a wide range of criminological research. Its applications have been extended to many problems of crime and disorder in a wide variety of contexts. The threat presented by displacement has receded with an improvement in theoretical understanding and an accumulation of empirical observations. Finally, it is increasingly recognized that focused preventive efforts may sometimes result in the "diffusion of benefits" in terms of reductions in crimes not directly addressed by the measures.

Particularly important has been the development of the rational choice perspective, which has provided a means of articulating the link between the two main groups of explanatory variables—offender and situational—and which has opened up a new line of policy-relevant research into offender decision making. As a consequence, situational prevention should become more attractive to criminologists, and its academic future ought to be secure, as least as judged by Colander's (1991) three requirements of publishability, teachability, and communicability. It has the potential to generate an almost unending stream of scholarly papers and dissertations. Its theoretical base is sufficiently broad and complex to satisfy the teaching requirements of a broad range of academic social scientists and to engage the interest of some, such as economists and geographers, whose assistance in developing situational prevention is needed. Its action research methodology and broad armory of practical techniques permits it to be communicated to the broad range of people—police, local officials, and managers in public and private agencies—who might have cause to investigate its relevance for their work.

The involvement of the private sector promises to extend the reach of situational prevention still further, and criminologists will have to become familiar with a host of behavioral settings—transportation systems, retail environments, factories, schools, and so forth—beyond the courts and the prisons. Indeed, it is not too fanciful to imagine that the wider application of situational prevention will result in criminologists being employed in a wide range of public and private agencies. If they are to be successful in these settings, however, they may need to adopt as mentors not sociologists and academics, but problem solvers such as traffic engineers and public health professionals.

The future reach of situational measures is also likely to be expanded by new technology (as it has been in the past decade by Caller-ID, photo radar, and many other devices) and, at least in the United States, by its growing convergence with problem-oriented policing. This convergence may help move it to a more central policy role, though implementation difficulties, ideological resistance, questions about displacement, and doubts about the capacity of situational measures to deal with violent and sexual offenses may continue to be impediments. Further loss of support from policy makers may result from its lack of dramatic effect on the totality of crime unless applied in the literally hundreds of settings that may be necessary. (It is already being criticized for not having reduced the crime rate when it has only been patchily applied in a comparatively few, and generally small-scale, projects.)

These various difficulties and criticisms will have to be addressed in the next generation of research. The need for a variety of "theoretical" studies has been identified in this essay, including research into the relationship between security and private space, into the supply of targets and crime facilitators, and into offender perceptions of the expansion of criminal opportunities resulting from social change and their contraction due to crime prevention activity. Such studies will help to clarify the theoretical limits of situational prevention, but they need to be complemented by more practically-oriented research into means of preventing particular crimes in particular contexts, into the limits of the various opportunity-reducing techniques, into ways of overcoming barriers to implementation, and into ways of containing displacement and enhancing diffusion. Research of this latter kind should help to deliver crime reductions in the increasingly efficient manner that seems likely to be demanded by the policy makers of the future.

Its future policy role may also depend, however, on the results of new work on developmental and community crime prevention directed at modifying criminal propensities. These approaches have broader appeal because they represent a more optimistic view of human nature. They do not manipulate or cajole people into compliance, but teach them to value conformity for its own sake. They lack only the evidence that they can be widely and effectively deployed, but were this forthcoming, they might readily eclipse situational prevention. However, if this evidence were not to emerge in any compelling form, it is unlikely that these approaches would fade from the policy scene since the desire to improve people is so strong and enduring. Rather, it may be that situational controls, sensitively and carefully designed to contain the unwanted results of the expanding personal freedom that accompanies technological and economic progress, will increasingly become accepted as an indispensable part of policy.

REFERENCES

Allatt, Pat. 1984. "Residential Security: Containment and Displacement of Burglary." *Howard Journal of Criminal Justice* 23:99–116.

Ardrey, Robert. 1966. *The Territorial Imperative.* New York: Dell.

Barr, Robert, and Ken Pease. 1990. "Crime Placement, Displacement, and Deflection." In *Crime and Justice: A Review of Research*, vol. 12, edited by Michael Tonry and Norval Morris. Chicago: University of Chicago Press.

Becker, Gary S. 1968. "Crime and Punishment: An Economic Approach." *Journal of Political Economy* 76:169–217.

Bell, John, and Barbara Burke. 1989. "Cruising Cooper Street." *Police Chief* (January) 56:26–29.

Bennett, Trevor. 1990. *Evaluating Neighbourhood Watch.* Aldershot, Hants: Gower.

Bennett, Trevor, and Richard Wright. 1984. *Burglars on Burglary.* Farnborough, Hants: Gower.

Berkowitz, Leonard, and A. LePage. 1967. "Weapons as Aggression-eliciting Stimuli." *Journal of Personality and Social Psychology* 7:202–27.

Biron, Louise L., and Carol Ladouceur. 1991. "The Boy Next Door: Local Teen-age Burglars in Montreal." *Security Journal* 2:200–204.

Bjor, Jill, Johannes Knutsson, and Eckhart Kuhlhorn. 1992. "The Celebration of Midsummer Eve in Sweden: A Study in the Art of Preventing Collective Disorder." *Security Journal* 3:169–74.

Bottoms, Anthony E. 1990. "Crime Prevention Facing the 1990s." *Policing and Society* 1:3–22.

Bourne, Michael G., and Ronald C. Cooke. 1993. "Victoria's Speed Camera Program." In *Crime Prevention Studies*, vol. 1, edited by Ronald V. Clarke. Monsey, N.Y.: Criminal Justice Press.

Braga, Anthony, and Ronald V. Clarke. "Improved Radios and More Stripped Cars in Germany: A Routine Activities Analysis." *Security Journal* (forthcoming).

Brantingham, Patricia L., and Paul J. Brantingham. 1988. "Situational Crime Prevention in British Columbia." *Journal of Security Administration* 11:17–27.

Brantingham, Paul J., and Patricia L. Brantingham. 1975. "The Spatial Patterning of Burglary." *Howard Journal of Criminal Justice* 14:11–23.

———. 1991. *Environmental Criminology*. 2d ed. Prospect Heights, Ill.: Waveland.

Briar, S., and I. M. Piliavin. 1965. "Delinquency, Situational Inducements and Commitment to Conformity." *Social Problems* 13:35–45.

Bright, Jon. 1992. *Crime Prevention in America: A British Perspective*. Chicago: University of Illinois at Chicago, Office of International Criminal Justice.

Brill, Harry. 1982. "Auto Theft and the Role of Big Business." *Crime and Social Justice* 18:62–68.

Brody, Stephen R. 1976. *The Effectiveness of Sentencing*. Home Office Research Study no. 35. London: H.M. Stationery Office.

Burbidge, Michael. 1984. "British Public Housing and Crime." In *Coping with Burglary*, edited by Ronald V. Clarke and T. Hope. Boston, Mass.: Kluwer-Nijhoff.

Burrows, John. 1991. *Making Crime Prevention Pay: Initiatives from Business*. Crime Prevention Unit Paper 27. London: Home Office.

Burt, Cyril. 1925. *The Young Delinquent*. London: University of London Press. Reprinted 1969.

Carr, Kerri, and Geoff Spring. 1993. "Public Transport Safety: A Community Right and a Communal Responsibility." In *Crime Prevention Studies*, vol. 1, edited by Ronald V. Clarke. Monsey, N.Y.: Criminal Justice Press.

Carroll, John, and Frances Weaver. 1986. "Shoplifter's Perceptions of Crime Opportunities: A Process-tracing Study." In *The Reasoning Criminal*, edited by Derek B. Cornish and Ronald V. Clarke. New York: Springer-Verlag.

Chaiken, Jan M., Michael W. Lawless, and Keith A. Stevenson. 1974. *The Impact of Police Activity on Crime: Robberies on the New York City Subway System*. Report no. R-1424-N.Y.C. Santa Monica, Calif.: RAND.

Challinger, Dennis. 1991. "Less Telephone Vandalism: How Did It Happen?" *Security Journal* 2:111–19.

Clarke, Ronald V. 1977. "Psychology and Crime." *Bulletin of the British Psychological Society* 30:280–83.

———. 1980. "Situational Crime Prevention: Theory and Practice." *British Journal of Criminology* 20:136–47.

———. 1983. "Situational Crime Prevention: Its Theoretical Basis and Practical Scope." In *Crime and Justice: An Annual Review of Research*, vol. 4, edited by Michael Tonry and Norval Morris. Chicago: University of Chicago Press.

———. 1984. "Opportunity-based Crime Rates." *British Journal of Criminology* 24:74–83.

———. 1990. "Deterring Obscene Phone Callers: Preliminary Results of the New Jersey Experience." *Security Journal* 1:143–48.

———, ed. 1992. *Situational Crime Prevention: Successful Case Studies*. Albany, N.Y.: Harrow & Heston.

———. 1993. "Fare Evasion and Automatic Ticket Collection on the London Underground." In *Crime Prevention Studies*, vol. 1, edited by Ronald V. Clarke. Monsey, N.Y.: Criminal Justice Press.

Clarke, Ronald V., Ronald Cody, and Mangai Natarajan. 1994. "Subway Slugs: Tracking Displacement on the London Underground." *British Journal of Criminology* 34:122–38.

Clarke, Ronald V., and Derek B. Cornish. 1983. *Crime Control in Britain: A Review of Policy Research*. Albany: State University of New York Press.

———. 1985. "Modeling Offenders' Decisions: A Framework for Research and Policy." In *Crime and Justice: An Annual Review of Research*, vol. 6, edited by Michael Tonry and Norval Morris. Chicago: University of Chicago Press.

Clarke, Ronald V., and Marcus Felson. 1993. "Introduction: Criminology, Routine Activity and Rational Choice." In *Routine Activity and Rational Choice: Advances in Criminological Theory*, vol. 5, edited by Ronald V. Clarke and Marcus Felson. New Brunswick, N.J.: Transaction Publishers.

Clarke, Ronald V., Simon Field, and Gerard McGrath. 1991. "Target Hardening of Banks in Australia and Displacement of Robberies." *Security Journal* 2:84–90.

Clarke, Ronald V., and Patricia M. Harris. 1992a. "Auto Theft and Its Prevention." In *Crime and Justice: A Review of Research*, vol. 16, edited by Michael Tonry.

———. 1992b. "A Rational Choice Perspective on the Targets of Automobile Theft." *Criminal Behaviour and Mental Health* 2:25–42.

Clarke, Ronald V., and David Lester. 1987. "Toxicity of Car Exhausts and Opportunity for Suicide: Comparison between Britain and the United States." *Journal of Epidemiology and Community Health* 41:114–20.

———. 1989. *Suicide: Closing the Exits*. New York: Springer-Verlag.

Clarke, Ronald V., and Gerard McGrath. 1990. "Cash Reduction and Robbery Prevention in Australian Betting Shops." *Security Journal* 1:160–63.

Clarke, Ronald V., and Patricia M. Mayhew. 1980. *Designing out Crime*. London: Her Majesty's Stationery Office.

———. 1988. "The British Gas Suicide Story and Its Criminological Implications." In *Crime and Justice: A Review of Research*, vol. 10, edited by Michael Tonry and Norval Morris. Chicago: University of Chicago Press.

Clarke, Ronald V., and David Weisburd. 1994. "Diffusion of Crime Control Benefits: Observations on the Reverse of Displacement." In *Crime Prevention Studies*, vol. 2, edited by Ronald V. Clarke. Monsey, N.Y.: Criminal Justice Press.

Cohen, Lawrence E., and Marcus Felson. 1979. "Social Change and Crime

Rate Trends: A Routine Activity Approach." *American Sociological Review* 44:588–608.

Colander, David. 1991. *Why Aren't Economists as Important as Garbagemen? Essays on the State of Economics.* Armonk, N.Y.: M. E. Sharpe.

Coleman, Alice. 1985. *Utopia on Trial: Vision and Reality in Planned Housing.* London: Hilary Shipman.

Cook, Phillip J. 1991. "The Technology of Personal Violence." In *Crime and Justice: A Review of Research*, vol. 14, edited by Michael Tonry. Chicago: University of Chicago Press.

Cornish, Derek B. 1993. "Theories of Action in Criminology: Learning Theory and Rational Choice Approaches." In *Routine Activity and Rational Choice: Advances in Criminological Theory*, vol. 5, edited by Ronald V. Clarke and Marcus Felson. New Brunswick, N.J.: Transaction Publishers.

Cornish, Derek B., and Ronald V. Clarke. 1986. *The Reasoning Criminal.* New York: Springer-Verlag.

———. 1987. "Understanding Crime Displacement: An Application of Rational Choice Theory." *Criminology* 25:933–47.

Cromwell, Paul F., James N. Olson, and D'Aunn Wester Avary. 1991. *Breaking and Entering: An Ethnographic Analysis of Burglary.* Newbury Park, Calif.: Sage.

Cusson, Maurice. 1986. "L'Analyse Strategique et Quelques Developpements Recente en Criminologie." *Criminologie* 19:51–72.

———. 1993. "Situational Deterrence: Fear during the Criminal Event." In *Crime Prevention Studies*, vol. 1, edited by Ronald V. Clarke. Monsey, N.Y.: Criminal Justice Press.

Davis, Mike. 1990. *City of Quartz: Excavating the Future in Los Angeles.* London: Verso.

Decker, John F. 1972. "Curbside Deterrence: An Analysis of the Effect of a Slug Rejectory Device, Coin View Window and Warning Labels on Slug Usage in New York City Parking Meters." *Criminology* 10:127–42.

Department of Environment. 1977. *Housing Management and Design.* Lambeth Inner Area Study IAS/IA/18. London: Department of Environment.

DesChamps, Scott, Patricia L. Brantingham, and Paul J. Brantingham. 1991. "The British Columbia Transit Fare Evasion Audit: A Description of a Situational Prevention Process." *Security Journal* 2:211–18.

Downes, David, and Paul Rock. 1982. *Understanding Deviance.* Oxford: Clarendon.

Dwyer, Jim. 1991. *Subway Lives.* New York: Crown.

Eck, John, and William Spelman. 1988. *Problem Solving: Problem-oriented Policing in Newport News.* Washington, D.C.: Police Executive Research Forum and National Institute of Justice.

Ekblom, Paul. 1987. "Crime Prevention in England: Themes and Issues." Paper presented at the Australian Institute of Criminology, November 24. London: Home Office Crime Prevention Unit.

———. 1988. "Preventing Post Office Robberies in London: Effects and Side Effects." *Journal of Security Administration* 11:36–43.

———. 1991. "Talking to Offenders: Practical Lessons for Local Crime Prevention." In *Urban Crime: Statistical Aproaches and Analyses*, edited by Oriol Nel-lo. Barcelona: Institut d'Estudis Metropolitans de Barcelona.

Engstad, Peter A. 1975. "Environmental Opportunities and the Ecology of Crime." In *Crime in Canadian Society*, edited by R. A. Silverman and J. J. Teevan, Jr. Toronto: Butterworth.

Engstad, Peter A., and John L. Evans. 1980. "Responsibility, Competence and Police Effectiveness in Crime Control." In *The Effectiveness of Policing*, edited by Ronald V. G. Clarke and J. M. Hough. Farnborough, Hants: Gower.

Farrell, Graham. In this volume. "Preventing Repeat Victimization."

Farrell, Graham, and Ken Pease. 1993. *Once Bitten, Twice Bitten: Repeat Victimisation and Its Implications for Crime Prevention*. Crime Prevention Unit Paper 46. London: Home Office.

Farrington, David P., Sean Bowen, Abigail Buckle, Tony Burns-Howell, John Burrows, and Martin Speed. 1993. "An Experiment on the Prevention of Shoplifting." In *Crime Prevention Studies*, vol. 1, edited by Ronald V. Clarke. Monsey, N.Y.: Criminal Justice Press.

Fattah, Ezzat A. 1993. "The Rational Choice/Opportunity Perspectives as a Vehicle for Integrating Criminological and Victimological Theories." In *Routine Activity and Rational Choice, Advances in Criminological Theory*, vol. 5, edited by Ronald V. Clarke and Marcus Felson. New Brunswick, N.J.: Transaction Publishers.

Feeney, Floyd. 1986. "Robbers as Decision-Makers." In *The Reasoning Criminal: Rational Choice Perspectives on Offending*, edited by Derek B. Cornish and Ronald V. Clarke. New York: Springer-Verlag.

Felson, Marcus. 1986. "Linking Criminal Choices, Routine Activities, Informal Control, and Criminal Outcomes." In *The Reasoning Criminal*, edited by Derek B. Cornish and Ronald V. Clarke. New York: Springer-Verlag.

———. 1992. "Routine Activities and Crime Prevention: Armchair Concepts and Practical Action." *Studies on Crime and Crime Prevention* 1:31–34.

———. "Integrative Crime Prevention." In *Crime Problems and Community Solutions*. Toronto: York University, ABL (forthcoming).

Field, Simon. 1993. "Crime Prevention and the Costs of Auto Theft: An Economic Analysis." In *Crime Prevention Studies*, vol. 1, edited by Ronald V. Clarke. Monsey, N.Y.: Criminal Justice Press.

Gabor, Thomas. 1981. "The Crime Displacement Hypothesis: An Empirical Examination." *Crime and Delinquency* 26:390–404.

———. 1990. "Crime Displacement and Situational Prevention: Toward the Development of Some Principles." *Canadian Journal of Criminology* 32:41–74.

Gladstone, Francis J. 1980. *Co-ordinating Crime Prevention Efforts*. Home Office Research Study no. 47. London: H.M. Stationery Office.

Goldstein, Herman. 1979. "Improving Policing: A Problem-oriented Approach." *Crime and Delinquency* 25:234–58.

———. 1990. *Problem-oriented Policing*. New York: McGraw-Hill.

Gottfredson, Michael R., and Travis Hirschi. 1990. *A General Theory of Crime*. Stanford, Calif.: Stanford University Press.

Grandjean, Christian. 1990. "Bank Robberies and Physical Security in Switzerland: A Case Study of the Escalation and Displacement Phenomena." *Security Journal* 1:155–59.

Griswold, David B. 1984. "Crime Prevention and Commercial Burglary: A Time Series Analysis." *Journal of Criminal Justice* 12:493–501.

Hall, Jerome. 1952. *Theft, Law and Society*. New York: Bobbs-Merrill.

Harding, Richard W. 1993. "Gun Use in Crime, Rational Choice and Social Learning Theory." In *Routine Activity and Rational Choice, Advances in Criminological Theory*, vol. 5, edited by Ronald V. Clarke and Marcus Felson. New Brunswick, N.J.: Transaction Publishers.

Harris, Patricia M., and Ronald V. Clarke. 1991. "Car Chopping, Parts Marking and Motor Vehicle Theft Law Enforcement Act of 1984." *Sociology and Social Research* 75:228–38.

Hartshorne, Hugh, and Mark A. May. 1928. *Studies in the Nature of Character*. Vol. 1, *Studies in Deceit*. New York: Macmillan.

Hawley, Amos. 1950. *Human Ecology: A Theory of Community Structure*. New York: Ronald.

Heal, Kevin, and Gloria Laycock. 1986. *Situational Crime Prevention: From Theory into Practice*. London: H.M. Stationery Office.

Hemenway, David, and Douglas Weil. 1990. "Phasers on Stun: The Case for Less Lethal Weapons." *Journal of Policy Analysis and Management* 9:94–98.

Hindelang, Michael J., Michael R. Gottfredson, and James Garofalo. 1978. *Victims of Personal Crime: An Empirical Foundation for a Theory of Personal Victimization*. Cambridge, Mass.: Ballinger.

Hirschi, Travis. 1969. *Causes of Delinquency*. Berkeley: University of California Press.

Homel, Ross. 1993. "Drivers Who Drink and Rational Choice: Random Breath Testing and the Process of Deterrence." In *Routine Activity and Rational Choice, Advances in Criminological Theory*, vol. 5, edited by Ronald V. Clarke and Marcus Felson. New Brunswick, N.J.: Transaction Publishers.

Hope, Tim. 1985. *Implementing Crime Prevention Measures*. Home Office Research Study no. 86. London: H.M. Stationery Office.

———. 1991. "Crime Information in Retailing: Prevention through Analysis." *Security Journal* 2:240–45.

———. 1994. "Problem-oriented Policing and Drug Market Locations: Three Case Studies." In *Crime Prevention Studies*, vol. 2, edited by Ronald V. Clarke. Monsey, N.Y.: Criminal Justice Press.

Hope, Tim, and Dan Murphy. 1983. "Problems of Implementing Crime Prevention: The Experience of a Demonstration Project." *Howard Journal of Criminal Justice* 22:38–50.

Hunter, Ronald D., and C. Ray Jeffery. 1992. "Preventing Convenience Store Robbery through Environmental Design." In *Situational Crime Prevention: Successful Case Studies*, edited by Ronald V. Clarke. Albany, N.Y.: Harrow & Heston.

Jacobs, Jane. 1961. *The Death and Life of Great American Cities*. New York: Random House.

Jeffery, C. Ray. 1971. *Crime Prevention through Environmental Design*. Beverly Hills, Calif.: Sage.

————. 1977. *Crime Prevention through Environmental Design*. 2d ed. Beverly Hills, Calif.: Sage.

Jones, Barnie, and Nita Wood. 1989. *Traffic Safety Impact of the 1988 Ignition Interlock Pilot Program*. Portland, Oregon: Motor Vehicles Division.

Karmen, Andrew A. 1981. "Auto Theft and Corporate Irresponsibility." *Contemporary Crises* 5:63–81.

————. 1984. *Crime Victims: An Introduction to Victimology*. Belmont, Calif.: Brooks/Cole.

Klepper, Steven, and Daniel Nagin. 1987. "The Anatomy of Tax Evasion." Paper presented at the annual meeting of the American Society of Criminology, Montreal, November.

Knutsson, Johannes, and Eckart Kuhlhorn. 1981. *Macro-Measures against Crime: The Example of Check Forgeries*. Information Bulletin no. 1. Stockholm: National Swedish Council for Crime Prevention.

Kube, Edwin. 1988. "Preventing Bank Robbery: Lessons from Interviewing Robbers." *Journal of Security Administration* 11:78–83.

Landes, William M. 1978. "An Economic Study of U.S. Aircraft Hijacking, 1961–1976." *Journal of Law and Economics* 21:1–31.

Lateef, Barry A. 1974. "Helicopter Patrol in Law Enforcement: An Evaluation." *Journal of Police Science and Administration* 2:62–65.

Law Enforcement News. 1990. "Trouble on the Line: Phone Companies Hang Up on Druggies." 16(316/7):5.

————. 1992. "NJ Slams the Brakes on Photo-Radar Test." 18(360):7.

Laycock, Gloria K. 1991. "Operation Identification, or the Power of Publicity?" *Security Journal* 2:67–72.

Laycock, Gloria, and Claire Austin. 1992. "Crime Prevention in Parking Facilities." *Security Journal* 3:154–60.

Laycock, Gloria, and Nick Tilley. In this volume. "Implementing Crime Prevention."

Lejeune, R. 1977. "The Management of a Mugging." *Urban Life* 6:123–48.

Levi, Michael. 1992. "Preventing Credit Card Fraud." *Security Journal* 3: 147–53.

Levi, Michael, Paul Bissell, and Tony Richardson. 1991. *The Prevention of Cheque and Credit Card Fraud*. Crime Prevention Unit Paper 26. London: Home Office.

Lewin, Kurt. 1947. "Group Decisions and Social Change." In *Readings in Social Psychology*, edited by T. M. Newcomb and E. L. Hartley. New York: Atherton.

Lowman, J. 1992. "Street Prostitution Control: Some Canadian Reflections on the Finsbury Park Experience." *British Journal of Criminology* 32:1–17.

Maguire, Mike. 1980. "Burglary as Opportunity." *Home Office Research Unit Bulletin* 10:6–9.

————. 1982. *Burglary in a Dwelling*. London: Heinemann.

Marisco, Ron. 1992. "Lens Cap: Measure Advances to Ban Photo Radar." *Star Ledger* (June 2), pp. 1, 18.

Markus, Charles L. 1984. "British Telecom Experience in Payphone Management." In *Vandalism Behaviour and Motivations*, edited by C. Levy-Leboyer. Amsterdam: Elsevier North-Holland.

Marx, Gary T. 1986. "The Iron Fist and the Velvet Glove: Totalitarian Potentials within Democratic Structures." In *The Social Fabric: Dimensions and Issues*, edited by J. F. Short, Jr. Beverly Hills, Calif.: Sage.

Masuda, Barry. 1992. "Displacement vs. Diffusion of Benefits and the Reduction of Inventory Losses in a Retail Environment." *Security Journal* 3:131–36.

———. 1993. "Credit Card Fraud Prevention: A Successful Retail Strategy." In *Crime Prevention Studies*, vol. 1, edited by Ronald V. Clarke. Monsey, N.Y.: Criminal Justice Press.

Matthews, Roger. 1990. "Developing More Effective Strategies for Curbing Prostitution." *Security Journal* 1:182–87.

Matza, David. 1964. *Delinquency and Drift*. New York: Wiley.

Mayhew, Patricia. 1979. "Defensible Space: The Current Status of a Crime Prevention Theory." *Howard Journal of Penology and Crime Prevention* 18:150–59.

Mayhew, Patricia, Ronald V. Clarke, John N. Burrows, J. Mike Hough, and Stuart W. C. Winchester. 1979. *Crime in Public View*. Home Office Research Study no. 49. London: H.M. Stationery Office.

Mayhew, Patricia, Ronald V. Clarke, and David Elliott. 1989. "Motorcycle Theft, Helmet Legislation and Displacement." *Howard Journal of Criminal Justice* 28:1–8.

Mayhew, Patricia, Ronald V. Clarke, Andrew Sturman, and J. Mike Hough. 1976. *Crime as Opportunity*. Home Office Research Study no. 34. London: H.M. Stationery Office.

Meredith, Colin, and Chantal Paquette. 1992. "Crime Prevention in High-Rise Rental Apartments: Findings of a Demonstration Project." *Security Journal* 3:161–69.

Miethe, Terance D. 1991. "Citizen-based Crime Control Activity and Victimization Risks: An Examination of Displacement and Free-Rider Effects." *Criminology* 29:419–40.

Mischel, Walter. 1968. *Personality and Assessment*. New York: Wiley.

Moore, J. 1987. "Safeguarding Patient Valuables: A Case Study." *Journal of Security Administration* 10:52–57.

Moore, Mark H. 1992. "Problem-Solving and Community Policing." In *Modern Policing*, edited by Michael Tonry and Norval Morris. Vol. 15 of *Crime and Justice: A Review of Research*, edited by Michael Tonry. Chicago: University of Chicago Press.

Morris, Norval, and Gordon Hawkins. 1970. *The Honest Politician's Guide to Crime Control*. Chicago: University of Chicago Press.

Morse, Barbara J., and Delbert S. Elliott. 1990. "Hamilton County Drinking and Driving Study: 30 Month Report." Boulder: University of Colorado, Institute of Behavioral Science.

National Roads and Motorists' Association Insurance Ltd. 1990. *Car Theft in New South Wales*. Sydney: National Roads and Motorists' Association.

Nee, Claire, and Max Taylor. 1988. "Residential Burglary in the Republic of Ireland: A Situational Perspective." *Howard Journal of Criminal Justice* 27:80–95.

Newman, Oscar. 1972. *Defensible Space: Crime Prevention through Urban Design.* New York: Macmillan. (Published in London: Architectural Press, 1973).

New South Wales Bureau of Crime Statistics and Research. 1987. *Robbery.* Sydney: Attorney General's Department.

Nugent, Stephen, Donald Burnes, Paul Wilson, and Duncan Chappell. 1989. *Risks and Rewards in Robbery: Prevention and the Offender's Perspective.* Melbourne: Australian Bankers' Association.

Painter, Kate. "The Impact of Street Lighting on Crime, Fear and Pedestrian Use." *Security Journal* (forthcoming).

Pease, Ken. 1979. "Some Futures in Crime Prevention." Research Bulletin no. 7. London: Home Office, Home Office Research Unit.

———. 1991. "The Kirkholt Project: Preventing Burglary on a British Public Housing Estate." *Security Journal* 2:73–77.

Poyner, Barry. 1988. "Video Cameras and Bus Vandalism." *Security Administration* 11:44–51.

———. 1991. "Situational Prevention in Two Car Parks." *Security Journal* 2:96–101.

———. 1993. "What Works in Crime Prevention: An Overview of Evaluations." In *Crime Prevention Studies*, vol. 1, edited by Ronald V. Clarke. Monsey, N.Y.: Criminal Justice Press.

Poyner, Barry, Caroline Warne, Barry Webb, R. Woodall, and R. Meakin. 1988. *Preventing Violence to Staff.* London: H.M. Stationery Office.

Poyner, Barry, and Barry Webb. 1987. *Successful Crime Prevention: Case Studies.* London: Tavistock Institute of Human Relations.

———. 1991. *Crime Free Housing.* Oxford: Butterworth Architect.

Press, S. J. 1971. *Some Effects of an Increase in Police Manpower in the 20th Precinct of New York City.* New York: Rand Institute.

Ramsay, Malcolm. 1991a. *The Influence of Street Lighting on Crime and Fear of Crime.* Crime Prevention Unit Paper 28. London: Home Office.

———. 1991b. "A British Experiment in Curbing Incivilities and Fear of Crime." *Security Journal* 2:120–25.

Rengert, George F., and John Wasilchick. 1985. *Suburban Burglary.* Springfield, Ill.: Chas. C. Thomas.

Reppetto, T. A. 1974. *Residential Crime.* Cambridge, Mass.: Ballinger.

———. 1976. "Crime Prevention and the Displacement Phenomenon." *Crime and Delinquency* (April), pp. 166–77.

Rosenbaum, Dennis. 1988. "A Critical Eye on Neighborhood Watch: Does It Reduce Crime and Fear?" In *Communities and Crime Reduction*, edited by Tim Hope and Margaret Shaw. London: H.M. Stationery Office.

Samdahl, D., and H. Christiansen. 1985. "Environmental Cues and Vandalism." *Environment and Behavior* 17:446.

Sampson, Alice, Paul Stubbs, David Smith, Geoffrey Pearson, and Harry Blagg. 1988. "Crime, Localities and the Multi-Agency Approach." *British Journal of Criminology* 28:478–93.

Scarr, Harry A. 1973. *Patterns of Burglary.* 2d ed. Washington, D.C.: U.S.

Department of Justice, National Institute of Law Enforcement and Criminal Justice.

Scherdin, Mary J. 1986. "The Halo Effect: Psychological Deterrence of Electronic Security Systems." *Information Technology and Libraries* 5:232–35.

Scottish Council on Crime. 1975. *Crime and the Prevention of Crime.* Scottish Home and Health Department. Edinburgh: H.M. Stationery Office.

Shearing, Clifford D., and Phillip C. Stenning. 1984. "From the Panoptican to Disney World: The Development of Discipline." In *Perspectives in Criminal Law: Essays in Honour of John Ll. J. Edwards*, edited by A. Doob and E. Greenspen. Aurora: Canada Law Book.

Shepherd, Jonathan, and Mark Brickley. 1992. "Alchohol-related Hand Injuries: An Unnecessary Social and Economic Cost." *Journal of the Royal College of Surgeons* 75:69.

Sherman, Lawrence W. 1990. "Police Crackdowns: Initial and Residual Deterrence." In *Crime and Justice: A Review of Research*, vol. 12., edited by Michael Tonry and Norval Morris. Chicago: University of Chicago Press.

———. 1992. "Attacking Crime: Policing and Crime Control." In *Modern Policing*, edited by Michael Tonry and Norval Morris. Vol. 15 of *Crime and Justice: A Review of Research*, edited by Michael Tonry. Chicago: University of Chicago Press.

Sherman, Lawrence W., Patrick R. Gartin, and Michael E. Buerger. 1989. "Hot Spots of Predatory Crime: Routine Activities and the Criminology of Place." *Criminology* 27:27–56.

Short, J. F., Jr., and F. L. Strodtbeck. 1965. *Group Processes and Gang Delinquency.* Chicago: University of Chicago Press.

Sloan-Howitt, Maryalice, and George Kelling. 1990. "Subway Graffiti in New York City: 'Gettin Up' vs. 'Meanin It and Cleanin It.'" *Security Journal* 1:131–36.

Stanford Research Institute. 1970. *Reduction of Robbery and Assault of Bus Drivers.* Vol. 3, *Technological and Operational Methods.* Stanford, Calif.: Stanford Research Institute.

Temple, Riley K., and Michael Regan. 1991. "Recent Developments Relating to Caller-ID." *Western State University Law Review* 18:549–63.

Tien, J. M., V. F. O'Donnell, A. Barnett, and P. B. Mirchandani. 1979. *Phase 1 Report: Street Lighting Projects.* Washington, D.C.: U.S. Government Printing Office.

Tilley, Nicholas. 1993a. "Crime Prevention and the Safer Cities Story." *Howard Journal of Criminal Justice* 32:40–57.

———. 1993b. *Understanding Car Parks, Crime and CCTV: Evaluation Lessons from Safer Cities.* Crime Prevention Unit Paper 42. London: Home Office.

Tizard, Jack, Ian Sinclair, and Ronald V. G. Clarke. 1975. *Varieties of Residential Experience.* London: Routledge & Kegan Paul.

Tonso, William R. 1982. *Gun and Society.* Washington, D.C.: University Press of America.

Trasler, Gordon. 1986. "Situational Crime Control and Rational Choice: A Critique." In *Situational Crime Prevention: From Theory into Practice*, edited by K. Heal and Gloria Laycock. London: H.M. Stationery Office.

————. 1993. "Conscience, Opportunity, Rational Choice and Crime." In *Routine Activity and Rational Choice, Advances in Criminological Theory*, vol. 5, edited by Ronald V. Clarke and Marcus Felson. New Brunswick, N.J.: Transaction Publishers.

Tyrpak, Steven. 1975. *Newark High-Impact Anti-Crime Program: Street Lighting Project Interim Evaluation Report.* Newark, N.J.: Office of Criminal Justice Planning.

van Andel, Henk. 1989. "Crime Prevention That Works: The Case of Public Transport in the Netherlands." *British Journal of Criminology* 29:47–56.

Veno, Arthur, and Elizabeth Veno. 1993. "Situational Prevention of Public Disorder at the Australian Motorcycle Grand Prix." In *Crime Prevention Studies*, vol. 1, edited by Ronald V. Clarke. Monsey, N.Y.: Criminal Justice Press.

Waller, Irvin, and Norman Okihiro. 1978. *Burglary: The Victim and the Public.* Toronto: University of Toronto Press.

Walsh, Dermot P. 1978. *Shoplifting: Controlling a Major Crime.* London: Macmillan.

————. 1980. *Break-ins: Burglary from Private Houses.* London: Constable.

Webb, Barry. 1994. "Steering Column Locks and Motor Vehicle Theft: Evaluations from Three Countries." In *Crime Prevention Studies*, vol. 2, edited by Ronald V. Clarke. Monsey, N.Y.: Criminal Justice Press.

Webb, Barry, and Gloria Laycock. 1992. *Tackling Car Crime: The Nature and Extent of the Problem.* Crime Prevention Unit Paper 32. London: Home Office.

Wilkins, Leslie T. 1964. *Social Deviance.* London: Tavistock.

Wilkinson, Paul. 1977. *Terrorism and the Liberal State.* London: Macmillan.

————. 1986. *Terrorism and the Liberal State.* 2d ed. New York: New York University Press.

Wilson, James Q. 1975. *Thinking about Crime.* New York: Basic.

Wilson, James Q., and George L. Kelling. 1982. "Broken Windows." *Atlantic Monthly* 249(3):29–38.

Wilson, Sheena. 1978. "Vandalism and 'Defensible Space' on London Housing Estates." In *Tackling Vandalism*, edited by Ronald V. G. Clarke. Home Office Research Study no. 47. London: H.M. Stationery Office.

Wise, James. 1982. "A Gentle Deterrent to Vandalism." *Psychology Today* (September 16), pp. 31–38.

Wright, James D., and Peter H. Rossi. 1982. *Armed and Considered Dangerous: A Survey of Felons and Their Firearms.* New York: Aldine de Gruyter.

Yablonsky, L. 1962. *The Violent Gang.* New York: Macmillan.

Young, Jock. 1988. "Radical Criminology in Britain: The Emergence of a Competing Paradigm." *British Journal of Criminology* 28:289–313.

Zimbardo, P. G. 1973. "A Field Experiment in Auto-Shaping." In *Vandalism*, edited by C. Ward. London: Architectural Press.

Richard E. Tremblay and Wendy M. Craig

Developmental Crime Prevention

ABSTRACT

Prevention experiments with children have targeted the development of antisocial behavior and confirm the hypothesis that early childhood factors are important precursors of delinquent behavior and that a cumulative effect model best fits the data. Experiments have aimed to prevent criminal behavior or one of three important delinquency risk factors: socially disruptive behavior, cognitive deficits, and poor parenting. Experiments with juvenile delinquency as an outcome demonstrate that positive results are more likely when interventions are aimed at more than one risk factor, last for a relatively long period of time, and are implemented before adolescence. Experiments featuring early childhood interventions with socially disruptive behavior, cognitive deficits, or parenting as an outcome generally have positive effects. The majority of studies, small-scale confirmation or replication experiments, need to be followed by large-scale field experiments that test the efficacy and cost of implementation in regular service systems.

Crime prevention from a developmental perspective is largely based on the idea that criminal activity is determined by behavioral and attitudinal patterns that have been learned during an individual's development. The developmental perspective can be long-term—for example, when early childhood behavior is linked to adult criminal behavior—or short-term—for example, when behaviors learned in a

Richard E. Tremblay is professor of psychology and psychiatry and director of the Research Unit on Children's Psychosocial Maladjustment, University of Montréal. Wendy M. Craig is professor of psychology at Queen's University. This work was made possible by a team grant to Tremblay from the Quebec government (Fonds pour la Formation de Chercheurs et l'Aide à la Recherche). We benefited from detailed comments on earlier drafts from David P. Farrington, Paul Ekblom, John Graham, and Michael Tonry.

treatment situation are linked to a six-month follow-up of recidivism. In both cases, the assumption is that earlier experience determines later behavior.

Most theories of human development have addressed the issue of criminal behavior. Analytical, behavioral, and sociological theories have concluded that the differences in criminal behavior could be explained by differences in earlier experiences (e.g., Eysenck 1964; Feldman 1969; Sutherland and Cressey 1978). Situational determinants of criminal behavior are recognized by developmentalists. However, developmental theories suggest that not only are some individuals more prone than others to commit crimes, given the same situation, but they are also more prone than others to place themselves in situations that favor criminal activity (e.g., delinquent peer association; see Cairns et al. 1989; Gottfredson and Hirschi 1990). Thus, individuals create their own environment, and the forces behind this phenomenon can be found in their genetic and ontogenetic history (see, e.g., Scarr and McCartney 1983; Rowe 1994).

Longitudinal studies, whether prospective or retrospective, have attempted to document these phenomena. Adoption studies have shown that adopted children with biological parents who had a criminal history were more at risk of criminal behavior themselves, compared to adopted children with biological parents who did not have a criminal history (e.g., Mednick, Harway, and Finello 1984). By controlling for the biological parents' antecedents, these studies have also shown the effects on criminality of the social environments in which the children were raised (Van Dusen et al. 1983; Gabrielli and Mednick 1984; Cloninger and Gottesman 1987; Duyme 1989). Longitudinal studies of children raised by their biological parents have systematically shown that a significant part of the variance in antisocial behavior during adolescence and adulthood can be predicted from childhood family characteristics and child behavioral characteristics (e.g., Huesmann et al. 1984; McCord 1986; Farrington 1991; Tremblay, Mâsse, et al. 1992; Moffitt 1993; Farrington 1994). There are still many questions to be answered concerning the development of antisocial behavior (see Farrington, Loeber, Elliot, et al. 1990; Tonry, Ohlin, and Farrington 1991; Farrington 1992), but there is no doubt that prior experience can increase or decrease the risk of later antisocial behavior.

Ideas concerning the prevention of crime should follow ideas concerning the causes of crime. If criminal activity is believed mainly to be influenced by proximate events, interventions should target proximate risk factors. But if distal influences are thought to be key risk factors, interventions should focus on long-term factors. Prevention experiments may be the best way to test theories of the causes of crime (see Schwartz, Flamant, and Lellouch 1980; Farrington 1986; Gottfredson and Hirschi 1990; Robins 1992). If an intervention has repeatedly been successful in preventing criminal behavior by modifying a factor that was hypothesized to be a causal factor of criminal behavior, then we have a better test of that theory than a simple correlation between two variables in a longitudinal or cross-sectional study. By contrast, if an intervention has repeatedly been successful in changing a phenomenon hypothesized to be a causal factor of criminality without a consequent reduction in criminal behavior, then one can doubt the validity of the causal hypothesis.

This essay reviews prevention experiments with children targeting the development of antisocial behavior. Our aim was to review prevention experiments with preschool and school-age children to understand the extent to which they indicate the possibility of preventing criminal behavior and contribute to our understanding of its development. Although a relatively large number of preventive experiments have addressed risk and protective factors for delinquency with children, relatively few have assessed their effect on delinquent behavior. Thus, the aim of the review is, not to quantify the effect of these prevention experiments on delinquent behavior, but to describe the types of studies that have been conducted, identify those that appear to give the most promising results, and suggest what further types of studies are needed to contribute to a science of developmental prevention.

Section I summarizes the current status of knowledge gained from prevention experiments with juvenile and adult offenders and concludes that the lack of positive effects from crime prevention experiments with offenders justifies attempts to prevent criminal behavior by interventions with children, before they become offenders. Section II gives an overview of theoretical and methodological issues that crime prevention work with children has attempted to solve and needs to tackle. Section III reviews prevention experiments with children that have assessed delinquency as an outcome and concludes that interventions that target more than one risk factor, last for a relatively long period of time, and are implemented early in life have the best chance of preventing delinquency involvement. The fourth, fifth, and sixth sections review prevention experiments that aim to prevent three important risk factors for delinquency: socially disruptive behavior, cognitive deficits, and poor parenting. Results indicate that most interventions with young children have positive effects on these risk factors. From a methodological perspective, the small-scale randomized experiments presented in this review must be considered a first step in a prevention research agenda. The next steps should be large-scale field experiments to test efficacy, cost, and effectiveness.

I. The Effectiveness of Prevention Experiments with Offenders

Most of the work to prevent crime has been done with adjudicated adults, young adults, or juveniles. The main aim is to prevent recidivism. The logic of this social choice is partly explained by parsimony. If an individual who commits a first crime can be prevented from recidivating, we need not worry about those who are still too young to commit crimes and the majority of people who will never commit crimes. In other words, if recidivism can be prevented by working with adults, why spend a lot of energy trying to identify and help children who are too young for criminal behavior?

The issue of earlier versus later prevention centers around the debate concerning the plasticity and rigidity of human behavior (see Wilson and Herrnstein 1985; Gottfredson and Hirschi 1990). If behavioral patterns that are associated with criminal behavior are relatively plastic throughout life, then preventive interventions should be focused on individuals at the time of adolescence when they are most likely to commit crimes. This life-span plasticity hypothesis implies that no intervention will have long-term effects since the plasticity rule implies that the individual will always be receptive to influences that could lead to criminal behavior. The advocates of childhood interventions to prevent adolescent and adult criminal behavior have relied on the hypothesis that patterns of behavior are plastic in early childhood but become more and more rigid as the individual grows older (Condry 1983; Parke and Slaby 1983; Eron 1990; Gottfredson and Hirschi 1990). Prevention experiments could confirm this hypothesis if it were found that interventions with adolescents and adults had few or short-term effects, while interventions with children had long-term effects.

The effectiveness of interventions with adult criminals to prevent recidivism has been, and still is, a controversial topic. In a review of outcome studies, Lipton, Martinson, and Wilks (1975) concluded that available evaluation data did not provide evidence that correctional interventions reduced recidivism. A committee of the National Academy of Sciences (Sechrest, White, and Brown 1979) later came essentially to the same conclusion. Almost twenty years after the Lipton et al. report, there is still a general impression that programs to prevent adult and young adult criminals from recidivating are and will be largely unsuccessful (Gottfredson and Hirschi 1990). Gendreau and Ross (1987) have argued that some types of programs are successful. Interestingly, they optimistically emphasize prevention with at-risk children.

Juvenile offenders have been the focus of systematic crime preventive interventions for more than a century and a half. In 1851 Mary Carpenter published a book with the aim of demonstrating that reformatory schools "will produce the desired effect of checking the progress of crime in those who have not yet subjected themselves to the grasp of the law, and of reforming those which are already convicted criminals. Such schools occupy a middle ground between educational and penal establishments" (Carpenter 1968, p. vi). Half a century later, Hart (1910) wrote that juvenile reformatories were then recognized as the last resort, after everything else had failed, and that "the practice of claiming that 90 percent of the children who are cared for turn out well will go out of fashion" (p. 12). He also underlined that those who were interested in helping children recognized "the family home as the most practical and efficient reformatory in the world" (p. 11).

It was only in 1974 that the Juvenile Justice and Delinquency Prevention Act in the United States required that states remove juvenile status offenders from institutions that treat individuals who violate the criminal code if they wanted to receive federal funds for juvenile justice programs. This was part of the deinstitutionalization movement that gained force during the 1960s (Land, McCall, and Williams 1992). From the beginning of the century to the 1970s there were a number of reported accounts of apparently successful residential treatments for juvenile delinquents (e.g., Aichhorn 1925; Healy and Bronner 1936; Friedlander 1947; Eissler 1949; Weeks 1963; Guindon 1971). These institutions used "milieu therapy" models that were largely based on psychoanalytic principles and attempted to create a residential environment that was therapeutic. In 1909 a White House Conference on the Care of Dependent Children (Rothman 1971) had recommended the "cottage plan" for delinquent children placed in residential institutions. This recommendation was an attempt to group small numbers of children in homelike environments. The milieu therapy model appears to have been built on this idea. To paraphrase Mary Carpenter's 1851 description of reformatory schools, the cottage plan and the therapeutic milieu model occupied the middle ground between the family and reformatory establishments. Thus, although it was recognized more than eighty years ago that residential treatment was a last resort for juvenile delinquents, most industrialized societies are still using residential institutions to "help" juvenile delinquents in order to prevent recidivism.

Lipton, Martinson, and Wilks (1975) were not much more encouraging about the effectiveness of juvenile interventions than they were about adult interventions. A number of reviews of experiments have followed (e.g., Garrett 1985; Whitehead and Lab 1989). Lipsey (1992) reviewed 443 studies and concluded that there was a small general positive effect that could be attributed to a large extent to method variables (e.g., randomization, sample size, attrition, instruments) and to a smaller extent to treatment variables (e.g., subjects treated, intensity of treatment, treatment modality). Lipsey also concluded that, although his meta-analysis did not confirm that nothing works, the "grand mean effect size is perilously close to zero" (p. 126).

The extent to which interventions with juvenile delinquents are effective can be compared to the effectiveness of other behavioral, psychological, and educational treatments. From an analysis of 156 meta-analyses in these domains, Lipsey and Wilson (1993) found that "the average treatment group scored 0.47 SDs [standard deviations] higher on the average outcome measure than did the average control group" (p. 1198). The mean effect size found by Lipsey (1992) for the treatment of juvenile delinquents was 0.18 SDs. Table 1 presents a selection of meta-analysis results from the 156 used by Lipsey and Wilson (1993). The selection represents treatment of patients hospitalized for mental illness and interventions for children at risk. The average effect size in these domains is at least twice as large as the average effect size found by Lipsey (1992) in his meta-analysis of treatments for juvenile delinquents. From this table, it is clear that juvenile delinquency interventions have had much less effect than most interventions that attempt to help individuals with other adjustment problems.

II. Toward a Science of Prevention during Childhood

Developmental prevention refers to interventions aiming to reduce risk factors and increase protective factors that are hypothesized to have a significant effect on an individual's adjustment at later points of his

TABLE 1

Selected Meta-analysis Results of Treatment Studies

Treatment Area (Reference)	Mean Effect Size	No. of Studies
Treatment for juvenile delinquents (Lipsey 1992)	.18	443
Innovative outpatient programs vs. traditional aftercare for mental health patients released from hospitals (Straw 1982)	.36	130
Deinstitutionalization programs for chronically mentally ill (Harris 1987)	.36	130
Cognitive behavioral modification strategies with children (Duzinski 1987)	.47	45
Cognitive behavioral therapy with dysfunctional children (Durlak, Fuhrman, and Lampman 1991)	.53	64
Parent effectiveness training (Cedar 1986; Cedar and Levant 1990)	.33	26
Head Start (early childhood education program, cognitive outcomes) (Administration for Children, Youth, and Families 1983)	.34	71
Early intervention for disadvantaged infants (Utah State University Exceptional Child Center 1983; Casto and White 1984)	.43	26
Early intervention for handicapped preschoolers (Utah State University Exceptional Child Center 1983; Casto and Mastropieri 1986)	.68	74
Educational interventions for students in danger of failing to complete their education (Slavin 1989)	.63	28

SOURCE.—Lipsey and Wilson (1993).

development. Childhood experiences have been identified as key predictors of later life events at least since the Greek philosophers (McCord 1993). The unique contribution of the twentieth century has been the use of longitudinal and experimental studies to test these ideas. It has been suggested recently (Coie et al. 1993) that a science of prevention is taking form. This body of knowledge has three main sources: longitudinal studies, experimental studies, and theory building.

A. *Longitudinal Studies*

Since the 1920s, investigators have conducted a number of long-term prospective longitudinal studies of children's development in industrialized countries (e.g., Sears 1975; Kagan and Moss 1983; Caspi, Elder, and Herbener 1990; Eron, Huesmann, and Zelli 1991; Farrington 1991; McCord 1991; Power, Manor, and Fox 1991; Wadsworth 1991). These longitudinal studies have shown that there are relatively good childhood predictors of later dysfunctions, including juvenile and adult crime involvement (for reviews, see Loeber and Dishion 1983; Rutter and Giller 1983; Wilson and Herrnstein 1985; Loeber and Stouthamer-Loeber 1986; Yoshikawa 1994).

Three broad categories of risk and protective factors have been identified: individual characteristics, family characteristics, and environmental characteristics. Among individual characteristics, those that have been found to be most strongly associated with later delinquent behavior are childhood disruptive behavior (opposition, aggression, and hyperactivity) and cognitive deficits (low IQ, inattentiveness, poor school performance). Among family characteristics, parental deviance, parental rejection, parental discord, ineffective discipline, and poor supervision appear to be the key risk factors. Among environmental characteristics, the key factors appear to be poor, disorganized neighborhoods, where criminality is higher, schools are less well organized, and association with deviant peers is more likely.

B. Experimental Studies

Having identified these risk and protective factors, the task for developmentalists is to determine the causal relations between these factors, identify those that are amenable to change, and identify the changes that have most effect on the prevention of delinquency. These are the goals of the prevention science that is taking form for both social and medical dysfunctions (Bock and Whelan 1991; Coie et al. 1993). This prevention science aims to prevent dysfunctions by acting on early causes—by reducing risk factors and reinforcing protective factors during childhood. Preventive interventions are thus used with at-risk subjects not only to identify the most effective interventions but also to test causal theories of dysfunction development (Farrington, Ohlin, and Wilson 1986; Tonry, Ohlin, and Farrington 1991; Robins 1992; Tremblay, Mâsse, et al. 1992; Coie et al. 1993; Dodge 1993).

The potential contributions of these experiments are important to both practice and theory development. Schwartz, Flamant, and Lellouch (1980) have shown how clinical trials can indeed reach "explanatory" and "pragmatic" goals. Experiments with an "explanatory" goal attempt to understand the causal links that lead to a given outcome. The focus is on understanding the mechanisms in a given process. In the same way that replacing a gene on a chromosome can help in understanding the role of that gene in the development of an organism (Capecchi 1994), modifying an individual's environment or behavior can help in understanding the role of that environment or behavior in his or her development. Experiments with a "pragmatic" goal attempt to attain a given outcome without requiring understanding of the process.

In the present review of prevention experiments with children, our first interest was to answer the pragmatic question, Can interventions with children prevent criminal involvement during adolescence and adulthood? We found few studies that could help answer that question clearly because few prevention studies with children followed their subjects up to the age of serious delinquency involvement. However, other prevention studies manipulated putative delinquency risk and protective factors and assessed changes on the same or other factors at follow-up. From an explanatory perspective, these studies can provide evidence that hypothesized causal factors of criminal behavior can be modified during childhood and can reduce later criminal behavior.

C. Theories

Longitudinal and experimental studies can be generated and supported from theoretical frameworks. It has been suggested that there are now no adequate theories of delinquency, mainly because each available theory has focused on a limited set of factors (Farrington, Loeber, Elliott, et al. 1990; Tonry, Ohlin, and Farrington 1991). However, from the knowledge accumulated by longitudinal, cross-sectional, and experimental studies of antisocial behavior, a number of developmental theories or models have been suggested in recent years. An exhaustive review of these theories is not our purpose, but a brief look at three types of proposed developmental theories will help to understand the contribution of the prevention studies that are reviewed in later sections of this essay (see fig. 1).

The first type of developmental theory of delinquency is exemplified by Gottfredson and Hirschi's (1990) general theory of crime. This theory proposes that people differ in their capacity to resist temptations. It explains why individuals faced with the same opportunity for deviant behavior will differ in their response. The central concept is self-control. Individuals with strong self-control will resist criminal opportunities more often than those with weak self-control. Gottfredson and Hirschi propose that self-control is acquired during child-

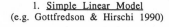

1. Simple Linear Model
(e.g. Gottfredson & Hirschi 1990)

Child-rearing ———————▶ Self-control ———————▶ Crime

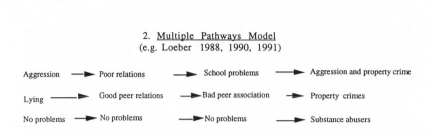

2. Multiple Pathways Model
(e.g. Loeber 1988, 1990, 1991)

Aggression ——▶	Poor relations ——▶	School problems ——▶	Aggression and property crime
Lying ——▶	Good peer relations ——▶	Bad peer association ——▶	Property crimes
No problems ——▶	No problems ——▶	No problems ——▶	Substance abusers

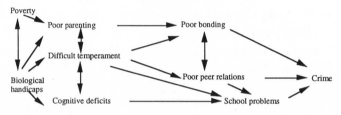

3. Cumulative Effect Model
(e.g. Yoshikawa 1994)

Fig. 1.—Three theoretical models for the development of criminal behavior from early childhood to adulthood.

hood and is mainly the product of child rearing. Such a theory clearly leads to the hypothesis that improving parents' child-rearing practices will increase children's self-control and prevent later criminal behavior.

Loeber's (1988, 1990, 1991) developmental pathways model is a second type of theory for the development of antisocial behavior. Loeber (1990), like Gottfredson and Hirschi (1990), specifically identifies low impulse control as a major determinant of criminal behavior, but he also hypothesizes that there are different paths leading to different types of offending in adolescence and adulthood. Loeber identifies three types of adult offenders (versatiles who engage in both aggressive and property offenses, exclusive property offenders, exclusive substance abusers) and suggests that they can be differentiated by the type of behavior problems they had in childhood, the age of onset of these problem behaviors, the rate of progression towards criminal behavior, and the probability that they will desist from criminal behavior. Similar models have been suggested by Moffitt (1993) and Patterson,

DeBaryshe, and Ramsey (1989). These developmental path models suggest that preventive interventions should focus on different risk and protective factors and at different ages, depending on which developmental path a child is assumed to be following. Prevention experiments to test these models, or simply to use their conceptual framework, clearly need to be much more complex than those that start from the Gottfredson and Hirschi (1990) model.

The third type of theoretical framework can be described as a cumulative risk model for diverse disorders (Coie and Jacobs 1993; Yoshikawa 1994). Longitudinal studies that focus on more than one risk factor and more than one disorder show that exposure to many risk factors has additive effects and that diverse disorders have common risk factors. This framework suggests complex interactions among early risk factors, among later disorders, and between risk factors and disorders. However, because of the cumulative nature of the risk factors, and their negative effect on diverse outcomes, it is suggested that early intensive interventions that target multiple risk factors will have long-term positive effects on diverse disorders (Coie and Jacobs 1993; Dodge 1993; Yoshikawa 1994). Clearly, experiments to untangle the multiple causal feedback loops suggested by this theoretical model will need to be quite complex.

D. From Theory to Experiments to Theory

If the three types of theories described above were used to plan prevention experiments, they would lead to somewhat different prevention strategies. The self-control theory would lead to an early intervention fostering parenting skills that would nurture self-control. The pathways model would probably lead to early childhood interventions for subjects at risk for the versatile pathway, early adolescent interventions for those at risk for the exclusive property offense pathway, and interventions in middle adolescence for the third group at-risk exclusively for substance abuse. The cumulative risk model would lead to interventions targeting numerous risk factors during early childhood to prevent most dysfunctions. Because these developmental theories are comparatively recent, they have not yet generated prevention experiments that could be considered good explanatory tests of their hypotheses. Our review attempts to understand to what extent previous experiments have been successful in preventing delinquency and to investigate how much support is provided for different models of antisocial behavior development.

Prevention studies with preschool and school-age children were classified according to the manipulated factors, the assessed outcomes, the age at which the intervention started, the duration of the intervention, the implemented treatment model, and the subjects' risk characteristics (see table 2). Three of these variables (the assessed outcomes, the age at which the intervention started, and the subjects' risk characteristics) were used as the main basis for the classification of experiments. The association between the manipulated factor and the assessed outcome was used to identify the putative causal links. Age at the time of the intervention and age at the time of the outcome assessment were used to locate the putative causal links on the developmental trajectory.

Figure 2 is a representation of a number of possible links between manipulated factors and outcomes from the prenatal period to adulthood. Each arrow represents one or a series of experiments where the variable at the beginning of the arrow is the manipulated factor and the variable at the end of the arrow is the assessed outcome. Arrows that link the same variable at two points in time (horizontal arrows) indicate that the experiment simply assessed whether the manipulation of a given variable created change in the variable over a defined period of time. For example, a parent training program for parents of infants could assess two years later whether the manipulation of parenting during infancy had an effect on parenting at age three years. Similarly, training children for anger control in preschool could be followed by an assessment of anger control at the end of elementary school. Arrows that link two different variables at two points in time (diagonal arrows) indicate that the experiment manipulated the first variable and assessed its later effect on another variable. For example, an experiment could assess whether a prenatal parent training program had an effect on children's cognitive performance or disruptive behavior three years later. Similarly, a training program for anger control in elementary school could be followed by an assessment of delinquency during early adolescence. For simplicity, figure 2 does not attempt to represent studies that manipulate more than one variable at the same time. These multimodal treatments, however, were included in the review.

Each of the following sections focuses on a given outcome. The order of presentation was based on the conceptual proximity of the variables to delinquent behavior. The first section presents experiments with delinquency as an outcome. It is followed by experiments with socially disruptive behavior as an outcome, then cognitive skills, and parenting.

TABLE 2

Studies with Juvenile Delinquency as an Outcome

Authors	Age at Treatment (in Years)	Type	Risk Factors Manipulated	Context of Intervention	No. of Subjects	Length of Treatment	Type of Treatment	Length of Follow-up	Results at Posttest or Follow-up — Delinquency	Results at Posttest or Follow-up — Others
1. Hawkins, Doueck, and Lishner (1988)	12	Universal	Teaching practices	Middle school classroom	1,166 boys and girls	1 year	Teacher training	0	Self-reported delinquency 0 (−.06)	Teaching practice +, school attachment +, educational expectations +, behavior +, achievement 0
2. Bry (1982)	$\bar{x} = 12.5$	Indicated	School commitment	Middle school	44 boys, 22 girls	2 years	Group, school attendance, school monitoring	5 years	Court records + (.51)	School problems +, employment +
3. Gottfredson and Gottfredson (1992)	12–17	Indicated	School curriculum	High school	247 boys and girls	1 year	Social studies	0	Self-reported delinquency + (.42)	School achievement +, attachment to school +, peer influence +
4. Arbuthnot and Gordon (1986)	$\bar{x} = 14.5$	Indicated	Moral reasoning	High school	35 boys, 13 girls	16–20 weeks	Group discussions	1 year	Police and court contact 0*	School behavior +, discipline +

TABLE 2 (*Continued*)

Authors	Age at Treatment (in Years)	Type	Risk Factors Manipulated	Context of Intervention	No. of Subjects	Length of Treatment	Type of Treatment	Length of Follow-up	Results at Posttest or Follow-up Delinquency	Others
5. Gottfredson (1987)	14–17	Indicated	Peer group	High school	360 boys and girls	15–30 weeks	Peer counseling	0	Self-reported delinquency 0 (.01)	Negative peer influences 0, school achievement 0, school suspensions 0
6. Gottfredson (1986)	11–17	Universal, indicated	School organization and behavior	High school	869 boys and girls	2 years	Monitoring, education, academic achievement, problem solving, peer counseling	0	Self-reported delinquency 0 (.12)	Promotion +, graduation +, school attachment 0, delinquent friends 0, attendance +
7. Lochman (1992)	9–12	Indicated	Social behavior	School	145 boys	4–5 months	Cognitive-behavioral, anger control	2.5–3.5 years	Self-reported delinquency 0 (.08)	Problem solving +, self-esteem +, substance use +
8. McCord (1978)	$\bar{x} = 10.5$	Selective	Social support	Family, community	506 boys	5.5 years	Home visits, tutoring, parent training	37 years	Court records (−.25)	Adjustment problems −
9. Kazdin, Siegel, and Bass (1992)	$\bar{x} = 10.3$	Indicated	Problem solving, parenting	Clinic, parents	76 boys, 21 girls	6–8 months	Cognitive-behavioral, parent training	1 year	Self-reported delinquency + (.55)	Antisocial behavior +, parental stress +

164

Study	Age	Type	Target	Setting	Sample	Duration	Intervention	Follow-up	Results at Posttest or Follow-up	Outcomes
10. Tremblay et al. (1994)	7	Indicated	Social behavior, parenting	Family, school	160 boys	2 years	Parent training, social skills training	6 years	Self-reported delinquency + (.25), courts records 0 (.07)	Aggression +, school adjustment +
11. Hawkins et al. (1992)	6	Universal	Family and school attachment	School, parent, classroom	1,659 boys and girls	4 years	Training of teachers, parents, students	5 months	Self-reported delinquency + (.14)	Academic achievement −, parenting +, attachment to family + and school +
12. Schweinhart, Barnes, and Weikart (1993)	3–4	Selective	Cognitive development	Day care, home	72 boys, 51 girls	1–2 years	Day care program, home visits	24 years	Police arrests + (.54)	IQ +, school achievement +, high school graduation +, social services +, wages +
13. Lally, Mangione, and Honig (1988)	Birth	Selective	Education, nutrition, family environment	Day care, home	82 children	5 years	Parent training, education, nutrition, health and safety, mother-child relationship	10 years	Court records + (.48)	IQ +, social behavior +, school achievement +

NOTE.—In the "Results at Posttest or Follow-up" column, a zero indicates no intervention effects, a plus sign indicates positive effects of the intervention, a minus sign indicates negative intervention effects, and the value in parentheses is the effect size. Tables 2–5 are ordered by decreasing age of treatment. Study numbers appear in more than one table but with their original numbers.
* Effect size could not be computed.

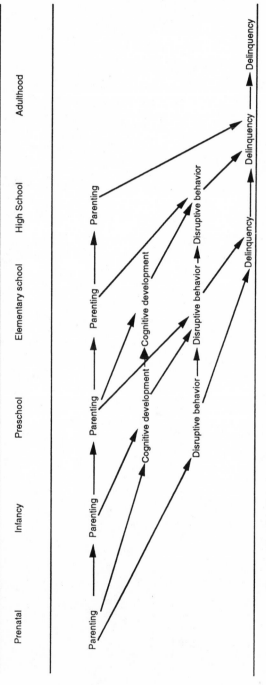

Fig. 2.—Possible links between manipulated factor and outcome for developmental prevention experiments

Tables 2, 3, 4, and 5 present summary information for all studies in each of the sections. Because the main focus of this essay is crime prevention, and because there are few studies with delinquency as an outcome, the latter are all presented in some detail. For the other sections, only a few examples of prevention studies are presented in some detail to give the reader an overview of the types of experiments involved.

III. Preventing Juvenile Delinquency
The prevention studies described in this section assessed the extent to which treated subjects were less involved in criminal activity during adolescence and adulthood compared to control subjects. The studies were identified by two different sources: a search of the Psycinfo and Medline data banks, and recent literature reviews. The data bank search identified 228 publications on delinquency prevention. However, only nine of these were prevention experiments targeted at subjects who were not already juvenile delinquents.[1] This finding confirmed that most delinquency prevention efforts are still aimed at preventing recidivism. These experiments were discussed in Section II above. It also confirmed that most prevention interventions with nondelinquent youths are not aimed at preventing delinquency or, at least, do not assess delinquency as an outcome.

The experiments that were included in this section (see table 2) fell into two categories. In the "selective" type (see Gordon 1983; Mrazek and Haggerty 1994), subjects were part of a subgroup whose risk of delinquency was above average (e.g., boys from poor inner-city neighborhoods). In the "indicated" type, individuals possessed an important risk factor (e.g., the boys were disruptive). The experiments manipulated social behavior, cognitive skills, school commitment, school curriculum, parenting skills, or peer influence. The age of the subjects at the start of the intervention ranged from prebirth to seventeen years of age. The length of the follow-up to assess outcome ranged from one year to thirty-seven years. Six of the prevention experiments that measured delinquency as an outcome were aimed at adolescents. Five studies were aimed at elementary school children, and only two prevention experiments with preschoolers had follow-ups that measured delinquency. A summary of the background, method, and results of

---

[1] Experiments with an exclusive focus on substance use or abuse prevention were not included in this review because they are described in the essay by Hawkins, Arthur, and Catalano (in this volume).

these thirteen studies follows. Experiments with adolescents are presented first, followed by experiments with elementary school children, then those with preschoolers. The effect size for prevention of delinquency was computed for all but one study that did not publish the necessary data. These effect sizes are presented in table 2.

A. Prevention of Delinquency with Adolescents

1. *Targeting Teaching Practices (Hawkins, Doueck, and Lishner 1988)*. This universal prevention experiment was implemented in Seattle middle schools (grade 7) during the 1981–82 school year. The intervention was based on a "social development" model (Hawkins and Weis 1985) that proposes that providing opportunities and rewards for school success will prevent juvenile delinquency. The "social development" model stresses the importance of maintaining low achievers in regular classrooms and modifying teaching practices to provide them with better learning opportunities. It suggests that students need opportunities for active involvement in the classroom, need to develop skills for successful participation, and need constant reinforcement for work involvement. The experiment tested the hypothesis that helping teachers acquire the necessary skills to provide these opportunities would have an effect on successful experiences in class, enhance social bonding to school, and consequently reduce misbehavior and delinquency. It was further hypothesized that these effects would be observed for all students, including low achievers.

Method. Five Seattle middle schools were chosen for the study. In three schools the students and teachers were randomly allocated to experimental and control classrooms. All the classes of one school were assigned to the experimental condition, and all the classes of the remaining school were assigned to the control condition. There were 520 experimental students, 653 control students, 15 experimental teachers, and 18 control teachers. Experimental classroom teachers were provided with training prior to the fall term and during the year (three booster sessions). They were also supervised in the instruction methods for two hours a month. The teacher training program had three components: "proactive classroom management," which trained teachers to create a learning environment, with appropriate student behavior; "interactive teaching," which, among other things, required that students master learning objectives before doing more advanced work; and "cooperative learning," which aimed to bring together as learning partners small groups of students with differing abilities. The intervention lasted one year, and the outcomes were assessed at the end of that year. Hawkins, Doueck, and Lishner (1988) focused their outcome report on students who had been assessed in the lower quartile of the math achievement test at the end of sixth grade. There were eighty-three subjects in the control condition and seventy-seven in the experimental condition. This analysis aimed to test the hypothesis that the experimental low achievers would benefit from better teacher practices and would have improved school success, leading to less delinquency involvement.

Results. Outcomes were measured at the end of the school year with standard achievement tests by the school district, a questionnaire to students measuring social bonding to school and delinquency, and school records for misbehavior. Implementation of experimental teaching practices was also assessed by direct observation of experimental and control classes for nineteen days over the school year. These observations revealed significant differences in the use of experimental instructional practices by experimental teachers compared to control teachers. The intervention was thus effectively implemented. School bonding assessment from students' questionnaires revealed that experimental low math achievers were reporting significantly more positive attitudes toward seventh grade math and school in general than the low math achievers in the control group. Their favorable attitude toward math was even higher than the general population. Significant differences in favor of the experimental subjects were also observed for expectations for future education, school suspensions, and expulsions. However, no significant differences were observed between the two groups for self-reported delinquency and drug use.

2. *Targeting School Commitment (Bry 1982).* Bry and George (1979) reported on the implementation of a delinquency prevention intervention in two U.S. school systems. The selection of subjects was based on the idea that adolescents' problem behaviors are preceded by a low sense of competence and cynicism about the predictability of the world. The intervention attempted to test the theory that cognitive processes mediate behavioral change (Bandura, Adams, and Beyer 1977). More specifically, it was hypothesized that if subjects were made to understand that their goals can be achieved through their own actions they would increase their sense of competence and reduce their cynicism.

Method. The intervention was implemented in two schools, one in a low-income urban area, the other in a middle-class suburban area.

Subjects were selected from sixth-grade records if they had "low academic achievement motivation, a disregard for rules and a feeling of distance from their families" (Bry 1982, p. 266). Subjects aged twelve to fifteen years were paired within each classroom and then randomly allocated to a control or a treatment group (total subjects at pretest was eighty). Sixty-six subjects (forty-four males, twenty-two females) were eventually followed up to five years after the end of the intervention, which lasted two years. The intervention was based on weekly group meetings and a reward system when the subjects were in seventh and eighth grade. The intervention staff met weekly with teachers to check on the subjects' behavior and school performance. They then met with the subjects in small groups to discuss individual report cards on behavior and achievement. Positive teacher ratings were praised and negative ones were discussed to identify subject behaviors which could improve the teacher's impressions, and points were accumulated to earn an extra school trip. Intervention staff were in contact with parents to keep them informed on the subject's progress. Outcome was assessed one year after the end of the two treatment years using school records and subject interviews. Five years after the end of treatment the county probation department files were checked to compare the treated and control groups.

Results. The school records obtained for fifty-eight subjects one year after the end of treatment showed that treated subjects had significantly fewer serious school problems. The interviews, obtained from sixty-three subjects, showed that significantly more of the treated subjects had held a job, fewer had reported abuse of drugs ($p < .09$), and fewer had reported criminal behavior ($p < .08$). Five years after the end of treatment, when the subjects had a mean age of 19.5 years, the probation department records indicated that significantly fewer of the treated subjects (10 percent) had serious or chronic delinquency files, compared to the control group (30 percent).

3. *Targeting the School Curriculum (Gottfredson and Gottfredson 1992).* The Student Training through Urban Strategies project was an attempt to prevent juvenile delinquency of high school students by providing a course specifically designed for high-risk youths. The intervention was designed to be consistent with strain and opportunity theory (Cloward and Ohlin 1960) and with the idea that, to become law-abiding citizens and develop moral reasoning, adolescents need to learn about responsibilities of individuals, the role of government, the justice system, and law. From the strain theory perspective, the inter-

vention was an attempt to decrease alienation of high school students by offering participatory instructional methods, a "high interest" curriculum, and the increased likelihood of academic success. School and community involvement, as well as the development of critical thinking abilities and problemsolving skills, were major components of the program.

Method. This experimental program was offered to two high schools (one for twelve to fourteen year olds, one for fifteen to seventeen year olds) in Pasadena, California, from 1980 to 1983. English and social studies teachers worked together and offered a one-year alternative class focused on school rules, human relations, the role of the family, social contracts, and the criminal justice system. Students eligible for the experiment were recruited through school staff referrals or self-nominations. Random allocation to the treatment and control conditions was planned but was not fully implemented because of scheduling problems. There were 120 subjects in the treatment condition, and 127 in the control condition. Treatment and control groups for the junior high school subjects (ages twelve to fourteen years) were equivalent on all demographic variables. However, in the treated senior high school group, there were significantly more African-American students and more females.

Results. Follow-up assessments appear to have been made only at the end of the school year during which the treatment was given. Delinquency was measured through self-reports and court contacts. Pretreatment variables for which significant differences were found between treatment and control groups were included in the statistical analyses as covariates. Analyses of variance and covariance indicated that the treated students in the senior high school reported significantly less serious delinquency than the control students. The same trend was observed for the junior high school students, but was not significant. A similar nonsignificant trend in the successful direction was also observed for court contacts of both junior and senior high school students. The results also indicate a short-term positive effect of this modification of the high school curriculum on negative peer influence, attachment to school, and school success.

4. *Targeting Cognitive Skills (Arbuthnot and Gordon 1986).* Moral reasoning has systematically been linked to delinquent behavior (Blasi 1980; Jurkovic 1980). Piaget (1965) showed that children's moral reasoning was associated with logical reasoning abilities such as perspective taking. He also proposed that reasoning abilities were developed

along fixed stages from early childhood to adolescence. Kohlberg (1969) built on these ideas to propose a cognitive developmental theory of moral reasoning. Arbuthnot and Gordon (1986) and Arbuthnot (1992) used this theoretical basis to suggest that adolescents at high risk for delinquent behavior were using less advanced moral reasoning skills and that training of proper skills could prevent delinquent behavior. They created an intervention program for adolescents at high risk of delinquent behavior. The purpose of their study was to show that appropriate training in moral reasoning would help adolescents with behavior disorders advance in their moral reasoning stage, improve their social behavior, and prevent delinquency involvement.

Method. The subjects (thirty-five males, thirteen females) in this study were between ages thirteen and seventeen. They were attending four different school systems in a rural U.S. county. The subjects were nominated by their teachers as behavior-disordered. After having been paired on the basis of their level of behavior problem, the subjects were randomly allocated to treatment or control conditions. The treatment consisted of one session per week (forty-five minutes) over a period of sixteen to twenty weeks. The sessions included five to eight subjects and were led by one or two trainers. The first sessions were used to build rapport between the leaders and subjects. The other sessions were centered on moral dilemma discussions. The dilemmas were chosen by the leaders from different sources, including the subjects' own experiences. The leaders focused the discussion on moral reasoning and perspective taking, and they also used role playing. Moral norms that were discussed included property, truth, affiliation, law, civil rights, and authority. Outcome data were obtained from teacher ratings, subject assessments, and school and court records, both at the end of the intervention and twelve months later. Unfortunately, data were obtained for less than half the sample at the twelve-month follow-up because of poor school cooperation.

Results. Arbuthnot and Gordon (1986; see also Arbuthnot 1992) reported that the treated group, compared to the control group, showed a significant increase in sociomoral reasoning both at the end of the treatment and at the twelve-month follow-up. Significant differences were also observed at both assessments for disciplinary referrals, school absenteeism, tardiness at school, and grade point average. In each of these cases, the treated subjects were doing better than the control subjects. Delinquency data were obtained from court records. At the end of the treatment, the treated group had significantly fewer police and court contacts than the control group. However, at the twelve-month follow-up period, there were no significant differences between the two groups.

5. *Targeting Peers (Gottfredson 1987).* The Peer Culture Development project (see also Gottfredson and Gottfredson 1992) attempted to prevent students' delinquency by offering group counseling meetings within the high school curriculum. The intervention program was meant to be consistent with the differential association theory (Sutherland and Cressey 1978) and the subcultural perspective on delinquency (Miller 1958). From these perspectives juvenile delinquency is seen as the product of a lower-class subculture that values toughness and excitement. Law violation values are learned through the peer culture. The intervention was an attempt to offer an alternative law-abiding model by integrating positive role model peers in groups of troublesome students. The Peer Culture Development program intended to provide confrontation and examination of inadequate behavior and beliefs using conventional role models during counseling sessions.

Method. The experimental program was offered to groups of fifteen single-sex students (ages fourteen to seventeen years) in three Chicago public high schools between 1980 and 1983. The counseling sessions were offered as a social studies course leading to credits. Attempts were made to create groups having an equal number of students in trouble and students who could serve as positive role models. The groups were heterogeneous in cultural background, age, and socioeconomic status. They met daily for fifteen weeks. The first sessions were focused on participants' life histories, while later sessions focused on specific problems the students were having. Problem-solving discussions were followed by a summary from the teacher. Participants were volunteers, often referred by teachers and peers. Random allocation to treatment and control groups was carried out separately by gender and within the following categories: conventional students, students in trouble, positive leaders, and negative leaders. There were 184 treatment subjects and 176 control subjects. Approximately half of the treated subjects participated in the treatment for one semester, while the other half participated for two semesters.

Results. Assessments of delinquent behavior appear to have been done at the end of treatment, using self-reports of delinquency and court appearances. The analyses of variance comparing the treated and control groups revealed no significant differences for self-reported serious delinquency and court appearances, but there was a clear trend for the treated subjects to have a worse outcome than the control subjects. There was also a significant difference for drug use, indicating that treated students were using more drugs than control students. Attachment to school and school achievement were assessed and showed no significant differences between the groups.

6. *Targeting Multiple Risk Factors (Gottfredson 1986)*. The Positive Action Through Holistic Education project (see also Gottfredson and Gottfredson 1992) was an attempt both to target individuals at high risk and to modify the school environment. The project was based on the social control theory (Hirschi 1969) hypothesis that social bonds will prevent delinquency involvement. These social bonds include attachment to law-abiding friends and commitment to conventional goals such as school success. The project aimed to help at-risk youths acquire such social bonds in the school system by increasing success in school and attachment to specific school staff.

Method. The experimental program was implemented in seven secondary schools for students aged eleven to seventeen years old in Charleston, South Carolina, between 1980 and 1983. The program included five components: teams composed of school staff, students, parents, and community members to revise school policies, school design, and manage school change; changes to increase academic performance for all students; changes to enhance school climate; programs to prepare students for careers; and special academic and other services for high-risk students. High-risk students were identified through academic and behavior records, as well as through teacher referrals. Approximately 10 percent of the schools' populations were targeted. Subjects were randomly assigned to treatment ($N = 468$) and control ($N = 401$) conditions. The program included diagnosis of individual needs, identification of services to meet the needs, and monitoring of progress. Each treatment subject was referred to a specialist (experienced teacher, guidance counselor, or assistant principal) who was provided with information on the subject's school experience. The specialist met with the student, and with his parents and teachers, if required, to set behavioral objectives. A program was devised to help attain these objectives. The program included individual counseling, tutoring, peer counseling, student leadership teams, field trips, and clubs. Specialists advised the student's teachers on instructional strategies and referred the families to community services. The treatment lasted two years.

Results. The effect of the intervention was measured both at the school level and at the individual level. Gottfredson (1986) reported that changes made in the management of the schools appeared to reduce disorders and increase social bonding for the entire school population. Delinquency for the whole school population was significantly reduced over a one-year period in the experimental high schools. Delinquency involvement was assessed by self-reports and court contacts at the end of the two-year treatment period for the high-risk control and treatment groups. Analyses of variance showed no significant differences for self-reported delinquency and court contacts between the treated and control groups. Although the school changes did reduce delinquent behavior in the general population, special services to the high-risk subjects did not have an effect on their delinquency or on their social bonding. However, high-risk treated subjects were significantly more successful than the untreated subjects in school achievement, including promotion and graduation rates. These results would appear to disconfirm the social control theory hypothesis that there is a causal link between school social bonds and delinquency, at least for high-risk subjects.

B. Prevention of Delinquency with Elementary School Children

Except for one study (Lochman 1992), all the other prevention experiments for elementary school and preschool children, with an assessment of delinquency as an outcome, targeted multiple risk factors. They are presented below under the names of the cities or universities where the studies took place.

1. *The Duke University Experiment (Lochman 1992).* This experiment with aggressive boys was initiated in the early 1980s, based on the premise that aggressive behavior in preadolescent boys is a risk factor predictive of subsequent levels of aggression and numerous other negative outcomes during adolescence. The intervention was based on social-cognitive research indicating that aggressive children tend to attribute hostility to other people's intentions and tend to misperceive their own aggressiveness and the degree of their responsibility for the conflict (e.g., Dodge 1986; Lochman and Lampron 1986). Cognitive-behavioral therapy procedures were developed to address these social cognitive deficits and distortions of aggressive children. Lochman (1992) implemented the prevention experiment with a three-year follow-up to test the hypothesis that cognitive-behavioral therapy with aggressive boys in elementary school would have a long-term effect on juvenile delinquency through its effect on aggressive behavior and moderating factors such as self-esteem.

Method. The subjects for the experiment were fourth-, fifth-, or sixth-grade boys rated aggressive and disruptive by their teachers (aggressive-treated sample = 31; aggressive-untreated sample = 52) and boys who were not rated aggressive by their peers (nonaggressive control sample = 62). There was a pool of 354 subjects who could have been included in the follow-up, but only the above 145 were retraced or had parental consent. There were no significant differences between the followed-up aggressive-treated and aggressive-untreated subjects on pretreatment aggression, IQ, and racial status. However, the aggressive-treated group were found to be significantly younger (by a mean of eight months) compared to the untreated boys. The intervention consisted of weekly sessions over a four-to-five-month period. The aggressive-treated boys met in groups for forty-five to sixty minutes. The sessions focused on learning to identify problems, learning to inhibit impulsive behavior, and generating alternative solutions to social problems. Discussions, role playing, and videotapes were the basic teaching techniques. A small subset of the aggressive-treated group (*N* = 12) was given a booster intervention one year after the first intervention. The booster included six weekly sessions similar to the previous sessions and five parent-training workshop sessions. Because of this parent training for a small subset of the subjects, this experiment could be considered a step toward a multimodal intervention including school and family contexts. Boys were assessed 2.5–3.5 years following treatment. Outcome variables (i.e., substance use, delinquent behavior) were assessed by structured interviews. Moderating variables such as self-esteem and social problem solving skills were assessed by paper-and-pencil questionnaires.

Results. Intervention effects were tested with a multivariate analysis of covariance for substance use, general behavior deviance, self-esteem, social problem solving, and classroom behavior as dependent measures. Race and IQ were the covariates. The aggressive-treated boys and the aggressive-untreated boys were not found to be significantly different on the self-reported delinquency measure—which included crimes against persons and theft—or on the classroom observations of behavior. However, the aggressive-treated boys displayed lower levels of substance use, higher levels of self-esteem, and better social problem-solving skills than the aggressive untreated boys. No significant differences were observed when the aggressive-treated boys who received a booster session were compared to the aggressive-treated boys who did not, except for passive off-task behavior in the classroom. The booster group showed less of these negative behaviors. The positive results provide some support for the assumption that targeting childhood aggression with a cognitive-behavioral approach will have a long-term effect on hypothesized moderating factors such as self-esteem and social problem-solving skills and on a negative outcome such as substance use. However, the absence of any effect on delinquency was disappointing.

2. *The Cambridge-Somerville Study (McCord 1978).* This prevention study for at-risk youths and their families was initiated in the 1930s. This was shortly after Glueck and Glueck (1934) had shown that 88 percent of juvenile delinquents sent to the Boston court had recidivated five years later and that recidivism rates were not much better for those who had been treated following the recommendations of the leading specialists at the Judge Baker Foundation (McCord 1992). The Cambridge-Somerville intervention program was influenced by the prevailing psychodynamic ideas that dominated social services in the 1930s. Healy and Bronner (1926) had underlined that most juvenile delinquents came from inadequate families where they were deprived of affection. The aim of the intervention program was to provide at-risk youths with emotional support, friendship, and guidance from an individual outside his family (McCord 1992).

Method. Subjects were selected from a poor, high-crime-rate area of Massachusetts. Boys aged twelve or younger were referred from different sources. A total of 650 boys were paired on a number of characteristics, including age, intelligence, and family environment, and were randomly allocated to a treatment and a control group. Each treated subject was given a counselor who tried to establish a close relationship with the boy and help his family as much as they could, by visiting them at home, in the street, or seeing them in the project headquarters. Counselors were supported by a team of psychologists, psychiatrists, and medical doctors, and they referred the boys and their families to specialists when they thought it appropriate. Boys received tutoring for school performance, they were sent to summer camps, and they joined community clubs, while families obtained help for medical problems and unemployment. Treatment lasted an average of 5.5 years with an average of two visits per month. The treated group was compared to the control group in 1942. At that time 253 boys were still in the program. Treatment for the other 72 boys had been stopped for a variety of reasons, including counselors joining the armed forces for World War II (McCord 1992). The comparison of the 253 treated boys to their controls indicated no significant differences on individual, family, and community variables.

Results. Results at the end of treatment (Powers and Witmer 1972) generally indicated no significant differences between the treated and control groups on criminal activity. A second assessment of effect was made some thirty years later when the subjects were on average forty-seven years old (McCord 1978). Court records up to 1975–76 were used to check criminal activities of treated and control boys. The results indicated no significant differences on criminal activity, but the treated group was found, significantly more often than the control group, to have alcoholism, serious mental illness, and stress-related physical health problems. McCord (1992) classified the men as having had an undesirable outcome if they had been convicted of an FBI index crime, if they had died before age thirty-five, and if they had been diagnosed alcoholic, schizophrenic, or manic-depressive; 37 percent of the subjects were classified as having an undesirable outcome. The comparison of the treated and control boys indicated that significantly more treated subjects than control subjects had an undesirable outcome. In sixty-three pairs of subjects (treated-control pairs) the treated subject had an undesirable outcome, while the control subject did not. The reverse was observed in only thirty-nine pairs. Thus, from a long-term perspective, this treatment appeared to have a negative effect on important adjustment problems.

3. *The University of Pittsburgh Study (Kazdin, Siegel, and Bass 1992).* This experiment was implemented with children who were referred for treatment to a psychiatric clinic for aggressive and antisocial behavior. The aim of the study was to verify the effect of three different intervention programs on antisocial children's functioning as well as on maternal stress and family relations. Kazdin, Siegel, and Bass (1992) argued that the reason there were so many different treatment approaches for antisocial children was the wide scope of the dysfunction. They also argued that the reason these treatments had not shown a significant effect on clinically referred antisocial youth was that they often addressed only one aspect of the dysfunction. They hypothesized that implementing two complementary types of treatment would have more effect than implementing either of those two treatments alone. They chose parent-management training and cognitively based problem-solving skills training because these treatments had been shown to have some effect on disruptive children and because they were directed toward important features of antisocial behavior: child-rearing prac-

tices and children's cognitive processes, which are conceptually complementary.

Method. The ninety-seven children in this experiment were aged between seven and thirteen years (mean = 10.3). They were referred to an outpatient psychiatric clinic for unmanageability at home or at school, including fighting, stealing, and running away. They were all above the ninetieth percentile on the aggression or delinquency scales of the Child Behavior Checklist (Achenbach and Edelbrock 1983), and they all had a diagnosis of conduct disorder, oppositional disorder, attention-deficit hyperactivity disorder, or adjustment disorder, based on the *Diagnostic and Statistical Manual of Mental Disorders* (American Psychiatric Association 1987). Sixty-nine percent were white, and 30 percent were black. Sixty-one percent came from two-parent families. They ranged from lower (21 percent) to upper (13 percent) socioeconomic classes, with a majority from the lower middle class (42 percent). Treatment was given within a six- to eight-month period after initial assessment. Individual treatment was provided for each family.

Subjects were allocated randomly to three treatment conditions. Problem-solving skills training (PSST) was given to twenty-nine subjects, who received individually administered weekly sessions for twenty-five weeks. The sessions combined cognitive and behavioral approaches to teach problem-solving skills and the management of interpersonal situations. Techniques such as modeling, role-playing, practice, and token reinforcement were used. Tasks were assigned to the child, parents participated in the sessions, and they were given written guidelines to help the child. Parent management training (PMT) was given to the parents of thirty-one subjects. One of the child's parents was seen individually for sixteen sessions of one and a half to two hours. The training program was inspired from work by Patterson et al. (1975) and Fleischman and Conger (1978). Using didactic instructions, modeling, and role-playing, parents were trained to observe their children's behavior, to reinforce positive behaviors, to provide reprimands and time out for negative behaviors, and to negotiate and make contracts with their children. The child and his teacher were also used to monitor school behavior, shape parent-child negotiations about reinforcement contingencies, and monitor the parent's execution of the program. The third treatment condition included both the PSST and PMT programs and was given to thirty-seven families. The outcome was assessed by comparing the three groups on pretreatment, posttreatment, and one-year follow-up measures of children's behavior (parent, teacher, and self-reports), parents' adjustment (stress, depression, psychiatric symptoms), and family functioning.

Results. Of the ninety-seven children who started treatment, there were seventy-six (78 percent) who completed treatment, seventy-five (77 percent) who were assessed at posttreatment, and seventy (72 percent) who were assessed at the one-year follow-up. Those who dropped out of the study were found to have significantly lower IQ, but there were no significant differences in the drop-out rate among the three conditions. For each outcome analysis, the pretreatment assessment was used as a covariate. Results for self-reported delinquency revealed significant differences between the combined treatment (PSST + PMT) and each separate treatment. Subjects from the PSST and PMT group reported significantly fewer delinquent behaviors than PMT subjects at posttreatment and fewer delinquent behaviors than both PSST and PMT at one-year follow-up. These results were confirmed by the parents' report of antisocial behavior. At posttreatment and one-year follow-up, parents from the PSST and PMT condition reported significantly less antisocial behavior from their children compared to the PMT and PSST conditions. Interestingly, the PSST and PMT condition appeared also to have a significantly greater effect on the parents' reports of stress and psychiatric symptoms. Both PMT only and PSST only had positive effects on some outcome measures, but only PSST and PMT had systematically and significantly better outcomes than the other two conditions.

4. *The Montréal Longitudinal Experimental Study (Tremblay, Vitaro, et al. 1992).* The Montréal Longitudinal Experimental Study was an attempt to nest an experimental prevention study within a longitudinal study of boys' social development from kindergarten to high school (Tremblay et al. 1991; Tremblay 1992; Tremblay, Vitaro, et al. 1992). The intervention was based on results from longitudinal studies showing the stability of aggressive behavior (Loeber and Dishion 1983) and showing that disruptive elementary school boys from low socioeconomic environments were at high risk of juvenile delinquency and adult criminality (West and Farrington 1973; Robins 1978; Pulkkinen 1982; McCord 1983). A multimodal, or "shotgun," approach to intervention was taken because it was felt that the effect could be increased by modifying more than one dimension of these boys' lives. Parent training and social skills training had been shown to have some effect with aggressive boys in the late 1970s and early 1980s (e.g., Camp et al. 1977; Patterson 1982; Patterson, Chamberlain, and Reid 1982;

Kettlewell and Kausch 1983). Parent training was selected to change the boys' home environment, while social skills training was selected to change the boys' school environment. Since parenting and child disruptive behavior had been identified as the most powerful predictors of later delinquent behavior (Loeber and Stouthamer-Loeber 1986), the early modification of these two dimensions was expected to have a preventive effect on school performance, peer interactions, and delinquent behavior.

Method. All the kindergarten teachers in the fifty-three schools with the lowest socioeconomic index of the main Montréal school board were asked to rate the disruptive behavior of all their male students. Ratings were obtained from 87 percent of the teachers for 1,161 boys. The 30 percent most disruptive were randomly allocated to a treatment group ($N = 46$), an attention-control group ($N = 84$), and a no-contact control group ($N = 42$). Subjects who were not born in Cànada from French-speaking Canadian-born parents were excluded to control for culture. The treatment lasted two years, starting when the boys were entering their second year of elementary school at age seven. Families were visited approximately once every three weeks for parent-training sessions. The mean number of sessions per family over the two school years was 17.4. The parent training program was based on the Oregon Social Learning Center's program (Patterson 1982) and included six components: giving parents a reading program, training them to monitor their son's behavior, training parents to reinforce positive behavior, training parents to punish effectively without being abusive, training parents to manage family crises, and training parents to generalize what they had learned. The social skills training program was implemented by professionals in the schools. The disruptive boys were included in small groups of prosocial peers who met for nine sessions during the first year and ten sessions in the second year. The first series of sessions was focused on learning prosocial skills, while the second series was focused on self-control. Coaching, peer modeling, self-instruction, behavior rehearsal, and reinforcement contingencies were used during these sessions. The original 1,161 boys were assessed yearly from age ten to fifteen, providing a follow-up of treated and control subjects, as well as a community sample comparison group.

Results. Six years after the end of the treatment, when the boys were age fifteen, the developmental trends of the treated and untreated boys were compared on teacher-rated disruptive behavior, school status, self-reported delinquency, and court records (Tremblay et al.

1994). For teacher-rated disruptive behavior, it was shown that the treated boys tended to be rated less disruptive than the untreated boys from age ten to thirteen, but that trend disappeared at age fourteen. For school status, being in an age-appropriate regular classroom was used as a criterion of school adjustment. Results showed that a significantly higher percentage of treated boys were in an age-appropriate regular classroom up to age twelve compared to untreated boys; however, that difference disappeared from age thirteen onward. For self-reported delinquency, the treated boys were shown to report significantly less delinquent behavior than the untreated boys from age ten to fifteen. Court records did not show any significant differences in the proportion of treated and untreated boys placed under the Young Offenders' Act between age twelve and fourteen. However, the proportion of boys placed under that law was very low (8 percent). In summary, this intervention had a significant effect on the social development of disruptive kindergarten boys, but it was not as successful with the more extreme cases.

5. *The Seattle Social Development Project (Hawkins et al. 1992).* This intervention was based on the social development model (Farrington and Hawkins 1991) and an integration of social control (Hirschi 1969) and social learning (Bandura, Adams, and Beyer 1977) theories. It follows the same logic as the Hawkins, Doueck, and Lishner (1988) study described in Subsection IIIA1 above. It was designed to reduce shared childhood risk factors for delinquency and drug abuse by enhancing school and family bonds. By promoting strong bonds to the family and school, it was hypothesized that children would be motivated to adhere to the behavior standards promoted by these agencies. The intervention was designed to increase the opportunities for prosocial interaction, to increase children's skills in their social interactions, and to increase reinforcements for prosocial behaviors and participation in the home and at school.

Method. This field experiment started in 1981 with children entering first grade in eight Seattle public schools. Two schools were assigned to the full control or full intervention. In the six remaining schools, classrooms were randomly assigned to intervention or control conditions. At posttest, ten more control schools were added. The intervention children were exposed to proactive classroom management, interactive teaching, and cooperative learning (see Hawkins, Doueck, and Lishner 1988). In addition, children in the first grade were given social cognitive problem-solving training. Two parent-training components were offered to families in the intervention on a voluntary basis. One taught parents to monitor and identify appropriate and inappropriate behavior, to set expectations, and to provide positive reinforcement for appropriate behaviors and negative consequences for inappropriate behavior in a consistent and contingent manner. The second parent-training component was designed to improve parent-child communication. The intervention was conducted over a four-year period. Data were collected at preintervention (fall 1981) and in the fall of 1985. There were 199 subjects (102 boys and 97 girls) in the intervention group (i.e., those who had received at least one semester of the intervention). The control group consisted of children who had not received the intervention in grades 1–4, plus students who were added to the project in the fall of the fifth grade when the panel was expanded to include ten additional schools (N = 709; 365 boys and 344 girls). Outcome measures included classroom observations and self-report measures on the family, school, academic achievement, beliefs and norms regarding drug use, and involvement in substance abuse and delinquency.

Results. Continuous measures were analyzed with analysis of covariance, controlling for ethnicity, socioeconomic status, and mobility. Students in the intervention group reported significantly more proactive family management by their parents, increased family communication and involvement, and more bonding than the control group. With regard to school variables, intervention group students reported that they perceived school as more rewarding; they had increased bonding but lower scores on the achievement test than the control group. There were no group differences on drug-related norms, but the intervention group reported significantly lower rates of alcohol use and delinquency initiation than the control group (intervention = 45.5 percent delinquents; controls = 52.2 percent delinquents). Overall, this intervention indicates that increasing family and school bonding and commitment can influence later delinquent and problematic behavior.

C. Prevention of Delinquency with Preschool Children

1. *The High/Scope Perry Preschool Project (Schweinhart, Barnes, and Weikart 1993).* The High/Scope Perry Preschool Project was implemented in the 1960s in the early period of the Head Start programs for disadvantaged children. The general hypothesis underlying these programs was that preschool programs could have a significant effect on later school achievement of children from economically deprived

families in the United States. The High/Scope Project was influenced by studies of environmental enrichment to stimulate the development of animals and by studies showing the importance of the preschool years for children's cognitive development. The program was not meant to prevent juvenile delinquency, but it can be argued from most social and psychological theories of delinquency that a program that increases children's cognitive development and school achievement should have a preventive effect on juvenile delinquency.

Method. The High/Scope program was implemented in a poor African-American neighborhood of Ypsilanti, Michigan. Most of the subjects' parents had not completed high school (79 percent) and close to half were single-parent families. A total of 123 children were selected for the study. They entered the program by small groups between 1962 and 1965. A sample of thirteen subjects attended the program from age four to five while all the other participants ($N = 45$) attended the program from age three to five. Subjects were first paired on IQ and then randomly allocated to two groups. After some modifications of group assignment to match the groups on sex and socioeconomic status, and to assign siblings to the same group, the membership of the treatment group was decided by flipping a coin. After five years, fifty-eight subjects had received the experimental program, and sixty-five had been placed in the control group. Children attended the preschool daily for two and a half hours on weekday mornings, and teachers visited each mother and child for one and a half hours a week in the afternoon. The program lasted thirty weeks a year. The program content was aimed at stimulating cognitive development by active learning based on Piaget's (1960) work. The program evolved over the five years but remained focused on a daily routine of active learning with systematic assessment of individual needs and interests. Subjects were followed up to age twenty-seven. There were yearly assessments from age three to eleven and assessments at age fourteen, fifteen, nineteen, and twenty-seven.

Results. The study documented the subjects' development in many areas, including educational performance, delinquency, and economic status. Results for cognitive development showed that the treated group scored higher than the control group on IQ tests from the end of the first year of treatment to age seven. That significant difference disappeared from age eight onward, but by age fourteen the treated subjects were performing significantly better than the controls on reading, arithmetic, and language achievement; by age twenty-seven significantly more treated subjects (71 percent) than controls (54 percent) had finished high school. The treated subjects by age twenty-seven were also earning significantly more money per year, a significantly higher percentage were home owners, and a lower percentage had received social services. The delinquency data indicated that the treated subjects had significantly fewer lifetime arrests (mean = 2.3) compared to the controls (mean = 4.6). The difference in arrest was observed mainly for adult arrests (adult misdemeanors and drug-related arrests). There were no significant differences for self-report measures of total acts of misconduct.

2. *The Syracuse University Family Development Research Program (Lally, Mangione, and Honig 1988).*[2] This prevention intervention was an attempt to break the link between poor education of parents and children's educational difficulties. The program was first implemented in 1969. It was aimed at poor pregnant young girls (mean age eighteen years) without a high school education. Five different theoretical perspectives were used to plan the intervention. Piaget's (1960) equilibration and active child participation theory was used to guide the development of a home and day care center curriculum for the child. Language theories (Bernstein 1954) were used to focus part of the program on language skills acquisition. Erikson's (1950) theory of personality development was used to focus the program on the child's development of trust in his abilities and environment. Help was given to the families only to the extent that they were stimulated to be active participants, according to Alinsky's (1971) theory of community organization. Finally, from John Dewey, the program staff took the idea of the importance of freedom of choice for the children, the stimulation of creativity, and the organization of an environment that stimulates exploration.

Method. The program was meant to help the families for the first five years of the child's life. A total of 108 pregnant women (mostly African-American) were recruited in the program over a three-year period. When the program children were thirty-six months old, a longitudinal control group was established. The control children were matched in pairs with program children with respect to sex, ethnicity, birth order, age, family income, family marital status, maternal age, and maternal education status (no high school diploma) at the time of

[2] This experiment was included, although it did not have random allocation of subjects, because it is the only intervention study from prebirth with longitudinal data on delinquency.

the infant's birth. Over 85 percent of the women were single parents, and all families had an income of less than $5,000 per year (in 1970 U.S. dollars). The intervention program was based on the premise that the parent was the primary caregiver and teacher of the child. Paraprofessionals made weekly home visits focused on parent-child interaction. Piagetian sensorimotor games were taught to the parents, nutrition and neighborhood services information was provided, and links with the day care staff were maintained. When the child entered the school system, mothers learned how to make contact with the teachers. From six months of age to sixty months, the children were taken daily by bus to a day care center at the university. The center had been specializing in preschool education since 1964. Special programs were developed for the children at different ages, using the concepts described in the background section above. Assessment of the children's development were made at different points in time up to age fifteen years.

Results. The five-year program was completed by 82 (76 percent) of the 108 children who started the program, and 74 (69 percent) of the matched controls remained in the study up to the fifth year. For the follow-up study, ten years after the end of treatment, 65 treated (60 percent) and 54 controls (50 percent) gave informed consent. The authors reported no bias caused by attrition. At age three the treated subjects had significantly higher IQ scores than control subjects. However, that difference had disappeared by age five at the end of the program. Data on delinquency when the children were between ages thirteen and sixteen were available from the probation department and court records. Six percent of the treated children (4 of 65) and 22 percent of the untreated children (12 of 54) had been probation cases ($\chi^2 = 6.54, p < .01$).

D. General Results and Discussion

The thirteen prevention experiments with delinquency outcomes summarized in this section were implemented over half a century, between the 1930s and the early 1980s. Six were aimed at adolescents, five at elementary school children, and two at preschoolers. Only two of the experiments with adolescents had follow-ups. One adolescent experiment had a twelve-month follow-up, while the other had a five-year follow-up. The elementary and preschool experiments had follow-ups ranging from one to thirty-seven years. The Seattle Social Development project has a follow-up, but data were available only for the posttest after four years of treatment. The mean effect size for delinquency outcomes was .20 (ranging from −.06 to +51) for the interventions with adolescents. The mean effect size for the interventions with preadolescents was .26, ranging from −.25 to +.55. The magnitude of these effect sizes should of course be viewed in the context of the length of follow-up and the quality of the design. The two preschool interventions had follow-ups of at least ten years and effect sizes of .48 and .54.

The adolescent studies tended to target only one risk factor as the manipulated variable in the experiment (e.g., teaching practices, or moral reasoning, or peer influence, or school commitment) and were all implemented in the schools. Experiments with elementary school children and preschoolers were all targeted at multiple risk factors, and in five of seven cases they were implemented in both schools (or day care facilities) and families. These differences probably reflect the idea that the family plays a greater role in children's development before adolescence. However, families continue to play an important role during adolescence, and schools are certainly not the only important influence on adolescents. If multimodal interventions are important to address the scope of dysfunctions that lead children to delinquency (Kazdin, Siegal, and Bass 1992), this should be at least as important for adolescents who are influenced by their families, schools, peers, and many other factors due to their increased autonomy.

Eight of the thirteen experiments have shown some positive effect on delinquent behavior. Half of the experiments with adolescents had some beneficial effect on delinquent behavior, while five of the seven experiments with preadolescents (elementary school and preschool) reduced delinquent behavior.

The beneficial effect on delinquency for adolescents came from two experiments with small numbers of treated subjects targeted at moral reasoning (Arbuthnot and Gordon 1986; twenty-four treated subjects) and school commitment (Bry 1982; thirty treated subjects) and from an experiment with a larger number of treated subjects that provided a special social studies course for 120 at-risk students (Gottfredson and Gottfredson 1992). However, methodological problems limit the significance of these results. The Gottfredson and Gottfredson (1992) study had some randomization problems, and there was no follow-up assessment after treatment. The Arbuthnot and Gordon (1986) study showed a significant effect only at the end of treatment; the one-year follow-up data were obtained for less than half of the sample (eleven treated subjects), and no significant difference was observed for delinquency.

The only study that appears to provide relatively good evidence of the long-term effect of a juvenile delinquency prevention effort with adolescents is thus Bry's (1982) study of an intensive (weekly for two years) cognitive-behavior oriented intervention, which targeted high-risk early adolescents (mean age = 12.5 years) who were entering seventh grade (effect size = .51). The intervention was aimed at the important transition period from elementary school to high school and gave intensive support by weekly meetings focused on problem-solving skills and links between the subject, his teacher, his parents, and his peers.

Interventions with elementary and preschool children all had multimodal programs and generally needed longer follow-ups to assess effect on delinquency. They showed statistically significant effects, except in one case (Lochman 1992). Five of the studies revealed beneficial effects on delinquency. The Cambridge-Somerville study indicated long-term negative effects on general adjustment. Although this finding was unexpected, it does show that interventions during childhood can have long-term effects and that these can be negative. The only other study that did not show a significant effect on delinquency was the Duke University experiment (Lochman 1992). It had the shortest and least intensive treatment of the six experiments. It appears, however, to have had a beneficial effect on substance use.

The common features of the five childhood prevention experiments that had an effect on juvenile delinquency were the scope and the intensity of the interventions with high-risk children. The shortest intervention lasted between six and eight months but had weekly individual sessions aimed at children, parents, and teachers. The longest intervention lasted five years from birth to school entry and aimed at both home and day care environments. Delinquency reductions were statistically significant. Effect sizes ranged from .14 to .55 with a mean of .39. However, the evidence for a significant reduction of serious criminal behavior remains weak. Because samples of treated subjects were small, the long-term statistically significant differences are impressive, but the small samples were generally followed only to midadolescence and, thus, could not generate high base rates of serious delinquency. There were also attrition problems in most of these studies.

The evidence provided by these studies should normally lead to experiments with larger number of subjects and longer follow-ups into the serious criminality age bracket. Such studies are very expensive. They need sponsors who are prepared to invest large sums of money and wait two to three decades to observe the effects. These sponsors are not easily found, and this might explain why there are only a handful of studies with small numbers of subjects that give some evidence that early intensive interventions can prevent some criminal involvement.

Most of the studies reviewed above show beneficial effects on outcomes other than delinquency. In some cases these effects confirm theoretical models of delinquency development (e.g., Bry 1982; Lally, Mangione, and Honig 1988; Arbuthnot 1992; Gottfredson and Gottfredson 1992; Hawkins et al. 1992; Kazdin, Siegel, and Bass 1992; Lochman 1992; Schweinhart, Barnes, and Weikart 1993), but in others they do not (e.g., Gottfredson 1986; Hawkins, Doueck, and Lishner 1988; Tremblay et al. 1994). Sections IV, V, and VI discuss experiments that have not used delinquency as an outcome but have attempted to modify some variables theoretically linked to this outcome. These studies suggest how much evidence is available that shows that interventions can have an effect on delinquency risk factors.

IV. Preventing Socially Disruptive Behaviors

A large number of the prevention experiments with children were attempts to prevent patterns of behavior considered disruptive at school and in the home: aggression, opposition, bullying, truancy, lying, hyperactivity, and impulsivity. These behaviors lead to frequent consultations with child specialists (Earls 1986; Mrazek and Haggerty 1994), and they are the best predictors of juvenile delinquency. These behaviors were the main criteria for the selection of subjects in the experiments to prevent juvenile delinquency described in the preceding section. This section presents experiments that aimed to prevent these disruptive behaviors but that did not assess the effect on delinquency.

Table 3 presents a summary of twenty-two such experiments; those in table 2 are not repeated in table 3, but they can all be considered experiments to prevent disruptive behavior. The subjects in these experiments were newborns to preadolescents, and most experiments were targeted on high-risk children or families. All ten experiments with preschoolers included some form of intervention with the parents, while three included day care programs. Of the twelve experiments with elementary school children, only three included interven-

TABLE 3

Studies with Socially Disruptive Behavior as an Outcome

Authors	Age at Treatment (in Years)	Type	Risk Factors Manipulated	Context of Intervention	No. of Subjects	Length of Treatment	Type of Treatment	Length of Follow-up	Results	
									Disruptive Behaviors	Others
14. Dishion, Patterson, and Kavanagh (1992)	10–14	Selective	Parenting, self-control	Clinic	58 boys, 61 girls	12 weeks	Parent training, self-regulation	0	Antisocial behavior +	Negative discipline +, home behavior −
15. Pelham et al. (1985)	$\bar{x} = 11.5$	Indicated	Inattentive behavior	Clinic	24 boys, 5 girls	12 weeks	Medication	0	Classroom behavior +	Academic performance +
16. Feldman (1992)	$\bar{x} = 11.2$	Indicated	Peer group	Community, peer	701 boys	32 weeks	Social learning, behavior modification	0	Antisocial behavior +	Prosocial behavior +
17. Rotheram (1982)	10–12	Selective	Social skills	School	202 children	12 weeks	Social skills training	1 year	Social relations +	Academic performance +, problem solving 0, assertive behavior +
18. Kendall et al. (1990)	$\bar{x} = 10.8$	Indicated	Problem solving	Clinic	26 boys, 3 girls	4 months	Cognitive behavior	0	Social competence +, impulsivity +, externalizing problems +	Prosocial behavior +
19. Pepler, King, and Byrd (1991)	$\bar{x} = 8$	Indicated	Social-cognitive skills	School, parent	34 boys, 6 girls	12 weeks	Social skills training	3 months	Externalizing problems +, social problem solving 0	Internalizing problems +

190

Study	Age	Type	Focus	Setting	Sample	Duration	Intervention	Follow-up	Outcomes	Outcomes
20. Coie et al. (1991)	$\bar{x} = 8$	Indicated	Social cognition, social behavior	School, peer	49 boys	7 months	Social skills, peer tutoring, emotion control	0	Aggression 0, peer rejection +	Self-concept 0, prosocial behavior +
21. Yu et al. (1986)	7–12	Indicated	Problem solving	Clinic, parent	35 boys	20 weeks	Social problem solving	0	Externalizing behaviors +, social competence +	Problem solving +, internalizing behaviors +
22. Kettlewell and Kausch (1983)	7–12	Indicated	Cognitive skills	School	31 boys, 10 girls	4 weeks	Behavior rehearsal, self-instruction	0	Aggression 0, fighting +	Anger 0, problem solving +
23. Horn et al. (1990)	7–11	Indicated	Parenting, social behavior	Parent, school	34 boys, 8 girls	12 weeks	Parent training, self-control therapy	8 months	Self-control +, hyperactivity +, externalizing behaviors +, conduct problems +	
24. Kolvin et al. (1981)	7	Selective	Academic training, parenting	School, peers, individual	574 children	3–15 months	Parent counseling, behavior modification, group therapy, academic work, play group therapy	20–32 months	Antisocial behavior +	Neurotic problems +
25. Kellam et al. (1994) Dolan et al. (1993)	6	Universal	Academic functioning, social behavior	School	590 children	2 years	Master learning, good behavior game	4 years	Aggression +	Depression +, shy +, school achievement +

191

TABLE 3 (*Continued*)

Authors	Age at Treatment (in Years)	Type	Risk Factors Manipulated	Context of Intervention	No. of Subjects	Length of Treatment	Type of Treatment	Length of Follow-up	Results	
									Disruptive Behaviors	Others
26. McNeil et al. (1991)	$\bar{x} = 4.9$	Indicated	Parenting	Home	30 children	14 weeks	Parent training	0	Inattention 0, aggression +, appropriate behavior +, compliance +, oppositional +	Peer relations 0
27. Packard, Robinson, and Grove (1983)	$\bar{x} = 4.3$	Indicated	Parenting	Home	34 mother-child pairs	2 weeks	Parent training	11 weeks	Problem behavior +	Positive behaviors 0
28. Shure and Spivack (1979)	$\bar{x} = 4.3$	Indicated	Interpersonal, cognitive problem solving	Home	10 boys, 10 girls	3 months	Social problem solving, parent training	0	Impulsivity +	Withdrawal +, problem solving +
29. Webster-Stratton, Kolpacoff, and Hollinsworth (1988) Webster-Stratton (1990)	$\bar{x} = 4.5$	Indicated	Parenting	Home	101 mothers, 70 fathers	4 months	Parent training	3 years	Externalizing problems +, total behavior problems +; hyperactivity +	Parenting +
30. Strain et al. (1982)	3–5	Indicated	Parenting	Home	33 boys, 7 girls	17 weeks	individual, parent training	3–9 years	Compliance +, oppositional behavior +	Positive behaviors +
31. Dadds, Schwartz, and Sanders (1987)	$\bar{x} = 4.2$	Indicated	Parent training, marital satisfaction	Home	24 families	6 weeks	Parent training, problem solving	6 months	Compliance +, oppositional behavior +	Marital satisfaction +

192

Study	Age	Type	Focus	Setting	N	Duration	Components	Follow-up	Results	Results
32. Strayhorn and Weidman (1991)	$\bar{x} = 3.7$	Selective	Parenting	Home	36 boys, 48 girls	5 months	Parent training	1 year	Hostility 0, hyperactivity +	Parenting +, attention +
33. Seitz, Rosenbaum, and Apfel (1985)	2.5	Selective	Family support	Home, day care	36 infants	2.5 years	Education, medical support, parent training, day care	10 years	Antisocial behavior +	Service usage +, socioeconomic status +, parenting style +, school attendance +, academic achievement +, learning patterns +
34. Johnson (1990)	1	Indicated	Parenting, cognitive development	Home, day care	47 girls, 41 boys	2 years	Education, parent training	8 years	Antisocial behavior +, impulsivity +	School achievement +, cognitive development +
35. Infant Health Program (1990)	Birth	Selective	Parenting, cognitive development	Home, day care	985 infants	3 years	Parent training, day care	0	Behavior problems +	Health status +, cognition +, I.Q. +

Note.—In the "Results" column, a zero indicates no intervention effect, a plus sign indicates a positive intervention effect, and a minus sign indicates a negative intervention effect. See table 2 note.

193

tions with parents, and seven were implemented in school settings. The treatment length varied from two weeks to three years. Two of the twelve experiments with elementary school children lasted more than one year, while three of the ten experiments with preschoolers lasted between one and three years. Twelve of the twenty-two interventions lasted less than five months. There were ten experiments with only a posttest. Five of the ten preschool experiments had follow-ups lasting between one and ten years (mean = 4.6 years), while three of the twelve elementary school experiments had follow-ups lasting between one and five years (mean = 2.4 years).

Three of the twenty-two experiments are outlined in the next few pages. They were selected to give an idea of the different types of interventions that have been experimented in different settings and at different ages. A summary of results from the twenty-two experiments follows the descriptions of the three programs.

A. Three Experiments

1. *The St. Louis Experiment (Feldman 1992).*   This intervention was based on the premise that peers play an especially important role in shaping an individual's behavior when the individual's relationship with his parents is weak. According to the theory of differential association (Sutherland and Cressey 1978), antisocial youths associate with similarly deviant others, and their deviant behaviors are consequently reinforced and encouraged. These youths have few same-age prosocial peers. The primary goal of this intervention was to treat antisocial youths among other adolescents who display positive social behaviors themselves and who reward and reinforce them when displayed by others (see Feldman, Caplinger, and Wodarski 1983).

Method.   In the early 1970s, a total of 701 boys, including 501 boys referred for antisocial behavior and 200 nonreferred boys between ages seven and fifteen, participated in the research (mean age was 11.2 years). According to parents, the referred boys had engaged in twenty-one or more antisocial acts. The nonreferred boys were youths who were enrolled in the community center in St. Louis where the intervention was taking place. The research employed a 3 × 2 × 3 factorial design. The three major variables examined were group composition (referred vs. nonreferred vs. mixed or integrated groups), group treatment method (social learning vs. traditional group therapy vs. minimal treatment), and the extent of the group leader's prior experience (experienced vs. inexperienced). All groups were stratified by age. The groups consisting entirely of referred boys totaled 237 boys, while the groups consisting entirely of nonreferred boys totaled 174 boys. The mixed group consisted of 264 nonreferred boys and 26 referred youths who had been assigned randomly. The social learning groups used group-level behavior modification techniques. The traditional groups were based on social psychological and social work practices. In the minimal treatment groups, there were no systematic interventions. The outcome variables were as follows: prosocial behavior, nonprosocial behavior, and antisocial behavior. Measures were completed by the boys, by referral agents, parents, and group leaders eight weeks before the intervention, at preintervention, and at postintervention. In addition, observational data were collected.

Results. The method of treatment did not change the subjects' behavior. The behavioral method had significantly better outcomes than the traditional method but was not different from the minimal treatment. A further assessment indicated that groups with experienced leaders achieved relatively positive outcomes, regardless of the type of intervention. Observed behavior of antisocial boys in unmixed groups did not decline over time, whereas it did for antisocial boys in mixed groups. In the unmixed groups, only 50.9 percent of the boys showed a discernible decline in antisocial behavior, whereas in the mixed groups 91.3 percent of the boys had such a decline. Therefore, prosocial peer influence caused a decrease in antisocial behavior. There was no significant change in the nonreferred boys' antisocial behavior. Hence, it is possible to conclude that these boys were not influenced adversely by interactions with the antisocial boys. This pattern of results was consistent for all informants except parents and referral agents. Unfortunately, the response rate at posttest was relatively low for parents and referral agents. The results of this study support current theories of peer group influence and differential association in the development of antisocial behavior.

2. *The Newcastle-upon-Tyne Experiment (Kolvin et al. 1981).* Kolvin and his colleagues designed this experiment in the early 1970s to evaluate the effectiveness of different treatment approaches with maladjusted elementary school children. Because different types of programs were implemented at different ages, it was possible to examine the effect of timing and content for different types of risks. In the senior elementary schools, the treatments offered were a behavior modification program, a parent counseling and teacher consultation program, and group therapy. In the junior elementary schools, there was a nur-

turing work program as well as the second and third programs offered in the senior schools. The behavior modification approach was based on social learning and reinforcement theories. Teachers were trained in instructional methods, feedback, social reinforcement, token reinforcement, and modeling to modify children's behaviors in the classroom. The group therapy was largely based on the work of Axline (1947). According to this perspective, the therapist develops a warm, friendly relationship with the child, accepts the child as exactly as he or she is, is permissive in the relationship, is alert to the feelings in the child, and is respectful and nondirective. The nurturing approach was designed to prevent the continuation or deterioration of behavioral and social disturbance and educational failure. In the parent counseling and teacher consultation intervention, social workers consulted the teachers about the management of children and worked with the parents of these children. This intervention focused on increasing the involvement of adults in a positive role in the children's lives. Over five school terms, teacher aides worked with children and provided them with the type of interactions characteristic of a healthy mother-child relationship, which include maternal warmth, interest, and acceptance, together with firmness when necessary. In addition, there was a behavioral shaping component to this intervention.

Method.   After an initial extensive screening process consisting of data on academic achievement, behavior control, and peer isolation or rejection, 592 children were identified as experiencing signs of social or psychiatric disturbance or learning problems. The study was carried out with two different age groups, seven-to-eight-year-olds and eleven-to-twelve-year-olds. Additional information was collected from parents, teachers, and these at-risk children. A total of 574 at-risk children were randomly assigned to various treatment or control conditions. There were two types of control groups—within-school and between-school. The length of the intervention depended on the type of treatment. For example, the behavior modification program was two school terms in duration, the nurture work program was five school terms in duration, and the group work program was ten sessions in duration. The control groups received no intervention. Follow-up assessments were conducted at the end of treatment, and at eighteen months and three years after the baseline. Ninety-five percent of the sample were assessed at the three-year follow-up. Outcome scores were based on aggregate scores (parent, teacher, and peer ratings) for the severity of emotional (neurotic) and conduct (antisocial) problems.

Results. At the three-year follow-up, only the age seven children in the play group treatment program were significantly different from the control group on ratings of antisocial behavior. This result confirms the hypothesis that interventions with younger children (ages seven to eight) will have a greater effect on antisocial behavior than interventions with older children (ages eleven to twelve). Surprisingly, the most effective program, the play group, was the shortest in duration (ten sessions). In addition, the play group intervention relied on the most permissive therapeutic approach (Axline 1947). A possible explanation for this result may be that girls tended to show more improvement than boys on antisocial behavior. Perhaps play groups are an effective treatment for those at less risk for antisocial behavior. Finally, and probably most significant, is the fact that the effects of treatment increased over time. Overall, the results indicated that it is the type rather than the amount of treatment that is a critical feature in intervention.

3. *The Houston Parent-Child Development Center Project (Johnson 1990).* This program was aimed at helping children develop optimal school performance (Johnson 1990). Intermediate goals were to reduce behavior problems and to promote self-esteem and social skills development. The program was designed in the tradition of other early childhood programs such as the Consortium for Longitudinal studies (Lazar et al. 1982) and the High/Scope Perry Preschool Project (Schweinhart, Barnes, and Weikart 1993).

Method. Families were recruited from low-income Mexican-American families who had one-year-old children. Families were randomly allocated to treatment conditions. Approximately one hundred families met the selection criteria each year from 1970 to 1978. The intervention was conducted over a two-year period. In the first year, paraprofessionals made home visits and provided information on child development, health, and safety. A significant part of the program was directed at promoting language development, curiosity, and inquiry. During the second year, mothers and children attended the Parent-Child Development Center four mornings a week for four hours each morning. At the center, mothers and their children attended separate sessions, in addition to joint sessions. The nursery school program was based on a Piagetian perspective (similar to the Perry Preschool Project), with an emphasis on the exploration of toys and development of relationships with others. The mother-training component focused on managing problem behaviors and developing an authoritative parenting

style. Assessments were carried out at preintervention, postintervention, at preschool age, and at elementary school age.

   Results.   Approximately 50 percent of the subjects completed the
two-year intervention. Mothers' reports from preschool indicated that
the intervention boys were less destructive and overactive than the
control boys. Teacher ratings in primary school indicated that the
boys and girls in treatment were less impulsive, obstinate, restless,
disruptive, hostile, and aggressive than the control group. Twenty-four
control children were classified as "referable" compared to only five
experimental children. In addition, the experimental subjects performed better on school achievement tests than the controls. The results of this study suggest that this intervention successfully improved
the behavior and school achievement of children from economically
and educationally disadvantaged families. Furthermore, the effects of
the program persisted for five to eight years following the intervention.

B. General Results and Discussion

   There has been a relatively large number of experiments with preadolescent children aiming to prevent the onset, maintenance, or increase
of disruptive behaviors. Thirty-five are summarized in tables 2 and 3.
Almost all report positive effects of treatments on disruptive social
behaviors such as fighting, opposition, impulsivity, and hyperactivity.
In many cases these effects were measured only at posttreatment or a
few months later, but a substantial number of studies had long-term
follow-ups and revealed important effects. Again, experiments with
long-term intensive interventions appear to have the most enduring
effects. However, some short-term studies have demonstrated long-
term effects. This was the case for the Newcastle-upon-Tyne experiment (Kolvin et al. 1981) and for the Webster-Stratton, Kolpacoff, and
Hollinsworth (1988) parent-training study that lasted only four
months. Although the general rule appears to be that an intensive
investment in changing the child's environment is needed to change the
course of disruptive behavior, in some cases only a short, well-focused
intervention may be needed to obtain a long-term effect. Further research with specific types of treatments matched to specific types of
disruptive subjects, and followed for long periods of time, could help
discriminate between those who need intensive interventions and those
who do not.

   The generally positive results obtained from the thirty-five studies
presented in tables 2 and 3 are promising, but that reaction must be

tempered by consideration of the methodological weaknesses of these studies. In many cases the number of subjects was small, attrition was large, numerous outcome variables were assessed, and only some revealed significant results at the end of a treatment that was targeting these variables. Although we made an effort to retain only studies that were methodologically sound, fifteen of the twenty-two studies in table 3 had less than one hundred subjects when control and treated groups were pooled, and twelve of these fifteen studies had follow-ups of less than one year.

V. Preventing Cognitive Deficits

Cognitive deficits of all kinds are associated with criminal behavior (Buikhuisen 1987; Moffitt 1993). Longitudinal studies have shown that preschoolers' and elementary school children's cognitive deficits predict later criminal behavior (e.g., Moffitt 1990; Farrington 1991; Stattin and Klackenberg-Larsson 1993). One would expect that preventive interventions that increase children's cognitive skills would have a reductive effect on delinquency. This hypothesis was supported by the two preschool prevention experiments discussed in Section III above. Both the High/Scope Perry Preschool project (Schweinhart, Barnes, and Weikart 1993) and the Syracuse University Family Development Research Program (Lally, Mangione, and Honig 1988) were aimed at fostering preschoolers' cognitive development, and both had significant reductive effects on delinquency. To understand the extent to which the positive outcomes of the High/Scope and Syracuse projects could be replicated, this section presents other studies aimed at fostering cognitive development. These experiments did not assess delinquency as an outcome, but the positive effect on cognitive skills would support the idea that this important precursor of delinquency can be modified.

Table 4 summarizes fifteen experimental interventions targeting children's cognitive skills. Three were implemented with elementary school children, nine were implemented with preschoolers, and three were implemented with expectant mothers. Four of the eight preschool interventions were implemented only in the children's home, while the other four were implemented in both the home and day care centers. Two elementary school children interventions were implemented in the school and one in a clinic, but two of the interventions were specifically targeted at high-risk children. One exception (no. 23) was a universal prevention experiment implemented for all first-grade children in selected schools. However, this study was specifically aiming

TABLE 4

Studies with Cognitive Skills as an Outcome

Authors	Age at Treatment	Type	Risk Factors Manipulated	Context of Intervention	No. of Subjects	Length of Treatment	Type of Treatment	Length of Follow-up	Results	
									Cognitive	Others
15. Pelham et al. (1985)	$\bar{x}$ = 11.5 years	Indicated	Inattentive behavior	Clinic	24 boys, 5 girls	12 weeks	Medication	0	Academic performance +	Classroom behavior +
17. Rotheram (1982)	10–12 years	Selective	Social skills	School	202 children	12 weeks	Social skills training	1 year	Academic performance +	Problem solving 0, social relations +, assertive behavior +
25. Kellam et al. (1994) Dolan et al. (1993)	6 years	Universal	Academic functioning, social behavior	School	590 children	2 years	Master learning, good behavior game	4 years	School achievement +	Aggression +, shy +, depression +
33. Seitz, Rosenbaum, and Apfel (1985)	2.5 years	Selective	Family support	Home, day care	36 children	2.5 years	Education, medical support, parent training, day care	10 years	Academic achievement +, school attendance +, learning patterns +	Antisocial behavior +, parenting style +, socioeconomic status +, service usage +
36. Madden, O'Hara, and Levenstein (1984)	21–33 months	Selective	Cognitive development	Home	164 families	2 years	Home visits, parent training	0–2 years	Cognitive +, I.Q. +	Positive mother interactions +, school problems 0
34. Johnson (1990)	1 year	Indicated	Parenting, cognitive development	Home, day care	47 girls, 41 boys	2 years	Education, parent training	8 years	School achievement +, cognitive development +	Impulsivity +, antisocial behavior +

Study	Age at start	Risk level	Focus	Setting	Sample	Duration	Intervention	Follow-up	Cognitive outcomes	Family outcomes
37. Garber (1988)	3–6 months	Selective	Education, parenting	Home, day care	11 girls, 9 boys	18 months	Education, parent training	10 years	I.Q. +, language +, school placement +	Sibling +, parenting +
38. Wasik et al. (1990)	6 weeks to 3 months	Selective	Parenting, cognitive development	Day care, home	62 families	3 years	Cognitive and social development, language development, parent training	4 years	Cognitive +	Family environment 0, family characteristics 0, attitudes to parenting +
39. Barrera, Rosenbaum, and Cunningham (1986)	Birth	Selective	Parenting	Home	83 infants	1 year	Parent training	1.3 years	Mental and motor scores +	Parent-child interaction +
40. Ross (1984)	Birth	Indicated	Parenting	Home	80 infants	1 year	Home visits, parent education, parent training	0	Mental and psychomotor development +	Home environment +, parent-child interactions +
41. Achenbach, Phares, and Howell (1990)	Birth	Selective	Parenting	Home	93 infants	3 months	Parent training	7 years	School achievement +, cognitive development +	Mother confidence +, mother satisfaction +, health 0
35. Infant Health Program (1990)	Birth	Selective	Parenting, cognitive development	Home, day care	985 infants	3 years	Parent training, day care	0	Cognition +, I.Q. +	Behavior problems +, health status +, child abuse +, child neglect +, punishment +

TABLE 4 (*Continued*)

Authors	Age at Treatment	Type	Risk Factors Manipulated	Context of Intervention	No. of Subjects	Length of Treatment	Type of Treatment	Length of Follow-up	Results		
									Cognitive	Others	
42. Pollitt et al. (1993)	Prenatal to 2 years	Primary	Diet	Home	1,410 children	3 years	Diet, high protein substitute	10 years	Cognitive +	Reaction time +	
43. Booth et al. (1992)	Prenatal	Indicated	Parenting, mother support	Home	147 mothers	1.5 years	Home visits, mother support, information	1.5 years	Attachment 0, I.Q. 0, motor 0	Mother-child relationship +, mother competence +	
44. Olds (1986) Olds and Kitzman (1990)	Prenatal	Indicated	Parenting, family planning	Home	400 families	2 years	Parent training, community support, family planning	4 years	I.Q. +	Abuse and neglect +, discipline +, parent-child relations +	

NOTE.—In the "Results" column, a zero indicates no intervention effects, and a plus sign indicates positive intervention effects. See table 2 note.

to prevent delinquency. The other exception was designed to change the diet of children and expectant mothers.

The types of interventions included day care participation, special learning opportunities, social skills training, medication for hyperactive children, parent education and training, and teacher training and supervision. The length of treatment varied from three months to three years. The mean length of treatment was twenty-five months for preschool experiments and ten months for the elementary school experiments. The mean length of follow-ups to assess outcomes after the end of treatment was 5.1 years for the preschool experiments and 1.6 years for the elementary school interventions.

Details of three selected programs are described below followed by a discussion of results obtained by the fifteen experiments.

A. Three Experiments

1. *The Johns Hopkins Research Center Project (Dolan et al. 1993; Kellam et al. 1994).* The Johns Hopkins Research Center has carried out a universal preventive trial aimed at reducing risk behaviors, such as aggression and school achievement, within the classroom context. The intervention was designed to target specific antecedents that have been shown to predict later problem behaviors. The Good Behavior Game (GBG) intervention focuses on reducing aggressive and shy behaviors, which are predictors of later antisocial behavior and heavy drug use. The Mastery Learning (ML) intervention is directed at increasing reading achievement that would reduce psychiatric symptoms, such as depression symptoms. The goals were to test the effect of the interventions and to test whether achievement was improved by improving aggressive or shy behaviors and whether aggressive and shy behaviors were improved by achievement.

The GBG intervention focuses on risk behaviors in the classrooms (i.e., time out of seats, disruptive behavior, talking out behaviors) and not at-risk individuals. It is based on a classroom team-based behavior management strategy. Children are placed in teams, and good behavior is rewarded at the team level. Students are encouraged to manage their own and their teammates' behavior through the processes of group activity and mutual self-interest. The ML intervention consisted of an extensive and systematically applied enrichment of the reading curriculum. Teachers received forty hours of training, curriculum materials, and time to prepare the materials. Elements in the ML intervention included setting clear instructional goals, high expectations of success, small sequenced instructional units, regular testing, corrective methods until mastery was reached, immediate feedback, and records of student progress (Dolan et al. 1993). In addition, there was a group-based approach to mastery: students did not proceed to the next learning unit until the majority of the group had met the learning objectives.

Method. Nineteen schools, matched on students' achievement levels, family socioeconomic status, and ethnicity, participated. Children in classrooms were randomly assigned to the three groups—GBG, ML, and no intervention. First-grade classrooms were assigned to the intervention at random. The sample for the GBG comprised 182 students from eight classrooms; the sample for the ML condition was 207 students from nine classrooms; and the control condition comprised 212 students from twelve classrooms. In addition to external controls (i.e., children in another school), there were internal controls (i.e., children in the same school where the intervention occurred). The samples for the GBG and ML internal controls consisted of 107 and 156 students, respectively. In total, 864 students participated. Outcome measures included teacher ratings of academic achievement and social behavior (i.e., aggression, shyness) and peer ratings, as well as a standardized reading test. The intervention was conducted over a two-year period. Evaluations were carried out at the end of the first year of the evaluation and four years after the intervention.

Results. The ML intervention significantly increased reading achievement success for males and females compared to the control condition after one year. Male low achievers benefited more from the intervention than high achievers. For females the opposite was true since high achievers benefited more than low achievers. At the end of the first year of the intervention, the ML students had higher reading competency scores than either the internal or external controls. The ML intervention did not directly influence aggressive behavior. For females only, there was a weak indication that ML intervention improved shy behavior, as rated by teachers. However, improving reading achievement was associated with a decrease in depression. Children who had been in the GBG were more successful at adapting to their new school and the demands of social tasks than those who did not receive the intervention at the four-year follow-up.

These results provide support for the idea that early increased repertoires of behaviors enhance transitions to a new school, a situation that requires social adaptation. The results showed individual variations. For example, the more aggressive first-grade children who participated in the GBG showed a reduction in aggression four years later, but the GBG did not prevent children who were not aggressive at the start from becoming aggressive. Differentiating the children who responded and benefited from the intervention from those who did not provides information about the development of behaviors as well as about the need for other types of interventions. There were no crossover effects of the intervention. For example, an improvement in aggressive and shy behaviors in the GBG was not associated with improvement in reading behavior. Similarly, ML improved its proximal target, of reading achievement, but did not affect aggressive or shy behaviors at the end of the first year. Hence, there seem to be independent effects of both interventions.

2. *Project CARE (Wasik et al. 1990).* Project CARE provided a multicontext intervention (home and day care) designed to promote preschool children's cognitive and behavioral development. This project was for families in North Carolina judged at risk for delayed development because of the disadvantaged educational or social circumstances of the parents. Children who grow up in poverty are at increased risk for school failure and lower cognitive performance. The combination of a home and day care intervention was designed to address a larger range of environmental variables that influence children's and parents' behavior. The study was in part based on the premise that parent-child interactions are influenced by the parent's knowledge and skill, as well as by the parent's own needs and coping strategies. By providing a family education program as well as a day care program, it was expected that the effect on children's development would be greater.

Method. Over an eighteen-month period beginning in July 1978, families were screened for an indication of risk by an interview and psychological assessment. The sixty-two families who met the risk criteria were randomly assigned at the time of the child's birth to one of the two interventions and control groups. One intervention group involved a day care program aimed at enhancing both cognitive and social development with a systematic curriculum, as well as a family education program. Children regularly attended day care; the curriculum emphasized activities that supported intellectual/creative, social, and emotional development. Language development was also a focus through promoting verbal interaction and modeling of what a nurturant and developmentally encouraging mother might do. Teachers provided opportunities for communication and for social, representational, syntactic, and semantic competence. The family education program was a home-based parent-training program with the specific goals of providing information, promoting effective coping, enhancing parent problem solving, and encouraging positive parent-child interactions. Home visitors facilitated the development of positive parenting practices and were advocates for the families in the community. In addition, the home visitor tried to help parents learn specific problem-solving strategies. Finally, the basic child curriculum taught in the day care center was also taught in the home. The home visits occurred on average 2.5 times a month for three years. During years 4 and 5, there was an average of 1.4 home visits per month. The second intervention group received only the family education intervention, while the control group received neither of the interventions.

There were fifteen subjects in the day care plus family education intervention, twenty-four in the family-education alone intervention, and twenty-three in the control group. Outcome measures included measures of children's cognitive abilities and observations of the quality of the mother-child relationship, quality of the environment in the home, types of parenting strategies, attitudes to parenting, and parent responsiveness. Assessments were conducted regularly over a fifty-four-month period during which the intervention was implemented.

Results. A repeated multivariate analysis of variance assessed the group differences over time. Children in the educational day care program with the family education component responded significantly better on measures of cognitive performance than the other groups. The family intervention group did not differ significantly from the control group on measures of parenting, parent responsiveness, quality of mother-child relationship, and parent satisfaction. Thus, overall, the addition of the family education component did not affect the home environment, nor did it change the parents' or child's behaviors in the home. This experiment supports the effectiveness of high-quality day care in improving children's cognitive development, but the value of family support programs in the home was not supported. These researchers suggest that the lack of success of the family support program may be in part a consequence of design variables such as not enough intensive training and supervision of home visitors and not initiating home services in the prenatal period.

3. *The Vermont Intervention Project (Achenbach, Phares, and Howell 1990).* This experiment for low-birth-weight (LBW) infants was implemented in the Vermont Hospital Medical Center between April

1980 and December 1981. These children were followed for seven years. It has been repeatedly documented that low-birth-weight infants tend to manifest biological, cognitive, and psychosocial disabilities in their development. The risk for cognitive deficits is present throughout the full spectrum of birth weights less than or equal to 2,500 grams, although the risk increases as birth weight decreases. The likelihood of adverse developmental and scholastic outcomes is further increased by low socioeconomic status. The intervention, the Mother-Infant Transactional Program, was designed to enhance the mothers' adjustment to the care of a LBW infant by educating the mother on the infant's specific behavioral and temperament characteristics. The program was aimed at sensitizing the mother to the infant's cues, such as stimulus overload, stress, and readiness for interaction, and teaching the mother to respond appropriately to the infant's specific cues. A neonatal care nurse worked with the mother daily prior to discharge from the hospital and in four home sessions at three, fourteen, thirty, and ninety days after discharge. The intervention took place in the home. Achenbach and his colleagues hypothesized that increasing the mother's knowledge, skill, confidence, and satisfaction through contact with the nurse would improve the mother-child interactions and consequently reduce the risk of later developmental delays and problems.

Method. Subjects were eligible for the study if they were born between April 1980 and December 1981, weighed less than 2,250 grams, and were free from congenital anomalies and neurological deficits. Subjects were randomly assigned to either the LBW experimental or LBW control conditions. A control group of normal-birth-weight infants was also used. One of the important measured outcomes of the program was academic progress. The infants were followed up at ages six and twelve months and ages four and seven years (adjusting for the short gestations of the LBW children). At the seven-year follow-up there were twenty-four LBW children in the experimental condition, thirty-seven LBW control children, and thirty-seven normal-birth-weight children. At this follow-up, children were assessed with the Kaufman Assessment Battery for Children and the Peabody Picture Vocabulary Test.

Results. The LBW children who received the experimental intervention program performed significantly better than LBW controls seven years following treatment on the Kaufman Mental Processing Achievement scales and the Peabody Picture Vocabulary Test. Compared to the LBW control children, the LBW experimental group did not differ from the normal-birth-weight children on any of these measures. The results of this intervention suggest that an intervention designed to enhance the skill and confidence of mothers significantly improves the cognitive development of LBW children. Achenbach and his colleagues provided support for their transactional model of development, whereby changing the mother's behaviors and attitudes contributed to more favorable transactional patterns between mothers and their children, which optimized children's cognitive development.

B. General Results and Discussion

Twenty studies aimed at facilitating the cognitive development of preadolescents are summarized in tables 2 and 4. Eleven were targeted on preschool children and nine on children before they had started their second year after birth. The rationale for these early interventions is that cognitive skills are very stable from early childhood (McCall and Carriger 1993). Most of these studies are thus based on the hypothesis that interventions must stimulate cognitive development early to obtain a significant effect.

Two complementary intervention strategies have been used to achieve this aim. The first is parent training to foster adequate caring behaviors. The second is day care to offer a stimulating environment to the child. Results from studies using one or both of these strategies show positive long-term outcomes. The studies are difficult to compare because the subjects are from different populations. Some studies aim at premature children, some aim at high-risk pregnant teenagers, and others aim at immigrant families. The majority had fewer than a hundred subjects, but three experiments with large samples (studies 25, 35, and 43) and low attrition indicated significant positive effects.

If cognitive skills are a protective factor for criminal behavior, these experiments indicate that helping at-risk families around the birth period should have a positive long-term effect. The High/Scope Perry Preschool project study (no. 12) has shown that such interventions can also be effective with three-year-old children from deprived environments. Interventions with elementary and secondary school children have shown that helping children adjust to their social environment can have a positive effect on their cognitive achievement (see studies 2, 4, 5, 6, and 10 in table 2, and studies 15, 17, and 25 in table 4). There is clearly an interaction between cognitive and behavioral problems throughout development. It appears wiser to prevent early negative interactive effects between these two dimensions than to wait for development on one dimension to have prejudiced development on both. Adequate parenting starting from the prenatal period appears to be a sound investment.

VI. Preventing Inadequate Parenting

The quality of parenting has been systematically associated with delinquent behavior over the past century (Healy and Bronner 1936; Carpenter 1968; McCord 1979; Loeber and Stouthamer-Loeber 1986). Interventions have attempted to support families (e.g., Cabot 1940) and train parents (e.g., Patterson et al. 1975) to help prevent onset of serious delinquent behavior. Section III above presented seven of these studies with follow-ups assessing delinquency outcomes (see table 2). Other experiments have aimed to prevent inadequate parenting but without follow-ups on delinquency. Nineteen of these studies are summarized in table 5.

Most of these experiments were carried out with parents during the prenatal period (four studies), from birth (six studies), or during the first year of life (two studies). Six of the remaining seven were implemented when the children were between two and five. Only one (no. 14) was implemented with pre- and early adolescents. As we have seen in other sections, many intervention experiments with elementary school children included parent training to have an effect on children's development. However, few of those studies focused on parenting skills as the outcome. The situation is different with perinatal studies, where parenting is the main manipulated variable and one of the main immediate outcomes. Interestingly, although the perinatal parenting interventions are "early" forms of intervention, they are relatively intensive. Of the nine perinatal studies, six lasted at least one year. In contrast, the intervention with pre- and early adolescents lasted twelve weeks. Outcome assessments were made at times varying from posttreatment (four of nineteen studies) to seven or more years later. All the parent interventions were mostly implemented in the family home, except the preadolescent study (no. 14), which was implemented in a clinic. The interventions included information programs, education programs, parent training, job training, medical support, and family support. Three of these experiments are described in more detail below. These descriptions are followed by a discussion of all the results.

A. Three Experiments

1. *The Adolescent Transitions Program (Dishion, Patterson, and Kavanagh 1992).* This study examined the effects of an experimental interven-

TABLE 5

Studies with Family Characteristics as an Outcome

Authors	Age at Treatment	Type	Risk Factors Manipulated	Context of Intervention	No. of Subjects	Length of Treatment	Type of Treatment	Length of Follow-up	Results Parenting	Results Others
14. Dishion, Patterson, and Kavanagh (1992)	10–14 years	Selective	Parenting, self-control	Clinic	58 boys, 61 girls	12 weeks	Family management, self-regulation	0	Negative discipline +, home behavior −	Antisocial behavior +
29. Webster-Stratton, Kolpacoff, and Hollinsworth (1988); Webster-Stratton (1990)	$\bar{x} = 4.5$ years	Indicated	Parenting	Home	101 mothers, 70 fathers	4 months	Parent training	3 years	Parenting +	Externalizing problems +, total behavior problems +, hyperactivity +
27. Packard, Robinson, and Grove (1983)	$\bar{x} = 4.3$ years	Indicated	Parenting	Home	34 mother-child pairs	2 weeks	Parent training	11 weeks	Mother attitudes to child +, commands +, praise 0	Problem behavior +, positive behavior 0
31. Dadds, Schwartz, and Sanders (1987)	$\bar{x} = 4.2$ years	Indicated	Parenting, marital satisfaction	Home	24 families	6 weeks	Parent training	6 months	Marital satisfaction +	Compliance +, oppositional behavior +
32. Strayhorn and Weidman (1991)	$\bar{x} = 3.7$ years	Selective	Parenting	Home	36 boys, 48 girls	5 months	Parent training	1 year	Parenting +	Hostility 0, attention +, hyperactivity +

Study	Age at start	Type	Focus	Setting	Sample	Duration	Program components	Follow-up	Mediating variables	Outcomes
33. Seitz, Rosenbaum, and Apfel (1985)	2.5 years	Selective	Family support	Home, day care	36 infants	2.5 years	Education, medical support, parent training, day care	10 years	Service usage +, socioeconomic status +, parenting style +	Antisocial behavior +, school attendance +, academic achievements +, learning patterns +
34. Johnson (1990)	2 years	Indicated	Parenting, cognitive development	Home, day care	47 girls, 41 boys	1 year	Education, parent training	8 years	Parenting +	School achievement +, antisocial behavior +, impulsivity +, cognitive development +
37. Garber (1988)	3–6 months	Selective	Parenting, education	Home, day care	11 girls, 9 boys	1.5 years	Education, parent training	10 years	Parenting +	Sibling +, I.Q. +, language +, school placement +, cognitive development +
38. Wasik et al. (1990)	6 weeks to 3 months	Selective	Parenting, education	Home, day care	62 families	3 years	Cognitive and social development, language development, parent training	4 years	Family environment 0, family characteristics 0, attitudes to parenting +	Cognitive development +
35. Infant Health Program (1990)	Birth	Selective	Parenting, cognitive development	Home, day care	985 infants	3 years	Parent training, day care	0	Child abuse +, child neglect +, punishment +	Health status +, cognition +, I.Q. +, behavior problems

TABLE 5 (*Continued*)

Authors	Age at Treatment	Type	Risk Factors Manipulated	Context of Intervention	No. of Subjects	Length of Treatment	Type of Treatment	Length of Follow-up	Results	
									Parenting	Others
39. Barrera, Rosenbaum, and Cunningham (1986)	Birth	Selective	Parenting	Home	59 preterm and 24 full-term infants	1 year	Parenting skills	1.3 years	Parent-child interaction +	Mental and motor scores +
45. Field et al. (1982)	Birth	Selective	Parenting, schooling	Home, school	120 mothers	6 months	Parent training, job training	1.5 years	Pregnancy rates +, return to work +	Cognitive development +, motor +
46. Jacobson and Frye (1991)	Birth	Selective	Social support	Home	46 mothers	1 year	Social support, education, child development	14 months	Stimulation 0, play 0	Attachment +
41. Achenbach, Phares, and Howell (1990)	Birth	Selective	Parenting	Home	93 infants	3 months	Parent training	7 years	Mother confidence +, mother satisfaction +, health 0	Achievement +, cognitive +, motor skills +
47. Ross (1984)	Birth	Indicated	Parenting	Home	80 infants	1 year	Home visits, parent education, parent training	0	Home environment +, parent-child interactions +	Mental and psychomotor development +
48. Larson (1980)	Prenatal	Selective	Social environment	Home	115 mother-infant dyads	1.5 years	Parent education, parent support	0	Positive interactions +, father participation +, medical +, accidents +, feeding +	

									Results
43. Booth et al. (1992)	Prenatal	Indicated	Parenting, mother support	Home	147 mothers	1.5 years	Home visits, mother support, information	1.5 years	Mother-child relationship +, mother competence +; Attachment 0, I.Q. 0, motor 0
49. Barth, Hacking, and Ash (1988)	Prenatal	Selective	Social support	Home	50 mothers	6 months	Parent training, home visits, parent education	0	Child welfare calls +, child abuse +, well-being −, prenatal care +, birth outcomes +
44. Olds et al. (1986); Olds and Kitzman (1990)	Prenatal	Indicated	Parenting, family planning	Home	400 families	2 years	Parent education, parent support, community support, family planning	4 years	Abuse and neglect +, I.Q. +, discipline +, parent-child relations +

NOTE.—In the "Results" column, a zero indicates no intervention effects, a plus sign indicates a positive intervention effect, and a minus sign indicates negative intervention effects. See table 2 note.

213

tion with parenting behaviors on young adolescent antisocial behavior. Dishion and his colleagues took the social interactional view that poor parent disciplinary practices increase the likelihood of child coercive responses. High rates of child coercion make it difficult to implement even-handed, consistent, effective discipline. Thus, the parent and the child reciprocally influence one another. The coercive behavior by the child is transferred to other contexts, such as school and peers. Intervening by focusing on the parent's behavior may deflect children from an antisocial life trajectory. From Patterson's (1982) coercion model it was hypothesized that family management training for at-risk youths would improve parenting practices (i.e., discipline) and be followed by less antisocial behavior.

Method. A total of 119 families with children at risk participated in the field experiment. The sample consisted of fifty-eight boys and sixty-one girls between the ages of ten and fourteen (the mean age was twelve years). Children were judged at risk based on parents' reports for the following dimensions: closeness to parents, emotional adjustment, academic engagement, involvement in positive activities, experience seeking, problem behaviors, substance abuse, peer substance abuse, family history of substance abuse, and stressful life events. Families were randomly assigned to one of four intervention conditions: parent focus only; teen focus only; parent and teen focus; or parent and teen self-directed. The "parent focus" treatment targeted family management practices and communication skills. The "teen focus" treatment targeted early adolescent self-regulation and prosocial behavior in the context of parent and peer environments. Subjects in these two treatments had weekly meetings, lasting ninety minutes at the treatment center for twelve weeks. The self-directed intervention did not involve contact with a therapist. This group received by mail the information materials (six newsletters and five videotapes) that the other groups received in person. Outcomes of the evaluation were based on pretest-posttest observations of the mother's negative discipline as well as teacher and mother ratings of child antisocial behavior.

Results. The results of the short-term assessment of the intervention indicated that mothers in the "parent focus" group used less negative discipline after the intervention. Observer impressions of the mother's disciplinary practices revealed a deterioration for boys and an improvement for girls as a function of parent training. For teacher ratings of antisocial behavior of both males and females together, there was a significant effect of the parent intervention. Children with parents who were directly involved in the training (parent focus) had significantly lower antisocial behavior ratings. Examining males and females separately indicated that the improvements were statistically reliable for males only. Parent reports of the child's antisocial behavior indicated an improvement, regardless of the intervention received. However, examining males and females separately revealed that there was a greater improvement in parent-reported antisocial behavior in girls whose parents did not receive parent training. Thus, the study showed that a parent training program for high-risk adolescents can have some effect on disciplinary practices, but this effect was small and observed only at the end of twelve intervention sessions.

2. *The Prenatal/Early Infancy Project (Olds et al. 1986)*.   Olds et al. examined the effects of a home-visit intervention in Rochester, New York, as a means of preventing child maltreatment and a range of childhood health and developmental problems. The randomized trial was an effort to prevent the development of long-term negative outcomes and increase understanding of underlying causal influences on maternal and child outcomes. Nurse home-care visitors are in an optimal position to identify and change factors in the family environment that interfere with maternal health habits, infant caregiving, and personal accomplishments in the areas of work, education, and family planning. The intervention was designed to address these processes.

Method.   Women were recruited if they had no previous live births and had one or more of the following problems that predispose to infant health and developmental problems: young age, single-parent status, or low socioeconomic status. Families were randomly assigned to one of the following conditions. In the control condition, no services were provided ($N = 90$). In the second condition, families ($N = 94$) were provided with transportation for prenatal and infant medical visits. In the third condition ($N = 100$), a nurse home-visitor was provided during pregnancy, in addition to screening and transportation. The nurses visited on average every two weeks. In the fourth condition, families ($N = 116$) received the same treatment as in the third condition, but in addition the nurse continued to visit until the child was two years of age. The nurses provided parent education regarding fetal and infant development, the involvement of family members and friends, and the linkage of family members with other health and human services. Data were collected at the thirtieth week of pregnancy and at six, ten, twenty-two, twenty-four, and forty-six months after birth. Sources of information included medical records of the infant, social services records, maternal reports of child behavior, standardized testing, and observations.

Results. Depending on the assessment phase, the rates of attrition varied during the first four years from 15 to 21 percent. There were no differences across treatments in the proportion of subjects with complete assessments. The results indicated significant group differences at the forty-six-month follow-up for reported child abuse and neglect, infant temperament, behavioral problems, conflict, use of punishment, play materials, developmental quotients, emergency room visits, and maternal sense of control. Infants in intervention conditions three and four had fewer problems than infants in the other conditions. For example, the nurse-visited mothers were less likely to restrict and punish their children, visited the emergency room fewer times, and had fewer episodes of child maltreatment than those in the control condition. In addition, the nurse-visited mothers showed an increase in the number of months they were employed and fewer had subsequent pregnancies.

The pattern of results from this study provides evidence that nurse home-care visitors are capable of preventing a large number of caregiving dysfunctions, including child abuse and neglect. Frequent home visits designed to establish a rapport with families and to identify and reinforce family strengths, combined with parent education, improved not only the quality of caregiving but also pregnancy outcomes and maternal life course development, such as rates of employment, education, and fertility. Moreover, there were demonstrable improvements in child functioning, thereby reducing the risk of unfavorable outcomes. Only a long-term follow-up of these children will confirm the hypothesis that crime can be prevented by giving support to pregnant women.

3. The Infant Health Program (1990). This study was an eight-site clinical trial designed to evaluate the effectiveness of an early intervention aimed at reducing the developmental and health problems of low-birth-weight premature infants. Low-birth-weight infants are at increased risk for developmental delay, a variety of medical complications, cognitive functioning difficulties, low scholastic achievement, and behavioral problems, compared to normal-birth-weight infants. The Infant Health and Development Program combined medical, child, and family services in an effort to reduce developmental, behavioral, and health problems among LBW premature infants.

Method.   A total of 985 infants were randomly assigned to treatment and control groups. The intervention program was initiated on discharge from the neonatal nursery and continued until the infants were three years of age. Both groups participated in the same pediatric follow-up, which comprised medical, developmental, and social assessments. In addition, the intervention group received home visits, attended a child developmental center, and participated in parent group meetings. The home visitor provided families with health and developmental information, family support, and family education on parent management and understanding of developmental issues. In the child development centers, educational and learning activities were provided five days a week. Finally, every second month parents attended parent group meetings that provided information on child-rearing, health and safety, and other parent concerns. Infants were assessed at four, eight, twelve, eighteen, twenty-four, thirty, and thirty-six months. Sources of information included mothers' reports (about health and developmental functioning and family sociographic and demographic information), physical measurements, cognitive assessments, and behavioral and observational data. Outcome measures included cognitive development, behavioral competence, health status, and quality of caregiving (e.g., child abuse and neglect).

Results.   Ninety-three percent of subjects were assessed at the thirty-six-month follow-up. The results indicated that there was a reduction in the incidence of caregiving dysfunction for the intervention groups. The incidence of verified cases of child abuse and neglect was reduced. The incidence of maltreatment increased in the comparison group (to 19 percent), but not in the nurse-visited group (remaining at 4 percent). The nurse-visited high-risk mothers were observed to restrict and punish their children less frequently than those in the control group. In addition, the intervention infants at thirty-six months had significantly higher cognitive scores, fewer maternally reported behavior problems, and a small but significant increase in maternally reported morbidity than those in the control group. The largest treatment effect was the significantly higher cognitive scores obtained by the intervention group. Thus, this research indicated that comprehensive and intensive early intervention decreases the number of LBW infants at risk for later developmental problems. The long-term significance of these results is currently being examined. It may be that as a consequence of the intervention children had higher academic achievement and lower rates of grade retention and school dropout. These positive outcomes tend to be associated with reduced juvenile delinquency and increased employment.

B. General Results and Discussion

The nineteen studies summarized in table 5 attempted to assess the effect of experimental interventions on family characteristics. To the extent that family characteristics are important factors in the development of criminal behavior (Loeber and Stouthamer-Loeber 1986; Yoshikawa 1994), the results of these experiments are useful to understand the possibility of a developmental prevention approach to crime. In Section III above, four studies (see table 2, nos. 9, 10, 11, and 12) were described that indicated that parent education and training were an important part of successful interventions to prevent juvenile delinquency. In this section it can be seen that a large number of perinatal and preschool studies have shown that interventions with high-risk families can change the parenting behavior many theories identify as the first part of a chain of events that lead to antisocial behavior.

Positive effects of the intervention were observed for a variety of outcomes, from attitudes to parenting, mother satisfaction, family communication, and father participation to child abuse and neglect, as well as return to work and pregnancy rates. To the extent that these effects can be maintained over long periods, they are likely to have a significant effect on children's development. Again, most studies had small samples (twelve of the nineteen studies had fewer than one hundred subjects), and most of the significant positive effects were of a moderate magnitude. We will need well designed large-scale, long-term studies, beginning before birth to conclude confidently that changes in parenting early in life will have a substantial effect on children's criminal behavior.

VII. Conclusions

This essay has examined prevention experiments with children targeting the development of antisocial behavior. The aim was to understand the extent to which these experiments could prevent later criminal behavior and contribute to theories of the development of criminal behavior. Studies were identified through computer searches of standard social sciences and medical abstracts, as well as recent reviews of prevention studies. Studies were classified according to the assessed outcomes, the manipulated variables, the age of the subjects at the time of the intervention, and their age at the outcome assessment. Only thirteen randomized prevention experiments were found to have used a nondelinquent population and included delinquency as an assessed outcome. Thirty-six other prevention experiments with nondelinquents were used to assess to what extent interventions could have an effect on three important risk factors for criminal behavior: disruptive social behavior, cognitive skills, and parenting. A summary of the findings with conclusions is given below, followed by a discussion of methodological problems, a discussion of the contribution of the reviewed experiments to developmental theories of criminal behavior, and a discussion of some policy implications.

A. Summary of Results

Delinquency prevention experiments with youths not referred by the courts (table 2) tend to be successful (with statistically significant differences between treated and control groups) mainly when the intervention aims at more than one risk factor (e.g., children's disruptive behavior and parenting), lasts for a relatively long period of time (at least one year), and is implemented before adolescence. If these interventions are powerful enough to have positive long-term effects, they can also be powerful enough to have negative long-term effects in some cases (see McCord 1978).

Prevention experiments for elementary and preschool children with disruptive behavior as an outcome (tables 2 and 3) all tend to show some beneficial effect. Most studies with elementary school children did not have long-term follow-ups, but both the elementary and preschool studies with long-term follow-ups (eight studies with three or more years of follow-up) indicated desirable outcomes. Most of these studies aimed at more than one risk factor, but some targeted at only one risk factor showed some positive effect.

Experiments to prevent cognitive deficits (tables 2 and 4) were mostly aimed at infants and toddlers. Parent training and day care programs were most often used. All experiments except one showed some positive outcome, with nine showing positive outcomes for more than three years.

Prevention experiments that used family characteristics as an outcome (mainly parenting) (table 5) were generally aimed at high-risk mothers or children during the perinatal period. Information, education, and parent training were the main intervention strategies. All experiments showed some positive effect, with six studies showing positive effects after more than three years of follow-up.

The general impression from examination of the forty-nine prevention experiments is that early childhood interventions can have a positive effect on the three most important risk factors for juvenile delinquency: disruptive behavior, cognitive skills, and parenting. Furthermore, experiments with long-term follow-ups that have targeted at least two of these risk factors in childhood have shown a significant effect on criminal behavior. From these results it can be concluded that early, intensive preventive interventions can have the desirable effect that appears to be so difficult to achieve with juvenile delinquents.

B. *Methodological Issues*

The Committee on Prevention of Mental Disorders of the United States Institute of Medicine has recently published recommendations for the design of preventive interventions (Mrazek and Haggerty 1994). These recommendations are useful to assess to what extent the studies reviewed in this essay come close to the state of the art in prevention studies. The committee differentiates between two types of experiments: small-scale studies that are either pilot, confirmatory, or replication trials; and large-scale field trials. Pilot studies are used to explore the feasibility of a given type of intervention. Confirmatory trials are used to determine if the intervention can produce beneficial results under ideal conditions. Replication trials ensure that the beneficial results can be obtained in new experiments using the same approach. The large-scale field trials try to implement interventions that were successful in small-scale trials to assess the generality of the intervention *efficacy* and its costs. A second large-scale trial is recommended to assess *effectiveness;* that is, does the intervention do what it is meant to do for a defined population once it is implemented in the field? This last trial should be implemented by the organization that will from then on run the intervention, but an assessment design should be put in place.

Most of the experiments discussed in this essay were small-scale studies of the confirmatory or replication type. Only one study could be classified under the first category of large-scale studies (no. 35). The encouraging results from this trial have led to the planning of an "effectiveness" trial by the United States Centers for Disease Control and Prevention (see Mrazek and Haggerty 1994). The small-scale studies examined here were generally conducted by one investigator or a small team of investigators, who managed to implement difficult procedures and long-term follow-ups with small-scale, ad hoc funding.

Taken individually, each study has important methodological weaknesses: small samples of heterogeneous subjects, poor quality of implementation, numerous unreliable measures, sample attrition during treatment and follow-up, questionable statistical analyses, and so on. However, the general trend of results suggests a positive answer to the question, Can childhood interventions prevent criminal behavior? The next question should be, Can large-scale implementations of these interventions show a satisfactory efficacy? A few large-scale experiments are now under way in North America (Bierman et al. 1992; Coie et al. 1993; Peters and Russell 1993; Guerra, Tolan, and Hammond, 1994). We will need to wait a decade at least to assess the effects of these large-scale studies and to decide whether the final trials to test effectiveness should be implemented.

C. Theoretical Issues

It has often been claimed that intervention experiments are one of the best means to test causal hypotheses of the development of criminal behavior (Farrington, Ohlin, and Wilson 1986; Tonry, Ohlin, and Farrington 1991; Robins 1992; Dodge 1993). The present review provides occasion to consider to what extent the results from forty-nine experiments test some of the causal hypotheses from theories of crime. Figure 3 represents the main causal paths that have been studied by linking the manipulated variables and the outcomes in the experiments. The numbers on each arrow represent the number of different studies for a given link. The numbers in parentheses on the arrows represent the number of different studies that have shown a significant positive effect of a given manipulated variable on a given outcome. From these results it can be seen that modifying parenting skills has an effect on children's cognitive skills, disruptive behaviors, and delinquency; that stimulating children's cognitive skills has an effect on their disruptive and delinquent behavior; and that modifying their disruptive behavior has an effect on cognitive skills and delinquent behavior. It can also be seen that the ratio of positive outcomes to number of studies increases as we go backward from interventions during adolescence to perinatal interventions.

The major problem with these results, as a means of testing developmental hypotheses, is that the interventions that had the most effect

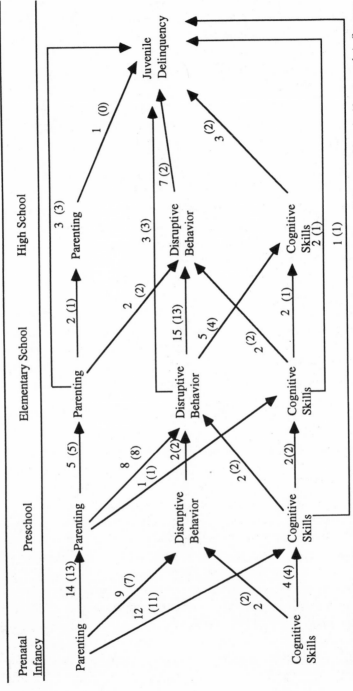

Fig. 3.—Number of experimental studies linking risk factors to outcomes (number in parentheses indicate positive significant results). See text for explanation.

were multimodal interventions targeted at more than one causal variable at the same time. The conclusion from these experiments is that the more a child's environment and behavior is changed to orient him toward better cognitive and social skills, the less he is at-risk of resorting to early and serious delinquency.

By returning to the three developmental models of criminal behavior of figure 1, we can verify to what extent the forty-nine experimental studies supported these models. The Gottfredson and Hirschi (1990) simple linear model from good child rearing to self-control and prevention of crime gets some support from the studies showing that parenting interventions reduced disruptive behavior and that reduction of disruptive behavior is followed by less delinquent behavior. However, surprisingly, no intervention has specifically attempted to train parenting skills specifically linked to children's self-control, and then to assess the children's self-control and later delinquent behavior. Considering that the most effective interventions were multimodal, it would be surprising if investigators would now undertake a large-scale experiment from early childhood targeting only the variables implied in this simple linear model.

The Multiple Pathways Model (Loeber 1988, 1990, 1991) has not been specifically tested by any of the experiments described in this essay. The general trend of the results confirms that the path from childhood aggression to juvenile aggression and property crime can be prevented for some children, with an intermediary effect on peer relations and school achievement. These results do not test the sequence of the events but show that these outcomes are associated over time. Most experiments were targeting subjects following the aggressive pathway. No study attempted to differentiate the three paths to see if an intervention had more effect on subjects following one particular path. Experiments to test this model would need to be specifically designed for this purpose and would need to be quite large. If the model gets support from further longitudinal work, it may be usefully integrated into the next round of large-scale experiments.

The Cumulative Effect Model appears to be supported by the experimental results that indicate that multimodal early intensive interventions have effects on most later social adjustment problems, including crime. The High/Scope Perry Preschool Project (Schweinhart, Barnes, and Weikart 1993) is probably the best example of this phenomenon. An early intervention program to help disadvantaged children achieve more in school had positive effects not only on school performance but also on most social adjustment measures during adolescence and early adulthood, including criminal behavior. The major problem with this model is that it implies specific effects between variables at specific times, but these probably could not and would not need to be disentangled. Indeed, from a pragmatic perspective, if this model is a valid description of human development, it implies that effective preventive interventions will need to be multimodal, early, and intensive. It follows that, from an explanatory perspective, prevention experiments will not be able to test specific causal links between individual variables because experiments with such aims would be unlikely to have a positive effect and would, thus, be ethically unjustifiable. Consequently, there is some tension between maximizing effectiveness and explanatory power.

Because this conclusion would prevent investigators from doing short-term prevention experiments targeting single causal factors (Dodge 1993), we need to assess carefully which theoretical models best describe early social development. Large-scale longitudinal studies from birth to school entry are urgently needed for this type of assessment (Tonry, Ohlin, and Farrington 1991).

D. Policy Implications

Successful preventive interventions with long-term follow-ups such as the High/Scope Perry Preschool Project described in Section III above (see table 2) have received a lot of public attention and are used to argue for an early prevention approach to most mental health problems (Mrazek and Haggerty 1994). This survey confirms that most prevention experiments show positive effects, and few show negative effects. This conclusion can be used to support the proposition that money invested in early prevention is money saved later on remedial services in school, social, physical, and mental health services for families and correctional services for juveniles and adults. Rigorous experimental studies with long-term follow-ups were not needed to understand that helping children get a good start in life increases their chance of better overall adjustment during the lifespan (see, e.g., Rodhe 1886). Research was needed to confirm this very old idea and to identify which types of intervention were more effective.

From a policy perspective, it does appear that money invested in early (e.g., preschool) prevention efforts with at-risk families will give greater payoffs than money invested in later (e.g., adolescence) prevention efforts with the same at-risk families. This general rule is not easy to apply because juvenile delinquents attract much more public attention than high-risk infants or toddlers. It is difficult to decide to invest fewer resources to extinguish fires in order to put more into preventing people from starting new fires. However, it is clear that, in the long run, the prevention strategy should reduce the amount of resources needed for corrective services from our education, health, and justice systems.

This conclusion is based on common sense as well as the trend of results observed in the present review. It should, however, be remembered that the research completed to date is only the first phase of what must be a long-term research process. A next generation of large-scale prevention experiments is needed to investigate to what extent small-scale experiments executed by investigators in somewhat ideal conditions can be transformed into effective large-scale public services.

This phase of research is certainly the most difficult because it implies cooperation among a large number of investigators, cooperation between investigators and practitioners, and large amounts of research funding to bring all these people together and maintain their cooperation. Enlightened policy makers committed to long-term goals are needed to achieve this program on the developmental prevention of crime.

REFERENCES

Achenbach, T. M. 1989. "Empirically Based Assessment of Child and Adolescent Disorders: Implications for Diagnosis, Classification, Epidemiology, and Longitudinal Research." In *Children at Risk: Assessment, Longitudinal Research, and Intervention*, edited by M. Bambring, F. Losel, and H. Skowronek. Berlin: Gruyter.

Achenbach, T. M., and C. Edelbrock. 1983. *Manual for the Child Behavior Checklist and Revised Child Behavior Profile*. Burlington: University of Vermont, Department of Psychiatry.

Achenbach, T. M., V. Phares, and C. T. Howell. 1990. "Seven-Year Outcome of the Vermont Intervention Program for Low-Birthweight Infants." *Child Development* 61(6):1672–81.

Administration for Children, Youth, and Families. 1983. *The Effects of the Head Start Program on Children's Cognitive Development, Preliminary Report*. Head Start Evaluation, Synthesis, and Utilization Project. Washington, D.C.: U.S. Department of Health and Human Services. (ERIC Document Reproduction Service no. ED 248 989.)

Aichhorn, A. 1925. *Wayward Youth*. New York: Viking Press.

Alinsky, S. D. 1971. *Rules for Radicals*. New York: Random House.

American Psychiatric Association. 1987. *Diagnostic and Statistical Manual of Mental Disorders: DSM-III-R*. Washington, D.C.: American Psychiatric Association.

Arbuthnot, J. 1992. "Sociomoral Reasoning in Behavior-disordered Adolescents: Cognitive and Behavioral Change." In *Preventing Antisocial Behavior: Interventions from Birth through Adolescence*, edited by J. McCord and R. E. Tremblay. New York: Guilford.

Arbuthnot, J., and D. A. Gordon. 1986. "Behavioral and Cognitive Effects of a Moral Reasoning Development Intervention for High-Risk Behavior-disordered Adolescents." *Journal of Consulting and Clinical Psychology* 54: 208–16.

Axline, V. M. 1947. *Play Therapy: The Inner Dynamics of Children*. Boston: Houghton Mifflin.

Bandura, A., N. E. Adams, and J. Beyer. 1977. "Cognitive Processes Mediating Behavioral Change." *Journal of Personality and Social Psychology* 35(3): 125–39.

Barrera, M. E., P. L. Rosenbaum, and C. E. Cunningham. 1986. "Early Home Intervention with Low-Birth-Weight Infants and Their Parents." *Child Development* 57(1):20–33.

Barth, R. P., S. Hacking, and J. R. Ash. 1988. "Preventing Child Abuse: An Experimental Evaluation of the Child Parent Enrichment Project." *Journal of Primary Prevention* 8(4):201–17.

Bernstein, B. 1954. "Social Class, Speech Systems and Psycho-therapy." In *Mental Health of the Poor*, edited by F. Riessman, J. Cohen, and A. Pearls. New York: Free Press of Glencoe.

Bierman, K. L., J. D. Coie, K. A. Dodge, M. T. Greenberg, J. E. Lochman, and R. J. McMahon. 1992. "A Developmental and Clinical Model for the Prevention of Conduct Disorder: The FAST Track Program." *Development and Psychopathology* 4:509–27.

Blasi, A. 1980. "Bridging Moral Cognition and Moral Action: A Critical Review of the Literature." *Psychological Bulletin* 88:1–45.

Bock, G. R., and J. Whelan. 1991. *The Childhood Environment and Adult Disease*. Ciba Foundation Symposium no. 156. Toronto: Wiley.

Booth, C. L., S. J. Spieker, K. E. Barnard, and C. E. Morisset. 1992. "Infants at Risk: The Role of Prevention Intervention in Deflecting a Maladaptive Developmental Trajectory." In *Preventing Antisocial Behavior: Interventions from Birth to Adolescence*, edited by J. McCord and R. E. Tremblay. New York: Guilford.

Bry, B. H. 1982. "Reducing the Incidence of Adolescent Problems through Preventive Intervention: One- and Five-Year Follow-up." *American Journal of Community Psychology* 10:265–76.

Bry, B. H., and F. E. George. 1979. "Evaluating and Improving Prevention Programs: A Strategy from Drug Abuse." *Evaluation and Program Planning* 2:127–36.

Buikhuisen, W. 1987. "Cerebral Dysfunctions and Persistent Juvenile Delinquency." In *The Causes of Crime: New Biological Approaches*, edited by S. A. Mednick, T. E. Moffitt, and S. A. Stack. New York: Cambridge University Press.

Cabot, R. S. de Q. 1940. "A Long-Term Study of Children: The Cambridge-Somerville Youth Study." *Child Development* 11:143–51.

Cairns, R. B., B. D. Cairns, H. J. Neckerman, L. L. Ferguson, and J. L. Gariépy. 1989. "Growth and Aggression: 1. Childhood to Early Adolescence." *Developmental Psychology* 25(2):320–30.

Camp, B. W., G. E. Blom, F. Hebert, and W. J. Van Doorminck. 1977. "Think Aloud: A Program for Developing Self-Control in Young Aggressive Boys." *Journal of Abnormal Child Psychology* 5:157–69.

Capecchi, M. R. 1994. "Targeted Gene Replacement." *Scientific American* 270: 52–59.

Carpenter, M. 1968. *Reformatory Schools for the Children of the Perishing and Dangerous Classes and for Juvenile Offenders*. London: Woburn Press. (Originally published 1851.)

Caspi, A., G. H. Elder, and E. S. Herbener. 1990. "Childhood Personality and the Prediction of Life-Course Patterns." In *Straight and Devious Pathways from Childhood to Adulthood*, edited by L. N. Robins and M. Rutter. New York: Cambridge University Press.

Casto, G., and M. A. Mastropieri. 1986. "The Efficacy of Early Intervention Programs: A Meta-analysis." *Exceptional Children* 52:417–24.

Casto, G., and K. White. 1984. "The Efficacy of Early Intervention Programs with Environmentally At-Risk Infants." *Journal of Children in Contemporary Society* 17:37–50.

Cedar, B., and R. F. Levant. 1990. "A Meta-analysis of the Effect of Parent Effectiveness Training." *American Journal of Family Therapy* 18:373–84.

Cedar, R. B. 1986. "A Meta-analysis of the Parent Effectiveness Training Outcome Research Literature." Doctoral dissertation, Boston University, 1985. *Dissertation Abstracts International* 47:420A. University Microfilm International no. 86-09263.

Cloninger, C. R., and I. I. Gottesman. 1987. "Genetic and Environmental Factors in Antisocial Behavior Disorders." In *The Causes of Crime: New Biological Approaches*, edited by S. A. Mednick, T. E. Moffitt, and S. A. Stack. New York: Cambridge University Press.

Cloward, R. A., and L. E. Ohlin. 1960. *Delinquency and Opportunity*. Chicago: Free Press.

Coie, J. D., K. A. Dodge, R. Terry, and V. Wright. 1991. "The Role of Aggression in Peer Relations: An Analysis of Aggression Episodes in Boys' Play Groups." *Child Development* 62:812–26.

Coie, J. D., and M. R. Jacobs. 1993. "The Role of Social Context in the Prevention of Conduct Disorder." *Development and Psychopathology* 5:263–75.

Coie, J. D., N. F. Watt, S. G. West, J. D. Hawkins, J. R. Asarnow, H. J. Markman, S. L. Ramey, M. B. Shure, and B. Long. 1993. "The Science of Prevention: A Conceptual Framework and Some Directions for a National Research Program." *American Psychologist* 48:1013–22.

Condry, S. 1983. "History and Background of Preschool Intervention Programs and the Consortium for Longitudinal Studies." In *As the Twig Is Bent: Lasting Effects of Early Education*, edited by the Consortium for Longitudinal Studies. Hillsdale, N.J.: Erlbaum.

Dadds, M. R., S. Schwartz, and M. Sanders. 1987. "Marital Discord and Treatment Outcome in Behavioral Treatment of Child Conduct Disorders." *Journal of Consulting and Clinical Psychology* 55(3):396–403.

Dishion, T. J., G. R. Patterson, and K. A. Kavanagh. 1992. "An Experimental Test of the Coercion Model: Linking Theory, Measurement, and Intervention." In *Preventing Antisocial Behavior: Interventions from Birth through Adolescence*, edited by J. McCord and R. E. Tremblay. New York: Guilford.

Dodge, K. A. 1986. "A Social Information Processing Model of Social Competence in Children." In *The Minnesota Symposia on Child Psychology*, vol. 18, *Cognitive Perspectives on Children's Social and Behavioral Development*, edited by M. Perlmutter. Hillsdale, N.J.: Erlbaum.

Dodge, K. A. 1993. "The Future of Research on the Treatment of Conduct Disorder." *Developmental Psychopathology* 5:311–19.

Dolan, L. J., S. G. Kellam, C. H. Brown, L. Werthamer-Larsson, G. W. Rebok, L. S. Mayer, J. Laudoff, J. Turkkan, C. Ford, and L. Wheeler. 1993. "The Short-Term Impact of Two Classroom-based Preventive Interventions on Aggressive and Shy Behaviors and Poor Achievement." *Journal of Applied Developmental Psychology* 14:317–45.

Durlak, J. A., T. Fuhrman, and C. Lampman. 1991. "Effectiveness of Cognitive Behavior Therapy for Maladapting Children: A Meta-analysis." Unpublished manuscript. Chicago: Loyola University.

Duyme, M. 1989. "Antisocial Behaviours and Postnatal Environment: A French Adoption Study." *Journal of Child Psychology and Psychiatry* 7:285–91.

Duzinski, G. A. 1987. "The Educational Utility of Cognitive Behavior Modification Strategies with Children." Doctoral dissertation, University of Illinois at Chicago. *Dissertation Abstracts International* 48:339A.

Earls, F. 1986. "Epidemiology of Psychiatric Disorders in Children and Adolescents." In *Psychiatry: Social, Epidemiologic, and Legal Psychiatry*, edited by G. L. Klerman, M. M. Weissman, P. S. Appelbaum, and L. H. Roth. New York: Basic.

Eissler, K. R. 1949. *Searchlights on Delinquency*. Madison, Conn.: International Universities Press.

Erikson, E. 1950. *Childhood and Society*. New York: Norton.

Eron, L. D. 1990. "Understanding Aggression." *Bulletin of the International Society for Research on Aggression* 12:5–9.

Eron, L. D., L. R. Huesmann, and A. Zelli. 1991. "The Role of Parental Variables in the Learning of Aggression." In *The Development and Treatment of Childhood Aggression*, edited by D. J. Pepler and K. H. Rubin. Hillsdale, N.J.: Erlbaum.

Eysenck, H. J. 1964. *Crime and Personality*. London: Routledge & Kegan Paul.

Farrington, D. P. 1986. "Stepping Stones to Adult Criminal Careers." In *Development of Antisocial and Prosocial Behavior*, edited by D. Olweus, J. Block, and M. Radke-Yarrow. New York: Academic Press.

———. 1991. "Childhood Aggression and Adult Violence: Early Precursors and Life Outcomes." In *The Development and Treatment of Childhood Aggression*, edited by D. J. Pepler and K. H. Rubin. Hillsdale, N.J.: Erlbaum.

———. 1992. "The Need for Longitudinal-Experimental Research on Offending and Antisocial Behavior." In *Preventing Antisocial Behavior: Interventions from Birth through Adolescence*, edited by J. McCord and R. E. Tremblay. New York: Guilford.

———. 1994. "Criminological Psychology: Individual and Family Factors in the Explanation and Prevention of Offending." In *Working with Offenders: A Psychological Sourcebook for Rehabilitation*, edited by C.R. Hollin. Chichester, N.Y.: Wiley.

Farrington, D. P., and J. D. Hawkins. 1991. "Predicting Participation, Early Onset and Later Persistence in Officially Recorded Offending." *Criminal Behaviour and Mental Health* 1:1–33.

Farrington, D. P., R. Loeber, D. S. Elliott, D. Hawkins, D. B. Kandel, M. W. Klein, J. McCord, D. C. Rowe, and R. E. Tremblay. 1990. "Advancing Knowledge about the Onset of Delinquency and Crime." In *Advances in Clinical Child Psychology*, vol. 13, edited by B. B. Lahey and A. E. Kazdin. New York: Plenum.

Farrington, D. P., L. E. Ohlin, and J. Q. Wilson. 1986. *Understanding and Controlling Crime: Toward a New Research Strategy*. New York: Springer-Verlag.

Feldman, D. 1969. "Psychoanalysis and Crime." In *Delinquency, Crime, and Social Process*, edited by D. R. Cressey and D. A. Ward. New York: Harper & Row.

Feldman, R. A. 1992. "The St. Louis Experiment: Effective Treatment of Antisocial Youths in Prosocial Peer Groups." In *Preventing Antisocial Behavior: Interventions from Birth through Adolescence*, edited by J. McCord and R. E. Tremblay. New York: Guilford.

Feldman, R. A., T. E. Caplinger, and J. S. Wodarski. 1983. *The St. Louis Conundrum: The Effective Treatment of Antisocial Youths*. Englewood Cliffs, N.J.: Prentice-Hall.

Field, T., S. Widmayer, R. Greenberg, and S. Stoller. 1982. "Effects of Parent Training on Teenage Mothers and Their Infants." *Pediatrics* 69: 703–4.

Fleischman, M. J., and R. E. Conger. 1978. "An Approach to Families of Aggressive Children: Procedures for Didactic Parent Training Groups." Eugene, Oreg.: Castelia Publishing Co.

Friedlander, K. 1947. *The Psycho-analytical Approach to Juvenile Delinquency: Theory, Case-Studies, Treatment*. New York: International Universities Press.

Gabrielli, W. F., and S. A. Mednick. 1984. "Urban Environment, Genetics, and Crime." *Criminology* 22:645–52.

Garber, H. L. 1988. *The Milwaukee Project: Preventing Mental Retardation in Children at Risk*. Washington, D.C.: American Association on Mental Retardation.

Garrett, T. M. 1985. "Factors Affecting the Initial Diagnosis of Emotionally Disturbed Mentally Retarded Clients in Mental Health Settings." *Dissertation Abstracts International* 44(11-B):3525.

Gendreau, P., and R. R. Ross. 1987. "Revivification of Rehabilitation: Evidence from the 1980's." *Justice Quarterly* 4(3):349–407.

Glueck, S. E., and E. T. Glueck. 1934. *One Thousand Juvenile Delinquents: Their Treatment by Court and Clinic.* Cambridge, Mass.: Harvard University Press.

Gordon, R. 1983. "An Operational Definition of Prevention." *Public Health Reports* 98:107–9.

Gottfredson, D. C. 1986. "An Empirical Test of School-based Environmental and Individual Interventions to Reduce the Risk of Delinquent Behavior." *Criminology* 24:705–31.

Gottfredson, D. C., and G. D. Gottfredson. 1992. "Theory-guided Investigation: Three Field Experiments." In *Preventing Antisocial Behavior: Interventions from Birth through Adolescence,* edited by J. McCord and R. E. Tremblay. New York: Guilford.

Gottfredson, G. D. 1987. "Peer Group Interventions to Reduce the Risk of Delinquent Behavior: A Selection Review and New Evaluation." *Criminology* 25:671–714.

Gottfredson, M. R., and T. Hirschi. 1990. *A General Theory of Crime.* Stanford, Calif.: Stanford University Press.

Guerra, N. G., P. H. Tolan, and R. Hammond. 1994. "Interventions for Adolescent Violence." In *American Psychological Association Commission on Youth Violence,* vol. 2, edited by L. D. Eron, G. Gentry, and P. Schlegel. Washington, D.C.: American Psychological Association.

Guindon, J. 1971. *Les étapes de la rééducation des jeunes délinquants et des autres.* Paris: Fleurus.

Harris, L. C. 1987. "Deinstitutionalization via Community-linked Programs: A Meta-analysis." Doctoral dissertation, University of Texas at Austin, 1986. *Dissertation Abstracts International* 47:3956B.

Hart, H. H. 1910. *Preventive Treatment of Neglected Children: Correction and Prevention.* New York: Arno Press.

Hawkins, J. D., M. W. Arthur, and R. Catalano. In this volume. "Preventing Substance Abuse."

Hawkins, J. D., R. F. Catalano, D. M. Morrison, J. O'Donnell, R. D. Abbott, and L. E. Day. 1992. "The Seattle Social Development Project: Effects of the First Four Years on Protective Factors and Problem Behaviors." In *Preventing Antisocial Behavior: Intervention from Birth through Adolescence,* edited by J. McCord and R. E. Tremblay. New York: Guilford.

Hawkins, J. D., H. J. Doueck, D. M. Lishner. 1988. "Changing Teaching Practices in Mainstream Classrooms to Improve Bonding and Behavior of Low Achievers." *American Educational Research Journal* 25(1):31–50.

Hawkins, J. D., and J. G. Weis. 1985. "The Social Development Model: An Integrated Approach to Delinquency Prevention." *Journal of Primary Prevention* 6(2):73–97.

Healy, W., and A. F. Bronner. 1926. *Delinquents and Criminals: Their Making and Unmaking.* New York: Macmillan.

———. 1936. *New Light on Delinquency and Its Treatment: Results of a Research Conducted for the Institute of Human Relations.* Westport, Conn.: Greenwood Press.

Hirschi, T. 1969. *Causes of Delinquency*. Berkeley: University of California Press.

Horn, W. F., N. Ialongo, G. Greenberg, T. Packard, and C. Smith-Winberry. 1990. "Additive Effects of Behavioral Parent Training and Self-Control Therapy with Attention Deficit Hyperactivity Disordered Children." *Journal of Clinical Child Psychology* 19(2):98–110.

Huesmann, L. R., L. D. Eron, M. M. Lefkowitz, and L. O. Walder. 1984. "Stability of Aggression over Time and Generations." *Developmental Psychology* 20(6):1120–34.

Infant Health Program. 1990. "Low-Birth-Weight Infants." *Journal of the American Medical Association* 263(22):3035–42.

Jacobson, S., and K. Frye. 1991. "Effect of Maternal Social Support on Attachment: Experimental Evidence." *Child Development* 62:572–82.

Johnson, D. L. 1990. "The Houston Parent-Child Development Center Project: Dissemination of a Viable Program for Enhancing At-Risk Families." In *Protecting the Children: Strategies for Optimizing Emotional and Behavioral Development*, edited by R. P. Lorion. London: Haworth Press.

Jurkovic, G. J. 1980. "The Juvenile Delinquent as a Moral Philosopher: A Structural-Developmental Perspective." *Psychological Bulletin* 88:709–27.

Kagan, J., and H. A. Moss. 1983. *Birth to Maturity: A Study in Psychological Development*. New Haven, Conn.: Yale University Press.

Kazdin, A. E., T. C. Siegel, and D. Bass. 1992. "Cognitive Problem-solving Skills Training and Parent Management Training in the Treatment of Antisocial Behavior in Children." *Journal of Consulting and Clinical Psychology* 60(5):733–47.

Kellam, S. G., G. W. Rebok, N. Ialongo, and L. S. Mayer. 1994. "The Course and Malleability of Aggressive Behavior from Early First Grade into Middle School: Results of a Developmental Epidemiologically-based Preventive Trial." *Journal of Child Psychology and Psychiatry* 35(2):259–81.

Kendall, P. C., M. Reber, S. McLeer, J. Epps, and K. R. Ronan. 1990. "Cognitive-Behavioral Treatment of Conduct-disordered Children." *Cognitive Therapy and Research* 14(3):279–97.

Kettlewell, P. W., and D. F. Kausch. 1983. "The Generalization of the Effects of a Cognitive Behavioral Treatment Program for Aggressive Children." *Journal of Abnormal Child Psychology* 11:101–14.

Kohlberg, L. 1969. "Stage and Sequence: The Cognitive-Developmental Approach to Socialization." In *Handbook of Socialization Theory and Research*, edited by D. Goslin. Chicago: Rand McNally.

Kolvin, I., R. F. Garside, A. R. Nicol, A. MacMillen, F. Wolstenhome, and I. M. Leitch. 1981. *Help Starts Here*. New York: Tavistock.

Lally, J. R., P. L. Mangione, and A. S. Honig. 1988. "The Syracuse University Family Development Research Program: Long-Range Impact of an Early Intervention with Low-Income Children and Their Families." In *Parent Education as Early Childhood Intervention: Emerging Directions in Theory, Research, and Practice*, edited by D. R. Powell. Norwood, N.J.: Ablex.

Land, K. C., P. L. McCall, and J. R. Williams. 1992. "Intensive Supervision of Status Offenders: Evidence on Continuity of Treatment Effects for Juveniles and a 'Hawthorne Effect' for Counselors." In *Preventing Antisocial Behavior: Interventions from Birth through Adolescence*, edited by J. McCord and R. E. Tremblay. New York: Guilford.

Larson, C. P. 1980. "Efficacy of Prenatal and Postpartum Home Visits on Child Health and Development." *Pediatrics* 66(2):191–97.

Lazar, I., R. Darlington, H. Murray, J. Royce, and A. Snipper. 1982. "Lasting Effects of Early Education: A Report from the Consortium for Longitudinal Studies." *Monographs of the Society for Research in Child Development* 47: 2–3, serial no. 195.

Lipsey, M. W. 1992. "Juvenile Delinquency Treatment: A Meta-analytic Inquiry into the Variability of Effects." In *Meta-analysis for Explanation*, edited by T. D. Cook, H. Cooper, D. S. Cordray, H. Hartman, L. V. Hedges, R. J. Light, T. A. Louis, and F. Mosteller. New York: Russell Sage Foundation.

Lipsey, M. W., and D. B. Wilson. 1993. "The Efficacy of Psychological, Educational, and Behavioral Treatment: Confirmation from Meta-analysis." *American Psychologist* 48:1181–1209.

Lipton, D., R. Martinson, and J. Wilks. 1975. *The Effectiveness of Correctional Treatment: A Survey of Treatment Evaluation Studies*. New York: Praeger.

Lochman, J. E. 1992. "Cognitive-Behavioral Intervention with Aggressive Boys: Three-Year Follow-up and Preventive Effects." *Journal of Consulting and Clinical Psychology* 60(3):426–32.

Lochman, J. E., and L. B. Lampron. 1986. "Situational Social Problem-solving Skills and Self-Esteem of Aggressive and Nonaggressive Boys." *Journal of Abnormal Child Psychology* 14:605–17.

Loeber, R. 1988. "Behavioral Precursors and Accelerators of Delinquency." In *Explaining Criminal Behaviour*, edited by W. Buikhuisen and S. A. Mednick. Leiden: Brill.

———. 1990. "Development and Risk Factors of Juvenile Antisocial Behavior and Delinquency." *Clinical Psychology Review* 10:1–41.

———. 1991. "Questions and Advances in the Study of Developmental Pathways." In *Models and Integrations: Rochester Symposium on Developmental Psychopathology*, vol. 3, edited by D. Cicchetti and S. Toth. Rochester, N.Y.: University of Rochester Press.

Loeber, R., and T. J. Dishion. 1983. "Early Predictors of Male Delinquency: A Review." *Psychological Bulletin* 94:68–99.

Loeber, R., and M. Stouthamer-Loeber. 1986. "Family Factors as Correlates and Predictors of Juvenile Conduct Problems and Delinquency." In *Crime and Justice: An Annual Review of Research*, vol. 7, edited by M. Tonry and N. Morris. Chicago: University of Chicago Press.

McCall, R. B., and M. S. Carriger. 1993. "A Meta-analysis of Infant Habituation and Recognition Memory Performance as Predictors of Later IQ." *Child Development* 64(1):57–79.

McCord, J. 1978. "A Thirty-Year Follow-up of Treatment Effects." *American Psychologist* 33:284–89.

———. 1979. "Some Child-rearing Antecedents of Criminal Behavior in Adult Men." *Journal of Personality and Social Psychology* 37:1477–86.

———. 1983. "A Longitudinal Study of Aggression and Antisocial Behavior."

In *Prospective Studies of Crime and Delinquency*, edited by K. T. Van Dusen and S. A. Mednick. Boston: Kluwer-Nijhoff.

———. 1986. "Instigation and Insulation: How Families Affect Antisocial Aggression." In *Development of Antisocial and Prosocial Behavior: Research, Theories and Issues*, edited by D. Olweus, J. Block, and M. Radke-Yarrow. Orlando, Fla.: Academic Press.

———. 1991. "Family Relationships, Juvenile Delinquency, and Adult Criminality." *Criminology* 29(3):397–417.

———. 1992. "Understanding Motivations: Considering Altruism and Aggression." In *Facts, Frameworks, and Forecasts: Advances in Criminological Theory*, edited by J. McCord. New Brunswick, N.J.: Transaction.

———. 1993. "Conduct Disorder and Antisocial Behavior: Some Thoughts about Processes." *Development and Psychopathology* 5:321–29.

McNeil, C. B., S. Eyberg, T. H. Eisenstadt, K. Newcomb, and B. Funderburk. 1991. "Parent-Child Interaction Therapy with Behavior Problem Children: Generalization of Treatment Effects to the School Setting." *Journal of Clinical Child Psychology* 20(2):140–51.

Madden, J., J. O'Hara, and P. Levenstein. 1984. "Home Again: Effects of the Mother-Child Home Program on Mother and Child." *Child Development* 55:636–47.

Mednick, S. A., M. Harway, and K. M. Finello. 1984. "Genetic Influences in Criminal Convictions: Evidence from an Adoption Cohort." *Science* 224: 891–94.

Miller, W. B. 1958. "Lower Class Culture as a Generating Milieu of Gang Delinquency." *Journal of Social Issues* 14:5–19.

Moffitt, T. E. 1990. "Juvenile Delinquency and Attention Deficit Disorder: Developmental Trajectories from Age 3 to Age 15." *Child Development* 61: 893–910.

———. 1993. "Adolescence-limited and Life-Course Persistent Antisocial Behavior: A Developmental Taxonomy." *Psychological Review* 100(4):674–701.

Mrazek, P. J., and R. J. Haggerty. 1994. *Reducing Risks for Mental Disorders: Frontiers for Preventive Intervention Research*. Washington, D.C.: National Academy Press.

Olds, D. L., C. R. Henderson, R. Chamberlin, and R. Tatelbaum. 1986. "Preventing Child Abuse and Neglect: A Randomized Trial of Nurse Home Visitation." *Pediatrics* 78:65–78.

Olds, D. L., and H. Kitzman. 1990. "Can Home Visitation Improve the Health of Women and Children at Environmental Risk?" *Pediatrics* 86: 108–16.

Packard, T., E. A. Robinson, and D. Grove. 1983. "The Effect of Training Procedures on the Maintenance of Parental Relationship Building Skills." *Journal of Clinical Child Psychology* 12(2):181–86.

Parke, R. D., and R. G. Slaby. 1983. "The Development of Aggression." In *Handbook of Child Psychology*, vol. 4, *Socialization, Personality and Social Development*, edited by P. H. Mussen. New York: Wiley.

Patterson, G. R. 1982. *Coercive Family Process*. Eugene, Ore.: Castalia Publishing Co.

Patterson, G. R., P. Chamberlain, and J. B. Reid. 1982. "A Comparative Evaluation of a Parent-training Program." *Behavior Therapy* 13:638–50.

Patterson, G. R., B. D. DeBaryshe, and E. Ramsey. 1989. "A Developmental Perspective on Antisocial Behavior." *American Psychologist* 44:329–35.

Patterson, G. R., J. B. Reid, R. R. Jones, and R. R. Conger. 1975. *A Social Learning Approach to Family Intervention: Families with Aggressive Children*, vol. 1. Eugene, Oreg.: Castalia Publishing Co.

Pelham, W. E., M. E. Bender, J. Caddell, S. Booth, and S. H. Moorer. 1985. "Methylphenidate and Children with Attention Deficit Disorder." *Archives of General Psychiatry* 42:948–52.

Pepler, D. J., G. King, and W. Byrd. 1991. "A Social Cognitively-based Social Skills Training Program for Aggressive Children." In *The Development and Treatment of Childhood Aggression*, edited by D. J. Pepler and K. H. Rubin. Hillsdale, N.J.: Erlbaum.

Peters, R., and C. Russell. 1993. *Better Beginnings, Better Futures Project, Model, Program and Research Overview.* Ontario: Ministry of Community and Social Services.

Piaget, J. 1960. *The Psychology of Intelligence.* Totowa, N.J.: Littlefield, Adams.

———. 1965. *The Moral Judgment of the Child.* New York: Free Press.

Pollitt, E., K. S. Gorman, P. L. Engle, R. Martorell, and J. Rivera. 1993. "Early Supplementary Feeding and Cognition." *Monographs of the Society for Research in Child Development* 58:7, serial no. 235.

Power, C., O. Manor, and J. Fox. 1991. *Health and Class: The Early Years.* London: Chapman & Hall.

Powers, E., and H. Witmer. 1972. *An Experiment in the Prevention of Delinquency: The Cambridge-Somerville Youth Study.* Montclair, N.J.: Patterson Smith. (Originally published 1951.)

Pulkkinen, L. 1982. "Self-Control and Continuity from Childhood to Late Adolescence." In *Life-Span Development and Behavior*, vol. 4, edited by P. B. Baltes and O. G. Brim. New York: Academic Press.

Robins, L. N. 1978. "Sturdy Childhood Predictors of Adult Antisocial Behavior: Replications from Longitudinal Studies." *Psychological Medicine* 8:611–22.

———. 1992. "The Role of Prevention Experiments in Discovering Causes of Children's Antisocial Behavior." In *Preventing Antisocial Behavior: Interventions from Birth to Adolescence*, edited by J. McCord and R. E. Tremblay. New York: Guilford.

Rodhe, B. C. 1886. *The New Reader for Infant Schools.* Gothenberg: n.p. (Referenced in I. Nylander, 1981, "The Development of Antisocial Behaviour in Children," *Acta Paedopsychiatrica* 47(2):71–80.)

Ross, G. S. 1984. "Home Intervention for Premature Infants of Low-Income Families." *American Journal of Orthopsychiatry* 54(2):263–70.

Rotheram, M. J. 1982. "Social Skills Training with Underachievers, Disruptive, and Exceptional Children." *Psychology in the Schools* 19:532–39.

Rothman, D. J. 1971. *Proceedings of the Conference on the Care of Dependent Children.* New York: Arno Press. (Originally published 1909.)

Rowe, D. C. 1994. *The Limits of Family Influence: Genes, Experience, and Behavior.* New York: Guilford.

Rutter, M., and H. Giller. 1983. *Juvenile Delinquency: Trends and Perspectives.* New York: Guilford.

Scarr, S., and K. McCartney. 1983. "How People Make Their Own Environments: A Theory of Genotype-Environment Effects." *Child Development* 54: 424–35.

Schwartz, D., R. Flamant, and J. Lellouch. 1980. *Clinical Trials.* New York: Academic Press.

Schweinhart, L. L., H. V. Barnes, and D. P. Weikart. 1993. *Significant Benefits: The High/Scope Perry Preschool Study through Age 27.* Ypsilanti, Mich.: High/Scope Press.

Sears, R. R. 1975. "Your Ancients Revisited: A History of Child Development." In *Review of Child Development Research*, vol. 5, edited by E. M. Hetherington. Chicago: University of Chicago Press.

Sechrest, L. B., S. White, and E. Brown, eds. 1979. *The Rehabilitation of Criminal Offenders: Problems and Prospects.* Washington, D.C.: National Academy of Sciences.

Seitz, V., L. K. Rosenbaum, and H. Apfel. 1985. "Effects of Family Support Intervention: A Ten-Year Follow-up." *Child Development* 56(2):376–91.

Shure, M. B., and G. Spivack. 1979. "Interpersonal Problem Solving, Thinking, and Adjustment in the Mother-Child Dyad." In *Primary Prevention of Psychopathology*, edited by M. W. Kent and J. E. Rolf. Hanover, N.H.: University Press of New England.

Slavin, R. E. 1989. "Students at Risk of School Failure: The Problem and Its Dimensions." In *Effective Programs for Students at Risk*, edited by R. E. Slavin, N. L. Karweit, and N. A. Madden. Boston: Allyn & Bacon.

Stattin, H., and I. Klackenberg-Larsson. 1993. "Early Language and Intelligence Development and their Relationship to Future Criminal Behavior." *Journal of Abnormal Psychology* 102(3):369–78.

Strain, P. S., P. Steele, T. Ellis, and M. A. Timm. 1982. "Long-Term Effects of Oppositional Child Treatment with Mothers as Therapists and Therapist Trainers." *Journal of Applied Behavior Analysis* 15(1):163–69.

Straw, R. B. 1982. "Meta-analysis of Deinstitutionalization in Mental Health." Doctoral dissertation, Northwestern University, 1982. *Dissertation Abstracts International* 43:2006B. University Microfilms International no. 82-26026.

Strayhorn, J. M., and C. Weidman. 1991. "Follow-up One Year after Parent-Child Interaction Training: Effects on Behavior of Preschool Children." *Journal of the American Academy of Child and Adolescent Psychiatry* 30(1):138–43.

Sutherland, E. H., and D. R. Cressey. 1978. *Principles of Criminology*, 10th ed. Philadelphia: Lippincott.

Tonry, M., L. E. Ohlin, and D. P. Farrington. 1991. *Human Development and Criminal Behavior: New Ways of Advancing Knowledge.* New York: Springer-Verlag.

Tremblay, R. E. 1992. "The Prediction of Delinquent Behavior from Childhood Behavior: Personality Theory Revisited." In *Facts, Frameworks, and Forecasts: Advances in Criminological Theory*, vol. 3, edited by J. McCord. New Brunswick, N.J.: Transaction.

Tremblay, R. E., L. Kurtz, L. C. Mâsse, F. Vitaro, and R. O. Pihl. 1994. "A

Bimodal Preventive Intervention for Disruptive Kindergarten Boys: Its Impact through Mid-adolescence." Unpublished manuscript. Montreal: University of Montreal, Research Unit on Children's Psychosocial Maladjustment.

Tremblay, R. E., J. McCord, H. Boileau, P. Charlebois, C. Gagnon, M. LeBlanc, and S. Larivée. 1991. "Can Disruptive Boys Be Helped to Become Competent?" *Psychiatry* 54:148–61.

Tremblay, R. E., B. Mâsse, D. Perron, M. LeBlanc, A. E. Schwartzman, and J. E. Ledingham. 1992. "Early Disruptive Behavior, Poor School Achievement, Delinquent Behavior and Delinquent Personality: Longitudinal Analyses." *Journal of Consulting and Clinical Psychology* 60:64–72.

Tremblay, R. E., F. Vitaro, L. Bertrand, M. LeBlanc, H. Beauchesne, H. Boileau, and H. David. 1992. "Parent and Child Training to Prevent Early Onset of Delinquency: The Montreal Longitudinal-Experimental Study." In *Preventing Antisocial Behavior: Interventions from Birth through Adolescence,* edited by J. McCord and R. E. Tremblay. New York: Guilford.

Utah State University Exceptional Child Center. 1983. *Early Intervention Research Institute: Final Report, 1982–83.* Logan: Utah State University. (ERIC Document Reproduction Service.)

Van Dusen, K. T., S. A. Mednick, W. F. Gabrielli, and B. Hutchings. 1983. "Social Class and Crime in an Adoption Cohort." *Journal of Criminal Law and Criminology* 74(1):249–69.

Wadsworth, M. E. J. 1991. *The Imprint of Time: Childhood, History, and Adult Life.* Oxford: Clarendon.

Wasik, B. H., C. T. Ramey, D. M. Bryant, and J. J. Sparling. 1990. "A Longitudinal Study of Two Early Intervention Strategies: Project CARE." *Child Development* 61(6):1682–96.

Webster-Stratton, C. 1990. "Long-Term Follow-up of Families with Young Conduct Problem Children: From Preschool to Grade School." *Journal of Clinical Child Psychology* 19(2):144–49.

Webster-Stratton, C., M. Kolpacoff, and T. Hollinsworth. 1988. "Self-administered Videotape Therapy for Families with Conduct-Problem Children: Comparison with Two Cost-effective Treatments and a Control Group." *Journal of Consulting and Clinical Psychology* 56(4):558–66.

Weeks, H. A. 1963. *Youthful Offenders at Highfields: An Evaluation of the Effects of the Short-Term Treatment of Delinquent Boys.* Ann Arbor: University of Michigan Press.

West, D. J., and D. P. Farrington. 1973. *Who Becomes Delinquent?* London: Heinemann.

Whitehead, J. T., and S. P. Lab. 1989. "A Meta-analysis of Juvenile Correctional Treatment." *Journal of Research in Crime and Delinquency* 26:276–95.

Wilson, J. Q., and R. J. Herrnstein. 1985. *Crime and Human Nature.* New York: Simon & Schuster.

Yoshikawa, H. 1994. "Prevention as Cumulative Protection: Effects of Early Family Support and Education on Chronic Delinquency and Its Risks." *Psychological Bulletin* 115:28–54.

Yu, P., G. E. Harris, B. L. Solovitz, and J. L. Franklin. 1986. "A Social Problem-solving Intervention for Children at High Risk for Later Psychopathology." *Journal of Clinical Child Psychology* 15(1):30–40.

Mark H. Moore

Public Health and Criminal Justice Approaches to Prevention

ABSTRACT

The public health perspective on interpersonal violence complements that of criminal justice by focusing on violence as a threat to community *health*, not only as a threat to community *order;* on victims, not only on offenders; and on violence between intimates, not only on violence among strangers. The public health perspective views violence as emerging from a complex causal system, not only offenders' intentions, motivations, and characters. Favored interventions take place at the level of primary prevention—the prevention of harms before they occur. This complements criminal justice efforts, which mostly take place at secondary and tertiary levels, when the risk of violence has been identified or when violence has already occurred. The public health approach brings a new platform for observation and intervention, additional resources for developing and using data, and a new constituency. It reminds us we cannot rely only on concepts of justice to achieve change among those involved in violent offenses.

Violence, particularly criminal violence, has long been the focus of intense public concern. For the most part, society's response has been guided by a criminal justice approach—one that views the motivations of offenders as an important cause of violence and the sanctioning of offenders as an effective and just response. Recently, however, the public health community has proposed an alternative approach—one that emphasizes prevention over reaction and the reduction of "risk factors" over the incapacitation of criminal offenders (Prothrow-Stith 1991).

Mark H. Moore is Daniel and Florence V. Guggenheim Professor of Criminal Justice Policy and Management at the John F. Kennedy School of Government, Harvard University.

The idea seems to be catching on. Increasingly, violence is described as an "epidemic" that is striking down young people—particularly young, minority men. Instead of clamoring for more effective prosecutions and longer jail terms, experts quoted in the media often stress the importance of "violence prevention" through more stringent gun control, more intensive and earlier interventions with violence-prone families, and the training of adolescents in nonviolent methods for resolving disputes (Applebome 1993; Goleman 1993).

The purpose of this essay is to analyze what the public health approach brings to society's efforts to understand and respond effectively to interpersonal violence that is different from the traditional criminal justice approach.[1] The method is to compare two different approaches along five separate dimensions: how each tends to view the problem of interpersonal violence, and what particular aspects of the problem attract their interest and concern; the analytic framework each uses to analyze the principal causes of interpersonal violence; the entering assumptions, rooted in professional experience, that guide each approach's search for effective interventions; the resources each community can mobilize to deal with the problem; and finally the values each community believes should be important in guiding society's response to interpersonal violence. Separate sections of the essay discuss each of these five dimensions.

This analysis is primarily an exercise in phenomenology. I implicitly assume that coherent sets of ideas exist that can properly be described as the "criminal justice approach" and the "public health approach." Further, I assume that these distinct approaches can be inferred from the writings of the intellectual leaders in these fields and from the distinctive responses of the two professional communities to questions about how best to deal with interpersonal violence.[2]

It is quite possible that neither assumption is true. There may be no distinctive criminal justice or public health approach to violence. Even if one approach can be distinguished conceptually, it might turn out that no individual or professional community really embraces the views in their pure form.

---

[1] This essay draws on a paper prepared for the National Academy of Sciences Panel on Violence (Moore et al. 1994).

[2] For the key writing on criminal justice approaches to violence, see National Academy of Sciences reports on career criminals (Blumstein et al. 1986), deterrence and incapacitation (Blumstein, Cohen, and Nagin 1978), and violence (Reiss and Roth 1993). For key writing about public health approaches, see Mercy and O'Carroll (1988). See also Report of the Surgeon General's Workshop on Violence and Public Health (1986).

My experience, however, indicates that there *are* important conceptual differences between the criminal justice approach to violence prevention and control and the public health approach and that the differences are worth explicating.[3] That is what makes the public health community's entry into this field potentially important and this essay worth writing.

Whether the pure forms of these views are held by any particular individual or community, however, is far more speculative. So, in characterizing the "criminal justice approach" and the "public health approach," I am not really claiming to be representing accurately the views of any particular individual or community. I am simply trying to present two *gestalt*s: two quite different but nonetheless coherent sets of ideas about how best to understand and respond to interpersonal violence. The exercise may be helpful even if the views are held by no one in particular, since it may help stimulate thought about the best way to analyze and respond to the violence that now plagues us.

I. What Is the Problem?

The criminal justice and public health communities share a common concern: occasions in which one citizen attacks and injures another. To the criminal justice community, these interpersonal attacks are viewed as "crimes"; to the public health community, as "intentional injuries." In these distinctions lies a world of difference.

A. *"Crimes" versus "Intentional Injuries"*

The criminal justice community views interpersonal attacks as one component of a larger problem called "crime." Included in the larger category are "violent crimes" such as homicide, rape, robbery, and aggravated assault and also "property crimes" such as burglary, larceny, and auto theft. What joins these disparate events is that one citizen willfully inflicts a loss on another in a way that exposes the actor to criminal prosecution. They are all "crimes."

To the public health community, the very same attacks are viewed as "intentional injuries" (National Committee for Injury Prevention and Control 1989, p. 192). These, in turn, are viewed as part of a larger category of "health problems" that includes "disease" and "injuries." Included in the larger category of "injuries" are both "intentional injuries" and "unintentional injuries" such as falls, fires, or auto accidents.

[3] For evidence on this point, see Committee on Law and Justice (1994).

What joins these disparate events in the minds of the public health community is that they, like cancer and the common cold, all affect the morbidity and mortality of citizens.

B. The Relative Importance of Interpersonal Attacks

Although the criminal justice and public health communities share a concern about interpersonal attacks, the relative importance accorded interpersonal attacks differs. The criminal justice community has always viewed "violent crime" and "violent criminals" as a particularly important part of its overall responsibilities (Moore et al. 1984). Intuitively, it seemed obvious that crimes resulting in physical injury to victims were worse and more reprehensible than those that produced only property losses. This seemed true not only because the consequences for the victims were worse but also because violence spread fear more widely and virulently than property offenses.

What was intuitively obvious has now been confirmed by systematic surveys of public attitudes toward specific crimes (Reiss and Roth 1993, p. 404). Presented with a series of different kinds of crime and asked to judge their relative seriousness, citizens place a great deal of weight on injury or the threat of injury. The criminal law also reflects these views, so that violent crimes are punished far more harshly than property crimes. All this tends to push violent crime to the center of the criminal justice community's concerns.

The public health and medical communities, by contrast, have not always viewed "intentional injury" as an important part of the nation's health problem. They have been far more focused on diseases such as cancer and coronary heart disease. To the extent that they were interested in injury and trauma, they tended to focus on "unintentional" injuries such as accidents on the road and in workplaces.

What has recently forced them to take "intentional injury" far more seriously are findings that reveal interpersonal violence to be a far more important contributor to the nation's overall health problems than was previously understood. Public health epidemiologists have shown that violence is a principal cause of death among young people and one of the most important destroyers of "quality years of life" (Rosenberg, Stark, and Zahn 1986, pp. 1399–1400). It is also becoming increasingly clear that healing the wounds of violence is an expensive part of the nation's overall health bill (Miller, Cohen, and Rossman 1993). Thus, when viewed from the public health perspective, violence emerges as an important health problem as well as a crime problem—an important and surprising new reason for society to be focused on reducing interpersonal violence.

C. The Relative Importance of Offenders and Victims

Viewing interpersonal attacks as a health problem rather than as a crime, and attacking the problem through health care as well as criminal justice institutions, has a subtle but powerful effect on the relative emphasis that society gives to offenders and victims in responding to interpersonal violence.

Of course, the traditional criminal justice approach saw the victims as an important focus of attention. It was their suffering, and the injustice inflicted on them that gave the criminal justice system its predicate for action. Moreover, the victims often remained important as witnesses in criminal justice proceedings against their attackers (Finn and Lee 1988; Bureau of Justice Statistics 1993). And, increasingly, under political pressure from victims' rights organizations, the criminal justice system has moved to become more responsive to victims' concerns and to provide limited amounts of financial compensation for their losses (Smith and Freinkel 1988, pp. 1–28, 167–86).

But what surprises many in the public health community who observe the operations of the criminal justice system is how quickly the attention of the criminal justice system turns away from the victim and toward the offender. The questions of who committed the crime and how they might be apprehended and prosecuted quickly become paramount.

In contrast, the public health and medical approach to violence (at least in theory) tends to stay focused on the suffering of the victims. In their view, the essential task in responding to violence is to repair the damage of the attack rather than assess the blame (Shepherd 1991). The victim's physical and emotional wounds must be healed. And the social bonds that connect individuals to one another must be reestablished. Assuring justice may help with some part of assuaging victims, but this alone is probably not enough, particularly not given the way that justice is now meted out. Physicians, psychiatrists, and social workers are required as well as police, prosecutors, and judges.

D. Violence among Strangers and Intimates

The sustained focus on victims and the implied need to repair relationships damaged by the interpersonal attacks, which seems common to the public health approach to violence, may be at least partly related to the particular kinds of violence that the public health community tends to see and therefore emphasize.

The criminal justice system has long been primarily focused on violence that occurs among strangers in public locations: serial killings, drive-by shootings, armed robberies, and barroom assaults. This focus can be justified and explained in several ways: such violence is the most common form; it is the kind that threatens the average citizen (Bureau of Justice Statistics 1992, p. 53); and, in any case, it is the kind of violence that the agencies of the criminal justice system are particularly adept at handling (Moore 1983a, pp. 17–42).

In contrast, the public health community has been particularly attentive to a different kind of violence: the kind that occurs in private settings among people who know one another well. This includes domestic violence, child abuse and neglect, and the abuse of elderly relatives (National Committee for Injury Prevention and Control 1989, pp. 192–203, 213–42). This kind of violence tends to be "invisible" to the criminal justice system because the victims tend not to report it (Moore 1983a). Without a report, the criminal justice system has no basis on which to proceed. Yet, this kind of violence is visible to the public health community because it shows up in emergency rooms and schools—at least once physicians and teachers have learned to recognize it (Shepherd, Shapland, and Scully 1989, pp. 251–57).

Moreover, this kind of violence is arguably more serious than violence among strangers. True, violence among strangers may spread fears more widely. But what intimate violence loses in its ability to *spread* terror, it more than makes up for in its ability to *concentrate* it. For the victims of intimate violence, life becomes a living hell. Violence among intimates also tends to recur, making preventive interventions seem particularly important (Sherman 1992). And, insofar as children become witnesses or victims of this kind of violence, their risks of growing up to be violent tend to escalate (Widom 1989, 1992; Reiss and Roth 1993).

Since this kind of violence is particularly and uniquely visible to the public health and medical community, they tend to see this form in high relief, and it influences their perceptions of how other kinds of violence might best be handled. Thus, they assume that ongoing care for victims should be an important part of the response to any kind of violence (Shepherd 1991) and that part of that response should be designed to prevent future violence by repairing the relationships within which the violence occurred (Prothrow-Stith 1991).

In sum, the criminal justice approach sees violence primarily as a threat to community order; the public health approach sees it as a threat to community health. The criminal justice approach tends to focus social attention on the offender; the public health approach on the victim. The criminal justice system has long put violence among strangers, and the apprehension of offenders, at the center of its concerns. The public health approach, in contrast, sees violence among intimates as an important neglected piece of the problem and the task of healing victims and communities as an important part of the response. Self-evidently, the public health approach adds a great deal that is important and useful to traditional criminal justice perspectives on the problem.

II. What Is the Cause?

Just as the criminal justice and public health approaches have usefully contrasting views of the socially significant aspects of violence, they also tend to have somewhat different views of its important causes. The differences may have more to do with the philosophical requirements of the criminal justice system than actual disagreements about the important empirical causes, but the differences seem important nonetheless.

A. The Criminal Justice Focus on Offenders

Philosophically, the criminal justice system is committed to finding the primary cause of violent offending in the intentions, motivations, and characters of offenders. Unless there is some intent, any violence that occurs would be treated as accidental rather than criminal (Kaplan and Skolnick 1982, pp. 4–12). But many criminal justice practitioners go beyond this philosophical position and see the intentions of individuals as the primary empirical cause of violence (Moore et al. 1984, pp. 24–30). In this view, if the offenders had not gotten angry, or if they were not so vicious and ruthless, the violent offenses would not have been committed.

If the motivations of offenders are the key causal factors shaping incidents of violence, then effective policy responses would be those that focused on this variable. In particular, it would be effective to threaten potential offenders with punishment for violent acts (Zimring and Hawkins 1973). It would also be effective to hold those who had shown themselves willing to commit violent offenses despite the moral injunctions against such conduct in close confinement so that they would be physically prevented from committing such acts again (Greenwood with Abrahamse 1982). And, it would be effective to try to alter offenders' attitudes and feelings so that they would be less inclined to commit violent acts in the future (Sechrest, White, and Brown 1979). Thus, the criminal justice community's commitment to deterrence, incapacitation, and rehabilitation flows quite naturally from its focus on the intentions of individual offenders as an important cause of interpersonal violence.

It also follows that if motivations to commit crimes are the important factors determining levels of criminal violence, then policies designed to intervene early in the development of potential criminal offenders would become an important preventive response (Hawkins, Arthur, and Catalano, in this volume). Thus, the criminal justice approach has long encompassed special efforts to deal with juvenile offenders who not only pose current problems for the community but also seem headed for more serious criminal careers. The challenge has been to find effective ways of interrupting these tragic trajectories.

B. The Public Health Focus on Risk Factors

The public health community acknowledges the role of the offender's intentions in causing the violence. That is implicit in categorizing assaultive behavior as "intentional injuries." But the public health community is far less concerned about the moral culpability of the offender and therefore much less committed to seeing the offender's motivation as the important cause. Instead, the public health approach tends to see violence as emerging from a more complex causal system than one dominated solely by the settled intentions of the offender.

Instead of focusing on specific causes of violence, the public health community focuses on "risk factors" that make it more likely that individuals will commit or be victimized by interpersonal violence. Mercy and O'Carroll describe the method as consisting of four steps (Mercy and O'Carroll 1988, p. 290): (1) public health surveillance (i.e., the development and refinement of data systems for the ongoing and systematic collection, analysis, interpretation, and dissemination of health data); (2) risk group identification (i.e., the identification of persons at greatest risk of disease or injury and the places, times, and other circumstances that are associated with increased risk); (3) risk factor exploration (i.e., the analytic exploration of potentially causative risk factors for the disease or death as suggested by the nature of the high risk population and other research); and (4) program implementation and evaluation (i.e., the design, implementation, and evaluation of preventive interventions based on our understanding of the population at risk and the risk factors for the outcome of interest).

Many things about this approach differ from criminal justice approaches. One is that it is determinedly empirical and experimental rather than theoretical. In the public health approach, theory is not used primarily to understand the phenomenon for its own sake but instead as a way of identifying plausibly important targets of intervention (Hawkins, Arthur, and Catalano, in this volume). Moreover, theories are tested at least partly by trying interventions to see if they work.

Similarly, the public health approach is attuned to the possibility that relatively small risk factors might exist that are important in shaping some acts of violence and could serve as easy points of intervention as well as large structural factors. Thus, a pediatrician from Washington, D.C., reported that after sitting for a year on an Infant Death Review Board and learning that several of the deaths occurred among children shortly after their mothers went to jail, the board recommended a program that would ensure greater continuity of care for convicted women with young children. Implementation of the program eliminated deaths of the type that had previously occurred (Moore, Roth, and Kelly 1994). Similarly, another public health practitioner, after examining assaultive injuries, recommended that plastic cups be substituted for traditional bar mugs to reduce some of the damage that emerged from drunken fights. The ad hoc, opportunistic, preventive aspects of these efforts becomes apparent only when one looks, as many public health epidemiologists do, at the details of violence as well as at broader structural factors.

Although risk factors for violence are numerous and hard to categorize, they can be distinguished among three broad classes—all of which are easily embraced by the public health approach. Some risk factors are *structural* or *cultural*. Thus, for example, insofar as poverty exposes children to early trauma or poor health that makes it harder for them to succeed, they may be nudged onto tracks that cause them to become youthful offenders or easy victims of others (e.g., Farrington 1990, 1991). And insofar as the historical legacy of the frontier or the daily onslaught of violence on television makes violence seem either virtuous or commonplace, then individuals may be more inclined to use violence in dealing with their problems (Prothrow-Stith 1991; for the impact of television on behavior, see Slaby and Roedell 1982, p. 119).

A second important class of risk factors concerns the availability of *criminogenic commodities* such as guns, alcohol, or drugs (Moore et al. 1984; Reiss and Roth 1993, p. 404). All of these commodities have been importantly linked to violence, and each represents a potentially important target of intervention.

A third class of risk factors could be described as *situational*. A subclass of situations that might be particularly important are those that point to festering, unresolved disputes, such as those among spouses, landlords and tenants, or youth gangs. Another important subclass may be those situations that produce short bursts of anger or frustration such as crowded bars or traffic jams. Even many nonviolent offenses can be thought of as situations that may lead to violence if a citizen comes across them while they are occurring and seeks to intervene or becomes angry and seeks retribution.

What is interesting to those wedded to a criminal justice approach to violence is that nowhere in the public health approach to causation is any explicit recognition given to the idea that interpersonal violence may be caused by "dangerous offenders"—the idea that is most common in criminal justice approaches to the problem. Instead, the problem is seen as emerging from "risk factors" tied to social structures, to criminogenic commodities, and to particular situations that blossom into violence.

This approach usefully complements the criminal justice approach for two somewhat different reasons. At a practical level, the approach widens the lines of attack that can be made on violence. It identifies opportunities for preventing and controlling violence through means other than deterring, incapacitating, and rehabilitating offenders. That is worth a great deal since we are all (more or less gradually) losing our confidence in these traditional measures.

At a philosophical level, the approach is useful because it challenges our common moral intuitions about who might justly be blamed for instances of violence. The idea that some interpersonal violence may be accidental and emerge from tragic circumstances rather than the moral depravity of the offenders tempers society's general hostility to those who commit violence. Nobody is suggesting that criminal culpability be eliminated, but it might be reexamined in individual cases in light of the more sophisticated understandings of the complex ways in which violence might occur. That, too, can be counted as an advantage.

III. What Are Effective Interventions?

Since the criminal justice and public health approaches have somewhat different views of the causes of violence, it is hardly surprising that they differ in their preferred interventions. But there is more to their differences in preferred interventions than different conceptions of causal processes. Different professional competencies and experiences have led the two different communities to prefer some interventions over others.

A. *Reactive versus Preventive Approaches*

From the perspective of public health advocates, the principal difference between the public health approach to violence and that of the criminal justice system is that the criminal justice system's approach is *reactive* while the public health approach is *preventive*. The criminal justice approach waits until violence occurs before taking action. In contrast, the public health community seeks to intervene before violence occurs.

To help identify preventive opportunities, the public health community distinguishes among three kinds of prevention. (There is inconsistency within the public health community in use of these terms; I am following the usage proposed by Last [1980], pp. 3–4.) *Primary* prevention seeks to prevent the occurrence of disease or injury entirely—usually by operating on broad features of the environment that make the disease or injury possible or likely to occur. *Secondary* prevention is concerned with identifying cases or situations relatively early in some developmental process that will lead to serious problems if not altered. *Tertiary* prevention intervenes after an illness has been contracted or an injury inflicted and seeks to minimize the long-term consequences of the disease or injury.

Among these forms of preventive interventions, the public health community has always had a particularly strong commitment to *primary* prevention. It is there that their epidemiological methods have the greatest leverage. And it is there that the public health community has scored its greatest successes in the health field by complementing the strictly medical approaches (Institute of Medicine 1988). For these reasons, it is natural for the public health community to think that their commitment to prevention, and particularly to primary prevention, is the most valuable thing they bring to discussions about effective interventions.

Moreover, this claim seems to be particularly likely to be true in responding to violence, for the criminal justice approach that now dominates the field does seem far too reactive. Like the medical community (as distinguished from the public health community) in the health field, the criminal justice community is focused far too much on reacting to individual cases rather than understanding and controlling the broad, structural factors that determine the overall flow of cases. Moreover, everything that the criminal justice system does—respond to calls for service, arrest offenders, and so on—seems to occur *after* rather than before an intentional injury has occurred. Thus, like the medical community, the criminal justice community seems limited to *tertiary* rather than primary or secondary prevention.

B. Preventive Approaches in Criminal Justice

To a degree, the criminal justice community would share the public health community's view of how the justice system operates. They, too, think of themselves as largely case-oriented and reactive. However, those who embrace criminal justice approaches to violence prevention and control do not necessarily agree that a "preventive approach" is always desirable in controlling violence, nor that it is particularly new to the criminal justice field.

Many in the criminal justice community (particularly those attuned to concerns about the intrusiveness of the law and the criminal justice system into ordinary social life) often see the reactive nature of the criminal justice system's response to violence as a virtue rather than a limitation. In their view, the reactive, case-oriented focus is a key device for limiting the reach of the criminal law. With this reactive approach, the criminal justice system is restricted to intervening in situations where it is urgent that it do so. Vast areas of social life are thereby protected from the intrusions of law and public policy. A more proactive or preventive approach, and one justified in terms of its practical impact on levels of violence, threatens a more intrusive, overreaching, and less principled public intervention in the lives of people than now exists.

Those who take a criminal justice approach would also observe that, while it is true that the criminal justice system must wait for a crime to be committed before acting, that does not necessarily mean that they cannot prevent future crimes. Some minor crimes may be preludes to serious crime, and if the criminal justice system intervenes effectively after a minor crime is committed, then it may succeed in preventing the more serious crime. Moreover, many violent offenders are repeat offenders. Consequently, effective interventions after the first offense may often prevent subsequent offending. Thus, although the criminal justice system may have to allow some crimes to occur before being able to act, it does not follow that its efforts are not preventive of future violence.

Indeed, to many in the criminal justice system, what the public health community views as reactive, they view as preventive. They think that arresting, prosecuting, and jailing violent offenders prevents crime through four important mechanisms: (1) general deterrence (i.e., the effect that comes from threatening everyone in the population with criminal prosecution if they violate laws); (2) specific deterrence (i.e., the effect on an individual criminal offender that comes from punishing him for a specific offense); (3) incapacitation (i.e., the effect that comes from holding an offender under such close supervision that it is impossible for him to commit offenses); and (4) rehabilitation (i.e., the effect that comes from using periods of confinement for rehabilitative activities such as psychological counseling, drug treatment, vocational skills training, and general education to reduce the likelihood that offenders will continue to commit crimes in the future).

The empirical evidence on the efficacy of these traditional criminal justice approaches in preventing violence is not particularly strong. It has been reviewed by three different panels of the National Academy of Sciences. One panel, assigned to review the evidence on general deterrence concluded that while the evidence drawn from both quasi experiments and natural variation tended to support the deterrence hypothesis, the evidence was not strong enough to prove that deterrence prevented crime, nor to indicate the magnitude of the effect (Blumstein, Cohen, and Nagin 1978, pp. 6–7). The panel also noted that it was difficult to disentangle the effects of general deterrence on crime from the effects of both incapacitation and specific deterrence that occurred when offenders were jailed.

A second panel, convened to estimate the impact of incapacitation on crime concluded that "[u]nder 1970 incarceration policies, incapacitation was estimated to have reduced the number of FBI index crimes by 10–20 percent. For robberies and burglaries, incapacitation is estimated to have reduced their number by 25–30 percent in 1973; in 1982 after the national inmate population had almost doubled, the incapacitative effect for these offenses is estimated to have increased to about 35–45 percent" (Blumstein et al. 1986, p. 6).

It is worth noting, however, that the method for making this estimate was a calculation based on an assumption that current imprisoned offenders would have committed crimes according to their estimated career trajectories if they had not been jailed. There has been no direct empirical test of the effect of incapacitation on a jurisdiction.

Finally, the panel on rehabilitation concluded that "the entire body of research appears to justify only the conclusions that we do not now know of any program or method of rehabilitation that could be guaranteed to reduce the criminal activity of released offenders. Although a generous reviewer of the literature might discern some glimmers of how [to do so], those glimmers are so few, so scattered, and so inconsistent that they do not serve as a basis for any recommendation other than continued research" (Sechrest, White, and Brown 1979, p. 3).

So although the criminal justice community has a *theory* of crime prevention through the mechanisms of deterrence, incapacitation, and rehabilitation, it is by no means clear that its theory is empirically validated.

The criminal justice community also thinks that it has long sought to prevent crime by intervening early in the lives of potential offenders. In the early decades of the twentieth century, state after state authorized the creation of juvenile courts and juvenile justice systems to deal with the problem of crimes committed by children (Platt 1969). To a degree, this movement was animated by concerns for justice. It seemed wrong as a matter of principle to hold children accountable for criminal conduct to the same degree, and in the same way, as adults were held accountable.

But there were also practical reasons to be interested in treating children differently from adults. The emerging disciplines of sociology, psychology, and criminology focused society's attention on developmental factors that might influence a child's path toward a life of crime or honesty. This work suggested the potential for intervening into the developmental processes that led to violent offending, thereby preventing future crime. This was the mission given to the juvenile justice system, and it was this institution that carried the criminal justice system's principal secondary prevention effort for most of the twentieth century.

More recently, of course, the debate over the propriety and effectiveness of the juvenile justice system has changed a great deal (Moore et al.

1987). The concern that inattentive parents and desperate communities might be producing violent offenders has gradually been supplemented by the view that the juvenile justice system was itself criminogenic: that by overreaching into conduct that was not in itself criminal, and by taking children out of their communities, the juvenile justice system stigmatized children and placed them in "schools of crime" (Platt 1969). Still more recently, some have sought to shift the focus of the juvenile justice system from its rehabilitative purposes to greater reliance on deterrence and incapacitation to control juvenile crime (Springer 1986).

The only point of reviewing this history is to illustrate that the criminal justice community has had a long tradition of thinking about how to prevent crimes by intervening early in the development of violent offenders, and that tradition has been located principally in the debates about the proper jurisdiction and approaches of the juvenile justice system.

C. Public Health Approaches to Violence Prevention

Still, from the public health perspective, much is missing from the criminal justice community's approach to prevention. At best, prevention is an additional thought in criminal justice; in public health, prevention is everything. In criminal justice, prevention is primarily tertiary and secondary; in public health, primary prevention is always the goal. Indeed, it is the emphasis on primary prevention that focuses the attention of the public health community on preventing first offenses as well as reoffending and on finding ways to affect the broad social factors now causing violence to occur.

1. *Preventing First Offenses.*   One of the most interesting points of difference has to do with the value of preventing first offenses. As noted above, the public health community seems to think that the criminal justice community's efforts to prevent crime are limited by the fact that they have to wait for at least one crime to be committed. That does not seem like too great a loss to the criminal justice community because they recognize that there is a great deal of reoffending and that the subsequent crimes committed by offenders would be worth preventing through an effective intervention.

The public health community has not really addressed this question yet, but there is one interesting and important thing that one can observe on their behalf. Preventing a *first* offense may be important not only to avoid the loss to the victim but *also to prevent an individual from becoming an offender*. The public health community's interests in reducing violent offenses are not limited to reducing victimization; they are also interested in interrupting the processes that produce offenders. If something could be done to stop first offenses, then the benefits would be recorded not only in reduced victimization but also in preventing the emergence of a criminal offender.

That benefit is not at the forefront of the criminal justice community's concerns. Whether or not people choose to offend is their decision. The criminal justice community's job is to catch people who have chosen to offend in the interests of doing justice and to prevent future victimization by the same or other offenders.

2. *Technological Manipulations of the Environment.* One idea close to the core of public health thought about primary prevention is the hope that they might find some simple, technological manipulations of the wider social world that would make it less vulnerable to violence. The reason is that some of the public health community's most dramatic successes in the health field have been scored in areas in which technology provided a broad, permanent solution to a problem. For example, municipal sewer and water systems solved the problem of typhoid epidemics (Blake and Feldman 1986). Immunizations solved the problems of polio and smallpox (Gregg and Nkowane 1986; Henderson 1986). Improvements in automobile and road design ameliorated the problem of traffic accidents (National Committee for Injury Prevention and Control 1989, pp. 120–38).

The lesson that the public health community learned from these experiences was that if they could find a way to reduce risk factors that did not depend on producing widespread cultural or behavioral changes, then that approach should be the primary one relied on, since we know from experience that changing the attitudes and behaviors of large numbers of people through persuasion or coercion is extremely difficult (Dennis and Draper 1983). Of course, all technological changes require some people to change their behavior. Somebody had to build the sanitary water systems. Someone had to invent the vaccines, and each year new people must be persuaded to take them. And the automobile companies had to be compelled to produce safe cars in a world in which consumers were more impressed by tail fins than safety.

So the point is not to eliminate efforts to change behavior but to minimize them. The aim is to focus the responsibility for producing safety-increasing actions on a relatively small number of people who are paying close attention and to ensure that the actions they take are efficacious because they produce a permanent, physical change in the social environment that reduces its vulnerability to violence.

That seems like an important principle. What is unclear, however, is precisely how this principle might be applied to preventing interpersonal violence. The public health community seems to think that it is this principle that is being applied when it recommends the more stringent control of criminogenic commodities such as guns and alcohol (Reiss and Roth 1993, p. 150). To a degree, the analogy to automobiles and other consumer product safety issues is apt. These commodities *do* look like consumer products that are unsafe and might be redesigned or regulated to produce fewer acts of interpersonal violence.

But to say that there are some commonly used products that could be redesigned or regulated to produce less violence is not quite like making safer cars, or inventing a vaccine, or building a sanitary water system. There is a much larger behavioral component to the production of interpersonal violence than there is in any of these other domains. Consequently, the effective reach of any particular product change in controlling the level of interpersonal violence is much less.

Take, for example, the issue of guns and their role in interpersonal violence in the current U.S. context. It might be possible to legislate a ban on new production of certain kinds of weapons. Or, it might be possible to design guns that are less dangerous by making them less easy to discharge or less lethal if accidentally discharged. But these interventions alone, without other behavioral changes, would probably have only a limited effect on levels of gun violence. The reason is primarily that there are already so many guns in private possession that these efforts might not decrease the availability of the weapons very much or increase the average safety of the guns that were in private hands (Moore 1983*b*).

The point is not that these interventions are useless. The point is that these "technological" changes must always be joined with efforts to change behavior through laws or educational programs or mass media campaigns.

The more apt analogies might be those efforts to make the physical environments of cities more "violence resistant." That could include reductions in density, or the creation of "defensible spaces" (Newman 1972), or the reduction in the number of bars and liquor stores, or the creation of more effective surveillance and responding systems to mobilize police agencies. While such efforts may well have promise, they do not look like quick, inexpensive fixes to the problem of violence. It seems that it is hard to get the behavioral element out of a problem that is so closely tied to human devices and desires.

3. *Cultural Approaches to Violence Prevention.* The effort to focus on broad social and behavioral factors represents the public health community's other main approach to primary prevention of violence. One part of the public health community's interest in primary prevention is broadly familiar to those in the criminal justice community. When the public health community reports that criminal violence is disproportionately located among the nation's poor minority communities and concludes that crime must be caused by poverty and racial discrimination and that the only long-term solution is to alleviate these "risk factors," they are merely echoing the conclusions of those in the criminal justice community who have long focused on the "root causes" of crime (Silberman 1978; Curtis 1985).

To some degree, in recent years, many in the criminal justice research and practitioner community have turned away from these concerns. They have done so not so much because these observations were judged to be wrong or inaccurate but because they seemed irrelevant to much criminal justice policy-making (Wilson 1983). To have these issues now return as a new approach to crime prevention is not necessarily unwelcome, but it is hardly a new contribution. The question that remains to be answered by the public health community (and the criminal justice community, and society in general) is whether they have any ideas about how to eliminate poverty and racial discrimination. Presumably, any such proposal in any public forum is always in order.

The other part of the public health community's primary prevention approach is less familiar to the criminal justice community: the focus on broad cultural factors that encourage violence. Some in the public health community see risk factors for violence in particular parts of the popular culture such as horror movies, violence on television, or even sports such as ice hockey and football (Reiss and Roth 1993, p. 404). They also see danger in corporal punishment because it embodies a primitive, retributivist view of justice and celebrates rather than condemns violence in general (Prothrow-Stith 1991, p. 143). Some in the public health community would like to see such activities reduced so that there was less support for a culture of violence.

Such proposals are greeted with a certain amount of skepticism in the criminal justice community. The rational reasons are that so far there has been little convincing evidence produced that such things do actually encourage a culture of violence and that regulating such conduct requires the state to intrude in sensitive areas such as freedom of expression and family privacy. Beneath the rational reasons, however, is probably a deeper skepticism about whether all violence is environmentally or culturally determined.

After all, many criminal justice practitioners have seen truly awful deeds. They have seen savage mutilations, vicious rapes, and horrible injuries. Often, the victims were both innocent and defenseless. They experience such events and the people who commit them as evil. The evil they observe *may* be the product of bad social conditions or a culture of violence or mental illness. But these factors are not always evident on the scene of the crime. Nor are they always seen as morally relevant.

As a consequence, the criminal justice practitioner community tends to accept the inevitability of some evil in the world and the need to combat it. They do not imagine that all tendencies to violence are caused by society and could be eliminated by altering environmental circumstances. The public health community's reliance on goodness and rationality seems far too hopeful for the world that the criminal justice practitioner community inhabits.

4. *Law versus Education in Behavioral Approaches.* One last point of contrast between the public health and criminal justice communities' approaches to the primary prevention of violence concerns their slightly different attitudes toward the use of the criminal law to regulate conduct. The criminal justice practitioner community believes that it is operating on broad social conditions and attitudes through the moral and instrumental impact of the law. In their eyes, when a criminal law is passed, it becomes a general standard of conduct—a moral obligation—binding on all citizens. It is supposed to affect citizens' attitudes and beliefs as well as their calculations. The combination is supposed to produce important changes in behavior.

Many in the public health community are more reluctant to trust the criminal law to effect broad changes in attitudes and behavior. This reluctance reflects their long experience in trying to control behavior in ways that would limit the spread of epidemics—particularly those involved with sexually transmitted diseases. What they have learned in such areas is that when certain forms of conduct are criminalized, the behavior is not eliminated but simply driven underground. Those who engage in the risky behavior are discouraged from seeking treatment. The net result is that the epidemics become harder rather than easier to control. Thus, in trying to shape attitudes and behavior, the public health community often prefers educational to legal approaches.

They are not entirely consistent on this. If there is a law that can be enacted against a producer or advertiser of a dangerous product, they are often in favor of such a law. And if there is a bit of behavior in the general population that seems to have little intrinsic value and poses a harm to health (such as riding a motorcycle without a helmet or gun owning), they are willing to legislate against such conduct. But in general, and particularly where the behavior of large numbers of citizens is involved, they would prefer to use educational approaches rather than coercive legal approaches.

There is nothing wrong with preferring educational approaches over legal approaches. In many cases, that seems entirely appropriate. The error is in forgetting that the law is often an important instrument of education as well as a device for authorizing state intervention and control. Viewed from this perspective, the two should be seen as complementary rather than competitive. Sometimes it may be wise for the criminal justice community to seek to widen the effective force of criminal laws by supplementing the laws with education programs (as we are now doing in the domain of drug abuse). In other cases, it may be wise for the public health community to strengthen its ability to control risk-taking behavior by adding the weight of the criminal law to its educational efforts (as has been done in the domain of drunk driving) (Laurence, Snortum, and Zimring 1988; Jacobs 1989).

IV. What Resources Can Be Mustered?

One important question a criminal justice practitioner might ask when the public health community offers to join the fight against criminal violence is what additional resources the public health community brings to the problem beyond a new appreciation of its significance and a new methodology for exploring causes and lines of attack.

At first blush, the answer seems to be relatively little. At last count, only two states had committed parts of their public health departments to give explicit attention to "intentional injuries," and these units existed primarily to gather information and provide advice rather than do anything operational. Thus, to hard-pressed criminal justice officials, it may seem that the public health community has relatively little to offer.

In reality, however, the public health community brings three key assets to social efforts to prevent and control violence: a new platform for observation and intervention into the problem; new data and analytic capabilities; and, most important, a new and powerful constituency for acting on the problem.

A. A New Platform for Observation and Intervention

One of the least commonly acknowledged but most important contributions that the public health community brings to efforts to prevent violence is a new platform to use in observing its occurrence and from which to launch interventions. That new platform includes the engagement of physicians and health practitioners lodged in emergency rooms, private offices, and schools. From this vantage point, they are uniquely positioned to see instances of assault that are never reported to the police (Shepherd 1990). They are also able to intervene in ways that are less formal and more potentially supportive of existing relationships than the criminal justice system can be.

This makes the public health and medical community particularly important in dealing with domestic and family violence. And since that is a very important component of the current violence problem, and an important risk factor for violent offending and victimization in the future, having this platform adds a great deal of operational capability to society's violence prevention efforts. An army of white coats can join the blue coats in dealing with violence.

B. New Analytic Capabilities

Almost as important is the fact that the public health community brings a commitment to developing and using hard data about the occurrence of violence to efforts to devise effective interventions. Most public health practitioners are trained epidemiologists who know how to gather and use data. They also know how to design multidisciplinary programs to deal with specific problems. While these skills also exist in the criminal justice research and practitioner community, they are less common, and less commonly deployed, than they are in public health agencies.

C. A Different Constituency

Probably the most important contribution that the public health approach brings to society's efforts to prevent and control violence is a new constituency. Indeed, what has been most striking to me personally about the public health approach to violence is that by changing the perception of the problem from a crime problem to a health problem, a new constituency is created to support preventive actions.

When violence was viewed primarily as a crime problem, to be handled through enforcement and confinement, only a limited constituency was mobilized. Those who paid the most attention were criminal justice practitioners. The discussion was mostly about the extent to which deterrence, incapacitation, and rehabilitation could be expected to work. Many in the minority community, and those employed in "helping" professions such as educators, psychologists, and social workers, were alienated from the discussion.

Once the problem was redefined as a health problem, however, a much different community appeared in the discussions. The minority community, which is most often the victim of criminal offending, seemed to find it much easier to talk about the problem as a health problem than as a crime problem. The health profession, educators, and social workers also found the public health formulation of the problem easier to understand and use. Thus, a new constituency interested in controlling violence was created.

This new constituency is particularly important because it is visible, articulate, and activist. Their interest will provide a basis for passing new laws, raising additional funds, mobilizing volunteer efforts, and inventing new approaches.

V. What Are the Key Values?

In the background of much of the technical issues that have been discussed so far is a larger issue—the question of what values society ought to have in mind as it responds to interpersonal violence. As noted in the introduction, the criminal justice approach to violence is importantly guided by concepts of justice: of what people properly owe to one another, and what should be done in instances where people fail to live up to their responsibilities. In this frame, the questions of blame and punishment are central.

Many in the public health community view these ideas as relatively primitive ideas of social organization, almost indistinguishable from concepts of vengeance and retaliation. Yet that outright rejection of concern for justice ignores the fact that victims of interpersonal violence (and other citizens) are angered when violence occurs not simply because the victims were injured but also because an injustice occurred. They want reassurances that the social order will be restored, that their expectations about social norms will be reinforced. The ceremonies of

the criminal justice system—the trial, the judgment, the punishment—are arguably an important part of providing that reassurance.
To ignore the values associated with doing justice is to miss the key
thing that distinguishes *intentional* injury from *unintentional* injury.

As the public health community consistently reminds us, however,
it is probably best not to rely too much on blame to achieve important
behavioral results among those who are blamed. It attracts too much
emotional heat, and blots out reasoning and analysis. It is not always
just to impose it. It will not do all the practical work that it is supposed
to do.

The public health approach to violence redirects our attention to
care for the victims. It encourages us to see the causes of violence in
different places than the mind of the offender and therefore to resist
the natural tendency to find a scapegoat when something bad happens
even if that is not always just. And it encourages new preventive lines
of attack that can prevent not only victimization but also the production
of more offenders. It emphasizes persuasion and education over coercion, reason over emotion, and analysis over the mobilization of over-
whelming force. In these broad ways, the public health community
may make its largest and most important contribution to society's understanding of, and effective and just response to, the problem of "intentional injuries."

REFERENCES

Applebome, Peter. 1993. "C.D.C.'s New Chief Worries as Much about Bullets
as about Bacteria." *New York Times* (September 26), p. E7.
Blake, P. A., and R. A. Feldman. 1986. "Typhoid Fever." In *Public Health
and Preventive Medicine*, 12th ed., edited by J. M. Last. New York: Appleton-
Century-Crofts.
Blumstein, Alfred, Jacqueline Cohen, and Daniel Nagin, eds. 1978. *Deterrence
and Incapacitation: Estimating the Effects of Criminal Sanctions on Crime Rates.*
Washington, D.C.: National Academy Press.
Blumstein, Alfred, Jacqueline Cohen, Jeffrey A. Roth, and Christy A. Visher,
eds. 1986. *Criminal Careers and "Career Criminals."* Washington, D.C.: Na-
tional Academy Press.
Bureau of Justice Statistics. 1992. *Criminal Victimization in the United States,
1991.* Washington, D.C.: U.S. Department of Justice, Bureau of Justice
Statistics.

————. 1993. *Victim and Witness Assistance: New State Laws on the System's Response*. Washington, D.C.: U.S. Department of Justice, Bureau of Justice Statistics.

Committee on Law and Justice; Commission on Behavioral and Social Sciences and Education; National Research Council; and the John F. Kennedy School of Government, Harvard University. 1994. *Violence in Urban America: Mobilizing a Response, Summary of a Conference*. Washington, D.C.: National Academy Press.

Curtis, Lynn. 1985. *American Violence and Public Policy*. New Haven, Conn.: Yale University Press.

Dennis, J., and P. Draper. 1983. "Preventive Medicine." In *Encyclopedia of Occupational Health and Safety*, edited by Luigi Parmeggiani. Geneva: International Labor Office.

Farrington, D. P. 1990. "Age, Period, Cohort, and Offending." In *Policy and Theory in Criminal Justice*, edited by D. M. Gottfredsen and R. V. Clarke. Aldershot: Avebury.

————. 1991. "Childhood Aggression and Adult Violence: Early Precursors and Later-Life Outcomes." In *The Development and Treatment of Childhood Aggression*, edited by R. J. Pepler and K. H. Rubin. Hillsdale, N.J.: Erlbaum.

Finn, Peter, and Beverly N. W. Lee. 1988. "Establishing and Expanding Victim-Witness Assistance Programs." Washington, D.C.: National Institute of Justice.

Goleman, Daniel. 1993. "Hope Seen for Curbing Youth Violence." *New York Times* (August 11), pp. A7, A10.

Greenwood, Peter W., with Allan Abrahamse. 1982. *Selective Incapacitation*. Santa Monica, Calif.: RAND.

Gregg, M. B., and B. M. Nkowane. 1986. "Poliomyelitis." In *Public Health and Preventive Medicine*, 12th ed., edited by J. M. Last. New York: Appleton-Century-Crofts.

Hawkins, J. David, Michael W. Arthur, and Richard F. Catalano. In this volume. "Preventing Substance Abuse."

Henderson, D. A. 1986. "The Eradication of Smallpox." In *Public Health and Preventive Medicine*, 12th ed., edited by J. M. Last. New York: Appleton-Century-Crofts.

Institute of Medicine. Division of Health Care Services. Committee for the Study of the Future of Public Health. 1988. *The Future of Public Health*. Washington, D.C.: National Academy Press.

Jacobs, James B. 1989. *Drunk Driving: An American Dilemma*. Chicago: University of Chicago Press.

Kaplan, John, and Jerome H. Skolnick. 1982. *Criminal Justice: Introductory Cases and Materials*. Mineola, N.Y.: Foundation Press.

Last, John M. 1980. "Scope and Methods of Prevention." In *Public Health and Preventive Medicine*, 11th ed., edited by John M. Last. New York: Appleton-Century-Crofts.

Laurence, Michael D., John R. Snortum, and Franklin E. Zimring. 1988. *Social Control of the Drinking Driver*. Chicago: University of Chicago Press.

Mercy, James A., and Patrick W. O'Carroll. 1988. "New Directions in Violence Prevention: The Public Health Arena." *Violence and Victims* 3(4): 285–301.

Miller, Ted R., Mark A. Cohen, and Shelli B. Rossman. 1993. "Victim Costs of Violent Crime and Resulting Injuries." *Health Affairs* 12(4):186–97.

Moore, Mark H. 1983*a*. "Invisible Offenses: A Challenge to Minimally Intrusive Law Enforcement." In *ABSCAM Ethics: Moral Issues and Deception in Law Enforcement*, edited by Gerald M. Caplan. Washington, D.C.: Police Foundation.

———. 1983*b*. "The Bird in Hand: A Feasible Strategy for Gun Control." *Journal of Policy Analysis and Management* 2(2):185–95.

Moore, Mark H., with Thomas Bearrows, Jeffrey Bleich, Francis X. Hartmann, George L. Kelling, Michael Oshima, and Saul Weingart, eds. 1987. *From Children to Citizens: The Mandate for Juvenile Justice*, vol. 1. New York: Springer-Verlag.

Moore, Mark H., Susan R. Estrich, Daniel McGillis, and William Spelman. 1984. *Dangerous Offenders: The Elusive Target of Justice*. Cambridge, Mass.: Harvard University Press.

Moore, Mark H., Deborah Prothrow-Stith, Bernard Guyer, and Howard Spivak. 1994. "Violence and Intentional Injuries: Criminal Justice and Public Health Perspectives on an Urgent National Problem." In *Understanding and Preventing Violence: Consequences and Control of Violence*, vol. 4, edited by Albert J. Reiss, Jr., and Jeffrey A. Roth. Washington, D.C.: National Academy Press.

Moore, Mark H., Jeffrey A. Roth, and Patricia Kelly. 1994. "Responding to Violence in Cornet City: The Problem-Solving Enterprise." Unpublished manuscript. Cambridge, Mass.: Abt Associates.

National Committee for Injury Prevention and Control. 1989. *Injury Prevention: Meeting the Challenge*. New York: Oxford University Press.

———. Commission on Behavioral and Social Sciences and Education. Panel on High-Risk Youth. 1993. *Losing Generations: Adolescents in High-Risk Settings*. Washington, D.C.: National Academy Press.

Newman, Oscar. 1972. *Defensible Space: Crime Prevention through Urban Design*. New York: Macmillan.

Platt, Anthony M. 1969. *The Child Savers: The Invention of Delinquency*. Chicago: University of Chicago Press.

Prothrow-Stith, Deborah. 1991. *Deadly Consequences*. New York: Harper Collins.

Reiss, Albert J., Jr., and Jeffrey A. Roth, eds. 1993. *Understanding and Preventing Violence*. Washington, D.C.: National Academy Press.

Report of the Surgeon General's Workshop on Violence and Public Health. 1986. "Violence and Public Health." Report sponsored by U.S. Department of Health and Human Services and U.S. Department of Justice. Washington, D.C.: Health Resources and Services Administration, U.S. Public Health Service, and U.S. Department of Health and Human Services.

Rosenberg, Mark L., Evan Stark, and Margaret Zahn. 1986. "Interpersonal Violence: Homicide and Spouse Abuse." In *Public Health and Preventive*

Medicine, 12th ed., edited by John M. Last. New York: Appleton-Century-Crofts.

Sechrest, Lee, Susan O. White, and Elizabeth D. Brown, eds. 1979. *The Rehabilitation of Criminal Offenders: Problems and Prospects.* Washington, D.C.: National Academy of Sciences.

Shepherd, Jonathan. 1990. "Violent Crime in Bristol: An Accident and Emergency Department Perspective." *British Journal of Criminology* 30:289–305.

———. 1991. "Violent Crime and Victim Support." *Archives of Emergency Medicine* 8:83–86.

Shepherd, J., M. Shapland, and C. Scully. 1989. "Recording by the Police of Violent Offences: An Accident and Emergency Department Perspective." *Medical Science Law* 29(3):251–57.

Sherman, Lawrence W. 1992. *Policing Domestic Violence: Experiments and Dilemmas.* Washington, D.C.: Crime Control Institute.

Silberman, Charles E. 1978. *Criminal Violence, Criminal Justice.* New York: Random House.

Slaby, R. G., and W. C. Roedell. 1982. "The Development and Regulation of Aggression in Young Children." In *Psychological Development in the Elementary Years*, edited by J. Wovell. Orlando, Fla.: Academic Press.

Smith, Steven R., and Susan Freinkel. 1988. *Adjusting the Balance: Federal Policy and Victims Services.* New York: Greenwood.

Springer, Charles E. 1986. "Justice for Juveniles." Washington, D.C.: Office of Juvenile Justice and Delinquency Prevention.

Widom, Cathy Spatz. 1989. "Child Abuse, Neglect, and Adult Behavior: Research Design and Findings on Criminality, Violence, and Child Abuse." *American Journal of Orthopsychiatry* 59:355–57.

———. 1992. "The Cycle of Violence." *Research in Brief.* Washington, D.C.: National Institute of Justice.

Wilson, James Q. 1983. *Thinking about Crime.* 2d ed. New York: Basic.

Zimring, Franklin E., and Gordon J. Hawkins. 1973. *Deterrence: The Legal Threat in Crime Control.* Chicago: University of Chicago Press.

Joanna Shapland

Preventing Retail-Sector Crimes

ABSTRACT

The prevalence of crime in the retail sector is higher than for residents, and multiple victimization is common. Shops and stores have major exposure to external crime such as theft, burglary, robbery and threats, and violence to staff. Internal crime, such as fraud and theft by employees, is less of a problem. The location, siting, and design of a store significantly affects its crime risk, as does the type of neighborhood in which it is situated. Expenditure on security measures is high, but evaluated and published accounts of crime-prevention experiments are rare. Nonetheless, there are documented and cost-effective examples of prevention against all the major crime risks; the most useful approach to implementing these will require development and dissemination of crime audit methods and good practice in crime prevention. Cooperative methods of crime prevention in local areas, involving changes in security management within companies, and participation of public agencies, are likely also to be required.

What image does retail-sector crime conjure up in our minds? Perhaps the most immediate is shoplifting. We know that shoplifting is a relatively common offense for male adolescents, at least in Western countries (West and Farrington 1977; Shapland 1978; Junger-Tas 1988). We are aware, as we do our shopping, of some of the crime-prevention precautions taken by stores—notices warning that shoplifters will be

Joanna Shapland is professor of criminal justice and director of the Institute for the Study of the Legal Profession, Faculty of Law, University of Sheffield, United Kingdom, and editor of the *British Journal of Criminology*. She is grateful to all those who commented on earlier drafts of this essay or provided fugitive materials, particularly John Burrows, Lawrence Sherman, Albert J. Reiss, Jr., David Farrington, and Michael Tonry.

prosecuted, closed-circuit TV cameras, mirrors. We remember reading articles in the newspapers about the amount of "shrinkage" retail companies suffer. If we explore further the stereotype of retail-sector crime, however, we find that it soon becomes insubstantial; we are not sure whether we are correct or how serious a problem other types of crime are. Armed robbery, yes, but is it a problem for all stores or just liquor and convenience stores? Do retail stores suffer greatly from burglary, or their employees from assault? Is internal crime, such as theft or fraud by employees, a problem?

Our fuzzy picture of retail-sector crime is a result of the dearth of published empirical research on the problems of crime and the possibilities for crime prevention in the retail sector. Criminological research has concentrated in recent years on the residential sector, and our national statistics and victimization surveys, our theories, and our view of crime are informed by the pattern of crime there. It is as though we are only interested in people while they are in their homes or out in bars, restaurants, and places of entertainment—but lose interest immediately when they go to work, or go shopping.

Crime prevention in the retail sector is less advanced than crime prevention in the residential sector, though there are many similarities in their development. Both started out with individuals and local groups trying to do their best to protect themselves against crime, with little help from research or government initiatives on prevention. The reliance at this stage is on the traditional criminal justice system measures of apprehending offenders, prosecuting them, and attempting to scare them off by these means (what the French call the "repressive" approach: see King [1988] for a history of the development of crime prevention in France).

Then a growing realization dawns that crime is having major effects on people's lives (or on the operation of companies) and that it continues to increase despite the best efforts of the traditional system. Increasing awareness of the need for more effective preventive techniques leads to the first studies on the patterned nature of crime in different localities and against slightly different targets. This is hampered by difficulties in categorization of crime, by a lack of data on offenders and their perspectives, and by technical problems with software and mapping. Simultaneously, considerable publicity about the need for potential victims to take action (awareness raising) occurs, though often without much help as to what they might actually do. Nonetheless, the first sponsored and localized attempts at experimentation in prevention take place, though often without adequate evaluation (and commonly without any cost-benefit analysis of their effects on the public, on the property owner, or on the state). A store of knowledge begins to build up, though there are major difficulties of disseminating this knowledge and of replicating successful projects in other places (usually because the locational requirements have not been carefully documented). Campaigns to raise awareness slowly begin to transform into "how to do it" sessions, which draw on examples of evaluated good practice. Public funding and sponsorship becomes more selective, dependent on evaluation of the proposed activity and on previous evaluation results. Negative results are no longer seen as unhelpful but contribute to an understanding of what techniques should be used in which conditions. The wider ethical and societal implications of pursuing different paths become clearer and are more widely discussed.

Crime prevention in the residential sector has reached the later stages of this evolution, as can be seen in other essays in this volume, with different countries being at slightly different points. Crime prevention in the retail sector is mostly way back at the awareness-raising and first tentative projects stage. This has considerable implications for the topics that can be examined in this essay. We do not have a plethora of well-evaluated crime-prevention initiatives from which we can draw conclusions on the effectiveness of different techniques and the consequences for theoretical views of crime prevention. Not only are there few methodologically sophisticated evaluations, but the ambit of crime and crime prevention in the retail sector is itself ill-defined.

The task is, hence, first to define what is meant by the retail sector and outline some of the distinctions which need to be made between different parts of that sector, which may affect shops' proneness to victimization and their ability to take preventive precautions (Sec. I). In Section II, I consider what "crime" would be for this sector, looking both at criminologists' or researchers' definitions and at retailers' own views, and, in Section III, I examine the possibilities for crime analysis. I draw together the studies that delineate the extent of the crime problem affecting retailing in Section IV. These need to be discussed both in terms of their methodological adequacy and in terms of the variation they show is occurring for different parts of the retail sector. In Section V, I turn to crime-prevention precautions per se, examining the case studies and evaluations that are publicly available on the use of different preventive techniques for the most common retail crimes and attempting to draw some lessons from these. Finally, in Section

VI, I reconsider the history of crime prevention in the retail sector, setting out what seem to be the major questions that still need to be addressed and looking at how different research techniques could examine these.

The need for an injection of research and publicly available evaluation reports in relation to crime prevention in the retail sector does not just stem from academic curiosity about a relatively unexplored area. A great deal of effort and money is now being put into new technological developments in security. If this is not accompanied by adequate evaluation, or if those evaluation results are not made public, then not only will direct victims suffer (companies, staff, and customers), but shoppers themselves will have to continue to bear the costs, both of crime and of the security measures taken to prevent it.

I. Defining the Retail Sector

The retail sector is not a homogeneous mass of similar companies and similar business opportunities (and illegal opportunities). The pattern of development of retail business has differed considerably in different countries and is changing rapidly over time. This has significant consequences for the ways in which we should think about crime and victimization in retailing, for the ways in which crime prevention can be organized and which kinds of initiatives are possible, and for the measures we can take to measure the amount and impact of crime (and hence the success or failure of crime prevention).

A. Shops, Outlets, and Companies

As shoppers, we view retail premises as a collection of shops. They vary in size, location, layout, and the goods they sell. For the retailer, however, the important variable is the company itself and its financial health and viability. Though most companies have just one shop or retail outlet, the retail sector is dominated by the multiples or chains—companies that have a large number of outlets with a national or regional spread. They include the familiar main (or high) street names and food stores, but increasingly such companies include within their overall financial empire several chains of shops. Though the proportion of multiples will vary between different countries, the extent of the influence of multiples can be seen from the United Kingdom, where retail businesses with ten or more outlets generate over 60 percent of total sales, while only accounting for some 0.5 percent of retail concerns/premises (*Business Monitor* 1993). The financial muscle of the multiples is hence considerable, and they are likely to dominate any national or regional federation of retailers in which crime prevention and security concerns will be discussed.

We have, therefore, different basic units by which to categorize retailing—outlets, premises, and companies. If we now think in terms of crime and offending, the most relevant unit is likely to vary with the type of crime. Local kids or other offenders thinking about burglary of shops will be interested in a particular shop, its location, its contents, and the crime-prevention devices in or on the shop. Many shoplifters will have the same perception—but those who are more professional in organization and who work in a team to strip considerable amounts of goods (often clothing) from each store have been found likely to target certain chains of stores, moving from town to town, because they have worked out how to outwit the particular crime-prevention precautions taken by that multiple retailer. If we consider fraud by employees or by suppliers and distributors, offenders will be interested in the financial processes and safeguards of the company, which are likely to be uniform across all its outlets or shops.

If, however, we turn to the ways in which retailers consider crime and crime prevention, we can see that the retailer is generally working and thinking at the level of the company. Policy on sales and marketing techniques, on brand image, on financial controls and, thereby, on security and crime prevention will be made at the level of the company. The aim is often to create a retailing environment that customers can feel is as similar as possible wherever they encounter that particular named store. Crime-prevention strategies and initiatives are hence often applied at the level of the whole company, though some account may be taken of the level of particular kinds of crime that individual stores notified company-level security managers of, and new initiatives may be piloted first in a few stores.

The challenge to criminologists is hence considerable. If we are thinking of the levels of crime and of crime-prevention initiatives in retailing, we need to consider in each case and for each crime whether our unit of analysis should be at the company or the premises level. If we take figures for the retail sector as a whole, we need to be aware that crime figures, if expressed as per outlet, will primarily reflect the experience of small retailers (corner shops and other one-outlet businesses), whereas financial data for the sector as a whole, such as the cost of crime, will primarily reflect the experience of the large multiples (because of their vastly greater turnover).

B. Management Perspective and Resources

The distinction between multiples and small one-outlet retailers also indicates differences in management perspectives, in the potential effect of crime, and in the resources available to deal with crime. There are corresponding differences in the information that may be available about crime and the cost of crime and in the crime-prevention initiatives that are likely to be possible.

Essentially, the multiple retailer will have considerable resources available in terms of personnel and money for crime-prevention hardware (if senior managers become convinced that particular kinds of crime are posing a significant risk to profit—see Sec. II below). Multiples will normally have specialist personnel for crime prevention, including store detectives and, possibly, uniformed security guards (who may be employed by the company or contracted in from a security company). There will be a reporting policy for criminal incidents, in which certain kinds of incidents (such as robberies and burglaries) are supposed to be reported by store/outlet managers to regional or national security managers, who operate a companywide database. The corollary, however, is that data on *all* the crime affecting the company may not be easily available to any one person in the company (see Shapland and Wiles 1989). Certain incidents will be collated by the security manager, but fraud by employees may be held by the finance department, whereas many minor assaults on staff may remain known only to the store managers and employees. With a relatively high turnover of managers in some multiples, the memory of what offenses have happened, and in what manner, can rapidly be lost, and the ability of many householders, for example, to recall victimization and so consider the adoption of particular crime-prevention devices, does not have its equivalent in the retail sector. One of the major difficulties bedeviling the development of effective crime-prevention policies in the retail sector has been the problem of collecting an adequate database on the crime and victimization risks.

If we turn to small outlets, then, typically, the company consists only of the owner or manager and a few employees. Company records will emphasize financial and stock details, rather than including details of criminal incidents, but managers and some employees are likely to have a much lower turnover and so will be able to remember victimization over the previous year or two years. The ability to consider which are effective crime-prevention measures, however, may well be much smaller. Shop owners and managers will not be able to be specialists or experts in crime-prevention hardware, nor can they necessarily be expected to be able to keep up-to-date with what is proving effective. Nor will they have the resources to buy in such help—an option available to the multiples. Often, small shop managers and owners work long hours (convenience stores, news agents, and tobacconists, etc.) and will also not have the time to attend seminars or training courses. Much of the concern in relation to crime prevention at this end of the retailing sector has been to find means to *deliver* crime-prevention advice and services to the large number of such small businesses, which tend to be relatively isolated from each other and from sources of advice.

For the researcher, therefore, the paradox is that the part of the retailing sector in which it is relatively easy to obtain victimization and crime data (small retailers) is not the part that has the resources of management or skill to think about and implement crime-prevention measures. Small retailers need to be advised about already-proven packages of crime-prevention measures suitable for their premises— but it is difficult for the chains and large multiples to compile their crime and victimization data in order to produce such a package.

C. Layout and Location

The development of the retail sector has been subject to relatively rapid change. In terms of the location in which we expect to find retail premises, the shopping environment has changed significantly during our lifetime—to a far greater extent than in the residential sector. The use of shopping precincts dates only from thirty to forty years ago. Shopping precincts have, more recently, often become enclosed as shopping malls, which can be shut to the public at night. Shopping malls may be built as stand-alone developments but may also now be enclosed within office buildings or attached to public buildings or leisure facilities (such as theaters, cinemas, or bowling alleys). Shopping malls increasingly contain restaurants, sandwich bars, and licensed premises serving alcohol, so that people can spend the whole day or half day there. Supermarkets themselves are a relatively recent occurrence, with their spread being more prominent in North America, and still not a major factor in many parts of Europe. The out-of-town development, whether of supermarkets, or large retail complexes, is taking retailing away from its previous close connection with city centers, and its earlier conjunction with housing.

The locational factors for retailing would be expected to have significant implications for crime risks and crime prevention. At the most basic, if an outlet is within a shopping mall that is closed at night and that has its own security precautions, then any burglar will first have to penetrate the shopping mall and only then penetrate the outlet. The outlet may not have to take antiburglary precautions of its own, relying on those of the mall. Malls and precincts may also have their own security staff, who are likely to supplement any policing input in dealing with incidents and in moving on "undesirable" customers. In a large shopping mall, the mall's plainclothes security staff, the shop's store detective, and neighboring shops' store detectives may all be mobilized to track and finally arrest a shoplifter first seen in one shop. Typically, the mall will itself require particular policies in relation to opening hours and layout of shops of its tenants, which will have crime-prevention consequences. In an open-air precinct, however, it is possible for next-door shops to have little communication with each other, so that the manager of one shop will not know of a burglary to the next-door shop or have any warning system if a suspicious person or possible robber is seen (Hibberd and Shapland 1993).

The location of the store is also potentially important in terms of the kinds of buildings and neighborhoods around. If the store is in a high-crime neighborhood, next to housing, it is highly likely to be one of the targets for property crime in that area. If it is on an out-of-town site, with just fields or roads around the collection of five or six big stores, then any burglar or out-of-hours predator will need to have transport (though the crime-prevention disadvantage is that any surveillance of the building will have to rely on electronic means, rather than there being neighbors to "protect" the store or police or guards nearby to respond to an alarm signal). Hence, varying the land-use pattern and siting retail premises in different places is likely to affect crime. Unlike for residential premises, offenders for retail-sector premises cannot live at the site of the crime. So if retail premises are placed elsewhere, then the types of potential offenders nearby will change, and the cultural pattern of types of offending may also change. For example, in England, "ram-raiding" has spread over a period of two to three years from two parts of the north of England to many other areas. "Ram-raiding" is the term given by the media to burglary out of shopping hours in which (normally stolen) vehicles are used to ram the plate-glass windows or roller-shutter doors of retail or wholesaling premises or the brick walls of banks or building societies. The "raiders" then quickly gather up racks of clothing or goods, or the wall cash-dispensing machine of banks, and make off with the goods in a second vehicle. The essence of the offense is speed (before the police respond to the alarm), and it is targeted at shops and other outlets where there is a considerable amount of high-value goods in the window or front wall or at the front of the store. Prevention tactics are either to strengthen the front walls or windows (which has been adopted by banks and some shops, but is expensive) or to move high-value goods much further into the store where they are not easily accessible in the time available to the burglars.

One of the difficulties in relation to crime risks and crime prevention for multiples is that, typically, data on criminal incidents are not accompanied by data on the locational variables of that store, which would make it possible to interrogate a database and discover the relative importance in crime-reduction terms of the locational variables discussed above. Equally, few multiples are big enough to have enough stores in sufficiently different locations to permit such an analysis. The retail concern in opening new outlets is to ensure that they are sufficiently far away from existing outlets not to take business away. Once the market is saturated, a new type of store appealing to different consumers needs to be started, which itself, if successful, becomes a chain. This process does not easily sit with the need of crime-risk analysis and crime-prevention evaluation to have enough of the *same* kind of location or store design to permit analysis of the factors affecting crime and successful crime prevention. It means that, in practice, crime-risk analysis and crime-prevention evaluation need to be undertaken as an independent research exercise, which selects the stores to be included on research criteria. The difficulty is that such research is only of immediate, obvious benefit to the stores included, which will tend to be from most of the multiples and also smaller companies. The opportunities for finding a single funder or a small number of funders for such research from the retailing sector thus are slim and depend on the trade associations for retailers themselves becoming convinced that there is a need for such overall work.

As well as location, certain aspects of the layout of stores are also of potential importance in influencing crime and crime prevention. Some of the more obvious variables are the siting of displays and tills (which may affect shoplifting and robbery), the visibility of all parts of the store to employees or electronic means of surveillance (affecting shoplifting and, potentially, burglary in the case of closed-circuit television [CCTV] or alarm systems that monitor audio or visual signals), the ease of removing stock from the front of the store with "walk-in" or "open" designs, and the ease of removing stock from the storeroom. Size, layout, and number of employees are likely also to affect the risk from violent assault and robbery. It is interesting how, in the United Kingdom, armed robbery has decreased in banks (with the more stringent security precautions put in place there) and has increased in smaller building societies and saving societies and in small shops (particularly those selling alcohol and open after normal shop hours), but *not* in larger shops.

Though stores are constantly changing their interior layout and design to attract customers and sales, the ability to do so for crime-prevention purposes will be linked with the management structure. We cannot presume that a national chain will be more effective in crime-prevention terms since the national chain will have a necessary uniformity for sales promotion, training, and the "look" of the store— and each retail outlet or shop will be similar in the criminal opportunities the layout of the store, the financial systems, and the training of the staff provide. It may well not be able to tailor its crime-prevention precautions to the needs of that area and that shopping precinct.

To what extent do these factors of size, management structure, location, and layout affect crime patterns and crime-prevention needs? Obviously, this is an empirical question, which I explore in Sections IV and V. They are addressed here because the reader will need to assess how far such factors have been covered in the existing state of research on crime prevention in the retail sector and to what extent they should be included in a future program of work.

II. Considering Crime in the Retail Sector

Criminologists or people interested in crime prevention naturally think in terms of "crime." "Crime" has moral connotations and, for most people, is indissolubly linked with ideas based on the criminal law and associated with the criminal justice system. Many of our stereotypes of what is "crime" concern offenses affecting individuals and include burglary and violent assaults. In the retail sector, the relevance of moral frames of reference is less clear.

A. Crime, Loss, Shrinkage, and Risk

The word "crime" itself, however, may be foreign to companies in relation to the terminology they use in internal auditing and risk-management procedures. Indeed, the term "crime prevention" may not be the most suitable one. The debate as to whether one should be talking of "crime" and "crime prevention," or of "risk" and "risk management," or of "shrinkage," or of "lost profit opportunities" is a heated one because each of these terms has connotations and symbolism that suggest which paths might be followed if a "crime" or "loss" or "lost profit opportunity" is discovered.

"Loss" and "lost profit opportunities" have few moral connotations but are clearly important in business terms, with their unit of measurement being financial. The kinds of crimes that leap to mind as "loss" are property crimes—theft, fraud, robbery. It is difficult to calculate the "loss" associated with violent crime, though it is there in the possible indirect costs of staff time off work to recover from injury and increased staff turnover, as well as deterring customers if the shop acquires a reputation as a dangerous place. "Shrinkage" is the retail equivalent of the more general commercial world's usage of "loss" and "lost profit opportunities." "Shrinkage" generally means the disparity between the financial value of stock acquired and sold and the financial value of stock left on the shelves (though one of the major problems in producing a national estimate of the cost of retail crime has lain in different retailers having slightly different operational definitions of shrinkage [British Retail Consortium 1994]). It includes stock that has been stolen (by customers or by staff) and losses within the stores' financial and merchandising procedures that have not been identified (poor accounting procedures on returns by customers, e.g., can cause apparently high levels of shrinkage, as can failure to account for stock marked down because it is damaged). Clearly, "shrinkage" cannot include assaults and normally would not include losses through burglary (because the goods stolen tend to be identified and recompensed by insurance).

"Risk management" is a far more likely term for retailers to use than "crime prevention." The "risks" that are to be considered and managed are much wider than criminal incidents and commonly include fire, failure of distribution mechanisms, and product liability, as well as theft and burglary—anything that poses a threat to the *financial* viability of the business. Management of risks is an effort to minimize the effect of common, but low-level, threats to financial success (theft and burglary, for example) and also to attempt to eliminate or reduce to a very low level those threats that strike at the viability of the whole business (such as arson, fire, major fraud—all of which can shut down a business). *Managing* the risk in relation to the first category, however, means weighing up the cost of possible security precautions against the cost of those events occurring and their consequences. Moreover, it involves weighing up the effect of potential security measures on sales and marketing (security is often seen in retailing as tending to reduce the opportunity for sales). It does not mean trying to eliminate crime. In contrast, much crime prevention in other sectors has had the aim of preventing that kind of offending completely, rather than deliberately accepting certain levels of crime in certain sites against certain kinds of victims.

The term used is not a mere matter of definition. The terms in which people become used to thinking affect what kinds of event are typically thought to be occurring and the ways in which they are likely to be measured and dealt with. Clarke (1990), for example, has suggested that the effect of calling crime "loss" or "shrinkage" is to tend to decriminalize it and to render it less morally serious. He regards companies as essentially amoral profit calculators, which may happily tolerate crime as long as it leads overall to the best "bottom-line" result for the company. There is, of course, some element of truth in this. The demands of increased security *may* conflict with the needs of promotion or sales (although much of this view is due to historical prejudice, unsupported by experimentation, and remediable by more innovative security measures). More commonly, it may not be commercially effective *initially* for a company to spend money on doing a crime audit and tightening its risk management because in so doing it may become less profitable for a time than its competitors, all of which have been relying on equal inefficiency with regard to crime loss in the sector. In the long term, however, the companies that have controlled losses in this way *and measured the results* have found it profitable even within their existing security budget (which may go down but may be just as effective).

B. Dealing with Crime, Loss, and Risk

The terms used and their connotations also affect the ways in which retailers and researchers will tend to deal with offending and the security precautions ("crime prevention," or "risk management") they will think first to put in place. "Crime" implies thinking about notifying the police and considering using a criminal justice system response—an offender-based reactive response. "Loss" or "risk" may imply considering first tightening up on financial procedures or installing preventive devices—an offense-based preventive response. "Shrinkage" has certainly tended to mean thinking about procedures in relation to customer theft (store detectives, layout of displays, mirrors, CCTV) and, more recently, the realization that employee theft is also important. The concentration on "shrinkage" may lead to underestimation of the losses caused by fraud and damage through burglaries (because they tend not to affect stock levels).

It has been found that companies do not necessarily rely on the criminal justice system to deal with the offenders they uncover—and that calling crimes "losses" and so forth may naturally promote the use of civil law or internal company measures (see, e.g., the discussion by Stenning [1989] on corporate policing in North America and the results of the recent Australian survey of business crime—see Walker [1994]). Walker found that 81 percent of food retailers and 58 percent of nonfood retailers had not reported thefts by employees (73 percent overall), and 93 percent of food retailers and 44 percent of nonfood retailers had not reported fraud by employees (83 percent overall). Major reasons included "lack of evidence," "inappropriate," and "police could do nothing," with "not serious enough," a common reason in residential victimization surveys, playing a smaller role. Stenning (1989) argues that most business people do not see "crime" as a useful label for dealing with the problems they and their businesses face.

From the limited amount of research that is available, it seems correct that companies will tend to use disciplinary or civil law measures to deal with internal crime, such as theft or fraud by staff (dismissal, suing to regain moneys taken through fraud, etc.—see Johnston et al. 1990). However, companies still routinely use the criminal justice system to deal with much external crime (including using the police to respond to alarm activation once it has passed through a central alarm station, and prosecuting those outsiders who steal, rob, burglarize, or set fire to business premises). Several retailers in Britain, for example, still have a policy of privately prosecuting shoplifters—and almost all will wish to use the police and the courts when armed robbery, assaults on staff, and arson are involved.

Prosecution policies in relation to customer theft are constantly under discussion. Retailers' policies as they relate to the employment of store detectives and whether detected offenders should be referred to the police or given "instant cautions" by shop managers are now being discussed with local police chiefs, whose officers may be tied up for a long time for every offender caught. The police in Milton Keynes, England, calculated in 1993 that each juvenile shoplifter they were notified about required over five hours of police time to process for the initial arrest, collection of evidence, and questioning, leading to a significant reduction in the number of patrolling officers available on the streets. A joint policy has now been worked out by police and the local large shopping center to increase deterrent value by notifying police, while minimizing processing time, and allowing more time for consideration of the appropriate final result (a warning/formal caution, diversion to a juvenile program, or prosecution; see Shapland, Wiles, and I'Anson 1994).

Ekblom (1986) found that in 1984 arrests by store detectives from one large music store in the center of London totaled 1,456. Of these, about 80 percent were referred to the police, who decided that about 26 percent should be prosecuted. This one store in 1985 had accounted for as many as 39 percent of the arrests for shoplifting by the local police station. This study illustrates many of the dilemmas about the decisions as to whether offending should be seen as "crime" or as "risk." The store suffered a relatively high rate of customer theft. It sold easily pocketable and highly attractive items, which were at that time easily picked up by customers (since tapes and records were left in their sleeves on the stands). Its rationale was that the sales advantages of such merchandising outweighed the financial risk through theft (a "risk" policy). However, the parallel policy of using store detectives and referring most detected offenders to the police (a "crime" response) imposed considerable cost on the public purse. However, more systematic crime analysis indicated that only a few parts of the store were showing this high-loss pattern and that store detectives were having to cope with an apparently inexhaustible stream of fresh, previously unknown, offenders (largely juveniles). The effectiveness of relying mainly on store detectives was seen by both the researcher and the store as limited. The store wished to continue its sales-enhancing display policy but decided to move to the more obvious deterrent of using some uniformed security staff as well as store detectives and installing preventive devices on the high-risk sites. The case study indicates the continuing prevalence of "risk"-based thinking on prevention, together with "crime"-based thinking on detected offending. It also shows the consequences of limiting risk for one body (the store) on the increased costs for others (the police). Similar cost-displacement effects can occur between one store and others nearby. It is clearly important that any cost-benefit analysis of adopting particular techniques specifies the base over which it is done (and that we start to examine the effects, both financial and moral, of the adoption of particular risk-management policies on other parties).

Depending on the balance within the sector and within the company between external crime and internal crime, it is likely that the terminology used by retailers will vary. If there is perceived to be more external crime (which often is seen to need a criminal justice response), it seems that the word "crime" may be used. If there is perceived to be a greater internal crime problem, then "loss" (or "lost-profit opportunity") is more likely to be used. The disputed use of these terms, however, is also slowly being affected by the move toward a total risk-management policy for companies, in which crime, default by suppliers, machinery breakdown, and natural disasters are all studied together as threats to the profitability and survival of the business. In its method of initial risk analysis, this is an amoral calculus (talking about "loss")—but in then working out how to deal with the source of the threat and what might be done in relation to the image and ethos of the company, moral questions often come into play (as does the use of the word "crime").

C. Researching Crime and Risk

Although a number of large retail concerns now have sophisticated databases on incidents of crime and disorder in their stores, few are prepared to talk about their overall crime problems openly. One major exception to this in the United Kingdom is Dixons PLC, which is why many of the case-study examples in this essay come from this company. The reasons for this reluctance are clearly set out in Burrows's survey of businesses' prevention practices (1991a). He states that "companies voiced skepticism that openness about crime problems could achieve anything positive, and corresponding concern that it could risk alerting potential criminals of their vulnerabilities, or earn the opprobrium of shareholders and the City [stock exchange]. Companies were concerned that publicizing the details of precautions taken against crime could render them invalid. Some believed that disclosure could reduce the competitive edge they had achieved by effective precautions. Finally, and most obviously, many companies—though content with the impact of preventive actions they have taken—were unable to provide supportable evidence to this effect" (pp. 4–5).

With regard to large companies, particularly large companies in the retail sector (whether they own large stores or chains of smaller stores), these sentiments fall in exactly with the author's experience. Small shops are happy to take part in research projects or collaborate in multiagency projects with the police, and so forth (providing that these do not conflict with the time constraints of running a small shop). In contrast, the senior management, particularly the security management, of large companies has been highly suspicious of research, fearing that it will affect their reputations or their profit margins (particularly since they have often not been able to isolate, and hence always realize, the extent of losses due to crime). Recently, however, there has been much greater interest in effective risk management in several countries (e.g., the United Kingdom, the Netherlands, and Australia), perhaps allied to recessionary pressures, and the major retailing associations have been prepared to talk with government and researchers much more openly about the levels of victimization that are occurring.

D. National Variation

Unfortunately, we have next to no knowledge of retail-sector crime and crime prevention in countries other than Western ones, with almost all our empirical research base stemming from the United States, Canada, the Netherlands, and the United Kingdom. This essay is necessarily confined to that research base, but it is quite clear that crime problems have distinctive cultural and geographic aspects. For example, labor relations, terrorism, civil unrest, kidnapping, and corruption are lower in the portfolio of concerns of security managers in Western European countries and North American countries than they are in some other parts of the world. Security managers of large multinational groups will stress their differing jobs in different parts of their company's empire. Equally, the rare self-report and detailed empirical studies of crime in Asia indicate that there may be very different parameters for delinquency there. In Hong Kong, predominant adolescent delinquent activity is concentrated on acquisition of property, rather than on the typical "street crime" model familiar from European and North American studies (Chan 1988). Hence stealing from jewelry stores, illegal gambling, and stealing consumer goods is predominant over obtaining alcohol, drugs, tobacco, theft from small general shops, criminal damage, and assault. It must not necessarily be assumed that the patterns of crime and the opportunities for crime prevention set out in this essay will apply to other countries. Indeed, in writing this essay, I have been well aware that the words used to describe the same kind of layout of retail-sector premises are different in different countries (the shopping precinct/mall; the street-corner shop/neighborhood store).

E. Different Perspectives

The reader will be aware from the above discussion that considering crime prevention in retailing is a rather more complex task than considering residential crime prevention. The complexity stems from the very different perspectives of those who are looking at crime or crime prevention in retailing and the necessity of using different terms, different measures, and often different methods when researching particular offenses in the retail sector or when advising retailers.

Take, for example, burglary, theft by customers, assault on staff, and credit card fraud. A burglary is highly likely to be noticed as an individual incident. It will be noted in company records as an incident (if company reporting procedures require notification of headquarters or security by local managers—as they probably will), as loss (with stock loss and damage cost being in separate ledgers), and (probably) as an insurance claim. It may also take up management time in liaison with the police, in considering security procedures, and in supporting staff. If researchers question local managers or staff, they are likely to remember it and so it will show up as an incident in victimization surveys. It is highly likely to be reported to the police, and both managers and criminological researchers will see it as "crime" (managers will also see it, if prevalent, as "loss"). We can express its incidence and prevalence on a base either of the number of retail premises or the number of retail companies—but we shall obtain very different apparent perceptions of its frequency from these two. Since burglars work to geographically defined patterns of search (Brantingham and Brantingham 1984), we would expect variations by location (and also by type of goods).

By contrast, a single incident of theft by a customer is unlikely to be detected. Burrows (1993) estimates, on the basis of the database being gathered by the British Retail Consortium, that known losses from crime (witnessed or judged unequivocal acts of crime) only account for 10–15 percent of total shrinkage. Retailers, therefore, may simply be unaware how many incidents of theft they are suffering. Unlike many individuals, they will be unable to realize, at the time, whether they have suffered an incident causing loss. They cannot survey all their property continuously. Nor will conventional victimization surveys (which rely on estimates by number of incidents) tap most customer theft. From a criminological perspective, customer theft is "crime," but for retailers, incidents of theft may be "crime" when detected but can only be "loss" when undetected. Detected and undetected incidents are often considered separately from a crime-prevention viewpoint. We can depict risks either in terms of premises and outlets or by company, if detected. Shrinkage losses could be portrayed in either way as well, but retailers often regard shrinkage per outlet as a matter that should be kept confidential for commercial reasons, so, since obtaining the figures requires access to their financial records, the few figures we have are often by company.

Staff themselves will of course remember and be vividly aware of assaults on them—if they see them as serious or as not part of the normal pattern of working. It is a very similar situation to the perception of violence in other settings. Local management will also be aware, but assaults may well not be included in centrally organized company databases because they cannot be expressed in direct financial loss terms (unless they are robberies) and because they usually do not require any central action on insurance. Assaults on staff, unless very serious, can be relatively invisible to central management. It is the contrast between the reaction to customer theft and assault at the senior management level that has also underpinned charges of "amoral profit calculators." Once aware, however, both staff and management see assaults as definitely in the "crime" category (Retail Action Group 1994a), though the same may not be true of threats and abuse. Recently, however, assaults are also coming to be seen as a health and safety issue (Health and Safety Executive 1989, 1994; Health and Safety Commission 1994). Victimization surveys will pick up incidents of assault in the same way as in residential surveys, but the evidence is that assault will vary with layout and location, as well as type of goods and working hours. It is unclear whether assaults should be expressed on the basis of number of employees per company, or by premises, or by company.

Who suffers the loss in credit card fraud is itself a disputed area and depends on the conditions of the contract between the credit card company and the retailer (and the credit card holder). Shops are only liable currently for cases in which their staff are negligent in not noticing or retaining the card (though the numbers of these may be growing—and certainly the potential for violence when retaining cards is worrying retailers). Most of the loss of the use of stolen cards is borne by the credit card company—but whether this will be seen as a significant risk by that company is less clear. Between 1980 and 1987 in the United Kingdom, credit card losses (from stolen and fraudulently used cards) to Visa and Access (the main U.K. credit cards) rose between three- and fourfold. However, for both companies these losses declined when seen as a proportion of card turnover—and so were seen as a diminishing problem, requiring little significant internal control or collaborative work between the companies (Home Office 1988). By 1990, Levi, Bissell, and Richardson (1991) documented that card losses had exploded to total £150 million—and there had been a similar explosion in both internal controls by the credit card companies and collaborative work. Crime prevention/risk management is work—and cost. It will only be undertaken if it is seen to be necessary (either in "loss" terms or in moral "crime" terms). Fraudulent use of credit cards poses problems of whether it is seen as "crime" or "loss" and who is seen to have the responsibility and cost for taking preventive measures. It is also difficult to research its extent without special studies because much of the data is held by the credit card companies, not the shops, so data on variation by locational shop variables (as opposed to geographical location) can be hard to acquire.

There are some very different perspectives among those who study and attempt to prevent retail crime. Criminologists using an opportunity theory or a routine activity theory would concentrate on risk and on the variation in risk in terms of location, layout, the goods sold, possible targets, and displacement. From the retailing viewpoint, it may be about loss and cost, and the difficulty or sheer inadvisability of separating loss and cost due to crime from that due to other risks. For an assaulted or burglarized employee, or his or her local manager, or often the customers of that store, the reactions and the viewpoints are incident-based and are similar to those of residents. When reviewing what we know about retail crime and how we could prevent it, and when suggesting future research, we must bear in mind these radically varied viewpoints.

III. Analyzing the Problem

Given the difficulties and variation outlined above, retailers may be wondering whether it is worth attempting to pull together their scattered company data sources and find out the scale of their problem in order to consider how best to manage the risk. It is a major task to define the losses from crime as opposed to other sources. Is this worth it? For some major companies, the exercise has in fact shown up exactly how much is being lost through crime—and the scope for prevention. A two-year British Telecom study of its losses through crime started with an awareness within the company of a figure less than £10 million per annum. The report to the board after the study showed the losses (including indirect losses) were more on the order of £290 million (see Burrows 1991*a* for a description of this exercise).

A. Within the Company: Risk Management

We have few published case studies of the effects of risk management in individual companies, but major retailers, government, and researchers have collaborated to advise companies how to analyze their crime problems, in order to equip them to produce targeted solutions. The model advocated by researchers, government, and business organizations is similar: in the words of the Confederation of British Industry (CBI), businesses should take action to determine the true cost of crime to their organization and their employees, produce a written strategy on crime prevention that includes the company's attitude to the offense, to offenders, and to victims, and make crime prevention a core responsibility of all managers and staff (CBI 1990, p. 8).

Determining the true cost of crime means doing a crime audit. The CBI/Crime Concern working party delineated this as requiring management to assign clear responsibility and provide appropriate resources; define precisely what it means by a "crime"; obtain relevant information, including comparative data where possible, on the various categories of crime in business; involve employees in the analysis, both to tap their expertise and commitment to tackling a problem that affects them and also to show that it has been taken seriously; and consolidate the findings into a report for the board of directors, thereby providing a clear picture of the cost of crime to their business (CBI 1990, p. 9).

This is the model that has been followed in the more successful attempts by large firms to conduct their own crime analysis (e.g., the major exercise by British Telecom, reported in Burrows [1991*a*]). It is also the kind of exercise carried out under the auspices of the Treadway Commission (1987) to illuminate the nature and causes of fraudulent financial reporting in the United States and is entirely compatible with the recommendations they make to minimize its occurrence. Ekblom (1988), from his work in both residential and retail settings, advocates a similar five-step process: collect good-quality information about crime in the area/company generally, analyze known incidents and see whether they form patterns, devise relevant preventive strategies, implement those strategies, and evaluate the impact of the preventive strategies.

In order to ensure that all types of crime (or risks through crime) are taken into account in doing such an analysis, it is important to develop a typology that allows each company to identify its major risks and to compare those both to the risk for the sector as a whole and the risk to other kinds of commercial, residential, and public premises in the vicinity. This will allow the company (and public agencies, where appropriate) to consider the measures it will take in relation to its own business activities and also cooperative action that might be taken with other nearby premises.

Shapland (1991) has set out a preliminary typology that separates threats to premises (burglary, theft, damage, arson, etc.), crimes related to financial dealings (fraud, etc.), personnel crime (committed directly against employees, such as assault, theft of personal belongings, theft of or from employees' cars), vehicle crime (against vehicles belonging to the company), terrorism and industrial espionage, theft or damage by employees, and health and safety offenses (by the company and by employees). Each of these needs to be analyzed in relation to its effects on the *costs* of the company, on the *viability* of the company, on *employees' morale and performance*, and on the *public*, including customers and consumers.

Most companies do not have the skills and tools in-house to carry out such an analysis (the main reason why they are so slow to appreciate the extent of their losses through crime, and the main reason why so few adopt effective and targeted crime-prevention measures). Very recently, therefore, there have been attempts to help smaller businesses by providing relatively detailed guides (e.g., Crime Concern 1991) and by "cascading" awareness raising, information, and expertise through industry groups and associations. In Britain at least, however, these attempts have been relatively unsuccessful. Most retail-sector managers have few staff and work relatively long hours in the shop, thereby reducing their time and their willingness to attend "events." There are few published and reliable empirical studies of the extent of crime, which allows complacent attitudes to persist. The consultancy sector (for large businesses) and packaged materials like guidebooks and checklists (for managers of small shops) are relatively underdeveloped, so there are few advisers around to help managers carry out such tasks. Crime is still seen as a commercial secret, as described by Burrows

(1991*a*, see above). Many small retail concerns do not belong to any sectoral organization.

Although attitudes are clearly changing in the retail sector—which has been stung by the recession and by some well-publicized examples of crime causing major financial effects on companies in general (such as the effect of major fraud on Ferranti), leading even to bankruptcy or forced takeovers. In some instances, it will take several years for the climate of change now beginning to affect larger concerns to percolate down to smaller ones.

The crime audit described above relates to within-company risks. It needs to be supplemented by analysis of the company's place in relation to the extent of crime affecting other, nearby premises. For example, that shop may not have been subject to armed robbery, or an attempted arson, but if 90 percent of the other shops in the precinct have been so victimized in the past year, it would be highly advisable for that shop to take precautions—and it may be that a cooperative solution may be the most effective (e.g., a temporary private security patrol, joint approach to the police for more police patrolling at night).

For this kind of analysis, however, the company cannot rely on its own resources. The most sensible way to address a crime audit of the neighborhood is to use routinely gathered data collected by others. My colleagues and I have attempted to research and to set out the most useful kinds of data local groups might use to address the problem of formulating neighborhood crime-reduction strategies (Shapland, Wiles, and Wilcox 1994). Our results are very similar to those of an American project also looking at the best strategies for formulating community development crime-reduction plans (Skogan 1992). We found the most crucial data to be detailed mapping of the area, police offense data, brief periods of observation, and small numbers of interviews with aware people in the locality (which included community leaders, church leaders, youth group workers, local police, and shopkeepers themselves).

Progress in crime audits and in risk-management analysis has only reached the stage of starting to set out the best ways to accomplish it and exhorting the retail sector to take these on board. The next, and crucial stage, is to test the effectiveness—and particularly the cost-effectiveness—of the risk-management plans drawn up on the basis of these analyses. They have the potential not only to reduce crime (as several companies have found), but also, more important, to redirect the very substantial sums now being spent on security more effectively.

B. Researching Crime and Crime Prevention in Retailing

The task of a researcher evaluating crime prevention in retailing is similar in its *process* to that of a company addressing the losses caused by crime. We, too, need to gain access to or gather adequate baseline data on the level of crime, to consider whether the crime-prevention initiative has addressed the major problems, to describe the implementation of the initiative, and to evaluate whether it has affected the level of crime and in what ways. The difference is that we are not confined within the boundary of the company's stores and processes. We can choose the kinds of retailers, shops, crimes, and crime-prevention initiatives to survey and evaluate. The only question is whether retailers will allow us the access we need to the time of their staff and, sometimes, to their records, bearing in mind that those records are often financial records, whose disclosure can affect the way in which the company may be viewed by potential shareholders and the market.

The first step has to be to consider what kinds of base data on crime should be used. I explore the results of the studies done so far in Section IV but discuss here first the advantages and disadvantages of using different methods to document crime in retailing. The choice will be dependent on the decisions made in regard to the kinds of crime and crime prevention to be investigated, the sample to be used (including whether crime is to be thought of in terms of companies, premises, or numbers of employees), and the extent to which location and layout are important variables.

The major research decisions are whether one should use already existing data (held by the company or by the police or by insurers), whether one should ask staff about what has happened (crime surveys), or whether an observational prospective method should be employed.

Police data in this field are very partial. Because they are normally locally held, they are also only suitable for a local area study of retailing, rather than exploring the effects of location, for instance, on a national chain. Official statistics commonly do not distinguish between the types of owner of any property taken, or the exact place where the offense occurred. So, for example, neither the English and Wales *Criminal Statistics 1990* (1991), nor their equivalents in the United States distinguish between property crimes committed against individuals in their private dwellings and those in the commercial sector, except for a few historical exceptions. In England and Wales, shoplifting is distinguished from other forms of theft (but employee theft in shops is not so specified). Equally, burglary in a dwelling is distinguished from nonresidential burglary, but all nonresidential premises are lumped together, with manufacturing industry, retailing, and public premises being put together with garden sheds and garages not attached to houses.

The result is that, in order to look at official statistics for retail premises, we have to rely on a few specially commissioned research studies that have painstakingly separated the crime records of such premises from all others (often using manual searches because computer coding of crimes by the police will not include a code for the type of owner). It is now coming to be accepted that one of the biggest limiting factors in the development of targeted crime prevention is the lack of coding for crime-prevention variables on official crime reports and, hence, the difficulty in producing accurate data for small areas or for particular business sectors (Johnston, Shapland, and Wiles 1994; Shapland, Wiles, and Wilcox 1994).

Company data suffer from all the problems of nonreporting and nonrecording of *incidents* that afflict police data, but in terms of *financial data* (the "cost of crime"), they are likely to be far more accurate than staff memories and perceptions. Financial data are the means by which companies themselves control their operations. Financial tracing of sales and loss patterns, and attempts to link them with company procedures and criminal opportunities, are the major weapons employed by companies themselves for crime analysis and crime prevention. Through looking at the returns by different premises, retail chains can see where losses are very different from the average. Through changing certain aspects of security or financial procedures, the effect on management accounts can be seen, and the effectiveness of the procedures judged. Note that, in doing this, companies are working, not in a currency of numbers of crimes, but in one of financial losses, with all the implications for the visibility of different kinds of crimes discussed in Section II (see Buckle et al. [1992] for a comparison of numbers of crimes and financial losses). Offenses with low levels of loss per offense and few separate incidents will have low priority on this measure (physical assault or threats, for instance). There are few examples of this method being used in academic research on crime in the retail sector.

It might be thought that *insurers' records* would be likely to surmount these drawbacks as far as incidents resulting in claims are concerned. However, many major insurers' databases are unfortunately unable to be accessed and analyzed on the basis of how many individual incidents have been the subject of claims by individual premises (and do not necessarily have locational information attached). Insurers are concerned with levels of premiums and claims records for each insured body—and, typically, one chain of retailers will be one insured body. Often, a large insured body will have an agreement to process the details of claims itself if they are below a certain limit, providing only aggregate details to the insurer. If an incident goes above that limit, a loss adjuster may be used—and their report will not be on the database.

For incident-based data (the incidence or prevalence of crime), therefore, there is usually no alternative to tapping the memories of staff (aided by whatever recorded internal incident data are available)—*crime surveys*. Increasingly, this is being done using telephone interviews, rather than face-to-face interviews or postal questionnaires. Each method has its benefits and drawbacks. For each, it is important to introduce the research first by sending a letter, explaining its purpose, its funding, and the kind of sample being used, and discussing confidentiality.

Retailers and business people generally are used to using the *telephone* to discuss business matters, so they do not find telephone interviews strange. In most Western countries, there is also high telephone penetration, especially for retailing (though it is necessary to conduct interviews face-to-face in certain rural regions and in central Europe, as the International Crime Survey has found for residential and personal crime [Zvekic 1993]). Indeed, it may be easier to acquire a telephone database of all the retailing companies and premises in the country than a similar address list, in order to select the sample to be included. In many countries, in fact, there is no list of which companies have premises where, comparable to the lists of residents and houses normally produced for market research and similar reasons. Researchers on retailing have to be prepared to spend long hours walking the streets noting down the names and addresses of companies and gaining some clue as to their activities. Computer-assisted telephone interviewing can also be used: questions are programmed into a computer and shown to the interviewer, with answers being directly recorded. This reduces the scope for coding and routing errors but requires considerable expertise to program correctly and to deal with more open-ended matters. Telephone interviews are typically relatively short (twenty to thirty minutes maximum) and so it is not possible to include lengthy lists of questions or explore detailed perceptions. They are most suited to victimization surveys or surveying crime-prevention precautions (particularly for national or widely spread samples) and can be used for costs *if* companies are prewarned about the information sought and the definitions to be used (e.g., by being provided with a chart, as in the Australian survey [Walker 1994] and the forthcoming International Commercial Crime Survey).

Face-to-face interviews remain the most effective for longer interviews, or where more confidential details are sought, or where it is desired to pool experiences in order to find out different people's perceptions of particular kinds of crime or crime-prevention precautions (group discussion sessions, especially for assaults or threats). They are also useful to "brainstorm" what might be effective in terms of new initiatives and to gauge reaction to new proposals. The drawback is obviously the need for skilled interviewers, the time and travel costs involved, and the resulting costs, both for the research and the respondents. They may still be the best choice for small shops, however, where there are few staff available and where the interview is often conducted at the counter, while customers are being served (see Hibberd and Shapland 1993).

The effectiveness of *postal questionnaires* depends largely on the extent to which the respondent thinks it sufficiently important to devote time to completing the questionnaire. Hence questionnaires that come from obviously important sources and that explain clearly how they will be useful have attracted reasonable response rates (from government or major retailing associations, in terms of finding out the scale of the problem; from local government in terms of proposed crime-prevention plans affecting local areas). Researchers not authorized by such organizations have had more mixed experiences.

In a similar fashion to personal or household crime, we can not only ask victims (companies or employees) about the incidence of crime but also ask potential offenders. *Self-reported delinquency studies* can give us some perspective on the choices offenders make in respect of different kinds of property and in patterns of committing offenses. There is no large-scale recent self-reported delinquency study that has separated out types of target for offenses (e.g., separating burglary of shops from burglary of factories or of houses), but there are again a few specialized research studies on burglars (usually convicted burglars) and shoplifters. The idea of doing research on *patterns of offending* through tracing the output of certain offenders has very considerable potential for crime prevention, but there are only a few examples, notably on credit card fraud (Tremblay 1986; Levi, Bissell, and Richardson 1991).

Observational methods have to date mainly been used in relation to customer theft (following randomly selected customers to see if they steal (e.g., Buckle and Farrington 1984) or systematic repeated counting of tagged items to see if they disappear (e.g., Buckle et al. 1992)). There is no reason, however, why they should not be used to consider neighborhood problems (such as the incidence of vandalism or threats by youths) or why the recent introduction of CCTV could not also be used as an observational tool for research in the retailing environment. Audio or visual identification alarm systems (which enable the alarm station to listen or look at what is happening when an alarm activates) have the same potential. Observational methods, however, require the consent and active participation of the retailers and, in the climate of concern about access and confidentiality discussed in Section II, have proved difficult to arrange in the past, especially if the research is to be published.

IV. The Pattern of Crime in the Retail Sector

In this section, I look first at the incidence and prevalence of crime in the retail sector, nationally and locally, and then turn to studies of the cost of crime.

A. National Crime Surveys of Retailing

There have been only a handful of national studies of businesses' victimization by crime. We need many more. Those now available show that victimization rates for businesses are much higher than those for households.

1. *Early Studies in the United States.* An early pioneer of work on retailing was the survey of crime against small businesses in the United States conducted by Albert J. Reiss, Jr., for the U.S. Senate's Review of Small Business Administration Programs and Policies in 1969 (Reiss 1969; Small Business Administration 1969). With the cooperation of the tax authorities, Reiss contacted a sample of 2,532 businesses selected from 1965 corporate and business tax returns. This was *all* businesses, not just retailers, but he found that, except in "ghetto" areas, retailers experienced about the same magnitude of losses as other businesses (in the ghetto, retailers had significantly worse problems).

His problems in doing the survey illustrate the difficulties of sampling and contacting retailers that have been faced by all researchers since (often not solved with the methodological rigor that Reiss applied—his discussion of the difficulties of determining units for expressing crime against businesses has hardly been added to by subsequent work). His sampling frame was stratified by the type of business ownership (determined by the tax categories, which enabled him to separate sole proprietorships from partnerships and corporations) and by receipts in dollars as reported to the tax authorities (a measure of size in financial terms, normally not available to researchers, who have to rely on numbers of employees or floor area as substitutes). The sampling frame contained 8,039,657 tax returns, and one in every 1,400 was selected for potential interview, which took place in summer 1968. As many as 17 percent of all the 1965 businesses were by that time no longer in business. Another 12 percent could not be contacted because of technical sampling problems or because the name and address was not contactable. Similar problems are being faced in the 1990s in relation to telephone surveys (companies that have folded, moved, or that are not contactable). Interviews were face-to-face, using Small Business Administration personnel from field offices, and it proved difficult to obtain completed interviews. Of the original sample selected from the sampling frame, only 48 percent resulted in completed interviews. The smaller the business, the more difficult it was to obtain an interview.

The survey concentrated on businesses' experience with burglary, robbery, shoplifting, employee theft, bad checks, and vandalism. Both incidence and losses were covered, though the survey found difficulties with shoplifting since "most businesses have no reliable form of inventory control" (Small Business Administration 1969, p. 73). The estimated business burglary prevalence rate for retailers in 1967 (the proportion experiencing one or more burglaries) was 15 percent, ranging from 32 percent in the ghetto (defined as a location whose surrounding area qualified as an "urban slum"), through 20 percent in other parts of the central city and in suburban locations, down to 10 percent in rural locations and towns under 2,500 population. This clearly shows the effect of location (and the surrounding neighborhood). Multiple victimization was common, with the overall burglary rate (all incidents of burglary reported divided by retailers interviewed) being 27 percent. Robbery was a much rarer crime, with 3 percent of businesses reporting they had had one or more robberies (again higher in the ghetto, but here bus and taxi drivers were much more vulnerable than retailers). Property damage was divided into that due to civil disorders or riots and that stemming from other causes. Damage was primarily to glass and external fittings, but costs were certainly not negligible. Seventeen percent of retailers reported damage to glass, 8 percent to fixtures, 7 percent to merchandise, 7 percent to vehicles, and 6 percent to buildings on one or more occasions. Shoplifting rates cover only those premises seen by their owners as susceptible at all to shoplifting (because of merchandise being readily available to customers, according to 85 percent of retailers in the survey). Known incidents of customer theft had afflicted 35 percent of all retailers, with 54 percent having problems with bad checks and 12 percent suffering employee theft. There was relatively little variation by location on any of these rates, with shoplifting in the ghetto only apparently affecting 43 percent of retailers.

Given the date of this survey, there is little point in giving all the cost figures directly, but Reiss also worked out the proportion of crime losses to receipts. For *all* types of business, the total dollar losses from these crimes was $3 billion, but this accounted for only 0.25 percent of receipts. However, small businesses and retail businesses took a disproportionate share of these costs, with 46 percent of total business crime losses falling against retail establishments including higher than average losses on all types of crime.

Aldrich and Reiss (reported in Small Business Administration 1969, app. B) also did a follow-up survey of small businesses in eight high-crime areas in three cities over two years, with particular reference to the effects of civil disorder and riot. Of 800 establishments surveyed in 1966, 659 remained to be resurveyed in 1968, with a 66 percent success rate in obtaining the second interviews. The areas had shown continuing decline over this period, and it was found that the crime rate of an area affected the rate of business survival. Retail establishments were the most vulnerable. Civil disorders and riots affected both loss and survival prospects, with again the majority who suffered damage or looting being retailers (97 out of 111, with 24 percent overall suffering some material loss or damage from the disorder). These are all important findings and badly need replication and further study today.

Work in the United States continued with the National Crime Survey surveying businesses, including retailers, until 1977 (reported in the annual *Sourcebook of Criminal Justice Statistics* sponsored by the U.S. Bureau of Justice Statistics), but unfortunately we do not have any recent national data from the United States. Given changes in overall crime rates and in patterning of types of crime since then, as well as changes in the retail environment, this is a major gap in our knowledge.

2. *Recent National Surveys: The Netherlands and Australia.* The only countries for which recent national overviews of the different kinds of crime that may affect the retail sector exist in published form are the

Netherlands and Australia. At the time of writing, however, an International Commercial Crime Survey organized from the Ministry of Justice in the Netherlands is in the field, with results expected by the end of 1994. Using the same questionnaire and a telephone survey method, it will cover retailing in the Netherlands, England and Wales, Germany, and small samples in France and other European countries, as well as manufacturing and some other types of business. Face-to-face interviews will take place in Hungary.

The Netherlands undertook a survey of companies in nine business sectors in 1989, asking them whether they had been the victim of crime during 1988 (van Dijk and van Soomeron 1990). This was a telephone survey, using the national business database of business premises. The business premises were taken as the unit, with results weighted up over that sector and size of business nationally, to show the overall vulnerability and cost of crime to companies nationally, according to the same database. Four different types of "external crime" (crime likely to have been committed by those not employed by the company) were covered: vandalism, burglary, theft, and "menaces" (threats, assaults). Table 1 shows the percentage of companies who said they had been the victim of one of these external crimes at least once in 1988.

It is immediately clear that, at least in the Netherlands, the crime risk of all sections of industry was considerable—and that it varied significantly by sector. For external crimes, retailing (both food and nonfood) is in a high-risk group of sectors for external crime, with over

TABLE 1

Percentage of Companies Who Had Been the Victim of an "External Crime" in the Netherlands in 1988, by Sector

Sector	Vandalism	Burglary	Theft	Menaces	Total
Industry	16	18	13	3	31
Construction	15	13	8	4	30
Wholesale	22	14	10	1	35
Car repair	28	26	12	15	45
Food retailing	24	20	14	2	42
Nonfood retailing	21	27	14	10	48
Hotel and catering	36	17	12	20	48
Transport	16	16	10	5	32
Business services	24	27	9	11	48
Total	23	21	13	8	42

SOURCE.—Van Dijk and van Soomeron (1990).

40 percent of the companies sampled (209) falling victim to at least one kind of external crime (a similar picture, though with much higher rates, than in the earlier U.S. work). Multiple victimization was common, with a company falling victim to external crime on average being affected on eight occasions per year. Theft and menaces were the most common repeated offenses, as would be expected. Although there was a clear connection between the size of the company and the likelihood of its victimization, there seemed to be no correlation between its location and the likelihood of victimization, with small and large cities giving similar results. For retailers, theft was the most costly crime overall, with burglary not far behind. The total cost in 1988 over the whole retail sector in the Netherlands was estimated to be f 540 million (spread over 121,500 establishments), with vandalism contributing f 85 million; burglary, f 186 million; theft f 220 million; "menaces," f 4 million; and arson, f 42 million. Although arson was rare, the cost per incident was high. (f = guilders; as of June 5, 1994, there were f 1.86 to $1.)

The study also considered "internal crime" (crime committed by the company's own employees). A victimization survey is not the ideal way to find out about internal crime (which really needs an in-depth investigation of the procedures and financial records of the company, employing financial tracing methods and possibly supplemented by other means such as confidential interviews with employees or surveillance). The results are, therefore, clearly just the tip of the iceberg but are the only industrywide study that exists. Companies were asked about vandalism and sabotage by employees (willful damage to company property); the appropriation of money, securities, or both through fraud, theft, and embezzlement; the appropriation of company property through theft or embezzlement of supplies, materials, and stocks; and industrial espionage (the theft or sale of company information). The latter is, of course, not always a criminal offense in all countries (though it is a major worry for several sectors).

Most companies professed themselves to be not very well informed as to the scale of internal crime being committed by their employees. Retailing, however, seemed to be at relatively low risk in this area, with 10 percent of companies surveyed saying they had been victimized in 1988 (15 percent for food retailing). The overall cost for the retailing sector in the Netherlands was estimated at f 58 million. This was low, both in frequency and in cost, in comparison with hotels and catering (21 percent), and the overall losses for retailing, particularly food retailing, were much lower than for construction, wholesaling, and hotels and catering. The kinds of internal crime uncovered were largely relatively simple crimes to commit, such as stealing cash from tills and stealing stock. Fraud was relatively rarely reported. As far as this study could uncover, therefore, the retailing sector in the Netherlands was more at risk from external crime than from internal crime.

The figures in table 1 may give the impression that crime in the retail sector is not necessarily a significant problem. If less than half the establishments surveyed were the victims of a crime in one year, and given that much of this is shoplifting, then how does it compare with other crime risks? Van Dijk and van Soomeron have used other studies by the Ministry of Justice and other ministries in the Netherlands to compare the risk and costs of crime in the commercial sector overall with those for other kinds of victims (the national victimization survey of individuals/households, for example). Looking first at the scale of criminal activity, their calculations indicate that the proportion of the overall number of offenses being committed against the public sector (central and local government, utilities) was 9 percent, those against private individuals were 37 percent, and those against the commercial sector overall were a staggering 55 percent (van Dijk and van Soomeron 1990). In other words, businesses were the victims of 55 percent of offenses committed in the Netherlands. Translating this into cost terms, the overall cost of "frequent crime" (the kinds asked about in victimization surveys) fell 17 percent on the public sector (6 percent on central government, 11 percent on local authorities, including educational establishments, and less than 1 percent on public corporations), 33 percent on private individuals, and 50 percent on businesses. In 1988 the overall cost of "frequent crime" in the Netherlands was at least f 8,190 million. Given that the retail sector has a higher crime risk than many, this indicates that crime in retailing is a very significant problem indeed, both in terms of the losses to companies and, from the perspective of the state, in terms of the proportion of criminal events in the commercial (and retailing) sector.

In September 1991, a similar victimization survey (with identical methodology) was carried out for a bigger sample of retail establishments in the Netherlands (about 1,000 retail shop owners, covering almost 2,000 establishments) in order to be able to specify further the extent of the crime risk among different kinds of shops (van Dijk and van Soomeron 1992). The survey covered theft (of stock and of money), burglary, graffiti, other forms of vandalism, robbery, and threats to employees (a larger selection of offenses than the previous survey, so the surveys are not directly comparable on overall crime risk).

It found that 63 percent of the shops had been the victim of at least one of these offenses during the one-year period. Theft of merchandise was the most common complaint (48 percent), with burglary (19 percent), graffiti (14 percent), other damage (14 percent), and theft of money (10 percent) also being significant. Robbery (2 percent) and threats (7 percent) were relatively rare. About 65 percent of the burglaries were attempts.

The cost figures are not entirely in line with the frequency figures. Estimating up to the total size of the retail sector in the Netherlands, the total cost of crime in one year was f 1,400 million (at that time $790 million). Theft of stock contributed f 500 million; burglary, f 450 million; theft of money, f 190 million; other damage, f 91 million; robbery, f 21 million; graffiti, f 19 million; and threats, a relatively small monetary loss. However, 20 percent of the threats were quite serious, with physical violence and a weapon being used.

The risk varied by the kind of shop. Merchandise carrying a higher risk included department stores, office stationers, and shops selling household appliances (including electrical and electronic goods).

We can compare these results with those from the First Australian National Survey of Crime against Businesses (Walker 1994), which used similar methods to the forthcoming International Commercial Crime Study (a telephone survey of a random sample of businesses stratified by sector and size, culled from the main national index of business premises). The sectors covered were retail food (184 respondents), retail other (210 respondents), primary industry (agriculture/mining, 187 respondents), tourism and recreation (179 respondents), and manufacturing (206 respondents). The size bands were 1–10 staff, 11–49 staff (11–99 for manufacturing), and 50+ staff (100+ for manufacturing). The samples are of course small, and the grossed up figures provided in the report need treating with caution. The unit was the premises. It was found that 38 percent of food retailers had been victims of burglary in 1992; with 20 percent being victims of vandalism; 1 percent of thefts of vehicles; 4 percent of thefts from vehicles; 35 percent of known incidents of thefts by customers, employees, or anyone else from the premises (23 percent customer theft, 11 percent employee theft); 5 percent of frauds by employees; 17 percent of other kinds of fraud (including check and credit card fraud); 4 percent of

robberies; 17 percent of assaults on employees; 1 percent of bribery/
extortion—and only 29 percent had no victimization by these offenses
at all in 1992. Equivalent figures for the nonfood sector were 26 percent
for burglary, 24 percent for vandalism, 4 percent for theft of vehicles,
7 percent thefts from vehicles, 43 percent thefts from premises (37
percent customer theft, 7 percent employee theft), 1 percent employee
fraud, 27 percent other fraud, 2 percent robberies, 12 percent employees assaulted, 1 percent bribery/extortion, and 31 percent suffering no
victimization of these types. Businesses with more staff were more
likely to suffer from almost all these crimes than were smaller businesses (an opposite finding from that of Reiss).

It is difficult to make comparisons from studies stemming from such
diverse countries and times—but it is quite clear both that retail victimization is high (we would be extremely worried if our average national
residential burglary rate reached 37 percent, the figure for small food
retailers in Australia) and that there are potentially substantial differences by type of goods sold and by location. We badly need more
national studies with reasonably large samples to understand this
variation.

B. The Pattern of Crime in Small Shops in England

At the other end of the scale, there are a number of smaller English
studies that have looked at particular areas of cities or at particular
companies. There are a small number of studies on small neighborhood
stores ("corner shops," or small shops generally) that have concentrated
on large towns (London, the West Midlands/Birmingham area) and
one published study of a shopping precinct. We also have good data
from one large retail chain, Dixons, which sells electronic high-value
goods (stereos, computers, calculators, video cameras). Dixons has set
up its own database and has made public the overall results.

Ekblom and Simon (1988) surveyed 240 grocery and news agent
stores with not more than two service tills (corner shops or neighborhood stores) in four areas of London and asked their managers or
owners about a range of "external crime." This included theft, robbery, till snatches, violence and threats, damage, burglary, disputes
with customers, abuse, and arson. They found that shopkeepers in
their areas were predominantly Asian, and the figures they give are
for this group only (which, nonetheless, constituted between 69 percent and 90 percent of shopkeepers in the four areas). Again the unit
was the premises.

The overall victimization risk in this kind of shop was very high. Eighty percent had experienced one or more of these offenses during their tenure of the shop, with many experiencing crime several times a year, a quarter even daily. In contrast to most residents' experience of crime, shopkeepers can regard it, not just as a common event, but as a continuous occurrence. The most prevalent offenses were theft of stock/shoplifting (54 percent ever, 39 percent a few times a year, 28 percent daily, figures not exclusive), window smashing (33 percent ever, 9 percent a few times a year), threatening behavior (28 percent ever, 25 percent a few times a year, 3 percent daily), verbal abuse (27 percent ever, 13 percent daily), till snatches (24 percent ever, 11 percent a few times a year), and burglary (22 percent within the past year). The results show that shopkeepers' experiences of crime were extremely varied, with some seeming to be immune from crime and some finding it very common. Nonetheless, these are high rates of victimization, higher than those from the overall Netherlands sample, with the rates of threats and abuse being particularly greater.

If we turn to the more serious, but rarer, forms of crime, the Asian shopkeepers from London reported very significant rates of violent and potentially violent crime. As shown above, around a quarter had experienced a till snatch, and several many till snatches. Seventeen percent had experienced a robbery (5 percent a few times a year). Fourteen percent had been assaulted (9 percent a few times a year). It is not surprising, given this rate of violent crime, and the likelihood of multiple victimization, that 21 percent of shopkeepers said that they worried "a lot" about crime.

There were some relationships between the type of shop and the kind of crime. Shops selling alcohol had more disputes about credit and more check fraud. The few shops that contained sub-post offices had a disproportionate amount of threats and robberies but little theft or till snatches (due to the nature of the goods and the layout of the shops).

We can compare the results from this study with one that focused on violent crime (although all other victimization was also studied) for all small shops with two tills or less in one area of London and one area of the West Midlands (both of which were densely populated and relatively poor areas but not the most deprived inner-city areas; see Hibberd and Shapland 1993). It showed again relatively high rates of violent crime—both serious crime, such as robbery, and lesser serious behaviors, such as continuing argumentativeness—and verbal abuse. The shopkeepers were again predominantly Asian, though the study covered all racial groups. In the past year, 17–26 percent of shopkeepers had had a robbery (figures for both areas are given), and 9–13 percent had had the till snatched. The level of general abuse was high: 26–36 percent indicated general violence or argumentativeness from customers; 22–47 percent, abuse from drunk or disturbed people (depending on the location of the shop compared to mental health facilities); 24–25 percent, racial abuse; 11 percent, threats; 11 percent, customers arguing or fighting among themselves; and 29–36 percent, customers shoplifting so openly that they were effectively daring the shopkeeper to intervene (and then to be assaulted). However, the level of actual physical assault was low (4 percent in both areas), although 17–21 percent of shopkeepers had had trouble apprehending shoplifters. These figures for violent crime compared with 7–16 percent who had been burglarized. Although ordinary shoplifting was very common (and not specifically measured in the study), other forms of crime, such as damage, were rare.

The offenders in both small shops studies were predominantly young. Those committing the robberies and till snatches in the Hibberd and Shapland (1993) study were usually on their own, often quite nervous, and a majority of the robberies involved weapons, usually knives, though occasionally guns. The abuse, quarreling, and fighting tended to involve groups of youngsters who would regularly visit the shop and plague the shopkeeper. There was great variation in shopkeepers' experience of these forms of violence, but it was clear that, for shopkeepers who were "picked on" by these groups of youths, the effect was as serious or more serious than for those who were victims of robbery. For these small shops, the effect of crime was measured more by wear and tear on the shopkeeper than direct effects in terms of monetary loss, although, as we shall see in Section V below, the cost of security measures taken against burglary and shoplifting was quite high.

C. England, the United States, and the Netherlands: The Shopping Precinct

We have three published case studies of crime and nuisance in shopping precincts or shopping centers: these were complexes of shops rented from a landlord and situated alongside or around semipublic space often patrolled by private security guards. All were in the city center of large cities, with the shopping precinct separated from the public road and pavements. These projects undertook a period of crime analysis in order to implement crime-prevention measures following feelings of rising crime and disorder.

The English center had 190 businesses in it, the tenants of which were sent questionnaires (Phillips and Cochrane 1988). As Phillips and Cochrane note, there are many groups of users of such shopping precincts, all of whom can be victims, and all of whom can be offenders. They include the management of the center, security personnel, police, tenants of the businesses, young people, and shoppers. Crime-management policy for such a center has to include the problem of creating a social order that has a place in it for all these groups and that, at least minimally, recognizes and respects their various needs in that space. The Phillips and Cochrane study, as reported to date, has concentrated on the tenants, management, police, and security—but there will be crime problems affecting the shoppers and young people as well.

Security staff in the precinct logged all incidents over a four-week period, revealing sixty-eight crimes, broadly defined, and 644 "nuisances" (such as loitering, misbehavior, disorder, fighting, glue sniffing, and members of the public being found in private areas). One hundred of the 190 tenants (shop managers) responded to a questionnaire, revealing at least 280 criminal or potentially criminal incidents of theft, using stolen credit cards, violence, or harassment in the previous month. For both groups, theft was the most numerous problem, with many more incidents of theft by the public than by staff being reported. For example, eighteen incidents of shoplifting were reported to security staff, thirty-one shoplifters were arrested by the police, and tenants reported arresting seventy-one shoplifters themselves. It is quite clear from the findings that tenants' policies on reporting shoplifters to other agencies varied significantly, as did their security policies and activities to catch them. Although youths were the largest group involved in incidents of any sort, only a very small proportion of the youths using the center were in any way associated with any incident of crime or nuisance. The management, security, and tenants' beliefs that the groups of youths using the center were loitering to commit thefts was not borne out by the analysis of incidents. Similarly, although the groups of youths complained about substantially involved groups of black or Asian youths, they were only minimally involved in incidents of theft.

In the English shopping center, therefore, the crime problems isolated were theft (primarily shoplifting, with some theft from cars in the car park attached to the center) and violence to and harassment of staff. Burglary and damage were minimal, reflecting the enclosed nature of the premises and the patrolling security presence when it was open.

The U.S. study is the case of Tysons Corner, a shopping center in northern Virginia, where the security records were examined by Sherman (1992). The advantage of this study is the comparison made between incidents occurring and the population at risk and its focus on crime relevant to customers, as opposed to crime relevant to retailers. Tysons Corner received more than fourteen million visitors annually, with an average of about 4,200 at any one time. Robberies from *customers* were perceived by the management as being potentially the most significant problem, though in the twenty-two months ending with October 1992, when the records were examined, it was found there were only eighteen robbery victims out of more than twenty-five million visits. Other criminal incidents also seemed at a relatively low level: ten cars being stolen in 1991, and sixty-one fights, assaults, and indecent assaults during the first ten months of 1991. Sherman concludes that the worry by customers about serious violent crime is not borne out by the actual levels, given the population at risk.

Staff, however, are at risk for longer periods, and it is interesting to juxtapose the figures from recent U.S. studies of workplace violence. Looking first at homicide, Davis (1987; Davis, Honchar, and Suarez 1987) has reviewed Texas death certificates for civilian men and women between 1975 and 1984. Of the 779 workplace male deaths, 81 percent were caused by firearms. Taxi drivers had the highest risk (seventy-eight per 100,000 per year), but gasoline station attendants (fourteen per 100,000 per year) and food store clerks (twelve per 100,000 per year) were also significantly at risk. Women gasoline station attendants had the same risk rates as men, though their risk in food stores was lower (four per 100,000 per year). Gasoline station employees were also picked out as having high homicide and injury rates in the Hales et al. (1988) study of Ohio workers' compensation scheme claims from 1983–85. Grocery store employees, specifically those working in convenience stores (together with real estate employees), suffered the most reported rapes.

The Dutch study (van Soomeron 1989) was spurred by tenants' worries about groups of youths congregating in the shopping precinct and, as tenants believed, worrying and disturbing customers, though there were no records of numbers of incidents of threats, and so forth (although figures did exist on vandalism, burglary, etc.). The first tactic tried was to use relatively harsh and repressive police measures. The problems increased because the youngsters reacted in a more aggressive way and some started to come to the shopping center hoping to have a "good fight with the cops." In 1984, after the establishment of a working group involving local and district authorities, the town youth association, shopkeepers, police, and the town crime-prevention bureau, a coordinated action plan was created. Strict (but reasonable) rules for what the youths could and could not do (without intervention by the police) were published by the police and widely disseminated. A case worker was appointed by the town youth association, and a place within the shopping center was cleared for her activities, where youngsters could have a cup of coffee and talk about their problems. Some "dropouts" went back to school, and employment was found for some older youths (in some cases in the shopping center itself!). As a result, the major crime problems of vandalism, shoplifting, and perceived aggression/threats (to shoppers and shopkeepers) decreased, with vandalism in that center reducing by some £10,000 in the next year and shoplifting decreasing below the normal rate in the Netherlands. In this study, the interest is not only in the imaginative interagency response to the center's problems but in the determination to specify the relevant crime problems and to evaluate the progress of the initiative as well.

D. The Cost of Crime: The U.K. National Database and Big Retail Chains

I referred earlier to the difficulties of persuading the larger retailers to allow research on their records, when that research is to be made publicly available, and particularly when it involves access to financial records (as opposed to incident-based surveys). One notable exception has been the recent setting up of the British Retail Consortium's (1994) *Retail Crime Initiative*. This involved a postal survey of companies (not premises), asking them for the cost of certain specified crimes. The data received are being transformed into a database with ongoing input from retailers, which is seeking to create a comprehensive continuing picture of the cost of crime, with the consortium's researchers working with the companies to refine the definitions used so that they become absolutely comparable (a very important issue in relation to shrinkage, in particular).

The initial postal survey drew responses from companies with over 54,000 outlets, with a combined turnover of £62 billion, and accounting for 44 percent of total U.K. retail sales. The responses were, however, biased strongly toward the major retailers (chains, groups, and big stores) and, although some smaller trade associations (such as pharmacists) participated, experiences must be seen to be strongly weighted toward those of bigger companies. Equally, responses were provided on the basis of data notified to company records and, as Section II demonstrated, certain kinds of incidents (particularly assaults and threats) are less likely to be reported to regional or national security managers. The survey covered detected crime incidents of burglary, theft by customers, criminal damage, arson, robbery, violence against staff, theft by staff, and terrorist incidents (bombs, bomb hoaxes). Incidents involving property were expressed as a proportion of outlets or premises surveyed; incidents involving violence were expressed as a proportion of numbers of staff; and cash was reported as a proportion of turnover. The figures given below have been extrapolated up to the full year for the industry as a whole *nationally* and are expressed as incidence figures (the total number of incidents divided by the number of outlets, etc.).

The importance of the survey lies in its cost figures, since these were derived from probably the most accurate source, company records, but the incident figures are also given, for comparison with other studies. The gross cost of burglary in 1992–93 was £331 million (£231 million loss of stock, £62 million repair costs, and £39 million consequential losses), giving an average loss per burglary incident of £683 loss of stock (the bias toward large outlets is clear here). Only 3 percent was subsequently recovered, giving a net burglary loss figure of £332 million, compared to £461 million for all recorded residential burglaries in England and Wales in 1991. The incidence rate for burglary was high, at fifty-seven per hundred retail premises, with grocery stores; those in the electrical, gas, and music sectors; do-it-yourself and hardware stores; and confectioners, tobacconists, and news agents having the highest risks. In comparison, the gross value of stock *recorded* as stolen *by customers* (shoplifting) was only £105.8 million (detected incidents); the gross value of criminal damage was £47 million (fifty-four incidents per hundred retail outlets in the year, but clearly each incident has a much lower average value than for burglary); the gross loss for arson (counted separately from criminal damage) was £26 million (one incident per hundred outlets); the gross loss for robbery was £24 million (six incidents per hundred outlets); the gross loss for fraud by staff in detected incidents was £11 million (no risk figure given); the gross loss *falling on retailers* for check, payment card, and other frauds was £22 million (the loss to the financial institutions in 1992 was £129 million where the place of misuse was a retail store); and the gross loss from terrorism was as much as £53 million (including consequential loss from lost trading—there were 7,098 incidents of terrorism related to retail outlets). In relation to such incident-based crime, burglary was clearly the major threat in cost terms and in incident terms, with many incidents of criminal damage also being reported, but with a much lower average cost. The amount of check and credit card loss falling on retail businesses is perhaps lower than many would expect.

If we look at shrinkage, however, the average shrinkage level was 1.18 percent of total sales at retail prices, grossing up to an industry shrinkage total of £1,745,236 million. Different sectors of the retail trade, however, have different conventions in defining shrinkage. Some include losses from damaged or wasted stock (passed sell-by date, etc.), and some do not. Companies were asked to estimate the amount of shrinkage attributable to crime—this was thought to be 57 percent. Unrecorded staff crime was thought to total £411 million and unrecorded customer theft £545 million, with £21 million attributable to vendor fraud. Shrinkage is a purely stock-based measure, and retailers also suffered from unexplained cash losses, which totaled £194 million, with 47 percent attributed to crime.

As well as these global figures from the British Retail Consortium, we also have some published figures from Dixons PLC, which operates primarily in the electrical/electronic sector and which we can use as a case study. In 1988, senior management from Dixons commented that the first prerequisite for effective management of losses through crime was recognition of the problem (Andrews and Burrows 1989). This needed to be recognition not only of the extent of loss recorded by systems within the company but also of unreported loss. Equally, it was important to consider losses, not just against turnover, but as against profit. This reflects the economic reality that, for theft, the business has lost not only the margin, handling charges and similar overheads, but the cost price itself. They quoted an estimate that, for retailing generally, losses were running at around 1–2 percent of turnover but that this equated to around 25 percent of profit (crime losses compared to overall profit levels before tax, noting that profit is much lower than markup of stock between retail and delivery price because of the operating costs involved). This figure of 25 percent is very similar to the 24 percent estimate in the Touche Ross (1992) shrinkage survey (which ranges from 195 percent to just under 0.7 percent of net profit before tax), where shrinkage was 1.09 percent of turnover (ranging from 4 percent to just under 0.1 percent). At this stage, Dixons had recently set up a computerized recording database for all criminal incidents (Burrows 1988).

In 1992, Dixons was losing 1–1½ percent of sales (or £12 million–£18 million) a year from the theft or unexplained disappearance of stock (Hosking 1992). The fastest growing component of theft was burglary by nonemployees—around £3 million at retail prices each year. As the group managing director commented: "Every night, somebody somewhere is trying to break into a Dixons or Currys store." Dixons is clearly taking the potential losses due to crime seriously: "If there's one message we want to get out, it's that a lot of people are underestimating retail crime and its explosive threat, both to business and to the fabric of society."

In another study done in 1990, Dixons surveyed the nature of violence to staff in its stores (Bushell et al. 1990) following the discovery in a limited survey in 1989 (Burrows 1991*b*) that around eight times as many incidents of threats and physical violence were occurring as were being reported to company security. The aim was to consider how best to respond to such incidents, rather than to measure their prevalence, and hence the sampling base was the incidents of violence recorded by the company's security department. Fifty-three victims of violence or abuse were interviewed. Defining violence is very difficult, and it is hard to know whether to include threats and abuse, though staff perceptions are often that threats and routine abuse are more unnerving than isolated incidents of physical violence (Hibberd and Shapland 1993). In the United Kingdom, threats and abuse would now be investigated as well as physical violence, on health and safety grounds. Forty-three percent of the incidents had occurred in relation to theft by customers, with 15 percent related to fraud (e.g., when a customer tries to use a stolen credit card). However, a significant number of incidents were associated with customers wishing to exchange items, obtain refunds, have goods repaired, or make complaints. They were, therefore, related to company policy on such matters. Forty-four percent of the incidents were threats, and 19 percent verbal abuse, but 36 percent involved physical contact.

It should not be concluded that Dixons is in any way unusual among retail companies in relation to its crime profile. Marks & Spencer, a larger retailer, primarily of clothing, for example, estimates that it loses nearly £60 million a year from unaccounted loss, more than half of which is thought to be from shoplifting (Hosking 1992). Equally, the overall incidence of violence to retail staff shows up in victimization surveys of individuals and householders, which allows classification of occupations by their risk of victimization (Mayhew, Elliott, and Dowds 1989; Phillips, Stockdale, and Joeman 1989; Skogan 1990; see also the U.S. homicide studies mentioned in the section on shopping malls). All these studies show that employees in the retail sector have an above average risk of suffering violence at work because they fall squarely within the categories of having considerable contact with a cross section of the public and work in a relatively unstructured environment. Several studies have noted the influence of conflict situations (such as refunds) on the incidence of violence.

E. The Crime Profile of Retailing

When the results discussed above are compared with the kinds of studies proposed in Sections I–III, it can clearly be seen that there are considerable holes in the research coverage in this area. We have national surveys for only a very few countries, compared to the extent of household and personal crime surveys, and our cost data come from very few sources, although those sources provide relatively uniform results. What is more problematical, we do not have a systematic profile of retailing crime according to location, layout, and type of goods, although the case studies done in different locations on different types of premises indicate clearly that there is such variation.

To summarize the results discussed above, it is necessary to make a number of large conceptual leaps to cover the considerable holes in the research coverage in this area. Readers will be able to judge for themselves whether they agree, from the detailed results reported above. We can tentatively conclude that:

The major *volume* crime problems affecting retail premises are burglary, theft (shoplifting by customers and theft by employees), criminal damage, and violence to staff.

In *cost* terms, retailers are suffering losses equivalent to 1–2 percent of turnover (which may be 20–25 percent of profits). These stem mainly from burglary and (often unrecorded as a detected incident) theft (since the loss in credit card fraud falls mainly on the credit card company).

However, exposure to property crime varies significantly by the location of the premises and, to some extent, by the type of goods sold.

Shops in enclosed shopping precincts have low risks of burglary (since they have considerable protection out of shopping hours), whereas stores in isolated out-of-town shopping centers and industrial parks are considerably at risk. Small "corner shops" appear to have risks midway between the two.

Shops selling high-value consumables are more at risk of theft and burglary, compared to food stores.

There is a serious risk of violence to staff in all retail premises, but (at least in Europe) this stems mainly from robbery and till snatches and from threats and general harassment, rather than from physical assault per se. Conflict situations (such as apprehending shoplifters, apprehending fraudulent users of credit cards, and disputes over refunds, etc.) produce one set of circumstances in which violence can occur—and these may be the major sources in bigger stores and in large chains. Shopping precincts (security staff) and small neighborhood stores may, however, be the target of generalized aggression by groups of young people and disturbed/drunk people. Some of this, in certain societies, has racial overtones.

The amount of property crime affecting retail premises is higher overall than that affecting domestic premises. From the English and the Dutch studies and the earlier U.S. work, the average *burglary* rate for shops not in shopping precincts is far higher than that for houses. If one-in-five or one-in-four English or Dutch houses were being burgled every year, many several times, there would be a considerable political outcry. It could be argued that, as a proportion of the property put at risk, the rates are more comparable (since some shops will clearly contain a greater value of property)—but here we need to consider from what viewpoint or perspective we wish to think about crime risks. As discussed in Section II, an opportunity or routine activity theorist would focus on property at risk. In terms of effects on individuals and effects on communities, however, the unit would need to be premises and households *or* staff plus customers aware of the burglary versus residents plus friends. We do not have enough research to know the comparative emotional impact of retail burglary when compared with residential burglary (though the impact on small shopkeepers is certainly considerable—see Hibberd and Shapland 1993). Given the greater visibility of retail burglary than residential burglary on communities, and the effect of crime on survival of retailers (Reiss 1969), the impact on communities is likely to be higher than that of residential burglary. The rate of robbery of small shops (equivalent or sometimes even higher than that for burglary) is obviously considerably higher than for residential premises.

Our lack of knowledge of the crime patterns of the rest of the commercial sector almost parallels that for retail premises. We do have, however, a major survey of manufacturing and wholesaling premises on industrial estates over the North of England (Shapland et al. 1991), together with data from a number of companies in the service sector (as well as the Dutch victimization survey described in table 1). From this it is possible to conclude that manufacturing premises as well may have higher crime rates than residential premises—but that their crime profile is very different from that of the retail sector (see Shapland [1991] for a summary of the crime profiles of the different sectors and a classification of their targets). Manufacturing and wholesaling premises suffer primarily from burglary, with smaller amounts of damage and theft (theft from and of vehicles, and theft of stock where the stock is consumer goods, such as clothing or electrical goods). They also worry considerably about the (real, though low) risk of arson. The risk of violence is extremely low, but the amount of theft by employees depends considerably on the goods being made (automobile, furniture, and clothing plants, e.g., have the potential for considerable theft, whereas component manufacturers usually do not make goods that are attractive targets).

However, the existence of these large surveys (as yet lacking for retailing) allows us to consider whether there is a significant variation in crime between geographical areas, as well as possibly between types of premises. We know that there is significant variation in residential crime rates between even small neighboring areas (Bottoms and Wiles 1986; Skogan 1991). Is this true of the commercial sector, at least for manufacturing and wholesaling?

The North of England survey of predominately manufacturing and wholesaling companies (with some retail "factory shops") compared the significance of geographical, locational, design, crime prevention, and policing factors in predicting crime rates for 585 businesses on forty-one industrial estates (Shapland et al. 1991). The sample of estates was stratified according to the number of units on them and by region, with 400 units to be drawn randomly from estates owned by the major development landlord using public money (English Estates: response rate, 85 percent) and a matching sample of 200 from those owned by other owners in the same town (as judged by the town council; response rate, 74 percent). Interviews were face-to-face with the manager of the unit, with the researchers also carrying out a site survey of the physical characteristics of the estate and the units. Victimization rates were calculated per unit and as an average rate per estate. It was found that the risk of victimization varied at least as much as it does for residential areas in England. On the best estate, units were likely to be victimized once every eight years, on average, whereas, on the worst, a unit was likely to be victimized five times each year (on the average, a unit would be victimized slightly less than once a year). The average rate of victimization was twice that for individual dwellings in residential areas (comparing the data with the British Crime Survey; see Mayhew, Elliott, and Dowds 1989). It is not possible to give a comparison taking into account the value of the property at risk. Using multivariate analysis, the industrial estate design, the estate layout, and the nature of the surrounding area were found to be significantly related to the estate's crime rate, but the crime-prevention precautions taken by units and policing showed few significant relationships. It is interesting that Reiss's (1969) early work on commercial crime, including retailing, in the United States also found no relationship between crime-prevention precautions taken and victimization rates (though he was not able to carry out such multivariate analysis). In the U.K. study, crime rates in the surrounding area, and the kind of buildings (or open space) near the estate thus seemed significantly to affect victimization on the estate (particularly burglary). Crime-prevention precautions taken by managers did not seem to be related well to the risks they ran or the likely predators—in particular, the installation of alarm systems was not correlated with the crime rate.

We have no reason to suppose that similar results in relation to design, layout, and geographical location will not pertain to retail premises (Brantingham, Brantingham, and Wong [1990] make the same point). Indeed, the small shops survey by Hibberd and Shapland (1993) found that shopkeepers' reports of victimization tallied well with local factors (such as preferred offending patterns by local youth, and local facilities attracting particular kinds of people). Informal evidence from some large chain store security managers would also support a locational and geographic effect for victimization.

The conclusions we can draw from the above review are that, first, we cannot try to produce crime-prevention packages for the commercial field as a whole, and, second, effective crime-prevention strategies will need to take into account locational and geographic factors, as well as the type of merchandise sold. It is quite possible that it may be helpful to take solutions developed in one sector, whose risk from that type of crime is high, and apply them in another sector. So, for example, the precautions against burglary developed for manufacturing industry or wholesaling on industrial estates may benefit retailers setting up in out-of-town locations. However, in general, it will be essential for preventive strategies to be designed to fit that particular sector's crime risks and needs.

V. Preventing the Different Types of Crime That Affect Retail Premises

The reader may be wondering why so much of this essay is devoted to delineating the crime problem in the retail sector, rather than addressing preventive solutions. The reason is that effective prevention requires targeted solutions. In the residential field, the pattern of crime is relatively well known. The state of development of crime prevention has therefore passed beyond working out what the crime profile to be addressed is, and how one might take action, to considering the results of evaluations of that action.

The position in the retail sector, and indeed throughout the commercial sector, is quite different. A large number of preventive strategies and devices have been put in place (costing a great deal of money—e.g., the respondents to the British Retail Consortium [1994] survey had spent £370 million in the 1992–93 year, against losses of £1,999 million as a result of crime). The consequence of the secrecy that has surrounded data gathering on crime, and the relative lack of crime analysis throughout the sector (except in some large companies), has, however, meant that measures have often been put in place without regard to the actual crime problem and certainly without any evaluation of their effects. Crime prevention in the retail sector, particularly for small retailers, has largely proceeded on the stable door accretion model: preventive action is taken after a crime has occurred, to prevent that particular kind of occurrence, and is added on to previous attempts at prevention, thereby providing an uncoordinated historical patchwork of preventive measures. It is now the case that some of the larger companies have taken a more informed and long-term look at risk management in general, and crime prevention in particular—but, as we have seen, they tend to wish to keep what they consider their more successful innovations to themselves.

This is a short-sighted policy. If crime risk is often affected more by the location of the store (both in terms of store type, and of geographical location) than by the type of business, then no one company can by itself produce a successful crime-prevention plan. It simply will not have the data on crime trends in that area or for that type of store. Crime prevention may need to be designed in terms of a package for all the different stores in a precinct, or a row, or an out-of-town estate, rather than for all the premises a company has throughout the country. The traditional company hierarchical management process may actively work against effective prevention, when what may be needed is encouragement to local managers to cope with their local crime patterns in consultation with the police, or the landlord of the precinct, or a multiagency local group, or a local association of stores, supported by the company's expertise at risk analysis and its library of successful schemes tried out elsewhere in the country from which to pick.

A. *Preventing Burglary*

Burglary is a relatively common experience for shopkeepers, though the risk varies by the location of the store. Neighborhood shops have a substantial risk of burglary, as do chains of stores (particularly those selling valuable consumer items), whereas the risk is negligible in shopping malls and precincts. I begin discussion of prevention methods with burglary, however, because it is the offense that many of stores' security precautions are designed to prevent, and one which almost all stores do *something* about.

There are almost no evaluated and published studies of crime-prevention precautions and their effectiveness in the retail sector (though see Laycock [1985] on chemists' shops). The cost of the security measures being taken against burglary, however, is high. In Ekblom and Simon's (1988) study, around two-thirds of their Asian shopkeepers of neighborhood stores in London had grilles or shutters, 53 percent had burglar alarms, 49 percent had security door locks, and 33 percent had security window locks. Most shopkeepers who had been victims of burglary had themselves taken additional preventive precautions, almost all of which were target-hardening approaches. One-fifth, for example, had themselves installed a burglar alarm after a burglary. It could be argued that this reflected extra requirements by insurance companies, but only one-third had been influenced by insurance companies. These measures were, however, costly in terms of these very small shops' profit levels: all had cost over £100 and half over £1,000.

Very similar use of precautions was seen in the London and West Midlands survey of small shopkeepers by Hibberd and Shapland

(1993). Burglar alarms were installed by 54–60 percent of shopkeepers, security locks on doors by 64–70 percent, grilles or shutters by 73 percent in both places, and a minority had other forms of protection (window locks where windows had no shutters or bars, protection of mailboxes against arson, etc.). The cost of this crime hardware in the last two years was lower, however, with about a quarter spending over £100 and 10–14 percent spending over £1,000. Running costs for a third, however, were over £200 per year. This reflects the use of burglar alarms and the date of their installation. Insurance companies had not played a significant role in crime-prevention activities, either in giving advice or in insisting on particular precautions.

Laycock (1985) concentrated solely on chemists' shops, attempting by the use of target-hardening measures to reduce the risk of burglary by drug addicts. She found that the installation of alarms was effective in reducing burglary rates, although there was some evidence of some displacement to violent encounters in the store instead.

Turning to the United States, Skogan (1990) makes the significant point, which I endorse, that it is extremely difficult to assess effectiveness of security measures through cross-sectional studies at one time— since businesses tend to put in more target-hardening measures as a *result* of victimization. The continuing finding of lack of relation between crime-prevention measures adopted and victimization rates in cross-sectional studies could be due either to some of the measures being put in after the crime or to lack of effectiveness of the measures (either in themselves or because of inadequate targeting or maintenance). We, therefore, need longitudinal (time-series) studies. These are currently available only as case studies of particular areas or companies.

Lavrakas and Kushmuck (1986; see also Griswold 1992) provide evaluations of the Portland Commercial Demonstration Project, which sought to reduce commercial crime in a 3.5-mile-long urban arterial commercial strip through a combination of physical redesign of certain streets and intersections, improved street lighting, road improvements, and various social measures (including the police's creation of an active Crime Prevention Bureau that carried out security surveys of the businesses and the formation of a business proprietors' association). It is difficult to evaluate such a complicated program of measures, particularly when they are implemented at different times. The first 1977 evaluation concluded that, primarily due to the security surveys and follow-ups by the police, the levels of physical security for commercial premises (though not the residential premises) had increased. It was found that lighting levels had also significantly improved. The methods used to look at effects on crime were to analyze reported crimes and to interview business proprietors, residents, community leaders, and police officers (though all the interviews involved relatively small numbers). Time-series analysis over thirty-six months showed that there had been a significant 48 percent decrease in recorded commercial burglaries following the security surveys but much smaller falls in residential burglary (14 percent) and commercial robbery (17 percent), with the city showing an overall burglary decrease of 10 percent over the same period. The 1980 reevaluation over sixty months confirmed the decrease in commercial burglary (which might, it was thought, have been due either to the survey-inspired security precautions or the street lighting) but did not find changes in street crime, residential burglary or commercial robbery. However, this shows that there was no displacement of the commercial burglary.

Dixons (1994) provides a recent case study of the effectiveness of different alarm systems on retail burglary. The aims were to reduce security costs, to enhance deterrence of burglars, and to reduce burglary. The initiative needs to be seen against the background of high false-alarm rates, which prior to 1990 were running at an average of 98.5 percent nationally. Though a unified policy by the police throughout England and Wales to insist on national technical standards for alarms and their installation then led to a smaller proportion of false calls (a 12 percent reduction in 1992, for example), police resources in responding were still being increasingly stretched by a rapidly increasing rate of installation of alarm systems. Dixons Group decided to experiment with audio verification and, more recently, video verification of alarms through an in-house alarm monitoring system. This means that the monitoring center can listen to (and, for video, see) what is going on in the vicinity of the alarm when it goes off. In 1993 a comparison of conventional and verification alarms was carried out. The results were dramatic. The 261 conventional systems produced 2,925 activations, of which only 247 proved to be genuine on arrival (a 91 percent false-alarm rate). The 690 audio verification systems produced 3,124 activations, of which 2,457 were screened out at the center (with only one genuine burglary missed), and, on arrival, 528 were found to be genuine and only 49 false (a 9 percent false-alarm rate). The conventional sites were attacked at a rate 20 percent above the verification sites, and interviews with remand and convicted burglars indicated this was because the criminal network and media publicity had stressed the greater security and greater likelihood of arrest on verification sites. For Dixons as a whole, burglaries decreased by 36 percent, and there was 60 percent less loss from such crimes, which, added to the removal of charges for engineering resets of £480,000, produced substantial savings. However, the alarm-monitoring station costs £300,000 per annum. The experiment was clearly successful for Dixons, both in cost and in crime-prevention terms. What is less clear is the extent of displacement that resulted and the time period over which the decreased crime savings will continue. Such audio systems are relatively rare, even among big retailers, and the (possibly slightly more organized) burglars of large quantities of electrical and electronic goods that Dixons may have attracted may have turned to other shops. A one-chain study cannot look at this kind of displacement. Even if the crime-prevention savings prove less durable as others follow this lead, however, the security cost savings will remain considerable.

Are the target-hardening measures typically thought of and used by smaller shopkeepers useful in preventing burglary? We have few published results—but the weight of evidence would suggest not. Skogan (1990) found that the correlation between physical security measures and commercial burglary was positive (i.e., they were a reaction, not a preventive device). His multivariate analysis of different kinds of precautions suggested that the willingness of people in the area to summon the police was consistently linked to lower levels of burglary and vandalism—but security precautions were not. Multivariate analysis of Johnston et al.'s (1990) industrial estate premises found that the possession of a burglar alarm showed no correlation at all with the rate of burglary, and nor did any other hardware precaution (a similar result to Reiss [1969] in the United States). Levels of crime were being driven by location, design, and maintenance characteristics, not by preventive precautions bolted on after the premises had been built. Skogan (1990) similarly found that burglary in his small neighborhood shopping centers was higher in poorer areas and those characterized by obvious physical decay but did not show any positive effect of having target hardening measures. In the United Kingdom, another major retailer with a chain of stores has taken the bold step of removing almost all the (active) burglar alarms and installing security lighting and dummy alarm boxes instead. Burglary rates did not increase—indeed, by targeting the lighting and adding messages to the burglars, it seems to have decreased.

Precautions against burglary are probably the most expensive ones that stores undertake. Managers' natural thoughts, on being victimized, are to turn to physical hardware, particularly burglar alarms. The very small amount of evidence we have suggests, however, that this is *only* an effective solution if the alarms installed are the more modern systems with lower failure rates (or verification alarms), if their use is properly targeted, and if there is an effective response to activation. Why? It seems that the burglar alarm box may be a deterrent to the less sophisticated burglar, but the response to the alarm itself is often not in time significantly to affect modern burglars (particularly those targeting more isolated premises). Hence, using lighting (thereby drawing attention to the burglars) and increasing guardianship (mobilizing neighbors, siting flats above shops, and including security patrols on large developments and verification alarms) may be more useful—and often less expensive.

B. Preventing Robbery

There are only a few studies of the use of preventive devices against robbery and their likely effectiveness. One group of measures involves reducing opportunities or proceeds by reducing either the amount of cash held in the store or the ease with which it can be taken. Simply taking care with cash handling is one of the simplest precautions and one that all shops, however small, can do—to keep only a small amount in the till, to count up money out of sight of customers, and to vary one's route to the bank. Most of these were commonplace—routine—for the small British shopkeepers in Ekblom and Simon's (1988) and Hibberd and Shapland's (1993) studies, though some shopkeepers seemed never to have thought about these potential problems. So, 80–84 percent limited the cash in the till, 52–63 percent closed the shop before counting up, and 37–57 percent took special precautions when going to the bank (Hibberd and Shapland 1993). More precautions were taken in the areas known to have a robbery problem. For larger companies, cash-handling precautions are built into the company procedures.

Clarke and McGrath (1990) examined the effectiveness of cash-reduction measures that appeared to be responsible for a decrease in armed robbery of Australian betting shops. They compared the number of robberies occurring in a ten-year period covering the implementation of such measures by the off-track betting authority with robberies of banks and robberies of all other commercial premises. Though police data were used, it was established that there was a very close fit with security records of the stores and banks. The number of robberies and the average amount taken declined in the betting shops in a pattern consistent with the introduction of the cash handling measures, whereas robberies in the banks and other commercial outlets increased. The most important individual measure seemed to be time-locking cash boxes. The cost of installation of these boxes was in fact outweighed by the decrease in robbery losses. The effectiveness of these measures corresponds with the effect of introduction of safes in buses in American cities (Chaiken, Lawless, and Stevenson 1974).

Another aspect of robbery prevention is deterrence through increased surveillance (by people or by cameras) and through there being simply more employees in the store (which may work through the staff being more able to alert the police, or remember identification details about the robbers, or intervene to stop the robbery). The literature on increased staff numbers and surveillance shows mixed results in terms of reducing the number of robberies occurring but indicates that staff feel much safer in greater numbers if they feel there is a significant robbery risk. Hunter and Jeffery (1992) describe the use of principles of Crime Prevention through Environmental Design in several studies that attempted to reduce armed robbery of convenience stores in the United States. The early study by Crow and Bull (cited in Hunter and Jeffery 1992) used a variety of techniques, including reducing cash, enhancing visibility, using security devices, enhancing employee alertness, and encouraging visits by police and cab drivers, in sixty convenience stores in Southern California owned by the Southland Corporation. They found the sixty experimental stores suffered fewer robberies than a similar sample of sixty control stores. This was followed by well-known studies in the Florida cities of Gainesville and Tallahassee, and in Florida overall. Summarizing the results of these, Hunter and Jeffery conclude that the strategy receiving the most support was having two or more clerks (staff) on duty, followed closely by good cash-handling practices, elimination of concealed access points to the store (unobserved back doorways, etc.), and location in areas with evening commercial activities. The scale of the effects is shown in the substantial reduction in commercial robbery in Gainesville in the year following the implementation of a statute requiring two clerks to be present in the store, which continued to decrease year on year, and the 65 percent reduction in Jacksonville, Florida, following limiting cash handling, enhancing lighting, removing visual impediments, and training of staff, with a further 26 percent reduction the following year.

Though staff increases seem to be effective (though, of course, costly), using cameras and alarms for surveillance may be less useful in deterring robberies, though cameras and alarms did make staff feel safer (Crow and Erickson 1984).

Sherman (1991), however, has cast some doubt on the findings in the Gainesville studies. He argues that, though there was clearly a reduction in the incidence of robberies, it may be false to attribute this to a deterrent effect on robbers of the ordinance requiring two clerks to be present. There are, he feels, a number of rival hypotheses. One is that active armed robbers were apprehended and taken off the "market" over that time period (there was some evidence of this). Another would be a simple regression to the mean since the rates before the changes were higher than normal. Some credence for this arises in the fact that, as Jerry V. Wilson (cited in Sherman 1991) subsequently found, the robberies dropped *prior* to the ordinance being implemented. Again, the previously high rates may have been partially clerks reporting robbery in order to hide their own fraudulent activities, which were made more difficult by having two clerks (though this does not dispute the reduction in reported robbery—merely that the "robberies" were by robbers). This illustrates the very real difficulties in evaluating the effectiveness of crime-prevention measures historically in the retail environment—even when there is a clear effect (decrease in crime), it can be extremely difficult to work out what caused the effect. The lesson is that there is a real need for experimentation set up deliberately to evaluate the effectiveness of *individual* measures (rather than a complete package). Figlio and Aurand (1991) indicate the additional difficulties of working out the effectiveness of measures when the event being studied is rare. They looked at robbery rates in convenience stores in the United States operated by twelve companies, over the period from 1985 to mid-1991, concentrating on the one clerk/two clerks dimension. In mid-1988, 230 stores started to have two clerks on the third shift, while another 346 stores remained with one clerk. Almost one half of the stores *never* experienced a robbery, either before or after implementation of the experiment. Of those that had a robbery before the experiment, even fewer had another robbery (or more) after the experiment. Hence the findings have to be based on an extremely small proportion who are multiple victimization targets (which makes them prone to have other special factors as well). They found that, given these evaluative problems, there was some suggestive evidence of a preventive effect of two clerks—but this could not be disentangled conclusively from regression to the mean, changes in store operating practices, and fluctuations in neighborhood crime levels.

Robbers cannot be assumed to be similar to burglars—and the measures that may affect one may not affect the other. There have been studies of the factors that appear to influence robbers in the United States, particularly in relation to convenience stores and neighborhood shopping precincts. Some of these have interviewed incarcerated or apprehended robbers (and have found cash-handling procedures to be important, with some contradictory evidence about the number of staff being relevant—see Hunter and Jeffery 1992). Others have looked at the locational and opportunity factors that appear to affect robbery. Skogan (1992) found commercial robbery in neighborhood shopping centers in the United States to be influenced by characteristics of the business (opportunity, i.e., long hours, selling consumer goods) but, unlike burglary, not by area characteristics. He hypothesizes that robbers are more mobile and see robbery as more of a "profession" (since they tend to have to procure a gun). By contrast, Hibberd and Shapland's (1993) perhaps rather more amateur U.K. robbers, in their study of different shopping environments and small areas for small shops in two cities, were almost certainly local since robbery rates varied considerably by area, rather than by type of target. The major preventive tactics by shopkeepers in relation to robbery and till snatching were installing panic buttons associated with burglar alarms (which made staff feel better but seemed not to have deterrent value) and, in contrast to the U.S. project, siting tills out of sight and certainly out of reach (which was definitely of use against till snatching).

Geason and Wilson (1992), in their advice to shopkeepers in Australia, include as an appendix the advice on armed robbery prepared by the National Police Research Unit, in conjunction with the Australian Bankers' Association. This includes a long list of precautions and tactics, which do not seem to have been subject to separate evaluation. They emphasize limiting cash and publicizing this, improving the layout of the store so that all corners are visible, reporting suspicious characters to the police, and, particularly, training staff to react correctly after a robbery, so that the scene is preserved, evidence gathered, and identification of the robbers made most likely. The emphasis seems to be more on detection than prevention—and it must be remembered that this may itself place staff at higher risk. It is true that many robbers are highly nervous and essentially amateur (and can be deterred or displaced by locational and small rewards precautions). But those with more practice may adjust their tactics to counteract some precautions. However, the available studies tend to suggest that, at least in Switzerland and Australia, there has been little displacement from more highly guarded targets (banks) to other kinds of targets (stores) or escalation of tactics by robbers in banks, though there may have been displacement within the banking sector from more protected banks to less protected banks (Grandjean 1990; Clarke, Field, and McGrath 1991). We do not have adequate studies of this in relation to displacement within the retail sector.

Robbery is relatively rare (both in the United States—see Figlio and Aurand 1991; and in the United Kingdom—see British Retail Consortium 1994), but when it does occur it is a traumatic event for the staff concerned (though it may not lead to significant financial losses). It is important to consider from which perspective we wish to prevent robbery. Is the prime concern prevention of financial loss? (In which case, cash-handling measures, particularly procedural ones, are relatively cheap, but staff-based measures may be far more expensive, particularly increasing staff numbers.) Or is the prime concern avoidance of robbery completely as far as possible because of its effects on staff and customers? (In which case, increasing staff numbers may be important, and preventive effects that reassure staff, such as panic buttons and postincident support, become of major import.) Few large retailers have yet taken on board the need to have policies for staff counseling and victim support after robberies—nor have trade associations provided this for smaller retailers. Given the difficulty of pinpointing physical antirobbery measures that do not significantly affect retail profitability and viability, postincident measures may be the major current need in respect of this kind of crime.

C. Preventing Theft

1. *Preventing customer theft.* The extent of customer theft or shoplifting cannot be judged from recorded crime figures, due to changes in prosecution policies and employment of store detectives over time by large chains and large stores (Farrington and Burrows 1993). Essentially, the more store detectives, the larger the recorded shoplifting figures—but this equates almost perfectly to the employment hours of such detectives, suggesting that, at current employment rates for store detectives, there is so much shoplifting that detectives merely have to pluck the nearest shoplifter. Recorded data are also unreliable in relation to the kinds of offenders since the picture will be influenced by

the type of shoppers targeted by store detectives and store staff, store policies in passing suspects to the police (the very young and the very old are less likely to have the police involved), and police prosecution policies (which err toward the prosecution of men rather than women, at least in the United Kingdom; see Retail Action Group 1994b). This impression of a large pool of shoplifters is reinforced by the small number of studies that have randomly followed shoppers to watch their behavior (Buckle and Farrington 1984) or counted the disappearance of marked items (Buckle et al. 1992), and, of course, the high figures for shoplifting from self-report studies on adolescents (such as West and Farrington 1977; Shapland 1978).

Buckle and Farrington (1984), for example, followed shoppers randomly and, in 115 person-hours of observation, found nine shoplifters. Nonetheless, this suggested a high rate of shoplifting, given the throughput of shoppers. The alternative technique of systematic, repeated counting of target objects is potentially subject to the same potential limitations as shrinkage estimates per se (i.e., that they have disappeared for reasons other than shoplifting), but the surveillance by those doing the repeated counting will tend to reduce employee theft, unless there is collusion. However, it is probably the only method where small, relatively inexpensive items are concerned. Buckle et al. (1992) used management trainees to put sticky labels on relevant items in Dixons/Currys stores (audio tapes, videotapes, headphones, film, plugs, batteries, etc.) and monitor their removal from sale, use in the store, and so forth. From this they calculated the amount of items that were missing and compared them with the till rolls and the overall financial results from the stores. There were very significant differences in the proportion of goods shoplifted to goods sold or used plus shoplifted in different stores, but the average over twenty-nine stores was 11 percent (with a range of 0–35 percent). This was 14 percent of the value of these items sold in Dixons stores and 7 percent in Currys stores (a very high proportion). Only a small fraction of these losses, however, had been reported and recorded using security procedures (which tended to concentrate on larger-value items). The stores with the highest shoplifting rates tended to be located in shopping centers or poor inner-city areas and to have a relatively "rough" clientele. Stores in out-of-town locations suffered less.

Another method of identifying losses through customer theft is using electronic point of sale figures, which are routinely gathered and can be used to spot unusual patterns across stores. Hope (1991) provides brief details of the efforts of one (unnamed) company, which is trying to develop an expert system to scan transactions across stores. In the longer term, once indicators are developed, this has the potential to link numbers of incidents in different stores (with different layouts or security staff procedures) with losses and sales and will allow much more effective experimentation.

Security managers for large retailers have spent a considerable amount of time altering the physical layout of the store and the way in which goods are displayed in order to influence both selling rates and loss rates (which tend to be positively correlated). Unfortunately, most of these experiments, being commercially sensitive, are not reported, with the knowledge gained being kept within the company. The Retail Action Group (1994b) describes a list of measures that are currently thought by retailers to be effective in preventing or minimizing customer theft. They include:

target removal, including using dummy or "disabled" goods on display (only having empty record sleeves/CD boxes in the shop, removing key components), holding expensive goods in cabinets, and selling from catalogs with the stock held in back rooms;

target hardening, including security-conscious display stands (e.g., designing garment racks so that large quantities of garments cannot be slipped off quickly, or putting coat hangers on alternating ways), improving security of cabinets (locks, glass not able to be slipped out, access to keys), and locking goods in place (chains, supergluing display items, electronic systems);

situational measures, including store layout (putting self-selection items in easily seen areas, putting most vulnerable products in least vulnerable places), warning notices and signs about the consequences of theft, mirrors or CCTV or 35 mm cameras to increase surveillance (35 mm or good CCTV is necessary if there is to be the possibility of identification of thieves and use as evidence in court), tagging goods to activate an alarm if taken out of the shop, store detectives and guards, surveillance of changing rooms and procedures to limit numbers of garments taken in, encouraging police presence in shops, radio-link/ringroad/Shop Watch schemes to connect adjacent stores so that they can warn each other and the police about suspected thieves, and town-center CCTV; and

staff training, including encouraging vigilance (and recognizing likely kinds of thieves), knowing what to do when a suspect is detected, and making arrests.

Given the number and variety of these measures and the amount of experimentation (albeit not always rigorous experimentation) that has taken place within stores, the number of published evaluations in relation to customer theft is, frankly, pathetic.

McNees et al. (1976) showed that marking frequently stolen items with a red star and posting warning notices identifying these items as frequently taken by shoplifters caused a significant decrease in the rate of theft of the items. Similar positive effects of identifying vulnerable items to shoppers were found in Sweden (Carter et al. 1979) but not in the United States (Thurber and Snow 1980).

Poyner and Webb (1987) have evaluated, using financial figures, the amounts of shrinkage in different departments of a major department store in London, Selfridges, and compared them with new management regimes instituted during that period. They found that increased management interest and tighter supervision of stock reduced shrinkage (significantly, e.g., from 7 percent of sales to 1–2 percent of sales), but it was clear that this could be because of its effect on stock counting, employee theft, or shoplifting. In terms of layout, both better visibility (staff and particularly supervisors being able to see the stock) and restraining chains on stock had effects.

Farrington et al. (1993) compared electronic tagging, store redesign, and deployment of a uniformed guard as preventive devices against customer theft. Customer theft was measured by systematic counting of specified items, comparing the missing items with the number sold, given away, and used in the store. The experiments took place in nine electrical goods stores of the Dixons and Currys chains in the United Kingdom, each of which had high shoplifting rates (identified in the Buckle et al. [1992] study). Electronic tagging was introduced in two stores, store redesign in two, a uniformed guard in two, and the remaining three served as controls. Shoplifting was measured during the week before the intervention, the week after, and three to six weeks later. All items counted (audio tapes, videotapes, films, headphones, and small domestic appliances) had a small, sticky label attached, were on open display, and were not protected by a loop alarm. Counting and attaching labels were the job of management trainees, who were *not* there as sales staff. Though there were some problems in carrying out the study (due to lack of trainees and snow), this is one of the most methodologically sophisticated studies. The amount of shoplifting of this kind of item varied from 7 percent to 37 percent in different stores before the measures were taken (illustrating the scale of the problem).

Electronic tagging caused a significant decrease in shoplifting rates (31 percent to 7 percent in one store, 17 percent to 1 percent in the other), and this was maintained for several weeks. Redesign of the store to increase visibility also caused a significant decrease immediately after it was introduced (37 percent to 15 percent in one store, 24 percent to 5 percent in the other), but this did not persist, and levels of theft rose again in the following weeks. It is important to realize that preventive measures in stores, like preventive measures for community crime reduction in local areas, have a life span. It is not possible to put in one measure and expect continuing success at the same rate for the foreseeable future. What is important is to look at the half-life (or some equivalent concept) and to compare this with the disruption and cost caused by the need to then change preventive measures. Clearly, a half-life of one or two weeks does not denote a helpful measure. There was no significant effect of introducing the uniformed guard at all.

In this experiment, tagging was found to be effective, but it did have disadvantages. One, of course, is cost (estimated at about £10 per day per store over five years). Another is the willingness of staff to respond to alarm activation when tagged goods are taken through the barriers. This is an illustration of the need, when considering alarms of any kind, to think about the response to alarm activation. Without a good response, habitual thieves will soon learn they can continue to steal (which is what happened in one store). Another major problem with tagging is the experience of several major retailers that more professional thieves can easily learn to foil or remove tags.

Geason and Wilson (1992) report a Swedish evaluation (Carter et al. 1979) that employed the marking of small, frequently stolen items and placing of warning signs that these were being specially monitored. They found reductions in losses by a half or two-thirds over a short period—but, of course, this measure as well could be due to employee theft or shoplifting (although it was ascribed to shoplifting). Geason and Wilson also cite a U.S. experiment in which raising staff awareness and employing consultants to reduce employee theft through surveillance and targeting reduced shrinkage by 40 percent (Gabbard, Montang, and Leonard 1986). Burrows (1991a) describes the experience of B&Q, a major retailer of do-it-yourself goods (paints, wallpaper, tools, etc., for maintenance of residential properties), when it set up a top-level task force to reduce losses through crime. The task force developed an action plan for which a crucial element was increasing the motivation of staff at branch level to tackle loss. Overall, stock losses reduced by 25 percent—but it is not quite clear which of the 95 elements of the action plan caused this. Targeting the worst stores and increasing audit and security support were, however, clearly effective. Increasing staff awareness and passing this on to potential thieves by notices, new activity, and so on, seems to have a significant preventive effect. Management attention to customer theft is also vital in motivating staff.

Small shopkeepers tend to rely mostly on physical hardware devices (this time, mirrors and CCTV) to prevent shoplifting. There are no evaluation studies for these small stores, but Tescos, a major food supermarket chain in the United Kingdom, has evaluated the introduction of CCTV in their worst stores as part of a total security package (Burrows 1991a). The initial reason for considering CCTV was as a possible protective device against robbery at tills and of cash carriers outside stores (in a similar way to the use of CCTV in loading bays and distribution points, though it is intended here as a deterrent to staff cheating as well), but they found that, though it was difficult to quantify its effect in minimizing any violent incidents (which were rare), the amount of loss from theft (by customers and staff) dropped immediately from some £12,000 per week to £5,000 per week. Closed-circuit television is very expensive (about £150,000 in capital costs and £15,000–£20,000 per year in running costs for an average superstore), but here it had paid back its installation costs in six months. It must be commented, however, that this is not an effect of CCTV alone—the program also raised staff awareness of loss (and staff awareness of management interest in loss).

2. *Preventing employee theft.* The routine measure available to retailers to measure losses through theft—shrinkage—includes both losses through customer theft and losses through employee theft. Retailers often estimate that there is as much employee theft as customer theft. We saw above also that incidents reported as robberies in single-manned stores may also sometimes be theft by staff (Sherman 1992).

Unfortunately, there are even fewer evaluations of preventive measures in relation to employee theft than there are of customer theft, largely because retailers, like other business people, regard it as an internal matter that they do not wish to reveal. In this field, strategies need to be designed to prevent such theft through selection of staff, to deter theft within stores through financial checking procedures, and to send the right messages to other staff if an incident is detected.

The subject of selection of staff has been a controversial one, with disputed views about the reliability and validity of "honesty" scales. The discussion is technical, and I cannot review it adequately here. The American Psychological Association and the U.S. Congress Office of Technology Assessment have recently compiled reports that examine the measurement and scientific issues involved in honesty/integrity tests (Camara and Schneider 1994). Both reviews had considerable difficulty in finding reliable data on all the tests on the market, particularly the more recent ones, and so concentrated on a small number of tests and a small number of studies. The Office of Technology Assessment concluded that the studies done were inconclusive in supporting or dismissing the assertion that integrity tests can reliably predict dishonest behavior in the workplace. The American Psychological Association said that for the few tests for which validity information is available, the preponderance of the evidence is supportive of their predictive validity, compared to other ways of selecting employees. Camara and Schneider themselves call for publishers to become more open about submitting their tests to independent validity measurement, without which it will remain extremely difficult to conclude that such tests should be used to the extent this is currently occurring.

Electronic point of sale systems are also a useful tool to detect staff theft, and Hope (1991) briefly describes their use in conjunction with video monitoring (of specific cashiers on which suspicion falls) by a large (unnamed) supermarket chain to tackle cash register fraud, particularly through collusion between till staff and accomplice shoppers. It has been piloted in eight stores, and here losses from unknown sources have apparently been cut by half.

Many of the techniques to motivate staff to prevent theft and to deal with any suspected incidents are not specific to the retail environment. They are the same as those identified by Morgan (1989) and the Treadway Commission (1987) in relation to fraud in larger businesses—to set the right tone at the top, to analyze the problem and the ways in which employee theft and fraud could be occurring, to examine procedures to ensure that abnormal patterns and incidents are detected, to have a policy as to what to do with apprehended staff, and to have the courage to carry out that policy and so send the right messages to staff. Again, however, we have few case studies that have been made available so that others can learn from them (none in the retail environment), and only greater openness in general will enable more general lessons to be drawn for crime prevention.

3. *Preventing theft.* It is certainly possible to reduce the current

level of loss through theft in retail premises. There is, however, no magic universal prescription for the most effective package—that will depend on the circumstances of the individual store and the willingness of management and staff to apply the measures.

The most effective first step must therefore be for the store itself to institute a thorough examination of its losses, its circumstances, and its procedures (see Burrows 1988; Ekblom 1988; Geason and Wilson 1992; and Sec. III above). For this, it will almost certainly be necessary for top management interest to be obtained and for that to be conveyed to staff. It has been argued that management is often not really interested in tackling theft—since the measures that reduce theft may also reduce sales. The evaluations described in this section, however, do not indicate any drop in sales through taking crime-prevention measures. The American Management Association, as long ago as 1977, estimated that 30 percent of all business failures could be attributed to employee theft (American Management Association 1977). More recent cost surveys, such as that by the British Retail Consortium (1994), may have produced additional motivation for top management—but it remains true that the overall lack of interest by business in crime prevention is shared by some of the retail sector. As more of the major companies both take action and make public their successes, the amount of motivation for their competitors will grow.

The survey of loss will itself point up the most effective strategies for prevention, but the evaluations above would point to the need to motivate staff, to encourage really accurate stock control, and to increase surveillance by staff. Other strategies include changes in layout to increase visibility, the use of restraining devices for valuable items, surveillance of particular articles using electronic means, and, in big stores, the use of CCTV to discourage more professional thieves.

D. Preventing Violence

The risk of violence at work (including threats) is significant for the retail sector, as shown in relation to homicide in the United States in the section on preventing robbery and from the surveys discussed in Section IV. The Health and Safety Executive in the United Kingdom has issued guidance for employers on ways to prevent such violence, which is seen as a public health issue (Health and Safety Executive 1989). It requires that employers produce a policy for their company that is relevant to the risks of violence for that business and that, in order to do so, they should have a system of classifying incidents and using the experience of those incidents to suggest and implement measures to prevent violent attack. They have recently issued guidance for the retail sector in particular (Health and Safety Executive 1994), following the guidance notes for banks and building societies.

The guidance stresses that the preventive procedures that should be adopted depend very much on the particular problems of that retailing environment. The emphasis is therefore on the need for management to follow the right process in analyzing and assessing risk, rather than an advocation of particular preventive measures. The process is very similar to that for crime analysis in general and involves establishing the scale of the problem (talking to staff, managers, and victims and collecting, investigating, and analyzing evidence and information; implementing a recording system—collecting, classifying, and analyzing data on incidents—and establishing reporting procedures that are clear, easy to follow, and confidential), developing and implementing suitable preventive measures and good practice, training all staff, monitoring and reviewing, communicating and involving staff throughout the process, and providing staff with adequate support, help, and guidance.

It should be emphasized that assessing the risk in the retail environment is seen as a duty on employers (as is required in the Framework Directive of the European Union)—to be backed up by visits by inspectors—and that it is now proposed that violence at work resulting in a relevant level of injury will be a reportable offense in the United Kingdom, in a similar fashion to that resulting from accidents at work from other causes (unguarded machines, etc.; see Health and Safety Executive 1994).

For retailers—given that it is customer contact, and often customer contact in relation to disputes that produces the context for violence—evaluated preventive action has concentrated on training staff to deal with difficult customers, improving visibility (through CCTV, etc.), evaluating store procedures to minimize friction with customers, and employing security staff. It is still the case, however, that most retail staff do not receive any particular training in relation to the risk of violence (see Bushell et al. 1990). Poyner and Warne (1988) have described nine case studies in which authorities or companies have developed recording systems, training programs, or physical protection for employees, but unfortunately none of these involves the retail sector.

Hibberd and Shapland's (1993) study of small shops indicated that some shopkeepers, and in particular those who had more trouble dealing with groups of youths, seemed to employ defective strategies for dealing with the youths. Physical presence and visibility was important, so that the shopkeeper felt in charge—and so it was recommended that shopkeepers might consider installing a platform behind the counter to give them greater height and improve sight lines. Equally, however, shopkeepers clearly needed strategies to deal with difficult groups and mentally disordered people. The researchers considered that shopkeepers could be trained to do this, using packaged instructional materials (such as videos)—but that there was no currently available material that was suitable for shopkeepers. By the nature of their trade, shopkeepers cannot take days off to go on courses—so the method of delivery of this crime-prevention advice is very important.

Violence is, of course, not a problem peculiar to the retail sector. Guidance and advice on preventive techniques have tended to develop more rapidly for other areas, such as health care and social services personnel, and for operators and employees of pubs and bars. In working out what preventive measures would be suitable for the particular retail environment, in the course of discussions with staff, we might find it helpful to look at the checklists and questions produced for other contexts. So, for example, Greaves (1994) includes a list of questions regarding safe systems of work and working practices for the health-care sector. Some of these would be very pertinent for the retail environment, such as,

> Why is any job always done in a particular way? Is it because it has always been done that way? Has the working method just developed over time or has experience shown that it is the only way to do the job well? When decisions are made about working methods, is any consideration given to the risk of violence? The workplace . . . includes areas set aside for the public to wait. Can these be changed in any way to reduce tension levels . . . [e.g., can] lighting, decoration, number of seats available, the arrangement of seating, access to refreshments, etc. [be changed]? How easy is it for members of the public to wander about the workplace unnoticed and unchecked?

Similarly, McDonnell, McEvoy, and Dearden (1994) offer a brief summary of what is known about the effectiveness of different methods of dealing with violent situations when they occur (low arousal vs. assertiveness, etc.). This is very much a new and developing field of prevention, which requires both the production of materials and evaluated trials to move further.

E. Preventing Fraud

Fraud affects retailers in two different ways: through the normal susceptibility of all companies to fraud by employees and management, and through check and credit card fraud.

Fraud by employees and management is one of the most dangerous crimes for any company—such frauds can involve greater loss than any other source and can lead to the collapse of the company. Only arson has greater potential for threatening the company's viability. Retailers are no more at risk than any other commercial sector and will be less at risk than the financial services sector. The real danger is not from sales staff or accounts staff (payroll frauds, expenses claims, invoices) but from frauds committed by senior management in relation to the financial records and shares of the company. Morgan (1989) has shown that this is relatively common. The best advice in preventing fraud remains that of the Treadway Commission (1987), which recommends a strong ethical line by top management, clear rules for all employees, and effective internal auditing procedures. Essentially, companies where sales drives are rewarded whatever their methods, where management bend the rules, where employees who take more than the normal perks are not disciplined, and where there are few checks built into the system are very much at risk of systematic and serious fraud.

Preventing check and credit card fraud involves making sure all issued cards reach their proper user and are used on the correct account, fast notification of retailers when a card is stolen and lost, and intercepting attempted fraudulent use both to retain the card and, preferably, also to detain the user. The locus at which such preventive action can take place varies. Preventive action on issuing cards can only be a matter for the card company (and the distributors). Notification is equally a matter for card companies. The retailer is important at the third stage, when the card has already been stolen and an attempt at fraud is occurring. However, making it easier to prevent fraudulent transactions depends on both retailer and card company. The retailer can train staff (see below). The card company can make identification of an incorrect user easier (via card design, photographs) and also make it less likely that retailers will incorrectly challenge genuine customers (which loses retailers customers). Much of the lively debate about combating check and credit card fraud revolves around the responsibilities and costs that fall on retailer and card company in this third category of prevention.

One of the reasons for that debate is that the balance of cost does not necessarily follow the current locus of responsibility. Check and credit card fraud are not serious sources of *direct* financial loss to retailers (see, e.g., British Retail Consortium 1994). Such frauds are, however, major sources of loss for credit card companies, whose charges to retailers will of course reflect this loss (though retailers will pass this on to customers). Retailers can be liable if they do not carry out the checks on cards required by the credit card companies. Equally, if more checks were to be required, retailers would complain that the cost of enforcement (in lost sales through the potential for "unpleasantness" and in assaults on staff) would fall on them (Gill 1992). Retailers are the "response" to the sign of crime for credit card fraud, just as alarm companies and the police are for burglar alarms (and the arguments about which preventive strategies should be adopted are very similar). It is retailers who have to detain those who try unsuccessfully to use fraudulent cards. Clearly, this creates tension between advocates of different forms of prevention. Putting photographs on cards, or installing "smart chips" in them, will be more expensive for the credit card companies. Doing more checks on customers will be more expensive for retailers.

What are the preventive actions that retailers are asked to undertake in relation to check and credit card use, and how effective are they? Levi, Bissell, and Richardson (1991) have reviewed the debate in the United Kingdom. Data from Barclaycard in relation to credit cards indicate that an average of 6.8 transactions are made on a lost or stolen card. It is, therefore, of importance to retain stolen and lost cards as early as possible in their use pattern. To assist this, banks offer a reward of £50 for each card retained by shop staff (though not all stores pay the till staff the reward, which may not improve the likelihood of detection, though it does improve store profitability). Levi, Bissell, and Richardson found that the variance in check-guarantee card recovery per fraudulent checks used was considerable, both between different stores in the same chain and between different chains. Examples were 1 in 268 for one large chain and 1 in 24 for another in a similar part of the retail sector. They comment that "the inconsistency almost certainly results from differences in management attitudes which permeate through to their staff" (1991, p. 29).

Clearly, staff training and staff attitudes are important. An initiative in Manchester's Arndale Centre in 1990 by the Association of Payment and Clearing Services (reported in Levi, Bissell, and Richardson 1991) aimed to inform cashiers about check cards, what to look for, and what action to take if they found a suspected fraudulent card. The suggestions for identifying such cards included observing that signatures do not compare or that the person does not match the name on the card, presigned checks in the book, a slow, deliberate signature or a thick felt-tip pen signature, a damaged or defaced signature strip, indiscriminate or hurried purchases or unusual combinations of goods, and the type or value of goods being just under the check card limit (since about 90 percent of fraud on checks with a limit of £50 are between £40 and £50).

A market research organization surveyed till staff to see the effectiveness of the training. They found that the awareness of cashiers about the reward rose substantially after training (from 81 percent to 97 percent), while managers' awareness was high both pre- and posttraining. Over 90 percent of cashiers stated that the free help-line card provided, giving details of telephone numbers to ring if fraud was suspected, was quite or very useful. Cashiers' views of the seriousness of fraud also changed, from 49 percent to 69 percent saying it was a very serious problem. Clearly, the training had had some immediate effect. However, one such initiative cannot be the sole training input, given the high turnover of staff and the pressure for throughput on tills, which conflicts with the need to examine cards carefully. Indeed, deliberate attempts by Levi, Bissell, and Richardson to cause suspicion (slowly written, felt-tip signatures looking very unlike the original on the card, etc.) were never picked up by cashiers in the stores. They conclude that the signature alone is not a reliable means of crime prevention against fraudulent check card use (and similar conclusions must apply to credit cards).

Another scheme has been the setting up of a telephone verification service by a card issuer, in which retailers who have become suspicious can ring up and have card details checked. Although it has been cost-effective for the issuer in terms of transactions prevented (it is not clear how often the card would have been retained anyway), it has foundered on delays in getting through to the service. As Levi, Bissell, and Richardson (1991) comment, it is unlikely that a fraudulent user would wait around for nine minutes for verification—and it is also unlikely that a genuine customer would be happy about such delays. Such systems will enable retailers to retain the card but not arrest the fraudulent user. A more effective scheme is the "Cardcast" type scheme, in which the card is "swiped" through a machine that compares the details against a register of lost and stolen cards and offers instant verification. Since Levi, Bissell, and Richardson's study, this kind of system has grown considerably in use and will be offering some deterrent value, at least in displacing fraudulent use to stores without such a system (which are becoming rarer). We do not, however, have current published data on its effectiveness.

Becoming aware of suspect cards and then taking appropriate action are preventive actions for the retailer. The design of cards, however, is a card company issue—and cost. Whether photographs or any other details should be included on cards is a contentious issue. Unfortunately, until experiments are done and the results reported, it is impossible to know whether photographs and related design elements could be forged, whether till staff will become more prepared to challenge users, whether losses decrease more than costs increase, and whether fraudulent users are deterred from using that brand of card (and whether burglars and pickpockets are deterred from stealing them). Given the scale of losses on credit and check card fraud, it seems strange that governments, police, and users, as well as retailers, are not able to exert more persuasive power on card companies to require such experiments.

Where the interests of card companies and retailers coincide, however, is when retailers issue in-house cards. However, the small amount of work done on this tends to indicate that, compared with the use of stolen check or credit cards, the rate of usage of *stolen* store cards is very low (Levi, Bissell, and Richardson 1991). The problem of *interception* of cards in the post is much greater (with losses of £271–£800 per store card intercepted and fraudulently used). Over all card issuers, the average amount of loss sustained by interception is 30 percent of all loss caused by fraudulent use. Preventive action here is to make more secure the route of transfer of card to customer, either by using more secure delivery services or by requiring the customer to come into the store (though this can generate considerable consumer resistance).

F. Knowing about Retail Crime-Prevention Initiatives

I have attempted to cover the major kinds of crime in the retail sector and the published evaluations of preventive techniques. On thumbing through the references to this essay, the reader will notice that the sources are not, in general, the standard journals on which researchers (or retailers) rely. Another general finding about the current state of crime prevention in retailing is that there is a difficulty in becoming aware of what crime-prevention initiatives have been done and of their results. It is highly likely that this review does not contain all the relevant literature, though considerable efforts have been made to acquire this (with considerable assistance from the editors and the other contributors to this volume). For the researcher or the retailer, however, much of the literature remains "gray," "fugitive," or just straightforwardly invisible. Though major efforts are being made to remedy this situation, notably in the United Kingdom by the Home Office Crime Prevention Unit and in the United States through new initiatives such as *Security Journal*, there remains a difficulty both for specialists and, particularly, for the individual managers and trainers who need to have in mind what they might pursue, as they become aware of the extent of their crime problems. As a conclusion, therefore, I discuss in the next section not only a possible future research agenda in this area but also the problems of dissemination of information in what is still a nascent area.

VI. The Progress of Crime Prevention in the Retail Sector

In Section III above, I outlined the kind of process that both researchers and retailers need to undertake to prevent crime in retailing. It involved, first, analyzing the extent of the crime problem and, second, devising and implementing measures to reduce that problem (and, of course, monitoring them and feeding the results of that monitoring back into the preventive effort).

A. A Research Agenda for Crime Prevention in Retailing

The first priority for a retail-sector research agenda is to continue to develop our baseline data on the extent and character of the crime problem. We are only at the beginning of appreciating the extent and nature of the retail-sector crime problem. Though there are now a few national retail surveys, they do not as yet permit analysis by geographical or retailing location or by type of goods sold. We cannot answer such questions as, What is the effect of location within an enclosed shopping mall? Do the mall's policies on security affect the individual shop's crime profile, and, if so, in what ways? What is the effect of out-of-town location? What is the influence of being situated next to residential property on crime profiles, on surveillance, and in relation to where offenders come from? What is the influence of company size on crime profile? Does greater local autonomy for shop managers affect the losses from crime? Do losses on crime relate to sales? (The stereotypical view is that there is a positive correlation, but this may vary by type of location and type of store.)

The answers to these questions will start to allow us to work out how to make different types of crime more visible to retailers and researchers. How can we pinpoint suspicious patterns through analysis of financial data? Can insurance data be specified in a different way (perhaps at the reporting stage) so that it can be used as a crime data source? Can electronic point of sales data be fed back to stores to permit managers and staff to contribute to crime prevention? Can we develop methods to unify the definition of shrinkage and to start, using electronic point of sales and other financial data, to provide more reliable estimates of customer theft and staff theft? Can we routinely use tagged items and repetitive counting in weekly stock checks to estimate theft more accurately? Could store detectives randomly follow shoppers to make profiles of shoplifters more accurate and to provide better estimates of the extent of customer theft?

In and of itself, making crime more visible, both in its overall extent and in companies' own records, will provide a spur to the development of effective preventive practice. The second major research effort is then to carry out the experiments needed to work out what is effective. The work already done has alerted us to the difficulties of retrospective evaluative studies. What ideally is now needed are prospective experiments. It would not be difficult for major retailers and researchers to team up to try out possible tactics one at a time in particular stores of the chain, with others being used as controls. Compared to the overall security budget for target hardening and physical security alone, doing two such experiments per year is a very minor cost. (Obviously, only a few experimental and control stores are needed for experiments on high-frequency crimes such as customer theft and credit and check card fraud; rather more are needed for medium frequency crimes such as burglary and damage; and a whole chain of stores for robbery— which I suspect is so rare that it will require experiments organized by government and police regionally.) The results could be used to create a portfolio of effective crime-prevention measures, which could be applied to stores as particular crime problems arise. The benefit in raising staff awareness of crime problems as each store in the chain participates would, on its own, probably cover any installation costs (particularly since security hardware manufacturers would probably supply the needed hardware).

The candidates for such experiments are numerous. What are the effects of security surveys on burglary? Is it worth doing such a survey, or is it better to install audio verification alarms? What is the time interval before a security survey needs to be done again (because crime patterns or store layout have changed)? What are the relative advantages of deterring customer theft through notices, stickers on goods, increasing surveillance using mirrors, increasing surveillance through CCTV, or tagging? Do photographs on check and credit cards lead to till staff noticing disparities? (Laboratory experiments could be used here as a pilot.) How long do training effects last in terms of staff attitudes? How often do staff use help lines for fraud, and why are they reluctant to use them? Does staff training on diffusing violent situations lead to greater staff confidence and to fewer violent incidents?

Acquiring the answers to those questions means, however, confronting the reluctance of retailers to participate in such data-collection exercises and to publish the results. As I observed in Sections II and IV above, though we can mount one-off research exercises to obtain incidence data, we still rely on retailers' time to answer surveys and their financial data to obtain costs and losses.

However, in my view, though retailers have clearly not been as alive as they might have been to the costs of crime and the need for crime prevention, the difficulty has been just as strong on the research and public-sector side. It is not possible to expect retailers to organize themselves in the optimal way to permit crime and cost surveys—they are not expert researchers. Researchers need to set out to retailers the best ways to conduct such surveys and studies.

Equally, it does not seem to me to be correct for government to indicate that retail crime prevention is a matter for retailers (because they are the "private sector"). Given the considerable extent of crime in the retail sector and its effects on the national economy (as well as its share of the offending market), it is as true to say that retail crime prevention is a matter for retailers as it is to say that residential crime prevention is a matter solely for householders, who should police themselves and acquire their own guidance on effective crime prevention. Government has an interest in minimizing offending, in minimizing the underground economy, and in minimizing the effects on publicly funded services (such as the police) as a result of retail-sector crime. All three of those interests need to be acknowledged (not just the last one), and those interests need to be communicated to researchers and to retailers. It implies government or other public funding for research that investigates the extent of retail crime and determines good practices in crime prevention—and how to disseminate the resulting findings. That acknowledgment and funding have so far been extremely patchy.

B. Cascading Advice and Good Practice: The Difficulty of Disseminating Prevention

Even if the attitude of larger retailers to research were to change, and resources found to produce more business victimization surveys (from government) and to do more evaluation studies of crime-prevention experiments (from business), it will still not be possible to implement those results without some solution to the problems of disseminating crime-prevention advice to businesses. The difficulties are twofold.

First, there is no natural lead agency or group that is seen by all the relevant participants as the natural organization to concern itself with crime prevention for business. Essentially, business itself is relatively uncoordinated. The national organizations for larger companies and smaller shops are separate, yet chain stores exist alongside small shops in the same environments. Most small shops do not belong to any organization. Hence, there are real difficulties in trying to cascade knowledge of risks or good practice in prevention down to individual managers. Development of crime prevention in the retail sector will need several different approaches to be adopted. Skills and risk aware-ness will have to be conveyed using packaged instructional materials for small shops. The more complex plans and surveys needed for large companies need to be facilitated within industry fora.

Second, business cannot organize this all for itself. If crime preven-tion requires constantly updated, good data to produce targeted plans (as I have argued it does), then only routinely gathered and accessible information on crime in the local area will be useful. It may be possible to hold a national or local business victimization survey every few years (in a similar fashion to the residential surveys—and these business surveys are sorely needed), but these surveys cannot give the really localized data that companies need to update their crime-prevention plans. For this, one has to turn to the police and fire services and to recorded crime and fire statistics (as far as external crime, such as burglary, arson, etc., is concerned). Hence, public bodies have a vital role in enabling business to perform the risk assessment process that has to precede crime-prevention action.

Public bodies are also crucial to good crime-prevention practice for business. The few studies we have indicate that crime risks are influenced by location, by design, and by the characteristics of the local population. This means that an interagency approach to crime prevention will be necessary—between local government, police, shopkeepers, and local residents' and youth groups.

The consequence of these two factors is that, just as one would not leave crime prevention in the residential sector solely as the responsibility of residents, with no help from anyone else, so one cannot leave crime prevention for business solely up to business. Quite simply, business does not have the information or the skills to learn about the best crime-prevention tactics for itself, nor is it possible to rely on business organizations to cascade information down to individual managers and owners.

For the residential sector, the delivery of crime-prevention advice and skills is aided by local public officials (police crime-prevention officers, fire prevention officers, local community police officers, local government officials), backed up by national research and publicity. For public health measures in the business sector, a similar approach has been adopted (a localized inspectorate of health and safety measures, backed up by national standards and regulations—although a fierce debate is ongoing in different countries as to the relative effectiveness of regulations, as compared with the prosecutorial and advice-giving functions of inspectors). Why should we consider crime prevention in the business sector to be any different in its requirements?

C. Cooperative Action in Crime Prevention

The thrust of the findings on the crime profile of the retailing sector is that crime risks are affected by local factors, as well as by the nature of the merchandise sold. The crime profile of the shop will depend on where it is situated, its design, and the other kinds of premises nearby. This has major implications for the organization of crime prevention in retailing.

The first implication is that, although a chain of stores may guide store managers nationally as to likely avenues for effective crime prevention, the package of measures adopted must be selected at the local level. Store managers and regional/national security have to work together to be effective. Currently, security policy tends to be decided at headquarters level—this may not be the most effective solution (though it will require much greater management skills to organize it at store level).

If the shop is situated together with other shops or commercial/ public concerns (factories, libraries, employment offices), as is increasingly likely to occur, then crime-prevention plans need really to be drawn up by involving as many as possible of the managers and author-ities on that site. It is highly likely that only landlords of major develop-ments, or local public officials (local government, police), will be seen as having the status to organize such cooperative planning between different companies. The Dutch shopping center experiment (van Soomeron 1989) is an example that this can occur. Similar (though unpublished and often unevaluated) experiments have taken place in other countries.

In the residential sector, it is now commonplace that crime preven-tion means community safety—and so involves everyone living in that small area. In the retail sector, the difficulty—and the challenge—for crime prevention is to overcome the suspicion and worry that a cooper-ative approach would entail.

Currently, our surveys show that managers and employees of indi-vidual retail businesses think of crime, risk management, and security as something that is necessary (since they are well aware they can be victimized), but terrifying, and very difficult—and so something that should be firmly pushed to the back of one's mind. If they do become victims, and they feel they have to do something (because of loss, because of insurance demands, because it is necessary to show employ-ees that management cares), then they will take emergency action and put in the first measure they can think of, or one that a consultant recommends. It may be costly, it may be ineffective, but they've been seen to manage the situation. It is now a trite truism to say that re-searchers always end by recommending more research. For the devel-opment of crime prevention in the retail sector, however, it is not just more research that is needed but publicly available surveys of the whole sector, detailed analysis of the lost profit opportunities of individual com-panies, and evaluations of the measures put in place in individual compa-nies and in retail precincts to reduce and to manage crime.

REFERENCES

American Management Association. 1977. *Summary Overview of the "State of the Art" regarding Information Gathering Techniques and Level of Knowledge in Three Areas concerning Crimes against Business*. Washington, D.C.: National Institute of Law Enforcement and Criminal Justice, Law Enforcement Adminis-tration.

Andrews, D., and J. Burrows. 1989. "Key Elements in Fostering Prevention."

In *Business and Crime: A Consultation*, edited by J. Shapland and P. Wiles. Swindon: Crime Concern.

Bottoms, A. E., and P. Wiles. 1986. "Housing Tenure and Residential Community Crime Careers." In *Communities and Crime*, edited by A. J. Reiss, Jr., and M. Tonry. Vol. 8 of *Crime and Justice: A Review of Research*, edited by M. Tonry and N. Morris. Chicago: University of Chicago Press.

Brantingham, P. L., and P. J. Brantingham. 1984. "Burglar Mobility and Crime Prevention Planning." In *Coping with Burglary*, edited by R. Clarke and T. Hope. Boston: Kluwer-Nijhoff.

Brantingham, P. L., P. J. Brantingham, and P. Wong. 1990. "Malls and Crime: A First Look." *Security Journal* 1:175–81.

British Retail Consortium. 1994. *Retail Crime Costs: 1992/93 Survey*. London: British Retail Consortium.

Buckle, A., and D. Farrington. 1984. "An Observational Study of Shoplifting." *British Journal of Criminology* 24:63–73.

Buckle, A., D. Farrington, J. Burrows, M. Speed, and T. Burns-Howell. 1992. "Measuring Shoplifting by Repeated Systematic Counting." *Security Journal* 3:137–46.

Burrows, J. 1988. "Retail Crime: Prevention through Crime Analysis." Crime Prevention Unit Paper 11. London: Home Office.

———. 1991a. "Making Crime Prevention Pay: Initiatives from Business." Crime Prevention Unit Paper 27. London: Home Office.

———. 1991b. "Violence and Threats in Branches." Paper given to the Victim Support annual conference, Warwick University.

———. 1993. Personal communication with Morgan Harris Burrows, Kineton, Warwickshire, United Kingdom, January 10.

Bushell, A., J. Chapman, G. Hughes, and S. Wightwick. 1990. *Victims of Violence*. Leicester: University of Leicester, Centre for the Study of Public Order.

Business Monitor. 1993. *SDA25*. London: Central Statistical Office.

Camara, W., and D. Schneider. 1994. "Integrity Tests: Facts and Unresolved Issues." *American Psychologist* 49:112–19.

Carter, N., L. Hansson, B. Holmberg, and L. Melin. 1979. "Shoplifting Reduction through the Use of Specific Signs." *Journal of Organisational Behavior Management* 2:73–84.

Chaiken, Jan M., Michael W. Lawless, and Keith A. Stevenson. 1974. "The Impact of Police Activities on Subway Crime." *Urban Analysis* 3:173–205.

Chan, T.-F. 1988. "Juvenile Delinquency in Hong Kong." Ph.D. dissertation, University of Oxford, Faculty of Social Studies.

Clarke, M. 1990. Personal communication with author. Liverpool University.

Clarke, R., S. Field, and G. McGrath. 1991. "Target Hardening of Banks in Australia and Displacement of Robberies." *Security Journal* 2:84–90.

Clarke, R., and G. McGrath. 1990. "Cash Reduction and Robbery Prevention in Australian Betting Shops." *Security Journal* 1:160–63.

Confederation of British Industry (CBI). 1990. *Crime—Managing the Business Risk*. London: CBI/Crime Concern.

Crime Concern. 1991. *Bottom Line Disappearing? That's a Crime!* Swindon: Crime Concern.

Criminal Statistics 1990. 1991. London: H.M. Stationery Office.

Crow, W., and R. Erickson. 1984. *Cameras and Silent Alarms: A Study of Their Effectiveness as a Robbery Deterrent.* Wilson, N.Y.: Athena Research Corporation.

Davis, H. 1987. "Workplace Homicides of Texas Males." *American Journal of Public Health* 77:1290–93.

Davis, H., P. Honchar, and L. Suarez. 1987. "Fatal Occupational Injuries of Women, Texas, 1975–84." *American Journal of Public Health* 77:1524–27.

Dixons Group PLC. 1994. "Reducing False Alarms." Internal document. London: Dixons Group PLC.

Ekblom, P. 1986. "The Prevention of Shop Theft: An Approach through Crime Analysis." Crime Prevention Unit Paper 5. London: Home Office.

———. 1988. "Getting the Best out of Crime Analysis." Crime Prevention Unit Paper 10. London: Home Office.

Ekblom, P., and F. Simon, with the assistance of S. Birdi. 1988. "Crime and Racial Harassment in Asian-run Small Shops." Crime Prevention Unit Paper 15. London: Home Office.

Farrington, D., S. Bowen, A. Buckle, T. Burns-Howell, J. Burrows, and M. Speed. 1993. "An Experiment on the Prevention of Shoplifting." In *Crime Prevention Studies*, vol. 1, edited by R. V. Clarke. Monsey, N.Y.: Criminal Justice Press.

Farrington, D., and J. Burrows. 1993. "Has Shoplifting Really Decreased?" *British Journal of Criminology* 33:57–69.

Figlio, R., and S. Aurand. 1991. "An Assessment of Robbery Deterrence Measures in Convenience Stores: Multiple Clerk Staffing, Central Station Based Interactive Television and Bullet-resistant Barriers." In *Convenience Store Security*, edited by the National Association of Convenience Stores. Alexandria, Va.: National Association of Convenience Stores.

Gabbard, R., J. Montang, and K. Leonard. 1986. "What To Do When the Shrink Hits the Fan." *Security Management* 30:97–101.

Geason, S., and P. Wilson. 1992. *Preventing Retail Crime.* Canberra: Australian Institute of Criminology.

Gill, M. 1992. Personal communication. University of Leicester, Centre for the Study of Public Order, November.

Grandjean, C. 1990. "Bank Robberies and Physical Security in Switzerland: A Case Study of the Escalation and Displacement Phenomena." *Security Journal* 1:155–59.

Greaves, A. 1994. "Organizational Approaches to the Prevention and Management of Violence." In *Violence and Health Care Professionals*, edited by T. Wykes. London: Chapman & Hall.

Griswold, D. 1992. "Crime Prevention and Commercial Burglary: A Time-Series Analysis." In *Situational Crime Prevention: Successful Case Studies*, edited by R. V. Clarke. New York: Harrow & Heston.

Hales, T., P. Seligman, S. Newman, and C. Timbrook. 1988. "Occupational Injuries due to Violence." *Journal of Occupational Medicine* 30:483–36.

Health and Safety Commission. 1994. "Draft Proposals for the Reporting of

Injuries, Diseases and Dangerous Occurrences Regulations." Consultative document. London: Health and Safety Commission.

Health and Safety Executive. 1989. *Violence to Staff.* London: Health and Safety Executive.

———. 1994. "Guidance on Preventing Violence to Staff in the Retail Sector." London: Health and Safety Executive.

Hibberd, M., and J. Shapland. 1993. *Violent Crime in Small Shops.* London: Police Foundation.

Home Office. 1988. "Report of the Working Group on the Prevention of Arson." Standing Conference on Crime Prevention, December 6. London: Home Office.

Hope, T. 1991. "Crime Information in Retailing: Prevention through Analysis." *Security Journal* 2:240–45.

Hosking, P. 1992. "Wire-Cutters Raise the Alarm." *Independent* (November 4), p. 25.

Hunter, R. D., and C. R. Jeffrey. 1992. "Preventing Convenience Store Robbery through Environmental Design." In *Situational Crime Prevention*, edited by R. V. Clarke. New York: Harrow & Heston.

Johnston, V., M. Leek, J. Shapland, and P. Wiles. 1990. *Crimes and Other Problems on Industrial Estates: Stages Two and Three.* Sheffield: Faculty of Law.

Johnston, V., J. Shapland, and P. Wiles. 1994. "Developing Police Crime Prevention: Management and Organisational Change." Crime Prevention Unit Paper. London: Home Office.

Junger-Tas, J. 1988. "Patterns in Delinquent Behavior." In *Juvenile Delinquency in the Netherlands*, edited by J. Junger-Tas and R. L. Block. Berkeley, Calif.: Kugler.

King, M. 1988. *How to Make Social Crime Prevention Work: The French Experience.* London: National Association for the Care and Resettlement of Offenders.

Lavrakas, P., and J. Kushmuk. 1986. "Evaluating Crime Prevention through Environmental Design." In *Community Crime Prevention: Does It Work?* edited by D. Rosenbaum. Beverly Hills, Calif.: Sage.

Laycock, G. 1985. "Reducing Burglary: A Study of Chemists' Shops." Crime Prevention Unit Paper 1. London: Home Office.

Levi, M., P. Bissell, and T. Richardson. 1991. "The Prevention of Cheque and Credit Card Fraud." Crime Prevention Unit Paper 26. London: Home Office.

McDonnell, A., J. McEvoy, and R. Dearden. 1994. "Coping with Violent Situations in the Caring Environment." In *Violence and Health Care Professionals*, edited by T. Wykes. London: Chapman & Hall.

McNees, M., D. Egli, R. Marshall, J. Schnelle, and T. Risley. 1976. "Shoplifting Prevention: Providing Information through Signs." *Journal of Applied Behaviour Analysis* 9:399–405.

Mayhew, P., D. Elliott, and L. Dowds. 1989. "The 1988 British Crime Survey." Home Office Research Study no. 111. London: H.M. Stationery Office.

Morgan, J. 1989. "Fraud—How to Fight It." In *Business and Crime: A Consultation*, edited by J. Shapland and P. Wiles. Swindon: Crime Concern.

Phillips, C. M., J. E. Stockdale, and L. M. Joeman. 1989. *The Risks in Going to Work.* London: Suzy Lamplugh Trust.

Phillips, S., and R. Cochrane. 1988. "Crime and Nuisance in the Shopping Centre." Crime Prevention Unit Paper 16. London: Home Office.

Poyner, B., and C. Warne. 1988. *Preventing Violence to Staff.* London: Health and Safety Executive.

Poyner, B., and B. Webb. 1987. *Successful Crime Prevention: Case Studies.* London: Tavistock Institute of Human Relations.

Reiss, A. J., Jr. 1969. "Minority Entrepreneurship." Report submitted to the Office of Planning, Research and Analysis of the Small Business Administration. Hearings before the Select Committee on Small Business, U.S. Senate, Ninety-first Congress. Washington, D.C.: U.S. Government Printing Office.

Retail Action Group. 1994*a*. "Violence to Retail Staff." Briefing Paper 3. London: Home Office National Board for Crime Prevention.

———. 1994*b*. "Customer Theft." Briefing Paper 4. London: Home Office National Board for Crime Prevention.

Shapland, J. 1978. "Self-reported Delinquency in Boys Aged 11 to 14." *British Journal of Criminology* 18:255–66.

———. 1991. "What Should Crime Audits Contain?" Paper presented at the consultation on "Business and Crime: Setting Standards," St. George's House, Windsor, September.

Shapland, J., and P. Wiles. 1989. *Business and Crime: A Consultation.* Swindon: Crime Concern.

Shapland, J., P. Wiles, and J. I'Anson. 1994. "Crime and Social Control in Semipublic Spaces." Ongoing research. Sheffield: Faculty of Law (forthcoming).

Shapland, J., P. Wiles, V. Johnston, and M. Leek. 1991. "Crime at Work: The Victimisation of Factories and Employees." In *Victims and Criminal Justice*, vol. 52, edited by G. Kaiser, H. Kury, and H.-J. Albrecht. Freiberg: Max-Planck-Institut für ausländisches und internalisches Strafrecht.

Shapland, J., P. Wiles, and P. Wilcox. 1994. "Targeted Crime Reduction." Crime Prevention Unit Paper. London: Home Office.

Sherman, L. 1991. "Book Review of Problem-oriented Policing by H. Goldstein." *Journal of Criminal Law and Criminology* 82:690–707.

———. 1992. *Tysons Corner Center: Safety Awareness.* Washington, D.C.: Crime Control Research Corporation of America.

Skogan, W. 1990. "Crime and Survival of Small Businesses in Urban Communities." Paper presented at the 1990 annual meeting of the American Society of Criminology, Baltimore, November.

———. 1991. *Disorder and Decline: Crime and the Spiral of Decay in American Cities.* New York: Free Press.

———. 1992. Personal communication, based on National Institute of Justice report "Appendix A: Study Areas and Survey Methodology." Northwestern University, March.

Small Business Administration. 1969. "Crime against Small Business." Report of the Small Business Administration to the Select Committee on Small Business, United States Senate, April 3. Washington, D.C.: U.S. Government Printing Office.

Stenning, P. 1989. "Corporate Policing: Some Recent Trends." In *Business and*

Crime: A Consultation, edited by J. Shapland and P. Wiles. Swindon: Crime Concern.

Thurber, S., and M. Snow. 1980. "Signs May Prompt Antisocial Behavior." *Journal of Social Psychology* 112:309–10.

Touche Ross. 1992. *Retail Shrinkage and Other Stock Losses: Results of the Second UK Retail Survey, January 1992*. London: Touche Ross Management Consultants.

Treadway Commission. 1987. *Report of the National Commission on Fraudulent Financial Reporting*. Washington, D.C.: Treadway Commission.

Tremblay, P. 1986. "Designing Crime." *British Journal of Criminology* 26: 234–53.

U.S. Bureau of Justice Statistics. Annual. *Sourcebook of Criminal Justice Statistics*. Washington, D.C.: U.S. Bureau of Justice Statistics.

van Dijk, B., and P. van Soomeron. 1990. *Bedrijfsleven en Criminaliteit*. The Hague: Ministry of Justice, Directie Criminaliteitspreventie.

———. 1992. *Criminaliteit en de Detailhandel*. The Hague: Ministry of Justice, Directie Criminaliteitspreventie.

van Soomeron, P. 1989. "Business and Crime—a Foreigner's View." In *Business and Crime: A Consultation*, edited by J. Shapland and P. Wiles. Swindon: Crime Concern.

Walker, J. 1994. *The First Australian National Survey of Crimes against Businesses*. Canberra: Australian Institute of Criminology.

West, D. J., and D. P. Farrington. 1977. *The Delinquent Way of Life*. London: Heinemann.

Zvekic, U. 1993. *Understanding Crime: Experiences of Crime and Crime Control*. Rome: UN Interregional Crime and Justice Research Institute.

J. David Hawkins, Michael W. Arthur,
and Richard F. Catalano

Preventing Substance Abuse

ABSTRACT

Although the prevalence of drug use among high school students and
household members has been declining in recent years, high rates of
substance use among arrestees, homeless individuals, and school dropouts,
and an increasing trend in the number of drug-related hospital emergency
room incidents, suggest that substance abuse among some populations has
not declined. Prospective longitudinal studies have identified a number
of risk factors that consistently predict greater likelihood of substance
abuse. Individuals experiencing multiple risk factors and few protective
influences during infancy, childhood, and early adolescence are at greatest
risk for abusing substances during late adolescence and early adulthood.
Efforts to reduce risk and enhance protective factors in multiple domains
hold promise for effective substance abuse prevention among high-risk
populations.

In the United States today, fewer people are using illegal drugs than
a decade ago. Yet, more people are being arrested and incarcerated for
drug-related offenses and admitted to treatment and emergency rooms
for drug-related crises now than ten years ago. These observations
underscore the complexity of the problem of drug abuse and efforts to
prevent it in a free society. While it appears that some of the tactics

J. David Hawkins is professor in the School of Social Work and director of the Social
Development Research Group at the University of Washington, Seattle. Michael W.
Arthur is research assistant professor, and Richard F. Catalano is associate professor in
the School of Social Work; both are associated with the Social Development Research
Group. The authors thank David Farrington, Helene White, and Michael Tonry for
comments on an earlier draft, Patricia Huling and Erin Weible for their assistance in
the preparation of this manuscript, and the Robert Wood Johnson Foundation, the
National Institute on Drug Abuse, and the Center for Substance Abuse Prevention for
supporting the preparation of this essay.

employed in the "War on Drugs" declared by the U.S. government during the 1980s may have been successful at reducing the prevalence of illicit drug use among high school students and the general population, there is less evidence of a reduction in the number of alcoholics, addicts, and drug abusers in the United States.

Since the early 1980s the U.S. government has adopted policies designed to reduce the availability of certain drugs through law enforcement and interdiction (supply reduction), whereas many Western European countries and Canada have concentrated more on reducing the negative consequences of drug abuse (harm reduction) (Reuter, Falco, and MacCoun 1993). The U.S. government's "War on Drugs" resulted in a tremendous expansion of resources applied to supply reduction and interdiction efforts focused on illegal drugs and in increasingly harsh criminal sanctions against users, including those caught in possession of relatively small amounts of illegal drugs. These policies have apparently had little effect on the availability of addictive drugs or on reducing abuse. They have also fueled higher costs associated with prison construction and a tremendous increase in the prison population, leading some to call for legalization of currently proscribed drugs such as marijuana and cocaine.

Recognition of the costs of substance abuse and of the costs and limitations of both supply reduction efforts and drug abuse treatment has also stimulated interest in preventive approaches focused on reducing demand for drugs. School-based prevention programs have flourished since the 1970s, providing students with information about the negative effects of drug abuse, promoting self-esteem and self-awareness, and teaching skills for social problem solving and for resisting social influences to use drugs. Methodological issues and challenges have weakened evaluations of many of these interventions (Gerstein and Green 1993). Where rigorous evaluations of these drug abuse prevention programs have been mounted, the evidence for effectiveness has usually been weak (Bangert-Drowns 1988; Moskowitz 1989), although it has been consistent with the hypothesis that the early initiation of tobacco, alcohol, and marijuana use can be prevented by school-based programs that emphasize the creation of social norms antithetical to use (Hansen and Graham 1991) and the development of skills to resist drug offers (Ellickson and Bell 1990).

Concurrently, researchers concerned with the health consequences of alcohol and tobacco use have investigated the effects of laws and regulatory mechanisms for reducing consumption of those substances that can be legally possessed and used by adults. High taxes on alcohol, legal restrictions on age of purchase, and outlet licensing restrictions have been shown to be effective in reducing rates of consumption of alcohol as well as negative consequences of alcohol use, including cirrhosis rates and drinking and driving among eighteen- to twenty-year-olds, suggesting that legal regulation remains an important tool in drug abuse prevention for "legal" drugs.

Both epidemiological and etiological investigations have revealed substance abuse to be a health and behavior problem with multiple causal roots. A number of wide-ranging factors have been shown to predict higher probability of substance abuse in longitudinal prospective studies (Kandel, Simcha-Fagan, and Davies 1986; Newcomb, Maddahian, and Bentler 1986; Simcha-Fagan, Gersten, and Langner 1986; Hawkins, Catalano, and Miller 1992). These findings suggest that the prevention of substance abuse may ultimately require a multiple component strategy with elements focused on different predictors thought to be causal. The complexity of such an undertaking is daunting.

However, advances in the understanding and prevention of cardiovascular disease have provided a promising model for comprehensive substance abuse prevention. Comprehensive communitywide programs focused on reducing environmental and behavioral risks for heart and lung disease have demonstrated positive effects on health behaviors, including reductions in cigarette smoking (Jacobs et al. 1986; Lefebvre et al. 1987; Puska et al. 1989; Farquhar et al. 1990; Vartiainen et al. 1990). As with heart and lung disease, alcohol and other drug abuse is predicted by many risk factors in the individual and the environment. These converging lines of evidence support the hypothesis that interventions reducing multiple risk factors in family, school, peer, and community environments hold promise for alcohol and other drug abuse prevention. This essay reviews current progress and prospects in substance abuse research from this perspective.

Our aims are to summarize what is currently known about the problem of substance abuse in the United States, to review the effectiveness of current prevention strategies, and to suggest promising directions for the future in terms of policy, intervention, and research. Current knowledge about drug use and abuse patterns and trends is summarized in Section I. Section II discusses the advances and limits of recent drug abuse prevention efforts, which have sought primarily to change laws and norms and to teach social influence resistance skills to young people. Section III discusses the research base of knowledge about the epidemiology and etiology of substance abuse and the effectiveness of various prevention strategies. Methodological and measurement problems are described, and their implications for prevention research are discussed. Section IV introduces emerging principles of prevention science based on the public health model of risk reduction and reviews risk and protective factors for substance abuse. Section V explores research and policy directions for the future in light of current knowledge about prevention and risk and protective factors for substance abuse. Interventions that reduce identified risks and enhance protective factors against substance abuse are reviewed with respect to their promise for substance abuse prevention. Emerging trends such as the emphasis on community ownership of prevention initiatives are explored.

I. Current Knowledge about Drug Use and Abuse

Data from two national surveys provide evidence that the prevalence of drug use decreased in the general population during the ten years from 1982 through 1992. The National High School Senior (NHSS) Survey, an annual survey of nationally representative samples of high school seniors conducted since 1975 by researchers at the University of Michigan (Johnston, O'Malley, and Bachman 1992), has documented substantial declines in the percentage of students who report having used marijuana or cocaine during the previous month and somewhat smaller declines in the percent reporting current use of alcohol and cigarettes (fig. 1), although in 1993 the prevalence of marijuana use increased after more than a decade of decline. The National Household Survey of Drug Abuse, a survey of a nationally representative sample of U.S. household members aged twelve and over (National Institute on Drug Abuse [NIDA] 1991) showed similar declines in the prevalence of drug use during the 1980s and early 1990s (fig. 2).

Currently, the most widely used and widely accepted drug in the United States and Great Britain is alcohol. Just under 90 percent of American high school seniors report having used alcohol in their lives. Over 80 percent report having used alcohol in the past year. About one-third report having consumed five or more drinks in a row in a two-hour period within the two weeks preceding the survey. Whereas the prevalence of illegal drug use has decreased dramatically since the early 1980s, the prevalence of alcohol use has decreased only slightly

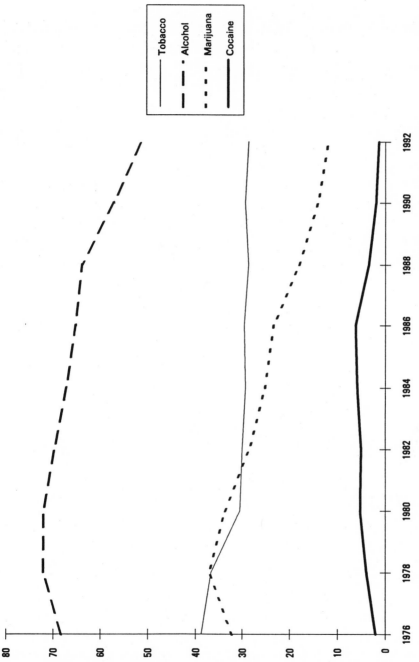

Fig. 1.—Trends in high school senior monthly use. Sources: Johnston, O'Malley, and Bachman (1991); Johnston, Bachman, and O'Malley (1993).

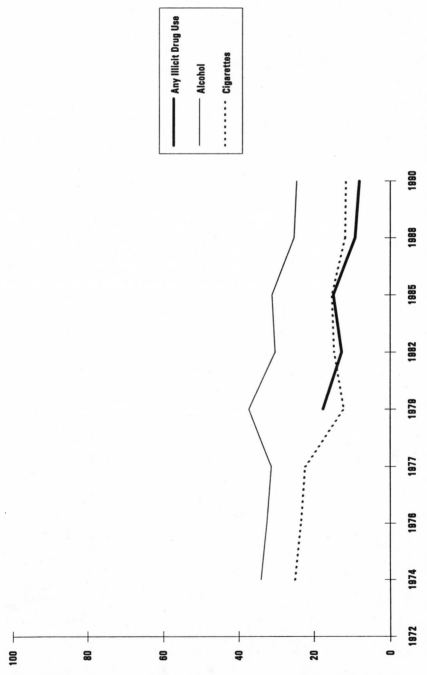

Fig. 2.—Trends in the percentage of youth ages twelve to seventeen reporting use of any illicit drugs, alcohol, and cigarettes in the past month. Source: National Institute on Drug Abuse (1974–90).

during the same period, and the prevalence of tobacco use among high school seniors has remained relatively stable.

In contrast to the findings indicating that the prevalence of illegal drug use is down, however, data from other sources suggest that the abuse of drugs in some segments of the population has not decreased. Reports of emergency room visits involving substance abuse from the Drug Abuse Warning Network (DAWN)—a representative sample of hospital emergency rooms located throughout the United States, including twenty-one oversampled metropolitan areas (Substance Abuse and Mental Health Services Administration [SAMHSA] 1993)—have increased during this same period (fig. 3).[1] Similarly, urine tests of persons arrested for non-drug-related crimes in twenty-four metropolitan areas participating in the Drug Use Forecasting System (DUF) reveal that recent drug use among this population is quite prevalent and has not decreased during the past five years (fig. 4) (Center for Substance Abuse Research [CESAR] 1993). Moreover, each of these sources of data indicates that there are pronounced differences in both levels of use and types of substances used most frequently in different demographic groups and geographic regions of the country (Johnston et al. 1991; NIDA 1991; SAMHSA 1993).

Despite these demographic and geographic variations, however, heavy drug use and abuse consistently appear to be much more prevalent among the most disaffected and disadvantaged populations (Gerstein and Green 1993). For example, studies of the homeless (Breakey et al. 1989; Fors and Rojek 1991) reveal that these populations exhibit rates of alcohol and other drug use up to twenty-five times higher than do school- or household-based populations. Urine tests of residents of homeless shelters in New York City conducted in January 1992 revealed a 54 percent prevalence of recent cocaine use and a 20 percent prevalence of recent marijuana use (New York City Commission on the Homeless 1992). Rates of recent self-reported drug use in a sample of 253 homeless and runaway youths in shelters in the Southeast were two to seven times higher than in comparison school samples (Fors and Rojek 1991). A survey of 1,436 chronic absentee students and dropouts aged fifteen to seventeen from two urban areas in California found that the prevalence of heavy alcohol and other drug use

---

[1] Prior to 1988 the sample of hospitals participating in the DAWN was not representative of all hospitals in the coterminous United States. The national estimates presented in figure 3 below are comparable between the period preceding 1988 and the period after but were estimated using different procedures to account for the sampling differences.

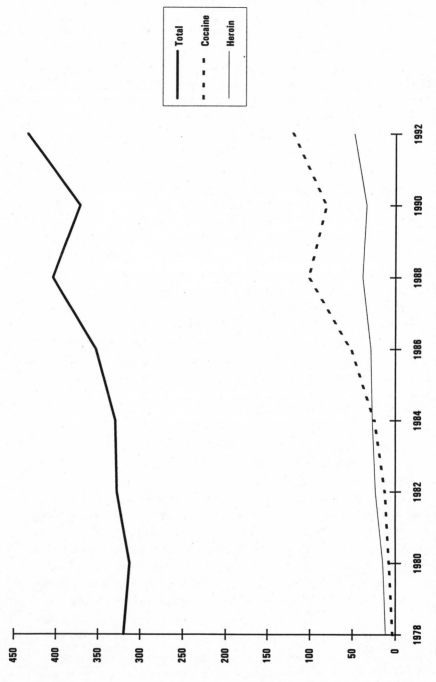

Fig. 3.—Estimated number of emergency room episodes, cocaine-related and heroin-related episodes. Episodes are in thousands. Source: Substance Abuse and Mental Health Services Administration (1993).

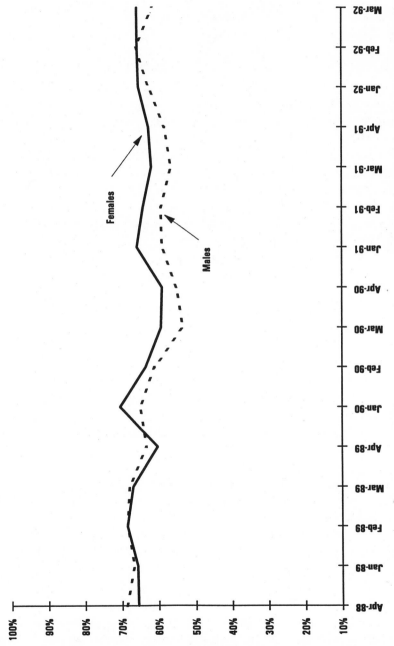

FIG. 4.—DUF-24 Site Index (fourth quarter, 1988, to third quarter, 1992). To summarize urinalysis results for adult arrestees participating in the National Drug Use Forecasting (DUF) program, the Center for Substance Abuse Research (CESAR) has developed the DUF-24 Site Index, which computes the average of individual site percentages for arrestees testing positive for drugs across all participating DUF sites. Source: CESAR (1993).

among survey respondents was more than five times that obtained from school surveys (Horowitz 1992). The apparent concentration of substance abuse among the disadvantaged is a challenging problem (Sawhill 1989; Johnson et al. 1990; Wish 1990–91; Gerstein and Green 1993).

Drug use is also related to criminal and violent behavior. Heavy use of alcohol and other drugs appears to increase risk for both commission and victimization of homicide and other acts of violence, as well as predatory crimes (Chaiken and Chaiken 1990). A study of 2,000 inmates in California, Michigan, and Texas revealed that 83 percent of prisoners incarcerated for violent offenses were taking drugs daily during the month prior to their committing an offense (Chaiken and Chaiken 1982). Another study reported that up to 50 percent of homicides in New York City were believed to be drug-related (Goldstein, Brownstein, and Ryan 1992). Although drug use is very prevalent among high-rate criminal offenders, the relationship between drugs and crime is complex (Chaiken and Chaiken 1990). Existing evidence suggests that involvement in criminal activity often precedes heavy drug use and that personality factors, situational factors, sociocultural factors, and the nature of the specific drug itself mediate the relationships among drug use, crime, and aggression (Chaiken and Chaiken 1990; Nurco, Kinlock, and Balter 1993).

These data suggest that there are different categories of drug users in this country and that current U.S. prevention policies have been differentially effective with different populations. Given the high costs associated with drug abuse, the apparent imperviousness of some segments of the population to current prevention policies and practices raises important policy issues.

A. Drugs of Abuse

A large number of psychoactive substances hold potential for abuse. These include tobacco and alcohol, drugs that are legally purchased and used by adults in both the United States and Great Britain. These are, not surprisingly, as figures 1 and 2 showed, the drugs most widely used by both adolescents and adults in the United States. In school and household samples, marijuana is the most widely used illicit drug (NIDA 1991), although rates of cocaine use are higher than marijuana use among individuals arrested by law enforcement agencies (Wish 1990–91). Other drugs—including both illegal substances such as cocaine and crack cocaine, heroin and LSD, and medically prescribed substances such as amphetamines, other opiates, tranquilizers, and barbiturates—are often lumped together in drug abuse prevention studies under a single category of "hard" drugs.

Because of their status as drugs that can legally be purchased and used by adults, tobacco and alcohol have not been a major focus of research on drug abuse conducted by criminologists, with the exception of those concerned with adolescent populations. However, from the perspective of drug abuse prevention, tobacco and alcohol are important substances for two reasons. First, they are the drugs most widely abused in the United States. In 1992, 400,000 Americans died of tobacco-related causes and 100,000 died of alcohol-related causes, whereas 30,000 died from the abuse of illegal drugs (Schroeder 1993). From a public health perspective, tobacco and alcohol abuse clearly require preventive attention. Much of the research on the prevention of abuse of these substances over the past thirty years has been done by public health researchers.

Second, research has revealed a predictable pattern of stages of drug use (Yamaguchi and Kandel 1984; Kandel, Yamaguchi, and Chen 1992). In the United States, initiation of tobacco use often precedes initiation of alcohol use. In turn, initiation of alcohol use virtually always precedes initiation of marijuana use, which almost always precedes initiation of use of cocaine and other "hard" drugs. For these reasons, tobacco, alcohol, and marijuana have been referred to as "gateway" drugs. Onset of use of these "gateway" drugs in early adolescence is an important predictor of subsequent drug abuse (Kandel 1982; Robins and Przybeck 1985). These findings have influenced many scientists and practitioners working on drug abuse prevention to concentrate on delaying the initiation of alcohol, tobacco, and marijuana use rather than on preventing the use of a specific category of "hard" drug. For these reasons, this review of prevention strategies does not classify prevention approaches by drug addressed. However, where an approach has focused on a specific drug or where results of prevention efforts differ by substance, these are indicated.

B. Substance Use versus Substance Abuse

The conflicting trends in the prevalence of drug use in the general population and indicators of drug abuse in emergency room admissions and treatment statistics, as well as among homeless and prison populations, underscore the importance of defining the terms "drug use" and "drug abuse." Data from Johnston, O'Malley, and Bachman's (1992) high school senior surveys reveal that a relatively large proportion of individuals use alcohol or marijuana at least once during adolescence without becoming involved in the frequent use of these substances and without developing drug-related problems. These findings have been consistently confirmed in longitudinal studies of the etiology and consequences of drug use (Newcomb and Bentler 1988; Shedler and Block 1990). Similarly, a large proportion of adults in the United States drink alcohol, whereas alcohol abuse and dependence are estimated to occur in about 14 percent of the population over the life course (Helzer, Burnam, and McEvoy 1991). It is reasonable to hypothesize that behaviors with such different rates in the population may arise from somewhat different causes. In short, the causes of drug initiation, casual or occasional drug use, frequent drug use, and drug abuse may well be different (Hawkins et al. 1986).

What distinguishes substance use from substance abuse? The answer depends on the normative, legal, and medical definitions dominant in the society. In the United States, substance abuse has been defined by the American Psychiatric Association (APA 1987) as a pattern of pathological use that persists for at least a month and that causes impairment in social or occupational functioning in the family, at school, or in a work setting. However, a single instance of possession or use of certain illegal substances such as cocaine or heroin can bring criminal charges and sanctions and may be viewed as an indication of substance abuse. In this essay, the APA's definition is used to distinguish substance abuse from substance use.

In seeking to understand the field of substance abuse prevention, it is important to recognize that different prevention efforts have focused on different drug-related outcomes. Some initiatives have tried to reduce the incidence of new cases of drug use in young adolescents. In school curricula, community media campaigns, and state laws raising the legal drinking age from eighteen to twenty-one, for example, the goal has often been to prevent the initiation of drug use in the general population. Other efforts have tried to reduce the prevalence of use in general or in specific populations without specific attention to the goal of preventing or delaying drug use initiation. Efforts to reduce drug supplies and incarcerate drug dealers, for example, seek to prevent substance abuse by decreasing the availability of substances.

Unfortunately, even though most substance abuse prevention workers might agree that their ultimate goal is the prevention of substance abuse, very few studies of the effectiveness of drug abuse prevention interventions have assessed their effectiveness in reducing impairment or other negative consequences of drug use. Few have, in short, assessed their effectiveness in preventing drug abuse as defined by the American Psychiatric Association. Although this is a serious limitation in substance abuse prevention research, important progress has been made toward understanding the promise and limitations of a number of approaches to prevention, and, as discussed later, the field of prevention science has developed a set of commonly shared empirically based principles that are guiding current work in substance abuse prevention research.

II. Drug Control Policy and Prevention through the 1980s

Initiatives to reduce substance abuse are conventionally, if misleadingly, said to focus on drug supply and drug demand. The former consist mostly of law enforcement activities, the latter mostly of prevention and treatment programs.

A. Law Enforcement and Interdiction

The association between drug use and crime has influenced U.S. drug control policy over the last fifteen years to focus the preponderance of resources on interdiction and "user sanctions" (i.e., incarceration) rather than on treatment or prevention (Reuter, Falco, and Mac-Coun 1993). From 1981 to 1989, the number of individuals arrested and committed to state prisons for drug offenses increased nearly eight times (Bureau of Justice Statistics 1992). In 1981, 11,487 individuals were committed to state prisons in the United States for drug offenses. In 1989, 87,859 individuals were committed for drug offenses. In 1981, 7.7 percent of the individuals admitted to state prisons were drug offenders. By 1989, 29.5 percent of those admitted to state prisons were drug offenders. Much of the recent demand for prison construction in the United States has been fueled by the incarceration of increasing numbers of drug dealers and drug users. Moreover, given the concentration of drug dealing and abuse in the inner cities (Johnson et al. 1990) and the disproportionate numbers of persons of color who reside in inner-city neighborhoods, the crackdown on drug offenders has contributed to a disproportionate number of persons of color being arrested and imprisoned for drug offenses (Blumstein 1993).

The current focus on user sanctions emerged during the past fifteen years. During the 1960s and 1970s the primary focus of U.S. drug control policies was to treat heroin addiction and prevent drug-related crime. Methadone treatment of addicted Vietnam veterans and the urban poor, the groups most affected by heroin addiction, was widely used (Wish 1990–91). The casual use of drugs such as marijuana and cocaine was generally tolerated and a few states decriminalized possession of small amounts of marijuana. These policies were similar in many respects to current policies in Canada and most Western European countries where the emphasis of drug control policies is on treatment and harm reduction (Reuter, Falco, and MacCoun 1993). An increase in use of marijuana among broad sectors of U.S. society during the 1970s and of cocaine during the early 1980s has been attributed to normative changes brought about by the Vietnam War and a rejection of governmental regulation and ideology among middle- and upper-class youth (Johnston 1991). This was followed by a reaction against casual drug use and the federally declared "War on Drugs" during the 1980s and early 1990s.

Although treatment and law enforcement have had some effect in limiting drug abuse in the United States (for reviews, see Anglin and Hser 1990; Moore 1990), they are not a focus of this essay. Treatment studies focusing primarily on alcohol and heroin and, more recently, cocaine abuse have demonstrated that addicts and drug abusers can achieve abstinence but that relapse following treatment occurs in one-third to two-thirds of cases (U.S. Surgeon General 1988). Those who remain in treatment longer typically have the best outcomes; however, dropout rates from treatment programs are high. The characteristics of the environments that addicts return to following completion of treatment appear to have an important role in maintaining or undermining achieved abstinence.

Foreign policy and interdiction efforts focusing on reducing the quantity of illegal drugs entering the country have sought to reduce drug abuse through reducing availability and increasing prices, particularly for heroin and marijuana (Moore 1990). These efforts have not been effective in eliminating the supplies of prohibited drugs or in raising the retail price of illegal drugs. To illustrate, in spite of more than doubling federal spending on interdiction and law enforcement from $1.8 billion in 1986 to $3.7 billion in 1989, the average street price of cocaine was estimated by the federal Drug Enforcement Agency to have fallen from $100 to $75 dollars per gram during that period. The availability of drugs in the United States has not declined, nor have prices for drugs on the street increased significantly. These findings confirm an analysis by the Rand Corporation (Polich et al. 1984) indicating that interdiction and law enforcement efforts should not be expected, in the face of strong demand, to eliminate illegal drug supplies, to significantly raise the price of illegal drugs, or to deter drug dealing. Taken together, the bulk of the evidence suggests that reducing demand for drugs is a more effective preventive strategy than supply reduction (Wilson 1990; Blumstein 1993).

It should be noted that interdiction and law enforcement can be viewed as efforts to convey a strong normative message regarding the unacceptability of the use of illegal drugs, thereby reducing demand for these drugs. The law enforcement efforts in the "War on Drugs" may have been more effective in reducing demand for illegal drugs among certain groups than in reducing drug supplies. Well-publicized enforcement actions communicate social norms of disapproval against the distribution and use of illegal drugs or drinking and driving. Those individuals who have a strong stake in their roles in family, work, and the community may be deterred from illegal drug involvement or drinking and driving by perceptions of risk associated with these behaviors. Those with less commitment to roles in the larger society are less likely to be deterred by legal sanctions (Sherman et al. 1992). Individuals with weak commitments to socially acceptable roles may view the relative reinforcements of drug dealing and use as worth the risks, even in the face of a normative consensus against the use of illegal drugs in the larger society. In short, enforcement efforts may have a deterrent effect in reducing demand for drugs, but they are most likely to deter those least likely to engage in drug abuse.

B. Major Approaches to Demand Reduction

Most recent substance abuse prevention research has focused on two factors that predict higher rates of substance use: norms favorable to drug use, and social influences to use drugs. Broad normative change campaigns using the media and classroom-based social influence resistance curricula in school classrooms were widely implemented in the 1980s and early 1990s. These prevention initiatives sought to foster strong norms against the use of drugs and to develop skills in young people to resist social influences to use. Developmentally, these factors have their greatest effects at the point of drug use initiation. Thus, their preventive effects on early drug use initiation should be detectable over relatively short time periods.

1. *Changing Social Norms.*   Direct attacks have been made on social norms favorable to drug use. Normative changes during the 1980s were symbolized by the Red Ribbon week of the National Federation of Parents for Drug Free Youth; the Reagan administration's "Just say NO!" campaign; the National Media Partnership's advertising campaigns ("This is your brain on drugs"); the proliferation of antismoking and antidrug curricula in the schools; and smoking restrictions in airplanes, schools, offices, and public places. The media and advertising industries have cooperated in a national project to encourage negative attitudes toward the use of illegal drugs through the use of antidrug advertising. Results of mall intercept surveys indicate that saturation advertising in ten markets was accompanied by significant changes in norms and by attitudes less favorable to marijuana and cocaine when compared with other markets over a one-year period (Black 1989). Similarly, school policies regulating smoking have shown effects on the amount of smoking by students (Pentz, Brannon, et al. 1989).

2. *Social Influence Resistance Strategies.*   During the 1960s and 1970s, substance abuse prevention approaches in schools provided information about drugs and their effects, promoted affective development or intrapersonal growth, and provided alternative activities to replace opportunities for drug use and to remediate social and academic skill deficits. Tobler's (1986) meta-analysis of 143 prevention programs using one or more of these approaches concluded that drug information and intrapersonal growth programs were not effective at reducing drug use.

In the late 1970s and early 1980s, school-based prevention efforts began to focus on teaching children in grades 5–10 the skills to recognize and resist social influences to use drugs. Classroom-based training in skills to resist influences to use drugs has become the most heavily studied strategy for preventing substance abuse. The social influence resistance approach views drug use as a socially acquired behavior (Bandura 1977). These curricula teach children through instruction, modeling, and role play to identify and resist influences to use drugs and, in some cases, to prepare for associated stresses anticipated in the process of resisting such influences (Botvin 1986).

Whereas virtually all interventions of this type offer skills in resisting social influences to use drugs, many also seek to promote norms negative toward drug use (Perry 1986; Hansen et al. 1988). These normative-change components have included efforts to depict drug use as socially unacceptable, identify short-term negative consequences of drug use, provide evidence that drug use is not as widespread among peers as children may think, encourage children to make public commitments to remain drug free, and, in some instances, use peer leaders to teach the curriculum (Botvin 1986; Klepp, Halper, and Perry 1986).

Social influence resistance approaches have also been combined with training in problem-solving and decision-making skills, skills to increase self-control and self-efficacy, adaptive coping strategies for relieving stress and anxiety, interpersonal skills, and general assertive skills (Flay 1985; Botvin 1986). Projects have also combined classroom-based social influence resistance curricula with mass-media programming and parent involvement strategies in comprehensive interventions seeking to change norms regarding drug use and increase resistance to drug-promoting influences among adolescents (Pentz, Dwyer, et al. 1989).

Several published studies of classroom curricula that focus on changing student norms and enhancing students' skills to resist drug influences, primarily in grades 6 and 7, have found modest but significant reductions, in comparison with controls, in the onset and prevalence of cigarette smoking after training (Murray et al. 1988; Schinke et al. 1988; Moskowitz 1989; Hansen 1992). A few studies have reported beneficial effects in preventing or delaying the onset of alcohol or marijuana use (McAlister et al. 1980; Botvin 1986; Hansen et al. 1988; Pentz, Dwyer, et al. 1989; Ellickson and Bell 1990). Unfortunately, longer-term follow-ups of programs of this type usually have shown that the positive short-term effects disappear over time (Hansen et al. 1988; Flay et al. 1989; Murray, Hannan, and Zucker 1989). Those few interventions that have sought to address norms and social influences in multiple domains of school, family, and the larger community (Johnson, Hansen, and Pentz 1986; Pentz, Dwyer et al. 1989; Vartiainen et al. 1990; Perry et al. 1992) or have used booster sessions to maintain consistency in normative commitments over time (Ellickson and Bell 1990; Arthur, Weissberg, and Caplan 1991; Perry et al. 1992) have shown the most durable positive effects.

Some unanticipated results from these prevention studies have suggested the importance of preventive interventions addressing a broader range of factors contributing to substance use. For example, Ellickson and Bell (1990) found that exposure to their classroom prevention curriculum was associated with greater smoking among children who were already smokers at the beginning of the study. In addition to their early initiation of cigarette smoking, these students were characterized by a number of other problems including low school achievement, poor family communication, school truancy, and conduct problems. For these children, a drug curriculum offered in seventh grade was not enough to reduce or prevent smoking. These findings suggest that a broader range of interventions focused on family, school, and community and delivered prior to the seventh grade may be required in order to prevent drug abuse among children at greatest risk.

The Federal Drug Free Schools and Communities Act restricted federal education funds to schools that enacted a drug policy and that instituted a drug abuse prevention curriculum. Partly in response to this requirement, the Drug Abuse Resistance Education (DARE) curriculum, Here's Looking at You 2000, Quest's various skills curricula, and other classroom-based curricula have been widely used in schools across the United States.

As noted earlier, the prevalence of alcohol, marijuana, and cocaine use decreased dramatically during the 1980s and early 1990s among high school students in the United States. Bachman, Johnston, and O'Malley have attributed this change to increased perceptions of risk and social disapproval of drug use. During the 1980s, as young people perceived greater risk—whether legal, social, health, family, or personal—in using drugs, they were less likely to initiate drug use (Bachman, Johnston, and O'Malley 1991). It is plausible that well-publicized enforcement, norm change strategies, and school antidrug curricula all contributed to this change in social norms and attitudes regarding drug use.

3. *Regulation of Alcohol Availability and Price.*   Since the repeal of the prohibition of alcohol, its supply has been controlled by taxation, restrictions on liquor-by-the-drink sales, age restrictions on consumption, and restrictions on hours of purchase. Increasing the price of alcohol by increasing taxes on retail sales of alcohol has been effective in reducing alcohol consumption rates (Levy and Sheflin 1985; Saffer and Grossman 1987) and related health problems, including cirrhosis mortality (Cook and Tauchen 1982) and alcohol-related traffic fatalities (Blose and Holder 1987). Similarly, increasing the legal age for alcohol purchase and consumption from age eighteen to twenty-one has been shown to decrease rates of teen drinking and driving and alcohol-related traffic fatalities among teens (Krieg 1982; Cook and Tauchen 1984; Saffer and Grossman 1987; Decker, Graitcer, and Schaffner 1988; Joksch 1988). Generally, efforts to restrict the use of alcohol and cigarettes through increased taxes, regulation of retail outlets, regula-

tion of public smoking, and minimum age requirements for legal alcohol and tobacco use have reduced the use of these substances (Cook and Tauchen 1982; Holder and Blose 1987; Pentz, Brannon, et al. 1989; O'Malley and Wagenaar 1991).

However, there are limits to the effectiveness of these regulatory approaches. For example, anecdotal evidence suggests that, when regulation increases cost or reduces availability of alcohol beyond a certain point, displacement may occur, especially among the most economically disadvantaged. Some users switch to illegal means of obtaining legal substances, such as the manufacture and sale of corn liquor currently reported in some urban inner-city areas.

It is a mistake to conclude from the evidence regarding alcohol and tobacco regulation that illegal drugs should be legalized so that they could be regulated in this way. From a public health perspective, legalization of cocaine or other illegal drugs is a bad idea. Legalization of illegal substances would inevitably increase the prevalence of use of these substances, exposing larger percentages of the population to health risks associated with use.

III. Methodological Issues in Drug Prevention Research
It is not the purpose of this essay to critique the methodological and measurement adequacy of specific drug abuse research studies. However, a number of issues that pertain to drug abuse prevention research should be considered when weighing the evidence, individually and cumulatively, from the studies available. Drug abuse research involves study designs that are challenged by measurement constraints, mixed units of analysis, differential attrition, and differential implementation as well as the interpretive challenge presented by heterogeneous effects across populations and along the developmental life course. Careful theoretical specification, multiple measurement sources, and multiple and varied statistical analysis techniques can be employed to meet these challenges.

A. Measurement Issues
Much of what has been learned about the etiology and epidemiology of alcohol and other drug use has come from surveys of individuals' knowledge, attitudes, and behaviors regarding alcohol and other drugs. Longitudinal studies using self-report data have provided information about childhood precursors of adolescent drug and alcohol use (Kandel 1978; Hawkins, Lishner, and Catalano 1985; Brook et al. 1986; Block,

Block, and Keyes 1988), patterns of progression in use involving different drugs and movement from experimentation to heavy use (Kandel, Kessler, and Margulies 1978; Yamaguchi and Kandel 1984; Newcomb and Bentler 1986), and adult consequences of adolescent drug use (Newcomb and Bentler 1988; Shedler and Block 1990). The extensive reliance on self-report survey data is not surprising given the nature of the behavior in question. Whereas use of tobacco and alcohol products often occurs in public settings, use of illicit drugs is clandestine behavior. Other variables typically examined in these studies include personal attitudes, beliefs, and perceptions about drug use. The most direct method of measuring these constructs is to ask the individual.

This is not to say that survey research methods are free from criticism (e.g., Johnston and O'Malley 1985). National and regional surveys of high school students have been criticized for missing those at greatest risk for exhibiting behavior problems (e.g., school dropouts and absentees, runaways, and those confined to institutions) (Cernkovich, Giordano, and Pugh 1985; Fors and Rojek 1991). Moreover, the validity of self-reports of illegal behavior has been questioned (U.S. General Accounting Office [USGAO] 1993). There is evidence that adults tend to underreport socially undesirable behavior (Harrell 1985; Wish 1990–91), whereas children and youth may be inclined to either underreport or overreport such behavior, depending on the circumstances. Problems with self-report surveys also include ambiguous definitions of the behavior in question and inaccuracies in recalling whether and how often a behavior occurred during the specified response period (Elliott and Huizinga 1988).

Self-report surveys also may have differential validity with different demographic and age groups (Huizinga and Elliott 1986). Despite concerns about possible differences in the meaning and predictive utility of different constructs with different racial and ethnic groups, existing research suggests that the validity of many constructs does not vary across demographic groupings (Austin and Pollard 1993; Gottfredson and Koper 1993; G. D. Gottfredson 1993; Vega et al. 1993). Other research has indicated that most distortions in self-report research are minor and do not pose a threat to the internal validity of prevention program evaluations since errors are equally distributed across the intervention and control groups (Reinisch, Bell, and Ellickson 1991). However, more work is needed to establish the conditions under which self-report inaccuracies are most and least likely to occur.

In response to these criticisms, a number of techniques have been suggested to improve the accuracy and validity of self-report surveys for measuring drug use. National household surveys of youth and adults have been developed to avoid the sampling limitations inherent in classroom-based surveys (e.g., NIDA 1991). Physiological methods of assessing alcohol and tobacco use (e.g., saliva thyiocyanate, expired air carbon dioxide, urinalysis, and hair testing) have been advocated as methods for improving the accuracy of self-reports (Murray et al. 1987; USGAO 1993). Parent, teacher, and peer ratings of a child's behavior are frequently used to assess problem behaviors but have not been widely used to measure drug use. Each of these measurement approaches has its own limitations (Forman and Linney 1991).

Research comparing different measurement strategies has indicated that self-report surveys, when administered privately and confidentially with adequate attention paid to the clarity of item meanings and reporting period boundaries, can provide data with adequate reliability and validity. Moreover, self-report surveys can be administered widely with relatively little cost and can minimize sampling problems caused by lack of consent to participate in more invasive procedures. For these reasons, self-report surveys will continue to be widely used in drug abuse prevention research.

Two basic strategies can be used to improve the validity of measurements used in prevention research. The first is to use multiple measurement strategies and informants to examine the validity of key constructs through their relationship to theoretically similar and dissimilar constructs (Campbell and Fiske 1959). Multiple measures of the same construct using different measurement strategies and informants are expected to correlate much more strongly than measures of theoretically different constructs using the same measurement strategy. Using these techniques, variance due to bias in a particular measurement strategy can be distinguished from variance in the construct itself (Campbell and Fiske 1959), and a "nomological net" can be developed that defines and validates a construct by placing it in a web of relationships to various measures (Patterson and Bank 1986). Prevention research should incorporate assessments from different sources, including student, parent, peer, teacher, and household surveys and archival indicators of risk factors and outcomes.

The second strategy is to examine patterns of relationships among a standard set of measures of the various constructs in different samples and in different contexts. Replication of research findings plays a central role in the validation of those findings in any scientific endeavor, yet so far replication studies have been rare in prevention research. Although many studies have examined risk and protective factors for alcohol and other drug abuse, few have used consistent sets of constructs and measures. Thus, it is difficult, if not impossible, to compare findings across studies, which severely limits the usefulness of the body of findings as a whole. Without comparable data across studies, it is impossible to distinguish the impact of different interventions, samples, or measures on study findings. A core set of psychometrically sound measures of those constructs that have emerged as consistent predictors of alcohol and drug abuse, used in multiple studies with different populations, would allow more rigorous testing of prevention effects and hypothesized relationships among variables in different population subgroups.

To some extent, standardization of instruments has begun to occur with regard to measures of alcohol and other drug abuse. Propelled by a desire to compare local trends in drug use prevalence to national trends, many states have adopted items from the NHSS Survey. However, in a recent examination of survey items from statewide classroom surveys of alcohol and other drug use administered by six states with whom we are collaborating, we found more differences than similarities in the ways questions were phrased and response options presented. These differences, although often subtle, can have substantial impact on the distributional characteristics of responses that, in turn, can change patterns of observed correlations among the variables dramatically. Careful definition of the key baseline, intervening, and outcome variables relevant to the prevention approach employed, along with the use of standardized and validated instruments and multiple data sources, can help strengthen the conclusions to be drawn from studies of preventive interventions.

B. Mixed Units of Analysis

In many published studies of drug abuse prevention programs, a basic premise of experimental design—that the unit randomized to experimental condition is the unit of analysis—is violated. Schools or classrooms are often the unit of random assignment to experimental or control condition, but analyses of the effect of the intervention are typically assessed using the individual student as the unit of analysis. School or classroom differences are thus confounded with program effects on individuals (Biglan and Ary 1985). Some studies have addressed this problem by assigning multiple schools or classrooms to each condition, then analyzing at the classroom level (Botvin et al. 1984; Biglan et al. 1987; Hansen et al. 1988; Pentz, MacKinnon, et al. 1989).

When scarce resources impose limits on the number of units that can be randomly assigned, some alternative solutions have been suggested. Randomized block and factorial designs can be employed to stratify schools by factors known to affect key outcomes (McKinlay, Stone, and Zucker 1989). Mixed model analyses of variance (Koepsell et al. 1991) and generalized estimating equations (Liang and Zeger 1986) can be used to estimate both the individual and group level components of variation. Alternatively, to account for variability attributable to the school, multiple investigators conducting similar studies with different populations in comparable or contrasting school settings could build a collective case for the general effectiveness of a given approach. Clear specification of the relevant features of the school settings and careful attention to implementation integrity are critical elements of this approach. Murray and Hannan (1990) have concluded that the most prudent course continues to be to assure that the unit of analysis and unit of assignment are the same.

C. Homogeneity of Effect across Different Populations

One problem with the current status of substance abuse prevention research comes from the variation and inconsistencies in study findings (Leukefeld and Bukoski 1991). Existing prevention studies have shown differential effectiveness with different demographic groups. When sample sizes are sufficiently large, researchers can investigate directly the differential effects of preventive interventions on different groups. When subgroups are not large enough for such analysis, Dwyer et al. (1989) have proposed statistical methods using combined logistic and multiple regression models to estimate interaction effects between intervention condition and baseline risk levels. Although this solution is proposed for assessing differential effects across baseline drug use levels, it may be applicable to other quantifiable risk factors as well. Oversampling of smaller demographic groups can also be used to generate large enough samples to investigate differential program impact. Ultimately, replication studies are needed to confirm the utility of specific prevention strategies with different populations.

D. Systematic Attrition

Problems of attrition are acute in school-based studies that are designed to follow longitudinal cohorts of students but use the school or classroom as the unit of random assignment (Hansen, Tobler, and Graham 1990; Biglan et al. 1991). The ecology of schools is such that many students move in and out of the system during any given year. This is especially true in schools located in neighborhoods with high rates of alcohol and other drug use. The external validity of results from school-based preventive interventions has been compromised in many studies by systematic attrition of those at highest risk for drug abuse.

Many published studies of school-based drug abuse prevention interventions have not addressed attrition, reporting results only for students remaining in experimental and comparison classrooms (Biglan et al. 1987). Where attrition has been investigated, studies have consistently shown that subjects with higher baseline levels of tobacco, alcohol, marijuana, and hard drug use are most likely to be lost at follow-up (Biglan et al. 1987; Hansen et al. 1988; Ary et al. 1990; Tebes, Snow, and Arthur 1992), raising questions as to the generalizability of reported results to those at greatest risk. Several solutions to this problem have been proposed. McKinlay et al. (1989) recommend the "intention-to-treat" approach, in which all subjects in the original cohort are retained for the analysis to avoid the bias of differential attrition and preserve the integrity of the randomization. Alternatively, direct observation of the effects of missing data due to attrition may be obtained by including a dummy-coded variable for subjects lost to the study in the analysis (Raymond 1987). Recent advances in statistical methods for imputing missing data (e.g., McArdle and Hamagami 1991; Graham and Donaldson 1993) provide another alternative for adjusting estimates of program effect that are threatened by participant attrition.

E. Intervention Implementation and Intensity

Prevention studies should also investigate the effects of differential intervention implementation and intensity (McKinlay et al. 1989; Institute of Medicine [IOM] 1994). By randomly and independently selecting samples of classrooms or schools in the intervention condition at each measurement point, factors hypothesized to influence the effect of the intervention may be examined (e.g., length of exposure, level of teacher training, variety of media employed). In our own substance abuse prevention studies, we have proposed and used three steps in examining implementation: collection of data to assess degree of implementation, reporting of data on implementation for each dimension of the intervention, and inclusion of implementation data in the tests of efficacy (Hawkins and Lam 1987; Hawkins, Abbott, et al. 1991).

F. Measuring Developmental Change and Intervention Effects

Designs nesting cross-sectional intervention studies within longitudinal panel studies have special relevance and appeal for prevention research. Such designs are well suited to explore questions of group differences as well as change over time, thus providing for tests of intervention effectiveness and for estimation of developmental sequences. Cross-sequential designs, conceived particularly to study developmental problems (Schaie 1965; Tonry, Ohlin, and Farrington 1991), allow estimation of age, cohort, and period effects, thereby producing data both on the development of and changes in drug risk and use patterns over time and on the effects of interventions across cohorts of adolescents (Hawkins, Abbott, et al. 1991).

A major challenge for substance abuse prevention research at this time is to overcome methodological weaknesses. Much work is proceeding along the lines described above. Meanwhile, the failure of substance abuse prevention strategies to establish durability of effects or to show consistent results with substances other than tobacco, as well as the questions remaining about the strategies' effects on abuse as opposed to initiation or occasional use, all suggest that a second major line of prevention research should be pursued.

IV. Prevention Science: The Emergence of Risk
Reduction as a Strategy for Prevention

Public health research offers a model for prevention that seeks to reduce risk factors for disease or disorder and promote processes that protect or buffer against risk (IOM 1994). This risk reduction model offers a promising strategy for the prevention of alcohol and other drug abuse. The risk reduction approach was pioneered by investigators concerned with cardiovascular disease who carried out longitudinal studies to identify risk factors for heart disease. They found that factors such as smoking, diet, stress, lack of exercise, and family history of heart disease all contributed to risk for cardiovascular disease (Farquhar et al. 1985). Risk factors are characteristics of individuals or their environments that, when present, increase the likelihood that individuals will develop a disorder or disease (Garmezy 1983). To qualify as a risk factor, a variable must occur before the onset of the disorder and be associated with an increased probability of disorder. Risk reduction trials that addressed several of the risk factors for cardiovascular disease found that it was possible to lower risk (Farquhar et al. 1990). Evidence has also emerged that morbidity is reduced by prevention strategies that use a risk reduction approach to prevent cardiovascular disease (Vartiainen et al. 1990; IOM 1994).

Recent longitudinal research has identified risk and protective factors in the individual and the environment that consistently predict drug involvement (Kandel, Simcha-Fagan, and Davies 1986; Newcomb, Maddahian, and Bentler 1986; Simcha-Fagan, Gersten, and Langner 1986; Hawkins, Catalano, and Miller 1992). Moreover, the evidence indicates that the likelihood of drug abuse is higher among those exposed to multiple risk factors (Bry, McKeon, and Pandina 1982) and that the risk of drug abuse increases exponentially with exposure to more risk factors (Newcomb et al. 1986). The higher rates of drug abuse among criminal and homeless populations are consistent with studies of personal, social, and environmental risk factors that are predictive of substance abuse. This line of research suggests that interventions to prevent drug abuse should focus on reducing multiple risk factors in family, school, peer, and community environments.

There is also increasing evidence that the effects of exposure to risk can be mitigated by a variety of individual and social characteristics that can be viewed as protective factors. Protective factors may directly decrease dysfunction; they may interact with a risk factor to buffer dysfunction; they may disrupt the mediational chain through which a risk factor operates to cause the dysfunction; or they may prevent the initial occurrence of a risk factor (Coie et al. 1993). To the extent that protective factors are identified that lower the likelihood of drug abuse among those exposed to risk factors, strategies can seek to reduce risk by enhancing these protective factors. Research with populations exposed to multiple risks has identified subgroups of individuals who are able to negotiate risk exposure successfully, escaping relatively unscathed (Werner 1989). These observations have led to interest in the etiological importance of factors that may protect against health problems including drug abuse.

Another important finding from research on risk and protective factors for drug abuse lies in the overlap among problem behaviors (e.g., Donovan and Jessor 1985; Elliott, Huizinga, and Ageton 1985; Barone et al., forthcoming) and the use of some common factors for predicting multiple outcomes (Osgood et al. 1988; Dryfoos 1990). A number of risk and protective factors for drug abuse are also predictors of delinquency (Hawkins et al. 1987), teen pregnancy (Dryfoos 1990), and school dropout (Slavin 1990). This suggests that prevention efforts focused on risk reduction may have a direct effect on diverse disorders that are predicted by these common risks. An important objective of substance abuse prevention research focused on risk reduction is to understand and assess the broader effects of prevention interventions seeking to address these common risk factors. The potential benefit to society of addressing common precursors of a wide range of health, mental health, and behavior problems that lead to nonproductiveness and to the costly utilization of health, mental health, drug and alcohol, and criminal justice services may be greater than simply decreasing the incidence of diagnosable cases of substance abuse. At least, it is important that effects on school achievement, on criminal behavior, and on other measures of adjustment be measured in substance abuse prevention studies using a risk reduction approach.

Most evaluated substance abuse prevention programs have addressed two risk factors that are salient developmentally just prior to or simultaneous with initiation of drug use (e.g., norms favorable to use and social influences to use drugs). It is not known whether these approaches can protect children made most vulnerable by previous exposure to other risk factors. Ellickson's social influence resistance curriculum, which demonstrated significant reductions in tobacco use for baseline experimenters and nonsmokers, was associated with increases in tobacco use among baseline smokers (Ellickson and Bell 1990). It is possible that these youngsters, having already defined themselves as part of a smoking subculture with attachments to tobacco-using peers, rejected drug resistance skills as antithetical to their social group identity. Learning skills to resist prodrug social influences may be important but insufficient to prevent substance use among those who have been "set up" for drug involvement by exposure to individual, family, or community risk factors earlier in their development (Block, Block, and Keyes 1988; Shedler and Block 1990). This possibility suggests a search for prevention strategies effective in reducing other factors, developmentally prior to social influences to use drugs, that predict drug abuse. Such strategies should be investigated for their long-term effects in preventing drug abuse.

A risk-focused approach to the prevention of substance abuse seeks to prevent drug abuse by eliminating, reducing, mediating, or moderating risk factors for substance abuse. As with cardiovascular disease, longitudinal studies have identified multiple biological, psychological, and social factors at several levels that contribute in some degree to the prediction of drug use. Knowledge regarding the causal status of many of these risk and protective factors is far from complete. Clayton (1993) recently identified key subjects on which little is known concerning the etiology of substance abuse: (a) which risk factors are predictive of the various stages in drug use other than initiation, including continuation, progression within drug classes, progression across drug classes, regression, cessation, and relapse; (b) the causal pathways connecting risk factors to later drug use and abuse; (c) the dynamic interactions between various risk and protective factors and behavior at different developmental stages; and (d) the reasons why most people who experience multiple risk factors do not end up abusing drugs. Despite the limitations in our understanding of the causal pathways that may or may not link specific risk and protective factors to subsequent drug abuse, to the extent that they are malleable, they represent the most promising targets currently available for preventive intervention (Lorion and Ross 1992; Coie et al. 1993). Eliminating or reducing those risk factors that play a causal role in etiology should reduce the prevalence of substance abuse.

Risk factors for substance abuse have been identified both within individuals and in the environments within which they develop, including families, schools, peer groups, and the broader community. These risk factors have been described elsewhere (Newcomb, Maddahian, and Bentler 1986; Simcha-Fagan, Gersten, and Langner 1986; Hawkins, Catalano, and Miller 1992) and are summarized here in table 1. These risk factors are predictive of the frequent use of alcohol or other drugs during adolescence and early adulthood, dysfunction associated with substance use, or both.

A. Individual Characteristics

Some children appear to be at greater risk for alcohol and drug abuse by virtue of their family histories, their temperament, and their early and persistent display of behavior problems. A family history of alcohol and other drug abuse has been well established as a risk factor for substance abuse (Schuckit 1987; Tarter 1988; Merikangas, Rounsaville, and Prusoff 1992). Some evidence supports the hypothesis of a genetic predisposition both for alcoholism (Murray, Clifford, and Gurling 1983; Blum et al. 1990; Merikangas 1990) and other drug abuse (Grove et al. 1990; Pickens et al. 1991). Studies of twins and adoptees have provided the strongest evidence of a genetic risk factor for alcoholism,

TABLE 1

Risk Factors for Adolescent Substance Abuse

Risk Factor	Etiological Study	Evidence (Findings)
A. Individual factors:		
1. Family history	Goodwin 1985	About half of hospitalized alcoholics do not have a family history of alcoholism.
	Pollock et al. 1983	More slow-wave electroencephalogram activity was found in children of alcoholics than nonalcoholics.
	Schuckit, Parker, and Rossman 1983; Schuckit 1980; Schuckit and Rayes 1979; Schuckit 1987	Differences were found between children of alcoholics and nonalcoholics in serum prolactin response, muscle response, and levels of acetaldehyde after administration of alcohol.
2. Genetic factors	Blum et al. 1990	Genetic susceptibility to at least one form of alcoholism is suggested by polymorphic pattern of dopamine D2 receptor gene.
	Grove et al. 1990	Significant concordance was found among monozygotic twins raised apart for diagnosis of drug-related problems, antisocial behavior. No concordance has been found for alcohol-related problems.
	Pickens et al. 1991	Higher concordance rates were found among monozygotic than among dizygotic twins for alcohol and drug abuse. Results were stronger for males than females.
	Kaij 1960; Hrubec and Omenn 1981	Monozygotic twins were more than twice as likely as dizygotic twins to be concordant for alcoholism (all males).
	Goodwin et al. 1974; Goodwin et al. 1977; Bohman 1978; Cadoret, Cain, and Grove 1980; Cadoret and Gath 1978	Rates of alcoholism ranging from 18–27 percent were found for adopted sons of alcoholics compared with 5–6 percent for adopted males without biological alcoholic parent.

TABLE 1 (*Continued*)

Risk Factor	Etiological Study	Evidence (Findings)
3. Biochemical factors	Cloninger, Sigvardsson, and Bohman 1988	Sensation seeking and low-harm avoidance predict early-onset alcoholism.
	Zuckerman 1987; van Knorring, Oreland, and von Knorring 1987; Tabakoff and Hoffman 1988	Sensation-seeking, early-onset alcoholism was linked to platelet monoamine oxidase activity.
	Suwacki and Ohara 1985; Schuckit 1987	Aldehyde dehydrogenase differences were found in Asians with lower rates of alcoholism than controls.
4. Early and persistent problem behaviors	Robins 1978	More variety, frequency of child antisocial behavior portends adult antisocial behavior.
	Lerner and Vicary 1984	"Difficult" temperament in 5-year-olds contributes to drug problems in adulthood.
	Shedler and Block 1990	18-year-old frequent marijuana users had emotional distress in childhood.
	Kellam and Brown 1982; Lewis, Robins, and Rice 1985; Nylander 1979; Loeber 1988; Spivack 1983	Aggressiveness in boys ages 5–7 predicts frequent drug use, delinquency in adolescence, problems in adulthood.
	Loeber and Dishion 1983	Only 30–40 percent of boys with problem aggressive behavior maintained it 4–9 years later.
	Loeber 1988; McCord 1981; Barnes and Welte 1986; Kandel 1982	Early aggressive or antisocial behavior persisting into early adolescence predicts later adolescent aggressiveness, drug abuse, and alcohol problems.
	Milich and Loney 1980	Hyperactivity or attention-deficit disorder raises delinquency risk if combined with conduct problems.
	Gittelman, Mannuzza, and Bonagura 1985	Hyperactivity in children, especially accompanied by conduct problems, increases substance abuse risk in late adolescence.

372

Factor	References	Description
	Brook et al. 1990	Children who are irritable or distractible, have temper tantrums, fight with siblings, or engage in predelinquent acts are more likely to use drugs in adolescence.
5. Alienation and rebelliousness	Jessor and Jessor 1977; Kandel 1982; Penning and Barnes 1982; Jessor, Donovan, and Windmer 1980; Robins 1980	Alienation from dominant societal values and low religiosity are positively related to drug use and delinquent behavior.
	Bachman, Johnston, and O'Malley 1981; Kandel, 1982; Smith and Fogg 1978	Rebelliousness and resistance to traditional authority are positively related to drug use and delinquent behavior.
	Jessor and Jessor 1977; Jessor 1976; Paton and Kandel 1978	High tolerance of deviance, resistance to authority, strong need for independence, and normlessness are linked with drug use.
	Shedler and Block 1990	Interpersonal alienation at age 7 predicted frequent marijuana use at 18.
6. Attitudes favorable to drug use	Kandel, Kessler, and Margulies 1978; Krosnick and Judd 1982; Smith and Fogg 1978	Initiation into substance use is preceded by values favorable to its use.
7. Early onset of drug use	Rachal et al. 1982; Kandel 1982; Fleming, Kellam, and Brown 1982; Robins and Pryzbeck 1985	Misusers of alcohol begin drinking earlier than users; earlier onset of drug use predicts greater and more persistent use of more dangerous drugs.
	Brunswick and Boyle 1979; O'Donnell and Clayton 1979	Earlier initiation of drug use increases probability of deviant activities.
	Kandel, Single, and Kessler 1976	Later onset of drug use predicts lower drug involvement and higher probability of discontinuation of use.
B. Family factors:		
8. Family drug behavior	Cotton 1979; Goodwin 1985; Cloninger et al. 1985; Johnson, Schoutz, and Locke 1984; Kandel, Kessler, and Margulies 1978; McDermott 1984	Parental and sibling alcoholism and use of illicit drugs increase risk of alcoholism, drug use initiation, and drug abuse in children.
	Ahmed et al. 1984	Drug salience in the household is the best predictor of children's expectations to use and actual use of alcohol, tobacco, and marijuana.

TABLE 1 (*Continued*)

Risk Factor	Etiological Study	Evidence (Findings)
	Hansen et al. 1987	Parental modeling was directly related to friends' use of drugs, which in turn was related to adolescent subjects' drug use.
	Brook et al. 1988	Oldest brothers as well as parents each had independent effect on younger brother's use. Both drug modeling and drug advocacy by older brothers had independent effects and interacted with parental drug use to provide a risk/protective effect.
	Brook et al. 1990	Fathers' nondrug use and emotional stability enhanced effects of peer nonuse of drugs.
	McDermott 1984; Hansen et al. 1987; Barnes and Welte 1986; Brook et al. 1986; Jessor, Donovan, and Windmer 1980	Perceived parent permissiveness toward drug and alcohol use was more important than actual parent drug use in determining adolescent drug, alcohol use.
	Kandel and Andrews 1987; Baumrind 1983; Penning and Barnes 1982	Lack of or inconsistent parental discipline and low parental educational aspirations for children predict initiation into drug use.
	Ziegler-Driscoll 1979; Kaufman and Kaufman 1979	Overinvolvement by one parent accompanied by distance or permissiveness by the other was associated with risk.
9. Family management practices	Baumrind 1983	Parent authoritativeness is related to children's prosocial, assertive behaviors; parent nondirectiveness and permissiveness is associated with higher drug use.
	Reilly 1979	Common characteristics of families of adolescent drug abusers: negative communication patterns; inconsistent, unclear behavior limits; and unrealistic parental expectations.

	Reference	Finding
	Norem-Hebeisen et al. 1984	Drug users saw fathers as more hostile, adversarial, and both parents as less caring, more rejecting.
	Tec 1974	Parental drug use in an unrewarding family structure is more linked to marijuana use than parental drug use in a rewarding family context.
	Brook et al. 1990	Parent-adolescent attachment is related to less marijuana use. The psychological stability of mothers offsets the effects of peer drug use.
	Shedler and Block 1990	The quality of mother's interactions with 5-year-olds is related to marijuana use at 18.
	Peterson et al., forthcoming	Good family management practices predicted less adolescent alcohol use, even when parents used alcohol.
10. Low bonding to family	Kandel, Kessler, and Margulies 1978; Brook et al. 1992; Braucht, Kirby, and Berry 1978; Penning and Barnes 1982; Kandel and Andrews 1987	Lack of parent-child closeness and lack of maternal involvement are related to drug use initiation.
	Hirschi 1969	Bonding inhibits delinquency.
	Elliott, Huizinga, and Ageton 1985; Brook et al. 1990	Family bonding interacts with peer variables to influence delinquency and drug use.
	Jessor and Jessor 1977; Kim 1979; Norem-Hebeisen et al. 1984; Gorsuch and Butler 1976; Selnow 1987; Brook et al. 1990; Brook et al. 1986; Hundleby and Mercer 1987	Family involvement and attachment discourage youth drug initiation and level of use.
11. Family conflict	Baumrind 1983; Penning and Barnes 1982; Robins 1980	Children from homes broken by marital discord are at higher risk of delinquency and drug use.
	Wilson and Hernstein 1985	There was no independent contribution of parents' marital dissolution to delinquent behavior.

TABLE 1 (*Continued*)

Risk Factor	Etiological Study	Evidence (Findings)
	McCord 1979; Rutter and Giller 1983; McCord and McCord 1959; Porter and O'Leary 1980; Hetherington, Cox, and Cox 1979; Wallerstein and Kelly 1980; Simcha-Fagan, Gersten, and Langner 1986	Family conflict is a stronger predictor of delinquency than family structure (intact parental marriage).
	Needle, Su, and Doherty 1990	Adolescents who experienced parental divorce during their adolescent years were more likely to use drugs than adolescents who experienced their parents' divorce during childhood.
C. School factors:		
12. Academic failure	Jessor 1976; Smith and Fogg 1978; Robins 1980	Failure in school predicted adolescent drug abuse, as well as the frequency and levels of use of illicit drugs.
	Feldhusen, Thurston, and Benning 1973	Early antisocial behavior may predict later academic failure.
	Hundleby and Mercer 1987	Good school performance reduced likelihood of frequent drug use in ninth graders.
13. Low commitment to school	Johnston, O'Malley, and Bachman 1985	The use of a variety of drugs is significantly lower among students expecting to attend college.
	G. D. Gottfredson 1988	4–6 percent of variance in truancy was associated with drug involvement, controlling for ethnicity, parent education, delinquency.
	Kelly and Balch 1971	How much students like school is related to levels of drug use.
	Friedman 1983	Time spent on homework and the perception of relevance of course work are related to levels of drug use.

D. Peer factors:

	References	
14. Peer rejection in elementary grades	Parker and Asher 1987; Coie et al. 1992	Low acceptance by peers seems to elevate risk for school problems and criminality.
	Kellam, Ensminger, and Simon 1980	Children who had been aggressive as first graders or aggressive and shy had higher levels of drug use than those who were just shy.
	Brook et al. 1986	Childhood traits of social inhibition, isolation, and aggression were not associated with an adolescent drug use stage, but aggression, lower inhibition, and lower isolation in adolescence was associated with a higher drug use stage.
	Cairns et al. 1988; Hartup 1983; Tremblay 1988	Aggressiveness may be associated with acceptance by other aggressive peers who could foster drug use; similarly, socially rejected children may form friendships with other rejected children in adolescence, leading to later delinquent behavior.
15. Association with drug-using peers	Barnes and Welte 1986; Kandel 1978, 1986; Kandel and Andrews 1987; Elliott, Huizinga, and Ageton 1985; Jessor, Donovan, and Windmer 1980; Brook et al. 1990	Peer use of substances is among the strongest predictors of substance use among youth.
	Newcomb and Bentler 1986; Gillmore et al. 1990	Influence of peers on drug use is stronger than that of parents for whites, African-Americans, Asians, and Hispanics.
	Harford 1985	Nondrinking African-American youths reported fewer drinking friends than African-American youths who drank.
	Dembo et al. 1979	Friends' use of alcohol and marijuana was related to use by African-American and Puerto-Rican youths.
	Brook et al. 1990, 1992	The most powerful linkage in the causal pathway to marijuana nonuse was association with nondrug-using peers.

TABLE 1 (*Continued*)

Risk Factor	Etiological Study	Evidence (Findings)
E. Contextual factors:		
16. Availability	Gorsuch and Butler 1976	Increased alcohol availability led to increases in drinking prevalence, amount of alcohol consumed, and heavy use of alcohol.
	Maddahian, Newcomb, and Bentler 1988; Dembo et al. 1979; G. D. Gottfredson 1988	Availability affected use of alcohol and illegal drugs.
17. Laws and norms:		
a) Taxation	Levy and Sheflin 1985	A one-dollar increase in tax on alcohol led to one-half percent decrease in consumption.
	Cook and Tauchen 1982	An increase in the alcohol tax led to a sharp decrease in consumption and cirrhosis mortality.
	Saffer and Grossman 1987	Higher taxes were associated with lower teen drinking and fatalities. A higher tax was more salient than drinking age.
b) Laws regulating to whom liquor is sold	Saffer and Grossman 1987; Krieg 1982; Cook and Tauchen 1982; Joksch 1988	Higher drinking age is associated with fewer teenage traffic fatalities and driving while intoxicated citations.
c) Laws regulating how liquor is sold	Holder and Blose 1987; Blose and Holder 1987	Liquor-by-the-drink sales increased consumption of distilled spirits but not the proportion of drinkers in the population.
d) Criminal laws making drugs illegal	Polich et al. 1984	Neither doubling of interdiction nor increased arrests of drug dealers affect retail prices or availability of illegal drugs.
e) Cultural norms	Watts and Rabow 1983; Flasher and Maisto 1984; Robins 1984; Vaillant 1983	Alcohol consumption and other alcohol-related effects are associated with sociodemographic factors, including ethnic and other group norms.

	Reference	Finding
	Johnston 1991	Changes in nationwide norms regarding the acceptability and harmfulness of marijuana and cocaine preceded decreases in prevalence.
	Atkin, Hocking, and Black 1984	Teens reporting higher drinking levels had more exposure to ads promoting alcohol.
	Bursik and Webb 1982; Farrington et al. 1985	Poverty was associated with childhood conduct problems, delinquency, chronic offenses.
	Bachman, Johnston, and O'Malley 1981; Zucker and Harford 1983; Murray et al. 1987	Parental education and occupation were positively correlated with teen alcohol and marijuana use.
	Robins and Ratcliff 1979	Extreme poverty is one of three factors increasing risk of adult alcohol and drug abuse in adults who were antisocial as children.
18. Extreme economic deprivation	Brook et al. 1990	Low socioeconomic status in childhood is related to greater drug use in adolescence.
19. Neighborhood disorganization	Murray 1983; Herting and Guest 1985; Wilson and Herrnstein 1985; Fagan 1988; Simcha-Fagan and Schwartz 1986; Sampson, Castellano, and Laub 1981; Sampson 1986	Characteristics of neighborhoods such as population density, mobility, physical deterioration, low attachment, and high crime are related to juvenile crime and drug trafficking.

379

particularly among males (Hrubec and Omenn 1981; Goodwin 1985). Recently, Kendler (1992) reported evidence for a similar genetic component in female alcoholism. However, these studies also indicate that most offspring of alcoholics do not themselves become alcoholic, while about half of hospitalized alcoholics do not have a family history of alcoholism (Clayton 1993; Goodwin 1985). Several researchers have suggested that different forms of alcoholism may have different levels of genetic influence (Cloninger et al. 1989).

Some studies suggest that inherited biological traits and temperament may provide the link between genetics and behavior (Schuckit 1987; Tarter 1988; Blum et al. 1990). High behavior activity level (Tarter et al. 1990), psychopathology (Weiss 1992), and sensation seeking (Cloninger, Sigvardsson, and Bohman 1988; Clayton 1993) have each been identified as predictors of early drug initiation or abuse. For example, hyperactivity and attention-deficit disorders in childhood have been found to predict substance abuse disorders in late adolescence, especially when combined with aggressive behaviors or conduct disorders (Gittelman, Mannuzza, and Bonagura 1985). These characteristics are hypothesized to influence the reciprocal interactions between the developing individual and his or her environment and, thus, influence acquired behavioral and habit patterns (Tarter 1988).

An early behavioral marker of risk for substance abuse is a pattern of persistent conduct problems in multiple settings. The greater the variety, frequency, and seriousness of childhood behavior problems, the more likely antisocial behavior is to persist into adulthood (Robins 1978). In a longitudinal study of five-year-olds followed into adulthood, Lerner and Vicary (1984) found that children with a difficult temperament, including frequent negative mood states and withdrawal and slow adaptability to change in childhood, were more likely to become regular users of alcohol, tobacco, and marijuana in adulthood than "easy" children, who evidenced greater adaptability and positive affect early in life. Similarly, aggressive behavior in boys as early as age five has been found to predict frequent drug use in adolescence (Kellam and Brown 1982; Brook et al. 1990) and drug problems in adulthood (Lewis, Robins, and Rice 1985).

Individual attitudes also predict higher risk for substance abuse. Shedler and Block (1990) found that interpersonal alienation measured as early as age seven predicted frequent marijuana use at age eighteen. Alienation from the dominant values of society (Jessor and Jessor 1977; Penning and Barnes 1982), low religiosity (Jessor, Donovan, and

Windmer 1980; Brunswick, Messeri, and Titus 1992), and rebellious-
ness (Bachman, Johnston, and O'Malley 1981; Kandel 1982; Block,
Block, and Keyes 1988) have been shown to predict greater drug use.
Favorable attitudes toward drug use precede the initiation of drug use
and have also consistently predicted drug use (Kandel, Kessler, and
Margulies 1978; Krosnick and Judd 1982).

B. Family Characteristics

Families affect children's drug use behaviors in a number of ways.
Beyond the genetic transmission of a propensity to alcoholism, family
modeling of drug use behavior and permissive parental attitudes toward children's drug use predict greater risk of alcohol and other drug
abuse (Johnson et al. 1984; Barnes and Welte 1986; Brook et al. 1986).
Generally, the more members of the household who use a drug, the
greater is a child's risk of early initiation of use of that drug (Ahmed
et al. 1984). Moreover, involving children in parental alcohol or drug
using behaviors (such as getting a beer or a pack of cigarettes for a
parent) also increases risk for early initiation of drug use (Ahmed et
al. 1984), which is, itself, one of the strongest predictors of alcohol
and other drug abuse (Robins and Przybeck 1985). Parents are not the
only family role models for their children's behavior, however. Brook
and her colleagues (1988) found that older brothers' drug behavior and
attitudes were more strongly related to younger brothers' use than was
parents' modeling of drug use.

More generally, poor parenting practices and high levels of conflict
in the family appear to increase risk for several adolescent health and
behavior problems including the abuse of alcohol and other drugs
(Brook et al. 1990). Kandel and Andrews (1987) found that lack of
maternal involvement in activities with children; lack of, or inconsistent, parental discipline (see also Penning and Barnes 1982; Baumrind
1983); and low parental educational aspirations for their children predict initiation of drug use. Stanton (1979), Kaufman and Kaufman
(1979), and Ziegler-Driscoll (1979) suggested that familial risk factors
include a pattern of overinvolvement by one parent and distance or
permissiveness by the other.

Parents' disciplinary techniques have also been related to adolescents' subsequent drug use. Brook and her colleagues (1990) found
that maternal control techniques were more important than paternal
techniques in explaining adolescent marijuana use. Baumrind (1983)
found that parental nondirectiveness or permissiveness contributed to

higher levels of drug use. Another study revealed that common characteristics of families with adolescent drug abusers included negative communication patterns (criticism, blaming, lack of praise), inconsistent and unclear behavioral limits, and unrealistic parental expectations of children (Reilly 1979).

In addition to parental disciplinary style, aspects of parent-child relationships have been shown to predict adolescent substance use. Shedler and Block (1990) found that the quality of mothers' interaction with their children at age five distinguished children who were frequent users of marijuana at age eighteen from those who had only experimented with marijuana use. Mothers of children who became frequent users were relatively cold, underresponsive, and underprotective with their children, giving their children little encouragement but pressuring them to perform in tasks. Brook and her colleagues (1992) found that maternal low attachment and paternal permissiveness predicted movement from low to moderate levels of alcohol and marijuana use. Norem-Hebeisen et al. (1984) also found that the quality of adolescents' relationships with their parents was related to patterns of drug use. Generally, drug users perceived their fathers as more hostile, rejecting, and adversarial than did nonusers.

Conversely, positive family relationships—involvement and attachment—appear to discourage youths' initiation into drug use (Gorsuch and Butler 1976; Jessor and Jessor 1977; Kim 1979; Norem-Hebeisen et al. 1984; Brook et al. 1986; Selnow 1987). Hundleby and Mercer (1987) found that adolescents' reports of parental trust, warmth, and involvement explained small portions of the variance in the extent of tobacco, alcohol, and marijuana use. Bonding to family may inhibit drug involvement during adolescence in a manner similar to the way in which family bonding inhibits delinquency (Hirschi 1969). Brook et al. (1990) reported a causal pathway in which parental internalization of traditional values led to the development of strong parent-child attachment; this mutual attachment led to the child's internalization of traditional norms and behavior, which in turn led the youngster to associate with non-drug-using peers, which led to nonuse.

Peterson et al. (1994) found that the effects of parental drinking on alcohol use of their children at ages fourteen to fifteen were mediated by family management practices and family proscriptions against involving children in adult family members' alcohol use (such as opening or pouring drinks). Good family management practices and refraining from involving children in adult alcohol use inhibited alcohol use among fourteen- to fifteen-year-olds, even when adults in the family drank alcohol. These effects were consistent for both African-Americans and whites, though African-American parents in the sample drank less frequently, held stronger norms against alcohol use by teenagers, and involved their children less in family alcohol use than did white parents.

In summary, the risk of drug abuse appears to be increased by family management practices characterized by unclear expectations for behavior, poor monitoring of behavior, few and inconsistent rewards for positive behavior, and excessively severe and inconsistent punishment for unwanted behavior. Both permissiveness and extremely authoritarian parenting practices predict later drug abuse in children (Baumrind 1983; Shedler and Block 1990). Moreover, recent longitudinal analyses indicate that the effects of parental drinking on alcohol use of adolescent offspring are mediated by both family management practices and parental norms with respect to adolescent involvement in the adults' alcohol use (Peterson et al. 1994).

Another aspect of family functioning that has been related to drug use is the level of family conflict. Children raised in families high in conflict appear at risk for both delinquency (Rutter and Giller 1983; Farrington et al. 1985) and illegal drug use (Simcha-Fagan, Gersten, and Langner 1986). Rutter and Giller have noted that parental conflict is associated with antisocial behavior in children even when the parental dyad is intact and, conversely, that, even in samples in which homes are broken by divorce or separation, the extent of continuing parental conflict is associated with the likelihood of antisocial behavior in the children. Needle, Su, and Doherty (1990) found in a longitudinal study of 508 families recruited from a large health maintenance organization that adolescents who had experienced parental divorce during their adolescent years reported greater drug use than adolescents who had experienced parental divorce during their childhood and adolescents whose parents had not divorced.

C. School Factors

While there appears to be no relationship between low intelligence and drug abuse, school failure beginning in late elementary grades increases risk for adolescent drug abuse. Achievement problems may result from early behavior problems, learning disabilities, the failure of teachers to motivate students, or other causes. Regardless of cause, the experience of not succeeding academically during late childhood appears to predict the early initiation of drug use (Bachman, Johnston, and O'Malley 1991), which, in turn, increases drug abuse risk. Poor school performance has been found to predict both frequency and levels of use of illegal drugs (Smith and Fogg 1978). Holmberg (1985), in a longitudinal study of fifteen-year-olds, reported that truancy, placement in a special class, and early dropout from school were prognostic factors for drug abuse. In contrast, outstanding performance in school reduced the likelihood of frequent drug use among a ninth-grade sample studied by Hundleby and Mercer (1987). Kandel and Davies (1992, p. 238) reported that "the present data indicate that successful school performance is a protective factor mitigating against escalation to a pattern of regular marijuana use. Working toward strengthening the educational system would have many beneficial effects, including a potential reduction in the number of students who go on to abusing drugs."

A low degree of commitment to education also appears to be related to adolescent drug use. Annual surveys of high school seniors by Johnston, O'Malley, and Bachman (1985) show that the use of hallucinogens, cocaine, heroin, stimulants, sedatives, or nonmedically prescribed tranquilizers is significantly lower among students who expect to attend college than among those who do not plan to go on to college. G. D. Gottfredson (1988) found that truancy for both males and females was associated with drug involvement after accounting for effects of ethnicity, parental education, and delinquency. Factors such as how much students like school (Kelly and Balch 1971), time spent on homework, and perception of the relevance of coursework are also related to levels of drug use (Friedman 1983), indicating a negative relationship between commitment to education and frequent drug use among junior and senior high school students.

D. Peer Factors

Peer relationships also are predictive of substance use and abuse. Although it would be premature to posit a direct link between peer rejection and substance abuse, low acceptance by peers seems to put an adolescent at risk for school problems and criminality (Parker and Asher 1987; Kupersmidt, Coie, and Dodge 1990; Coie et al. 1992), which are also risk factors for substance abuse (Hawkins et al. 1987).

Little research has been done on the direct link between peer rejection and substance use, but traits of the child that have been associated with peer rejection—aggressiveness, shyness, and withdrawal—have been examined for their relationship to drug use. For example, Kellam,

Ensminger, and Simon (1980) found that children who had been shy in first grade reported low levels of involvement in drug use, whereas those who had been aggressive or had shown a combination of aggressiveness with shyness in first grade had the highest levels of use. Brook et al. (1986) found that childhood traits relevant to peer rejection—social inhibition, isolation from peers, and aggression against peers—were not significantly associated with adolescent drug use stage. However, aggression against peers during adolescence was associated with stage of use, and teenagers who were less socially inhibited and less isolated from peers were likely to be at a more advanced stage of use.

These studies suggest that the link between peer rejection and subsequent drug use may not be a simple one. Shyness, by isolating a child from his or her peers, may protect the child against drug use by eliminating one source of influence to use: drug-using peers. Aggressiveness, on the other hand, while resulting for some children in exclusion from groups of conventional peers, may be associated with acceptance by other aggressive and perhaps delinquent peers who could foster drug use (Cairns et al. 1988). Hartup (1983) suggested that rejected children form friendships with other rejected children during the preadolescent years and that these friendship groups become delinquent during adolescence. However, this process is as yet unconfirmed (Tremblay 1988).

Peer use of substances has consistently been found to be among the strongest predictors of substance use among youth (Kandel 1978, 1986; Jessor et al. 1980; Elliott, Huizinga, and Ageton 1985; Barnes and Welte 1986; Kandel and Andrews 1987; Brook et al. 1990, 1992). Studies among specific ethnic groups confirm this relationship. Newcomb and Bentler (1986) reported that the influence of peers on adolescent drug use was stronger than that of parents for Caucasians, African-Americans, Asian-Americans, and Hispanic-Americans. Similar findings were reported by Byram and Fly (1984). Harford (1985) found that African-American youth who did not drink alcohol reported fewer school friends who drank than were reported by those who did drink, and Dembo et al. (1979) found that friends' use of alcohol and marijuana was related to a youth's own use for both African-American and Puerto Rican–American youth.

E. Early Onset of Drug Use

An early onset of drug use predicts subsequent misuse of drugs and drug abuse. The younger the child is when alcohol or other drug use is first initiated, the greater the frequency of drug use (Fleming, Kellam, and Brown 1982), the greater the probability of extensive and persistent involvement in the use of more dangerous drugs (Kandel 1982), and the greater the risk of drug abuse (Robins and Pryzbeck 1985). Conversely, a later age of drug use onset has been shown to predict lower drug involvement and a greater probability of discontinuation of use (Kandel, Single, and Kessler 1976).

F. Contextual Factors

Factors external to the individual in the broad social environment also affect rates of drug abuse. Contextual factors affect the levels of use and abuse of alcohol as well as illegal drugs. Community drug use patterns predict individual use (Robins 1984). Contextual factors that predict risk for abuse include the availability and price of alcohol and other drugs, broad social norms regarding alcohol or other drug use in the population (Vaillant 1983; Watts and Rabow 1983; Flasher and Maisto 1984; Robins 1984), poverty (Robins and Ratcliff 1979; Murray, Richards, et al. 1987), and neighborhood disorganization (Sampson 1986; Fagan 1988).

Rates of alcohol use, including heavy use and rates of illegal drug use, have been found to be higher in neighborhoods and schools where alcohol and other drugs are easily available (Gorsuch and Butler 1976; D. C. Gottfredson 1988; Maddahian, Newcomb, and Bentler 1988). Availability and price are influenced by legal restriction or regulation on purchase, by excise taxes, and by market forces. Legal restriction significantly limits the prevalence of use. This is true for all drugs including alcohol: "Contrary to the prevalent view that prohibition failed, there is substantial evidence that it reduced alcohol consumption substantially" (Goldstein and Kalant 1990, p. 1515). The epidemiological evidence from prohibition indicates that the prevalence of use of a drug increases with its legalization and decreases with legal restriction.

Demand for drugs, whether legal or illegal, drives the market. Drugs legally distributed to adults, including alcohol and tobacco, are advertised to build demand. There is limited evidence that rates of alcohol consumption among teens are associated with exposure to ads promoting alcohol (Atkin, Hocking, and Block 1984). Moreover, societal norms regarding the use of illicit drugs have been shown to affect both the incidence and prevalence of marijuana and cocaine use among high school seniors nationwide (Johnston 1991). Increased perceptions of social disapproval and harmfulness of marijuana and cocaine use among the seniors in the NHSS Survey preceded the downward trend in prevalence of use of these substances. Similarly, where laws and community norms express greater tolerance for the use of alcohol or illegal drugs, rates of alcoholism, alcohol abuse, and drug abuse are higher (Johnston 1991).

Finally, there is evidence that children who grow up in disorganized neighborhoods with high population density, high residential mobility, physical deterioration, and low levels of attachment to neighborhood may face greater risk for a range of behavior problems, including trafficking and drug abuse (Fagan 1988).

G. Generalizations and Implications from Research on Risk

Like risks for cardiovascular disease, risks for drug abuse exist in several domains. Family factors, school experiences, peers, individual attitudes and characteristics, and community norms all contribute to risk for drug abuse. The greater the number of risk factors to which the individual is exposed, the greater the risk of drug abuse (Bry, McKeon, and Pandina 1982; Newcomb, Maddahian, and Skager 1987). Thus, effective prevention of drug abuse may require coordinated intervention to reduce multiple risks, especially in areas where children are exposed to multiple risk factors early in life. The majority of individuals who experience risk factors, however, do not develop substance abuse problems, suggesting another, albeit related, line of research and intervention focusing on processes that buffer or protect against risk.

H. Protective Factors

Three broad categories of factors that protect against substance use even in the face of risk exposure in childhood have been identified. The first are individual characteristics including resilient temperament, positive social orientation, intelligence, and skills (Radke-Yarrow and Sherman 1990). Whereas some individual factors, such as behavioral skills, may be modifiable, others such as cognitive processing and the ability to concentrate may be more strongly influenced by genetic and biological factors. A second protective factor is cohesion, warmth, or bonding during childhood. This generally occurs in the family, but, in addition, other social supports from teachers, other adults, and peers that reinforce the individual's competencies and commitments and support a non-drug-using belief system appear to buffer risk exposure (Garmezy 1985; Werner 1989). Finally, norms, beliefs, or behavioral standards that oppose the use of illegal drugs or the use of alcohol by teenagers also appear to serve as protective factors (Hansen and Graham 1991). As distinct from risk factors, protective factors are hypothesized to operate indirectly through interaction with risk factors, mediating or moderating the effects of risk exposure (Rutter 1990; Hawkins, Catalano, and Miller 1992).

I. Principles of Prevention Science

The existing evidence suggests the following basic principles for designing preventive interventions.

1. *Focus on Reducing Known Risk Factors.* The goals of prevention may be accomplished by direct efforts to reduce exposure to risk factors or by enhancing protective factors that moderate or mediate the effects of exposure to risk. Prevention efforts should specify what risk factors are targeted and should specify the mechanism or process through which these risk factors are thought to operate. Some risk factors may not be causal but may be useful in identifying high-risk populations for intervention. These should be identified. Other, causal, risk factors should be the objects of preventive interventions that seek to modify them.

2. *When Reducing Risk, Enhance Known Protective Factors.* Further strength may be added to preventive interventions by enhancing mutable protective factors that moderate risk. For example, interventions that focus on reducing family management problems should do so in ways that enhance family bonding and the conventional or healthy belief structure in the family. In this way, not only is the negative risk reduced, but bonding is strengthened to provide motivation to continue sound management and to obey family rules.

Further, in some circumstances, it may be impossible to reduce or eliminate certain risk factors directly through preventive intervention, but the effects of these may be moderated by intervention to enhance protective factors. For example, even in families with an alcoholic parent, it may be possible to moderate the effects of parental alcoholism on children by intervening to provide supports for good family management, school achievement, and abstinence from alcohol use by children.

3. *Address Risk and Protective Factors at Appropriate Developmental Stages.* Some risk and protective factors appear to be relatively stable predictors across the life span, while others appear to predict dysfunction at specific periods of development. For example, poor parental

monitoring appears to predict conduct disorders across childhood, while association with drug using peers is predictive of drug use only in adolescence (Dishion 1990). Conduct and behavior problems in early elementary grades signal risk for later health and behavior problems. Early intervention is warranted for children with these problems. If children experience academic difficulties in grades 4–6, this is a predictor of drug abuse risk. Tutoring and academic enrichment programs are, thus, indicated during the elementary period.

4. *Intervene Early—before the Target Behavior Stabilizes.* Early initiation of drug use is a predictor of a prolonged course of involvement with drug use and of drug abuse. This suggests that preventive interventions should be delivered before the initiation of drug use. A viable goal for preventive intervention may be to delay the onset of initiation of alcohol or other drug use. This is the immediate goal of many recent drug abuse prevention initiatives, though few have been followed long enough to determine whether early delays in initiation translate into later reductions in diagnosable substance use disorders.

5. *Include Those at High Risk.* Given the additive or perhaps multiplicative effect of exposure to multiple risk factors, it is important to design preventive interventions to reach those exposed to multiple risk factors. This may be accomplished by selecting for intervention communities or schools in which there are elevated levels of risk or by identifying individuals exposed to multiple risks for special attention.

6. *Address Multiple Risks with Multiple Strategies.* A viable prevention strategy may require attention to individual vulnerabilities, poor child rearing, school achievement, social influences, social skills, and broad social norms, all of which are implicated in the development of adolescent drug abuse. Because risks are present in several social domains and cumulate in predicting drug abuse, multicomponent prevention strategies focused on reducing multiple risks and enhancing multiple protective factors may be required. Such strategies would be designed to build up protection while reducing or moderating risk exposure.

In sum, the evidence suggests a need for a developmentally adjusted, multicomponent risk reduction strategy that cuts across traditional health, education, and human service delivery systems. The strategy must reach those at highest risk by virtue of exposure to multiple risk factors and address the most significant risk factors they face, seeking, where possible, to increase protection as well as to reduce risk.

A risk-focused perspective on substance abuse suggests that the broad changes in social norms regarding the use of illegal drugs noted earlier are affecting those who are most bonded to the current social order. Social norms against drug use may inhibit the initiation of drug use only among children who are bonded to those promoting the norms. Children who are alienated from their families by high levels of family conflict and poor family management practices, who are alienated from school as a result of misbehavior and little academic success, and who are rejected by normative peer groups are less likely to be inhibited by parental, school, or classroom norms against the use of drugs. If not securely attached to parents, committed to school, or committed to a set of beliefs or values, young people may be unresponsive to changes in normative expectations in the larger society. It is likely that those at greatest risk of drug abuse by virtue of exposure to multiple risk factors during infancy and childhood are the least likely to be prevented from drug use initiation by current strategies promoting norms against drug use such as "Just say NO" clubs or drug abuse prevention curricula that teach skills to resist drug prone social influences.

For this reason, it is important to assess the effects of law enforcement, normative change strategies, and social influence resistance curricula in deterring substance abuse among those characterized by multiple risk factors predictive of heavy drug use. This has rarely been done. Even if such programs are successful in reducing the prevalence of drug use in the general population, these strategies may have little or no effect on the prevalence of drug abuse as defined in this essay. To illustrate, the lifetime prevalence of alcohol use among U.S. high school seniors in 1991 was 89.5 percent, but only 3.7 percent used alcohol daily (Johnston et al. 1991). Preventive interventions focused on changing social norms and social influences could show positive effects in reducing the prevalence of alcohol use in the general population without affecting those at greatest risk for alcohol-related problems. Learning skills to resist social influences to use drugs may be a necessary, but not sufficient, element of prevention for children who have been "set up" for drug involvement by exposure to individual, family, or community risk factors (Block, Block, and Keyes 1988; Shedler and Block 1990).

If norm change and social influence resistance strategies are to be effective with those most exposed to risk, the preventive task during infancy and childhood is to reduce developmentally salient risk factors while simultaneously encouraging the development of strong social bonds to family, school, and prosocial peers. From a social development perspective, this is accomplished by creating, for developing children, environments rich in opportunities and positive reinforcement, where they may master the cognitive and interpersonal skills appropriate for their developmental age (Catalano and Hawkins, forthcoming). These considerations suggest investigation of intervention strategies that have been effective in reducing other risk factors for substance abuse that occur earlier in the life cycle than norms favorable to use and social influences to use drugs.

V. Promising Prevention Approaches

A number of interventions have shown promise for drug abuse prevention because they address risk factors for drug abuse at appropriate developmental stages, enhance prosocial bonding directly and indirectly by promoting prosocial opportunities, promote cognitive and interpersonal skill development and reinforcement for skillful performance in prosocial situations, and use intervention techniques that have demonstrated positive effects (e.g., Botvin 1990; IOM 1994; USGAO 1994). These interventions include prenatal and infancy programs, early childhood and family support programs, programs for improving parenting skills, social competence skills training programs, programs to promote academic achievement and commitment to school, and programs to change social norms regarding use of alcohol and other drugs. The relevant literatures have been reviewed elsewhere (Hawkins, Catalano, and associates 1992; Hawkins, Catalano, and Miller 1992; IOM 1994; Yoshikawa 1994), although few such interventions have been studied specifically for drug abuse prevention effects. When well implemented, all have reduced known risk factors for drug abuse and have been shown to promote bonding to family and/or school. Examples are described in the following sections.

A. Perinatal Interventions

Interventions with pregnant women and neonates typically have not been designed to prevent drug abuse by the infant many years later. However, some have targeted characteristics of the perinatal experience and the early health and development of the infant, often associated with economic deprivation, that have been linked to higher risk for chronic delinquency and substance abuse in adolescence (Hawkins, Catalano, and Miller 1992; Nyberg et al. 1992; Yoshikawa 1994). Prenatal exposure to alcohol and other drugs, premature birth and very low birthweight, and poor early infant-caregiver relations have emerged as predictors of a number of health and behavior problems in early childhood, including aggressiveness and conduct disorder, hyper-activity and attention disorders, and low IQ and developmental delay (Telzrow 1990; Bates et al. 1991). These childhood characteristics, in turn, may interact over time with environmental conditions such as family stress associated with poverty to increase the likelihood of per-sistent conduct problems, school failure, poor family relations and high levels of family conflict, and alcohol and other drug abuse (Sameroff and Chandler 1975; McGee, Silva, and Williams 1984; Werner 1987). Thus, perinatal interventions that improve the chances of healthy births and infant development while increasing parents' capacity for positive, nurturing caregiving are recognized as a priority for public health policy in the 1990s (Department of Health and Human Services 1990) and should be considered in terms of their promise for prevention of alcohol and other drug abuse and chronic delinquency (Hawkins, Catalano, and associates 1992; Yoshikawa 1994).

One example of a comprehensive perinatal intervention designed to prevent a wide range of maternal and infant health and behavior prob-lems is the Prenatal/Early Infancy Project (Olds et al. 1986, 1988). The project targeted a sample of pregnant women in a high-risk geo-graphical area characterized by high rates of poverty, teen and unmar-ried parents, and child abuse and neglect. The experimental test of the intervention included 394 women, most of whom were European-American and of whom 47 percent were nineteen years or younger, 61 percent lived in poverty, and 62 percent were unmarried. The intervention test compared randomly assigned groups who received either developmental screening of the children at one and two years of age, referral for services, and transportation to well child care clinics or these services combined with home nurse visitation during preg-nancy and until the children were two years old.

The intervention demonstrated positive effects for both mothers and infants (Olds et al. 1986, 1988). At the forty-six-month follow-up, mothers who received nurse visitation had 43 percent fewer additional pregnancies, had worked 82 percent more months, and had spent fewer days on welfare than the mothers who had not been visited. Nurse-visited mothers also reported greater perceived social support and were significantly more likely to improve their diets and stop smoking during pregnancy than mothers in the control condition. Moreover, the young teenage mothers in the experimental condition had a 75 percent reduc-tion in preterm delivery and had 75 percent fewer verified reports of child abuse or neglect than control group mothers. Thus, the intervention had positive effects on risk factors for chronic delinquency and substance abuse, including severe economic deprivation, birth complications, and poor parenting behavior. Long-term effects on the intervention group children were, unfortunately, not assessed.

The Yale Child Welfare project is a second example of a risk reduction intervention during the perinatal period. The goal was "to help disadvantaged young parents to support the development of their children and to improve the quality of family life" (Provence and Naylor 1983, p. 3, as quoted in Seitz 1990). The intervention targeted twenty-five families expecting their first child who registered at the women's clinic of a large city hospital located in a depressed inner-city area and met the following criteria: the families resided in the inner-city area and had incomes less than the federal poverty level; there were no serious complications of pregnancy; and the mothers were not seriously retarded or acutely psychotic. Seventeen of these families met the criteria and agreed to participate (Trickett et al. 1982).

The intervention that began during the mother's pregnancy lasted until thirty months postpartum and included four components: home visits, pediatric care, day care, and developmental exams. The home visits were conducted by professionals (five clinical social workers, two psychologists, and one nurse) and were intended to provide close, personalized help with parents' concerns including food, housing, physical dangers, and educational, marital, and career decisions. Home visitors also acted as liaisons to other community service providers. Intervention families averaged twenty-eight visits during the course of the intervention.

The pediatric care began with daily visits during the postdelivery hospital stay and one home visit during the first week after birth, then continued with house calls (if needed), telephone consultations, and thirteen to seventeen hour-long well-baby exams during the first thirty months. Intervention families received an average of 13.2 months of high-quality day care: staff were highly trained; there were no more than three children to one caregiver; each child had a primary caregiver; and an effort was made to match child-care practices with those of the parents and to work out mutually agreed upon methods of handling issues of emotional and social development. The children also received seven to nine developmental exams using the Yale Child Development Schedule (similar to the Bayley Scales of Infant Development). The four components were coordinated to address basic health, social, and developmental needs of both parents and children comprehensively.

Experimental families demonstrated positive outcomes at the ten-year follow-up, including significantly higher levels of maternal education, fewer children, children spaced farther apart, greater likelihood of full-time employment, and greater likelihood of initiating contact with their child's school teacher than a group of matched comparison families recruited from the same clinic after the intervention had ended. Children in the experimental group were rated less negatively in terms of their behavior by their teachers, were less likely to be excessively absent without a valid excuse, showed significantly better overall adjustment to school, and were less likely to have been referred for school services such as being placed in a class for emotionally disturbed children than children in the comparison group. The authors calculated that the program cost about $20,000 for each child for the full 30 months and achieved a savings of $40,000 per year (in family support costs and additional school services costs) for the total sample by the ten-year follow-up (Seitz, Rosenbaum, and Apfel 1985). These results must be interpreted with some caution, however. Although the intervention and control families were similar, they were not randomly selected or assigned. Thus, alternative explanations of the results due to nonrandomization cannot be ruled out.

These and other studies of early family support and high-quality day-care interventions (e.g., Horacek et al. 1987; Lally, Mangione, and Honig 1988; Rauh et al. 1988) have demonstrated positive effects on family functioning and cognitive and social development that appear to lead to substantial long-term benefits, including significantly reduced risk for chronic delinquency and abuse of alcohol and other drugs (Hawkins, Catalano, and Associates 1992; Zigler, Taussig, and Black 1992; Yoshikawa 1994). These studies demonstrate both the relevance and potential power of early preventive interventions. Some of the implications of these studies are that improving access to prenatal care, providing social support to high-risk families during the transition to parenthood, and providing high-quality day care for infants and children in high-risk environments can be effective strategies for reducing risk and enhancing resilience that have an enduring positive effect on social development (IOM 1994; Yoshikawa 1994).

B. Preschool Interventions

The next category of interventions designed to reduce risk and enhance protection addresses the major developmental tasks of early childhood: gaining the cognitive, language, and social skills necessary to succeed in school. The goal of the Houston Parent-Child Development Center (HPCDC) was to promote school competence among Mexican-American children from low-income families living in Houston. The HPCDC focused on improving parents' skills to facilitate their children's development as the means to achieve this goal. Risk factors addressed included family management practices, academic failure, and early problem behaviors. The program also sought to increase the children's self-esteem, IQ, social skills, and family bonding as protective factors.

The intervention targeted Mexican-American families with a one-year-old child who was not significantly neurologically impaired and in which the family met federal poverty guidelines and the mother was not employed regularly enough to interfere with participation in the intervention. Approximately one hundred families were recruited per year over an eight-year period, were fully informed about the project, and then were randomized into equal experimental and no-treatment control groups. Comparisons of the two groups on baseline data failed to indicate any differences between them. Boys and girls were about equally represented in the sample; nearly 90 percent of the families had the father present; yearly incomes averaged about $6,000; the families had an average of three children; and roughly equal thirds of the parents preferred to speak Spanish, English, or both languages. About 40 percent of the parents had been born in Mexico, and the parents averaged seven years of education.

The intervention was delivered in two phases, beginning when the target children were one year old and lasting for two years. A total of about 550 hours of family involvement was required over the two-year period. During the first year of the program, trained female paraprofessionals from the barrios where the participants lived conducted twenty-five visits to the homes covering child development issues and information about how the mothers could promote their children's development. Several family workshops were also held during the first year to encourage participation by fathers and siblings. Mothers were invited to attend English as a Second Language (ESL) classes, and community workers including a project nurse worked with each family to provide additional social and health services and to inform participants about how to obtain needed community services.

During the second year of the program, mothers and their children attended four-hour sessions four days per week at the center. During these sessions, children were taught cognitive and social skills in group settings while mothers continued to learn about child development and management skills, as well as home management, human sexuality, and drivers' education. Mothers also practiced teaching their children while being videotaped to help refine their skills. Fathers continued to be involved through monthly meetings of a Parent Advisory Committee (attended by about 80 percent of the program fathers), which offered suggestions for program content and assisted in program maintenance and advocacy. To encourage participation, transportation was provided to all activities, all teachers were bilingual (English and Spanish), and day care was provided for older siblings. However, due to the number of hours required for participation, attrition from the intervention was a serious problem, and about one-half of the families dropped out before the end of the intervention.

Postintervention measures (including videotaped mother-child interactions and home observations) indicated that the HPCDC had an immediate positive effect on mother-child interactions and a small but significant positive effect on the child's IQ. Follow-up interviews with 128 parents from the first four cohorts when the children were four to seven years of age indicated that mothers of control boys rated their behavior as significantly more aversive than the other three gender-by-condition groups (Johnson and Breckenridge 1982). A second follow-up of 139 children conducted when they were in grades 2–5 revealed that teachers rated control children (particularly boys) as having significantly greater behavior problems than children who had been in the experimental condition. Members of the experimental group were also only one-fourth as likely to have been referred for special services and scored significantly higher on the composite score of the Iowa Test of Basic Skills than children who had been in the control group. Finally, ratings of parent-child interactions at the end of each program year were significantly related to behavior ratings in elementary school (Johnson 1988). Thus, the intervention was successful at improving parent-child interactions and the children's subsequent behavior and academic competence up to eight years following intervention.

Another well-known example of a successful preschool intervention is the Perry Preschool Project (Berrueta-Clement et al. 1984; Schweinhart 1987). Based in an elementary school in a low-income, predominantly African-American neighborhood in Ypsilanti, Michigan, the preschool program targeted three- and four-year olds using the High/Scope curriculum. The intervention actively involved the children in planning their classroom activities and met every weekday for thirty weeks each year, coupled with weekly home visits by the preschool teachers. Families participated in the program over a one- to two-year period.

Long-term follow-ups comparing the randomly assigned experimental and control group participants revealed that program participants had lower rates of aggressive, disobedient, and disruptive behavior during elementary school than members of the control group. By age nineteen, program participants were less likely than control students to have been arrested, been arrested five or more times, had special education placements in school, dropped out of school, or been on welfare. Program students also had higher grade point averages and lower rates of self-reported fighting than control students (Berrueta-Clement et al. 1984). The long-term positive findings were related to teacher ratings of conduct and personal behavior in elementary school, suggesting that the intervention produced positive long-term outcomes by reducing risk factors and enhancing social competence during the elementary years (Schweinhart 1987).

These two examples suggest that preschool interventions that reduce risk and improve social behavior in elementary school can lead to improved developmental trajectories and more positive long-term outcomes (Yoshikawa 1994). While these programs did not assess alcohol and other drug abuse as outcomes, the programs did demonstrate significant reductions in risk factors and problem behaviors that frequently cooccur with substance abuse.

C. Interventions during the Elementary School Years

Elementary school is typically the first major social domain that a child encounters outside of the family. Developmentally, a child must learn how to function effectively in this new domain to succeed, which entails developing social and impulse control skills as well as academic skills. The extent to which a child succeeds or fails to master the skills needed to function effectively in this new social domain can exert a powerful influence on both the child's and others' expectancies of his or her ability to function in other social domains. Thus, it is not surprising that several of the social and behavioral predictors of later alcohol and other drug abuse, as well as chronic and serious delinquency, stabilize in their predictive ability during this period. Persistent conduct problems in multiple settings, peer rejection, and academic failure and low commitment to school during the elementary years join genetic, temperament, and family factors as consistent predictors of later substance abuse and chronic delinquency (Loeber and Dishion 1983; Farrington 1987; Hawkins, Catalano, and Miller 1992).

Risk reduction interventions during this period focus on enhancing parenting and family functioning, enhancing social and academic competence, and changing the school environment to be more supportive and inclusive of children who are having academic or social difficulties (e.g., IOM 1994). Two examples of such interventions are the Seattle Social Development Project (Hawkins, Catalano, Morrison, et al. 1992), which combined teacher training, parent training, and social skills training for students in the early elementary grades, and the School Development Program developed by Comer and his colleagues at the Yale Child Study Center (Comer 1985).

The Seattle Social Development Project targeted first graders in eight Seattle, Washington public schools. The schools were selected based on high crime rates in their catchment areas, but all students in the eight schools were targeted for the study regardless of their individual risk status. All students in one school were assigned to the intervention, all students in a second school served as controls, while students in the remaining six schools were randomly assigned to either experimental or control classrooms (Hawkins, Catalano, Morrison, et al. 1992). The initial intervention lasted for four years, following the cohort of students from first through fourth grade.

The intervention included training and supervision for teachers in experimental classrooms in grades 1–4 to use proactive classroom management, interactive teaching, and cooperative learning techniques to increase opportunities for all students to participate in the classroom, increase skills for successful involvement, and increase rewards for positive involvement. The intervention also included training for the first-grade teachers in the use of an effective social skills training curriculum, the Interpersonal Cognitive Problem Solving curriculum (Shure and Spivack 1988), and two programs for parents. Parents of first graders were offered a program that taught skills for monitoring and supervising children's behavior, for using appropriate and consistent rewards and discipline, and for involving children in family activities. Parents of second and third graders were offered a program that focused on providing support and encouragement at home for the children's academic development (Hawkins, Catalano, Morrison, et al. 1992).

Assessments of the effect of these interventions made at the end of the second grade (Hawkins, Von Cleve, and Catalano 1991) and soon after the students had entered the fifth grade (Hawkins, Catalano,

Morrison, et al. 1992) showed positive effects. Teacher ratings of aggressiveness in second grade were significantly lower for students in intervention classrooms than for students in control classrooms (Hawkins, Von Cleve, and Catalano 1991). By the start of fifth grade, students who had participated in an intervention classroom for at least one semester during grades 1–4 reported significantly higher levels of proactive family management, positive family communication and involvement, bonding to family, and commitment and bonding to school than control students. Students in the experimental group were also less likely to have initiated alcohol use or delinquent behavior by the fifth grade than students in the control group (Hawkins, Catalano, Morrison, et al. 1992).

Another example of an intervention designed to change the school environment in order to enhance the academic achievement of students is the School Development Program created by Comer and his associates at the Yale Child Study Center (Comer 1985, 1988). The intervention aims to increase the involvement of a broad range of stakeholders in the school to reduce school problems and create a positive school climate. Parents, teachers, school administrators, and mental health professionals join together to form a school management team, a mental health team, and a parent involvement program. The governance and management team meets weekly to address school issues, including needs and goals, school climate, curriculum, in-service training, program implementation, resources, and evaluation. The mental health team also meets weekly to consider student behavior problems from an interdisciplinary perspective, to determine whether the school is contributing to behavior problems, and to recommend changes in school policies and procedures intended to improve school climate and students' well-being. The parent involvement program creates a parent handbook describing the parents' roles in the school and opportunities for involvement through social activities and workshops, and in serving as classroom tutors or aides. The goals of the School Development Program are to improve the climate and atmosphere of the school and to increase the commitment of students and parents by improving the ties between the school and the community and the responsiveness of the school to the concerns of parents and students.

Quasi-experimental evaluations of the School Development Program applied to two inner-city elementary schools serving a predominantly low-income African-American population in New Haven, Connecticut, showed positive results. At the start of the intervention, the two schools ranked near the bottom of the city's schools in reading and mathematics achievement. A dozen years later with no change in the schools' population demographics, the two schools ranked third and fourth in the city on achievement scores, having surpassed national averages. Truancy and disciplinary problems had also decreased dramatically (Comer 1988). A follow-up study comparing children in the intervention schools with a matched comparison group found that the intervention group had higher reading and math achievement scores, school grades, and social competence scores than the comparison group (Cauce, Comer, and Schwartz 1987). A more rigorous, randomized controlled study of the intervention is now being conducted in Maryland (Jessor 1993).

D. Middle and High School Interventions

During the middle and high school years, peers begin to rival parents in their influence on the adolescent's behavior (Tao Hunter and Youniss 1982). Developmental tasks during this period of rapid cognitive and physical change include developing autonomy from one's parents and family while simultaneously learning how to relate intimately with others outside of the family, coping with pubertal changes in hormones and physical characteristics and one's emerging sexuality, and making significant life decisions about lifestyles and educational and vocational goals (Elliott and Feldman 1990). Since early first use of alcohol, tobacco, and other drugs predicts greater likelihood of later substance abuse (Robins and Przybeck 1985; Kandel, Yamaguchi, and Chen 1992), preventing or delaying the initiation of use is an important prevention goal during adolescence. Primary risk factor targets for interventions during this stage of development include the early onset of use, social influences to use drugs, social norms regarding use, and attitudes favorable to use.

Given the importance of social influences, two examples of interventions that have demonstrated promise for preventing substance abuse are those that focus on learning about social influences and changing social norms regarding use of alcohol and other drugs, and those that focus on enhancing social competence. Many of the school prevention curricula that have shown the most consistent reductions in onset and prevalence of cigarette smoking, alcohol use, and marijuana use have included lessons designed to teach and reinforce skills to recognize and resist social influences to use drugs along with lessons designed to correct students' overestimates of the prevalence and acceptability of drug use among their peers while promoting classroom norms against use (e.g., Hansen et al. 1988; Ellickson and Bell 1990; Hansen 1992).

The Adolescent Alcohol Prevention Trial examined the relative effect of social influence strategies and social norm change strategies in an experimental study of 3,011 seventh-grade students at twelve junior high schools (Hansen and Graham 1991). Schools were stratified by size, test scores, and ethnic composition and randomized to four conditions that received either information about drug use, training in skills to resist peer and advertising pressures to use alcohol and other drugs, a normative education program, or a combination of information, resistance skills training, and normative education. Results indicated that the normative education component had the greatest effect on reducing consumption of alcohol, cigarettes, and marijuana (Hansen and Graham 1991). Classrooms that received the normative education component had significantly lower rates of onset and prevalence of heavy drinking, marijuana use, and cigarette smoking than those that received either the information or resistance skills training components alone. The authors suggested that the reported positive effects of social resistance skills training curricula may have resulted from the normative education elements included in the curricula.

Other researchers have also suggested that establishing clear social norms against use is an important component of effective substance abuse prevention curricula (Ellickson and Bell 1990). Moreover, several studies have suggested that using peer leaders to assist in teaching the prevention curricula enhances their positive impact (e.g., Murray et al. 1984; Tobler 1986; Perry et al. 1989; Botvin et al. 1990). However, as noted earlier, establishing clear norms against use may be counterproductive in preventing use among students who have already initiated use (Ellickson and Bell 1990). Norm change strategies may also, however, serve to alienate or isolate those whose behavior already violates the desired norm and produce iatrogenic effects among those at greatest risk for abuse due to early exposure to multiple risk factors.

Social competence strategies, in contrast, focus on teaching a broader array of generic life skills, including social problem-solving skills, stress reduction skills, self-regulation skills, social interaction skills, and assertiveness skills in addition to social influence resistance skills (Botvin 1990). Based on social learning (Bandura 1977) and problem behavior (Jessor and Jessor 1977) theories, these interventions attempt to provide young people with the basic skills needed to function effectively in most social domains. They address many general risk factors including early and persistent conduct problems, family conflict, academic failure, peer rejection, alienation, and lack of social bonding, as well as attitudes favorable to drug use and peer norms and influences to use drugs. These curricula often teach students to use these general life skills and then include lessons on how to apply the skills specifically to avoid alcohol and drug use.

An example of a social competence promotion intervention is the Positive Youth Development Program (Caplan et al. 1992). Classrooms in one urban middle school (90 percent African-American, 8 percent Hispanic, and 2 percent mixed race) and one suburban middle school (99 percent European-American, 1 percent Hispanic) were randomly assigned to the intervention or control condition. The twenty-session curriculum included two lessons per week taught by university-based health educators along with the classroom teachers. The results indicated that students in the intervention classrooms had higher teacher-rated impulse control and conflict resolution skills following the intervention than control students. Intervention students also reported less intent to use alcohol and lower rates of heavy alcohol use than control students. The two conditions did not differ in the rates of initiation of alcohol, tobacco, or marijuana use.

Other studies by Botvin and his colleagues (Botvin et al. 1984, 1990; Botvin and Eng 1990) have also indicated the promise of social competence curricula for preventing substance abuse through reducing risk factors and enhancing protective factors. These studies have also revealed the importance of considering peer- versus adult-led interventions, the intensity (frequency) of the sessions, the importance of follow-up booster sessions to reinforce initial gains, and the integrity of implementation of the curricula. When these issues are addressed, a growing body of research suggests that school-based social competence promotion and social influence/social norm-setting curricula can delay initiation of alcohol and other drug use and lower risk for later abuse, at least among some populations.

E. Strategies for Coordinating Interventions in Multiple Domains

Despite the promise demonstrated by each of the preceding examples, it is probable that a combination of interventions will be required to influence those at highest risk for substance abuse. Given the breadth and persistence of risk exposure experienced by some segments of society (e.g., Wilson 1988; Garmezy 1993), along with the substantially higher rates of substance abuse among individuals exposed to multiple risk factors, it seems unlikely that programs that reduce one or two risk factors can appreciably lower the likelihood of abuse among these populations. For these populations, models of service delivery that link programs designed to reduce risk and increase protection in multiple domains across multiple developmental periods are needed to reduce cumulative risk. Such models require the coordination of resources of many historically and organizationally distinct social and educational service agencies and delivery systems.

Another issue complicating the development of effective drug abuse prevention strategies lies in the multiple pathways that can lead to abuse. Research on risk factors suggests that the number of factors present is more important in determining risk levels than the specific factors themselves (Bry et al. 1982; Newcomb et al. 1986; USGAO 1994). Thus, it is unlikely that any one prevention strategy will be effective with multiple populations in multiple situations (Gilchrist 1991; Gorman 1992). This suggests that prevention programs must be customized to some extent to meet the specific needs of the populations they target.

To make such a multistrategy approach work and to ensure that changes are institutionalized, community and participant "ownership" of prevention initiatives is essential. As people come to believe that particular forms of behavior are risky or unacceptable in their social group, they are more likely to avoid those behaviors. To the extent that community members are bound together by a culture or set of shared values and standards for behavior, the community should actively take responsibility for ensuring that such values and standards are known and understood by all members.

This community role and responsibility for prevention efforts highlights the importance of attending to diversity in communities so that all groups participate in preventive activities. The preventive interventions included in substance abuse risk reduction strategies require focusing on individuals, parents, teachers, community health and social service providers, and law enforcement personnel. Cultural perspectives of different groups, classes, ethnicities, and races affect their views on parenting, teaching, and drug use as well as the prevalence of drug use among their members (Catalano et al. 1993). To be adopted and used by a community, the preventive strategy must be acceptable to community members. This is best accomplished when community leaders and opinion shapers have the opportunity to take ownership of the strategy and make it their own and when diverse community members are involved in tailoring the intervention to the community. Community efforts can affect the entire local environment, including norms, values, and policies (Bracht 1990). The firm support of community leaders and their involvement in a prevention effort should lead to long-term change; the reallocation of resources to reduce risk becomes feasible with support from key community leaders. Thus, community ownership of preventive initiatives is important from both theoretical and practical perspectives.

Here, again, cardiovascular disease prevention and smoking prevention initiatives provide a model. Recognizing the importance of community norms in shaping behavior, planners of the major risk reduction trials have intervened at the level of the community (Farquhar et al. 1990). Moreover, they have designed and implemented the interventions to create community ownership of the preventive initiatives (Farquhar et al. 1985). They have found that program maintenance requires community mobilization in addition to changing individual behavior (Farquhar et al. 1977).

The evidence suggests that multistrategy approaches that address multiple risks while enhancing protective factors hold the most promise for preventing substance abuse. The current challenge for substance abuse prevention research is to test prevention strategies that empower communities to design and take control of their own efforts to explicitly assess, prioritize, and address risk and protective factors for substance abuse. Substance abuse prevention researchers have begun this work. In the Midwestern Prevention Project, Pentz and her colleagues collaborated with the Kauffman Foundation in developing a communitywide intervention component. A local project office, Project Star, was charged with program implementation including mobilizing drug abuse prevention task forces at the metropolitan and community levels and securing high visibility and news coverage for the program. The complete intervention included a curriculum of social influence resistance skills training for students in grades 6 or 7, with homework assignments to be completed with parents, booster sessions in the year after initial intervention, and organizational and training opportunities for parents in positive parent-child communication skills and in reviewing school policies, in addition to community task force and media interventions. The complete intervention was more effective than media exposure alone in reducing prevalence rates of weekly cigarette, alcohol, and marijuana use after the second year of intervention (Pentz, Dwyer, et al. 1989) and the prevalence of monthly cigarette and marijuana use three years after the original intervention (Johnson et al. 1990). However, the research did not allow investigation of the contribution of community or media mobilization to the strength or durability of effects. Studies currently being conducted by Cheryl Perry and her colleagues at the University of Minnesota and Dennis Ary and Tony Biglan at the Oregon Research Institute are also using community mobilization and empowerment models to address risks for alcohol and other drug abuse. They are expected to provide important information on the effects of this strategy.

Our own fieldwork in this area has been a collaboration with sixty communities in the states of Washington and Oregon. The overall goal has been to mobilize communities toward a self-defined health promotion outcome, that is, to achieve significant reductions in adolescent health and behavior problems. The mobilization process consists of three phases. In the first phase, key community leaders including the mayor, superintendent of schools, chief law enforcement officer, and business and other leaders are oriented to the project. If they commit to implementing it, they decide as a group to become the oversight body for the project and to appoint a prevention board of diverse members of their community. During the second phase, the community prevention board is constituted and trained to conduct a community risk and resource assessment. Over a six-month period the board gathers archival and survey data on indicators of the risk factors for adolescent health and behavior problems in the community. Based on these results, the board prioritizes risk factors for preventive action. The board then designs its prevention strategy to address targeted risk factors and enhance protective factors, selecting preventive interventions from a menu of programs and strategies that meet prevention principles as summarized earlier in this essay. In the third phase, the board implements and evaluates the preventive strategy, using task forces composed of community members with a stake in the outcome to insure implementation of each component. Baseline risk assessment data serves as the benchmark against which to judge community progress in risk reduction. This strategy has been successfully implemented in a range of communities but has not yet been evaluated in a controlled field trial.

VI. Conclusion

The casual use of illegal drugs in the United States is down. In the general population, norms and attitudes regarding the use of substances have become less favorable to the excessive consumption of alcohol and to the use of tobacco, marijuana, and cocaine. Unfortunately, at the same time, alcohol abuse and other drug abuse problems have remained stable or increased, as indicated by treatment and emergency room admissions. It appears that the use of drugs other than alcohol is becoming concentrated in high-risk groups. It is likely that the abuse of alcohol and other drugs will share increasing overlap or comorbidity with other legal and health behavior problems.

These findings indicate the importance of community participation in prevention initiatives. If communities are to become protective environments for healthy development, community members will have to take responsibility for identifying, prioritizing, and addressing risks in the community and for implementing strategies to reduce salient risks and enhance the development of social integration and bonding to the community and its standards. Preventive interventions seeking to reduce substance abuse prevalence among those at greatest risk must include a focus on the successful development of cognitive and social skills and social bonding from an early age and on the promotion of strong normative standards in opposition to drug abuse across the community.

REFERENCES

Ahmed, S. W., P. J. Bush, F. R. Davidson, and R. J. Iannotti. 1984. "Predicting Children's Use and Intentions to Use Abusable Substances." Paper presented at the annual meeting of the American Public Health Association, Anaheim, Calif., November.

American Psychiatric Association. 1987. *Diagnostic and Statistical Manual of Mental Disorders.* 3d ed. Washington, D.C.: American Psychiatric Association.

Anglin, M. D., and Y.-I. Hser. 1990. "Treatment of Drug Abuse." In *Drugs and Crime,* edited by M. Tonry and J. Q. Wilson. Vol. 13 of *Crime and Justice: A Review of Research,* edited by M. Tonry and Norval Morris. Chicago: University of Chicago Press.

Arthur, M. W., R. P. Weissberg, and M. Z. Caplan. 1991. "Promoting Social Competence in Young, Urban Adolescents: A Follow-up Study." Poster presented at the ninety-ninth annual convention of the American Psychological Association, San Francisco, Calif., August.

Ary, D. V., A. Biglan, R. Glasgow, L. Zoref, C. Black, L. Ochs, H. Severson, R. Kelly, W. Weissman, E. Lichtenstein, P. Brozovsky, R. Wirt, and L. James. 1990. "The Efficacy of Social-Influence Prevention Programs versus 'Standard Care': Are New Initiatives Needed?" *Journal of Behavioral Medicine* 13:281–96.

Atkin, C., J. Hocking, and M. Block. 1984. "Teenage Drinking: Does Advertising Make a Difference?" *Journal of Communication* 34:157–67.

Austin, G., and J. A. Pollard. 1993. *Substance Abuse and Ethnicity: Recent Research Findings*. Prevention Research Update no. 10. Portland, Oreg.: Western Regional Center for Drug-free Schools and Communities.

Bachman, J. G., L. D. Johnston, and P. M. O'Malley. 1981. *Monitoring the Future: Questionnaire Responses from the Nation's High School Seniors*. Ann Arbor, Mich.: Survey Research Center.

———. 1991. "How Changes in Drug Use Are Linked to Perceived Risks and Disapproval: Evidence from National Studies That Youth and Young Adults Respond to Information about the Consequences of Drug Use." In *Persuasive Communication and Drug Abuse Prevention*, edited by L. Donohew, H. E. Sypher, and W. J. Bukoski. Hillsdale, N.J.: Erlbaum.

Bandura, A. 1977. "Self-Efficacy: Toward a Unifying Theory of Behavioral Change." *Psychological Review* 84:91–215.

Bangert-Drowns, R. L. 1988. "The Effects of School-based Substance Abuse Education: A Meta-analysis." *Journal of Drug Education* 18:243–64.

Barnes, G. M., and J. W. Welte. 1986. "Patterns and Predictors of Alcohol Use Among 7–12th Grade Students in New York State." *Journal of Studies on Alcohol* 47:53–62.

Barone, C., R. P. Weissberg, W. J. Kasprow, C. K. Voyce, M. W. Arthur, and T. P. Shriver. "Involvement in Multiple Problem Behaviors of Young Urban Adolescents." *Journal of Primary Prevention* (forthcoming).

Bates, J. E., K. Bayles, D. S. Bennet, B. Ridge, and M. M. Brown. 1991. "Origins of Externalizing Behavior Problems at Eight Years of Age." In *The Development and Treatment of Childhood Aggression*, edited by D. J. Pepler and K. H. Rubin. Hillsdale, N.J.: Erlbaum.

Baumrind, D. 1983. "Why Adolescents Take Chances and Why They Don't." Invited address for the National Institute for Child Health and Human Development. Bethesda, Md., October.

Berrueta-Clement, J. R., L. J. Schweinhart, W. S. Barnett, A. S. Epstein, and D. P. Weikart. 1984. *Changed Lives: The Effects of the Perry Preschool Program on Youths through Age 19*. High/Scope Educational Research Foundation, Monograph 8. Ypsilanti, Mich.: High/Scope Press.

Biglan, A., and D. V. Ary. 1985. "Current Methodological Issues in Research on Smoking Prevention." In *Prevention Research: Deterring Drug Abuse among Children and Adolescents*, edited by C. Bell and R. J. Battjes. National Institute of Drug Abuse Research Monograph no. 63. Washington, D.C.: U.S. Government Printing Office.

Biglan, A., D. Hood, P. Brozovsky, L. Ochs, D. Ary, and C. Black. 1991. "Subject Attrition in Prevention Research." In *Drug Abuse Prevention Intervention Research: Methodological Issues*, edited by C. G. Leukefeld and W. J. Bukoski. National Institute of Drug Abuse Monograph no. 107. Washington, D.C.: U.S. Government Printing Office.

Biglan, A., H. Severson, D. Ary, C. Faller, C. Gallison, R. Thompson, R. Glasgow, and E. Lichtenstein. 1987. "Do Smoking Prevention Programs Really Work? Attrition and the Internal and External Validity of an Evaluation of a Refusal Skills Training Program." *Journal of Behavioral Medicine* 10:159–71.

Black, G. S. 1989. *The Attitudinal Basis of Drug Use—1987* and *Changing Attitudes toward Drug Use—1988: Reports from the Media Advertising Partnership for a Drug-free America, Inc.* Rochester, N.Y.: Gordon S. Black.

Block, J., J. H. Block, and S. Keyes. 1988. "Longitudinally Foretelling Drug Usage in Adolescence: Early Childhood Personality and Environmental Precursors." *Child Development* 59:336–55.

Blose, J. O., and H. D. Holder. 1987. "Liquor-by-the-Drink and Alcohol-related Traffic Crashes: A Natural Experiment Using Time-Series Analysis." *Journal of Studies on Alcohol* 48:52–60.

Blum, K., E. P. Noble, P. J. Sheridan, A. Montgomery, T. Ritchie, P. Jagadeeswonan, H. Nogami, A. H. Briggs, and J. B. Cohen. 1990. "Allelic Association of Human Dopamine D2 Receptor Gene in Alcoholism." *Journal of the American Medical Association* 263:2094–95.

Blumstein, A. 1993. "Making Rationality Relevant." *Criminology* 31:1–16.

Bohman, M. 1978. "Some Genetic Aspects of Alcoholism and Criminality." *Archives of General Psychiatry* 35:269–76.

Botvin, G. J. 1986. "Substance Abuse Prevention Research: Recent Developments and Future Directions." *Journal of School Health* 56:369–74.

———. 1990. "Substance Abuse Prevention: Theory, Practice, and Effectiveness." In *Drugs and Crime*, edited by M. Tonry and J. Q. Wilson. Vol. 13 of *Crime and Justice: A Review of Research*, edited by M. Tonry and N. Morris. Chicago: University of Chicago Press.

Botvin, G. J., E. Baker, L. Dusenbury, S. Tortu, and E. M. Botvin. 1990. "Preventing Adolescent Drug Abuse through a Multimodal Cognitive-Behavioral Approach: Results of a 3-Year Study." *Journal of Consulting and Clinical Psychology* 58:437–46.

Botvin, G. J., E. Baker, N. L. Renick, A. D. Filazzola, and E. M. Botvin. 1984. "A Cognitive Behavioral Approach to Substance Abuse Prevention." *Addictive Behaviors* 9:137–47.

Botvin, G. J., and A. Eng. 1982. "The Efficacy of a Multicomponent Approach to the Prevention of Cigarette Smoking." *Preventive Medicine* 11:199–211.

Bracht, N. 1990. *Health Promotion at the Community Level.* Beverly Hills, Calif.: Sage.

Braucht, G. N., M. W. Kirby, and G. J. Berry. 1978. "Psychosocial Correlates of Empirical Types of Multiple Drug Abusers." *Journal of Consulting and Clinical Psychology* 46:1463–75.

Breakey, W. R., P. J. Fischer, M. Kramer, G. Nestadt, A. J. Romanski, A. Ross, R. M. Royall, and O. C. Stine. 1989. "Health and Mental Health Problems of Homeless Men and Women in Baltimore." *Journal of the American Medical Association* 262:1352–58.

Brook, J. S., D. W. Brook, A. S. Gordon, M. Whiteman, and P. Cohen. 1990. "The Psychosocial Etiology of Adolescent Drug Use: A Family Interactional Approach." *Genetic, Social, and General Psychology Monographs* 116 (whole issue no. 2).

Brook, J. S., P. Cohen, M. Whiteman, and A. S. Gordon. 1992. "Psychosocial

Risk Factors in the Transition from Moderate to Heavy Use of Abuse of Drugs." In *Vulnerability to Abuse*, edited by M. Glantz and R. Pickens. Washington, D.C.: American Psychological Association.

Brook, J. S., A. S. Gordon, M. Whiteman, and P. Cohen. 1986. "Some Models and Mechanisms for Explaining the Impact of Maternal and Adolescent Characteristics on Adolescent Stage of Drug Use." *Developmental Psychology* 22:460–67.

Brook, J. S., M. Whiteman, A. S. Gordon, and D. W. Brook. 1988. "The Role of Older Brothers in Younger Brothers' Drug Use Viewed in the Context of Parent and Peer Influences." *Journal of Genetic Psychology* 151: 59–75.

Brunswick, A. F., and J. M. Boyle. 1979. "Patterns of Drug Involvement: Developmental and Secular Influences on Age at Initiation." *Youth and Society* 2:139–62.

Brunswick, A. F., P. A. Messeri, and S. P. Titus. 1992. "Predictive Factors in Adult Substance Abuse: A Prospective Study of African American Adolescents." In *Vulnerability to Abuse*, edited by M. Glantz and R. Pickens. Washington, D.C.: American Psychological Association.

Bry, B. H., P. McKeon, and R. J. Pandina. 1982. "Extent of Drug Use as a Function of Number of Risk Factors." *Journal of Abnormal Psychology* 91: 273–79.

Bryam, O. W., and J. W. Fly. 1984. "Family Structure, Race, and Adolescents' Alcohol Use: A Research Note." *American Journal of Drug and Alcohol Abuse* 10:467–78.

Bureau of Justice Statistics. 1992. *National Update.* Vol. 2, no. 1. Washington, D.C.: Bureau of Justice Statistics.

Bursik, R. J., and J. Webb. 1982. "Community Change and Patterns of Delinquency." *American Journal of Sociology* 88:24–42.

Cadoret, R. J., C. A. Cain, and W. M. Grove. 1980. "Development of Alcoholism in Adoptees Raised Apart from Alcoholic Biologic Relatives." *Archives of General Psychiatry* 37:561–63.

Cadoret, R. J., and A. Gath. 1978. "Inheritance of Alcoholism in Adoptees." *British Journal of Addiction* 132:252–58.

Cairns, R. B., B. D. Cairns, H. J. Neckerman, S. D. Gest, and J. L. Gariépy. 1988. "Social Networks and Aggressive Behavior: Peer Support or Peer Rejection?" *Developmental Psychology* 24:815–23.

Campbell, D. T., and D. W. Fiske. 1959. "Convergent and Discriminant Validation by the Multitrait-Multimethod Matrix." *Psychological Bulletin* 56: 81–105.

Caplan, M., R. P. Weissberg, J. S. Grober, P. J. Sivo, K. Grady, and C. Jacoby. 1992. "Social Competence Promotion with Inner-City and Suburban Young Adolescents: Effects on Social Adjustment and Alcohol Use." *Journal of Consulting and Clinical Psychology* 60:56–63.

Catalano, R. F., and J. D. Hawkins. "The Social Development Model: A Theory of Antisocial Behavior." In *Delinquency and Crime: Current Theories*, edited by J. D. Hawkins. New York: Cambridge University Press (forthcoming).

Catalano, R. F., J. D. Hawkins, C. Krenz, M. Gillmore, D. Morrison, E. Wells, and R. Abbott. 1993. "Using Research to Guide Culturally Appropriate Drug Abuse Prevention." *Journal of Consulting and Clinical Psychology* 61:804–11.

Cauce, A. M., J. P. Comer, and D. Schwartz. 1987. "Long-Term Effects of a Systems-oriented School Prevention Program." *American Journal of Orthopsychiatry* 57:127–31.

Center for Substance Abuse Research (CESAR). 1993. "Criminal Population in U.S. Continues to Be Plagued by Drug Abuse." CESAR FAX vol. 2(46), November 22.

Cernkovich, S. A., P. C. Giordano, and M. D. Pugh. 1985. "Chronic Offenders: The Missing Cases in Self-Report Delinquency Research." *Journal of Criminal Law and Criminology* 76:705–32.

Chaiken, J. M., and M. R. Chaiken. 1982. *Varieties of Criminal Behavior.* Santa Monica, Calif.: Rand.

———. 1990. "Drugs and Predatory Crime." In *Drugs and Crime*, edited by M. Tonry and J. Q. Wilson. Vol. 13 of *Crime and Justice: A Review of Research*, edited by M. Tonry and N. Morris. Chicago: University of Chicago Press.

Clayton, R. R. 1993. "Basic/Etiology Research: Drug Use and Its Progression to Drug Abuse and Drug Dependence." Unpublished manuscript. Lexington: University of Kentucky, Center for Prevention Research.

Cloninger, C. R., M. Bohman, S. Sigvardsson, and A. L. von Knorring. 1985. "Psychopathology in Adopted-out Children of Alcoholics: The Stockholm Adoption Study." *Recent Developments in Alcoholism* 3:37–51.

Cloninger, C. R., S. Sigvardsson, and M. Bohman. 1988. "Childhood Personality Predicts Alcohol Abuse in Young Adults." *Alcoholism: Clinical and Experimental Research* 12:494–505.

Cloninger, C. R., S. Sigvardsson, S. B. Gilligan, A. F. von Knorring, T. Reich, and M. Bohman. 1989. "Genetic Heterogeneity and the Classifications of Alcoholism." In *Alcohol Research from Bench to Bedside*, edited by E. Gordis, B. Tabakoff, and M. Linnoila. New York: Haworth.

Coie, J. D., J. E. Lochman, R. Terry, and C. Hyman. 1992. "Predicting Early Adolescent Disorder from Childhood Aggression and Peer Relations." *Journal of Consulting and Clinical Psychology* 60:783–92.

Coie, J. D., N. F. Watt, S. G. West, J. D. Hawkins, J. R. Asarnow, H. J. Markman, S. L. Ramey, M. B. Shure, and B. Long. 1993. "The Science of Prevention: A Conceptual Framework and Some Directions for a National Research Program." *American Psychologist* 48:1013–22.

Comer, J. P. 1985. "The Yale–New Haven Primary Prevention Project: A Follow-up Study." *Journal of the American Academy of Child and Adolescent Psychiatry* 24:154–60.

———. 1988. "Educating Poor Minority Children." *Scientific American* 259: 42–48.

Cook, P. J., and G. Tauchen. 1982. "The Effect of Liquor Taxes on Heavy Drinking." *Bell Journal of Economics* 13:379–90.

———. 1984. "The Effect of Minimum Drinking Age Legislation on Youthful Auto Fatalities, 1970–1977." *Journal of Legal Studies* 13:169–90.

Cotton, N. S. 1979. "The Familial Incidence of Alcoholism: A Review." *Journal of Studies on Alcohol* 40:89–116.

Decker, M. D., P. L. Graitcer, and W. Schaffner. 1988. "Reduction in Motor Vehicle Fatalities Associated with an Increase in the Minimum Drinking Age." *Journal of the American Medical Association* 260:3604–10.

Dembo, R., D. Farrow, J. Schmeidler, and W. Burgos. 1979. "Testing a Causal Model of Environmental Influences on Early Drug Involvement of Inner City Junior High School Youths." *American Journal of Drug and Alcohol Abuse* 6:313–36.

Department of Health and Human Services (DHHS). 1990. *Healthy People 2000: National Health Promotion and Disease Prevention Objectives*. DHHS Publication no. PHS 91-50212. Washington, D.C.: U.S. Government Printing Office.

Dishion, T. J. 1990. "The Peer Context of Troublesome Behavior in Children and Adolescents." In *Understanding Troubled and Troublesome Youth*, edited by P. Leone. Beverly Hills, Calif.: Sage.

Donovan, J. E., and R. Jessor. 1985. "Structure of Problem Behaviors in Adolescence and Young Adulthood." *Journal of Consulting and Clinical Psychology* 53:890–904.

Dryfoos, J. G. 1990. *Adolescents at Risk: Prevalence and Prevention*. New York: Oxford University Press.

Dwyer, J. H., D. V. MacKinnon, M. A. Pentz, B. R. Flay, W. B. Hansen, E. Y. I. Wang, and C. A. Johnson. 1989. "Estimating Intervention Effects in Longitudinal Studies." *American Journal of Epidemiology* 130:781–95.

Ellickson, P. L., and R. M. Bell. 1990. "Drug Prevention in Junior High: A Multi-site Longitudinal Test." *Science* 247:1299–1305.

Elliott, D. S., and D. Huizinga. 1988. "Improving Self-reported Measures of Delinquency." Paper presented at the NATO Workshop on Self-reported Measures of Delinquency, Congress Center, the Netherlands, June 26–30.

Elliott, D. S., D. Huizinga, and S. S. Ageton. 1985. *Explaining Delinquency and Drug Use*. Beverly Hills, Calif.: Sage.

Elliott, G. R., and S. S. Feldman. 1990. "Capturing the Adolescent Experience." In *At the Threshold: The Developing Adolescent*, edited by S. S. Feldman and G. R. Elliott. Cambridge, Mass.: Harvard University Press.

Fagan, J. 1988. "The Social Organization of Drug Use and Drug Dealing among Urban Gangs." Unpublished manuscript. New York: John Jay College of Criminal Justice.

Farquhar, J. W., S. P. Fortmann, J. A. Flora, C. B. Taylor, W. L. Haskell, P. T. Williams, N. Maccoby, and P. D. Wood. 1990. "Effects of Communitywide Education on Cardiovascular Disease Risk Factors: The Stanford Five-City Project." *Journal of the American Medical Association* 264:359–65.

Farquhar, J. W., S. P. Fortmann, N. Maccoby, W. L. Haskell, P. T. Williams, J. A. Flora, C. B. Taylor, B. W. Brown, Jr., D. S. Solomon, and S. B. Hulley. 1985. "The Stanford Five-City Project: Design and Methods." *American Journal of Epidemiology* 122:323–33.

Farquhar, J. W., N. Maccoby, P. D. Wood, J. K. Alexander, H. Breitrose,

B. W. Brown, Jr., W. L. Haskell, A. L. McAlister, A. J. Meyer, J. P. Nash, and M. P. Stern. 1977. "Community Education for Cardiovascular Health." *Lancet* 1(June 4):1192–95.

Farrington, D. P. 1987. "Early Precursors of Frequent Offending." In *From Children to Citizens: Families, Schools, and Delinquency Prevention*, edited by J. Q. Wilson and G. C. Loury. New York: Springer-Verlag.

Farrington, D. P., B. Gallagher, L. Morley, R. J. Ledger, and D. J. West. 1985. *Cambridge Study in Delinquent Development: Long-Term Follow-Up. First Annual Report to the Home Office, August 31, 1985.* Cambridge: Cambridge University, Institute of Criminology.

Feldhusen, J. F., J. R. Thurston, and J. J. Benning. 1973. "A Longitudinal Study of Delinquency and other Aspects of Children's Behavior." *International Journal of Criminology and Penology* 1:341–51.

Flasher, L. V., and S. A. Maisto. 1984. "A Review of Theory and Research on Drinking Patterns among Jews." *Journal of Nervous and Mental Disease* 172:596–603.

Flay, B. R. 1985. "Psychosocial Approaches to Smoking Prevention: A Review of Findings." *Health Psychology* 5:449–88.

Flay, B. R., D. Koepke, S. J. Thomson, S. Santi, J. A. Best, and K. S. Brown. 1989. "Six-Year Follow-up of the First Waterloo School Smoking Prevention Trial." *American Journal of Public Health* 79:1371–76.

Fleming, J. P., S. G. Kellam, and C. H. Brown. 1982. "Early Predictors of Age at First Use of Alcohol, Marijuana and Cigarettes." *Drug and Alcohol Dependence* 9:285–303.

Forman, S. G., and J. A. Linney. 1991. "Increasing the Validity of Self-Report Data in Effectiveness Trials." In *Drug Abuse Prevention Intervention Research: Methodological Issues*, edited by C. G. Leukefeld and W. J. Bukowski. National Institute on Drug Abuse Monograph no. 107. Washington, D.C.: U.S. Government Printing Office.

Fors, S. W., and D. G. Rojek. 1991. "A Comparison of Drug Involvement between Runaways and School Youths." *Journal of Drug Education* 21:13–25.

Friedman, A. S. 1983. "High School Drug Abuse Clients." In *Treatment Research Notes*. Rockville, Md.: National Institute on Drug Abuse, Division of Clinical Research.

Garmezy, N. 1983. "Stressors of Childhood." In *Stress, Coping and Development in Children*, edited by N. Garmezy and N. Rutter. New York: McGraw-Hill.

———. 1985. "Stress Resistant Children: The Search for Protective Factors." In *Recent Research in Developmental Psychopathology*, edited by J. Stevenson. Oxford: Pergamon.

———. 1993. "Children in Poverty: Resilience despite Risk." *Psychiatry* 56:127–36.

Gerstein, D. R., and L. W. Green, eds. 1993. *Preventing Drug Abuse: What Do We Know?* Washington, D.C.: National Academy Press.

Gilchrist, L. D. 1991. "Defining the Intervention and the Target Population." In *Drug Abuse Prevention and Intervention Research: Methodological Issues*, edited by D. G. Leukefeld and W. J. Bukoski. National Institute on Drug Abuse Research Monograph no. 107. Washington, D.C.: U.S. Government Printing Office.

Gillmore, M. R., R. F. Catalano, D. M. Morrison, E. A. Wells, B. Iritani, and J. D. Hawkins. 1990. "Racial Differences in Acceptability and Availability of Drugs and Early Initiation of Substance Abuse." *American Journal of Drug and Alcohol Abuse* 16:185–206.

Gittelman, R. S., R. S. Mannuzza, and N. Bonagura. 1985. "Hyperactive Boys Almost Grown Up: I. Psychiatric Status." *Archives of General Psychiatry* 42:937–47.

Goldstein, A., and H. Kalant. 1990. "Drug Policy: Striking the Right Balance." *Science* 249:1513–21.

Goldstein, P. J., H. H. Brownstein, and P. J. Ryan. 1992. "Drug-related Homicide in New York: 1984 and 1988." *Crime and Delinquency* 38:459–76.

Goodwin, D. W. 1985. "Alcoholism and Genetics: The Sins of the Fathers." *Archives of General Psychiatry* 42:171–74.

Goodwin, D. W., F. Schulsinger, N. Moller, L. Hermansein, G. Winokur, and S. G. Guze. 1974. "Drinking Problems in Adopted and Nonadopted Sons of Alcoholics." *Archives of General Psychiatry* 31:164–69.

Goodwin, D. W., F. Schulsinger, N. Moller, S. Mednick, and S. Guze. 1977. "Psychopathology in Adopted and Nonadopted Daughters of Alcoholics." *Archives of General Psychiatry* 34:1005–7.

Gorman, D. M. 1992. "Using Theory and Basic Research to Target Primary Prevention Programs: Recent Developments and Future Prospects." *Alcohol and Alcoholism* 27:583–94.

Gorsuch, R. C., and M. C. Butler. 1976. "Initial Drug Abuse: A Review of Predisposing Social Psychological Factors." *Psychological Bulletin* 83:120–37.

Gottfredson, D. C. 1988. "An Evaluation of an Organization Development Approach to Reducing School Disorder." *Evaluation Review* 11:739–63.

Gottfredson, D. C., and C. S. Koper. 1993. "Race and Sex Differences in the Measurement of Risk for Delinquency and Drug Use." Paper presented at the annual meeting of the American Society of Criminology, Phoenix, October.

Gottfredson, G. D. 1988. "Issues in Adolescent Drug Use." Unpublished final report to the U.S. Department of Justice. Baltimore: Johns Hopkins University, Center for Research on Elementary and Middle Schools.

———. 1993. "Measurement Equivalence for African- and European-American Students: Empirical IRT Models." Paper presented at the annual meeting of the American Society of Criminology, Phoenix, October.

Graham, J. W., and S. I. Donaldson. 1993. "Evaluating Interventions with Differential Attrition: The Importance of Nonresponse Mechanisms and Use of Follow-up Data." *Journal of Applied Psychology* 78:119–28.

Grove, W. M., E. D. Eckert, L. Heston, T. J. Bouchard, N. Segal, and D. T. Lykken. 1990. "Heritability of Substance Abuse and Antisocial Behavior: A Study of Monozygotic Twins Reared Apart." *Society of Biological Psychiatry* 27:1293–1304.

Hansen, W. B. 1992. "School-based Substance Abuse Prevention: A Review of the State of the Art in Curriculum, 1980–1990." *Health Education Research* 7:403–30.

Hansen, W. B., and J. W. Graham. 1991. "Preventing Alcohol, Marijuana, and Cigarette Use among Adolescents: Peer Pressure Resistance Training versus Establishing Conservative Norms." *Preventive Medicine* 20: 414–30.

Hansen, W. B., J. W. Graham, J. L. Sobel, D. R. Shelton, B. R. Flay, and C. A. Johnson. 1987. "The Consistency of Peer and Parent Influences on Tobacco, Alcohol, and Marijuana Use among Young Adolescents." *Journal of Behavioral Medicine* 10:559–79.

Hansen, W. B., C. A. Johnson, B. R. Flay, J. W. Graham, and J. Sobel. 1988. "Affective and Social Influence Approaches to the Prevention of Multiple Substance Abuse among Seventh Grade Students: Results from Project SMART." *Preventive Medicine* 17:135–54.

Hansen, W. B., N. Tobler, and W. Graham. 1990. "Attrition in Substance Abuse Prevention Research: A Meta-analysis of 85 Longitudinally Followed Cohorts." *Evaluation Review* 14:677–85.

Harford, T. C. 1985. "Drinking Patterns among Black and Nonblack Adolescents: Results of a National Survey." In *Prevention of Black Alcoholism: Issues and Strategies*, edited by R. Wright and T. D. Watts. Springfield, Ill.: Charles C. Thomas.

Harrell, A. V. 1985. "Validation of Self-Report: The Research Record." In *Self-Report Methods of Estimating Drug Use: Meeting Current Challenges to Validity*, edited by B. A. Rouse, N. J. Kozel, and L. G. Richards. National Institute on Drug Abuse Research Monograph no. 57. Washington, D.C.: U.S. Government Printing Office.

Hartup, W. W. 1983. "Peer Relations." In *Handbook of Child Psychology*, vol. 4, *Socialization, Personality, and Social Development*, edited by P. H. Mussen. Toronto: Wiley.

Hawkins, J. D., R. Abbott, R. F. Catalano, and M. R. Gillmore. 1991. "Assessing Effectiveness of Drug Abuse Prevention: Long-Term Effects and Replication." In *Drug Abuse Prevention Research: Methodological Issues*, edited by C. Leukefeld and W. Bukoski. National Institute on Drug Abuse Research Monograph no. 107. Washington, D.C.: U.S. Government Printing Office.

Hawkins, J. D., R. F. Catalano, and associates. 1992. *Communities That Care: Action for Drug Abuse Prevention*. San Francisco, Calif.: Jossey-Bass.

Hawkins, J. D., R. F. Catalano, and J. Y. Miller. 1992. "Risk and Protective Factors for Alcohol and Other Drug Problems in Adolescence and Early Adulthood: Implications for Substance Abuse Prevention." *Psychological Bulletin* 112:64–105.

Hawkins, J. D., R. F. Catalano, D. M. Morrison, J. O'Donnell, R. D. Abbott, and L. E. Day. 1992. "The Seattle Social Development Project: Effects of the First Four Years on Protective Factors and Problem Behaviors." In *The Prevention of Antisocial Behavior in Children*, edited by J. McCord and R. Tremblay. New York: Guilford.

Hawkins, J. D., and T. Lam. 1987. "Teacher Practices, Social Development and Delinquency." In *Primary Prevention of Psychopathology*, vol. 10, *Prevention of Delinquent Behavior*, edited by J. D. Burchard and S. N. Burchard. Newbury Park, Calif.: Sage.

Hawkins, J. D., D. Lishner, and R. F. Catalano. 1985. "Childhood Predictors and the Prevention of Adolescent Substance Abuse." In *Etiology of Drug Abuse: Implications for Prevention*, edited by C. L. Jones and R. J. Battjes. National Institute on Drug Abuse Research Monograph no. 56. Washington, D.C.: U.S. Government Printing Office.

Hawkins, J. D., D. M. Lishner, R. F. Catalano, and M. O. Howard. 1986. "Childhood Predictors of Adolescent Substance Abuse: Toward an Empirically Grounded Theory." *Journal of Children in Contemporary Society* 18: 11–48.

Hawkins, J. D., D. M. Lishner, J. M. Jenson, and R. F. Catalano. 1987. "Delinquents and Drugs: What the Evidence Suggests about Prevention and Treatment Programming." In *Youth at High Risk for Substance Abuse*, edited by B. S. Brown and A. R. Mills. Washington, D.C.: U.S. Government Printing Office.

Hawkins, J. D., E. Von Cleve, and R. F. Catalano. 1991. "Reducing Early Childhood Aggression: Results of a Primary Prevention Program." *Journal of the American Academy of Child and Adolescent Psychiatry* 30:208–17.

Helzer, J. E., A. Burnam, and L. T. McEvoy. 1991. "Alcohol Abuse and Dependence." In *Psychiatric Disorders in America: The Epidemiologic Catchment Area Study*, edited by L. N. Robins and D. A. Regier. New York: Free Press.

Herting, J. R., and A. M. Guest. 1985. "Components of Satisfaction with Local Areas in the Metropolis." *Sociological Quarterly* 26:99–115.

Hetherington, E. M., M. Cox, and R. Cox. 1979. "Play and Social Interaction in Children following Divorce." *Journal of Social Issues* 35:26–49.

Hirschi, T. 1969. *Causes of Delinquency*. Berkeley: University of California Press.

Holder, H. D., and J. O. Blose. 1987. "Impact of Changes in Distilled Spirits Availability on Apparent Consumption: A Time Series Analysis of Liquor-by-the-Drink." *British Journal of Addiction* 82:623–31.

Holmberg, M. B. 1985. "Longitudinal Studies of Drug Abuse in a Fifteen-Year-old Population: I. Drug Career." *Acta Psychiatrica Scandinavica* 71: 67–79.

Horacek, H. J., C. T. Ramey, F. A. Campbell, K. P. Hoffmann, and R. H. Fletcher. 1987. "Predicting School Failure and Assessing Early Intervention with High-Risk Children." *Journal of the American Academy of Child and Adolescent Psychiatry* 26:758–63.

Horowitz, J. E. 1992. *Survey of Alcohol and Other Drug Use among Chronic Absentee Students and Dropouts in California: Selected Findings*. Los Alamitos, Calif.: Southwest Regional Laboratory.

Hrubec, Z., and G. S. Omenn. 1981. "Evidence of Genetic Predisposition to Alcoholic Cirrhosis and Psychosis: Twin Concordance for Alcoholism and Biological Endpoints by Zygosity among Male Veterans." *Alcoholism: Clinical and Experimental Research* 5:207–15.

Huizinga, D. H., and D. S. Elliott. 1986. "Reassessing the Reliability and

Validity of Self-Report Delinquency Measures." *Journal of Quantitative Criminology* 2:293–327.

Hundleby, J. D., and G. W. Mercer. 1987. "Family and Friends as Social Environments and Their Relationship to Young Adolescents' Use of Alcohol, Tobacco, and Marijuana." *Journal of Clinical Psychology* 44:125–34.

Institute of Medicine, Committee on Prevention of Mental Disorders (IOM). 1994. *Reducing Risks for Mental Disorders: Frontiers for Preventive Intervention Research.* Washington, D.C.: National Academy Press.

Jacobs, D. R., R. V. Luepker, M. B. Mittelmark, A. R. Folsom, P. L. Pirie, S. R. Mascoili, P. J. Hannan, T. F. Pechacek, N. F. Bracht, R. W. Carlaw, F. G. Kline, and H. Blackburn. 1986. "Community-wide Prevention Strategies: Evaluation Design of the Minnesota Heart Health Program." *Journal of Chronic Diseases* 39:775–88.

Jessor, R. 1976. "Predicting Time of Onset of Marijuana Use: A Developmental Study of High School Youth." *Journal of Consulting and Clinical Psychology* 44:125–34.

———. 1993. "Successful Adolescent Development among Youth in High-Risk Settings." *American Psychologist* 48:117–26.

Jessor, R., J. E. Donovan, and K. Windmer. 1980. "Psychosocial Factors in Adolescent Alcohol and Drug Use: The 1980 National Sample Study, and the 1974–78 Panel Study." Unpublished final report. Boulder: University of Colorado, Institute of Behavioral Science.

Jessor, R., and S. L. Jessor. 1977. *Problem Behavior and Psychosocial Development: A Longitudinal Study of Youth.* New York: Academic Press.

Johnson, B. D., T. Williams, K. A. Dei, and H. Sanabria. 1990. "Drug Abuse in the Inner City: Impact on Hard-Drug Users and the Community." In *Drugs and Crime,* edited by M. Tonry and J. Q. Wilson. Vol. 13 of *Crime and Justice: A Review of Research,* edited by M. Tonry and N. Morris. Chicago: University of Chicago Press.

Johnson, C. A., W. B. Hansen, and M. A. Pentz. 1986. *Comprehensive Community Programs for Drug Abuse Prevention: Childhood and Chemical Abuse.* New York: Haworth Press.

Johnson, C. A., M. A. Pentz, M. D. Weber, J. H. Dwyer, D. P. MacKinnon, B. R. Flay, N. A. Baer, and W. B. Hansen. 1990. "Relative Effectiveness of Comprehensive Community Programming for Drug Abuse Prevention with High-Risk and Low-Risk Adolescents." *Journal of Consulting and Clinical Psychology* 58:447–56.

Johnson, D. L. 1988. "Primary Prevention of Behavior Problems in Young Children: The Houston Parent-Child Development Center." In *14 Ounces of Prevention,* edited by R. H. Price, E. L. Cowen, R. P. Lorion, and J. Ramos-McKay. Washington, D.C.: American Psychological Association.

Johnson, D. L., and J. N. Breckenridge. 1982. "The Houston Parent-Child Development Center and the Primary Prevention of Behavior Problems in Young Children." *American Journal of Community Psychology* 10:305–16.

Johnson, G. M., F. C. Schoutz, and T. P. Locke. 1984. "Relationships between Adolescent Drug Use and Parental Drug Behaviors." *Adolescence* 19:295–99.

Johnston, L. D. 1991. "Toward a Theory of Drug Epidemics." In *Persuasive Communication and Drug Abuse Prevention*, edited by L. Donohew, H. E. Sypher, and W. J. Bukoski. Hillsdale, N.J.: Erlbaum.

Johnston, L. D., J. G. Bachman, and P. M. O'Malley. 1993. News release. Ann Arbor: University of Michigan News and Information Service (April 9).

Johnston, L. D., and P. M. O'Malley. 1985. "Issues of Validity and Population Coverage in Student Surveys of Drug Use." In *Self-Report Methods of Estimating Drug Use: Meeting Current Challenges to Validity*, edited by B. A. Rouse, N. J. Kozel, and L. G. Richards. National Institute on Drug Abuse Research Monograph no. 57. Washington, D.C.: U.S. Government Printing Office.

Johnston, L. D., P. M. O'Malley, and J. G. Bachman. 1985. *Drug Use, Drinking, and Smoking: National Survey Results from High School, College, and Young Adult Populations*. Washington, D.C.: U.S. Government Printing Office.

———. 1991. *Drug Use among American High School Seniors, College Students, and Young Adults, 1975–1990*, vol. 1, *High School Seniors*. Washington, D.C.: National Institute on Drug Abuse.

———. 1992. *Smoking, Drinking, and Illicit Drug Use among Secondary School Students, College Students, and Young Adults*, vol. 1, *Secondary School Students*. Washington, D.C.: U.S. Department of Health and Human Services.

Joksch, H. C. 1988. *The Impact of Severe Penalties on Drinking and Driving*. Washington, D.C.: AAA Foundation for Traffic Safety.

Kaij, L. 1960. *Alcoholism in Twins: Studies on the Etiology and Sequelae of Abuse of Alcohol*. Stockholm, Sweden: Alonguist & Winkell.

Kandel, D. B. 1978. "Convergences in Prospective Longitudinal Surveys of Drug Use in Normal Populations." In *Longitudinal Research on Drug Use: Empirical Findings and Methodological Issues*, edited by D. Kandel. Washington, D.C.: Hemisphere–John Witen.

———. 1982. "Epidemiological and Psychosocial Perspectives on Adolescent Drug Use." *Journal of the American Academy of Clinical Psychiatry* 21:328–47.

———. 1986. "Processes of Peer Influence in Adolescence." In *Development as Action in Context: Problem Behavior and Normal Youth Development*, edited by R. Silberstein. New York: Springer-Verlag.

Kandel, D. B., and K. Andrews. 1987. "Processes of Adolescent Socialization by Parents and Peers." *International Journal of the Addictions* 22:319–42.

Kandel, D. B., and M. Davies. 1992. "Progression to Regular Marijuana Involvement: Phenomenology and Risk Factors for Near-daily Use." In *Vulnerability to Abuse*, edited by M. Glantz and R. Pickens. Washington, D.C.: American Psychological Association.

Kandel, D. B., R. C. Kessler, and R. S. Margulies. 1978. "Antecedents of Adolescent Initiation into Stages of Drug Use: A Developmental Analysis." *Journal of Youth and Adolescence* 7:13–40.

Kandel, D. B., O. Simcha-Fagan, and M. Davies. 1986. "Risk Factors for Delinquency and Illicit Drug Use from Adolescence to Young Adulthood." *Journal of Drug Issues* 16:67–90.

Kandel, D. B., E. Single, and R. Kessler. 1976. "The Epidemiology of Drug Use among New York State High School Students: Distribution, Trends, and Change in Rates of Use." *American Journal of Public Health* 66:43–53.

Kandel, D. B., K. Yamaguchi, and K. Chen. 1992. "Stages of Progression in Drug Involvement from Adolescence to Adulthood: Further Evidence for the Gateway Theory." *Journal of Studies on Alcohol* September:447–57.

Kaufman, E., and P. N. Kaufman. 1979. *Family Therapy of Drug and Alcohol Abuse.* New York: Gardner Press.

Kellam, S. G., and H. Brown. 1982. *Social Adaptational and Psychological Antecedents of Adolescent Psychopathology Ten Years Later.* Baltimore: Johns Hopkins University Press.

Kellam, S. G., M. E. Ensminger, and M. B. Simon. 1980. "Mental Health in First Grade and Teenage Drug, Alcohol, and Cigarette Use." *Drug and Alcohol Dependence* 5:273–304.

Kelly, D. H., and R. W. Balch. 1971. "Social Origins and School Failure: A Re-examination of Cohen's Theory of Working-Class Delinquency." *Pacific Sociological Review* 14:413–30.

Kendler, K. F. 1992. "A Population-based Twin Study of Alcoholism in Women." *Journal of the American Medical Association* 268:1877–82.

Kim, S. 1979. *An Evaluation of Ombudsman Primary Prevention Program on Student Drug Abuse.* Charlotte, N.C.: Charlotte Drug Education Center.

Klepp, K. I., A. Halper, and C. L. Perry. 1986. "The Efficacy of Peer Leaders in Drug Abuse Prevention." *Journal of School Health* 56:407–11.

Koepsell, T. D., D. C. Martin, P. H. Diehr, B. M. Psaty, E. H. Wagner, E. B. Perrin, and A. Cheadle. 1991. "Data Analysis and Sample Size Issues in Evaluations of Community-based Health Promotion and Disease Prevention Programs: A Mixed Model Analysis of Variance Approach." *Journal of Clinical Epidemiology* 44:701–13.

Krieg, T. L. 1982. "Is Raising the Legal Drinking Age Warranted?" *Police Chief* (December), pp. 32–34.

Krosnick, J. A., and C. M. Judd. 1982. "Transitions in Social Influence at Adolescence: Who Induces Cigarette Smoking?" *Developmental Psychology* 18:359–68.

Kupersmidt, J. B., J. D. Coie, and K. A. Dodge. 1990. "The Role of Poor Peer Relationships in the Development of Disorder." In *Peer Rejection in Childhood*, edited by S. A. Asher and J. D. Coie. Cambridge: Cambridge University Press.

Lally, J. R., P. L. Mangione, and A. S. Honig. 1988. "The Syracuse University Family Development Research Program: Long-Range Impact on an Early Intervention with Low-Income Children and Their Families." In *Advances in Applied Developmental Psychology*, vol. 3, *Parent Education as Early Childhood Intervention: Emerging Directions in Theory, Research, and Practice*, edited by D. R. Powell and I. Sigel. Norwood, N.J.: Ablex.

Lefebvre, R. C., T. M. Lasater, R. A. Carleton, and G. Peterson. 1987. "Theory and Delivery of Health Programming in the Community: The Pawtucket Heart Health Program." *Preventive Medicine* 16:80–95.

Lerner, J. V., and J. R. Vicary. 1984. "Difficult Temperament and Drug Use: Analyses from the New York Longitudinal Study." *Journal of Drug Education* 14:1–8.

Leukefeld, C. G., and W. J. Bukoski. 1991. "Prevention Evaluation Research Methods: Findings and Consensus." In *Drug Abuse Prevention Intervention Research: Methodological Issues,* edited by C. G. Leukefeld and W. J. Bukoski. National Institute on Drug Abuse Research Monograph no. 107. Washington, D.C.: U.S. Government Printing Office.

Levy, D., and N. Sheflin. 1985. "The Demand for Alcoholic Beverages: An Aggregate Time-Series Analysis." *Journal of Public Policy and Marketing* 4: 47–54.

Lewis, C. E., L. Robins, and J. Rice. 1985. "Association of Alcoholism with Antisocial Personality in Urban Men." *Journal of Nervous and Mental Disorders* 173:166–74.

Liang, K. Y., and S. L. Zeger. 1986. "Longitudinal Data Analysis Using Generalized Linear Models." *Biometrika* 73:13–22.

Loeber, R. 1988. "Natural Histories of Conduct Problems, Delinquency, and Associated Substance Use: Evidence for Developmental Progressions." In *Advances in Clinical Child Psychology,* vol. 11, edited by B. B. Lahey and A. E. Kazdin. New York: Plenum.

Loeber, R. T., and T. Dishion. 1983. "Early Predictors of Male Delinquency: A Review." *Psychological Bulletin* 93:68–99.

Lorion, R. P., and J. G. Ross. 1992. "Programs for Change: A Realistic Look at the Nation's Potential for Preventing Substance Involvement among High-Risk Youth." *Journal of Community Psychology* OSAP (special issue), pp. 3–9.

McAlister, A. L., C. L. Perry, J. Killen, L. A. Slinkard, and N. Maccoby. 1980. "Pilot Study of Smoking, Alcohol, and Drug Abuse Prevention." *American Journal of Public Health* 70:719–21.

McArdle, J. J., and F. Hamagami. 1991. "Modeling Incomplete Longitudinal and Cross-sectional Data Using Latent Growth Structural Models." In *Best Methods for the Analysis of Change: Recent Advances, Unanswered Questions, Future Directions,* edited by L. M. Collins and J. L. Horn. Washington, D.C.: American Psychological Association.

McCord, J. 1979. "Some Child-rearing Antecedents of Criminal Behavior in Adult Men." *Journal of Personality and Social Psychology* 37:1477–86.

———. 1981. "Alcoholism and Criminality." *Journal of Studies on Alcohol* 42: 739–48.

McCord, W., and J. McCord. 1959. *Origins of Crime.* Montclair, N.J.: Columbia University Press.

McDermott, D. 1984. "The Relationship of Parental Drug Use and Parent's Attitude concerning Adolescent Drug Use to Adolescent Drug Use." *Adolescence* 19:89–97.

McGee, R., P. A. Silva, and S. Williams. 1984. "Perinatal, Neurological, Environmental and Developmental Characteristics of Seven-Year-old Children with Stable Behavior Problems." *Journal of Child Psychology and Psychiatry* 25:573–86.

McKinlay, S. M., E. J. Stone, and D. M. Zucker. 1989. "Research Design and Analysis Issues." *Health Education Quarterly* 16:307–13.

Maddahian, E., M. D. Newcomb, and P. M. Bentler. 1988. "Adolescent Drug Use and Intention to Use Drugs: Concurrent and Longitudinal Analyses of Four Ethnic Groups." *Addictive Behaviors* 13:191–95.

Merikangas, K. R. 1990. "The Genetic Epidemiology of Alcoholism." *Psychological Medicine* 20:11–22.

Merikangas, K. R., B. J. Rounsaville, and B. A. Prusoff. 1992. "Familial Factors in Vulnerability to Substance Abuse." In *Vulnerability to Abuse*, edited by M. Glantz and R. Pickens. Washington, D.C.: American Psychological Association.

Milich, R., and J. Loney. 1980. "The Role of Hyperactive and Aggressive Symptomatology in Predicting Adolescent Outcome among Hyperactive Children." *Annual Progress in Child Psychiatry and Child Development*, pp. 336–56.

Moore, M. H. 1990. "Supply Reduction and Drug Law Enforcement." In *Drugs and Crime*, edited by M. Tonry and J. Q. Wilson. Vol. 13 of *Crime and Justice: A Review of Research*, edited by M. Tonry and N. Morris. Chicago: University of Chicago Press.

Moskowitz, J. M. 1989. "The Primary Prevention of Alcohol Problems: A Clinical Review of the Research Literature." *Journal of Studies on Alcohol* 50:54–88.

Murray, C. A. 1983. "The Physical Environment and Community Control of Crime." In *Crime and Public Policy*, edited by J. Q. Wilson. San Francisco: Institute for Contemporary Studies.

Murray, D. M., M. Davis-Hearn, A. I. Goldman, P. Pirie, and R. V. Leupker. 1988. "Four- and Five-Year Follow-up Results from Four Seventh-Grade Smoking Prevention Strategies." *Journal of Behavioral Medicine* 11: 395–405.

Murray, D. M., and P. J. Hannan. 1990. "Planning for the Appropriate Analysis in School-based Drug Use Prevention Studies." *Journal of Consulting and Clinical Psychology* 58:458–68.

Murray, D. M., P. J. Hannan, and D. M. Zucker. 1989. "Analysis Issues in School-based Health Promotion Studies." *Health Education Quarterly* 16: 315–20.

Murray, D. M., C. A. Johnson, R. V. Luepker, and M. B. Mittelmark. 1984. "The Prevention of Cigarette Smoking in Children: A Comparison of Four Strategies." *Journal of Applied Social Psychology* 14:274–288.

Murray, D. M., C. M. O'Connell, L. A. Schmid, and C. L. Perry. 1987. "The Validity of Smoking Self-Reports by Adolescents: A Reexamination of the Bogus Pipeline Procedure." *Addict Behavior* 12:7–15.

Murray, D. M., P. S. Richards, R. V. Luepker, and C. A. Johnson. 1987. "The Prevention of Cigarette Smoking in Children: Two- and Three-Year Follow-up Comparisons of Four Prevention Strategies." *Journal of Behavioral Medicine* 10:595–611.

Murray, R. M., C. A. Clifford, and H. M. D. Gurling. 1983. "Twin and Adoption Studies: How Good Is the Evidence for a Genetic Role?" In

Recent Developments in Alcoholism, vol. 1, edited by M. Galanter. New York: Plenum.

National Institue on Drug Abuse (NIDA). 1974–90. *National Household Survey on Drug Abuse*. Washington, D.C.: U.S. Government Printing Office.

———. 1991. *National Household Survey on Drug Abuse: Highlights 1990*. Washington, D.C.: U.S. Government Printing Office.

Needle, R. H., S. S. Su, and W. J. Doherty. 1990. "Divorce, Remarriage, and Adolescent Substance Use: A Prospective Longitudinal Study." *Journal of Marriage and the Family* 52:157–69.

Newcomb, M. D., and P. M. Bentler. 1986. "Substance Use and Ethnicity: Differential Impact of Peer and Adult Models." *Journal of Psychology* 120: 83–95.

———. 1988. *Consequences of Adolescent Drug Use: Impact on the Lives of Young Adults*. Newbury Park, Calif.: Sage.

Newcomb, M. D., E. Maddahian, and P. M. Bentler. 1986. "Risk Factors for Drug Use among Adolescents: Concurrent and Longitudinal Analyses." *American Journal of Public Health* 76:525–30.

Newcomb, M. D., E. Maddahian, and R. Skager. 1987. "Substance Abuse and Psychosocial Risk Factors among Teenagers: Associations with Sex, Age, Ethnicity, and Type of School." *American Journal of Drug and Alcohol Abuse* 13:413–33.

New York City Commission on the Homeless. 1992. *The Way Home: A New Direction in Social Policy*. New York: New York City Commission on the Homeless.

Norem-Hebeisen, A., D. W. Johnson, D. Anderson, and R. Johnson. 1984. "Predictors and Concomitants of Changes in Drug Use Patterns among Teenagers." *Journal of Social Psychology* 124:43–50.

Nurco, D. N., T. Kinlock, and M. B. Balter. 1993. "The Severity of Preaddiction Criminal Behavior among Urban, Male Narcotic Addicts and Two Nonaddicted Control Groups." *Journal of Research in Crime and Delinquency* 30:293–316.

Nyberg, K., P. Allebeck, G. Eklund, and B. Jacobson. 1992. "Socio-economic versus Obstetric Risk Factors for Drug Addiction in Offspring." *British Journal of Addiction* 87:1669–76.

Nylander, I. 1979. "The Development of Antisocial Behaviour in Children." *Acta Paedopsychiatrica* 47:71–80.

O'Donnell, J. A., and R. R. Clayton. 1979. "Determinants of Early Marijuana Use." In *Youth Drug Abuse: Problems, Issues, and Treatment*, edited by G. M. Beschner and A. S. Friedman. Lexington, Mass.: Lexington Books.

Olds, D. L., C. R. Henderson, R. Chamberlin, and R. Tatelbaum. 1986. "Preventing Child Abuse and Neglect: A Randomized Trial of Nurse Home Visitation." *Pediatrics* 78:65–78.

Olds, D. L., C. R. Henderson, Jr., R. Tatelbaum, and R. Chamberlin. 1988. "Improving the Life-Course Development of Socially Disadvantaged Mothers: A Randomized Trial of Nurse Home Visitation." *American Journal of Public Health* 78:1436–45.

O'Malley, P. M., and A. C. Wagenaar. 1991. "Effects of Minimum Drinking

Age Laws on Alcohol Use, Related Behaviors and Traffic Crash Involvement among American Youth: 1976–1987." *Journal of Studies on Alcohol* 52: 478–91.

Osgood, D. W., L. D. Johnston, P. M. O'Malley, and J. G. Bachman. 1988. "The Generality of Deviance in Late Adolescence and Early Adulthood." *American Sociological Review* 53:81–93.

Parker, J. G., and S. R. Asher. 1987. "Peer Relations and Later Personal Adjustment: Are Low-accepted Children at Risk?" *Psychological Bulletin* 102: 357–89.

Paton, S., and D. B. Kandel. 1978. "Psychological Factors and Adolescent Illicit Drug Use: Ethnicity and Sex Differences." *Adolescence* 13:187–200.

Patterson, G. R., and L. Bank. 1986. "Bootstrapping Your Way in the Nomological Thicket." *Behavioral Assessment* 8:49–73.

Penning, M., and G. E. Barnes. 1982. "Adolescent Marijuana Use: A Review." *International Journal of Addictions* 17:749–91.

Pentz, M. A., B. R. Brannon, V. L. Charlin, E. J. Barnett, D. P. MacKinnon, and B. R. Flay. 1989. "The Power of Policy: Relationship of Smoking Policy to Adolescent Smoking." *American Journal of Public Health* 79:857–62.

Pentz, M. A., J. H. Dwyer, D. P. MacKinnon, B. R. Flay, W. B. Hansen, E. Y. I. Wang, and C. A. Johnson. 1989. "A Multi-community Trial for Primary Prevention of Adolescent Drug Abuse: Effects on Drug Use Prevalence." *Journal of the American Medical Association* 261:3259–66.

Pentz, M. A., D. P. MacKinnon, B. R. Flay, W. B. Hansen, C. A. Johnson, and J. H. Dwyer. 1989. "Primary Prevention of Chronic Diseases in Adolescence: Effects of the Midwestern Prevention Project on Tobacco Use." *American Journal of Epidemiology* 130:713–24.

Perry, C. L. 1986. "Community-wide Health Promotion and Drug Abuse Prevention." *Journal of School Health* 56:359–63.

Perry, C. L., M. Grant, G. Ernberg, R. U. Florenzano, M. C. Langdon, A. D. Myeni, R. Waahlberg, S. Berg, K. Andersson, K. J. Fisher, D. Blaze-Temple, D. Cross, B. Saunders, D. R. Jacobs, and T. Schmid. 1989. "WHO Collaborative Study on Alcohol Education and Young People: Outcomes of a Four-Country Pilot Study." *International Journal of the Addictions* 24:1145–71.

Perry, C. L., S. H. Kelder, D. M. Murray, and K. I. Klepp. 1992. "Communitywide Smoking Prevention: Long-Term Outcomes of the Minnesota Heart Health Program and the Class of 1989 Study." *American Journal of Public Health* 82:1210–16.

Peterson, P. L., J. D. Hawkins, R. D. Abbott, and R. F. Catalano. "Disentangling the Effects of Parental Drinking, Family Management, and Parental Alcohol Norms on Current Drinking by Black and White Adolescents." *Journal of Research on Adolescence* 4:203–27.

Pickens, R. W., D. S. Svikis, M. McGue, D. T. Lykken, L. L. Heston, and P. J. Clayton. 1991. "Heterogeneity in the Inheritance of Alcoholism: A Study of Male and Female Twins." *Archives of General Psychiatry* 48:19–28.

Polich, J. M., P. L. Ellickson, P. Reuter, and J. P. Kahan. 1984. *Strategies for Controlling Adolescent Drug Use*. Santa Monica, Calif.: RAND.

Pollock, V. E., J. Volavka, D. W. Goodwin, S. A. Mednick, W. F. Gabrielli, J. Knop, and F. Schulsinger. 1983. "The EEG after Alcohol Administration in Men at Risk for Alcoholism." *Archives of General Psychiatry* 40:857–61.

Porter, B., and K. D. O'Leary. 1980. "Marital Discord and Childhood Problems." *Journal of Abnormal Child Psychology* 8:87–295.

Provence, S., and A. Naylor. 1983. *Working with Disadvantaged Parents and Children: Scientific Issues and Practice*. New Haven, Conn.: Yale University Press.

Puska, P., J. Tuomilehto, A. Nissinen, J. T. Salonen, E. Vartiainen, P. Pietinen, K. Koskela, and H. J. Korhonen. 1989. "The North Karelia Project: 15 Years of Community-based Prevention of Coronary Heart Disease." *Annals of Medicine* 21(3):169–73.

Rachal, J. V., L. L. Guess, R. L. Hubbard, S. A. Maisto, E. R. Cavanaugh, R. Waddell, and C. H. Benrud. 1982. "Facts for Planning No. 4: Alcohol Misuse by Adolescents." *Alcohol Health and Research World*, pp. 61–68.

Radke-Yarrow, M., and T. Sherman. 1990. "Children Born at Medical Risk: Factors Affecting Vulnerability and Resilience." In *Risk and Protective Factors in the Development of Psychopathology*, edited by J. Rolf, A. S. Masten, D. Cicchetti, K. H. Nuechterlein, and S. Weintraub. Cambridge: Cambridge University Press.

Rauh, V. A., T. H. Achenbach, B. Nurcombe, C. T. Howell, and D. M. Teti. 1988. "Minimizing Adverse Effects of Low Birth Weight: Four-Year Results of an Early Intervention program." *Child Development* 59:544–53.

Raymond, M. R. 1987. "Missing Data in Evaluation Research." *Evaluation and the Health Professions* 9:395–420.

Reilly, D. M. 1979. "Family Factors in the Etiology and Treatment of Youthful Drug Abuse." *Family Therapy* 11:149–71.

Reinisch, E. J., R. M. Bell, and P. L. Ellickson. 1991. *How Accurate Are Adolescent Reports of Drug Use?* Santa Monica, Calif.: RAND.

Reuter, P., M. Falco, and R. MacCoun. 1993. *Comparing Western European and North American Drug Policies: An International Conference Report*. Santa Monica, Calif.: RAND.

Robins, L. N. 1978. "Sturdy Childhood Predictors of Adult Anti-social Behavior: Replications from Longitudinal Studies." *Psychological Medicine* 8:611–22.

———. 1980. "The Natural History of Drug Abuse." *Acta Psychiatrica Scandinavica* 62(suppl. 284):7–20.

———. 1984. "The Natural History of Adolescent Drug Use." *American Journal of Public Health* 74:656–57.

Robins, L. N., and T. R. Przybeck. 1985. "Age of Onset of Drug Use as a Factor in Drug and Other Disorders." In *Etiology of Drug Abuse: Implications for Prevention*, edited by C. L. Jones and R. J. Battjes. National Institute on Drug Abuse Research Monograph no. 56. Washington, D.C.: U.S. Government Printing Office.

Robins, L. N., and K. S. Ratcliff. 1979. "Risk Factors in the Continuation of Childhood Antisocial Behavior into Adulthood." *International Journal of Mental Health* 7:76–116.

Rutter, M. 1990. "Psychosocial Resilience and Protective Mechanisms." In *Risk and Protective Factors in the Development of Psychopathology*, edited by J. Rolf, A. S. Masten, D. Cicchetti, K. H. Nuechterlein, and S. Weintraub. Cambridge: Cambridge University Press.

Rutter, M., and H. Giller. 1983. *Juvenile Delinquency: Trends and Perspectives*. New York: Penguin.

Saffer, H., and M. Grossman. 1987. "Beer Taxes, the Legal Drinking Age, and Youth Motor Vehicle Fatalities." *Journal of Legal Studies* 16:351–74.

Sameroff, A. J., and M. J. Chandler. 1975. "Reproductive Risk and the Continuum of Caretaking Casualty." In *Review of Child Development Research*, vol. 4, edited by F. D. Horowitz, M. Hetherington, and S. Scarr-Salopatek. Chicago: University of Chicago Press.

Sampson, R. J. 1986. "Crime in Cities: The Effects of Formal and Informal Social Control." In *Communities and Crime*, edited by A. J. Reiss, Jr., and M. Tonry. Vol. 8 of *Crime and Justice: A Review of Research*, edited by M. Tonry and N. Morris. Chicago: University of Chicago Press.

Sampson, R. J., T. C. Castellano, and J. H. Laub. 1981. *Juvenile Criminal Behavior and Its Relation to Neighborhood Characteristics*. Washington, D.C.: Office of Juvenile Justice and Delinquency Prevention.

Sawhill, I. V. 1989. "The Underclass: I. An Overview." *Public Interest* 96:3–15.

Schaie, K. W. 1965. "A General Model for the Study of Developmental Problems." *Psychological Bulletin* 64:92–107.

Schinke, S. P., M. Y. Bebel, M. A. Orlandi, and G. J. Botvin. 1988. "Prevention Strategies for Vulnerable Pupils: School Social Work Practices to Prevent Substance Abuse." *Urban Education* 22:510–19.

Schuckit, M. A. 1980. "Biological Markers: Metabolism and Acute Reactions to Alcohol in Sons of Alcoholics." *Pharmacology, Biochemistry, and Behavior* 13:9–16.

———. 1987. "Biological Vulnerability to Alcoholism." *Journal of Consulting and Clinical Psychology* 55:301–9.

Schuckit, M. A., D. C. Parker, and L. R. Rossman. 1983. "Ethanol-related Prolactin Responses and Risk for Alcoholism." *Biological Psychiatry* 18: 1153–59.

Schuckit, M. A., and V. Rayes. 1979. "Ethanol Ingestion: Differences in Blood Acetaldehyde Concentrations in Relatives of Alcoholics and Controls." *Science* 203:54–55.

Schweinhart, L. J. 1987. "Can Preschool Programs Help Prevent Delinquency?" In *From Children to Citizens: Families, Schools, and Delinquency Prevention*, edited by J. Q. Wilson and G. C. Loury. New York: Springer-Verlag.

Seitz, V. 1990. "Intervention Programs for Impoverished Children: A Comparison of Educational and Family Support Models." *Annals of Child Development* 7:73–103.

Seitz, V., L. K. Rosenbaum, and N. H. Apfel. 1985. "Effects of Family Support Intervention: A Ten-Year Follow-up." *Child Development* 56: 376–91.

Selnow, G. W. 1987. "Parent-Child Relationships in Single and Two Parent Families: Implications for Substance Usage." *Journal of Drug Education* 17: 315–26.

Shedler, J., and J. Block. 1990. "Adolescent Drug Use and Psychological Health: A Longitudinal Inquiry." *American Psychologist* 45:612–30.

Sherman, L. W., D. A. Smith, J. D. Schmidt, and D. A. Rogan. 1992. "Crime, Punishment, and Stake in Conformity: Legal and Informal Control of Domestic Violence." *American Sociological Review* 52:680–90.

Shure, M. B., and G. Spivack. 1988. "Interpersonal Cognitive Problem Solving. In *14 Ounces of Prevention: A Casebook for Practitioners*, edited by R. H. Price, E. L. Cowen, R. P. Lorion, and J. Ramos-McKay. Washington, D.C.: American Psychological Association.

Simcha-Fagan, O., J. C. Gersten, and T. S. Langner. 1986. "Early Precursors and Concurrent Correlates of Patterns of Illicit Drug use in Adolescence." *Journal of Drug Issues* 16:7–28.

Simcha-Fagan, O., and J. E. Schwartz. 1986. "Neighborhood and Delinquency: An Assessment of Contextual Effects." *Criminology* 24:667–704.

Slavin, R. E. 1990. *Cooperative Learning: Theory, Research, and Practice*. Englewood Cliffs, N.J.: Prentice Hall.

Smith, G. M., and C. P. Fogg. 1978. "Psychological Predictors of Early Use, Late Use, and Non-use of Marijuana among Teenage Students." In *Longitudinal Research on Drug Use: Empirical Findings and Methodological Issues*, edited by D. B. Kandel. Washington, D.C.: Hemisphere-Wiley.

Spivack, G. 1983. *High Risk Early Behaviors Indicating Vulnerability to Delinquency in the Community and School*. National Institute for Juvenile Justice and Delinquency Prevention publication. Washington, D.C.: U.S. Government Printing Office.

Stanton, M. D. 1979. "The Client as Family Member: Aspects of Continuing Treatment." In *Addicts and Aftercare: Community Integration of the Former Drug User*, edited by B. S. Brown. Beverley Hills, Calif.: Sage.

Substance Abuse and Mental Health Services Administration (SAMHSA). 1993. *Estimates from the Drug Abuse Warning Network: 1992 Estimates of Drug-related Emergency Room Episodes*. Washington, D.C.: U.S. Department of Health and Human Services, Public Health Service.

Suwaki, H., and H. Ohara. 1985. "Alcohol-induced Facial Flushing and Drinking Behavior in Japanese Men." *Journal of Studies on Alcohol* 46:196–98.

Tabakoff, B., and P. L. Hoffman. 1988. "Genetics and Biological Markers of Risk for Alcoholism." *Public Health Reports* 103:690–98.

Tao Hunter, F. T., and J. Youniss. 1982. "Change in Functions of Three Relations during Adolescence." *Developmental Psychology* 18:806–11.

Tarter, R. 1988. "Are There Inherited Behavioral Traits Which Predispose to Substance Abuse?" *Journal of Consulting and Clinical Psychology* 56:189–96.

Tarter, R., S. Laird, M. Kabene, O. Bukstein, and Y. Kaminer. 1990. "Drug

Abuse Severity in Adolescents Is Associated with Magnitude of Deviation in Temperament Traits." *British Journal of Addiction* 85:1501–4.

Tebes, J. K., D. L. Snow, and M. W. Arthur. 1992. "Panel Attrition and External Validity in the Short-Term Follow-up Study of Adolescent Substance Use." *Evaluation Review* 16:151–70.

Tec, N. 1974. "Parent-Child Drug Abuse: Generational Continuity or Adolescent Deviancy?" *Adolescence* 9:350–64.

Telzrow, C. F. 1990. "Impact of Perinatal Complications on Education." In *Neuropsychology of Perinatal Complications*, edited by J. W. Gray and R. S. Dean. New York: Springer.

Tobler, N. S. 1986. "Meta-analysis of 143 Adolescent Drug Prevention Programs: Quantitative Outcome Results of Program Participants Compared to a Control or Comparison Group." *Journal of Drug Issues* 16:537–67.

Tonry, M., L. E. Ohlin, and D. P. Farrington. 1991. *Human Development and Criminal Behavior: New Ways of Advancing Knowledge*. New York: Springer-Verlag.

Tremblay, R. 1988. "Peers and the Onset of Delinquency." Unpublished paper prepared for the Onset Working Group of the Program on Human Development and Criminal Behavior. Castine, Me.: Castine Research Corporation.

Trickett, P. K., N. H. Apfel, L. K. Rosenbaum, and E. F. Zigler. 1982. "A Five-Year Follow-up of Participants in the Yale Child Welfare Research Program." In *Day Care: Scientific and Social Policy Issues*, edited by E. F. Zigler and E. W. Gordon. Boston: Auburn House.

U.S. General Accounting Office (USGAO). 1993. *Drug Use Measurement: Strengths, Limitations, and Recommendations for Improvement*. Report to the Chairman, Committee on Government Operations, U.S. House of Representatives. Washington, D.C.: U.S. General Accounting Office.

———. 1994. *Drug Use among Youth: No Simple Answers to Guide Prevention*. Report to the Chairman, Subcommittee on Children, Family, Drugs, and Alcoholism, Committee on Labor and Human Resources, U.S. Senate. Washington, D.C.: U.S. General Accounting Office.

U.S. Surgeon General. 1988. *The Health Consequences of Smoking: Nicotine Addiction. A Report of the Surgeon General*. Rockville, Md.: U.S. Department of Health and Human Services.

Vaillant, G. 1983. *The Natural History of Alcoholism*. Cambridge, Mass.: Harvard University Press.

Vartiainen E., U. Pallonen, A. McAlister, and P. Puska. 1990. "Eight-Year Follow-up Results of an Adolescent Smoking Prevention Program: The North Karelia Youth Project." *American Journal of Public Health* 80:78–79.

Vega, W. A., R. S. Zimmerman, G. J. Warheit, E. Apospori, and A. G. Gil. 1993. "Risk Factors for Early Adolescent Drug Use in Four Ethnic and Racial Groups." *American Journal of Public Health* 83:185–89.

von Knorring, L., L. Oreland, and A. L. von Knorring. 1987. "Personality Traits and Platelet MAO Activity in Alcohol and Drug Abusing Teenage Boys." *Acta Psychiatrica Scandinavica* 75:307–314.

Wallerstein, J. S., and J. B. Kelly. 1980. "Effects of Divorce on the Visiting Father-Child Relationship." *American Journal of Psychiatry* 137:1534–39.

Watts, R. K., and J. Rabow. 1983. "Alcohol Availability and Alcohol-related Problems in 213 California Cities." *Alcoholism: Clinical and Experimental Research* 7:47–58.

Weiss, R. D. 1992. "The Role of Psychopathology in the Transition from Drug Use to Abuse and Dependence." In *Vulnerability to Abuse*, edited by M. Glantz and R. Pickens. Washington, D.C.: American Psychological Association.

Werner, E. E. 1987. "Vulnerability and Resiliency in Children at Risk for Delinquency: A Longitudinal Study from Birth to Adulthood." In *Primary Prevention of Psychopathology*, vol. 10, *Prevention of Delinquent Behavior*, edited by J. D. Burchard and S. N. Burchard. Newbury Park, Calif.: Sage.

———. 1989. "High-Risk Children in Young Adulthood: A Longitudinal Study from Birth to 32 Years." *American Journal of Orthopsychiatry* 59:72–81.

Wilson, J. Q. 1990. "Drugs and Crime." In *Drugs and Crime*, edited by M. Tonry and J. Q. Wilson. Vol. 13 of *Crime and Justice: A Review of Research*, edited by M. Tonry and N. Morris. Chicago: University of Chicago Press.

Wilson, J. Q., and R. J. Herrnstein. 1985. *Crime and Human Nature*. New York: Simon & Schuster.

Wilson, W. J. 1988. *The Truly Disadvantaged: The Inner City, The Underclass, and Public Policy*. Chicago: University of Chicago Press.

Wish, E. D. 1990–1991. "U.S. Drug Policy in the 1990s: Insights from New Data from Arrestees." *International Journal of the Addictions* 25:377–409.

Yamaguchi, K., and D. B. Kandel. 1984. "Patterns of Drug Use from Adolescence to Young Adulthood: Part III. Predictors of Progression." *American Journal of Public Health* 74:673–81.

Yoshikawa, H. 1994. "Prevention as Cumulative Protection: Effects of Early Family Support and Education on Chronic Delinquency and Its Risks." *Psychological Bulletin* 115:28–54.

Ziegler-Driscoll, G. 1979. "The Similarities in Families of Drug Dependents and Alcoholics." In *Family Therapy of Drug and Alcohol Abuse*, edited by E. Kaufman and P. Kaufman. New York: Gardner Press.

Zigler, E., C. Taussig, and K. Black. 1992. "Early Childhood Intervention: A Promising Preventative for Juvenile Delinquency." *American Psychologist* 47:997–1006.

Zuckerman, M. 1987. "Biological Connection between Sensation Seeking and Drug Abuse." In *Brain Reward Systems and Abuse*, edited by J. Engel and L. Oreland. New York: Raven.

Per-Olof H. Wikström

Preventing City-Center Street Crimes

ABSTRACT

Prevention of crime and disorder in the city center is a neglected research topic. Few evaluations have been conducted of city-center street-crime prevention measures or programs. However, strategic insights for preventing crime and disorder in public in the city center can be gleaned from research into the patterns and causes of city-center crime and disorder. City centers are largely nonresidential areas where strangers from different social backgrounds mix in public space. City-center legal activities such as shopping and entertainment attract both conventional people and criminals, but they also create temptations and friction between people. Preventing crime in the city center is basically a question of influencing routine activities generating temptations and friction and of developing focused strategies of policing and surveillance.

There is a vast amount of research on city neighborhoods and crime (e.g., Taub, Taylor, and Dunham 1984; Reiss and Tonry 1986; Skogan 1990; Wikström 1991*b*; Bottoms, Claytor, and Wiles 1992; Bursik and Grasmick 1993). Studies on crime and disorder in urban areas have focused on residential areas (be they suburban or inner city), and very few have investigated nonresidential downtown areas (e.g., Poyner 1980; Hope 1985; Wikström 1985, pp. 259–70; Sherman et al. 1991). Crime prevention studies in cities have also largely focused on residential areas, for example, neighborhood watch programs and community policing (e.g., Skogan 1990; Bursik and Grasmick 1993), and rarely concerned the special type of environment that the city center consti-

Per-Olof H. Wikström is professor of sociology of crime in the Department of Sociology, University of Stockholm, and director of research at the Swedish National Council for Crime Prevention.

tutes (e.g., Reiss 1985; Sherman and Weisburd 1992). There are, to my knowledge, few careful evaluations of city-center street-crime prevention programs. So we do not have very much previous scientific experience to build on regarding what preventive measures work in the downtown environment.

In this essay, I examine research and theory of relevance for the understanding and prevention of city-center disorders and street crimes. By city center (or downtown area) is, somewhat loosely, meant the central business district (CBD). The concept of "street crimes" (or crimes in public) is used in a broad sense, including those crimes that take place not only in streets, squares, and parks, but also in places of public entertainment and on public transport. I focus particularly on crimes against the person.

In Section I, I provide background on the relationship between city centers, crime, and crime prevention. Preventing crime and disorder in the city center is a question of finding crime prevention measures that work in public places in a nonresidential environment in which myriad legal activities attract large numbers of visitors with widely diverse backgrounds and who generally are strangers to one another.

Section II sets out a theoretical discussion of a routine activity approach to city-center street-crime prevention. The basic strategies for preventing city-center crime should focus on reducing temptations and friction-producing encounters between people. Since the frequency of temptations and friction-producing encounters is a result of the social organization of everyday city-center activities, prevention efforts should be directed at influencing these activities.

The following three sections discuss youth and city-center crimes (Section III); public disorder, drinking, and drugs in the central city (Section IV); and violence in the city center (Section V). These three parts are organized in the same way; each begins with a problem definition followed by a section on prevention. Stockholm is used to illustrate the city-center street-crime problem. Stockholm is Sweden's largest city, having about 650,000 inhabitants, of whom 230,000 live in the inner city and fewer than 1,000 in the CBD. The inner city consists of 18 percent of the total Stockholm land area and has 35 percent of its residential population. The CBD area consists of 1 percent of the land area and has 0.1 percent of the population. The metropolitan area of Stockholm, including the city, has about 1.4 million inhabitants.

Three different strategies relating to youth crime in the city center are discussed in Section III: keeping youth out of the city center, keeping youth in the city center in "good" activities to keep them away from the "bad" ones, and surveillance and monitoring of youth in the city center.

In Section IV, three different approaches to reduce public disorder in the city center are considered: general policies to reduce alcohol and drug consumption; policing public drunkenness, drug use, and drug dealing; and problem-oriented measures targeted at disorders linked to the activities and running of licensed establishments.

The three strategies to prevent violence in the city center discussed in Section V are preventing disorder, reducing the availability and carrying of weapons, and surveillance.

The overall conclusion in Section VI is that an integrated crime prevention program, focusing on influencing routine activities generating temptations and friction and developing strategies of focused policing and surveillance, is the best way to attack city-center crime in public.

I. The City Center, Crime, and Crime Prevention

It is well established that crimes generally are more widespread in urban than in rural areas and that the rate of crime tends to increase with the size of the urban community (e.g., Christie, Andenaes, and Skirbekk 1965; van Dijk and Vivanen 1978; Wikström 1991a). The rate difference by degree of urbanization is generally greater for property crimes than for crimes against the person (e.g., Swedish Census Bureau 1981; Wikström 1989). For violent crimes, the difference is greater for crimes taking place in public than for those occurring in private (e.g., Wikström 1991a). Moreover, some types of crimes, for example, robbery and residential burglary, are strongly concentrated in big cities (e.g., Skogan 1978; Wikström 1991a).

The city center is likely to have a high supply of potential offenders. It is an area that is familiar to offenders, an area in which legal activities attractive to offenders occur, and an area that offers a rich supply of targets for crime.

The city has been characterized as being "*a market place*" (Weber 1966) and "*a world of strangers*" (Lofland 1973). The greater opportunities for property crimes (marketplace) and the weaker social control (world of strangers) are two dominant explanations for the increase in crime with rate of urbanization.

The bigger the city, the more of social life that will take place in public arenas and involve strangers. Fischer (1981, p. 308) has pointed out: "As urbanism increases, residents' public activities increasingly bring them into contact with unfamiliar, annoying, and threatening people. Their subjective reaction and public behavior expresses estrangement from, and even conflict with, members of foreign subcultures. However, urbanism does not estrange individuals from familiar and similar people. Conversely, urbanism's effects are specified: estrangement occurs in the public sphere—less helpfulness, more conflict—but not in the private one—personal relations and psychological well-being."

The city center, or the downtown area, is generally the environment of the city that is the most extreme as regards being "a market place" and "a world of strangers." Therefore, the city center is likely to be a key city environment for understanding the relationship between urbanization and crime.

A. The Crime/City-Center Concentration

In socioecological studies of urban crime, the city center is generally reported as the area of the city with the highest rate of crime (e.g., Schmid 1960a, 1960b, p. 660; Werner 1964; Pyle 1974; Baldwin and Bottoms 1976; Davidson 1981, p. 25; Wikström 1991a). Street crimes are among the types of crimes showing the strongest city-center concentration (e.g., Bullock 1955, p. 570; Curtis 1974, p. 147; Baldwin and Bottoms 1976, p. 81; Schwind, Ahlborn, and Weiss 1978; Wikström 1991a, p. 202, 1991b; McClintock and Wikström 1992).

That the city center tends to have the highest frequency of crime does not, however, necessarily mean that the victimization risk is highest in the city center. Boggs (1965) has questioned, with particular regard to property crimes, the finding that the central cities have the highest rates of crimes, on the grounds that when other denominators—more relevant than the commonly applied crime per residents—are used, the dominance of the city center is not so obvious. For example, if rates were calculated to take account of the number of possible victims, including employed commuters and day-tripping shoppers, the patterns might be considerably different. However, Boggs's argument is not likely to change the finding that for many crimes the city center is the area with the highest *density of crime* (crimes per land area unit), although the city center may not for all crimes be the area where the *victimization risk* is the greatest (i.e., rate of crimes per target). Although the overall crime density tends to be highest for the city center, the degree of city-center concentration varies substantially between types of crimes (see, e.g., Pyle 1974; Davidson 1981; Wikström 1991a).

B. Social Life in the City Center

Hunter (1985) distinguishes three types of social order: the private (the primary group—households, networks of households); the parochial (acquaintances—neighborhood); and the public (strangers—streets, squares, public transport). Public places are distinctive in "that they 'belong' to no one, are not parts of private and parochial orders, therefore belong equally to everyone" (Hunter 1985, p. 236).

Although all areas of the city have public spaces, the city-center area is the predominant public arena. The downtown area is likely to be the most densely built-up area, is characterized by a mixture of department stores, smaller shops, office complexes, hotels, pubs, clubs, and restaurants, and often is the focal point of the public transportation system. Generally the residential population is low, but at the same time the downtown area attracts numerous visitors for work, shopping, or entertainment. The social mix is likely to vary over the course of the day depending on the temporal variations in work and shopping going on in the day and entertainment in the evening.

The social life is predominantly *public*, compared to other areas of a city, which means that a high rate of interactions occur between *strangers* in streets, squares, public locales, and on public transport. What kinds of people interact, and what types of interactions occur, are likely to vary by the hour of the day. The city center is likely to be the site of the highest frequency of meetings between people with different social backgrounds.

While every city has many residential areas, in most there is only one distinct downtown area. Although there are some universal characteristics of the CBD, each city center displays more or less unique characteristics depending on factors such as the size of the city, its historically and geographically constructed form, and the social and economic characteristics of the larger metropolitan area. These differences are likely to influence the rate and structure of crime. One important example is whether slum areas (or "problem estates") are located near the downtown area (see, e.g., Brantingham and Brantingham 1981, pp. 40–41).

Moreover, the city structure has changed over time, and in that process the role of the city center has also in some respects changed, especially in relation to developments of transportation and the growing number of suburban local centers. These changes have influenced the overall crime patterns in the city and possibly also influenced crime in the downtown area—probably more so in North American cities than in European cities (see, e.g., Reiss 1985; Bursik 1986; Felson 1987).

C. Social Life in the City Center and Crime

Routine activity theory (Cohen and Felson 1979) proposes that there is a close relationship between the distribution in time and space of legal and illegal human activities. The latter are in many ways dependent on the former. To understand the spatial and temporal variations of crime, one therefore needs to understand the spatial and temporal variations of everyday legal activities.

That the city center is a major area of commerce and entertainment where many people who are strangers to each other are brought together should be reflected in the rate and structure of downtown criminality. It is hardly surprising, for example, that shoplifting is a major daytime crime and that different types of public disorder, vandalism, and stranger-to-stranger violent crimes are major nighttime crimes.

D. Social Life in the City Center and Crime Prevention

The distinction between private and public is crucial for crime prevention strategies. For instance, preventing assault in the home is in many ways a different task from preventing assault in the street. There are a number of relevant factors that may vary depending on whether a crime takes place in private or in public. There is an obvious relationship between different types of social orders and the conditions for different forms of social control. Controlling crime and disorder in the CBD area is a different problem from that of controlling crime and disorder in residential areas.

That the central city predominantly is a public arena has several important consequences for crime prevention strategies. First, the public space has traditionally been the main responsibility of the police (and more recently also of private security agencies). Second, although many crime prevention strategies build on involving the neighborhood in one way or another (e.g., defensible space, neighborhood watch, community policing), the CBD generally lacks a residential community. The actors who can be mobilized in the city-center area, besides the police and private security agencies, are people who work there in shops, restaurants, office buildings, on public transport, and so on. However, as Mayhew (1981, p. 128) has pointed out: "The crime prevention role of employees is a topic which has not featured greatly in the criminological literature."

The basic question thus becomes how to prevent crime in public places in a nonresidential environment in which diverse vocational and recreational activities attract large numbers of visitors with widely differing social backgrounds and who generally are strangers to each other.

II. Routine Activities and City-Center Street-Crime Prevention

In this section I discuss a routine activity approach to the prevention of city-center street crimes. I begin by discussing central dimensions of criminal behavior and crime sites and the key elements of the routine activity theory (motivated offenders, suitable targets, and capable guardians). Thereafter, I take up the key point made by the routine activities theory in relation to city-center street crimes and disorder, that "the probability that a violation will occur at any specific time and place might be taken as a function of the convergence of likely offender and suitable targets in the absence of capable guardians" (Cohen and Felson 1979, p. 590). Finally, against this background I discuss general strategies for preventing city-center street crimes from a somewhat modified routine activity theory conceptual framework.

A. *Routine Activities, Street Crimes, and Disorders*

Originally the routine activity approach (Cohen and Felson 1979) focused only on so-called predatory crimes. However, in a later work Felson (1987, p. 912) extends the scope of the approach to include a wider range of illegal behavior.

Some types of crimes and disorder are easier than others to fit into the conceptual framework of the routine activity approach, although the notions of dependence between legal and illegal activities and of the convergence of potential offenders with "criminogenic situations" for the occurrence of criminal events and disorders seem to apply to most types of crime and disorder.

1. *Dimensions of Criminal Behavior.* The circumstances of a criminal act are an important point of departure for the consideration of different prevention strategies. For instance, targeting crime prevention

measures to specific types of criminal events is central to the situational prevention approach (Clarke and Mayhew 1980).

Crimes have been classified according to two central dimensions: instrumental or expressive crime (McClintock 1974) and crimes with or without interaction (Knutsson 1984). An expressive crime is usually defined as an offense in which the criminal act is a goal in itself (e.g., injuring or causing pain to another person), whereas an instrumental crime is normally thought of as one in which the criminal act is merely a means toward an end (such as personal gain). However, particularly as regards crimes of violence, which may have both expressive and instrumental elements, the division of crimes into instrumental (robbery, rape) and expressive criminal acts (assault) is not without complication. Many expressive crimes of violence seem also to have an instrumental or controlling component (e.g., trying to make the other party comply with one's wishes or views), and some instrumental crimes of violence appear to have an expressive element (e.g., rape with a purpose of humiliating or dominating the victim). Following Reiss (1990), instrumental assaultive violence can be divided into proactive assault (e.g., beating up someone to scare them from testifying) and reactive assault (e.g., self-defense). Black (1984) has pointed out that many assaults can be viewed as "self-help." Empirical studies of assaults also show that, although the majority of assaults in public may be classified as hostile aggression arising from interpersonal situational conflicts, many assaults occur in what may be labeled "social control situations" and are reactive, for example, involving an intervening doorman (Wikström 1991a; McClintock and Wikström 1992). Combining the two dimensions provides the four general categories of crime shown in figure 1.

For understanding how crime events are generated and for finding ways to prevent them, the instrumental-expressive dimension is important; instrumental crimes can be expected to have a higher degree of planning than do expressive crimes. However, the instrumental-expressive dimension should be treated as a variable, and it is dichotomized here only for convenience.

Whether the crime is interactive influences the detection possibilities (both as regards whether a crime has been committed and who the offender is). Except for completed homicides, interactive crimes always involve at least a victim who knows that a crime has been committed and who normally has seen the offender and may be able to identify

INSTRUMENTAL

	YES	NO
INTERACTIVE **YES**	Robbery, rape (proactive and reactive assault)	Hostile assault
NO	Shoplifting	Vandalism

FIG. 1.—Examples of traditional crimes classified by dimension: instrumental or expressive crime, and interactive or noninteractive crime.

him. In noninteractive crimes such as shoplifting and vandalism, it may sometimes be difficult to know whether a lost item or damaged piece of property means that a crime has been committed or not, and it may be difficult in most cases to know who the offender may be.

2. *Public Crime Sites.* Another important crime circumstance is whether the crime takes place in public. The social circumstances of theft, assault, robbery, or rape are likely to differ depending on whether the act takes place in private or public. Violence in private tends to occur between people of similar social positions and lifestyles; violence in public tends to occur between people of different social positions (e.g., Wikström 1991a, p. 103). The private-public dimension of criminal behavior can also be regarded as crucial for crime prevention strategies.

Brown and Altman (1981, p. 59) describe public territories in the following way: "Public territories are usually occupied for short times and are typically not very central to the lives of their occupants (for instance, seats of a bus, tables in a restaurant). Occupancy of public territories is open to almost everyone and is usually determined on a 'first come, first serve' basis."

In discussions of neighborhoods and crime, it is generally reported that low social integration, heterogeneity of population, and high residential mobility are factors associated with high rates of crime and offending (e.g., Kornhauser 1978; Bursik 1988). The city center is characterized by low social integration (people are strangers to each other), by heterogeneity (people with different social backgrounds are brought together), and mobility (people do not stay long). In addition, the city center is characterized by alcohol- and drug-related activities that contribute to social instability. The downtown area, at least in European cities, and particularly at night, is the most socially unstable public environment in the city.

This makes it difficult to mobilize the city center's "population" for crime-prevention activities. Although bystanders generally cannot be assumed to be inclined to intervene in crime situations (e.g., Mayhew 1981), the public and socially unstable character of the city-center environment probably make bystanders even less willing to intervene.

The public character of the city center makes it difficult to keep "undesirables" out; they have the same right to be there as anybody else. The city center is likely to be attractive to socially marginalized groups. The anonymity of the downtown area may make potential offenders view this environment as attractive. This anonymity may interact with the rich supply of targets for property crimes.

The downtown is attractive also to conventional people. Public space, particularly in the city center, is where meetings between conventional and socially marginalized people are most frequent. This creates opportunities for instrumental crimes such as robbery.

The public character of the city-center environment can contribute to social frictions. Brown and Altman (1981) point out that bodily and verbal markings (e.g., marking one's table in a restaurant by hanging a jacket over a chair) are common in public territories. These markings (which at times may be perceived as insults), in combination with ambiguity about rights to public space, may generate conflict that can lead to aggression and violence. This is likely to be especially so at night when the activities are less organized than the work and shopping that go on during the day.

3. *Motivated Offenders.* The propensity to offend varies significantly in the urban population, ranging from the opportunistic offender who occasionally succumbs to an extreme temptation to the chronic offender who searches for opportunities to commit crimes (e.g., Wolfgang, Figlio, and Sellin 1972; Farrington 1983, 1988; Wikström 1987, 1990; Wolfgang, Thornberry, and Figlio 1987; LeBlanc and Fréchette 1989). This appears largely to hold true for violent behavior, although it is perhaps better to speak of a differential readiness to respond violently in different situations. Offenders with a high frequency of violent offending tend to be chronic offenders (e.g., Wikström 1985; Farrington and Wikström 1993).

Control theory predicts, and research shows, that individuals with a high propensity to offend tend to be adventuresome and action-seeking (e.g., Gottfredson and Hirschi 1990, p. 90). The downtown environment of a city with its concentration of restaurants, pubs, and red-light activities is an attractive environment for adventuresome and action-seeking people. Interviews of chronic offenders in prison (e.g., Åkerström 1983) have shown that they, while free, have high rates of participation in public entertainment activities. It is also well known that the club and pub business, as well as the red-light district business, attracts criminals.

The parts of a city in which a delinquent chooses to commit crime are those areas with which he is most familiar and where he spends most of his time (Brantingham and Brantingham 1981). Other than one's own neighborhood, the downtown is likely for most city dwellers to be the most familiar part of the city.

Offenders' residences are not evenly distributed over a city's neighborhoods (e.g., Wikström 1991a, pp. 130–84). Offenders who commit crimes in the CBD predominantly come from slum and public housing areas. The pattern of location of high-offender-rate neighborhoods varies between cities and countries, but two major areas of concentration are slum areas adjacent to the CBD or public housing (council estates) in the outskirts of the city. The former pattern is more common in the United States and the latter in Europe, although many cities have a mix of both.

In a study of land use, adult offenders' residence, and place of commission of rapes, robberies, and burglaries in the District of Columbia, Rhodes and Conly (1981, pp. 186–87) show that areas with concentrations of large businesses such as department stores, shopping malls, and large offices and special land uses such as public services, museums, and libraries "offer good targets and serve as magnets for offenders." They interpret their findings regarding crime and distance as follows: "Offenders living near business and commercial areas travel into those areas to commit their offenses, while offenders who live near transitional neighborhoods stay near home to commit most of theirs, and offenders who live near predominantly residential areas travel farther than individuals who do not live near such areas."

4. *Suitable Targets.* In instrumental crimes, there is usually a clear distinction between the offender and the victim, regardless of whether the crime is interactive as in rape or robbery or noninteractive as in shoplifting. In expressive interactive crimes such as assaults, the distinction between offender and victim is often unclear, since the circumstances in which the crime is committed frequently resemble more a

fight than a one-sided attack. In crimes that are neither instrumental nor interactive, such as vandalism, the distinction between offender and target is clear; but it may still be difficult to determine what constitutes an attractive target (after all, most things can be damaged or destroyed).

Research on the social context of criminal episodes (e.g., Wikström 1991a) indicates that the concept of a "suitable criminal target" can generally be applied without much difficulty to instrumental crimes but is less obviously applicable to expressive crimes. For the latter, the question of a considered "choice" of target hardly arises; it is a matter more of how situations arise that may lead to violence or damage. I refer to these situations as friction-producing meetings and reserve the concept of "suitable targets" for instrumental crimes for which there is planning and target choice.

Concerning instrumental crimes, it would be reasonable to suppose that the more an individual is involved in crime generally, the more often his instrumental crimes will result from an active search for favorable opportunities rather than from exploitation of opportunities that happen to present themselves.

Concerning expressive crimes, there is an obvious link between public disorders like public drunkenness and street harassment and friction-producing meetings that develop into aggression and violence. This may also hold for many cases of vandalism in public.

5. *Capable Guardians.* Capable guardians include any individual who may be regarded by the potential offender as able and willing to intervene should a crime be committed, intervention including not only direct physical action but also such steps as summoning the police or witnessing the crime.

Although the police are obvious capable guardians, they are primarily reactive rather than proactive; they seldom intervene except when summoned by others (Reiss 1971; Knutsson 1984). Recent emphases on "problem-oriented policing" (Goldstein 1990) may shift the police toward a more proactive approach. Besides the police, those with the highest potential for being capable guardians in the downtown area are those who work there.

Capable guardians are of particular significance to instrumental crimes. Their significance for expressive crime is less clear (e.g., many cases of violence in the downtown area involve intervening individuals). Some types of vandalism may be susceptible to the influence of guardianship.

B. "Hot Spots" and "Hot Times"

Sherman, Gartin, and Buerger (1989, pp. 30–31) point out that "the most important contribution of routine activities theory is the argument that crime rates are affected not only by the absolute size of the supply of offenders, targets, or guardianship, but also by the factors affecting the frequency of their convergence in space and time."

The city center is probably the prime public environment in the city that connects potential offenders with criminogenic situations. The variations that link motivated offenders with suitable targets and friction-producing encounters include the differentiation of legal activities in the city, people's patterns of movement, the street layout, and the structure of the public transport system.

Within the downtown environment, there is a great variation between places in the rate of crimes and disorder. Concentrations of crime or disorder in a specific place have been called "hot spots" (Sherman, Gartin, and Buerger 1989, p. 28), "trouble spots" (Hope 1985), or "black spots" (Wikström 1985, p. 237). Since these concentrations tend to appear at certain times of the day and in some cases on certain days of the week or even certain parts of the year (e.g., the summer), it may make sense to talk about "hot times." The hot spots/hot times approach has considerable implications for crime prevention. The more closely a type of crime or disorder can be related to specific places and times, the better the chances of relating the crime or disorder to specific aspects of the social life and of finding ways to prevent its occurrence.

An illustrative example of hot spots from a study of stranger-on-stranger outdoor assaults in the city center of a medium-sized Swedish city (Wikström 1980) is given in figure 2. These crimes tend to cluster around licensed establishments (restaurants, bars), and the clustering is much more pronounced around some licensed establishments than around others. Observational studies revealed that the major clusters of stranger-to-stranger violence were characterized by the conjunction of alcohol-intoxicated people from different social backgrounds; these meetings tended to cause friction and sometimes developed into aggression and violence. Many, but far from all, of the establishments located at the hot spots had high rates of violence inside the establishments.

One hot spot was a small cross street where the entrance to a restaurant, often frequented by pupils of upper secondary school, and a high-class dance restaurant, frequented by somewhat older people, were located on one side of the street, while a hamburger bar was located on the other side. The latter was a place where many of the

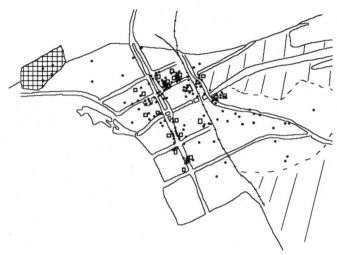

● = One case of assault outdoors between strangers.

◻ = Block with one or more licensed establishment.

▲ = The railway station.

⊞ = Hospital area.

||| = Industrial area.

FIG. 2.—Key map of city center: stranger-to-stranger outdoor assaults. Source.—Wikström (1980).

rockers (often working class) of the city spent time in the late evenings. The "hot spot" was peaceful during the day and most of the evening. It was only late in the evenings, especially on weekends, that it was a "hot spot" for stranger-to-stranger assault.

Another example is the pattern of assault at the major outdoor amusement park in Stockholm. In the summertime, while the park is open, there is a significant clustering of assaults in the park, while at wintertime, when the park is closed, there are virtually no assaults.

The conditions necessary for creating a hot spot probably vary with the nature of the crime or disorder in question. Instrumental crimes are probably more sensitive to the presence of capable guardians than are expressive crimes and disorders. Instrumental crimes are also probably more dependent on suitable targets than are expressive crimes and disorders. The generation of hot spots for instrumental crimes is likely to be a function of the convergence of potential offenders and suitable targets in the absence of capable guardians, while the generation of hot spots for expressive crimes is likely to be dependent on circumstances in which strangers are brought together and where intoxication and a high frequency of mixing of people with different social backgrounds is common.

One problem with the hot spots approach, however, is that conditions identified at the hot spots may spuriously be taken to be the causes of the crime or disorder concentration. For example, there may be many other places with similar characteristics that do not display a concentration of crime and disorder.

Since a basic assumption of the routine activity approach is that illegal acts are dependent on legal activities, certain types of legal activities may be predicted to be likely to attract crime and generate hot spots. A related, but reverse, approach is to analyze the links between legal and illegal activities in order to predict what legal activities are likely to generate crime and disorder. Since legal activities are closely linked to land use patterns, mapping out the land use of the downtown area would be a way to predict what places are likely to be hot spots, and at what times. This can then be compared with the actual distribution of hot spots of crimes and disorders. This approach would involve three steps: detailed mapping of city-center land use—relating different types of land use to different types of social activities and social mixes of people, typology—relating different types of social life to different types of crime and disorder, and dependence of legal and illegal activities—studying concentrations of crime and disorders in relation to variations in social life.

One benefit of making such a comprehensive analysis of the downtown area is that it may suggest possible alternative sites with similar characteristics as existing hot spots that may come into use, for instance, if effective policing of a hot spot takes place. This may have important implications for efforts to avoid displacement. For drug dealing and prostitution, for example, some places may be especially facilitative, but there are probably alternative sites with similar characteristics.

Displacement is probably a more relevant consideration for instrumental crimes than for expressive crimes. The risk of displacement is probably higher for crimes likely to be committed by chronic offenders since they are likelier to search for suitable targets than are occasional offenders, who may be more opportunistic.

C. Preventing City-Center Crime: General Strategies

There are basically two ways to prevent crime and disorder. One is to reduce people's propensity to offend. A social control theoretical approach assumes that the propensity to offend depends on the individual's degree of self-control and social bonds to conventional society (e.g., Gottfredson and Hirschi 1990; Wikström 1994*a*). Low self-control and weak social bonds increase the risk for offending. The other is to reduce the presence of criminogenic situations. A criminogenic situation is one in which an individual is tempted to commit a criminal act or in which the situation generates friction and conflict.

The ways in which people's propensities to offend or criminogenic situations may be reduced are numerous. But the overall goals are to strengthen self-control and social bonds, to reduce tempting circumstances, and to reduce friction-producing encounters. Successful efforts to strengthen self-control and social bonds should, other things being equal, mean a reduction in situations that are viewed as tempting and that cause friction.

Since the downtown area is a prime environment in which an individual's potential to offend is realized, a general strengthening of self-control and social bonds in the population is likely to reduce crime and disorders in the city center by reducing the supply of highly motivated offenders. This, however, is a task that is basically developmental (e.g., Farrington 1992; Tremblay and Craig, in this volume) and accomplished in the private and parochial social orders and not in the public social order that dominates city-center life.

Crime prevention strategies for the city center must focus on reducing temptations and friction-producing encounters, which result from the social organization of everyday life. Influencing downtown social life thus is the basic way to change the frequency of criminogenic situations.

III. Youth and City-Center Crime

The city center is for many reasons attractive to youth but is also an environment with great temptations: exposure and easy access to drinking and drug use, the presence of groups of socially marginalized youth and adults, and a friction-producing social mix of youth of different backgrounds. It is also an environment where youth are largely free from adult control.

TABLE 1

All Crimes Recorded by the Police and Committed by Youth (Aged
below Nineteen) in the City of Stockholm 1988 by Area of Crime
Scene: Total Crimes, and Selected Categories of Crime (in Percent)

Area of Crime	Total Crimes	Assault	Vandalism	Non-residential Burglary	Shop-lifting
CBD	31.3	23.1	16.5	36.4	50.0
Other inner-city area	25.7	32.7	31.9	22.0	16.0
Suburbs	43.0	44.2	51.6	41.5	34.0
N	1,200	104	91	118	412

SOURCE.—Author's unpublished data.
NOTE.—CBD = central business district.

A. Problem Definition

The downtown is generally attractive for youth. There is a lot going
on and a lot to do. Youth are relatively free from adult control since
the likelihood that they will come across family members, school teachers, or neighbors is quite small. This is certainly the case for most
European cities. However, for less affluent big-city U.S. youth, the
downtown area may not be so attractive, and they may be more likely
than European youth to remain in their own neighborhoods.

A recent study in Stockholm of crimes by offenders under age nineteen recorded by the police in 1988 found that youth crime was highly
concentrated in the inner city and especially in the downtown area
(Wikström 1994c). Almost one-third of Stockholm youth crime was
committed in the CBD area (table 1). Given that the CBD area has
0.1 percent of the city population and 1 percent of its land area, the
concentration is very strong. The concentration was stronger for property crime than for crimes against the person and vandalism.

Practically none (0.3 percent) of the youth offenders committing
crime in the CBD area resided in that area. Most resided outside the
city boundaries in more distant suburbs or in some cases even outside
the Stockholm metropolitan area. Thus, youth crime in the CBD area
of Stockholm is committed mostly by visiting youth who live in the
suburbs; most lived in nonprofit-housing-dominated areas (council estates, public housing). That most of the youth coming to the city center

reside at a distance also affects crimes and disorders in public transport since they normally use public transport to get to and from the central city. This "commuting to the city center" pattern may be different in other cities where residential slum areas or problem estates are located closer to the city center than is the case for Stockholm. Probably this pattern is more common in European than in U.S. cities.

The city-center area has been identified as an undesirable place, especially at night and during weekends, for young people to hang around. A study in 1978 in Stockholm of "bad youth environments," which asked police officers and social workers to name bad places for young people, produced a strong concentration of such places in the city center (Sarnecki 1983, pp. 99–100). The same study showed that the most criminal youth tend to engage more in commercial spare-time activities and spend more time in the city center than do other youth. This finding was largely replicated in a newer 1989 study of Stockholm youth (Dolmen and Lindström 1991). The city-center area, with its concentration of shops and big department stores, is an environment of many temptations.

Since there is substantial residential segregation in many cities—between neighborhoods dominated by immigrants and others, between affluent and less affluent neighborhoods—when youth commute to the city center, they are confronted with youth from other types of neighborhoods and with social backgrounds different from their own. In Stockholm, there are well-established meeting points for different groups of immigrant youth and for different groups of native youth. Further, some youth gangs are not neighborhood-based as in large U.S. cities. For example, youth from all over the metropolitan area claim certain places in the city center as their "turf." Moreover, the city center is an environment for bringing conventional youth in contact with criminally active youth. However, little is known about any "recruitment" to criminality that may result from this convergence, or the convergence of youth and older, socially marginalized people, although the question of "recruiters" is an extremely important one in the understanding of youth crime (Reiss and Farrington 1991).

B. Prevention

There appear to be three different and complementary strategies to prevent city-center youth crime: keeping youth out of the city center, keeping youth in the city center in "good" activities to keep them away from "bad" ones, and surveillance and monitoring of youth in the city center.

1. *Keeping Youth out of the City Center.* Given all the risks involved for youth in the city center, one preventive strategy is to try to keep them out. This could be accomplished by cooperation with schools and parents, by different kinds of curfews, or by creating attractive youth activities in their neighborhoods.

One strategy is for schools and parents to try to keep youth from the city center, especially at critical times. Since shoplifting is a major crime among youth, and a crime predominantly taking place during daytime, and concentrated in the city center, schools may have an important preventive role. Although not particularly concerned with the prevention of city-center crimes, Felson's suggestion that the school by its organization and monitoring of pupils may contribute to crime prevention is partly relevant in this context. Examples of school activities that may influence youth city-center shoplifting include "1. Uniform school schedules, so the community has no doubt when youth belong in school and when not. 2. Truancy enforcement and other efforts to keep adolescents in school. 3. After-school activities keeping youths under some degree of adult influence from soon after school lets out to soon before parents arrive home from work" (Felson 1992, p. 3).

Parents should be given information about the risks for youth of spending time (especially weekends and nights) in the city center, with the purpose of motivating parents to keep their children as much as possible away from the city center at critical times or, at least, to see that they are accompanied as much as possible by adults when visiting the city-center area. Measures like these may have some effect on conventional youth but are harder to apply to socially marginalized youth.

Curfew laws can help conventional parents keep their children out of city centers at night. Examples of more repressive possible measures directed principally toward criminal youths include so-called weekend prisons, meaning that the person in question, as a penalty, is held in an institution during critical periods such as weekend nights. Another measure directed at criminally active youth is for penalties for city-center crimes to include a prohibition against being in the city center, for example, on weekend nights. This could be enforced by normal police surveillance of the city center or by electronic monitoring. Little is known about the effectiveness of such measures.

A third way to approach the problem of keeping youth away from the city center at high-risk times is to create alternative attractive activities in their neighborhoods—youth clubs, rock concerts, sports events. If successful, this is likely to mean a reduction in youth crime in the city but possible displacement of crime to the neighborhood. The obvious advantage of having youth participate in public entertainment in their neighborhood is that the conditions to create effective social control are better in a young person's own neighborhood than in the city center. This may also reduce friction arising from bringing together groups of youth from different social backgrounds.

2. *Involving Youth in "Good" Activities to Keep Them away from "Bad" Ones.*   Given that a youth-free city center is hardly realistic, another strategy is to create positive activities for youth in the city center under some adult control: for example, drug-free youth clubs and discos. The main problem is that this approach may lead to an increase in the attractiveness for youths of the downtown area and bring a larger number of conventional youth to the central city and into contact with more deviant youths and with risky environments. It is also doubtful whether such activities can in any number attract the criminal youth hanging around in the city center. In general, experience with youth leisure activities as crime prevention measures is not very promising. In a review of evaluations of different types of crime prevention measures, Poyner (1993, p. 16) concludes, as regards a group of measures including providing youth leisure activities, "that none of the measures involving 'social or community services' can be claimed to have much direct impact on crime."

3. *Surveillance and Monitoring of Youth in the City Center.*   A third basic strategy is surveillance and monitoring of youth in the city center. Besides routine police surveillance, this approach involves focused policing and social work and different kinds of "citizen patrols." The latter consist both of patrols by adults and patrols by youths.

So-called parent walks consist of voluntary adults who patrol the city center. Parent walks may serve different purposes—to increase adult control, to give participating adults more knowledge of what is happening in the city center, and to offer assistance to youth in need. The best-known group of parent walkers in Stockholm call themselves "mothers and fathers on town," although they are not likely to be the mothers and fathers of the young people hanging around in the city center. Their aim is to try to interact with youth in the city center, to inform them about alternative activities, to help with contacts with social welfare authorities, and occasionally to get them a bed for the night (Alexandersson 1993).

There are also "youth patrols" in the central city of Stockholm. One group calls itself a "nonfighting generation" and patrols the central city to help prevent youth fights and violence. This group was started by former violent youth, and its activities have been highly debated as, I believe, have also been the activities of the "Guardian Angels" in New York City and similar movements elsewhere.

Although there is some evidence that "citizen patrols" in neighborhoods, and in particular in suburban neighborhoods, have some general preventive effect (e.g., Lab 1988, pp. 49–51), little is known about whether the adult or youth city-center "patrol" activities, as described here, have any effect on city-center youth crime.

Given that criminally active youth are attracted to the city-center area, a plausible police strategy is to collect information about these youth in the city center, where they hang around, with whom they mix, and what kinds of crimes they tend to commit. A related strategy is to create contact between the criminal youth and the police to make these youth less anonymous; one hypothesis is that youth would know that the police know them and that this would have some general preventive effect on their criminal behavior.

A plainclothes youth group of the Stockholm police works along these lines. Besides doing the things just mentioned, they share the collected information with the uniformed policemen patrolling the city center so they can adjust their patrolling to this knowledge; they also supply information to the social welfare authorities about problem youth in the city.

IV. Public Disorder, Drinking, and Drugs

"Drinking and disorderliness have traditionally gone hand-in-hand. In modern cities, the city center (or entertainment district) has become an arena for both. But the interrelationship between the use of alcohol, disorderliness, and the life of city centers is complex" (Hope 1985, p. 45).

In this section I discuss public disorder, drinking, and drugs in the city center. By public disorder I mean behavior such as vandalism, public drunkenness, and street harassment. Although in many cases it is difficult to separate disorder from violence, the latter is separately discussed in Section V.

A. Problem Definition

The downtown area is attractive to socially marginalized and conventional people for the same reasons (e.g., entertainment) and for different reasons (e.g., the socially marginalized may be attracted by the "anonymity" and target concentrations). The downtown area is the predominant public space of the city where socially marginalized and conventional people converge. This is likely to cause friction, and conventional people may in some circumstances become suitable targets for criminals. An important characteristic of the downtown entertainment activities is their link to drinking and, to a lesser extent, to drug use. This means that the city center has concentrations of interactions between alcohol-intoxicated people and sometimes also involving people under the influence of drugs.

In Stockholm, as in most other cities, there is a strong concentration of public drunkenness and drug abuse in the city center. A 1979 study (Wikström 1981) of the distribution of police interventions for drunkenness and illegal sales of alcohol and narcotics showed an extreme concentration in the CBD. As many as 42 percent of the interventions for illegal sales of alcohol or drugs and 37 percent of the interventions due to drunkenness occurred in the CBD.

Stockholm studies of street harassment also show concentration in the city center that is hardly surprising since those molesting other people in public often are alcoholics and drug addicts.

Street prostitution is often concentrated in the CBD. In a study of Stockholm prostitution, the author concludes that street prostitution has been concentrated in the same ten-block area of Stockholm since the 1930s even though great changes in the physical structure of the downtown area have taken place during this period (Ds S 1980, p. 534). The author describes the street prostitution activity as like an old town market. The peak hours are between 10 P.M. and midnight. The prostitutes are described as a mixture of drug abusers and nondrug abusers. The buyers mostly come by car, and sex acts typically take place elsewhere (Ds S 1980, pp. 535–36). Prostitution is legal in Sweden.

Vandalism is concentrated in the inner city of Stockholm, but the concentration in the CBD is not as strong as for public drunkenness, illegal alcohol, and drug sales and violence. Acts of vandalism cover a wide range of behaviors, for instance, scratching the paint off cars with a key while passing by, covering walls or subway cars with one's "tags," lighting a fire in a dustbin, and damaging street lights and windows of business establishments.

Vandalism in the city center can predominantly be described as "weekend vandalism," a concept used by Roos (1986, p. 119; my translation). Roos describes a typical case in the following way: "This type of vandalism often consists of youth, but also older persons, on a weekend evening or night, moving through the city on their way to areas of public entertainment after having been at a private party, and then, for instance, kicking against parked cars, throwing sausages and mashed potatoes in the face of a kiosk employee so her glasses break, kicking in doors to dance halls to which they are refused entrance, etc."

The proportion of youth offenders is quite high in cases of vandalism in streets, in squares, and on public transport. It is likely that the proportion of youth offenders for these cases is an underestimation.

In a recent interview study, covering all shopkeepers in the Stockholm CBD in 1989 (Torstensson 1994), it was shown that significant proportions of the shops reported persons coming into the shop being under the influence of drugs (27 percent) and threats to and harassment of the staff (14 percent) as "a big problem." The shops most likely to experience these kinds of disorders were those located close to well-known meeting points for abusers and places of illegal drug sales.

B. Prevention

The city-center public disorder problem is to a large extent an alcohol and drug problem. Prevention of downtown public disorder naturally focuses on influencing alcohol and drug use. There are at least three different approaches: general policies to reduce alcohol and drug consumption; policing public drunkenness, drug use, and drug-dealing; and problem-oriented measures targeted at disorders linked to the activities and running of licensed establishments.

1. *General Policies to Reduce Alcohol and Drug Consumption.* All successful general preventive measures against drinking and drug use are likely to influence the rate of public disorders in the city center. Such measures may include price policies and restrictions in the right to sell and use alcohol and drugs in general or for specific places, times, and groups of people.

"Social users" and the "down and out" are likely to be somewhat differently receptive to different types of alcohol and drug-use prevention programs. For instance, drinking patterns of alcoholics and social drinkers present different problems. These two groups are also likely to have different roles in city-center disorder, so different preventive measures may have different effects on specific disorders depending on which group is affected.

2. *Policing.*   Intoxicated people may generally be assumed to be less inhibited by the presence of capable guardians than are sober persons. Public-disorder-related conflicts often arise between drunken persons and capable guardians (shop employees, doormen, security personnel, police officers).

Dealing with and intervening against drunk persons or persons under the influence of drugs is not an easy task, and bystanders are likely to be reluctant to do so and to defer to the police and security personnel. Individuals working in establishments located in the downtown area may be more willing to take action. But, by and large, "policing" public drunkenness and persons under the influence of drugs is likely to be a task predominantly left to the police.

One factor that may influence the general level of disorder in the city center is what threshold for interventions the police choose. The lower the threshold, the fewer public disorders there are likely to be (although control-related conflicts may be higher than elsewhere). The choice of what behaviors are viewed as unacceptable in the city center need not be a police decision but may be decided by the local municipality or even through a referendum. It is probably important that the threshold is generally accepted by the public and is well-known.

The likelihood that the chosen threshold will be enforced is likely to be of importance. The character of the interventions (aggressive, nonaggressive) and the style of patrolling (by car or foot patrol) may also influence the effectiveness of police efforts. It may, for instance, be easier to recognize a disorder and do the right thing, or to detect a developing disorder, if the officer is on site than if he jumps into the scene from a patrol car.

Different public disorders may be concentrated in different places and related to different aspects of legal activities going on in these places. In Stockholm, there are, for instance, well-known places where socially marginalized people come together and where disorders are likely to occur. The analysis of the locations of hot spots and hot times and the reasons for these places to be hot spots at certain times may be an important point of departure for policing disorder (Sherman 1992). It will form a basis for focused policing and perhaps also a basis on which crime preventive cooperation with legal activities going on at these places can be established.

Successful focused policing of hot spots may lead to displacement of disorders. However, even if there is displacement, the activity displaced may have been displaced to a "better place," for instance, a place where there are fewer chances of contacts between conventional and socially marginalized people (perhaps decreasing recruitment and conflicts). This implies that even if a disorder cannot be eliminated, there may be value in controlling its location. For an in-depth discussion of the problem of displacement, see Barr and Pease (1990).

3. *Policing "Soft Crimes": The Case of Oakland.* Few published studies describe policing strategies for city-center areas and their effectiveness. One exception is the study by Reiss (1985) of a program for policing the central city of Oakland. This study gives some evidence that policing what Reiss labels "soft crimes" (i.e., harassment, panhandling, chronic loitering, offensive and threatening behavior) also may influence the rate of "hard crimes" (e.g., robbery, auto theft). Reiss (1985, pp. 8–37) describes the Oakland police program in terms of the strategies that are summarized below.

a. A diversified police patrol strategy—uniformed and plainclothes foot patrol and mounted patrol to assure people that they may safely move within the core area, and different types of motorized patrolling (motor scooters, motorcycles and cars) matched to meet specific needs (e.g., using small motorcycles to be able to move quickly around larger areas such as parks, vacant lots, and byways).

b. Private sector participation—private corporation financial support for policing the central city area (e.g., salary and fringe benefits for extra police officers), attention to importance of environmental design for crime prevention (e.g., design of interior space and parking spaces), and increased reporting to the police from private companies of soft crimes.

c. Enforcing laws relating to soft crimes—work with community agencies to ameliorate the problems associated with special populations that contribute to fear of crime or diminish the quality of life in the central area.

d. Deploy tactical police units to deal with special problems within the central core and its fringes (e.g., narcotic sales).

e. Obtain greater control over the sanctioning of offenders who create continuing problems in the central core.

Although the Oakland experience could not be evaluated in any rigorous sense, the evidence suggests that observed declines in the rates of some types of hard crimes may at least partly be attributed to program effects (Reiss 1985, pp. 39–43).

4. *Public Establishments.* Since the concentration of public entertainment facilities is one major reason for the high prevalence of alcohol and drug-related disorders in the city center (e.g., Ramsey 1983; Hope 1985; Tuck 1989), it is natural to focus on preventive measures in relation to licensed establishments. Ramsey (1983, p. 7) argued that a focus of crime prevention efforts on public entertainment establishments would have a great potential for reducing city-center crime: "Greater gains could be made preventing crime by concentrating on the pubs, clubs and perhaps other establishments which, collectively, are linked either directly or indirectly with, in volume terms, a considerable amount of city center crime."

Laws regulating drinking and drugs and drinking cultures (sometimes also drug cultures) are different in different countries and recommendations based on experiences from one country may not be transferable to others. However, Hope (1985), based on a study in Newcastle, has made a comprehensive list of possible time- and situation-specific preventive measures related to disorders directly or indirectly linked to the activities of licensed establishments. The majority of Hope's recommendations may be valid also for countries other than England.

Following are possible time- and situation-specific measures for preventing drink-related disorders in city centers that Hope proposes (1985, p. 57):

Time-specific Disorderliness. (a) Alter permitted hours—extend, abandon, or selectively stagger pub closing times to avoid a concentration of drinkers inside pubs and on the street; (b) Increase the number of late-night premises and public spaces at closing time to match the greater need for control; (c) Increase police supervision of premises and public spaces at closing time to match the greater need for control; (d) Train bar staff in interpersonal relations and management techniques—to lower the risk of confrontation with customers at closing time; (e) Facilitate the dispersal of people from the city center—increase public transport provision to speed the removal of people and avoid the gathering of disruptive crowds.

Situation-specific Disorderliness. (a) Revoke licenses or impose conditions on premises that have a record of disorder; (b) Alter the number and density of licensed premises; (c) Alter the character of pubs and clubs—encourage the development of premises where the facilities are unlikely to lead to disorder; (d) Discourage youth-oriented and age-specific leisure activity and facilities from concentrating in city centers; (e) Improve the ability of bar staff to cope with disorder, through better training and management practice; (f) Encourage management practices that will result in the keeping of orderly premises; (g) Improve the ability of the police to supervise licensed premises and respond to disorder; (h) Reduce the amount of indefensible public space in city centers by urban planning and design.

V. Violence in the City Center

Violence and public entertainment have long been associated. Aschaffenburgh (1911, p. 77) reports from a study in Germany in the first years of this century that "*two thirds of all fights occur in or outside an inn*" (my translation). A large number of studies show that much violence in public is linked to public entertainment activities (e.g., Bullock 1955; Downes 1958, p. 145; Wolfgang 1958; McClintock 1963, p. 40; Pittman and Handy 1964; Porkny 1965; Curtis 1974, pp. 143–45; Lenke 1974, 1978; Dunn 1976; Persson 1977; Wikström 1980, 1981, 1991*a;* Ramsey 1983; Roncek and Maier 1991; McClintock and Wikström 1992; Sherman, Schmidt, and Velke 1992). A significant proportion of crimes occur in places of public entertainment, and violence also often occurs in streets when people are on the way to or from places of public entertainment. In addition, much public entertainment is not connected with specific locales but occurs in the streets—places where youth groups gather. These outdoor meeting points are often located in areas with many places of public entertainment.

Several British victim surveys show that the risk of violence is closely related to participation in public entertainment. Sparks, Genn, and Dodd (1977, p. 105) report that of those interviewed who were never out in the evenings, 2.3 percent had been subjected to violence, whereas the corresponding figure for those out every evening was 22.2 percent. Similar results have been reported in a newer British study by Gottfredson (1984, p. 10). The downtown area is the predominant site of public entertainment, and it is therefore no surprise that violence in public is strongly concentrated in the city center.

A. Problem Definition

In a 1982 study of large samples of recorded assaults, robberies, and rapes, it was shown that violence in public was concentrated in the inner city and, further, showed extreme concentration in the CBD (Wikström 1991*a*). There was a strong area-level correlation between the rate per land-area unit of assaults, robbery, and, to a lesser extent, rapes in public.

Violence shows not only a strong concentration in the downtown area but also a remarkable concentration in certain places. For instance, a study of the locations of street assaults in the inner-city area of Stockholm in 1982 (Miller 1988) showed that 47 percent of all street assaults occurred on 3 percent of all streets. These streets were generally major thoroughfares, and most were located in the CBD or passed through the CBD. Another study, of a rarer crime, shows a remarkable stability of the violent hot spots. A study of all criminal homicides in Stockholm between 1951 and 1991 (Wikström 1994*a*) showed that street homicides showed concentration in a few places and that these places were practically the same over the whole forty-year period.

Interestingly, the street homicide hot spots were by and large the same as the hot spots identified in the study of violence in public in Stockholm in 1982 (Wikström 1991*a*). Further, the findings from a study of injuries from violence of those admitted to a city-center hospital emergency department show that these cases also tended to show concentration in the same places (Dysting et al. 1991). The latter study also showed that 10 percent of the cases occurred in or around sixteen restaurants, which is a remarkable concentration.

The circumstances of assault, robbery, and rape are different, and this has relevance for crime prevention strategies. Assaults occur in two major types of situations—situational conflicts and social control situations.

1. *Assaults—Situational Conflicts.* Assaults in public are predominantly male-to-male fights involving young males who are strangers. The great majority of the offenders have a previous criminal record. More than one-third have a previous record of violent crimes.

Situational conflicts are heterogeneous, but case descriptions and statements reveal common patterns. One set of cases is related to male-female relationships. One major activity of public entertainment is to meet persons of the opposite sex to establish casual or lasting relationships, efforts that may be disappointing and frustrating and that may cause rivalry among males (Kühlhorn 1984, p. 83). Another pattern involves the importance of defending one's self-esteem in a public setting when confronted with minor provocation such as being pushed or being passed in a queue.

Alcohol is a major ingredient in public entertainment and probably explains why often trivial conflicts develop into violent actions. Many assaults involve an offender and a victim who are both intoxicated. The proportion of cases involving intoxication is especially high in assaults in public. There are practically no cases of assault in public between two sober persons. However, there is general agreement among researchers that intoxication does not directly cause aggression and violence but rather is an important factor in specific milieus involving specific types of persons (e.g., Powers and Kutash 1978, p. 326; Taylor and Leonard 1983, p. 86). A high proportion of assaults involve socially marginalized persons, and some research indicates that people who become aggressive after drinking alcohol are especially prevalent among individuals with social problems, which is often related to low self-esteem (e.g., Boyatzis 1975, p. 1205; Deardorff et al. 1975, pp. 1193–94).

Most of the assaults in public in the CBD occur between people with different backgrounds. For instance, six out of ten assaults occur between one individual with a previous record and one who lacks such record, and four out of ten of the cases are between a Swede and a person of foreign nationality (see table 2).

2. *Assault—Social Control Situations.* A high proportion of violence in public involves people on duty or in the course of work. Of all reported cases of violence in public in the city center in Stockholm in 1982, as many as 38 percent involved someone during work—in roughly half of these cases as victim and in half as offender. However, those victimized while working may be likelier to report to the police than are those victimized as private persons. The five groups with the highest number victimized during work were, in rank order, doormen, police officers, shop employees, public transport employees, and restaurant personnel other than doormen. This finding is in line with findings from the Swedish Census Bureau's national victim survey (Swedish Census Bureau 1981). The five groups with the highest number of individuals offending in the course of their work were, in rank order, doormen and security personnel, restaurant personnel, public transport employees, police officers, and shop employees. These figures illustrate that many assaults in public are linked to social control situations. It also points to possible complications in trying to increase

TABLE 2

Aspects of Assaults in Public Occurring in the
CBD Area of Stockholm 1982:
Police-recorded Crimes

	CBD Assaults (in percent)
Scene of crime:	
Crimes in licensed establishments	33
Crimes in streets, squares	30
Crimes in public transport	23
Offender and victim residence:	
Both living outside the CBD	100
Involvement in crime during work:	
Victim or offender on duty	38
Previous record of crime:	
One of the parties	63
Both parties	20
Victim-offender demographics:	
Male-to-male	82
Swede-to-immigrant or vice versa	42

SOURCE:—Wikström (1985).
NOTE.—CBD = central business district.

employees' engagement in crime preventive activities since interventions may develop into violent incidents.

3. *Robberies.* Compared with assault in public places, robbery in public places typically involves more planning. Judging from the case descriptions and statements in the police investigations of Stockholm robberies in 1982, the most planned robberies are those in which the offender, or offenders, decide to rob someone and wait for a suitable target to rob. In other less planned cases, there appears to be a situational inducement to rob, that is, a good opportunity suddenly arises, such as when an older alcohol abuser passes a group of youth sitting on a park bench. A third type of robbery appears to involve no preplanning. Rather, a fight may end with the winner taking a wallet or other valuables from his antagonist after knocking him down. The last type of robbery is best regarded as equivalent to situational conflict assaults.

Robbery is by definition a crime of gain, although there is often reason to doubt whether theft really is the main motive. Pratt (1980, pp. 164–65) observes, in a London study of mugging, that "the actual financial gain from mugging is normally so small that it must be seen as totally incidental to the main object of the operation, which, I would suggest, must therefore be to demonstrate toughness and masculinity." Pratt also suggests that a street robbery is "not so much a criminal activity as an attempt to establish a social identity, and in this sense I would argue that mugging bears close resemblance to the mods/rockers/hippies/skinheads and other similar phenomena" (Pratt 1980, p. 62).

Pratt's (1980) discussion of London muggings appears mainly applicable to street robberies committed by youth. A large part of the street robberies in Stockholm are committed by youth; four out of ten offenders are below the age of twenty, and more than one-half are below the age of youth. There are good reasons to believe that the actual proportion of youth and youth groups in the street robberies is higher than appears in studies of reported crimes.

Even if the offender's profit in street robberies is normally small, it would of course be wrong to ignore the gain motive totally. Street robbers, especially older ones, include a large group of known drug addicts. Of all street robbers in Stockholm in 1982, 28 percent were known as intravenous drug abusers.

4. *Rapes.*   Most rapes in public appear to involve some kind of planning, although often it appears to be minimal. Most of the Stockholm rapes in public in 1982 were attempts (73 percent), and some of these were more of the character of a sexual molestation than a rape attempt (Wikström 1991a). In most cases (82 percent), the duration of the event was less than five minutes. This also means that most rapes in public are sudden attacks. The generally short time span of the act is related to the finding that most rapes in public are attempts (Wikström 1991a).

Compared to assaults and robberies in public, the offenders in rape cases are less concentrated in certain age groups, unlike their victims, who show a concentration in their twenties. A very high proportion of the cases involve a non-Swedish offender. The offenders to a high degree have previous records of violence (Wikström 1991a).

5. *Causes of the Concentration of Stranger Violence in the City Center.*   A major reason for the comparatively high rate of assaults in the course of public entertainment is that the combination of intoxication and large numbers of strangers with different backgrounds in a small area produces a high rate of friction and large numbers of social control situations that sometimes develop into violent actions.

While most assaults in the city center are likely to be caused by friction-producing encounters, robberies and rapes are typically at least somewhat planned, which suggests that the occurrence of these two types of crimes is influenced by the presence of poorly protected "targets." A lone drunk person walking the streets on his way back home from a public establishment is one example of a target who may be attractive for robbery.

B. Prevention

There is a clear link between public entertainment and disorder. There is a clear link between public entertainment and violence in public. So the link of public entertainment/disorder/street violence seems fairly obvious. However, the link between violence and disorder is predominantly a link between disorder and assaults. The majority of the robberies and rapes in the city center do not develop out of disorderly situations.

1. *Preventing Disorder.*   The best way to prevent assaults in the city center is to prevent disorder. This means that the strategies to prevent disorder discussed in Section IV above, if successful, should also reduce situationally induced assault incidents. Assaults developing out of social control situations are likely to become more frequent when implementing a disorder prevention program. Expressive crimes like assaults are not likely to be highly sensitive to guardianship; capable guardians do normally not have an inhibiting influence on individuals in an angry state of mind. Many encounters involve more formal guardians such as doormen.

2. *Reducing the Availability and Carrying of Weapons.*   The outcomes of assaults are highly dependent on the presence of weapons (e.g., Wikström 1989). Therefore, measures to reduce the availability of weapons and the carrying of weapons in public places are likely to reduce the number of assault incidents that result in serious injuries or become fatal. Moreover, in many cases of rape and robbery in Stockholm in 1982 (Wikström 1989), knives were used as a means to complete the crime by threatening the victim.

One way to reduce weapon availability is passage of restrictive legislation. Britain has long had a law against carrying offensive weapons, and Sweden has recently introduced a law that restricts the carrying of knives and pointed weapons in public places. However, these kinds of laws may sometimes be difficult to enforce.

3. *Surveillance.*   Perpetrators of assault are often not very sensitive to the presence of bystanders. However, in cases of robberies (with

some preplanning) and rapes, the potential offender is likely to pay more attention to the presence of capable guardians.

Jane Jacobs (1961, p. 44) has put forward a strategy for making safer streets. Her basic argument is that "a well-used city street is apt to be a safe street. A deserted city street is apt to be unsafe." A well-used street has guardianship properties. Jacobs's argument may very well be applicable to some types of crime, like robbery and rape, but it is a more questionable argument as regards crimes like assaults and some types of disorder. Jacobs (1961, p. 46) states that natural surveillance on the streets is best achieved by "a substantial quantity of stores and other public places sprinkled along the sidewalks of a district; enterprises and public places that are used by evening and night must be among them especially. Stores, bars, and restaurants, as the chief examples, work in several different and complex ways to abet sidewalk safety." Jacobs's description of what makes a safe street could also be a description of a street having characteristics that also may be associated with a hot spot of some types of disorder and assault.

A central concept in the defensible-space approach to crime prevention (e.g., Newman 1972) is to increase the number of eyes on the streets. This can be accomplished not only by increasing the presence of people in the streets but also by designing buildings so that people have a good view of public space. An alternative for a basically nonresidential area as the city center (to the old lady sitting in her window watching what is going on in the streets) is closed-circuit television covering public space and operated by the police or private security companies. The latter is likely to have a higher surveillance potential since even when buildings are created to give good views of surrounding public space, the residents are often not paying attention (e.g., Merry 1981).

An example of the use of closed-circuit television in the surveillance of the city center is the City Watch project in Birmingham (England) in which the police in a joint venture with the city-center business community have installed forty-eight cameras (West Midlands Police 1991).

It is likely that surveillance by closed-circuit television predominantly may act as a deterrent of instrumental types of violent crimes (rapes and robberies). However, even if it is less effective at preventing assaults, it may play an important role in identification and apprehension of assaulters.

Just as for public disorders, an important strategy to prevent instrumental types of violence is to identify hot spots and hot times for these types of crime and to focus surveillance efforts on these places and times. This is part of the strategy to reduce street robberies by youth used by the special youth group of the Stockholm police.

VI. Conclusion

In most studies of crime distributions in the city, the city center is reported as the area of the city with the highest frequency of crime and disorder. The city center is typically a nonresidential area where strangers with different social backgrounds mix in public space.

City-center activities like shopping and entertainment attract both conventional people and criminals. One major reason for the high frequency of crime in the city center is the high presence of motivated offenders. City-center activities also create temptations (shopping, merchandise, consumers with money) and frictions between people, the other major reasons for the high frequency of crime and disorder.

A crime prevention strategy for the city center must acknowledge that unlike residential areas, where a prevention program can build on involving the residents, prevention programs for the city center have to be built around the police (and private security personnel) and those who work in the area. This involves influencing the social organization of legal activities (shops, licensed establishments, etc.) in a way that reduces temptations and friction, and developing strategies for focused policing and surveillance. Probably the most powerful approach to preventing city-center crime is to develop an integrated and comprehensive preventive program building on cooperation between the police and the city-center business community.

Although we have a general understanding of what factors cause the high frequency of crime and disorder in the city center, more research is needed, especially observational studies into what could be referred to as the social psychology of hot spots. For instance, increased knowledge about how conflicts and frictions in real life develop into violence and other crimes could be crucial for the formulation of effective preventive measures.

Few crime prevention initiatives for the city center have resulted in published evaluations. If knowledge about the effectiveness of different strategies and tactics of city-center crime prevention is to accumulate, regular programs of evaluation will play a central role.

With the changing role of the city center in the urban system, for example, in relation to transportation and the growing number of suburban local centers, there is a need for more research into the consequences of such developments for the urban crime pattern and its implications for crime prevention. These changes in general have gone farther in the United States than in European cities.

REFERENCES

Åkerström, M. 1983. *Crooks and Squares.* Lund: Studentlitteratur; Stockholm: Liber Förlag.

Alexandersson, L. 1993. "Våld i nöjeslivet, vid idrottsevanemang, och på allmänna kommunikationer." BRÅ-PM 1993:2. Stockholm: National Council for Crime Prevention.

Aschaffenburgh, G. P. 1911. *Brottet och dess bekämpande.* Stockholm: Bonniers Förlag.

Baldwin, J., and A. E. Bottoms. 1976. *The Urban Criminal.* London: Tavistock.

Barr, R., and K. Pease. 1990. "Crime Placement, Displacement, and Deflection." In *Crime and Justice: A Review of Research*, vol. 12, edited by M. Tonry and N. Morris. Chicago: University of Chicago Press.

Black, D. 1984. "Crime as Social Control." In *Toward a General Theory of Social Control*, vol. 2, edited by D. Black. New York: Academic Press.

Boggs, S. L. 1965. "Urban Crime Patterns." *American Sociological Review* 30: 899–908.

Bottoms, A. E., A. Claytor, and P. Wiles. 1992. "Housing Markets and Residential Community Crime Careers: A Case Study from Sheffield." In *Crime, Policing and Place*, edited by D. J. Evans, N. R. Fyfe, and D. T. Herbert. London: Routledge.

Boyatzis, R. E. 1975. "The Predisposition towards Alcohol-related Aggression in Men." *Journal of Studies on Alcohol* 36:1196–1207.

Brantingham, P. J., and P. L. Brantingham. 1981. "Introduction: The Dimensions of Crime." In *Environmental Criminology*, edited by P. J. Brantingham and P. L. Brantingham. Beverly Hills, Calif.: Sage.

Brown, B. B., and I. Altman. 1981. "Territoriality and Residential Crime." In *Environmental Criminology*, edited by P. J. Brantingham and P. L. Brantingham. Beverly Hills, Calif.: Sage.

Bullock, H. A. 1955. "Urban Homicide in Theory and Fact." *Journal of Criminal Law, Criminology, and Police Science* 45:565–75.

Bursik, R. J. 1986. "Ecological Stability and the Dynamics of Delinquency." In *Communities and Crime*, edited by A. J. Reiss, Jr., and M. Tonry. Vol. 8 of *Crime and Justice: A Review of Research*, edited by M. Tonry and N. Morris. Chicago: University of Chicago Press.

464 Per-Olof H. Wikström

———. 1988. "Social Disorganization and Theories of Crime and Delinquency: Problems and Prospects." *Criminology* 26:519–51.

Bursik, R. J., and H. G. Grasmick. 1993. *Neighborhoods and Crime.* New York: Lexington.

Christie, N., J. Andenaes, and S. Skirbekk. 1965. "A Study of Self-reported Crime." *Scandinavian Studies in Criminology* 1:86–116.

Clarke, R. V. G., and P. Mayhew, eds. 1980. *Designing Out Crime.* London: H.M. Stationery Office.

Cohen, L. E., and M. Felson. 1979. "Social Change and Crime Rate Trends: A Routine Activity Approach." *American Sociological Review* 44:588–608.

Curtis, L. A. 1974. *Criminal Violence.* Lexington, Mass.: Lexington.

Davidson, R. N. 1981. *Crime and Environment.* London: Croom Helm.

Deardorff, C. M., F. T. Melges, C. N. Hout, and D. J. Savage. 1975. "Situations Related to Drinking Alcohol." *Journal of Studies on Alcohol* 36:1184–95.

Dolmen, L., and P. Lindström. 1991. "Skola, livsstil och brott." BRÅ-rapport 1991:3. Stockholm: Liber Förlag.

Downes, D. 1958. *The Delinquent Solution.* London: Routledge & Kegan Paul.

Ds S 1980:9. 1980. *Prostitutionen i Sverige. Del 1.* Stockholm: Socialdepartementet.

Dunn, C. S. 1976. *The Patterns and Distribution of Assault Incident Characteristics among Social Areas.* Analytic Report no. 14. Washington, D.C.: U.S. Department of Justice.

Dystig, M., E. Gauffin, A. Nilholm, and E. Westerling. 1991. "Gatuvåldets ansikte." Unpublished manuscript. Stockholm: Sabbatsbergs Akutklinik.

Farrington, D. P. 1983. "Offending from 10 to 25 Years of Age." In *Prospective Studies on Crime and Delinquency*, edited by K. T. Van Dusen and S. A. Mednick. Boston: Kluwer-Nijhoff.

———. 1988. "Social, Psychological, and Biological Influences on Juvenile Delinquency and Adult Crime." In *Explaining Criminal Behaviour*, edited by W. Buikhuisen and S. A. Mednick. Leiden: E. J. Brill.

———. 1992. "Criminal Career Research: Lessons for Crime Prevention." *Studies on Crime and Crime Prevention* 1:7–29.

Farrington, D. P., and P.-O. Wikström. 1993. "Criminal Careers in London and Stockholm: A Cross-National Comparative Study." In *Cross-National and Longitudinal Research on Human Development*, edited by E. Weitekamp and H. J. Kerner. Dordrecht: Kluwer.

Felson, M. 1987. "Routine Activities and Crime in the Developing Metropolis." *Criminology* 25:911–31.

———. 1992. "Routine Activities and Crime Prevention." *Studies on Crime and Crime Prevention* 1:30–34.

Fischer, C. S. 1981. "The Public and Private Worlds of City Life." *American Sociological Review* 46:306–16.

Goldstein, H. 1990. *Problem-oriented Policing.* New York: McGraw-Hill.

Gottfredson, M. R. 1984. *Victims of Crime: The Dimensions of Risk.* Home Office Research Study no. 81. London: Home Office.

Gottfredson, M. R., and T. Hirschi. 1990. *A General Theory of Crime.* Stanford, Calif.: Stanford University Press.

Hope, T. 1985. *Implementing Crime Prevention Measures.* Home Office Research Study no. 86. London: Home Office.

Hunter, A. 1985. "Private, Parochial and Public Orders: The Problem of Crime and Incivility in Urban Communities." In *The Challenge of Social Control,* edited by G. D. Suttles and M. N. Zald. Norwood, N.J.: Ablex.

Jacobs, J. 1961. *The Death and Life of Great American Cities.* Harmondsworth: Penguin.

Knutsson, J. 1984. *Polisen och brottspreventionen.* Stockholm: Stockholms Universitet, Kriminologiska Institutet.

Kornhauser, R. R. 1978. *Social Sources of Delinquency.* Chicago: University of Chicago Press.

Kühlhorn, E. 1984. "Den svenska våldsbrottsligheten." BRÅ Rapport 1984:1. Stockholm: Liber Förlag.

Lab, S. P. 1988. *Crime Prevention: Approaches, Practices and Evaluations.* Cincinnati: C. J. Anderson.

LeBlanc, M., and M. Fréchette. 1989. *Male Criminal Activity, from Childhood through Youth: Multilevel and Development Perspectives.* New York: Springer-Verlag.

Lenke, L. 1974. "Våldsbrottsligheten i Stockholm." Unpublished manuscript. Stockholm: Stockholms Universitet, Kriminologiska Institutet.

———. 1978. "Risker för våldsbrott i Sverige." Unpublished manuscript. Stockholm: Stockholms Universitet, Kriminologiska Institutet.

Lofland, L. H. 1973. *A World of Strangers.* New York: Basic.

Mayhew, P. 1981. "Crime in Public View: Surveillance and Crime Prevention." In *Environmental Criminology,* edited by P. J. Brantingham and P. L. Brantingham. Beverly Hills, Calif.: Sage.

McClintock, F. H. 1963. *Crimes of Violence.* London: Macmillan.

———. 1974. "Phenomenological and Contextual Analysis of Criminal Violence." In *Collected Studies in Criminological Research,* vol. 11, *Violence in Society,* edited by Council of Europe. Strasbourg: Council of Europe.

McClintock, F. H., and P.-O. Wikström. 1992. "The Comparative Study of Urban Violence: Criminal Violence in Edinburgh and Stockholm." *British Journal of Criminology* 32:505–20.

Merry, S. 1981. "Defensible Space Undefended." *Urban Affairs Quarterly* 16: 397–422.

Miller, J. 1988. "Brottsplatser i stadsrummet." In *Brottsutvecklingen,* edited by L. Dolmen. Stockholm: BRÅ Forskning.

Newman, O. 1972. *Defensible Space.* London: Architectural Press.

Persson, L. G. W. 1977. *Offer för tillgrepp, skadegörelse och våld—en redovisning av 1974 års offerundersökning.* Swedish Census Bureau Promemorior 1977:7. Stockholm: Swedish Census Bureau.

Pittman, D. J., and W. Handy. 1964. "Patterns in Criminal Aggravated Assault." *Journal of Criminal Law, Criminology and Police Science* 55:462–70.

Porkny, A. D. 1965. "Human Violence: A Comparison of Homicide, Aggravated Assault, Suicide and Attempted Suicide." *Journal of Criminal Law, Criminology and Police Science* 56:488–97.

Powers, R. J., and I. L. Kutash. 1978. "Substance-induced Aggression." In

Perspectives on Murder and Aggression, edited by I. L. Kutash, S. B. Kutash, and L. B. Schlesinger. San Francisco: Jossey-Bass.

Poyner, B. 1980. "A Study of Street Attacks and Their Environmental Settings." Unpublished manuscript. London: Tavistock Institute of Human Relations.

———. 1993. "What Works in Crime Prevention: An Overview of Evaluations." *Crime Prevention Studies* 1:7–34.

Pratt, M. 1980. *Mugging as a Social Problem*. London: Routledge & Kegan Paul.

Pyle, G. F. 1974. *The Spatial Dynamics of Crime*. Research Paper no. 159. Chicago: University of Chicago, Department of Geography.

Ramsey, M. 1983. *City Center Crime. Research Bulletin 16*. London: Home Office Research and Planning Unit.

Reiss, A. J., Jr. 1971. *The Police and the Public*. New Haven, Conn.: Yale University Press.

———. 1985. *Policing a City's Central District: The Oakland Story*. Washington, D.C.: U.S. Department of Justice, National Institute of Justice.

———. 1990. "Perplexing Questions in the Understanding and Control of Violent Behavior." *International Annals of Criminology* 28:23–39.

Reiss, A. J., Jr., and D. P. Farrington. 1991. "Advancing Knowledge about Co-offending: Results from a Prospective Longitudinal Survey of London Males." *Journal of Criminal Law and Criminology* 82:360–95.

Reiss, A. J., Jr., and M. Tonry, eds. 1986. *Communities and Crime*. Vol. 8 of *Crime and Justice: A Review of Research*, edited by M. Tonry and N. Morris. Chicago: University of Chicago Press.

Rhodes, W. M., and C. C. Conly. 1981. "Crime and Mobility: An Empirical Study." In *Environmental Criminology*, edited by P. J. Brantingham and P. L. Brantingham. Beverly Hills, Calif.: Sage.

Roncek, D. W., and P. A. Maier. 1991. "Bars, Blocks, and Crime Revisited: Linking the Theory of Routine Activities to the Empiricism of 'Hot Spots.'" *Criminology* 29:725–53.

Roos, H.-E. 1986. *Vandalism i storstad och glesbygd*. Stockholm: Byggforskningsrådet/Liber.

Sarnecki, J. 1983. "Fritid och brottslighet." BRÅ Forskning 1983:7. Stockholm: Liber Förlag.

Schmid, C. F. 1960*a*. "Urban Crime Areas: Part I." *American Sociological Review* 25:527–43.

———. 1960*b*. "Urban Crime Areas: Part II." *American Sociological Review* 25:655–78.

Schwind, H. D., W. Ahlborn, and R. Weiss. 1978. *Empirische Kriminalgeographie*. Wiesbaden: BKA-Forschungsreihe.

Sherman, L. W. 1992. "Attacking Crime: Police and Crime Control." In *Crime and Justice: A Review of Research*, vol. 15, edited by M. Tonry and N. Morris. Chicago: University of Chicago Press.

Sherman, L. W., P. R. Gartin, and M. E. Buerger. 1989. "Hot Spots of Predatory Crime: Routine Activities and the Criminology of Place." *Criminology* 27:27–55.

Sherman, L. W., J. D. Schmidt, and R. J. Velke. 1992. *High Crime Taverns:*

A RECAP Project in Problem-oriented Policing. Final report submitted to U.S. Department of Justice, National Institute of Justice, Washington, D.C. Washington, D.C.: Crime Control Institute.

Sherman, L. W., R. J. Velke, C. Bridgeforth, and D. Gaines. 1991. "Violent Crimes in Georgetown: Hotspots and Trends." Unpublished manuscript. Washington, D.C.: Crime Control Institute.

Sherman, L. W., and D. Weisburd. 1992. "Does Patrol Prevent Crime? The Minneapolis Hot Spots Experiment." Paper presented at the forty-seventh International Society of Criminology Course on "Urban Crime Prevention," Tokyo.

Skogan, W. G. 1978. "The Changing Distribution of Big-City Crime." *Urban Affairs Quarterly* 13:33–49.

———. 1990. *Disorder and Decline*. New York: Free Press.

Sparks, R. F., H. G. Genn, and D. J. Dodd. 1977. *Surveying Victims*. London: John Wiley & Sons.

Swedish Census Bureau. 1981. *Offer för vålds- och egendomsbrott*. (Rapport Nr. 24.) Statistiska centralbyrån. Levnadsförhållanden 1978. Stockholm: Swedish Census Bureau.

Taub, R. P., D. G. Taylor, and J. D. Dunham. 1984. *Paths of Neighborhood Change: Race and Crime in Urban America*. Chicago: University of Chicago Press.

Taylor, S. P., and K. E. Leonard. 1983. "Alcohol and Human Physical Aggression." In *Theoretical and Empirical Reviews*, edited by G. G. Russel and E. I. Donnerstein. New York: Academic Press.

Torstensson, M. 1994. *Brott i Butik*. Brå rapport 1994:2. Stockholm: Allmänna Förlaget.

Tremblay, R. E., and W. Craig. In this volume. "Developmental Crime Prevention."

Tuck, M. 1989. *Drinking and Disorder: A Study of Non-metropolitan Violence*. Home Office Research Study no. 108. London: H.M. Stationery Office.

van Dijk, J. J. M., and A. C. Vivanen. 1978. *Criminal Victimization in the Netherlands*. The Hague: Ministry of Justice.

Weber, M. 1966. *The City*. New York: Free Press.

Werner, B. 1964. "Den ekologiska fördelningen av tillgrepp och tillgreppsbrottslingar i Malmö." *Nordisk tidskrift for kriminalvidenskab* 29:132–65.

West Midlands Police. 1991. "Policing Central Birmingham: The Next Ten Years." Report no 4. Birmingham: West Midlands Police.

Wikström, P.-O. 1980. "Våldsbrott i Gävle." Research report. Stockholm: Stockholms Universitet, Kriminalvetenskapliga Institutet.

———. 1981. "Våldsbrottslighetens rumsliga fördelning i Stockholm." Unpublished manuscript. Stockholm: Stockholms Universitet, Kriminologiska Institutet.

———. 1985. "Everyday Violence in Contemporary Sweden: Ecological and Situational Aspects." BRÅ Report no. 15. Stockholm: Liber Förlag.

———. 1987. "Patterns of Crime in a Birth Cohort: Sex, Age and Social Class Differences." Project Metropolitan Research Reports no. 24. Stockholm: University of Stockholm, Department of Sociology.

————. 1989. "Utvecklingen av vapenanvändningen vid våldsbrott, 1970–1987—särskilt skjutvapen." SOU 1989:44. Stockholm: Liber Förlag.

————. 1990. "Age and Crime in a Stockholm Cohort." *Journal of Quantitative Criminology* 6:61–84.

————. 1991*a*. *Urban Crime, Criminals and Victims.* New York: Springer-Verlag.

————. 1991*b*. *Sociala problem, brott och trygghet.* Stockholm: Allmänna Förlaget.

————. 1994*a*. "Brotts, brottsprevention och kriminalpolitik." In *Brott, brottsprevention och kriminalpolitik,* edited by P.-O. Wikström, J. Ahlberg, and L. Dolmen. Stockholm: Allmänna Förlaget.

————. 1994*b*. *Dödligt våld.* Brå-rapport. Stockholm: Allmänna Förlaget.

————. 1994*c*. "Ungdomsbrott i Stockholm." Unpublished manuscript. Stockholm: National Council for Crime Prevention.

Wolfgang, M. E. 1958. *Patterns in Criminal Homicide.* Philadelphia: University of Pennsylvania Press.

Wolfgang, M. E., R. M. Figlio, and T. Sellin. 1972. *Delinquency in a Birth Cohort.* Chicago: University of Chicago Press.

Wolfgang, M. E., T. P. Thornberry, and R. M. Figlio. 1987. *From Boy to Man: From Delinquency to Crime.* Chicago: University of Chicago Press.

Graham Farrell

Preventing Repeat Victimization

ABSTRACT

Revictimization or repeat victimization of people and places represent
a large proportion of all victimization. Preventing revictimization
may prevent a large proportion of all offenses. Repeat crimes are
disproportionately likely in high-crime areas and in the period shortly
after a crime—suggesting that efficient crime prevention might be
achieved through rapid, transitory responses to victimization. The
extent of revictimization is typically underestimated. Knowledge of
revictimization patterns may provide bases for more effective prevention
of domestic violence, burglary, car crimes, and other offenses. Quick
response alarms, loaned to "high-risk" targets on a temporary basis, are
one possible way forward for efficient crime prevention and offender
detection.

The phenomenon of revictimization has been recognized in the criminological literature for over two decades. Small percentages of the
population, and of victims, suffer large percentages of all criminal victimizations. Only comparatively recently have the policy implications
of repeat victimization begun to be recognized. If revictimization constitutes a large proportion of all victimization, then preventing revictimization will prevent a large proportion of all offenses. Focusing
preventive resources on identified victims simultaneously uses past victimization as a justifiable rationale for allocation of crime prevention
resources, opens up a new set of strategies for preventing crime, poten-

Graham Farrell is senior research officer at the United Nations in Vienna and honor-
ary research fellow at Manchester University, Department of Social Policy and Social
Work. He is indebted to Ken Pease for comments on earlier versions of this essay and
to Alice Sampson, Coretta Phillips, Paul Ekblom, Mike Hough, Albert J. Reiss, Jr.,
Trevor Bennett, Lawrence Sherman, and the editors of this volume.

tially promises greater preventive efficiency than many strategies now in use, and highlights a new set of empirical and theoretical issues for analysis and understanding. Research on revictimization is in its early days, but results are promising and suggest that more energy and resources be invested in basic research and evaluation of prevention programs, and that investigation of victim careers, by analogy to the now maturing body of work on criminal careers, may yield considerable fruit.

Distinct patterns of the nature of revictimization have begun to emerge from the literature. The most obvious is that a relatively small proportion of the population experience a large proportion of all crime. There is a highly skewed distribution of crime in the population that is not due to chance. This observation holds up to rigorous testing from a variety of different sources. Table 1 (below) shows that research using at least nine different research methods has generated similar patterns. Similar patterns of revictimization have emerged from hospital records (Johnson et al. 1973), interviews generated from recorded crime (Zeigenhagen 1976), local victim surveys (Sparks, Genn, and Dodd 1977; Hope 1982; Jones, Maclean, and Young 1986; Farrell 1992), national victim surveys (Gottfredson 1984; Hough 1986; Trickett et al. 1992), comparative international victim surveys (Hindelang, Gottfredson, and Garofalo 1978; Fienberg 1980; Reiss 1980), a survey of hospitalized victims of assault (Shepherd 1990), participant observation (Genn 1988), victim referrals to a Victim Support scheme (Sampson 1991), police recorded crimes (Forrester, Chatterton, and Pease 1988a; Forrester et al. 1990; Polvi et al. 1990; Burquest, Farrell, and Pease 1992), and police incident logs (Farrell 1992; Lloyd, Farrell, and Pease 1994). In addition, the degree of skew in the distribution of victimization is such that the 2 or 3 percent of respondents to victim surveys who are the most victimized commonly report between a quarter and a third of all incidents.

Crime prevention has been defined as the securing of a future nonevent (Forrester et al. 1990). By inference, there are two necessary criteria for efficient crime prevention: a reliable predictor of future victimization, and a practical, cost-effective means of preventing the predicted crime. An extensive literature including work in several countries suggests that prior victimization may be a good predictor of future revictimization; hereafter I use the term "the revictimization predictor." The predictor can be refined according to differential char-

TABLE 1

Published Sources on Repeat Victimization and Crime Prevention

Source	Crime Type(s)	Data Source/ Method of Study
Sparks, Genn, and Dodd (1977)	various	local victim surveys
Hindelang, Gottfredson, and Garofalo (1978)	personal crime	U.S. cities survey
Johnson et al. (1973)	gunshot and stab wounds	hospital records
Zeigenhagen (1976)	violent crime	victim survey based on recorded crime
Fienberg (1980)	various	National Crime Survey
Reiss (1980)	various	National Crime Survey
Nelson (1980)	burglary and robbery	National Crime Survey
Sparks (1981)	general	discourse, based on Sparks, Genn, and Dodd (1977)
Gottfredson (1984)	various	1982 British Crime Survey
Hough (1986)	violent crime	1982 British Crime Survey
Jones, Maclean, and Young (1986)	various	local crime survey
Genn (1988)	domestic violence	participant observation
Shapland et al. (1991)	business crime	crime survey
Shepherd (1990)	violent crime	survey in hospital waiting rooms
Skogan (1990a, 1990b)	N.A.	discourse based on National Crime Survey and other survey experience
Sampson (1991)	various	victim support referrals
Hope (1982)	school burglary	survey
Forrester, Chatterton, and Pease (1988a, 1988b)	residential burglary	recorded crime
Forrester et al. (1990)	residential burglary	recorded crime
Polvi et al. (1990, 1991)	residential burglary	citywide recorded crime
Pease (1991, 1992)	residential burglary	recorded crime
Burquest, Farrell, and Pease (1992)	school burglary	recorded crime
Sampson and Phillips (1992)	racial attacks	weekly local victim survey
Trickett et al. (1992)	property/personal	British Crime Survey
Farrell, Buck, and Pease (1993)	domestic violence	calls to police
Farrell and Pease (1993)	various	review of prevention work
Tilley (1993a)	crime against small business	recorded crime

NOTE.—N.A. = not applicable.

acteristics to increase its accuracy. The literature also suggests that the circumstances and conditions produced by targeting revictimization may foster the development of new and innovative prevention techniques and more efficient deployment of existing ones. Thus, preventing victimization may satisfy the first condition while producing circumstances conducive to the attainment of the second. As a rider, however, the dearth of practical application to date means that the revictimization predictor has been used mostly to generate promising hypotheses rather than to test hypotheses.

Parallels exist between predictive uses of prior victimization and prior offending. Prior offending is the single most reliable predictor of future offending (see, e.g., Nuttall et al. 1977). Preventing recidivist offending would prevent a large proportion of all offending, just as, it appears, preventing revictimization would prevent a large proportion of all victimization.

An emphasis on victim-oriented prevention may be attractive to victims, practitioners, and policymakers. This may be particularly true in the light of a growing literature that portrays victims as neglected by the criminal justice system (Shapland, Willmore, and Duff 1985; Newburn and Merry 1990). With respect to the revictimization predictor, if, as Farrington and Tarling (1985) suggest, the most successful criminological predictors are usually those obtained using simple methods, then the one presented here may serve well.

Here is how this essay is organized. Section I is an introduction to the subject matter. It defines revictimization and discusses terminology, research that is not included, and some complexities of revictimization. Section II reviews the literature on the extent and nature of revictimization. Section III presents the first major application of preventive insights arising from a focus on revictimization—the Kirkholt Burglary Prevention Project. Section IV presents refinements of the revictimization predictor that may make crime prevention more efficient for predicting repeat crime in both time and space and even with respect to building design. Section V discusses possible disadvantages of the approach. Section VI discusses some of the methodological issues encountered in the study of revictimization and the evaluation of the approach to crime prevention. Section VII discusses the prevention of repeated domestic assault, developments in burglary prevention, and alternative applications of the preventive approach. Section VIII introduces the fruitful symbiosis that could develop between preventing revictimization and offender detection based around the revictimization predictor. Section IX presents conclusions.

I. Introduction

Revictimization or repeat victimization are the terms preferred here to refer to the repeated criminal victimization of a person or place. People subject to revictimization are here termed repeat victims. A variety of different terms have arisen to refer to the same phenomenon: revictimization, multiple victimization, repeat victimization, multivictimization, repetitive victimization, and recidivist victimization. There has been little consistent usage of terminology to date. The grounds for the choice of terminology deserve some explanation. "Revictimization" is preferable to multiple victimization because it makes clear that revictimization is distinct from incidents in which multiple offenders commit a crime or in which more than one victim is affected in a single incident. These have both been described as "multiple victimization" (Sparks 1981). The terms "revictimization" and "repeat victimization" can be used largely interchangeably with respect to crime prevention: both imply a link, however constituted, between one victimization and the next, thereby highlighting the potential for intervention. A preference for "revictimization" comes from the ease with which the parallels can be fashioned and recognized between revictimization and reconviction or recidivism, particularly with respect to criminological prediction.

A. "Preventing Revictimization" and "The Criminology of Place"

Parallels can be drawn between the works discussed in this essay under the theme of preventing revictimization and some of the work undertaken by Lawrence Sherman and his colleagues. Examples include the Repeat Call Address Policing experiments, which involved a focus of activity on locations from which calls are frequently made on police services (Sherman, Buerger, and Gartin 1988; Sherman and Weisburd 1988), and the emphases of "the criminology of place" (Sherman, Gartin, and Buerger 1989) and "hot spot" policing (Sherman 1989) in focusing policing activity. Similarly, work on domestic violence from the Minneapolis Domestic Violence Experiment (Sherman and Berk 1984) through to the replications (Sherman et al. 1991; Sherman 1992a) revolve around prevention of repeated crimes against a single victim. It would be difficult to draw a distinct line between crime "hot spots," repeat call address policing, and the prevention of revictimization. Some of the revictimization work discussed here bases crime analyses on calls to the police. Among common themes are the use of empirical data to identify crime patterns, a policy interest in prediction, and an interest in identifying the causal mechanisms of crime. However, there are differences; the emphasis on preventing revictimization, for example, is on crime and crime prevention rather than on reducing calls for police service. The link between the two might be that between problem-oriented policing (Goldstein 1979, 1990; Sherman 1991) and crime prevention through crime analysis (Ekblom 1988), both of which are manifestations of the epidemiological approach.

Because these developments have been comprehensively covered in a recent *Crime and Justice* volume (Sherman 1992b), findings from problem-oriented policing research are not detailed here, though they are discussed in the light of their implications for preventing revictimization.

B. Determinants of Revictimization

The term "revictimization" can refer to a variety of different circumstances and conditions in which one criminal victimization is followed by another. The probability of revictimization will vary according to the initial type of crime. Revictimization of a person or place may be related or unrelated to a prior incident. A subsequent crime may be of the same or a different type. The offender(s) may or may not be the same. The victim and offender may or may not know each other. The offender may know the victim but not vice versa. Two parties to a long-running dispute may be both repeat victims and repeat offenders. The probability of revictimization may be influenced by individual and environmental characteristics. Individual-level characteristics affecting revictimization probabilities may be ascribed or acquired. To go further still, the specific characteristics of and motivation behind the crime, be they instrumental, expressive, violent, nonviolent, or acquisitive, or a combination of these, may all influence revictimization probabilities. Sparks (1981) asks, "What is the typical time period between victimization and revictimization?" Undoubtedly this varies with any of the above differences between crimes, and more, and is a crucial issue. Do rates of repeats vary by area, and if so why? Is revictimization more likely at certain times of the day, week, month, or even year? Are certain types of household or building more prone to repeat burglary and vandalism? How do these factors relate to different car crimes?

The list of the factors that may influence revictimization is not intended to be exhaustive but to serve as an introduction to the intricacies of the subject. Some of these ingredients may be important to the development of more accurate revictimization predictors. The extent to which they refine the predictor will have direct implications for the optimal allocation of crime prevention resources.

C. Paradox and Prudence in Crime Prevention

A paradox of much crime prevention effort, highlighted by Harvey, Grimshaw, and Pease (1989) with respect to crime prevention officers, and Hussain (1988) with respect to Neighbourhood Watch, is that the distribution of crime prevention activity and resources is often inversely related to need. Those with the highest probability of victimization may also be those least likely to be provided prevention resources, and those resources that are in the public domain may inadvertently go elsewhere. In the United Kingdom at least, crime prevention officers can spend much of their time in public relations work and other tasks that have at best a tangential link to crime prevention.

Crime prevention policies based on the prevention of revictimization may bring about a more effective and defensible allocation of resources. If victimization is a good predictor of revictimization, targeting the latter is a practical and prudent strategy, in effect concentrating resources on those crimes that are the most predictable in time and space. By definition, it targets those who disproportionately experience crime—shifting supply of resources closer to demand.

D. Crime Rate Measures

To the extent that measurement determines the perception of the problem, measures of crime rates have direct implications for crime prevention policy. The two most commonly used measures of crime rates are prevalence and incidence. Crime prevalence refers to the estimated percentage of the population at risk who are victims in a given time period (victims per head). Crime incidence refers to the average number of crimes per 100 of the population at risk (crimes per head). A third measure is crime concentration which is the average number of victimizations per victim (crimes per victim) (Barr and Pease 1990; Barr et al. 1991). In short, prevalence counts victims, incidence counts crimes, and concentration counts average victimizations per victim.

There will almost always be more crimes than victims, so incidence is higher than prevalence, and concentration is greater than one.[1] This is because some people and places are victimized on more than one occasion. However, even when presented side by side, incidence and prevalence rates only suggest the extent of revictimization through a comparison of their differences and do not suggest the inequality of victimization found in all aspects of the literature. The concentration rate can be used to compare the rate of repeat victimization, between two areas or subgroups of the population for example, where it might not be otherwise apparent from differing incidence and prevalence rates. If revictimization is prevented, crime incidence will fall close or equal to crime prevalence.[2] The three measures are almost the sum total of progress in the measurement of victimization to date.

Barr and Pease (1990) suggest further measures that account for skewed or unequal distribution and might be applied to crime rates. These would not require any artificial limits to be placed on the number of victimizations a person can report to a crime survey for a given time period (this is discussed in more detail later), because the measures would not be distorted by a small number of people experiencing a large number of crimes. Barr and Pease (1990) suggest the Gini coefficient as a possibility taken from urban geography. The Gini coefficient measures inequality between zero (complete equality) and one (complete inequality). A measure of inequality has important potential applications: measuring change in inequality through time for instance. A crime prevention initiative might have different effects on prevalence and incidence, which would be effectively shown as a change in crime distribution through the population. Personal crime is more unequally distributed (has a higher Gini coefficient) than property crime, largely due to personal crime's higher prevalence. When victims only are considered however, personal and property crime are both more evenly distributed (as would be expected when nonvictims are taken out) but show greater similarity in the distribution of victimization (Farrell 1994a). If revictimization were reduced, the Gini coefficient would

---

[1] Possible exceptions to the rule will depend on counting procedures used. Crimes for which there is more than one victim may have greater prevalence.

[2] This is without considering the possibility of a dispersion of benefits (Clarke 1992, in this volume), a free-rider effect (Miethe 1991), or domino prevention (Farrell, Buck, and Pease 1993) that could make preventive inroads into crime prevalence. Essentially these all refer to occasions when the benefit of crime prevention spreads to areas or targets that were not directly designated for prevention, most likely through the perception of increased risk and effort or reduced rewards to offenders.

move closer to zero. Trickett et al. (1994) use the Gini coefficient to measure inequality of victimization between areas across the 1982, 1984, and 1988 British Crime Surveys and conclude that inequality in the distribution of victimization has increased through the 1980s but that the increase was largely due to an increase in repeat victimization.

More research into measures of distribution would improve our understanding of victimization. In economics, the concentration curve and ratio, the Herfindahl Index, and the entropy and relative entropy coefficients are commonly used measures of concentration, distribution, and inequality (see, e.g., George and Joll 1981), as is Atkinson's inequality index (Atkinson 1970). With respect to general methodology in the study of revictimization, just as Fienberg (1980) used a Markov-chain analysis to study revictimization, this is a method that has been used in the study of criminal careers (see, e.g., Stander et al. 1989). Studies of revictimization, insofar as they may be "victim careers," could benefit greatly from the method and analytical techniques of its more developed counterpart, the study of criminal careers. How does a victimization lambda vary by crime type, by area, over time, and by subgroups of the population, for example?

II. The Extent of Revictimization
Repeat victimization appears to be robust across types of crime and methods of study. Repeat victimization can be by the same or different types of crime, or both. A "survey of surveys" shows that five crime surveys have each demonstrated similar patterns of the extent of repeat victimization.

A. The Extent of Repeat Victimization
Revictimization constitutes a large proportion of all victimization. It is necessary to establish a firm empirical foundation in order to demonstrate why preventing repeat victimization may be an attractive general crime prevention strategy. Revictimization findings are restricted neither to types of crime nor to particular methods of study. Methodological limitations in the study of revictimization, discussed in a later section, suggest that the extent of revictimization is often understated.

Table 1 presents a list of published sources that distinguish the extent of revictimization in a variety of forms. They cover a variety of crimes and research methods and differ in the degree to which revictimization is the subject of discussion. Sparks, Genn, and Dodd (1977) and Hindelang, Gottfredson, and Garofalo (1978), both classic works, one British, one American, were the earliest works to undertake an extensive analysis of revictimization using crime survey data. They remain prominent among the existing literature for their breadth and thoroughness. However, it should be noted that they were preceded by the works of Johnson et al. (1973) and Zeigenhagen (1976).

The Johnson et al. study (1973) is the earliest work on revictimization found in an extensive literature review. It attempted to describe the social, medical, and criminal characteristics of victims and recidivist victims of gunshot and stab wounds from the records of a U.S. hospital. The study emerged from the authors' personal experiences that the same people returned to the hospital time and again, as repeat victims of these types of violence. Case histories were constructed that showed that some victims, while not always "frequently" returning to the hospital, did so every year or every other year throughout the 1960s. Since it can be supposed that only a small proportion of all violence reaches hospital records, most going unreported, the study might be seen to suggest that some people live with violent repeat victimization as part of their everyday lives, in some cases over their lifetime. The purpose of the study was to try to increase awareness of repeat victimization, with its cost to hospitals and public funds being of major concern. The earliest work to use a victim survey and concentrate on repeat victimization was Eduard Zeigenhagen's *The Recidivist Victim of Violent Crime* (1976). Zeigenhagen's study surveyed 268 victims of attempted homicide, assault, rape, robbery, and aggravated robbery. Seventy-five persons, 28 percent of those surveyed, reported more than one violent victimization within the five years prior to the survey. Of these, most had been victimized twice, but fifteen, or 5.6 percent, had been previously victimized between three and six times. "Thus," Zeigenhagen concludes, "victimization appears to be a chronic condition for a subset of the recidivist group." This is an observation that recurs throughout the literature.

Hindelang, Gottfredson, and Garofalo devote one chapter of their 1978 book on victimization to revictimization. Sparks, Genn, and Dodd (1977) devote the bulk of one chapter of their 1977 book to an analysis that is similar in many ways. The works concurrently introduced statistical modelling to the study of revictimization. Each attempted to fit the spread of revictimization to a Poisson distribution. Neither set of data fitted this model, suggesting that revictimization was not caused by "bad luck" or chance; that is, it did not correspond to a chance distribution of independent, single-incident victimizations in a population sampled with replacement. Sparks, Genn, and Dodd (1977) had conducted a victimization survey in three London boroughs and tried to fit a "contagious" Poisson model (where the probability of revictimization is increased by prior victimization), then moved on to a heterogeneous model. The heterogeneous model attempted to fit subgroups of the population, divided by, for example, age, gender, and ethnicity, to separate Poisson distributions, for which they had greater success, but concluded it was "far from perfect."

Hindelang, Gottfredson, and Garofalo (1978) used data from eight U.S. cities and over 165,000 interviews—though the chapter on revictimization combines data from twenty-six different city surveys to give a database of 600,000 cases. The book is mainly known for developing the lifestyle/exposure theory of victimization (see Meier and Miethe 1993). However, the chapter on repeat victimization (they use the term "multiple victimization") acknowledges methodological difficulties studying revictimization. This is perhaps not surprising in that they were charting difficult and unknown criminological territory while trying to wield a data set of 600,000 person-cases from over 250,000 households across twenty-six cities. The logistical problems must have been considerable by any standards, even before the particular nuances of the study of repeat victimization could be considered. A primary difficulty seems to have lain in the problem of reconciling "series" and "nonseries" repeat victimization. They define a series offense as "three or more similar victimisations that occur to the same person during the [six month] reference period and for which the victim cannot recall details of the individual event" (Hindelang, Gottfredson, and Garofalo 1978, p. 126).

A further point to note when data from the U.S. National Crime Victimization Survey (NCS) are compared to, for example, British Crime Survey data, is that the NCS typically uses a six-month reporting period for crimes. While the aim behind this is to try to reduce respondent memory problems or "telescoping" (see Skogan 1981, 1986a, for a discussion of these methodological issues), the effect is to reduce the apparent extent of repeat victimization that takes place over time. Some incidents would be repeats of incidents prior to the period, and some precursors to incidents after the six-month period. The effect of a shorter reporting period is to reduce the apparent extent of repeat victimization. In their analysis, series incidents were given a value of one (so that a series of five or ten incidents was counted as one incident). To have two "series" incidents therefore, a victim would have to have two series, each with three or more related incidents. The analysis separates these "series" incidents from nonseries repeated incidents. The exclusion of series incidents from the NCS analysis later prompted one of the consultants to the 1966–67 President's Commission on Law Enforcement and Administration of Criminal Justice (in which the NCS finds its origins), to calculate the effect during the course of developing his own work on repeat victimization: According to Albert J. Reiss, Jr. (cited in Skogan 1981, p. 9): "including series incidents (for analyses of the NCS) would increase the estimated number of crimes in the United States by 18 percent."

It is perhaps due to this that Hindelang, Gottfredson, and Garofalo state for both personal and property crime that the survey indicated "repetitive victimization" was an "extreme rarity" (1978, p. 127). Given their preamble about the rarity of repeat victimization—which was indeed borne out by their data and was the reason they increased the sample size for the analysis—it is perhaps a testimony to their largely unwritten recognition of these methodological issues that they devote a whole chapter of the book to the subsequent analysis. This seems the only plausible explanation, since otherwise it seems paradoxical to devote such extensive analysis, and not only analysis, but extensive publication space, to this "extreme rarity." It is further testimony to the work that, within the constraints imposed by the data set and method, some of the patterns that they discover and describe concur almost exactly with those that have been found by other studies. Hindelang, Gottfredson, and Garofalo established distinct patterns of repeat victimization that they summarized as follows:

> First, both once-victimised persons and once-victimised households
> were more likely to have suffered subsequent victimisation
> than were members of the population (persons or households
> respectively) selected at random. For personal victims, this is
> accounted for—but only in part—by the finding that repetitive
> victims were more likely than one-time victims to be victimised by
> persons known to them. Second, persons living in households in
> which another household member had been personally victimised
> had a greater risk of personal victimisation than persons living
> in households in which no other household member had been
> personally victimised. Third, persons living in households that had
> been victimised by a household crime had a higher risk of personal
> victimisation than persons living in households that had not been
> victimised by a household crime. [1978, p. 149]

For personal crime, Hindelang, Gottfredson, and Garofalo observed that "for simple assault, the unconditional likelihood of victimisation in the general population . . . was 15 per 1,000, but among victims of aggravated assault the likelihood was 103 per 1,000. Similarly, the unconditional likelihood of aggravated assault was 12, but among victims of simple assault it was nearly seven times as great (82)" (Hindelang, Gottfredson, and Garofalo 1978, p. 132).

The same probability patterns were evident in their findings for property crime—a victimization by one type of property crime was a good predictor of victimization by another type of crime. More spectacular still, the findings held across personal and property crimes, where they found that, "overall, regardless of the age, marital status, or sex of the respondent, the likelihood of having been a victim of at least one personal crime was about twice as great for members of households that were victims of household crimes as for members of households that were not victims of household crimes" (Hindelang, Gottfredson, and Garofalo 1978, pp. 138–39).

In 1980, James Nelson followed up some of this work with analysis of U.S. National Crime Survey data. Unlike Sparks, Genn, and Dodd (1977), Nelson found that the heterogeneous Poisson or negative binomial model provided a good fit for the distribution of repeated burglary and robbery. It does seem highly plausible that while the whole population is far from homogeneous, when different subgroups of the population are investigated, these would have similar rates of revictimization. This is consistent with the lifestyle/exposure model of victimization. Nelson concluded that "the negative binomial model is consistent with the hypothesis that the probability of being victimized is constant over time and does not depend upon the number of prior victimizations, but that not all persons, businesses, and households have the same probability of being victimized . . . [and that] regardless of the interpretation, the analysis shows that victimization rates are not unduly affected by small numbers of persons having unduly high rates" (1980, p. 870).

Nelson's paper presents a strong argument: the model fits the theoretical background of lifestyle theory, and the empirical evidence fits the model. However, Wesley Skogan (1990a, 1990b) suggests that the second of Nelson's conclusions may be due to the weakness of the data specifically with respect to repeat victimization, and this may in turn mean the good fit of the negative binomial model needs to be reexamined. Skogan has played a large role in the development of victim surveys to date (for examples, Skogan 1976, 1981, 1986*a*, 1986*b*, 1990*a*, 1990*b*), with a prominent role in the design and redesign of the NCS and a role in the design of the British Crime Survey. He has commented on the significance of repeat victimization in at least three papers. The first (Skogan 1990*a*) was an examination of the series incidents and the 18 percent of U.S. crime that (according to Albert J. Reiss, Jr.) went missing. Skogan summarizes the methodological limitations of the NCS for the study of revictimization when he writes: "[Series victimisations] were defined as groups of three or more similar incidents which respondents could not adequately differentiate in terms of their placement in time. Because incidents in this category are presumably too frequent and similar to be enumerated individually, they have been dealt with in the worst way possible—they are not counted at all. Series incidents (even the most recent episode, which is fully described in the interview) have always been excluded from analysis on the grounds their frequency is uncertain and that they might not all fall in the same NCS category. This of course makes a shambles of any effort to use the NCS to document the extent of multiple victimisation" (1990*a*, pp. 260–61).

So much for the U.S. National Crime Survey. Despite these criticisms, it is tempting to hope that the work which Hindelang, Gottfredson, and Garofalo (1978) presented (the U.S. Cities Survey and the NCS were closely linked) may have developed some useful patterns even if they were based on extreme underestimates of the extent of repeat victimization. The decisive factor would be to determine whether the extreme underestimates of revictimization produced a bias in the results or just a large underestimation of the extent of the problem. Skogan goes on to address the practical and policy implications of repeat victimization when he writes: "Repetitive victimisations are important for policy purposes because they are predictable from past reported crimes, they typically involve offenders who are immediately identifiable, intervention is possible, and they add disproportionately to the overall crime count" (1990*a*, pp. 259–60).

In a further paper, Skogan (1990*b*) draws attention to repeat victimization and business crime. Skogan's analysis of NCS data (presumably taking account of some of the methodological problems he had previously acknowledged) indicated that victimization of business establishments was heavily concentrated within a small pool of businesses. Skogan also cites Shapland et al.'s (1991) finding that "multiple victimisation drove the total crime count in English industrial estates, and that on the worst estates businesses could expect to be victimised five times per year" (Skogan 1990*b*, p. 9). The skewed distribution of victimization in business crime is reflected in further work by Shapland (in this volume). Preventing repeated business crime is touched on in the next section with respect to the work of Tilley (1993*a*).

Other attempts were made to investigate repeat victimization through mathematical and statistical techniques. In an article that was a decade ahead of its time, Albert J. Reiss, Jr. (1980—two years after his methodological criticisms), using data from the U.S. National Crime Survey wrote: "Evidence of repeat victimization makes it clear that victimization is not a random occurrence. . . . Moreover, in repeat victimization, there is a proneness to repeat victimization by the same type of crime" (1980, p. 52).

This was a finding echoed by Fienberg (1980), though using different methods of analysis. The two articles are complementary and were published in the same volume. Reiss constructed a crime-switch matrix to explore the difference between observed repeat victimization as reported in the NCS and repeat victimization that would be expected due to random chance. Fienberg used a semi-Markov model to observe the likelihood that a repeat victimization was of the same or a different crime type to a prior victimization. The recognition that one victimization incident may be followed by another of the same type has direct implications for crime prevention.

After 1980, revictimization does not seem to appear as a major subject of study for most of the next decade. Unfortunately, this was also the decade that saw a boom in victimological study, so a large body of conceptually related work has developed largely without recognizing or accounting for revictimization. Where it was studied, revictimization was usually revealed and presented as subsidiary to the main topic of analysis. However, the works listed in table 1 all contribute to the development of the picture of revictimization. While no single reference from the rest of table 1 may be convincing in its own right, the whole is greater than the sum of the parts. This is not intended as a criticism, since the works cited here are those exceptional ones that touched on the topic. It is difficult to state that table 1 presents an exhaustive list, since revictimization is often hidden within, or secondary to, another subject of study.

Repeat victimization is mentioned in the report of the first Islington Crime Survey (ICS) (Jones, Maclean, and Young 1986, p. 84). The survey showed that for all crimes, 47 percent of households reported repeat victimization, and that repeat victimization was most likely for assault (38 percent), followed by vandalism (37 percent) and burglary (24 percent). Much lower rates of repeat victimization were reported for theft from the person (17 percent), as might be expected for a relatively "anonymous" crime, though no information is provided with respect to repeat robbery. The apparently low frequency (15 percent) of repeat sexual offenses reported can probably be put down to the fact that those sexual assaults that are reported may be much more likely to be "stranger violence," with sexual assaults by men who are known, and which may be more likely to be repeated, going largely unreported. The higher rate of repeat victimization for all crime than for any of the individual types suggests repeat victimization can be by different types of crime as well as by the same type of crime.

Genn (1988) provides a shift away from the conventional definition of repeat victimization used so far in this essay. Genn provided an exacting critique of victim surveys that, she argues, impose a strict definition of "a crime" and "a victim" on the interviewee. In short, Genn's thesis was that most victim surveys undercount repeat victimization since they have only a one-year reporting period, limit the number of crimes that can be reported, and impose an artificial limit on those that are reported. Genn suggests that, in particular for certain types of crime such as domestic violence, some people are forced to live with almost continual victimization as part of their everyday lives. Genn returned to the research site of the survey detailed in Sparks, Genn, and Dodd (1977) to conduct some follow-up interviews. Genn's participant observation study of repeat victimization included spending several months with a group of victims on a high-crime estate in north London. Genn reports that, "after some months of association with this group of people, I no longer found it surprising that a structured questionnaire administered to one household should uncover some thirteen incidents of 'victimization' " (1988, p. 93).

Genn argued that for some households, victim surveys often picked up only a fraction of the total incidents. Without presenting a direct recommendation about how it should be developed, Genn argues that criminology may need to reconceptualize the understanding of "a crime" as a single, isolated, or discrete event and the understanding of "a victim" as the victim of an isolated event.

Hough (1986) indicated the presence of repeat victimization in his analysis of the 1984 British Crime Survey and violent crime. He presented both crime incidence and prevalence rates side by side, from which it could be seen that the extent of revictimization varied by type of violent crime and that, since the concentration rate (ratio of incidence to prevalence) for "all" violent crime was greater than that from the sum of the individual crime types, then repeat victimization could also be by different types of violent crime. More recent evidence regarding different types of crime is provided by Mayhew, Aye Maung, and Mirrlees-Black (1993) from the 1992 British Crime Survey. While only 5 percent of respondents reported a burglary, 83 percent of these reported only one, and the 6 percent of victims (1 percent of respondents) who reported three or more to the survey accounted for 17 percent of burglaries (Mayhew, Aye Maung, and Mirrlees-Black 1993, p. 49). Violent crime was analyzed by different types of violence for which rates of revictimization vary. The prevalence of violent crime was generally quite low, at or around 1 or 2 percent. However those people who were victims were much more likely to be repeat victims, with the 17 percent of victims who reported three or more violent incidents to the survey accounting for 45 percent of all incidents (1993, p. 86). Thefts involving cars in the United Kingdom were much more prevalent at 17 percent than either burglary or violent crime, but a similar pattern of revictimization occurs. The 8 percent of victims (1 percent of respondents) who reported three or more thefts involving cars accounted for 22 percent of all thefts involving cars (1993, p. 71). These findings are all subject to the conditions that a victim could report a maximum of five series of incidents (Mayhew, Aye Maung, and Mirrlees-Black 1993, p. 150), and series incidents were given an arbitrary top limit of five crimes (1993, p. 157), and that the BCS is a time-bounded survey (some incidents might be repeats of ones prior to the survey, and some may be predecessors of ones after the survey period). Each of these factors suggests the findings are underestimates of the extent of revictimization.

A report by Alice Sampson (1991) presents information about repeat victims referred to a "high-crime" estate-based Victims Support scheme. Of 289 referrals to the scheme over two years, Sampson found that forty-six households or residents (16 percent) were victims of more than one reported crime and that "these victims accounted for 38% of the crimes" (1991, p. 6). In addition, twenty of the repeat victim households suffered from both property and personal crimes, twenty from at least two property crimes, and eight people were victims of interpersonal crime only. Of the forty-six repeat victims, "in 10 cases it is not known if the incidents were related or unrelated; in 23 cases the (victim support) workers thought they were unrelated; and in 13 cases the incidents were related (they were either domestic attacks, neighbour disputes, or the offender was known but did not live in the same flat or next door)" (Sampson 1991, pp. 6–7).

Referrals to Victim Support are also subject to what Maguire (1991, p. 408) calls the "huge filtering process" whereby, for a variety of reasons, less than 1 percent of crimes committed result in a visit from Victim Support. There is reason to believe that the filtering process would disproportionately affect repeat crimes in a similar way to recorded crime (see Sec. VI), so that as a measure of the true extent of revictimization, Sampson's findings may be an extreme underestimate.

In a survey of victims of assault at an accident and emergency hospital in Bristol, Shepherd (1990) found that 43 percent of victims were repeat victims of assault. Of these, 27 percent reported involvement in more than two assaults, and 7 percent reported having been assaulted more than ten times. This distribution of violence mirrors the skewed distribution of crime found in other studies. Shepherd also studied social factors and suggested that repeat victims of assault are more likely to be unemployed, with 58 percent of unemployed respondents as repeat victims, compared to 38 percent of employed victims. In addition, Shepherd suggests that unemployed victims are twice as likely as employed victims to have experienced more than two previous assaults: 44 percent compared to 22 percent.

B. A "Survey of Surveys" Showing the Extent of Revictimization

Tables 2–6 show frequency distributions of victimization for five crime surveys, encompassing two decades. Table 2 shows the heavily skewed distribution of victimization found in the survey by Sparks, Genn, and Dodd (1977) that was conducted in 1973. Table 3 shows a previously unpublished distribution of victimization from a Home Office local crime survey on a "high-crime" estate in South London. Further details of the estate and the work are given in Sampson and Farrell (1990).[3] Tables 4–6 show frequency distributions from three sweeps of the British Crime Survey (BCS): 1982, 1988, and 1992. The BCS is a periodic survey averaging over 10,000 respondents. The comparison shows the similarity in the patterns between two local surveys and a national survey. While three tables from different British

[3] Table 3 excludes car crime, which was not the focus of the study, though the evidence from the British Crime Survey described above suggests this would only have increased rather than decreased the extent of revictimization.

TABLE 2

The Distribution of Repeat Victimization from a Survey of Three London Boroughs in 1973: All Offenses

Number of Times Victimized	Respondents (in Percent) ($N = 545$)	Incidents (in Percent) ($N = 582$)
0	54.7	.0
1	22.0	20.6
2	10.3	19.2
3	7.3	20.6
4	2.0	7.6
5 or more	3.7	32.0
Total	100.0	100.0

SOURCE.—Sparks, Genn, and Dodd (1977), p. 89.
NOTE.—The values do not correspond to those which would be generated solely from the table on p. 89 of Sparks, Genn, and Dodd (1977) but take account of the fact that it states "the total number of incidents reported by the sample in response to the screening questions was 582" (p. 74).

TABLE 3

Distribution of Repeat Victimization from a Survey of a "High Crime" Estate in South London: All Offenses

Number of Times Victimized	Respondents (in Percent) ($N = 600$)	Incidents (in Percent)
0	67.3	.0
1	16.5	21.2
2	6.5	16.7
3	3.7	14.1
4	3.5	18.0
5 or more	2.5	30.0
Total	100.0	100.0

Crime Survey sweeps may make this look less like a survey of five surveys, they show the same national patterns across the course of a decade.

In the 1973 London study shown as table 2, 45.3 percent of respondents had been victimized on one or more occasions, and 23.3 percent of the population had been victimized more than once. The 3.7 percent of the population who said they had been victimized five or more times accounted for 32 percent of all incidents reported. This is perhaps the earliest study from which a numeric value can be put on the heavily skewed distribution of victimization and the first from which it can be inferred that while the majority of the population are not victimized, even among those who are victimized, a small minority of the victimized population experience a vastly disproportionate amount of all crime. This is to anticipate the result that is found across the next four surveys.

Table 3 shows a distribution of victimization that is extremely skewed. Six hundred people were interviewed in the survey. Repeat victims accounted for 78.8 percent of all crimes reported. In addition, the higher rate of repeat victimization on the "high-crime" estate than in the British Crime Survey corresponds with the findings of Trickett et al. (1992) that repeat victimization is more intense in high-crime areas. Other findings derived from the survey with respect to repeat victimization were that 5 percent of the respondents reported 62 percent of the personal crimes. Of the victims of personal crime, a third were repeat victims of personal crime, and one in six had experienced at least two different types of personal crime in the last year. A person or household reporting a burglary or attempted burglary was more than twice as likely to report a personal crime. In the "high-crime" estate victim survey, fifteen people (2.5 percent of respondents) reported 141 incidents (30 percent of total incidents) (Farrell 1992). The proportionate distribution of repeat victimization is slightly more concentrated than that revealed by the survey of three London boroughs.

Table 4 is from Gottfredson's (1984) analysis of the 1982 British Crime Survey. The extent of repeat victimization in the BCS is evident when he writes: "Of the victims of personal crime in the BCS, 72% were one time victims while 28% were repetitively victimised. For all crimes in the survey, the corresponding percentages are 56% one-time victims and 44% multiple victims" (1984, p. 42).

Table 4 suggests that over 70 percent of all criminal incidents reported by the 1982 BCS were experienced by repeat victims, who

TABLE 4

Distribution of Repeat Victimization
from the 1982 British Crime Survey:
All Offenses

Number of Times Victimized	Respondents (in Percent) (N = 10,905)	Incidents (in Percent)
0	68.1	.0
1	17.8	29.1
2	6.2	20.3
3	3.1	15.2
4	1.8	11.8
5 or more	2.9	23.7
Total	99.9*	100.1*

SOURCE.—Gottfredson (1984).
* Total percentage does not add to 100 because of rounding.

made up only 14 percent of the population (total victimized respondents made up 32 percent). Further, 2.9 percent of the respondents reported 23.7 percent of the total incidents. From Gottfredson's original paper, similar patterns of the distribution of victimization for household offenses and personal offenses can also be generated.

Table 5 shows the distribution of victimization for the 1988 British Crime Survey. The method by which the data were produced differs slightly from that for the 1982 survey. The 1988 analysis, as with the 1992 analysis in table 6, was conducted using "screener" or "filter" questions to the survey on the main questionnaire. The 1982 data were calculated by Gottfredson from the victim-form responses of victims. This methodological difference probably accounts for most of the difference in findings between the 1982 survey and the two later sweeps of the BCS. It may also explain why the proportion of the population that is victimized at all is closer between table 2 (44.3 percent) and tables 5 (40.7 percent) and 6 (40.5 percent), since Sparks, Genn, and Dodd also used screener questions.

The 1988 and 1992 British Crime Surveys show almost an exact correspondence in the distribution of victimization—almost eerily so since for either the percentage frequency of respondents or the percentage frequencies of incidents, the results never differ by more than

TABLE 5

Distribution of Repeat Victimization from the 1988 British Crime Survey: All Offenses

Number of Times Victimized	Respondents (in Percent)	Incidents (in Percent)
0	59.3	.0
1	19.9	18.5
2	9.1	16.8
3	4.2	11.6
4	2.5	9.1
5 or more	5.0	43.9
Total	100.0	99.9*

SOURCE.—Shah (1991).
* Total percentage does not add to 100 because of rounding.

TABLE 6

Distribution of Repeat Victimization from the 1992 British Crime Survey: All Offenses

Number of Times Victimized	Respondents (in Percent)	Incidents (in Percent)
0	59.5	.0
1	20.3	18.7
2	9.0	16.5
3	4.5	12.4
4	2.4	8.8
5 or more	4.3	43.5
Total	100.0	99.9*

SOURCE.—Farrell and Pease (1993).
* Total percentage does not add to 100 because of rounding.

seven-tenths of a percentage point. This suggests that there was little change in the inequality of distribution of victimization between the two surveys, a finding that also occurs in Section III on area crime rates and the revictimization curve, though through a slightly different analysis.

III. The Kirkholt Burglary Prevention Project

This section describes the first crime prevention project based on a revictimization prevention strategy. The Kirkholt burglary prevention project (Forrester, Chatterton, and Pease 1988*a*, 1988*b;* Forrester et al. 1990; Pease 1991, 1992) is presented at this stage in the essay in order to track the chronological development of the applied study of revictimization. To a large extent, the Kirkholt project acted as a catalyst for much of the more recent work on the prevention on repeat victimization that is presented in following sections.

A. *Phase I: Devising Preventive Strategies and Implementation*

Crime prevention through crime analysis (Ekblom 1988) is the phrase that springs to mind when the literature of the Kirkholt project is studied. Data and evidence were collected, common themes and factors of the problem identified, and specific prevention measures devised and introduced.

The Kirkholt project was situated on a public housing estate in Rochdale in the northwest of England. The initial research phase combined interviews with known (detained) burglars, interviews with burglary victims and their neighbors, and the analysis of available burglary data to find that, "once a house has been burgled, its chance of repeat victimisation was four times the rate of houses that had not been burgled at all" (Forrester et al. 1988*b*, p. 2289). While of a housing stock which was of a type that nationally had a medium burglary rate (Hough and Mayhew 1985), the Kirkholt estate had a recorded burglary rate double that for both recorded and unrecorded burglary for a high-crime housing type. The data generated by the research phase showed that nearly half of those households burglarized in December 1986 had been burglarized earlier in the year. It was evident to the project team that the prevention of burglary revictimization would prevent a large proportion of all burglary.

The second crucial aspect of the strategy was that within the general revictimization framework, prevention would be by all locally appropriate means. Recognition of this point is crucial to an understanding of both developments that were to come and the earlier suggestion that preventing revictimization may produce the conditions for the development of new, innovative, and cost-effective means of crime prevention. The Kirkholt approach was not one single method or technique to prevent burglary. It was a package of measures that united under the general banner "the prevention of revictimization."

The strategies devised depended on the specific problems identified. The research phase showed that the taking of money from electricity and gas prepayment meters was a factor in many of the burglaries (49 percent). The meters were sitting targets for burglars since they were emptied only every three months and so could accumulate large amounts of money. To prevent revictimization, the relevant utility services agreed to replace meters after a burglary, with the agreement of the householder. A second factor in many burglaries was the relative ease with which burglars appeared to enter premises, invariably by the first route attempted. To prevent revictimization, when a household was burglarized, it would receive a security upgrade, and valuables in the home were property marked by postcoding. The security upgrading was not of a general nature but was specific to the means of entry that were described by both burglars and victims. An estate-wide burglary monitoring system was set up so that security upgrading could be revised to reflect changes in burglary practice. In order to reduce the opportunity for revictimization, around households that had been burglarized, small neighborhood watches were developed, consisting of immediate neighbors and called "cocoon" neighborhood watches. Neighbors were asked to watch out for burglars returning to the victimized household: the watches were specifically set up and specifically focused rather than general, as in the case of previous Neighbourhood Watch schemes. As an incentive, neighbors were also provided with security upgrading. Victims were provided with information on services available in the local area.

The rate of burglary on the Kirkholt estate fell to 40 percent of its previous level after five months of the start of the program. Revictimization fell to zero over the same period and did not exceed two in any of the following months.

B. Maintenance and Continuation

The second phase aimed to maintain and continue the practices developed in the first phase, to develop additional initiatives within the community, and to secure community ownership of the project. It became part of the local housing authority routine that burglarized properties were given priority for repairs. Other elements included a school-based crime prevention program, provision of offenders from the area to attend groups to address their problems, a cheap savings and loan scheme for residents, and better-informed probation officers and courts.

The lower burglary rate on the estate was maintained, and the project became "owned" by the community after the research team withdrew. The reports suggested that displacement of burglary did not occur to a great extent. The burglary rate in surrounding areas dropped, but not to the extent that it did in Kirkholt.

1. *Evaluations and Conclusions.*   The Kirkholt project was rigorously evaluated in the main Home Office reports (e.g., Forrester et al. 1990). However, this was by the researchers who were paid to develop the project. Consequently, as with any apparent success, critics soon challenged the findings. It was suggested that the reduction in the burglary rate was not due to the burglary prevention project but was due to other work undertaken on the estate at the time, particularly a "Warm and Dry" project that improved the condition of the homes of elderly people on the estate. Fencing on the estate was improved generally. More recently, an independent evaluator, David Farrington, was called in to assess the disagreements. After rigorous analysis of the data into different time periods and different properties according to when they received different treatments and were or were not burglarized, Farrington determined that the reduction in the burglary rate could not be attributed to the Wet and Dry program and that the reduced burglary rate was attributable to the burglary prevention program (Farrington 1992*b*). Farrington observed, however, that it would be preferable to identify the precise active ingredient in the prevention program. In searching for the active ingredient or mechanism by which prevention occurs, it should be evident even from this brief description that none of the techniques in the Kirkholt project were extraordinary. They were ordinary prevention methods. The most innovative was the focused or cocoon neighborhood watches, which consequently received most publicity. A retrospective analysis would suggest that it was the specific context of the strategies that led to the drop in burglaries. The innovation lay in the application of existing knowledge in a different context: that of the prevention of repeat victimization, and the tailoring of the technique to the specific problems identified in order to increase the risk and effort and reduce the awards to committing the most likely

burglaries. This is a view largely supported by Nick Tilley's appraisal of three putative replications of the Kirkholt project that are discussed below.

2. *Putative Kirkholt Replications.* Replication is a form of evaluation since it tests the external validity of a project. Tilley (1993*b*) evaluated three efforts at preventing residential burglary that purported to replicate the Kirkholt project and were undertaken as part of the United Kingdom Safer Cities Programme. The first project focused on burglary and experienced increases of 21.5 percent and 42.8 percent in burglary incidence in the two years of the project, though these rises were much lower than those of adjoining areas. The second produced an apparent large drop in burglaries, and the third a rise of 9 percent in burglary incidence compared to a rise of 139 percent in the rest of the police division. Tilley appraises the manner in which they attempted to "replicate" Kirkholt. None of the projects had nearly as high a burglary incidence rate as Kirkholt when they started, and Tilley concludes that

> [Putative Replication 1] is a replication of Kirkholt only in the sense that it used a similar repertoire of methods that were tailored to the local situation, which had been subject to systematic examination. The differing outcome patterns are to be expected. Whatever these had been they could neither confirm nor disconfirm the findings in Kirkholt.
> In the case of [Putative Replication 2], though the outcome pattern was similarly successful to that in Kirkholt, the context, measures and mechanisms differed radically. It cannot be considered a replication in scientific realist terms of any or all of Kirkholt, and thus its success is of no confirmatory value.
> [Putative Replication 3] . . . comprised an offer of security upgrading to those in the area already victimised whose risk of reburglary was shown thereby to be reduced. Though the crime rate was not as high as in Kirkholt, there was a similar decrease in burglary risk amongst those already victimised following target hardening. Some linked elements of context, measure, mechanism and outcome patterns are similar, and thus there is partial replication in scientific realist terms. [Tilley 1993*b*, p. 17]

Tilley concluded that strict replication is neither appropriate nor possible in different local contexts. At the other extreme, Tilley identifies relativist replication that he refers to as "anything goes" (Tilley 1993*b*, p. 13) replication, which is also not applicable since the definition of replication can be as narrow or as wide as the replicator so wishes. Tilley proposes scientific realist replication: "rather than attempting to mimic a large number of 'attributes,' 'variables,' 'conditions' and so forth from one trial to the next the trick is to recognise and to reproduce those salient features of the context which are needed for the [crime prevention] mechanism/s to be activated" (Tilley 1993b, p. 14).

3. *Preventing Revictimization as a General Crime Prevention Strategy.* Whatever the differing opinions about the Kirkholt project, it played a pivotal role in the development of subsequent research into revictimization and its prevention. The project prompted Pease (1991, 1992) to conclude that the prevention of revictimization might be an attractive general crime prevention strategy. The approach would have certain advantages, including

- Attention to dwellings or people already victimised has a higher "hit rate" of those likely to be victimised in the future.
- Preventing repeat victimization protects the most vulnerable social groups, without having to identify those groups as such, which can be socially divisive. Having been victimised already probably represents the least contentious basis for a claim to be given crime prevention attention.
- Repeat victimization is highest, both absolutely and proportionately, in the most crime-ridden areas (Trickett et al. 1992), which are also the areas that suffer the most serious crime (Pease 1988). The prevention of repeat victimization is thus commensurately more important the greater the area's crime problem.
- The rate of victimization offers a realistic schedule for crime prevention activity. Preventing repeat victimization is a way of "drip-feeding" crime prevention.
- Even from the unrealistic view that crime is only displaced, avoiding repeat victimization at least shares the agony around (see Barr and Pease 1990; Pease 1991, p. 76).

While the Kirkholt project focused solely on burglary prevention, Pease argued that its theoretical base provides a foundation for crime prevention of a general nature. This is not to argue that the opportunity reduction and situational measures used in the Kirkholt project are generally applicable—these were tailored for the specific project—rather, that crime prevention in general might concentrate on the phenomenon of repeat victimization. The "drip-feeding" of crime prevention is an analogy created to suggest that targeting repeat victimization is more practically viable—it is spread through time and hence less labor intensive and easier to maintain.

IV. Increasing the Accuracy of the Revictimization Predictor

This section presents the major refinements of the revictimization predictor that have arisen to date. A study that shows how design can be influential in determining the likelihood of revictimization in some instances is first covered. The evidence on the role that repeat victimization plays in the relationship between low- and high-crime areas is then reviewed, and it is suggested that the revictimization predictor might be refined according to the overall level of crime in an area. Last, existing studies showing that revictimization is likely in the immediate aftermath of a crime are covered and the implications for crime prevention are discussed.

A. Revictimization and Design

The influence of architectural and environmental design on the crime rate has long been the focus of attention in crime prevention (see, e.g., Clarke and Mayhew 1980). However the impact of design on repeat victimization is not well documented. That certain buildings may be more likely to be repeatedly victimized as well as victimized could have important prevention implications if they can be identified. Hope (1982) presented data on the extent of repeat victimization in schools that precedes other work on the subject by a decade (Burquest, Farrell, and Pease [1992] and Tilley [1993a] are discussed later in this section). Hope's first startling finding is that "a school or college is 38 times more likely to be burgled than a residential dwelling" (1982, p. 1).

If crime prevention were prioritized, this suggests that schools in general may be excellent sites for efficient prevention work. In addition, however, the statement may inadvertently disguise the extent of revictimization. It may have been the incidence rather than the prevalence of school burglary that was disproportionately higher than that of residential burglary, and the prevention emphasis should perhaps be on revictimization. The most likely explanation may be that the prevalence of school burglary was higher and that the rate of repeat victimization was disproportionately high. Restricting the definition solely to forced entries, Hope notes that recorded incidents probably provided a conservative estimate of the extent of the crime (Hope 1982, pp. 2–3). The extent of repeat school burglary is evident later in the text when Hope writes, "Some 38 schools (64%) had less than five burglaries between 1977 and 1978 including 11 schools (19%) which had no burglaries at all. In contrast, 19% had 10 or more burglaries each during this two year period. The most victimised school had 24 burglaries."

Moreover, Hope develops a "design continuum," grouping the schools in the study into one of three categories according to size, area of site, number of buildings, age, and so forth, using thirteen factors in total. The average number of burglaries per school was calculated for each design category. Schools within the three categories averaged 1.4, 5.1, and 7.9 burglaries each for the two-year study period. In essence, Hope had refined the predictability of revictimization in schools according to thirteen design criteria. Perhaps a study that updated Hope's 1982 work could use a revictimization predictor to inform the efficient allocation of resources for both crime prevention and offender detection. There is a need for other studies covering design factors and their importance in refining the predictability of revictimization. This could be true for both residential and commercial burglary. Similarly, design factors in relation to motor vehicles could also be important. While it has long been recognized that certain makes of car are more likely to be victimized (e.g., Clarke and Harris 1992), whether or not incidence increases disproportionately in relation to prevalence remains to be empirically determined.

B. High-Crime Areas and Repeat Victimization

Trickett et al. (1992), broach the important question whether certain areas have high crime rates because more people are victimized or because there is more revictimization of the same people. The evidence is presented here as figure 1 using area data from the first three sweeps of the British Crime Survey—1982, 1984, and 1988. The data were grouped into deciles according to crime incidence. The 10 percent of areas with the lowest crime incidence rate are decile 1, the 10 percent of areas with the next lowest incidence rates are decile 2, and so on.[4] The resultant curves are shown for personal and property crime. The raw data and the regression equations are presented in the Appendix.

[4] I am indebted to Dan Ellingworth of the Quantitative Criminology Group at Manchester University for providing me with the raw data grouped into deciles using the same method as the Trickett et al. (1992) paper.

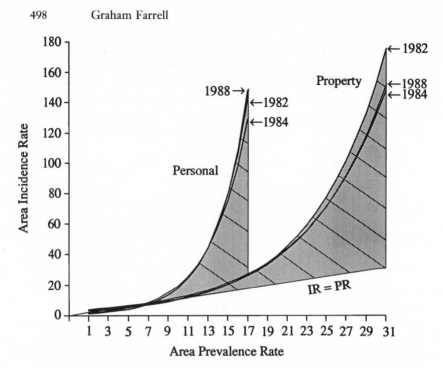

Fig. 1.—Area revictimization curves (British Crime Survey data—personal and property crime, 1982, 1984, 1988). Source: Farrell and Pease (1993).

For both of the crime types, there is consistency of both position and curvature across each of the surveys. This consistency suggests the findings can be viewed with a high degree of confidence.

In figure 1, revictimization exists where crime incidence is greater than crime prevalence. A state of no revictimization is shown by the line IR = PR (incidence rate = prevalence rate). Since the areas under each curve represent total victimization, at a glance it is evident that revictimization constitutes a large proportion of all victimization. However, for areas with higher crime prevalence (more victims per head), this is disproportionately the case. Trickett et al. (1992) conclude that there is a positive nonlinear correlation between the overall incidence of crime and the extent of revictimization (well beyond what would be expected by a random process). As a consequence, the accuracy of the revictimization predictor will correlate with area crime prevalence and incidence rates; or, the higher an area's crime rate, the higher the rate of repeat victimization.

Crime prevention focused on high-crime areas could be expected to prevent more crime per unit of investment merely because there is more crime. However, figure 1 shows that the rewards to the prevention of revictimization may be disproportionately high in high-crime areas. With an increasingly accurate predictor, the opportunity for preventing revictimization is commensurately greater. The identification and focusing of prevention on highly predictable crime appears potentially efficient in such areas. As a refinement of the predictor, a revictimization prevention policy in high-crime areas could be expected to be even more efficient in terms of crimes prevented (as well as per unit of labor and expenditure) than focusing on revictimization across all areas. Tables showing the area decile counts of crimes and victims and the incidence and prevalence rates used in figure 1 are in the Appendix. The greatest increase in revictimization appears between the ninth and tenth deciles, so that preventing revictimization would be at its most efficient in the 10 percent of areas with the highest crime incidence.

It may also be that across crime type, revictimization is more likely in higher-crime areas. Given the empirical finding that personal crime is more likely when property crime has been experienced and vice versa, in the light of the above evidence, it would not be unreasonable to expect that this relationship grows stronger as overall crime levels increase. Further research, for example, a development of the British Crime Survey area analysis, might be able to tease out the nature and interactive effects of this relationship. While the focus of this essay largely precludes the causes of repeat victimization (Farrell [1994*b*] addresses causality for specific crime types), a possible rationale for an "across crime-type revictimization area-effect" might be found through a quick look at recent criminal career research. Farrington writes of the London longitudinal survey that "it was concluded that offenders did not specialize in violence . . . [and] violent offenders are essentially frequent offenders" (1992*a*, p. 21).

This could provide one explanation for the likelihood that victims are revictimized both by a different type of personal crime or by a property crime.

A further explanation of disproportionate revictimization in high-crime areas might be found in routine activity theory. A crime occurs on the convergence in time and space of a suitable victim or target and a motivated offender in the absence of a capable guardian (Cohen and Felson 1979). If all three of suitable victims, motivated offenders, and the absence of guardians increase, then the effect may be to dispropor-

TABLE 7

Crude Model of Routine Activities, High Crime Rates, and Revictimization

	Input: Routine Activities			Output: Crime Rate		
Area	Number of Suitable Victims/Targets	Frequency of Motivated Offenders	Frequency of Interactions Where Guardians Absent	PR	IR	CR
A	1	1	1	1	1	1
B	2	2	2	2	8	4
C	3	3	3	3	27	9

SOURCE.—Farrell, Ellingworth, and Pease (1994).
NOTE.—PR = prevalence rate. IR = incidence rate. CR = concentration rate.

tionately increase revictimization. Table 7 shows a simplified model for three hypothetical areas with different levels of the variables that make up routine activities theory, based on the model of Farrell, Ellingworth, and Pease (1994).[5] A linear increase in the three constituent factors produces a linear increase in crime prevalence but a nonlinear increase in crime incidence.

Of course, table 7 is extremely crude. In most instances there will be an absence of one of the contributing variables—hence, crime does not take place everywhere all of the time. The model can be varied for the absence and differing levels of one or more factors, and the effects on the crime rates can be monitored. An absence of any one factor produces zero crime. In the model, relatively more suitable victims would increase prevalence and incidence but not necessarily concentration. Relatively more offenders increase concentration rather than prevalence. Routine activities theory suggests that when crime does take place, aggregate area rates may be in some way determined by the interaction effect of different levels of the constituent variables, and that, since incidence is the product of prevalence and concentration, repeat victimization may play a fundamental role in the picture. Where there are many suitable targets but few motivated offenders, repeat victimization might be expected to be lower. The aim of crime prevention is to reduce either or both the availability of suitable victims

[5] Table 7 reports work in progress that has been revised on the basis of probabilities of interactions occurring and the influence of a "contagion effect."

or the absence of guardians, and the aim of preventing criminality is the reduction of the supply of motivated offenders. The crude model could be made more realistic through, for example, introducing frequency of interactions as well as numbers of both victims and offenders (perhaps based on lifestyle theory), but in the present, largely illustrative context there would be diminishing marginal returns to such added complexities. Perhaps the model could be developed empirically through building the routine activities variables from information in victim surveys. The practical implications for crime prevention of the model would be to help determine which levels of which variables produce known crime rates and to tease out the effects of different policies designed to affect the different variables in different ways.

C. The Time-Course of Revictimization

This section discusses the most important refinement of the revictimization predictor to date: the length of time between one victimization and the next. A discussion of the pioneering work on residential burglary is followed by case studies of school burglary, racial attacks, domestic violence, and business crime. Each study demonstrates that the risk of revictimization is greatest in the period immediately after victimization and that this is robust across crime type, location, and the method and period of study. Based on this evidence, two main policy implications are developed: crime prevention measures need to be moved quickly into place following victimization, and temporary prevention measures that provide cover during the high-risk period after victimization might be an effective and efficient means of preventing crime.

When Albert J. Reiss, Jr., studied the likelihood of revictimization by type of crime in 1980, the available data sources were not sufficiently flexible to allow reliable conclusions to be drawn about the time period between one victimization and the next. Consequently, the policy implications of the findings about the nature of revictimization were not fully exploited.

A decade later, Polvi et al. (1990, 1991) published their findings from a study of residential burglary in Saskatoon, Canada, that showed there was a much greater chance of a repeat burglary in the period immediately after a burglary and that the magnitude of this risk declined with time: "The likelihood of a repeat burglary within one month was over twelve times the expected rate, but this declined to less than twice the expected rate when burglaries six months apart were considered. Analysis of the repeat burglaries within one month showed that half of the second victimisations occurred within seven days of the first" (Polvi et al. 1991, p. 412).

The Canadian study analyzed recorded crime data for a four-year period. To date this remains the largest and most comprehensive study of the time between victimizations, for which they coined the term the "time-course." However, as with all pioneering work, the results required replication and application in other contexts. In isolation it did not provide sufficient evidence to make generalizations across different types of crime, across different cities and countries, and through the use of different data sources. Four further, smaller-scale studies from the United Kingdom are described below. Each is of a different type of crime; two concerning different property crimes, and two different interpersonal crimes. Between them, the four studies use three different types of data.

1. *School Burglary and Property Crime.* Of the case studies, this is the most similar in crime type and data source to the work cited above. The data presented here were first published by Burquest, Farrell, and Pease (1992). The study was of the extent of police-recorded property crime at thirty-three schools in an area of Merseyside, England, in 1990. Seven schools reported only one crime, and the most victimized school reported twenty-eight crimes for the one-year period. Of the total of 296 crimes reported, 263 (97.6 percent) were repeat crimes. Of these, 208, or 79 percent, were revictimizations occurring within one month of a prior victimization. Figures 2 and 3 are graphs of the revictimization time-course for recorded school property crime. Figure 2 shows the decline in the likelihood of revictimization in the months following a crime. The period of highest risk is easily identifiable as the first month. Figure 3 shows the likelihood of revictimization within the first month and how even then it declines sharply with time. Revictimization is heavily skewed toward the date of the prior victimization.

Figure 2 shows two curves, one of the actual crimes, and one weighted to take account of the one-year time-period of study. The weighting accounts for the fact that some schools will have victimizations either immediately before or after the period of observation that may be repeats (or precursors) of crimes captured within the one-year window.[6]

[6] The formula used was $W = (T + R)/(T - R)$, where W is the weight applied to each point on the graph, T is the number of time periods of observation, R is the time period in which repeats are counted, subject to T and R being measured in the same

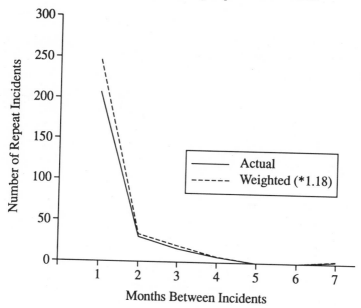

Fig. 2.—Time-course of repeat school crime (grouped thirty-day periods, Liverpool 1990). Source: Burquest, Farrell, and Pease (1992).

2. *Racial Attacks.*   The evidence is from a study by Sampson and Phillips (1992) of racial attacks on an estate in the East End of London. The data were generated through weekly interviews over a six-month period with the families potentially at risk of violent racial attacks. Of the thirty families in the study, the analysis showed that "67% of the families were multi-victims . . . many of the families have experienced attacks before and after this [six month] period. However . . . within any one time period some families suffered more than others. Seven families reported no incidents during this period. The most heavily victimised family was harassed on average once every six days. The second and third most victimised were attacked on average every nine days. Furthermore, subsequent victimisations were most frequent within the first week of the first attack" (Sampson and Phillips 1992, p. 6).

Figure 4 is reproduced from the original with authors' permission. The revictimization time-course for racial attacks shows identical pat-

units of time. In figure 2, a one-year study period ($T = 12$) looks at repeats within one month ($R = 1$), so that each point on the graph is weighted by $W = 13/11$.

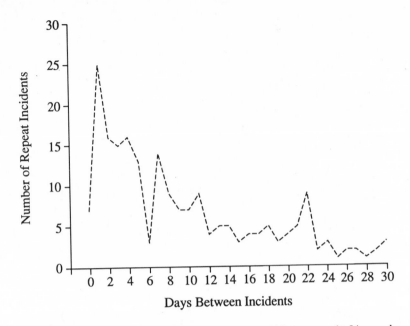

FIG. 3.—Time-course of repeat school crime (repeats within one month, Liverpool 1990). Source: Burquest, Farrell, and Pease (1992).

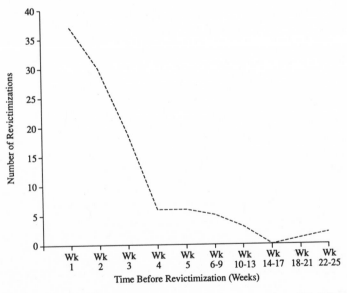

FIG. 4.—Time-course of racial attacks (six months' data, September 1990–February 1991). Source: Sampson and Phillips (1992).

terns to that of residential and school burglary. Families that are racially attacked are much more likely to be revictimized forthwith.

3. *Domestic Violence.* That domestic violence is likely to be a frequently repeated crime is well established. Smith (1988) provides a comprehensive review of the literature to that date, and more recently, Morley and Mullender (1994, p. 5) state that attacks by the same assailant are almost always repeated. In 1980, results of an American family violence survey showed that serious domestic assaults "took place at an annual rate of 38 per 1,000 married women. This is sixteen times the National Crime Survey rate of 2.3 per 1,000 . . . moreover, it was typically not an isolated instance; the mean number of beatings per year for such couples was 8, and the median was 2.4." Further research showed at least equivalent prevalence and incidence for those cohabiting, divorced, or separated (Strauss 1983). Sherman (1992*a*) presents a wealth of data on the topic and shows the increasing likelihood of repeat calls to the police once calls have been made. The Sherman analysis is much more extensive than the analysis presented here, and although the emphasis is slightly different, it provides strongly confirmatory evidence.

The data presented below were generated in the initial phase of a Home Office–funded crime prevention project (see Farrell, Buck, and Pease 1993; Lloyd, Farrell, and Pease 1994). The results are based on analysis of 1,261 calls to police over the two-year period 1989–91, from an area of approximately 1,500 households. One hundred and sixty-two calls to domestic disputes were analyzed. These are relatively small figures for analysis. However, based on the concurrence of the findings with those of the previous three sections and that of Sherman (1992*a*), it is not unreasonable to suggest that they might be viewed with a high degree of confidence.

Figure 5 shows the steep time-course of revictimization for domestic violence. Based on the evidence of the other three studies, it seems unlikely that this is an artifact of either reporting or recording of incidents. In this study the analysis of the incident logs was taken further to generate a specific revictimization predictor. The findings were summarized thus: "There exists a 'heightened risk period' for repeat domestic victimizations—when a woman has called the police she is more likely to call them again and within a short period of time. A household with one call to the police for a 'domestic' incident has a probability of 0.8 of another within one year. The typical period between incidents is much less than a year. After a first incident, 35 per cent of house-

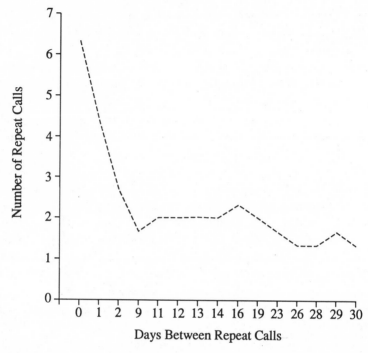

Fɪɢ. 5.—Time-course of domestic violence (calls to police, February 1989–March 1991). Source: Lloyd, Farrell, and Pease (1994).

holds suffer a second incident within five weeks of the first. After a second incident, 45 per cent of households suffer a third incident within five weeks of the second" (Farrell, Clarke, and Pease 1993).

Based on the revictimization predictor a package of measures were developed to try to prevent violent domestic revictimization, some of which are touched on again later.

4. *Business Crime.* Tilley (1993*a*) presents the revictimization time-course for business crime. The study was part of the Home Office evaluation of the United Kingdom Safer Cities Programme. In a similar manner to the previous four time-course studies, Tilley showed that repeat business crime was more likely to be soon after victimization. Tilley's study was methodologically innovative in that it overcame the problem of the time-window of revictimization to some extent through constructing a one-year study out of two year's data. After a burglary, victimization at each property was studied for the whole of the following year. This differs from a standard one-year time-bound study

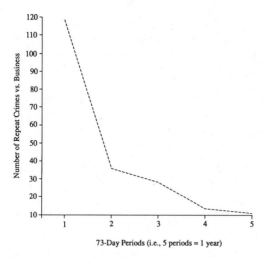

FIG. 6.—Time-course of business crime (repeat crimes within seventy-three-day periods). Source: Tilley (1993*a*).

where a property that was burglarized late in the year would only have available a short period in which revictimization could take place until the end of the study period. Figure 6 shows the time-course of commercial burglary revictimization for the rates generated by Tilley (1993*a*).

D. Future Developments of the Revictimization Time-Course

The time-course of revictimization will differ in its specifics by type of crime and other factors. The general pattern however seems to be consistent: that revictimization is most likely in the short period following victimization, and that risk remains artificially high for the longer period over which it decays. The time-course picture will also be complicated by the factor of crime prevalence. It does not seem unreasonable to suppose that an area with high crime prevalence and incidence will have a shorter average time until revictimization than a low-crime area—though again this will vary by crime type and local circumstance. Again, this presents a possibility for future research. How does the time-course of revictimization change as prevalence and incidence change between areas?

That the revictimization time-course was not found from victim survey analysis is not a criticism of victim surveys. Victim surveys have enabled many, great, and varied advances in knowledge about crime, but they are more revelatory in some areas than in others. Many of the findings of victim surveys have been used to develop limited insight gained from other data sources, and recognition of limitations of victim surveys can directly lead to progress through prompting new veins of research elsewhere.

E. Policy Implications of the Revictimization Time-Course

In Section I, the criteria outlined for efficient crime prevention were a reliable victimization predictor and a practical, cost-effective means of preventing crime. With respect to the first, the time-course is a refinement of the revictimization predictor. However, the time-course analysis also has major implications for achieving the cost-effectiveness element of criterion two. This breaks into two parts: the need for a quick response to victimization, and the need for a response that can be transient.

1. *Quick Response.*   Prevention resources should be mobilized immediately following victimization in order to maximize prevention. From the time-course analysis, for maximum prevention effect, they must be in place within twenty-four hours. After victimization there exists a "heightened risk period" for revictimization. The risk declines with time as the time-course smooths out at a low level of revictimization, and so a late response is less efficient. This may present logistical difficulties that, from the perspective of supporting victims as well as preventing crime, warrant effort to be overcome.

2. *Transient Response.*   If the risk of revictimization declines rapidly with time, then, given that crime prevention resources are finite, maximum efficiency would be achieved through reallocating the resources according to differential risk. If the crime prevention resource is, for example, a portable alarm, then it can be placed in one location immediately following victimization. When the risk of revictimization declines, the resource could then be relocated to a different "high-risk" location that has just been victimized. The implication of the time-course for the efficient allocation of limited crime prevention resources is therefore that temporary prevention measures moved rapidly into place will achieve maximum preventive efficiency. Returns on investment in crime prevention resources will be greatest where this occurs, since the return in terms of crimes prevented will be both high (due to the predictor) and constant over time (due to reallocation).

V. Cautions concerning Revictimization Prevention

There will never exist a perfect means of crime prevention. There are probably some "least worst" crime prevention options, though even those may be few and far between. The limitations of an approach must be acknowledged before problem solving and progress can take place. The subjects of crime displacement, deflection, "dispersion of benefit," and "free-rider effects" are more general crime prevention topics, not specific to revictimization, and are discussed in the Clarke, and Pease and Ekblom essays in this volume. (Also see Barr and Pease 1990; Miethe 1991; and Clarke 1992.)

A. Victim Blame

It has been suggested that victim-focused prevention based on past experience in some way blames the victim (see Meier and Miethe 1993). It is most likely that this criticism has evolved due to a few well-publicized cases in which judges have blamed rape victims of "provoking" rape through their particular comportment or attire. This is a criticism that is out of context when applied to the prevention of revictimization and can be likened to opposition to building crossings at accident "hotspots" because it would be blaming the pedestrians for being knocked down. The opposite is true, and from both economic and public safety motives, crossings are placed at the points where most pedestrians cross, providing greatest opportunity for accidents, or where conditions are such that a particular road is dangerous. Crossings do not prevent all pedestrian accidents, but they do lessen the incidence of the most predictable accidents at known accident locations and hazardous situations.

B. One Free Go! Everyone a Winner!

A revictimization prevention policy, by definition, is designed to move preventive strategies into place after a crime has taken place. This has led some to criticize the policy on the grounds that the criminals get "one free go" at every target, and therefore cannot lose. Unfortunately, this is a sad but true indictment of the success of criminology to date in terms of efficient crime prevention. However, there are at least two reasons why it is not an argument against a revictimization prevention policy. The primary reason is that revictimization policy does not have to be undertaken in isolation from other crime prevention strategies; they are neither mutually exclusive competitors nor substitutes. Second, using the "one free go" argument as an argument against a revictimization policy is similar to suggesting that a policy to prevent repeat offending should be dropped because it allows offenders a "free" first offense. The argument would be ignoring the consistent finding that reoffending and recidivism constitute a large part of all offending and, thus, that preventing revictimization may prevent a large part of all victimization.

C. Devising Preventive Strategies

The degree to which repeat victimization can be prevented will depend on the effectiveness of the preventive measures introduced. Situational prevention will fail if the "target hardening" of properties consists only of sticky tape around the front door. However, this would not constitute failure of the perspective, merely its specific application. This problem is what Ekblom (1988) identifies as the stage of "devising preventive strategies" in a crime prevention schema: the stage in the preventive process after data collection, data analysis, and interpretation. Chronologically, preventive strategy failure lies between theory failure and implementation failure, though it might not be recognized as such until the evaluation stage. In the context of revictimization, it might therefore be argued that a different perspective is of little advantage and of no practical benefit if it can only rely on "tried and tested" preventive measures. However, as suggested by the Kirkholt project and will become more evident when more recent practical applications are discussed, this is not necessarily the case. As was suggested in the introduction to the essay, the advantage of preventing revictimization is more efficient and practical allocation of those limited "tried and tested" resources. Additionally, as suggested by the discussion of the temporal and spatial focus of repeat victimization, the specific conditions that the analysis generates may be conducive to the development of both new preventive methods and innovative applications of existing methods. While the success of revictimization prevention in practice is never guaranteed, preventive strategy failure does not encroach on the recognition of the extent of revictimization or its potential for prevention under different circumstances.

D. The Problem of Low Crime Prevalence: Situations with Apparently Little or No Revictimization

At the bottom of the revictimization curve, where there is little revictimization, the approach outlined here will be less applicable. This will include areas that have low crime rates and crimes that are typically of low prevalence. However, this is a sweeping generalization that may not hold up to closer examination. Areas with apparently "general" low crime prevalence may still have high rates of revictimization under some circumstances. A specific example would be domestic violence, which cuts across social class and a variety of identifiable criminogenic factors (Smith 1988). The extent to which individual types of crime (though in reality there is often a grey area between "types") that are typically of low prevalence may interact in cross-crime revictimization does not preclude them from this approach. This is also true of crimes that, while of low prevalence, may, due to their specific circumstances, make them likely to be repeated. The obvious case would be crimes where the victim-offender relationship makes it likely that it will be repeated: neighbor disputes that result in assault or vandalism, for example. Robbery, a crime reputedly of general low prevalence, may be likely to result in revictimization; for example, where the same school bully extracts money from the same victim in the school yard each lunchtime.

E. False Positives and "Just Deserts"

Criticisms of predictive sentencing have largely concerned overprediction (false positives) and desert. In particular, two arguments against criminological prediction have been put forward. They have rarely, if ever, been discussed in relation to victims of crime.

1. *False Positives.* Following Blumstein et al. (1986), Sherman writes, "One major difficulty with using epidemiological data for policy purposes is the risk of false positives, or incorrect predictions of future criminality. . . . When the prediction is the basis for sentencing people to longer prison terms, the problem of false positives obviously becomes serious; even five or one percent may be unacceptable" (1992*b*, p. 4).

As it has been used almost wholly to date, this is the criticism that has most seriously dogged the advocates of criminological prediction. The problem as it is formulated is the moral dilemma of incarceration based on prediction, that some people would not have offended had they been sentenced to shorter terms or released earlier. However, to the extent that false positives will occur with any predictions (prediction without error being certainty), they can be argued to be at their least problematic in the case of preventing revictimization. A false positive is simply a misallocation of resources with no moral or other impediment. Any misallocation of resources might be reduced through future research to refine the predictability of revictimization according to different criteria, as the previous section suggested. Assuming that there will be false positives (though it may be difficult to determine which cases are false positives and which are true preventions when a crime does not take place), then a revictimization prevention policy may even have benefits in terms of alleviating the fear of crime that is at a peak for some time after a victimization (see, e.g., Corbett and Maguire 1988). As has been suggested, albeit in slightly different forms elsewhere, the best form of victim support may be crime prevention, particularly so when revictimization is the alternative (see Farrell and Pease 1994).

What this brief discussion suggests may be a fundamental development for predictive criminology. Despite the heated moral and philosophical debate around the use of prediction in the context of sentencing, parole, and selective incapacitation policies, they have flourished. When these philosophical objections need not arise at all, as may be the case for the revictimization predictor, the incentive to refine the predictor and promote its practical use may receive support from all sides.

2. *Just Deserts.*   The desert philosophy argues that criminal justice policy should not be based on predicted possibilities of what might happen but should be based on analysis of what has happened. An offender, the argument ran, should be sentenced on offenses that have been committed rather than on ones that might be committed in the future. This argument could be transferred to the allocation of crime prevention resources. By a process of "desert," crime prevention resources would be allocated on the basis of past experiences of victimization. The concept of desert can be viewed as one of the principal justifications for crime prevention activity. Virtually no one "deserves" to be victimized. A person deserves even less to be revictimized. Even behind a Rawlsian veil of ignorance, who would receive allocation of limited crime prevention resources? Should everyone receive a small and equal share when most will go unused and the limited coverage caused by the strain on resources renders it in most cases ineffective? Alternatively, should resources go to the person who has suffered victimization and is most likely to be victimized again?

VI. Methodological Issues in the Study of Repeat Victimization[7]

This section tackles a variety of methodological issues specific to repeat victimization. It does not cover more general methodological issues.

---

[7] The section title adapts that of Skogan (1986a).

Although they are based only on experience to date and will not be exhaustive, they are important considerations for both researchers and practitioners who investigate revictimization and evaluate attempts at its prevention. In particular, they highlight the importance of not underestimating the extent of revictimization.

A. Recorded Crime Data

The underreporting of crime to the police is compounded in the case of repeat victimization. Much crime goes unrecorded since it is unreported. Successive British Crime Surveys have also established that some crime is reported to the police but remains unrecorded. Taking both reasons together, much crime fails to appear in police data banks. This tends to the understatement of the extent of repeat victimization. For example, a household suffers a burglary. A burglary has roughly a 70 percent (or 0.7) chance of featuring as a recorded burglary in police statistics. The household suffers a second burglary. That too has roughly a 70 percent chance of featuring in police statistics. This means that the chance that they have both been recorded is 0.49 or 49 percent (that is, 0.7×0.7). Of households that have been burglarized twice, 49 percent will appear twice in police records. Nine percent (0.3×0.3) will appear never to have been burglarized, and 42 percent ($[0.7 \times 0.3] + [0.3 \times 0.7]$) will appear to have been burglarized once. This means that 3 percent of people suffering three burglaries will have no burglaries recorded. Nineteen percent (6.3 percent + 6.3 percent + 6.3 percent) will have one burglary recorded. Forty-four percent (14.7 percent + 14.7 percent + 14.7 percent) will have two burglaries recorded. Only 34 percent will have all three burglaries recorded. This analysis is somewhat artificial in regarding each incident as independent. In reality, people who report their first burglary may be more likely than average to report their second and third. Thus the analysis may exaggerate the degree of underestimation of repeat victimization, but it does not invent it. The truth may lie somewhere between small underestimation and underestimation of the extent described here and will vary by type of crime.

B. Police Incident Log Data

Incident logs are records of calls for police service, usually from the public. They are recorded for operational purposes but have been used as a source of data by many researchers (e.g., Sherman, Gartin, and Buerger 1989; Sampson 1991). The first of these used incident logs in the analysis of crime "hot spots" and describes counting and analysis problems similar to those discussed here.

The first important point with respect to incident logs is that in some instances they may give a more accurate indicator of the extent of repeat victimization than recorded crimes. This may be particularly true for crimes like domestic violence. Most domestic violence does not get recorded as a criminal offense. However, incident logs give one, albeit imperfect, indicator of the ongoing nature of domestic violence when repeat calls to the same addresses are analyzed. Obviously this is not perfect since it has been suggested that a woman has, on average, experienced violence thirty-five times before calling the police (cited in Horley 1988, p. 2). Despite this imperfection, incident logs display distinct patterns of repeat calls. Incident logs were the initial source of data used by Farrell, Buck, and Pease (1993) to analyze the extent and time-course of domestic violence. For that study, the incident log data were transferred on disk from the police mainframe computer to a personal computer for analysis using SPSS-PC, a standard data analysis package. The major drawback for the analysis of repeat calls to a household was that addresses are not necessarily recorded in the same format each time by police dispatchers—a fact that is not overly important for police use but was fundamental to this research. Computers do not recognize the same address if it is spelled differently in any way (some computer software packages may have a "like" facility for similar spellings, but not for data analysis, and in this instance it may lead to additional counting problems). For an example of the problem, these six fictional address records are all calls to the same address, but a computer recognizes them all as separate addresses: (1) 119 Turton Road; (2) 119, Turton Rd BL8 ; (3) 119 Turton Rd. ; (4) 119, Turton Rd. ; (5) 119, Turton Road; and (6) 119 TURTON ROAD.

There are many more variations that can occur, and even the difference of a comma, a space, an abbreviation, a spelling, or a difference between upper- and lowercase, may be enough for the computer to read them as separate addresses. In the Merseyside project (Farrell, Buck, and Pease 1993), calls were sorted (SORT command in SPSS) by address, and then discrepancies were edited where they obviously referred to the same address. These were resorted, and further editing conducted. Several iterations of the sorting and editing procedure were necessary. This was found to be a lengthy but necessary process. It reduces the falsely high number of "single-incident calls" and brings the number of "repeat calls" closer to the actual number. When results are aggregated, this procedure can make a huge difference to the findings.

A further point to note with respect to incident logs is that some events are not located to an address. An episode that may be a repeat call to an address may just be recorded as a call to the street name. These "unlocated" calls will increase the apparent number of single incidents at the expense of their true status as repeat occurrences.

C. Crime Survey Data

The pathbreaking paper by Genn (1988) has already been discussed, but a brief recap of the methodological issues she raises is warranted. Genn notes that many analyses of the British Crime Survey place an "artificial upper limit" on the number of criminal incidents that a person could report to the survey as a series. A series of incidents was usually given an artificial upper limit of five, regardless of whether this was one of five or fifty incidents. A limit was also placed on the number of series of incidents that could be reported. Each series of incidents was recorded on a questionnaire called a "victim form." However, any one respondent could only complete up to four victim forms. This is not limited to the BCS. I worked on a survey that placed an artificial limitation of six victim forms on a respondent, as well as failed to account for several other of the aspects considered here (see Sampson and Farrell 1990).

A further problem of crime survey data is the absence of accurate date and time of repeated incidents of crime. This makes it difficult to determine the length of time between victimizations.

The presentation of these limitations is not meant to belittle the enormous contribution that crime surveys have made to criminological research and knowledge. The British Crime Survey has dispelled many myths about crime, shed light on others, and opened up many new areas to research. It will make an important continuing contribution to British criminological research. Some recent analyses of British Crime Survey data have attempted to overcome the problem of the artificial limit placed on data through the use of victim forms by using the "filter" or screening questions that record the initial responses to questions about the amount of crime. While these are themselves not without problems, they may go some way toward indicating the extent of repeat victimization.

D. The "Time-Window" in the Study of the Time-Course

A study of crime in an area for a one-week period will show virtually no repeat victimization. This is because crimes observed as "single-incident" crimes during the observed week may be repeats of crime the week before or may be precursors of crimes in the subsequent week. Even if there are only six days between one incident and the next, only those in which the prior crime took place on the first day of the study would have the repeat recorded as such.

Repeat victimization is therefore undercounted, and single-incident crimes are overcounted. The extent of the problem of the "time-window" of the research is proportional to the length of the period of observation. A study with a long reporting or recording period—perhaps several years of crime with dates and times of occurrence—will have virtually excluded this problem. A study with a very short time period has this problem acutely. In the study of schools burglary and property crime covered in Section IV, a simple weighting formula was used to account for the underestimate. Alternatively, as mentioned, Tilley (1993a) imaginatively constructed a one-year time-course study from two years of crime data.

E. Attempted Crime

In victim surveys, the inclusion or exclusion of attempted crime may have important effects on the findings with respect to repeat victimization. This is not presented here as a statement of fact but as a hypothesis and an area that needs further study. Is an attempted crime more or less likely to be repeated than a completed crime? It has not, to the writer's knowledge, been the object of any repeat victimization research. Rates of repeat victimization for attempted crimes may vary greatly by type of crime. For example, a frustrated burglary attempt may be deflected to a different target. Conversely, attempted rapes and murders may be excellent predictors of completed rapes and murders. This may be particularly so when victim and offender are known to each other. While very few rapes are reported, the volume has increased in recent years. It might be the subject of empirical study. Given the necessary background research, it could be one uncharted area in which a preventive approach might develop.

F. "Eligibility" for Revictimization

By definition, in order for revictimization to take place it is necessary for the target or victim to exist and be "eligible" for revictimization.

The extent to which this does not take place needs to be considered in calculating the rate of repeat victimization. Repeated murder victimization is impossible. Webb and Laycock (1992) show that the proportion of cars that are stolen and not recovered in the United Kingdom has increased over two decades, so that this is now the fate that befalls about one-third of cars taken. This spectacularly reduces the maximum repeat victimization that can occur. The extent of repeat victimization must be assessed in relation to the vehicles remaining eligible for repeat victimization. Cars that are badly damaged as a result of crime may be "written off" or otherwise off the road for a prolonged period. During this time they are not eligible for repeat victimization. Cars that move between areas or are sold on to a different owner (which could be more likely after victimization) might not have repeated victimizations traced to them even if they were repeatedly victimized. A similar pattern of the systematic overrepresentation of single-incident victimizations and the undercounting of repeat victimization would be the outcome if eligibility factors are not considered. While here it largely takes the form of a hypothesis of methodological considerations, it could form a further interesting prospect for future research during the development of a car crime prevention program.

One of the few attributes held in common by all routinely available sources of data about crime is their tendency to understate the level of repeat victimization. Some police areas may not realize that they have a problem of this kind. While some areas and some crime types may truly be characterized as involving low levels of repeat victimization, evidence to this effect has yet to emerge. When they do, these will be of particular interest. The first possibility to be eliminated when such a prospect is being considered is whether the intrinsic tendency to understate repeats accounts for their nonappearance. For prevention programs, consideration of methodological issues is important in order that the correct baseline of revictimization is initially established and in order that changes in this level can be properly evaluated.

VII. Preventing Revictimization: Domestic Violence and Burglary

This section details two projects that have introduced innovative techniques into crime prevention through an approach developed around the prevention of revictimization. While it is by no means the only factor (particularly so in the case of preventing domestic violence), a factor common to the projects is the use of quick response alarms located at victimized targets during the period they are perceived as "high risk."

A. *The Merseyside Domestic Violence Prevention Project*

A Home Office–funded crime-prevention project, the immediate progenitor of which was the Kirkholt Burglary Prevention Project, the emphasis was on the prevention of repeated domestic assault by all locally appropriate means. Some of the findings of the initial research phase of the project were detailed in the section on the time-course of revictimization. The study showed that domestic violence was very concentrated: a large proportion of all calls to the police came from a small proportion of all households that repeatedly made calls. This concurred with the findings of all previous research. However, it also showed that a repeat call was likely to occur within a short period after a call. A package of prevention measures was introduced based on the probability that revictimization was likely and likely within a short time, based on the preference for a specifically tailored package of measures. This package of measures included the recognition that domestic violence was often a long-term process to which short-term prevention would not necessarily bring a halt and that preventive measures must be encased in a package of social support for the survivors of domestic violence. The package included two main aspects. The first consisted of portable alarm technology, and the second a computerized database of all calls for police service recorded as "domestic" incidents, recorded by household. The alarms were connected, via a telephone line or a cellular phone, directly to the local police station. They used technology that was already used for elderly people in sheltered housing. The location of the alarm and the history of problems and violence at the address were automatically recalled onto a computer screen in the police control room. This information was then relayed to officers sent to the scene. The alarms received a priority response. They were offered to victims (primarily women) based on certain criteria: the issuance of a court injunction, a recommendation by a police officer who had attended a domestic dispute, a referral from another agency (through a local interagency domestic violence forum), or a recommendation based on a history of violence at an address detected through the computerized database. Information about a history of violence at an address was relayed from the database to officers attending a call regardless of whether the address had an alarm. Addresses where an alarm had been placed but had been returned would also be placed in the database so that officers would know it was a location where there had previously been an alarm. Alarms were initially loaned for a period of thirty days, subject to recommendation for an extension (which was found often to be the case, as might be expected). A further main aspect of the prevention package was a Domestic Violence Prevention Worker who was employed to give support and information to women who received the alarms. This aspect of the package was crucial since an alarm would not necessarily solve many of the underlying problems of domestic violence; it produces a "breathing space" in which the victim can work, with the support of the domestic violence prevention worker, to achieve a situation where she would feel both safe and confident without the alarm. This is the reason why this section has been introduced prior to further discussion of the alarms for crime prevention: in the context of domestic violence, the alarms cannot be used in isolation. The package of measures also included "aide-memoires" for police officers about their powers to intervene at domestic incidents and information cards for victims (about local services available) that officers could distribute. Some of the initial results of the project are discussed in Lloyd, Farrell, and Pease (1994). Since undertaking that work, it came to light that a similar package of measures has been developed in a city in Canada, called DVERS (Domestic Violence Emergency Response Team), though with a different emphasis and infrastructure. The potential of the loaned alarms may still be further developed. Farrell, Clarke, and Pease (1993) suggest that they could be used to enforce court injunctions and family protection orders that have hitherto been largely unenforceable. Farrell, Jones, and Pease (1993) describe how alarms could be lent for witness and juror protection where necessary, a development that emerged due to demand as a by-product of the Merseyside project.

B. The South Yorkshire Burglary Prevention Project

South Yorkshire police developed the use of the portable alarm technology in a different crime prevention context (Fieldsend, Jones, and Pease 1992). Alarms were loaned to victimized properties immediately following victimization. These remained in place for a period of two months to give cover during the period when revictimization was most likely. While it is a refinement of the practices of the Kirkholt project, the technology used is the primary improvement. The service provided to the customer—the victim—is improved, due to the more effective and informed police response. The savings were also for the police who can use the same crime prevention resources at different locations. Aspects of the portable intruder alarms for crime prevention are discussed below.

C. Portable Intruder Alarms and Efficient Crime Prevention

The use of portable intruder alarms for crime prevention has advantages over permanent alarms. The problems of "conventional" (i.e., permanent) intruder alarms are twofold. The first is the high rate of false activations. It has been estimated that over 95 percent of intruder alarm activations are false (see Pease and Litton 1984, p. 190). A second problem that compounds the first is the proliferation of permanent alarms across household and commercial properties. False alarms are a drain of police resources. With the proliferation of alarms, this becomes a great drain on police resources. As a direct result of the problem, police in Britain removed all monitoring of alarms from the police station. In many force policies it is explicit that alarm monitoring is not undertaken by the police (with the exception of the very limited use of Home Office alarms loaned by Crime Prevention Officers). Security firms were obliged to set up centralized monitoring units for their alarms. This introduced an aspect of screening for false calls and reduced the labor required by the police to monitor calls. With the portable intruder alarms, the problems of proliferation and false activations are both overcome to some extent. The number of alarms issued is far lower, and the number of false alarms will be much less. This is not an irrational claim to make: alarms are loaned, based on the revictimization predictor, to "high-risk" recipients. A genuine activation is much more likely during the loan period than one from a permanent alarm where allocation is not determined by probability of victimization. The alarms will not proliferate because they are issued on a temporary basis by an agency that reclaims them. Even if they did receive wider usage, one personal computer, such as the one in use on Merseyside, can monitor several thousand alarms at any one time.

VIII. Dynamic Crime Prevention: The Offender Detection Predictor

Viewed from only a slightly different perspective, the revictimization predictor is an offender detection predictor. By definition, it is a predictor of the time and place of a future offense, where an offender or offenders can be found and may be apprehended. Moreover, it could be that a predictive "hit" would be more likely to be the detection of a frequent offender who has returned to repeat the crime. As a frequent offender detector, the predictor may also be a serious offender predictor. The potential is of placement of a minimum of preventive resources, efficiently allocated, to apprehend the most frequent and predictable offenders. If silent alarms were loaned to burglarized properties for the postburglary heightened-risk period, then all that remains is to harvest the offenders when they return. If one offender is responsible for several burglaries in an area, then based on the addition of revictimization probabilities, it may only be a matter of time until detection. Obviously this is a simplification, and the result may just be a crime prevented rather than an apprehension. If prevention resources were rapidly moved into place following each victimization, then the estimated time period before offender detection would be short. If the offender were to realize that alarms are being rapidly fitted and is deflected or displaced to a different target, almost by definition the choice of targets will involve increased risk. If it is not the same offenders who commit the revictimization of a particular target, this is not a problem.

A. Activity-sensitive Offender Monitoring Units

The revictimization/offender detection predictor holds the potential to become an antioffender policing strategy, a form of aggressive or proactive crime prevention, and for a variety of types of crime. This could be for domestic violence, residential and commercial burglary, and car crimes. Domestic violence and burglary have already been discussed.

1. *Dynamic Crime Prevention and Car Crime.* Unpublished results from the British Crime Survey suggest that car crime is even more concentrated in terms of rates of revictimization than personal and other property crime. As a means of prevention Sherman (1992b, p. 38) writes of the introduction of "Lo-Jack" car tracking devices that trace cars and have increased both car recoveries and offender detection in Massachusetts. The innovative combination suggested by the revictimization predictor would run thus: a pool of car tracking devices would be rotated between vehicles perceived to be at high risk (i.e., in the time just after victimization). This would be a more efficient allocation of alarms that are expensive when used on an individual basis. Even if there were not enough alarms for all cars to be tracked after victimization (or premises to be alarmed, etc.), as Sherman notes with respect to offenders and the possibilities for crackdowns, "by

keeping them guessing, we may have better luck at keeping them honest" (1990, p. 44).

2. *Implementation.*   The use of the revictimization predictor as a tool for dynamic crime prevention would have to be correctly implemented. It would need a coordinated policy: a rapidly mobilized response to victimization; prevention resources in place within twenty-four hours (ideally); and an informed, priority response to alarm activations. This would have to include a consistent policy for alarm withdrawal and reallocation when risk of revictimization declines for a particular target. As with domestic violence alarms, alarms can be reallocated to a particular target for a further period based on specified recommendation criteria (e.g., after further victimization or an attempted break-in that did not result in actual theft).

Officers deployed to the scene of an activation, for example, of a burglar alarm or car locator, would be informed by radio that it was a silent signal and that they might catch an offender unaware. The control room monitoring a widespread set of silent alarms on loan to locations at high risk of revictimization would in effect constitute a cheap and highly effective "offender monitoring unit." It would only be called into action when criminal activity takes place. Historically, the monitoring of frequent offenders is tedious and labor intensive (i.e., expensive), typically a round-the-clock vigil involving several officers for one offender. The results of such a strategy are by no means guaranteed. Sherman writes of the Washington, D.C., Repeat Offender Project (ROP), involving seventy officers, that "it began with the goal of focusing constant surveillance on stranger robbers, but couldn't identify enough of them to stay busy," and continues, "the [repeat robbers] they did identify had the unfortunate habit of going home at night and staying there for 12 to 16 hours, which made surveillance extremely expensive and very boring. ROP officers wound up making more 'serendipitous' arrests while watching their targets than actual arrests of the targets" (Sherman 1992b, p. 15).

Based on a constant supply of repeat offenses as predicted by the revictimization/offender detection predictor, a whole police division of frequent offenders could be monitored in the course of the everyday activities of a single control room. A computer would monitor the long hours of inactivity for all the loaned alarms in a force area, and it would not be bored or inattentive when called on to respond. In the Washington Repeat Offender Project, there was a consistent input of labor (twenty-four hour, day after day) regardless of the extent of criminal activity. The monitoring mechanism (i.e., the officers involved) cost the same amount in labor for the long periods of inactivity as for the periods of activity. Based on the revictimization predictor and the loan of silent alarms, human resources would only need to be allocated to sites of known potential offender activity when an alarm is activated. The expected outcomes of this for crime prevention would be doubly efficient per unit of labor expended: the prevention of revictimization and the increased likelihood of apprehension of frequent offenders.

B. Combined Crime Prevention and Offender Detection

Offender detection and apprehension is one form of crime prevention. However, other than implicitly, it does not traditionally overlap with a concern for the victim. Criminal careers research suggests that the returns to apprehending one offender would often be greater than one single crime prevented. To be realistic, it is likely that not all genuine activations will result in apprehension even if a crime is prevented. Perhaps the most effective practice would be both a crime prevention and an offender detection combination, not least to increase chances of implementation. Implementation of crime prevention initiatives is by no means easy (see Laycock, in this volume). In policing, as in all walks of life, the extent to which something is implemented and overseen will depend on self-interest. Policing is traditionally assessed on arrest rates, not on rates of crime prevention. This is because the first is a practical measure while the latter is more elusive for everyday monitoring purposes. If offender detection and the prevention of revictimization could be combined, the rewards will be greater for all concerned. The victim will receive a superior crime prevention service if there is an element of a potential tangible return to those who put it into place. The potential detection and apprehension of an offender will produce a more efficient crime prevention service than the potential securing of a future nonevent. The symbiotic relationship that could develop between preventing revictimization and offender detection (symbiotic because the "attractive" aspect—offender detection—could not take place without the crime prevention aspect) could be a potentially fruitful form of dynamic crime prevention. To be optimistic about the future, a productive Crime Prevention team based around the detection and prevention of revictimization could be an enviable posting.

IX. Conclusion

Revictimization prevention is beginning to catch on in the United Kingdom. In early 1993 all Chief Constables of Police and Force Crime Prevention Officers in England and Wales received a paper on the subject appended to a Home Office circular. One police area ordered nearly a thousand copies of a subsequent Home Office paper that was launched at a national conference on the subject. It is being considered as a national performance indicator for United Kingdom police work (Tilley 1994). This makes sense since most changes in crime rates are largely independent of the work of the police. Hence the level of crime per se is not a measure of police performance. Where policing is a response to victimization, it might be preferable to look for any crime prevention effect in the level of repeat victimization (Farrell and Buckley 1993). The rider to this would be the need to tackle the methodological issues in determining the extent of revictimization and in evaluating its prevention.

While this essay has endeavored to be sanguine, caution may need to be exercised in a variety of forms. There is no off-the-shelf prevention package, and each needs to be tailored to specific crimes and local circumstance. While preventing revictimization may suggest conditions conducive to the development of more efficient crime prevention, the demarcation of a sound preventive mechanism (Pawson and Tilley 1992) is a prerequisite to its achievement. The putative replications of the Kirkholt burglary project suggest that merely recognizing revictimization may not always be enough (Tilley 1993*b*).

Opinion may, as with any developments, remain divided on the potential of the revictimization predictor for general crime prevention strategy. This is not a problem. It will be determined almost solely by the extent to which the preventive strategies are devised. The revictimization predictor may in addition produce circumstances conducive to the development of new and innovative strategies, and, at worst, more efficient allocation of existing resources. The loan of alarms under certain circumstances may be one step toward efficient crime prevention. Specific examples have been illustrated, including domestic violence, residential and commercial burglary, and car crime. It should be stressed that in the case of domestic violence, alarms were not used in isolation but as part of a package of measures. Other possibilities for alarm loans will include racial attacks, and, moving away from revictimization predictors, alarms may have a variety of other potential uses, including, for example, witness and juror protection programs (Farrell, Jones, and Pease 1993).

As a means of focusing limited crime prevention resources where they are needed, "heightened risk" can be determined by a variety of methods. The extent of revictimization is an empirical fact. In time it will become a criminological commonplace.

APPENDIX

The tables show results for the 1982, 1984, and 1988 British Crime Surveys used to generate figure 1, the regression equations, and related information.

TABLE A1

1982 British Crime Survey: Area Decile Counts and Rates for Property Crime

Decile	Incidents	Victims	Respondents	IR	PR	CR
1	15	15	827	1.81	1.81	1.00
2	60	55	1,027	5.84	5.35	1.09
3	114	92	976	11.68	9.43	1.24
4	168	125	1,100	15.27	11.36	1.34
5	236	164	1,076	21.93	15.24	1.44
6	301	179	1,041	28.91	17.20	1.68
7	392	224	1,193	32.86	18.78	1.75
8	560	274	1,239	45.20	22.11	2.04
9	816	324	1,398	58.37	23.18	2.52
10	1,226	311	1,028	119.26	30.25	3.94
Total	3,888	1,763	10,905			

NOTE.—IR = incidence rate. PR = prevalence rate. CR = concentration rate.

TABLE A2

1984 British Crime Survey: Area Decile Counts and Rates for Property Crime

Decile	Incidents	Victims	Respondents	IR	PR	CR
1	33	32	1,052	3.14	3.04	1.03
2	88	74	981	8.97	7.54	1.19
3	145	121	1,090	13.30	11.10	1.20
4	192	142	1,109	17.31	12.80	1.35
5	229	158	1,150	19.91	13.74	1.45
6	288	186	1,163	24.76	15.99	1.55
7	371	206	1,149	32.29	17.93	1.80
8	497	220	1,092	45.51	20.15	2.26
9	674	309	1,086	62.06	28.45	2.18
10	1,302	322	1,157	112.53	27.83	4.02
Total	3,819	1,770	11,029			

NOTE.—IR = incidence rate. PR = prevalence rate. CR = concentration rate.

TABLE A3

1988 British Crime Survey: Area Decile Counts and Rates for Property Crime

Decile	Incidents	Victims	Respondents	IR	PR	CR
1	31	29	1,031	3.01	2.81	1.07
2	89	75	1,032	8.62	7.27	1.19
3	141	116	1,174	12.01	9.88	1.22
4	201	147	1,129	17.80	13.02	1.37
5	258	173	1,040	24.81	16.63	1.49
6	334	207	1,177	28.37	17.59	1.61
7	436	258	1,174	37.14	21.98	1.69
8	587	302	1,239	47.38	24.37	1.95
9	745	309	1,263	58.99	24.47	2.41
10	1,900	414	1,482	128.21	27.94	4.59
Total	4,722	2,030	11,741			

NOTE.—IR = incidence rate. PR = prevalence rate. CR = concentration rate.

TABLE A4

1982 British Crime Survey: Area Decile Counts and Rates for Personal Crime

Decile	Incidents	Victims	Respondents	IR	PR	CR
1	0	0	840	.00	.00	· · ·
2	6	6	936	.64	.64	1.00
3	37	37	969	3.82	3.82	1.00
4	67	60	1,094	6.12	5.48	1.12
5	105	89	1,135	9.25	7.84	1.18
6	135	89	1,196	11.29	7.44	1.52
7	189	122	1,256	15.05	9.71	1.55
8	272	138	1,172	23.21	11.77	1.97
9	439	166	1,351	32.49	12.29	2.64
10	1,145	161	956	119.77	16.84	7.11
Total	2,395	868	10,905			

NOTE.—IR = incidence rate. PR = prevalence rate. CR = concentration rate.

TABLE A5

1984 British Crime Survey: Area Decile Counts and Rates for Personal Crime

Decile	Incidents	Victims	Respondents	IR	PR	CR
1	0	0	1,073	.00	.00	...
2	14	14	1,082	1.29	1.29	1.00
3	33	33	1,102	2.99	2.99	1.00
4	60	51	1,052	5.70	4.84	1.18
5	86	70	1,116	7.71	6.27	1.23
6	113	86	1,149	9.83	7.84	1.25
7	155	102	1,118	13.86	9.12	1.52
8	203	113	1,105	18.37	10.23	1.80
9	321	136	1,107	29.00	12.29	2.36
10	1,130	181	1,125	100.44	16.09	6.24
Total	2,115	786	11,029			

NOTE.—IR = incidence rate. PR = prevalence rate. CR = concentration rate.

TABLE A6

1988 British Crime Survey: Area Decile Counts and Rates for Personal Crime

Decile	Incidents	Victims	Respondents	IR	PR	CR
1	5	5	1,046	.48	.48	1.00
2	30	30	1,093	2.74	2.74	1.00
3	54	50	1,092	4.94	4.58	1.08
4	86	66	1,126	7.64	5.86	1.30
5	117	84	1,040	11.25	8.08	1.39
6	170	99	1,208	14.07	8.20	1.72
7	238	142	1,153	20.64	12.32	1.68
8	337	150	1,276	26.41	11.76	2.25
9	506	172	1,290	39.22	13.33	2.94
10	1,290	217	1,417	91.04	15.31	5.95
Total	2,832	1,015	11,741			

NOTE.—IR = incidence rate. PR = prevalence rate. CR = concentration rate.

TABLE A7

Regression Equations for Area Crime
Revictimization Curves for 1982, 1984,
and 1988 British Crime Survey:
Personal and Property Crimes

Crime and Year	ln IR
Property:	
1982	.918212 + .135513PR
1984	1.183834 + .121597PR
1988	1.062117 + .126298PR
Personal:	
1982	−.09133 + .294031PR
1984	.19720 + .271399PR
1988	−.16572 + .301056PR

Note.—IR = incidence rate; PR = prevalence
rate.

TABLE A8

Supplementary Information to Regression Equations of Table A7

Crime and Year	Standard Error of the Intercept	R^2	df	Standard Error of X Coefficient
Property:				
1982	.267	.956	8	.010
1984	.263	.941	8	.010
1988	.224	.961	8	.009
Personal:				
1982	.303	.969	7*	.022
1984	.170	.984	7*	.129
1988	.474	.915	8	.032

* There are only seven degrees of freedom (df) because nine rather than ten area deciles
were used in analysis where decile 1 had no crime reported (see tables A4 and A5).

REFERENCES

Atkinson, Anthony B. 1970. "On the Measurement of Inequality." *Journal of Economic Theory* 2:244–63.
Barr, Robert, Graham Farrell, Fiona McCready, and Ken Pease. 1991. "Multiple Victimization in Northern Ireland." Unpublished report to the Northern Ireland Office. Manchester: University of Manchester, Department of Social Policy.

Barr, Robert, and Ken Pease. 1990. "Crime Placement, Displacement, and Deflection." In *Crime and Justice: A Review of Research*, vol. 12, edited by Michael Tonry and Norval Morris. Chicago: University of Chicago Press.

Blumstein, Alfred, Jacqueline Cohen, Jeffrey Roth, and Christy Visher, eds. 1986. *Criminal Careers and "Career Criminals."* Washington, D.C.: National Academy Press.

Burquest, Ralph, Graham Farrell, and Ken Pease. 1992. "Lessons from Schools." *Policing* 8:148–55.

Clarke, R. V. 1992. *Situational Crime Prevention: Successful Case Studies*. London: Heinemann.

———. 1994. "Situational Crime Prevention." In this volume.

Clarke, R. V., and Patricia M. Harris. 1992. "Auto Theft and Its Prevention." In *Crime and Justice: A Review of Research*, vol. 16, edited by Michael Tonry. Chicago: University of Chicago Press.

Clarke, R. V. G., and P. Mayhew, eds. 1980. *Designing Out Crime*. London: H.M. Stationery Office.

Cohen, Lawrence E., and Marcus Felson. 1979. "Social Change and Crime Rate Trends: A Routine Activity Approach." *American Sociological Review* 44:588–608.

Corbett, Claire, and Mike Maguire. 1988. "The Value and Limitations of Victim Support Schemes." In *Victims of Crime: A New Deal*, edited by Mike Maguire and John Pointing. Milton Keynes: Open University Press.

Ekblom, Paul. 1988. *Getting the Best Out of Crime Analysis*. Home Office Crime Prevention Unit Paper 10. London: H.M. Stationery Office.

Farrell, Graham. 1992. "Multiple Victimization: Its Extent and Significance." *International Review of Victimology* 2(2):85–102.

———. 1994a. "Measuring Crime Distribution: The Lorenz Curve and Gini Coefficient of Victimization." Unpublished manuscript. Manchester: University of Manchester, Department of Social Policy and Social Work.

———. 1994b. "Why Does Repeat Victimization Occur?" Manchester: University of Manchester, Department of Social Policy and Social Work.

Farrell, Graham, Wendy Buck, and Ken Pease. 1993. "The Merseyside Domestic Violence Prevention Project." *Studies in Crime and Crime Prevention*, vol. 2. Stockholm: Scandinavian University Press.

Farrell, Graham, and Alistair Buckley. 1993. "Repeat Victimization as a Police Performance Indicator: Case Study of a Domestic Violence Unit in Merseyside." Paper to the British Criminology Conference, University of Wales at Cardiff, July.

Farrell, Graham, Karen Clarke, and Ken Pease. 1993. "Arming the Toothless Tiger: Court Injunctions, Family Protection Orders and Domestic Violence." *Justice of the Peace* (February 6), pp. 88–90.

Farrell, Graham, Dan Ellingworth, and Ken Pease. 1994. "Repeat Victimization, High Crime Areas and Routine Activities." University of Manchester, Department of Social Policy and Social Work.

Farrell, Graham, Glynn Jones, and Ken Pease. 1993. "Witness and Juror Protection through Available Technology." *Magistrate* (forthcoming).

Farrell, Graham, and Ken Pease. 1993. *Once Bitten, Twice Bitten: Repeat Victimization and Its Implications for Crime Prevention.* Home Office Crime Prevention Unit Paper 46. London: Home Office.

———. 1994. "Repeat Victim Support." Unpublished manuscript. Manchester: University of Manchester, Department of Social Policy and Social Work.

Farrington, David. 1992*a*. "Criminal Career Research: Lessons for Crime Prevention." *Studies in Crime and Crime Prevention* 1:7–29.

———. 1992*b*. "Was the Kirkholt Burglary Project a Success?" Unpublished manuscript. Cambridge: Cambridge University, Institute of Criminology.

Farrington, David, and Roger Tarling. 1985. *Prediction in Criminology.* Albany: State University of New York Press.

Fieldsend, Terry, Glynne Jones, and Ken Pease. 1992. "Cellular Phones: Yuppies' Friend, Intruders' Foe?" Unpublished manuscript. Manchester: University of Manchester, Department of Social Policy and Social Work.

Fienberg, Stephen E. 1980. "Statistical Modelling in the Analysis of Repeated Victimization." In *Indicators of Crime and Criminal Justice: Quantitative Studies,* edited by Stephen E. Fienberg and Albert J. Reiss, Jr. Washington, D.C.: U.S. Department of Justice, Bureau of Justice Statistics.

Forrester, David, Mike Chatterton, and Ken Pease. 1988*a*. "Why It's Best to Lock the Door after the Horse Has Bolted." *Police Review* (November 4), pp. 2288–89.

———. 1988*b*. *The Kirkholt Burglary Prevention Project, Rochdale.* Home Office Crime Prevention Unit Paper 13. London: Home Office.

Forrester, David, Samantha Frenz, Martin O'Connell, and Ken Pease. 1990. *The Kirkholt Burglary Prevention Project: Phase II.* Home Office Crime Prevention Unit Paper 23. London: Home Office.

Genn, Hazel. 1988. "Multiple Victimization." In *Victims of Crime: A New Deal?* edited by Mike Maguire and John Pointing. Milton Keynes: Open University Press.

George, Kenneth D., and Caroline Joll. 1981. *Industrial Organization: Competition, Growth and Structural Change.* 3d ed. London: George Allen & Unwin.

Goldstein, Herman. 1979. "Improving Policing: A Problem-oriented Approach." *Crime and Delinquency* 25:234–58.

———. 1990. *Problem-oriented Policing.* New York: McGraw-Hill.

Gottfredson, Michael R. 1984. *Victims of Crime: The Dimensions of Risk.* Home Office Research Study no. 81. London: H.M. Stationery Office.

Harvey, Linda, Penny Grimshaw, and Ken Pease. 1989. "Crime Prevention Delivery: The Work of Police Crime Prevention Officers." In *Coming to Terms with Policing,* edited by Rod Morgan and David Smith. London: Routledge.

Hindelang, Michael, Michael R. Gottfredson, and James Garofalo. 1978. *Victims of Personal Crime: An Empirical Foundation for a Theory of Personal Victimization.* Cambridge, Mass.: Ballinger.

Hope, Tim. 1982. *Burglary in Schools: The Prospects for Prevention.* Home Office Research and Planning Unit Paper 11. London: H.M. Stationery Office.

Horley, S. 1988. *Love and Pain: A Survival Handbook for Women.* London: Bedford Square Press.

Hough, Mike. 1986. "Victims of Violent Crime: Findings from the British Crime Survey." In *Crime Policy to Victim Policy: Reorienting the Justice System*, edited by Ezzat A. Fattah. Basingstoke: Macmillan.

Hough, Mike, and Pat Mayhew. 1985. *Taking Account of Crime: Key Findings from the 1984 British Crime Survey*. Home Office Research Study no. 85. London: H.M. Stationery Office.

Hussain, Sohail. 1988. *Neighbourhood Watch in England and Wales: A Location Analysis*. Home Office Crime Prevention Unit Paper 12. London: Home Office.

Johnson, J. H., H. B. Kerper, D. D. Hayes, and G. G. Killenger. 1973. *The Recidivist Victim: A Descriptive Study*. Criminal Justice Monograph, vol. 4, no. 1. Huntsville, Texas: Sam Houston University, Institute of Contemporary Corrections and the Behavioral Sciences.

Jones, T., B. Maclean, and J. Young. 1986. *The Islington Crime Survey: Crime, Victimization and Policing in Inner-City London*. Gower: London.

Laycock, Gloria K., and Nick Tilley. In this volume. "Implementing Crime Prevention."

Lloyd, Sam, Graham Farrell, and Ken Pease. 1994. *Preventing Repeated Domestic Violence: A Demonstration Project on Merseyside*. Home Office Crime Prevention Unit Paper 49. London: Home Office.

Maguire, Mike. 1991. "The Needs and Rights of Victims of Crime." In *Crime and Justice: A Review of Research*, vol. 14, edited by Michael Tonry. Chicago: University of Chicago Press.

Mayhew, Pat, Natalie Aye Maung, and Catriona Mirrlees-Black. 1993. *The 1992 British Crime Survey*. London: H.M. Stationery Office.

Meier, Robert F., and Terance D. Miethe. 1993. "Understanding Theories of Criminal Victimization." In *Crime and Justice: A Review of Research*, vol. 17, edited by Michael Tonry. Chicago: University of Chicago Press.

Miethe, Terance D. 1991. "Citizen-based Crime Control Activity and Victimization Risks: An Examination of Displacement and Free-Rider Effects." *Criminology* 29:419–39.

Morley, Rebecca, and Audrey Mullender. 1994. *Preventing Domestic Violence to Women*. Home Office Crime Prevention Unit Paper 48. London: Home Office.

Nelson, James. 1980. "Multiple Victimization in American Cities: A Statistical Analysis of Rare Events." *American Journal of Sociology* 85(4):870–91.

Newburn, Tim, and Susan Merry. 1990. *Keeping in Touch: Police-Victim Communication in Two Areas*. Home Office Research Study no. 116. London: H.M. Stationery Office.

Nuttall, C. P., et al. 1977. *Parole in England and Wales*. London: H.M. Stationery Office.

Pawson, Ray, and Nick Tilley. 1992. "Re-Evaluation: Rethinking Research on Corrections and Crime." *Yearbook of Corrections Education 1992*. Vancouver: Simon Fraser University.

Pease, Ken. 1988. *Judgements of Crime Seriousness: Evidence from the 1984 British Crime Survey*. Home Office Research and Planning Unit Paper no. 44. London: Home Office.

———. 1991. "The Kirkholt Project: Preventing Burglary on a British Public Housing Estate." *Security Journal* 2:73–77.

———. 1992. "The Kirkholt Project: Preventing Burglary on a British Public Housing Estate." In *Situational Crime Prevention: Successful Case Studies*, edited by R. V. Clarke. London: Heinemann.

Pease, Ken, and Roger Litton. 1984. "Crime Prevention: Practice and Motivation." In *Psychology and Law*, edited by D. J. Mueller, D. E. Blackman, and A. J. Chapman. New York: Wiley & Sons.

Polvi, Natalie, Terah Looman, Charlie Humphries, and Ken Pease. 1990. "Repeat Break-and-Enter Victimization: Time-Course and Crime Prevention Opportunity." *Journal of Police Science and Administration* 17(1):8–11.

———. 1991. "The Time-Course of Repeat Burglary Victimization." *British Journal of Criminology* 31:411–14.

Reiss, Albert J., Jr. 1980. "Victim Proneness in Repeat Victimization by Type of Crime." In *Indicators of Crime and Criminal Justice: Quantitative Studies*, edited by Stephen E. Fienberg and Albert J. Reiss, Jr. Washington, D.C.: U.S. Department of Justice, Bureau of Justice Statistics.

Sampson, Alice. 1991. *Lessons Learnt from a Victim Support Crime Prevention Project.* Home Office Crime Prevention Unit Paper 25. London: Home Office.

Sampson, Alice, and Graham Farrell. 1990. *Victim Support and Crime Prevention in an Inner-City Setting.* Home Office Crime Prevention Unit Paper 21. London: Home Office.

Sampson, Alice, and Coretta Phillips. 1992. *Multiple Victimization: Racial Attacks on an East London Estate.* Home Office Crime Prevention Unit Paper 36. London: Home Office.

Shah, Rabindra. 1991. "Multiple Victimization: A Secondary Analysis of the 1988 British Crime Survey." Master's thesis. Manchester: University of Manchester, Department of Social Policy.

Shapland, J., J. Willmore, and P. Duff. 1985. *Victims in the Criminal Justice System.* Aldershot: Gower.

Shapland, Joanna. In this volume. "Preventing Retail-Sector Crimes."

Shapland, Joanna, Paul Wiles, Valeria Johnson, and Maria Leek. 1991. "Crime at Work: The Victimization of Factories and Employees." Unpublished paper. Sheffield: University of Sheffield, Faculty of Law.

Shepherd, J. 1990. "Violent Crime in Bristol: An Accident and Emergency Department Perspective." *British Journal of Criminology* 30:289–305.

Sherman, Lawrence W. 1989. "Repeat Calls for Service: Policing the 'Hot Spots.'" In *Police and Policing: Contemporary Issues*, edited by Dennis Jay Kenney. New York: Praeger.

———. 1990. "Police Crackdowns: Initial and Residual Deterrence." In *Crime and Justice: A Review of Research*, vol. 12, edited by Michael Tonry and Norval Morris. Chicago: University of Chicago Press.

———. 1991. "The Results of Police Work: A Review of *Problem Oriented Policing*, by Herman Goldstein." *Journal of Criminal Law and Criminology* 82:401–18.

———. 1992a. *Policing Domestic Violence: Experiments and Dilemmas.* New York: Macmillan.

————. 1992*b*. "Attacking Crime: Policing and Crime Control." In *Modern Policing*, edited by Michael Tonry and Norval Morris. Vol. 15 of *Crime and Justice: A Review of Research*, edited by Michael Tonry. Chicago: University of Chicago Press.

Sherman, Lawrence W., and Richard Berk. 1984. "The Specific Deterrent Effects of Arrest for Domestic Assault." *American Sociological Review* 49:261–72.

Sherman, Lawrence W., Michael E. Buerger, and Patrick R. Gartin. 1988. *Beyond Dial-a-Cop: A Randomized Test of Repeat Call Address Policing.* Report to the National Institute of Justice. Washington, D.C.: Crime Control Institute.

Sherman, Lawrence W., Patrick R. Gartin, and Michael E. Buerger. 1989. "Hot Spots of Predatory Crime: Routine Activities and the Criminology of Place." *Criminology* 27:27–55.

Sherman, Lawrence W., Janell D. Schmidt, Dennis P. Rogan, Patrick R. Gartin, Ellen G. Cohn, Dean J. Collins, and Anthony R. Babich. 1991. "From Initial Deterrence to Long-Term Escalation: Short-Custody Arrest for Poverty Ghetto Domestic Violence." *Criminology* 29:821–50.

Sherman, Lawrence W., and David Weisburd. 1988. "Policing the 'Hot Spots' of Crime: A Redesign of the Kansas City Preventive Patrol Experiment." Unpublished manuscript. Washington, D.C.: Crime Control Institute.

Skogan, Wesley. 1976. *Sample Surveys of the Victims of Crime.* Cambridge, Mass.: Ballinger.

————. 1981. *Issues in the Measurement of Victimization.* Washington, D.C.: U.S. Department of Justice, Bureau of Justice Statistics.

————. 1986*a*. "Methodological Issues in the Study of Victimization." In *Crime Policy to Victim Policy: Reorienting the Justice System*, edited by E. A. Fattah. Basingstoke: Macmillan.

————. 1986*b*. "The Fear of Crime and Its Behavioural Implications." In *Crime Policy to Victim Policy: Reorienting the Justice System*, edited by E. A. Fattah. Basingstoke: Macmillan.

————. 1990*a*. "The National Crime Survey Redesign." *Public Opinion Quarterly* 54:256–72.

————. 1990*b*. "Innovations in the Analysis of Crime Surveys." Paper to the Conference on Measurement and Research Design in Criminal Justice, Griffith University, Queensland, August.

Smith, Lorna J. F. 1988. *Domestic Violence.* Home Office Research Study no. 107. London: H.M. Stationery Office.

Sparks, Richard. 1981. "Multiple Victimization: Evidence, Theory and Future Research." *Journal of Criminal Law and Criminology* 72:762–78.

Sparks, Richard, Hazel Genn, and David Dodd. 1977. *Surveying Victims.* London: Wiley.

Stander, J., D. P. Farrington, G. Hill, and P. H. E. Altham. 1989. "Markov-Chain Analysis and Specialization in Criminal Careers." *British Journal of Criminology* 29:317–35.

Strauss, Murray A. 1983. "Violence in the Family: Wife Beating." In *Encyclopedia of Crime and Justice*, vol. 4, edited by Sandford H. Kadish. New York: Free Press.

Tilley, Nick. 1993a. *The Prevention of Crime against Small Businesses: The Safer Cities Experience*. Home Office Crime Prevention Unit Paper 45. London: Home Office.

———. 1993b. *After Kirkholt: Theory, Method and Results of Replication Evaluations*. Home Office Crime Prevention Unit Paper 47. London: Home Office.

———. 1994. Personal communication, Home Office Police Research Group, London, February 4.

Trickett, Alan, Dan Ellingworth, Tim Hope, and Ken Pease. 1994. "Changes in Area Crime Inequality in the 1980's: An Analysis of the British Crime Survey." Manchester: University of Manchester, Department of Econometrics and Social Statistics.

Trickett, Alan, Denise K. Osborn, Julie Seymour, and Ken Pease. 1992. "What Is Different about High Crime Areas?" *British Journal of Criminology* 32:81–90.

Webb, Barry, and Gloria Laycock. 1992. *Tackling Car Crime*. Home Office Crime Prevention Unit Paper 32. London: Home Office.

Winkel, Frans W. 1991. "Police, Victims and Crime Prevention: Some Research-based Recommendations on Victim-orientated Interventions." *British Journal of Criminology* 31:250–65.

Zeigenhagen, Eduard. 1976. "The Recidivist Victim of Violent Crime." *Victimology* 1:538–50.

Gloria Laycock and Nick Tilley

Implementing Crime Prevention

ABSTRACT

Situational crime prevention is increasingly proving its worth in crime control, but crime rates in many countries continue to rise. Existing small-scale, but effective, measures should be more widely duplicated. There is a need at all levels to identify mechanisms that will lead to more widespread implementation of situational approaches. Legislative mandates and publicity exhortation can be used, but the demonstration to those with the authority to act that situational measures result in cost savings may be more effective. A prerequisite of such a demonstration is the availability of good data and their analysis. This points to a considerable training task and the need to introduce criminological theory and good research and evaluation practice to those with the authority and responsibility to take action against crime.

Crime control is a major issue in all Western economies and of increasing concern in the former communist states. Crime is rising and has been doing so in the United Kingdom at least for most of the later part of this century. What appears to vary over time is the rate at which crime increases (Field 1990), with property crime rates increasing more quickly in times of recession and violent crime rates rising less quickly in such times.

Although the criminal justice system is a necessary component in crime control, it is clearly not sufficient. There are a number of reasons for this. First, using data from the United Kingdom, there is a great

Gloria Laycock is head of the Home Office Police Research Group. Nick Tilley is reader in sociology at the Nottingham Trent University in England. He is currently a consultant to the Home Office.

Published with the permission of the Controller of Her Britannic Majesty's Stationery Office.

deal of attrition in the system. For every 100 offenses committed, forty-nine are reported to the police, and thirty are recorded by them. Of this thirty, seven are cleared up, three result in a caution or conviction, and two result in a conviction (Barclay 1993). It seems at least inefficient to argue that crime can be controlled by the police, the courts, or the sentencing structure when half of "offenses" are not reported to the police and many of those that do come to attention are not cleared.

Second, as criminologists have argued from a number of perspectives, the criminal justice system has not been particularly successful in pointing to innovative or effective crime control strategies (Clarke 1983; Felson 1994). Police patrols are not ineffectual, but in the context of limited resources, their scope for increased efficacy is bounded; similarly, sentencing options, including the increased use of imprisonment, have a general deterrent effect to an extent, but within the limits of what is acceptable in a so-called civilized society, the deterrent effects have probably been reached. There is little scope for major crime control payoff by what would amount to tinkering with existing criminal justice options.

There is, however, potential for preempting criminal behavior by paying greater attention to the prevention of crime. Prevention can and does cover a vast array of activity from environmental design and situationally related measures through preschool programs, social control, and criminal justice system institutions. The interventions that may claim to make a contribution to the prevention of crime are almost as numerous as the number of initiatives themselves. In an early attempt to provide some structure to these myriad crime prevention activities, Brantingham and Faust (1976) described a conceptual model in which they distinguished between primary, secondary, and tertiary prevention. Primary prevention is directed at the modification of criminogenic conditions in the physical and social environment at large, secondary prevention at early identification and intervention in the lives of individuals or groups in criminogenic circumstances, and tertiary prevention at the prevention of recidivism. This model has been helpful in clarifying work areas within the United Kingdom; the organization of the central government's efforts in crime control is reasonably consistent with the Brantingham and Faust model. In particular, the Home Office Crime Prevention Unit is concerned with primary prevention. Secondary prevention is largely the responsibility of the

Departments of Health and Education, and tertiary prevention is the focus of the prison and the probation services, which are the responsibility of the Home Office.

The bulk of this essay is concerned with work that has arisen from the Home Office Crime Prevention Unit and is therefore limited to primary prevention. Furthermore, since it evolved from earlier work of Clarke and colleagues in the Home Office (Tilley 1991; Felson 1994), it concentrates on situational rather than social measures. Situational prevention covers a wide variety of strategies and techniques. From an original eight-category classification of opportunity-reducing techniques (Clarke and Mayhew 1980), Clarke has elaborated and refined the classification to cover twelve techniques under three major headings: increasing the effort, increasing the risks, and reducing rewards (Clarke 1992). (The essay by Clarke, in this volume, describes the techniques and provides examples of each.)

As Clarke describes in this volume, situational crime prevention has delivered some notable gains in crime management. It has not, however, been without its critics. Situational crime prevention has suffered disproportionately from what could be called a general lack of confidence in its ability to deliver permanent and significant reductions in crime. These criticisms fall under three headings.

Symptoms, Not Causes.   One of the most pervasive criticisms of situational crime prevention is that it tackles the symptoms of crime and not the causes. The reduction of opportunities is seen as a blocking mechanism—a mechanistic way of preventing crime from happening while not affecting the motivation to offend. There is, however, a sense in which opportunities do cause crime. This is particularly the case with relatively trivial offending, which is not uncommon across all classes of society (Felson 1994). In the United Kingdom, for example, 35 percent of the adult male population have a criminal conviction for an indictable offense by the age of thirty-five (Barclay 1993). If we assume an individual with at least a neutral attitude to offending in relation to trivial offenses finds himself or herself in the presence of an almost "too good to miss" opportunity, then an offense could well be committed and would have been in a sense *caused* by the opportunity.

The notion, however, that opportunities cause crime is one that has proved particularly unacceptable to many people. There are probably a number of reasons for this, including reluctance to accept the deterministic view of human behavior which is seen to follow from the opportunity reduction model of crime. Nevertheless, crime, at least at the individual incident level, is in many cases far more unstable than it should be were dispositional theories correct. The decision to offend or not can often hinge on relatively minor and chance events that push the individual in one direction or another. For example, the particular combination of alcohol, a group of excitable peers, and a vulnerable vehicle could well lead to an increased probability that any particular individual young person might commit a car crime offense (Cohen and Felson 1979). It is likely that many relatively trivial offenses fall into this opportunistic category. While, therefore, the argument that opportunities cause crime may not be tenable at the highly motivated end of the continuum where a well-motivated offender will seek out opportunities or even create them (Bennett 1986), this would not apply to a great number of individuals who may be convicted only once of committing any kind of offense.

There are of course an even greater number of individuals who commit offenses, as self-report studies have shown on many occasions, and who are not caught for the offense. We must assume, therefore, that criminal behavior is far more common than official records show, and it is not unlikely, unless we choose to assume that vast numbers of the general population are "motivated to offend," that many of those offenses that *are* committed by otherwise law-abiding individuals are committed on a relatively opportunistic basis.

Displacement.   Situational crime prevention has also been criticized as not preventing crime, but merely leading to its displacement. Far from displacement being "a nail in the coffin" of situational crime prevention, it is arguably one of the reasons it could indeed prove effective. It is *because* criminal behavior is open to displacement that it is open to prevention. For example, if we could accept that the blocking of a particular opportunity for crime reduces the probability of its occurrence at that time and place, it does not necessarily follow that the individual would *offend* elsewhere. He or she may, for example, find something else to do, as is hoped in establishing the various summer play school activities and diversionary schemes for young offenders and others. If displacement were not a possibility, then crime prevention would be an impossibility. The phenomenon of displacement has been comprehensively discussed by Barr and Pease (1990) who argue that displacement of crime following situational or other initiatives is neither inevitable nor necessarily a particularly bad thing. Indeed, going further, Clarke and Weisburd (1994) have discussed the extent to which crimes that were not the target of an initiative can be reduced as a by-product of preventive action elsewhere. They call this "diffusion of benefits" and suggest that the preoccupation of crime prevention research with the criticism of displacement has led to the neglect of a potentially useful program of work looking in more detail at the diffusion of benefits.

Nothing Works. There is a danger that crime prevention will fall victim to the same kind of nothing-works philosophy that befell the treatment of offenders in the 1970s (Lipton, Martinson, and Wilks 1975; Brody 1976) because, despite the increased attention to prevention, crime is continuing to rise. With the benefit of hindsight, negative conclusions in relation to correctional treatment programs seem to have been overstated, and more recent research, combined with developments in the conceptualization of scientific investigation, has led researchers and others to question the nothing-works conclusions drawn (Thornton 1989). Nevertheless, there remains a pervasively critical and negative ethos within social research traditions that risks oversimplistic and premature rejection of potentially fruitful innovations.

On the more positive side for the present generation of social researchers, there is now greater clarity in relation to the concept of program "failure." Program evaluators are alert to the need for sensitivity in distinguishing among theory, measurement, and implementation failure (Rosenbaum, Lewis, and Grant 1986; Ekblom and Pease, in this volume). Such sensitivity in relation to situational crime prevention is facilitated by the development since the 1970s in the United Kingdom and the United States of crime pattern analysis and problem-oriented policing, respectively (Goldstein 1979, 1990; Gladstone 1980; Ekblom 1986a). The U.K. emphasis on crime pattern analysis, and an essentially rational approach to the problem of developing preventive measures, helps in assessing the contribution of situational crime prevention to crime control and thus avoiding too early a pessimistic conclusion that nothing works (e.g., Tilley 1993).

These three criticisms are well recognized, have each been considered in the situational crime prevention literature, and to varying extent have been or are being dealt with. Another problem for opportunity reduction efforts, however, and one that constitutes the focus of the remainder of this essay, concerns implementation. A wide variety of situational measures effectively reduce crime on a small scale, including shop theft, vandalism, burglary, parking lot crime, robbery, car theft, racial attacks, and domestic violence. Two questions arise. First, why, if small-scale situational crime control measures are as effective as they seem, are there not more of them? Second, more important, how is political interest in situational prevention to be maintained, which itself relates to the extent to which situational measures can deliver large-scale reductions in, for example, national burglary or car crime figures? If national crime control is even to be approached, then national measures must be implemented—but what items need to be on such a national agenda and how can that agenda be activated? The sections that follow discuss small- and larger-scale situational crime prevention initiatives with particular emphasis on how the probability of successful implementation can be increased.

A paper by Engstad and Evans (1980) provides some useful concepts for this discussion. They took issue with the notion that the police *can* control crime and discussed the extent to which the locus of responsibility for crime control needed to shift to those competent to take action. This concept of competence is central to the debate on implementation. In a nutshell—while the police may usefully act as a catalyst for crime prevention, they are neither *responsible* for crime levels, nor do they in most cases have the *competency* to take remedial action. The identification of those with the competency to act, at both the local and national levels, is thus crucial to the implementation of measures—but there is more to it than that.

The remainder of this essay discusses these issues. It is divided into four major parts. Section I considers ways in which prevention can be promoted at the national level, generally by central government. This includes consideration of the roles of legislation and exhortation, together with the various effects of publicity which, although often transitory, can be positive. In Section II, the role of the private sector is considered. This is a difficult area both politically and practically, but if opportunity reduction is to be taken seriously in crime control, it cannot be ignored. Section III looks at a number of issues associated with implementation, but generally at the community or more local level, and Section IV attempts to draw conclusions from what has been learned with some cautions for the future.

I. Promoting Situational Prevention at the National Level

At the national level, a major contribution to the implementation of crime prevention measures can be made through persuading others that they should act. Three main ways in which this can be accomplished are illustrated in the subsections that follow. First, governments can simply instruct. This has occurred in relation to the introduction, in rather different ways, of legislation to compel the installation of steering wheel locks in the United States and the Federal Republic of Germany versus its voluntary introduction in the United Kingdom. In each case falls in car theft followed, though in the United Kingdom, where the voluntary adoption covered only new cars, there was some displacement to older ones. The government in the United Kingdom has also used existing powers in relation to the substitution of prepayment coin meters installed by electricity and gas utilities, which had been shown to be attractive targets either for real burglary or for residents' theft in the guise of burglary.

Second, exhortation can be used. This is illustrated in the United Kingdom through the introduction by the police of a "Secured by Design" award for house builders, encouraging them to consider and incorporate crime prevention when they erect new dwellings.

Third, publicity can be given to actions the public, agencies, and community groups can take to reduce crime. Various victim-focused examples are given. Though individual items of publicity may not have a measurable effect, efforts to convey crime prevention messages to potential victims can have a cumulative impact. For instance, there have been changes in the security behavior of drivers in Britain, who have over the past twenty years come much less often to leave their cars with an unlocked trunk or door or an open window. So far as offenders go, persuasive publicity indicating that risks of being caught are increased forms an important mechanism through which much crime prevention work has its impact. This is illustrated by reference to studies of the effectiveness of a project installing video cameras in buses and another introducing high-density operation identification in a rural area in South Wales. Finally, a balance needs to be drawn between raising anxieties unnecessarily through publicizing risks and stimulating precautions by alerting people to what they can do to make themselves safer. The aim is to make sensible security behavior a routine, almost unconscious and unintrusive feature of everyday life.

A. Legislative Mandates

The most obvious means of implementing a crime prevention strategy is to instruct those with the competency to act to do so. But simple "instruction" requires either considerable authority in the sphere in question or "levers" that can be applied to those competent to act.

One of the most powerful examples of the use of authority is the introduction of legislation. This can require action by, for example, the manufacturers of goods or the providers of services, which may be against their best financial interests. An example of this arose in the early 1970s in relation to the introduction of steering column locks on motor vehicles. The history of the steering column lock and crime has been relatively well documented (Webb and Laycock 1992; Webb 1993) and demonstrates the way in which its introduction affected the pattern of motor vehicle crime in the United Kingdom, the United States, and the Federal Republic of Germany as it then was. In Germany, legislation was introduced that required the provision of steering column locks on all vehicles in the late 1960s. This applied not only to newly manufactured vehicles but also to all vehicles on the road at that time. The effect on the German car crime rates was a substantial reduction in the following years. This reduction was maintained until 1989 (see fig. 1) and is only now beginning to rise as a consequence not of temporary loss of vehicles, but of their permanent loss, probably caused by changes in political organization between Eastern and Western Europe.

The situation in the United States and in the United Kingdom was quite different. In these jurisdictions, steering column locks were introduced on new vehicles at the manufacturing stage (on a voluntary basis by the manufacturers in the United Kingdom), but not on the vast majority of vehicles already on the road. The consequence, as reported in relation to the United Kingdom, was a reduction in the vulnerability of new vehicles, but no reduction in the theft of vehicles generally, because the crimes were displaced to older cars. More recent data from the United Kingdom (Webb and Laycock 1992) suggest that the effect of the introduction of steering column locks in 1970 has now begun to penetrate the vast bulk of vehicles on the road and has reduced the temporary loss of cars, presumably for "joyriding" (taking account of the number of vehicles on the road).

The preceding example illustrates that legislative mandates can reduce offending when directed at the manufacturers of goods that are particularly vulnerable to crime. In the example discussed below, which relates to domestic burglary, legislation was already in existence for reasons other than burglary control, but following a crime pattern

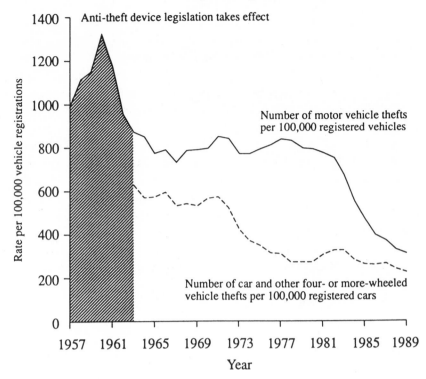

Fig. 1.—Rate of theft and unauthorized taking of motor vehicles in the Federal Republic of Germany, 1957–89, per 100,000 vehicle registrations. Source: Webb (1994).

analysis, it was possible to highlight the relevance of the legislation to prevention and to secure political commitment to national action.

The police in the United Kingdom had known for many years that prepayment coin meters are a source of crime-related problems. These meters were introduced by fuel companies as a means of collecting bad debts. The meter is installed in the home, and the occupant pays for the fuel as it is consumed. Payment is made in units of perhaps 50p or £1, and the meter can be adjusted to recover bad debts, while at the same time allowing the consumer to continue to have access to the fuel. They are, on the face of it, a reasonably helpful response by the fuel company to consumers with financial difficulties, and although their use was not popular with the companies themselves, they did provide a viable alternative to disconnection. The disadvantage from the fuel company's point of view is that meters have to be emptied regularly, because they accumulate considerable sums of money. The individuals emptying the meters were themselves vulnerable to attack during the course of collection, and this was made worse by the habit of the fuel companies of not emptying the meters more frequently than about every three months. A consequence of infrequent emptying was that the meters were an extremely lucrative source of ready cash in homes on many of the poorer housing estates, where the houses themselves were particularly vulnerable to burglary. Although the police were aware of this vulnerability, it was a popular belief among them that householders themselves broke into the meter and claimed a burglary (Hotson 1969). There is indeed some evidence that this happened, typically on a Wednesday or Thursday night, prior to payday, when the man of the house was presumed to need money to buy beer. The wife, with the responsibility for the children and for maintaining the home, was as much a victim in these circumstances as if she had been burglarized.

The consequence of this belief among police officers was a relative unwillingness to take the problem too seriously. In his analysis of this offense, Hill (1986) drew on evidence from victim support schemes and debt counselors that suggested that the frequency of "own goals," as they were called, was not as great as the police believed. Although the figures were difficult to measure accurately, it seemed a significant number of the burglaries were genuine. The status of these incidents as burglary, either self-inflicted or otherwise, was not, however, entirely the point in the context of the crime statistics. Hill showed that up to 40 percent of reported burglaries on some local authority housing estates were associated with losses from prepayment coin meters. When these figures were presented to the fuel companies, they were able to point out that although 40 percent was a significant problem for the police and arguably for the victims, these meters accounted for only, in the case of electricity, just over 7 percent of their customers and in the case of gas, just under 10 percent. They were also able to argue that until the beginning of the 1980s, the proportion of prepayment coin meter customers was declining as a matter of the fuel companies' policy. The economic difficulties of the 1980s, however, led to an increase in the number of customers with debt problems and therefore an increase in the number of meters being installed, particularly electricity meters. Although the proportion of householders using prepayment coin meters remained small, it was growing.

Despite the vulnerability of these meters to burglary, and their growing frequency of installation, there was little incentive for action on the part of the companies. This was because the installation of a prepayment coin meter was accompanied by an undertaking from the householder that the householder would make good the loss and would be responsible for repair of the meter should the meter money be lost or stolen. Victims were then caught in a vicious circle of having a bill to pay for fuel and up to £80, at the time of Hill's report, for the replacement, if necessary, of a standard electricity meter. This sort of situation caused enormous hardship, and it was not customary for the fuel companies to waive the charges. Thus, although the fuel companies, in the mid-1980s, were in the process of developing alternative means of collecting bad debts, including the development of token-operated meters, their implementation program was fairly relaxed.

When it came to trying to decide what could be done about this situation, it became clear that government departments other than the Home Office needed to become involved. The Department of Energy was responsible for certifying the use of all meters in domestic circumstances in the United Kingdom, and they discovered that legislation existed that would enable them to decertify any meter at any time. They could, therefore, had they chosen, have decertified all of the several million prepayment coin meters in use at that time and required the fuel boards to replace them forthwith. This issue was discussed at a seminar on crime prevention held by the Prime Minister of the day in the mid-1980s when the relative costs and benefits of the use of these meters and their relationship with crime was explained. The consequence of the seminar was that the Department of Energy, the government department with responsibility for fuel, was encouraged to take a rather more aggressive line with the fuel supply industry and required them to speed up the implementation program for the installation of token meters. This was done and led to a subsequent reduction of 49 percent in electricity meter breaks and a 20 percent reduction in breaks of gas meters (Cooper 1989).

This case study provides an example of the role that central government can play, and the levers it can exert, if armed with adequate data. The problem had been known to the police, of course, for many years, and they were well placed to provide supporting arguments for change. There are a number of reasons why they did not do so, including a lack of channels through which such communications could flow and to some extent a lack of expertise in analyzing and presenting data in this way. The information was far more readily available to the fuel companies where, whether or not the burglary or loss was reported to the police, it had to become known to the fuel company that there was a problem with their meter. It was of course an irritation to them rather than a serious problem, because of their requirement that the householder assume responsibility for the debts.

B. Exhortation

One of the constraints complained of by crime prevention officers in the United Kingdom (these are police officers with specialized skills in the areas of crime prevention) is that they do not have legislation in place comparable to that concerning fire prevention. Thus when buildings are being constructed, while there are very strict regulations regarding in-built fire security measures, there is no comparable requirement in relation to security. Indeed, fire and security requirements frequently conflict. For example, while the crime prevention interest might call for locked doors and windows, the fire regulations demand doors that can at least be opened from the inside and require external fire escape ladders which improve criminal access.

The approach in relation to crime prevention has of necessity, therefore, been characterized by carrots rather than by sticks. In the absence of legislation, the police themselves have introduced a system entitled "Secured by Design" that offers a design award to house builders if they meet minimum requirements laid down by the police and approved by architectural liaison officers (another police specialism—see Johnson, Shapland, and Wiles [1993] for a description of their work). This innovation, while lacking the force of legislation, encourages crime prevention considerations at the design stage that would otherwise not have occurred.

A similar initiative has been developed in relation to the design of parking lots in which the police in collaboration with the motoring organizations offer a design award (the more stars the better) according to the characteristics of the parking facility (Webb and Laycock 1992).

While there is some anecdotal evidence that these schemes do encourage implementation of security improvements, the police view is that they are inefficient and not universally adopted (Pengelly 1994). They are, nevertheless, unlikely to be replaced by legislative requirements in the United Kingdom in the immediate future because of a central government preference for deregulation and because in some cases, for example, in relation to car design, the United Kingdom government cannot introduce legislation without the agreement of the other member states of the European Union.

C. Publicity

Publicity can be used to persuade the public, agencies, and groups not only that they should take action but also what they should do and how it should be done. The relevance of publicity campaigns to crime prevention has, however, been questioned, and there are a number of difficulties both with their use and evaluation.

The role of publicity in crime prevention was extensively reviewed by Riley and Mayhew (1980) who noted that central government support for crime prevention publicity has had a number of aims. Although, at one level, a government-funded campaign is concerned to do no more than show official concern for crime or related issues, in the majority of cases it is intended to do more than that. Riley and Mayhew suggest four additional objectives: to encourage potential victims of crime to take better security precautions, to remind potential offenders of the consequences of their behavior, to reinforce and sustain the behavior of those who normally act in accordance with the advertised recommendations, and to shift attitudes or to create a climate of opinion in which legislation or other action may be introduced by central and local bodies to reduce crime.

These are illustrated in figure 2, which demonstrates that the encouragement of potential victims to take action can act as a method through which implementation can be increased. This should in theory result in a reduction in crime, as should reminders to potential offenders of the consequences of their actions. The reinforcement of present behavior clearly makes a contribution to the maintenance of security consciousness by potential victims and in a sense can be seen to encourage implementation in its continuance. While maintenance does not necessarily lead to a reduction in crime, it should contribute to its continued control in the sense of limiting rises.

Setting aside the declaratory function of showing official concern, publicity campaigns are generally oriented toward either potential victims or potential offenders.

1. *Victim-oriented Campaigns.* Victim-oriented campaigns are designed either to encourage potential victims to take preventive action or to reinforce the need for continued vigilance. In either case, the assumption is that crime rates will be affected as a result.

Looking at campaigns that aim to change the behavior of potential

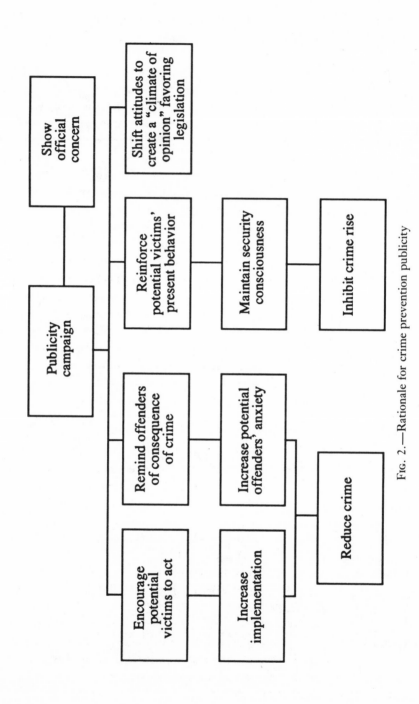

Fig. 2.—Rationale for crime prevention publicity

victims, the majority of which have been in relation to car theft and burglary, Mayhew and Riley note that such advertising has not been successful in promoting improved security behavior and cite a number of studies in support of this (Research Bureau Ltd. 1977; Burrows and Heal 1979; National Opinion Polls 1979; Riley and Mayhew 1980, chaps. 2 and 3). These results generally did not demonstrate changes in behavior following publicity campaigns. There was, however, evidence from some campaigns of increased knowledge of the recommendations in the campaign or a positive shift in attitude. This was seen as encouraging to the extent that changes in attitudes and awareness might lead to promises of behavioral change in the longer term. Although Riley and Mayhew concede that short-term evaluations may be incapable of measuring longer-term effects, or those apparent only after a lapse of time, they argued that the case for expecting such effects was not a strong one.

Subsequent evaluations have suggested grounds for greater optimism. To take the particular example of the extent to which drivers lock their vehicles on leaving the car, more recent evidence (Webb and Laycock 1992) suggests that drivers are now increasingly locking their vehicles. For example, data from a number of studies carried out over the last twenty years show that the proportion of cars found with an unlocked door or trunk, or an open window, declined from 22 percent in 1971 to 20 percent in 1977 to 16 percent in 1979 to 4 percent in 1992 (Webb and Laycock 1992). This has probably come about as a result of the view expressed by Marplan Limited (1973) that "regular if spasmodic exposure to crime prevention publicity acts in much the same way as water wearing away a stone." Not only has the publicity in relation to car security been relentless, it has been conducted in the context of publicized national reports showing an inexorable rise in car crime. Criminal statistics were made public on a quarterly basis in the United Kingdom until relatively recently (they are now made available on a six-month basis; Home Office 1989). So, although any one publicity campaign may be seen as making a relatively insignificant contribution to overall change, when seen as part of a program set in a context of rising crime, it can make a useful contribution to behavioral change.

Recent national campaigns have also been concerned to show official concern, to reinforce present behavior, to encourage potential victims to act, and to shift attitudes in preparation for legislative change—with greater emphasis on the last two aims. Victims or potential victims have been encouraged to take action in the context of national advertising and through the provision of a substantial handbook offering advice on crime prevention across a wide range of offenses. To date, over 6 million copies have been distributed together with an additional 13 million copies of a shorter version, largely through police forces but also following direct requests from members of the public.

The extent to which a campaign effectively achieves change in public attitudes is difficult to evaluate, but it is perhaps worth explaining the rationale underlying it. In the early 1980s, Home Office crime prevention publicity was associated with the image of an offender living outside the community—a shadowy figure portrayed as a running man who operated furtively and was to be feared. This image was changed during the mid-1980s at the time when Neighbourhood Watch was becoming popular in the United Kingdom. An advertising campaign was run at that time that suggested that the public needed to support the police in the "fight against crime," and a series of television and newspaper campaigns were run with supporting material for distribution through police forces and other crime prevention groups, which encouraged the public to act as the "eyes and ears of the police."

More recently, the key dimension to the advertising publicity related to the extent to which the public needed to work with the police and each other in preventing crime. Advertising both nationally and at local levels portrayed crime as an inherent part of life today. The community was asked to work together to prevent it and actively to support the police and other agencies including interagency groups. More particularly, members of the community were asked to take individual responsibility for crime prevention and to contribute to the development of communities within which, to quote the text, "my granny can walk the streets without being afraid."

These latest campaigns arguably better reflect the nature of crime as a fundamental part of the fabric of our society. Crime was presented as not inevitable but requiring individual action if it were to be prevented. This style of advertising was intended to shift the public's attitude away from the view that crime was something that the police ought to be left to deal with and far more toward the notion that we all share responsibility for it, both individually in terms of ensuring that we ourselves do not commit offenses, but also in the sense that we have responsibility for our children, neighbors, and those around, ensuring that we all work together to reduce offending behavior.

This type of publicity was also intended to create a national environment within which local initiatives could more effectively operate. Although it is exceptionally difficult to measure attitudinal changes in the general population, it is probably the case that the campaigns have had some measure of success. Surveys, for example, of the extent to which interagency groups operate at the local level suggest that there is far more activity under way now than there was even five years ago. Whether this activity is effective in reducing crime is a somewhat different matter, but there is some evidence to suggest that there is at least in place a framework within which appropriate crime prevention activity can be developed in some parts of the country (Safer Cities 1989–1993; Morgan 1991; Liddle and Gelsthorpe 1994*a*, 1994*b*).

Riley and Mayhew suggest that campaigns are more effective if they are more specific, both in the sense of targeting on a particular crime, but also in suggesting what specific activities would be helpful in reducing the probability of victimization. Taking this message forward, the 1992 national campaigns in the United Kingdom centered on reduction of car crime. The publicity associated with this campaign aimed to present car offenders as preying on the vulnerabilities of the community. The image used was a hyena, which market research had shown was not a popular animal, and which was seen as a scavenger and a cowardly acquisitive creature. The national advertising and associated publicity campaigns were particularly powerful in portraying this image, but again they were intended only as an umbrella for a great deal of local activity that was generated nationwide.

The question of whether, if implemented, a national campaign can be effective in reducing crime is almost impossible to answer. Whether an increase in implementation of a publicized measure leads to crime reduction depends not only on the extent to which implementation is achieved, which may be influenced by publicity, but also on the scope for displacement and the effectiveness of the measures proposed, which is not. So, for example, if the publicity campaign is directed at the general public and there is no evidence of which particular individuals choose to act on it, it is generally only overall crime levels that can be evaluated subsequently. This means, to take a concrete example, that if one million people started to lock their car doors as a consequence of a crime prevention advertising campaign, but if we do not know which one million people that was, while the campaign itself could be seen to have been effective in achieving its aims, it would not necessarily result in measurable reductions in crime levels because of the 21 million or so alternative vehicles available in the United Kingdom to which crime can be displaced. This also assumes that the act of locking the car is in itself an effective defense against theft. We know that this is not the case, as a variety of studies have shown to the rapidity with which offenders can break into vehicles (Webb and Laycock 1992; Spencer 1993).

Publicity, although not actively sought by any one agency, has also been instrumental in the widespread adoption of Neighbourhood Watch throughout the United Kingdom. There are now well over 100,000 schemes covering 4.1 million households (Dowds and Mayhew 1994), even though research results are at best equivocal in relation to the success of Neighbourhood Watch as a crime reduction measure (Titus 1984; Rosenbaum 1986; Bennett 1990). There are a number of difficulties associated with the interpretation of the Neighbourhood Watch figures which it is not appropriate to go into here. Suffice it to say that Neighbourhood Watch's *implementation* success in the United Kingdom at least is probably in part due to its facial validity. It makes sense to the public to suggest that watching out for crime is a useful and worthwhile activity; it also appeals to the public-spirited members of the community, particularly in the middle-class areas where it is known to flourish (Husain 1988). Neighbourhood Watch has undoubtedly been the flavor of the month, or perhaps the decade, and has caught on as a consequence.

2. *Offender-oriented Campaigns.* Riley and Mayhew quote a number of offender-oriented publicity campaigns that have led to some success. These campaigns were directed, however, at what was probably a relatively middle-class and relatively low-offending-rate population. For example, Riley and Mayhew cite television license campaigns and drinking-and-driving initiatives in the United Kingdom, Australia, Canada, and Holland as being particularly effective. One of the key elements of these offender-oriented campaigns has been not only to publicize changes in legislation but to imply that there is an increased risk of being caught. Publicity provides information about what is to happen and argues the case for the introduction of what might be regarded as initially unpopular measures—the enforcement of seat belt legislation being an example.

Offender-oriented publicity, when directed at individuals with potentially high risks of offending, can also be effective at the local level when targeted on a specific offense. Poyner's (1992) study of video cameras and bus vandalism provides an example. Poyner described the evaluation of the introduction of video cameras on buses in a northern town in the United Kingdom. The video cameras were introduced to reduce vandalism of buses, particularly by schoolchildren in the local area. After a pilot study in November 1985, involving one bus, more video buses were introduced. Significantly, this introduction was accompanied by a considerable amount of local publicity. In Poyner's view, one of the reasons for speed of improvement in behavior was that the video bus was well publicized. Two months after it began operation, Tyne TV's *Northern Life* magazine ran an item called "TV trap for vandals," which reported that the company was getting tough with hooligans. The initiative was also widely reported in local newspapers throughout the area. In parallel with this, a program of visits was introduced to local schools encouraging children to treat buses and the staff with more respect.

Initially, this scheme was called "our bus scheme," but after a few months, it was relaunched in a more developed form as "Bus Watch." In the course of promoting the scheme, the video bus would be taken to the school, and a short presentation to the children would describe the bus operation, the cost of damage to buses, and its implications. The children would then be taken for a ride on the bus to the bus depot where they would be shown around. They would also be taken through the bus wash, and the ride to the depot and the bus wash would be videoed. When the children were taken back to school, they were shown the video recording. In this way, it was hoped they would learn about the risk of being caught misbehaving on buses and the increased likelihood of their being seen to do so. 'Although this is not what is normally construed as "publicity," it does in practice have the same effect in heightening awareness and increasing sensitivity. Poyner's overall conclusion on the effectiveness of this scheme was that the number of seat repairs dropped dramatically to a third of what it had been during the previous year, and the number of cleaners had also been reduced by a similar proportion. The bus company claimed this was due to the video cameras and the program of school visits. As Poyner points out, the method by which these reductions were achieved was a combination of several powerful initiatives, including TV news features and the program of school visits. While it is not possible to disentangle the relative contribution of these different effects, including the effect of fairly rapid arrest and follow-up of young people caught in the act of bus vandalism, it is clear that collectively the measures led to a reduction in the problems.

A similar phenomenon was described in relation to the launch of operation identification in South Wales (Laycock 1986). In order to evaluate the operation identification scheme in this particularly rural part of Wales, the police were asked to ensure a high take-up rate. If they had not done so, it would have been extremely difficult to have demonstrated statistically or otherwise any reduction in the rates of burglary in the valleys. The police response was to visit every household in the area and to provide free of charge the necessary equipment for the marking of the property. The results subsequently showed an approximate 70 percent take-up rate across the area, including on the relatively high-crime central estate, which was a public housing area and which, according to the local police, housed the majority of young offenders and burglars. What subsequently proved remarkable was that burglary rates did indeed decline. As readers of this essay will know, there is relatively little evidence, nor is there a particularly persuasive rational reason, why operation identification should significantly reduce the rate of burglary. There is no evidence that marked goods are difficult to dispose of as a consequence, and there is no reason to suppose that households with marked property should be any more difficult to enter than others. What appeared to have happened in relation to the South Wales study was that in persuading people to mark their property, the police had spent a great deal of effort in coincidentally persuading them that it would be effective. They were not only, in the case of the central estate, persuading the householders of this, but were also persuading the burglars.

An additional feature to this study was that, prior to the introduction of the scheme, the loss of cash from prepayment coin meters (Hill 1986; Cooper 1989) was also significant. The subsequent reduction in this loss made no sense in the context of a property-marking scheme, although it made eminent sense when bearing in mind the police view that householders would steal from their own prepayment coin meter and subsequently claim to have been burglarized. By placing a property-marked sticker in their window, which was an indication of having joined the scheme, householders were acknowledging and accepting that they were thereby less vulnerable to burglary. It then subsequently became more difficult for them to argue that they had been burglarized in the course of losing the prepayment coin meter cash, a case of diffused benefits.

Further evidence in support of the power of local publicity arose in the year following the implementation of this initiative (Laycock 1992).

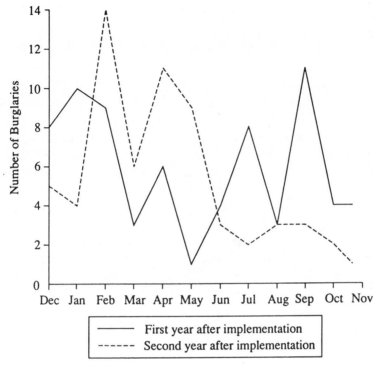

Fig. 3.—Burglaries by month, one and two years after implementation. Source: Laycock (1992).

The second-year follow-up data showed the burglary rates to have been reduced by an even greater extent than in the first year. This is illustrated in figure 3 which shows a drop mid-year and was coincident with the publication of the report of the first year's evaluation. This had been interpreted by the media as supporting property marking and had incurred extensive publicity on the estate itself. Publicity in this context, then, had an educative effect; it informed the local community that an "effective" scheme was in operation. This was indeed a self-fulfilling prophecy since, with the possible exception of some increased activity on the estate in June, it is difficult to see what could have led to the reduction in the second year other than the publicity.

D. Raising Fears

One of the more perplexing aspects of crime-related publicity is its effect on what is commonly called "the fear of crime" (Home Office 1989). There is a balance to be struck between worrying people about crime sufficiently to invoke action to protect themselves and worrying them unnecessarily and generating fear as a consequence. The worry would perhaps be less if the cure were more certain. To take an analogy with preventive medicine, we know the importance of washing our hands in the interest of preventing infection, but it is doubtful if many of us worry about the probability of infection when actually washing our hands. There are exceptions, and the clinical literature can point to obsessional neurotics whose behavior is abnormal in this respect, but the generality of people live their lives in a way compatible with the reduction in the probability of infection without unduly worrying about it. The trick to take in relation to crime prevention is to generate the same kind of sensible care in relation to one's property and oneself without simultaneously generating maladaptive anxiety. This does not necessarily mean living in a fortress, or curtailing lifestyles unduly for the majority of residents. For those in high crime areas, where this might be a consequence—it would indicate the need for targeted community and agency action to reduce risk, rather in the way that investment in the provision of drains and sewers provides a backdrop against which personal hygiene operates effectively.

II. Prevention in the Private Sector

There is much that the private sector can do to reduce both its own crime risks and to disable crimes that become possible because of the products and services provided. The prime concern of members of the private sector is to survive in a commercial environment and to maximize their profits. When it comes to expenditure of money and effort on crime prevention, these commercial considerations, of course, apply. If it is in the perceived economic best interests of companies to introduce crime prevention measures, they will do so. If to do so entails a net cost, private sector organizations will be loath to act. In some cases, however, the market can impede business cooperation in developing a collective good. Motor manufacturers, though for a long time able to ignore the vulnerability of their products to crime, are now having to take an interest in security, because insurance premiums in some cases may be influencing consumer decisions. They have not, however, found a way to work cooperatively in developing more effective devices, which would presumably on balance be cheaper. In other cases cooperation has been forthcoming and has been found to be highly effective. Prompted by huge losses, credit card companies have implemented measures that have quickly led to substantial reductions in those losses. The Tobacco Advisory Council has similarly achieved dramatic reductions in vehicle hijacks. Where economic forces do not demand attention to crime, however, businesses may continue to miss the economic benefit that could follow from crime prevention efforts. It was shown that in one record store high costs were being borne by the public purse because of the rate at which shoplifters were being arrested by store detectives and passed on to the police. Detailed analysis revealed cost-efficient crime prevention measures that also avoided the heavy calls on police time. It will not always be evident to those with a capacity to act that there are measures that they could take to reduce crime. Finally, clear channels of communication are needed between those dealing with crime and those in a position to do something about it. This is illustrated in the British Ministerial Group on Crime Prevention (1992) that is intended as a forum where government departments are asked to consider contributions they might make.

A. The Design of Goods and the Provision of Services

Motor manufacturers sell vehicles that are insecure and vulnerable to theft (Clarke and Harris 1992; Houghton 1992) in large part as a consequence of their design. But the cost of car crime is not borne by the manufacturers themselves, who are in a position to make cars less vulnerable at the design stage (Field 1993). The cost is carried instead by the car owner, either directly or through the increased costs of insurance. Because the insurance costs are spread and car crime although high is still a relatively low risk (Houghton 1992), the cost of crime, or at least the cost of any one crime, has not until relatively recently led to pressure for crime prevention measures. There is now an interesting dialogue between manufacturers and insurers: insurers are pinpointing particularly high-risk performance cars for punitive premiums while manufacturers are arguing that good quality security hardware fitted during manufacturing should attract reduced premiums.

As a consequence of the very high levels of car crime and the clear argument that to increase security on vehicles at the manufacturing stage would reduce it, meetings were held between government officials and motor manufacturers with the aim to encourage manufacturers toward greater action in this area. It became clear almost immediately that the manufacturers were in competition with each other (perhaps not surprisingly). The notion, therefore, that they might cooperate in developing a more secure vehicle for the better good of the

British public, or at least for the better good of the British crime figures, was quite foreign to them. This opened up two possible ways forward. First, the inevitable competition between manufacturers could be acknowledged, and exploited, if the public themselves could be persuaded to demand better security. This would then put security as an issue on the marketing agenda that would make manufacturers compete for the better-secured car: market forces would thereby be invoked in developing and improving car security. Second, the British public might be assumed to remain relatively indifferent to car crime risks (e.g., Mayhew and Hough 1983), not least because they are currently protected by insurance premiums. This would have left the manufacturers free to cooperate and to develop corporately, and at presumably considerably less expense, a sensible and cost-effective mechanism for securing the vehicle and its contents that could be introduced across the board—but there would be no incentive for them to do so other than public-spiritedness. The outcome was basically that market forces prevailed, not least because the car crime figures rose to such an extent that they began to affect insurance premiums for certain high-value vehicles. This emphatically introduced the need for better security, and the demand for it from certain sections of the public. The insurance industry had got to the point where they would refuse to insure vehicles in certain areas or of a particularly high-risk design. Although legislation has to remain a possibility in relation to improving the design of cars at the motor manufacturing stage, there are considerable practical difficulties stemming from the requirement to do so throughout Europe, with a political disinclination toward regulation generally. At present, however, the manufacturers are collectively inclined of their own volition to improve vehicle security—but on an individual rather than a collective basis.

The motor manufacturers are, nevertheless, removed from the victims of car crime. They can be contrasted with the banks, U.K. building societies, and other financial institutions whose development and handling of the credit system has brought them slightly closer to the victims of poor design. The cost of credit card fraud and its consequences have been reviewed by Levi, Bissell, and Richardson (1991) who carried out an exhaustive analysis of credit card fraud in the United Kingdom using data provided by the financial institutions themselves. They reviewed the options for prevention at a time when the losses to the banks and building societies—which they could of course, and were, passing on to their customers—had reached an unacceptable level. The relative proximity of the banks to the victims of the fraudulent use of check and credit cards meant that the banks were more inclined to take the problem seriously and to act on it; they were also prepared to act collectively. Following the publication of Levi's report, meetings were held in the United Kingdom with representatives of the financial institutions to discuss the report's implications. It is probably fair to say that the financial institutions were on the brink of action on their own behalf because losses had reached a level that they were collectively finding it difficult to pass on to the consumer, but nevertheless, the meetings initiated by central government and the publication of the Levi report (with its associated publicity) added considerable impetus to their work. It was announced in 1992 that the banks and building societies were to invest, collectively, £500 million over five years in order to develop improved methods of countering fraud through better-designed systems. The payoff began immediately. The loss from plastic card fraud in the United Kingdom for 1992 had been £165 million, but fell to £129.8 million in 1993.

B. Private Sector Organizations as Victims of Crime

Action on prevention is far more visible where the competent institutions are themselves the victims of the offending. In a wide-ranging review of crime prevention initiatives from business in the United Kingdom, Burrows (1991) was able to provide a number of illustrations where either singly or collectively companies had taken effective action to combat crime, largely of their own volition, across a wide field including the protection of assets in transit, designing out fraud, responding to violence, and the general management of crime risk at the workplace. Some of these initiatives had been in operation for a number of years, and it was possible to demonstrate considerable cost savings as a consequence. But in his review, Burrows came across a number of difficulties. For example, companies voiced considerable skepticism that openness about crime problems could achieve anything positive and were also concerned that it could risk alerting potential criminals to vulnerabilities or lead to difficulties with their shareholders and the city. They were also concerned that registering and publicizing the details of precautions taken against crime would render them invalid or that disclosure could reduce the competitive edge they had achieved by the introduction of effective preventive measures. Most obvious, however, many companies were unable to provide supportive evidence of the efficacy of the measures introduced. The companies collaborating in the work reported by Burrows came to terms with the difficulties that he outlined, although not in some cases without obtaining authority from relatively senior sectors of the organization. It is perhaps worth noting examples from Burrows's work as illustrative of what can be achieved.

At a general level, Burrows was able to report an increased sensitivity on the part of industrialists and commercial organizations in relation to crime and crime risk. This was particularly true of the larger corporations which were able to provide operating companies with in-house crime audits undertaken by specialists in the parent or holding company. The risk assessment and associated crime analysis allowed for a targeting of crime prevention developments. Another common route being pursued by many of the major companies consulted in the course of Burrows's work was the integration of security systems and controls both with each other (e.g., merging closed-circuit TV, alarms, and electronic surveillance) and with other trading systems. This trend was made feasible by a range of technological developments but also, more significantly, illustrated the extent to which security was becoming built-in, rather than an add-on afterthought, in the operating environments of the companies involved. Appropriate data analysis, therefore, combined with the promotion of awareness in staff and devolved responsibility, had collectively led to tangible gains in crime control.

One of the encouraging features of the work reported by Burrows was the increasing extent to which companies ostensibly in competition with each other were prepared to pool information and resources in the interest of reduced crime across the board. An example arose in the late 1960s, when the Tobacco Advisory Council achieved substantial success in tackling the major crime losses being sustained by the tobacco industry. One of the unique characteristics associated with the success of the Tobacco Advisory Council was its early decision to pool all reports of U.K. crime incidents experienced by the industry. Funding was provided for the analysis of these data that enabled the Advisory Council to monitor the performance of distribution companies, providers of alarms, and other security equipment, police forces, and indeed company anticrime strategies. It put the group in a powerful position in establishing a crime prevention program. Their experience in tackling vehicle hijacks during the 1980s illustrates the way in which this operated. In 1983, an increased number of vehicle hijacks prompted the Advisory Council to commission the development and evaluation of antihijack devices. These devices were fitted to vehicles operated by one of the largest independent carriers for the industry, but attacks were displaced to other fleets. It was possible to trace the extent of displacement, and, because of its extent, the antihijack devices had little impact on overall industry losses. This pattern changed in 1988, with the development and industrywide adoption of data track (a device that pinpoints with accuracy the location of any hijacked vehicle), which has reduced the number of attacks across the board. Burrows reports that hijacks of tobacco, which typically net a loss of at least £80,000 per incident, were reduced from twenty-two in 1988 to fourteen in 1989, four in 1990, and one in the first quarter of 1991. Similarly effective corporate action is reported by Burrows in relation to other commercial and industrial enterprises.

A further example of a private sector organization as crime victim arose in relation to a study reported by Ekblom (1986*b*) describing the early stages of a crime analysis exercise concerning shop theft. Ekblom's starting point was police data in one of the main police stations in central London with responsibility for policing Oxford Street, a well-known and very busy shopping center. Examination of the shop theft figures from the central police station showed that nearly 40 percent of arrests were coming from one relatively small store, HMV, on the main street selling recorded music. The records and cassettes were kept "live" within the boxes and sleeves on the shop floor. This was done because of the lack of storage space and the exceptionally high turnover of goods, which meant that more staff would have had to have been provided had the usual "masterbag" system been in operation. The crime control strategy adopted by the store was to provide extensive store detective coverage. In practice, this meant that a number of store detectives operated in the shop and arrested offenders who were then taken to the local police station for "processing." The outcome of this policy was the exceptionally high level of shop theft in the store and unfortunately a very high "recruitment" of young people into the criminal justice system, many of whom were first offenders. This could be contrasted with arrests on the remainder of Oxford Street where the majority of shop thieves tended to be older and frequently of non-British origin—there were many tourists, for example.

The initial response of the store to Ekblom's arrest findings was that it was an unfortunate consequence of their marketing strategy, but not something they could easily rectify. They argued that to change their marketing style by removing cassettes and records from the shop floor would have serious consequences for their turnover and was not acceptable on commercial grounds. It was nevertheless clear that something needed to be done about this situation, not least because, as Ekblom pointed out, the cost of the strategy was largely borne by the public purse in processing offenders at approximately £100 per head. This, Ekblom argued, at least raised the question of the extent to which this practice was acceptable in public policy terms.

Having clearly highlighted the problem, the police then informed the store that unless acceptable action was taken, they would exercise their discretion to caution all offenders following arrest and immediately release them. This was clearly not in the interests of the store managers who were then prepared to consider alternative solutions. As a first step in seeking alternative means of control, the store crime figures were analyzed in detail, although before this could be done it proved necessary to put in place a whole new data collection system with the help of the store detectives (Ekblom 1986b). The data analysis illustrated the vulnerable areas of the store and led to a series of proposals for implementation that kept the store's central marketing policy in place. These measures were implemented as described by Ekblom and subsequently evaluated. The results were reported briefly in Mayhew (1988) and are reproduced in table 1 below. They showed that the average monthly arrest figures in the store fell by 41 percent from 113 arrests per month averaged over two years before the implementation of measures to an average of 67 over the twelve months following implementation.

TABLE 1

Average Monthly Arrest Figures for Shop Theft Before and After
Implementation of Preventative Measures

	Average Monthly Arrest Figures		
	Before December 1983– November 1985	After November 1985– December 1986	Percent Change
HMV music shop	113	67	−41
Oxford Street stores	357	343	−4
Oxford Street stores less music shops	356	330	−8
Other central area	213	195	−8

SOURCE.—Mayhew (1988).

This case study illustrates a number of points: First, the "natural" method of crime control used by the store managers was not preventive, but was dependent on detection, and the managers felt that they had good commercial reasons for this. Second, when challenged by the police to look again at the crime control options, there was a total lack of good data available on which to base a rational crime management strategy. Third, the establishment of a crime analysis system did lead to commercially viable options that, when implemented, were effective. This illustrates the scale of the national challenge if preventive methods of crime management are to replace the first-thought detective methods that are heavily dependent on the backup of the criminal justice system and that, deterrence notwithstanding, address offending after it has occurred.

C. Coordinating Prevention in the Private Sector

The implications of analyses of this kind for the police and other agencies associated with the criminal justice system include the need for training both to be alert to the problems and to present them in an actionable manner and also the need for channels of communication through which information of this kind can be routed. Although any individual police officer at the local level could have told his immediate superior of the difficulty with prepayment coin meters, for example, effective preventive action could be initiated only at a national level working through the major fuel suppliers. This requires extremely efficient communication from local police force areas up through their command structure to central government. It is then for the center to package and present information to the industry, and also not infrequently to other government departments, in such a way that corrective action can be taken.

In order to facilitate this process, a ministerial group on crime prevention was established in the United Kingdom, following central government crime prevention seminars in the mid-1980s. This group, chaired by a Home Office minister with responsibility for crime prevention, has met regularly with colleagues in other government departments over a number of years. They have reviewed a variety of issues associated with the prevention of crime, including violence and social crime prevention, and completed blocks of work on the extent to which each particular government department's policies may or may not be criminogenic. For example, the group initiated a review of the incidence of and methods used in social security fraud and made a number of recommendations for its reduction (Home Office 1992). The group represents what might be seen as a high-level interagency working group on crime prevention with all the conflicts and difficulties associated with these groups. It does, nevertheless, provide an almost unique opportunity to raise the profile of crime prevention within other government departments since underlying the discussions at ministerial level is a whole series of meetings and exchanges of papers at official level. This gives Home Office staff the opportunity to discuss crime and crime prevention with colleagues in other government departments.

III. Implementation and Communities

Sections I and II have shown that there is much that can and has been done nationally in the United Kingdom and within the private sector to prompt the implementation of crime prevention measures that have scope for widespread effectiveness. There is also a need to put in place strategies to address crime issues that are important in particular localities or that are less susceptible to national action. There are important local dimensions to many crime problems, including burglary, racial attacks, and intimidation in high-crime neighborhoods. For many more general problems, such as domestic violence, it will be necessary to develop local responses where effective services can be provided for those at risk of victimization or repeat victimization. Even where broader responses are possible along the lines discussed, for example, prompting improvements in the security of motor vehicles, local action will be needed where the problems are most acute. Some of the problems and opportunities here are rather different from those already considered.

The keys to successful local crime prevention are to be found in no single agency. Multiagency cooperation is required, and the potential benefits can be illustrated by reference to the Kirkholt Burglary Prevention Project. Yet, it has also been argued that there are obstacles to the development of partnerships and difficulties in their delivering effective initiatives. The British Home Office's time-limited Safer Cities Programme represents an effort to establish arrangements for a partnership approach in relatively high-crime local authorities. These have achieved some success in catalyzing longer-term strategic approaches in which local agencies have been drawn into and become more confident in what can be achieved through interagency work. For individual projects to operate effectively, there needs to be both a clearly articulated purpose and rationale for the measures to be introduced and provision for implementation that is sensitive to the interests and motivations of those from participating agencies. Success is important in maintaining commitment, and poorly thought out or partially implemented projects risk conspicuous failure and loss of confidence. Finally, the effectiveness of most crime prevention measures fades over time, and this should be expected. This means that attention should be given to points at which new impetus is needed. Overselling what realistically can be achieved again jeopardizes credibility and hence the enthusiasm of agencies to play their part.

A. The Rationale for Multiagency Responses

Routine activities theory points out that for an offense to take place, *likely offenders*, *suitable targets*, and the *absence of capable guardians* must converge in time and space (Cohen and Felson 1979; Felson 1994). High-crime communities are those where these three conditions are concentrated (Farrell 1993, in this volume), and crime prevention requires the removal or reduction of one or more of them. Greater success may be expected where programs are implemented that affect all three, though efforts to achieve this will not always be practicable.

In order to plan and implement well-targeted crime prevention measures affecting likely offenders, suitable targets, and capable guardianship, differing local agencies need to act cooperatively, and they need to involve the local community. The various agencies have differing information relevant to understanding the extent and nature of crime problems. They are also differently placed to alter the crime conditions identified in routine activities theory. None has effective leverage on all three.

The Kirkholt Burglary Prevention Project illustrates what can be achieved when there is successful interagency work (Forrester, Chatterton, and Pease 1988; Forrester et al. 1990; Pease 1991; Hope, in this volume). The work took place on a public housing estate of some 2,280 dwellings in the North of England. The police were able to provide initial data on the burglary problem, though this was supplemented by the collection of extensive additional information. The police were not, however, in a position to implement required measures directly. By installing alternatives to coin meters, electricity and gas utilities removed suitable targets. By promptly repairing and upgrading the security of burglarized premises, the local authority reduced the suitability of those targets evidently found most attractive by motivated offenders—repeat victimization had been found by crime analysis to be a particular problem. By establishing cocoons (mini neighborhood watches) around the recently victimized, capable guardianship was improved by the local community. Finally, by developing programs for local burglars, efforts were made to reduce the supply of motivated offenders. The upshot was a reduction to zero in repeat victimization in the first seven months of the project and a 75 percent reduction in the overall burglary rate over three years. The package of Kirkholt measures appears to have functioned synergistically to affect the various conditions for burglary to achieve its apparent dramatic effects.

B. Commitment and Coordination in Partnerships

If local crime problems are to be addressed effectively, individual agencies have to be persuaded that there are preventive actions that they could take and that they should take them. They also need to be convinced that they should participate in multiagency partnerships, in which they will act cooperatively with others to address problems systematically.

This partnership approach to crime prevention has been advocated by the British government in two interdepartmental circulars (Home Office Circulars 8 [Home Office 1984] and 44 [Home Office 1990]) and still is promoted by the Home Office (Home Office 1993). Indeed, part of the initial rationale for the Kirkholt project, which received some government funding, was to show what could be achieved from interagency work following Circular 8/84.

A first problem in promoting interest and action concerns the cost-effectiveness of crime prevention efforts. Crime prevention can be exceptionally expensive. The lessons learned on the design side, for example, have been spelled out by a number of writers (Newman 1972; Poyner 1983). In some parts of both Europe and the United States, the remedy for some appallingly designed public housing estates of the 1960s has been to demolish them. Solutions to crime on this scale are difficult to justify in cost-effectiveness terms, and other reasons are likely to be invoked for this kind of response. Design changes can, however, be made in less extreme cases, and are often introduced in the United Kingdom under a variety of schemes for improving public sector housing estates. Some of these schemes have a crime prevention spin-off, although this is in general marginal to their primary purpose and often difficult to demonstrate (Coleman 1985; Hope and Foster

1992; Safe Neighbourhoods Unit 1993; Hope, in this volume). The possible crime prevention payoff on its own is thus unlikely frequently to persuade local authorities that it is in their interests to implement radical physical redesign programs.

It has, however, proved easier to persuade agencies, whose major mission is not concerned with crime, to devote resources to crime prevention where the payoff, financial or otherwise, is more certain. Where patterns of repeat victimization, for example, indicate that existing victims are at significantly greater risk, those organizations with a concern for the quality of life of residents may be persuaded that diversion of resources to their protection can be warranted because the funds are well targeted. The success in Kirkholt in obtaining an initial £75,000 to provide a rapid repair service to residents is a case in point. Research on patterns of repeat victimization suggests increasingly that, as Farrell and Pease (1993) put it, a focus on victims helps get the crime prevention grease to the crime squeak (see also Farrell, in this volume).

In Nottingham, a city with a population of about 300,000, a "crime audit" was undertaken to estimate the financial and other costs of crime (Peat Marwick 1991). It found, for example, that city center avoidance because of fear of crime could be costing the retail sector £12 million in turnover, 210 jobs, and £0.84 million profit. Within the leisure sector, a turnover forfeit of £12 million was estimated with a loss of 442 jobs. The overall review of costs has been used to demonstrate that it is in the interests of business and the local authority as well as the police to cooperate in crime prevention.

A further problem for achieving the required coordination of local crime prevention efforts is leadership. Without leadership, crime prevention work is apt to drift. The various Home Office notices and guidance circulated in relation to crime prevention failed to indicate a lead agency. There were a variety of reasons for this, not least that no particular agency stood out as being clearly appropriate. The police, for example, had a considerable amount of relevant information and no little expertise in relation to crime and crime problems, but they had no control over the various criminogenic elements in the society that they were policing, that is, in Engstad and Evans's (1980) terms, they were neither responsible for crime nor competent to act in its prevention. More relevant in terms of competency are architects and designers, banks, local government, sectors of commerce, and industry, all with the ability and competency to take preventive action, but lacking either a general remit to do so, motivation, expertise, or resources.

There is, nevertheless, an argument for the local authority to be seen as the lead agency, not least related to the fact that they have greater control of resources at the local level. This argument was put forward by an independent group established by the Home Office to look specifically at the issue (Morgan 1991). There are, however, also arguments against it (Liddle and Gelsthorpe 1994a, 1994b). Local authorities could not be held responsible for crime or all solutions to it, since as we have seen, national developments play a part, and national action is needed. In addition, the local authorities do not have all the information necessary to tackle crime (although in the interagency context they could obtain it, such as it is, from the police or others). Furthermore, they arguably do not have the expertise at this stage in their development. This, though, is being remedied, in the United Kingdom at least, first by an increasing number of university courses providing training in crime prevention and associated community safety techniques; second by advice being provided both by the Home Office itself (Home Office 1993) and by independent consultants, notably Crime Concern; and third through the experience being gained by a wide range of local authorities that have chosen to make community safety part of their work.

A final difficulty facing coordination concerns the achievement of cooperation among partners. While there may be initial and superficial enthusiasm, this often masks real problems in practice both at the strategic and at the practice level (Pearson et al. 1992). Large multi-agency groups are apt to be quite fragile. There are often histories of suspicion, ignorance, stereotyping, and noncooperation to overcome. The missions of differing agencies do not always at first sight harmonize well together. Crime prevention is often one of a number of concerns, and commitment to it has to compete for time, attention, and resources with what are often perceived to be higher priorities. Some agencies, particularly those from the voluntary sector, are often relatively weak and inexperienced. Ordinary members of the community, when they become involved, frequently find the ways of formal organizations alien and difficult to work with (Webb 1993). Community representatives are, in turn, often found awkward and narrowly self-interested by those in statutory agencies. Partnerships are easily undermined through the noncooperation of key personnel from key agencies (Foster and Hope 1993; Tilley and Webb 1994). In practice in Britain, the local authority and the police will characteristically be necessary players in any crime prevention partnership. If not obliged to take part, members are, of course, free to refuse to join or to withdraw or to undermine what is being attempted (Liddle and Gelsthorpe 1994*b*). This means that successful crime prevention work is more than usually dependent on the qualities and commitments of individuals taking part in it, in particular those from the key agencies whose position makes them extremely powerful. It is sometimes found that within smaller multiagency groups it is easier to maintain effective communication and commitment (Tilley and Webb 1994).

C. Community Safety Strategies/Safer Cities

In 1986, the Home Office set up the Five Towns Initiative, which ran for eighteen months. This involved establishing multiagency steering committees and putting locally seconded coordinators in each project area. The idea was that coordinated interagency crime prevention efforts would be stimulated. Though there was no formal evaluation at the time (see Liddle and Bottoms 1991), the experience was considered sufficiently encouraging to establish the larger and more generously resourced Safer Cities Programme in 1988.

Twenty Safer Cities were established between 1988 and 1991, in relatively deprived local authority areas in England (see Ekblom and Pease, in this volume). Each was given an initial three years to run, following which there would be a review. For each area, the government funded a locally based coordinator, an assistant and a secretary, allocating also £250,000 per year for initiatives to be chosen by those coordinators in consultation with a local interagency steering group. It was hoped that the grant moneys would act as a useful pump-priming source to generate further sponsorship and support at the local level. This was, in effect, what happened in a number of the Safer Cities areas (see Safer Cities 1989–93).

These Safer Cities projects were intended to act both as a focus for interagency organization and planning of local crime prevention work and as initiators of individual schemes designed to attack particular crime problems. By the end of March 1994, 3,500 schemes had been funded at a total cost of £21.5 million, to which some £15 million had been added from other sources.

The whole Safer Cities program is currently being evaluated (Ekblom 1992; also Ekblom and Pease, in this volume), and reports will be available in due course. Individual schemes launched by each of the twenty projects have also been assessed to varying extents either by the coordinators themselves or by associated academics and consultants.

Tilley (1992) reports the success of the various projects in creating interagency strategic approaches to crime prevention at the local level. He describes the way in which the introduction of a "stranger" into each project area, in the person of the Safer Cities coordinator, has been particularly well suited to the initiation of crime prevention activity within an existing structure where agencies were not always operating to best corporate effect for reasons already given. Tilley describes five stages in the process of generating an effective community safety strategy, some components of which are relevant to implementation and the generation of local resources. In their capacity as "strangers," the coordinators were able to stand aside from the local interagency conflicts and difficulties and to gain the trust of agencies independently. This comparative independence, together with the funding that they brought and the expertise that they had in relation to crime prevention, enabled them to generate effective strategies within the communities in which they operated with the support of the local people. As expertise was gained locally, the coordinators became less relevant to the local action, and the confidence of the communities developed sufficiently for them, Tilley speculates, to be no longer needed after three to four years. The way in which this process has developed illustrates the importance of training at the local level for the agencies wishing to join together to combat crime. The Safer Cities coordinators had acted as an effective catalyst and exemplar of what could be done. They were not only a resource in themselves, but brought with them and were able to generate financial sponsorship and other support in the form of personnel at the local level.

One of the many lessons learned from the experience of the Safer Cities program is the need for positive and supportive messages in relation to crime prevention at the local level. The morale of local people, particularly in high-crime areas where traditionally apathy has been seen to dominate, is vital if crime prevention measures are to be effectively implemented. Those from formal agencies beginning their involvement in interagency crime prevention work need early successes to be recognized if their enthusiasm is to be maintained. These needs are to some extent reflected in the various progress reports of Safer Cities, which may be seen as overoptimistic and uncritical. The objective rigor required by an academic evaluation of a project can often be received as criticism, dampening that enthusiasm and commitment of those involved which is essential if projects are either to be launched or to operate successfully. There is a fine balance to be drawn. Local evaluations need to be sensitively tuned to what can realistically be achieved by the measures implemented in the contexts in which schemes are operating and to be oriented to identifying points where corrective action can be taken. Bald conclusions to the effect that "it didn't work" are both discouraging and unhelpful to practitioners.

There is a further reason for overstating potential and achievement. Hyping accomplishments is not only unsurprising and a vehicle for creating and maintaining enthusiasm but also part of what leads to success itself. Within Kirkholt, part of the strategy was to convey positive, success messages to the local newspaper to improve the community's confidence (Forrester et al. 1990). As indicated above, a key part of the success found in Laycock's property-marking experiment in South Wales related to the effects of reports of the work (Laycock 1992). W. I. Thomas's famous aphorism certainly goes for crime prevention: "The definition of the situation is real in its consequences."

That said, there are certainly dangers in massaging findings on effectiveness to create the illusion of success. This happened within the Safer Cities Programme for the reasons given here, notably in regard to high-cost, flagship projects that had been used to encourage commitment and contributions from key local agencies. The risk is, of course, that apparent results will be taken at face value and time and additional resources wasted on more of the same.

D. *Planning and Implementing Individual Projects*

One of the problems for Safer Cities was, ironically, the very attraction of the grant money. Many groups were keen to take advantage of the funds and to represent their activities in ways that highlighted potential crime preventive consequences. Applications for funds for after-school clubs are an example, of which there were several that were successful. There may be many reasons for funding after-school clubs, and there may be many sources of funds. It did not prove difficult to frame funding applications to emphasize crime prevention. Yet, this can be expected to be a by-product in only rather particular situations, and it is likely that if this were to be part of their aim, modifications in targeting and service delivery might be needed.

Other more explicit crime prevention measures, with surface validity, have been uncritically adopted widely, with insufficient attention to what they might potentially achieve in any particular area. Neighbourhood Watch is a case in point. It has been very widely implemented with high initial enthusiasm, most commonly in low-crime areas (Husain 1988; Mayhew, Elliott, and Dowds 1989). Evangelism on behalf of Neighbourhood Watch has then apparently led to widespread apathy and indifference (McConville and Shepherd 1992). It is not surprising that failures to achieve crime reduction have been found (e.g., Bennett 1990).

What then is needed for the planning and implementation of successful crime prevention projects? The concerns that scientific realist evaluation methodology have for "contexts," "measures," "mechanisms," and "outcome patterns" (Pawson and Tilley 1994; see also Ekblom and Pease, in this volume) may give some clues. Let us return to after-school clubs.

First, what problem are they intended to address? Put another way, what crime prevention outcome patterns might they aim for? There is no point in implementing a crime prevention measure where there is no relevant crime problem. Crime prevention problems after-school clubs might address could include reducing the risks to children who would otherwise be on the streets after school, antisocial behavior of children at school, or crimes and incivilities that might be perpetrated by children in the time between leaving school and receiving care by parents or guardians. And so on. Unless there is a clear definition of the crime problems to be addressed, with evidence for them, it will not be possible to work out what to introduce or how to implement it.

Second, what is it about what after-school clubs do that might help solve the crime problem? That is, what crime prevention mechanisms could they be made to trigger that might produce the problem solution aimed at? After-school clubs may do all sorts of things that might affect crime problems. They might simply contain children at a time when they could otherwise be misbehaving. Those running after-school clubs are then both acting as capable guardians within the group and reducing the supply of motivated offenders elsewhere. A reduction in the supply of motivated offenders might be effected in other ways also. Hence, workers might provide the children with liked and trusted adult role models, where parents are absent or inadequate and teachers disliked as authority figures merely managing difficult children while teaching the rest. After-school clubs might act as bridges between the street and the school, showing children the positive side of authority and learning and reincorporating the disaffected into mainstream schooling. After-school clubs might establish new peer groups among children, away from the delinquents on the streets. After-school clubs may provide valued activities and valued regard from significant others which children would be loath to forgo through misbehavior. And so on.

Third, is the *situation* in which the after-school club is intended to work one in which the crime prevention mechanisms can be triggered and which can be expected to be effective in dealing with the crime problem? The context is crucial. It will comprise the mix of children who are recruited to the after-school club (including age, sex, race, class, culture, and previous behavior), the staff who are employed or who volunteer, the facilities provided, the numbers attending, the staff-child ratio, the stability of the staffing group, the relationship the club has with the school, the periods when the club is open and closed, the traveling times and arrangements for the children to go home, and so on. What aspects of the context matter depends on the mechanisms to be triggered in relation to the problems to be addressed.

It might, finally, also be that after-school clubs could be criminogenic. Nondelinquent children may be introduced to delinquent ones and the influence may be negative as well as positive, producing as well as removing motivated offenders. Attendance may mean that children go home in the dark, where they can misbehave with less chance of being seen by capable guardians. After-school clubs might be places where children are victimized either by bullies among the children or by predatory workers.

None of this peroration about after-school clubs involved much more than common sense. Planning and implementing successful crime prevention projects does, however, require the active deployment of common sense. It requires the systematic identification and diagnosis of crime problems and the tailoring of measures to deal with them effectively. There is no sense in deciding that after-school clubs are to be established as crime prevention devices or are not to be implemented because they do or do not work as general crime prevention devices. The issue is whether in relation to a given local crime prevention problem after-school clubs can be established and run in ways that enable them to trigger mechanisms, which will on balance produce the intended crime problem reduction outcomes commensurate with the effort and expenditure required without counterbalancing dysfunctional side effects. If they can be useful in crime prevention, implementation amounts to so operating them that the context provided most effectively triggers crime prevention mechanisms and avoids triggering crime production ones. And that will require considerable skill and sensitivity.

The Kirkholt Burglary Prevention Project is instructive precisely because here common sense of the kind just described was applied systematically (Forrester, Chatterton, and Pease 1988; Forrester et al. 1990; Farrell and Pease 1993). The initial research clarified the extent and nature of the problem. The local police inspector who first led the project made himself very familiar with the estate and the service providers within the estate. In these ways much was learned of the problems to be addressed and the background context for the initiative. Measures within that context were adopted that had some prospect of effectively triggering burglary prevention mechanisms. The project team were also alert to changes in the nature of the problem and in the context of their work, responding to emerging problems and taking advantage of new opportunities. The achievements are apparent.

The argument so far suggests that in planning crime prevention measures, some theory is needed to explain why they are expected to have some impact, though the theory need not necessarily be abstract, abstruse, or academic. Unless there is some "theory" that addresses the linked issues of measure, context, mechanism, and expected outcome pattern, to give the project a clear purpose, it will be difficult to target and implement effectively. Moreover, without an articulated theory it will not be possible to find out whether there has been "theory failure," as Rosenbaum, Lewis, and Grant (1986) put it.

There is a particular lack of clarity of purpose in relation to some social measures dedicated to crime prevention, which are of special relevance in the context of communities. This is partly because of a relative theoretical vacuum in the area of social crime prevention that precludes any clear statement of *why* any particular initiative should be effective. To take a concrete example, in the United Kingdom at present "wheels projects" are popular and are intended to divert young car crime offenders from further offending. They are "marketed" to those with the resources to fund them as a means by which car crime can be reduced. What is not clear, however, is the mechanism through which they might operate. It is possible to speculate, for example, that they are intended to divert known offenders from car crime and into more acceptable activity. Unfortunately, however, the usual recruitment mechanism into the schemes is through the probation service where known and relatively high-rate offenders are to be found. While it may be the case that in the better schemes these particular individuals are diverted from further offending, there is no evidence and it is difficult to see how there could be, that car crime in its entirety could be reduced as a consequence of these schemes. They are addressed at known high-rate offenders, possibly coming to the end of their careers, and not at the recruitment end of the chain when these offenders are first becoming involved in car crime. The only sense in which many of these "wheels project" could be effective is if they are reducing the reconviction rate of known offenders. It is, therefore, not sensible to market such schemes as likely to reduce car crime in a local area, although this tends to be what has been happening and as a consequence of which it is quite likely that the schemes will at some point be judged not to have worked.

Even where projects do have clarity of purpose—where the problem is known and understood and measures are introduced in a context in which crime prevention mechanisms will be triggered—this does not mean, of course, that they will be fully implemented.

Hope and Murphy (1983) report the implementation failures of a project to reduce vandalism in schools in Manchester. The scheme did have a clear purpose, and there was a lucid rationale for the range of proposed measures, most of which were of a physical kind. Only fifteen of the thirty proposals, however, had been implemented within two years. There were a variety of reasons. Some had to do with unanticipated technical obstacles. Others followed from difficulties in controlling and coordinating the behavior of the range of more or less independent agencies and departments that would need to act, each of which had its own aims and objectives. Hope and Murphy highlight the need to be flexible and actively to align implementation to a clear understanding of the realities, opportunities, and difficulties of workers and agencies in local situations, rather than simply to assume that if a rational course of conduct is laid out it will therefore naturally take place.

For crime prevention schemes to be successful they need not only to have a clear purpose with a worked-out rationale for the measures to be adopted, they need also to be implemented with an eye to the local political, organizational, and personal realities in which it is hoped that the proposed action will take place. Unsuccessful crime prevention initiatives risk undermining credibility and the often fragile commitment of those who need to be involved.

E. Maintaining Momentum

A further difficulty in relation to crime prevention, and also related to gaining the confidence of potential sponsors or providers of resources, is that, insofar as they have an effect, initiatives seldom work indefinitely. The effect generally wears off. This lack of long-term efficacy has been frequently used as a criticism of crime prevention generally. The issue is discussed by Berry and Carter (1992) who introduce the notion of a "life cycle" for a crime prevention initiative. This concept enables us to question quite openly the extent to which crime prevention measures *should* be seen to be permanent. Berry and Carter draw on analogies with industry and commerce in discussing a "life cycle" and argue that it is necessary to monitor the introduction of a crime prevention initiative in the expectation that the effect will diminish over time. They introduce these ideas in the context of managing crime and argue that the effective crime manager, in the course of appropriate monitoring, will be in a position to decide whether or not an initiative should be given a "boost" or whether it should be allowed to atrophy as it naturally otherwise would. The example quoted in Berry and Carter's research is of work carried out by interagency groups in Cambridgeshire in England which were attempting to reduce the incidence of school burglary. After an initial success, the rate at which schools were being burglarized began to rise. It is possible to speculate on the reasons for this: loss of key personnel, reduction in investment, or a new generation of young people coming to the age of increased criminal activity. The task for the crime manager is to decide whether to "revitalize" the initiative or move to another.

As is often the case with insights of this kind, it seems a fairly obvious point to make. To take an analogy, the manufacturers of a particular kind of candy bar may well launch what they regard as an exceptionally good product with an advertising campaign, at which point they would expect to see sales rise. What they would not expect, however, is that the sales will stay at a high level unless, to some extent, they continue to market their goods. This would be independent of how "good" the product was. It is, therefore, no criticism of the particular candy bar that sales start to fall off—it does not mean that it is reduced in quality or that the public has developed a sudden distaste for it. It simply means that if it is to continue to be sold, it needs to continue to be marketed. That is no more or less than good management practice in relation to sale of goods. It should come as no surprise, therefore, that good practice in relation to crime prevention involves similar marketing. Novelty and publicity for new initiatives are as likely in crime prevention as in the commercial field to bring their own short-term gains. It is, therefore, not sufficient to launch an initiative and expect it of its own momentum to continue in perpetuity both to be maintained and to be effective. This concept of a "life cycle" for crime prevention initiatives is therefore important, not only for the crime prevention manager, but also as an illustration of what needs to be explained by the would-be crime prevention implementer to those with the competence to act. It basically means that crime prevention initiatives should not be oversold as likely to lead to permanent reductions in crime unless they are of a very particular type, such as the total removal of the target of crime.

In "selling" a crime prevention initiative to a potential implementer, it is necessary, therefore, either to demonstrate that the initiative has worked in other places or that it has some potential to be effective in the present context. In some respects this is particularly difficult with social crime prevention measures that, insofar as they are argued to have an effect, in some cases do so only in the very long term. It is difficult to see, in addition, how others of these initiatives could work within the context of the consumer-based society within which they are introduced. So, for example, while the provision of a youth club on a local authority housing estate might reduce offending in the particular period of time over which it operates, it is unlikely to produce a net reduction in offending given the considerable periods of time available and the vast array of opportunities presented for offending outside the hours in which the youth club is open to young people. It is vital that the constraints on initiatives and the limits to potential effectiveness are spelled out clearly. There is otherwise a real danger that all crime prevention activity will be seen as futile and ineffective because of the overexpectations engendered, particularly in the minds of politicians, by would-be implementers.

IV. Conclusion

There are three main problems in implementation, which may take somewhat different forms at the national and local levels and within the business sector.

The first is that of putting crime prevention on the agenda. At the national level, crime prevention can be put on the agenda through new legislation and use of existing powers, through exhortation, and through well-directed and long-term publicity. Within the business sector, crime prevention comes on to the agenda when commercial pressures force it there or when businesses can be persuaded that it is to their economic advantage to attend to crime. If business-related costs of crime are borne by the public, and have an insufficient impact on business costs to persuade managers to attend to them, it may be necessary to apply external forces. Within communities, concerns for crime prevention among the agencies that need to cooperate can be catalyzed by a coordinator with pump-priming funds and by central government encouragement.

The second problem is to make action effective. Small-scale situational crime prevention initiatives can be effective. Why then are there not more? Perhaps in part because the "natural" response of both the public and agencies and organizations with a crime problem is to look to the criminal justice system for its solution. The realization that preemptive action is appropriate and necessary is not always welcome since it requires action and commitment from those involved rather than the devolution of responsibility to agencies of the state. Interestingly, banks and other financial institutions, as enormously attractive targets for crime, have not been slow to develop powerful situational protective measures with the criminal justice system as backup, but these have been the exception. While it is one thing to persuade people that there is a problem they should address, eliciting effective action is another.

Moreover, in most cases, it is likely that good quality information will be needed if the extent and nature of the problem are to be understood. Generally, this information is lacking. This can be seen at the national level in England and Wales, for example, in relation to prepayment coin meters for electricity and gas utilities, at the business level with the response to shop theft in the London record store, and at the local level with the Kirkholt Burglary Prevention Project. In all of these examples, data were collected and collated by the research teams; they were never readily available other than in crude form, and their preparation was resource-intensive. Better data and the appropriate training to handle them are required.

Effective action may also require coordination. That advantages can accrue can be seen in the response by credit card companies to plastic fraud, and at the local level again in the Kirkholt project. Finally, for crime prevention to be effective, not only do there have to be well thought out initiatives, they also need properly to be applied—which can often produce severe difficulties, particularly where several agencies are involved.

The final problem is that of maintaining impetus. Interest by organizations whose main purpose is not crime prevention can be difficult to maintain even when it has been stimulated in the first place. Other preoccupations supervene. At the local level, there are advantages in having local leadership which can act as a continuing focus for interest. The Home Office Crime Prevention Unit, which has played a part in much of the work described here, has since 1983 functioned as a national resource maintaining attention to crime prevention opportunities (Tilley 1991). In the business sector the credit card work is not once for all but depends on continuous attention. It will be interesting to see if it is maintained. The effects of many individual initiatives, especially at the local level, must be expected to fade over time and will need periodic injections of new action.

Situational crime prevention has demonstrated that there is a great deal that can be achieved in crime reduction. The trick is now to get it done. That said, it should not be expected that a "final solution" will be found. New crime opportunities become available with new products, increasing numbers of products, local and national policy developments, and changing lifestyles (see Felson 1994). What may be possible is "environmental scanning" which attempts to watch out for and anticipate new crime opportunities lying on the horizon and to implement situational crime prevention measures before the opportunities are delivered. It may also be possible to take advantage of new situational crime prevention opportunities with advances in technology.

REFERENCES

Barclay, G., ed. 1993. *Digest 2: Information on the Criminal Justice System in England and Wales.* London: Home Office Research and Statistics Department.

Barr, R., and K. Pease. 1990. "Crime Placement, Displacement, and Deflection." In *Crime and Justice: A Review of Research*, vol. 12, edited by M. Tonry and N. Morris. Chicago: University of Chicago Press.

Bennett, T. 1986. "Situational Crime Prevention from the Offenders' Perspective." In *Situational Crime Prevention: From Theory into Practice*, edited by Kevin Heal and Gloria Laycock. London: H.M. Stationery Office.

———. 1990. *Evaluating Neighbourhood Watch*. Aldershot, Hants: Gower.

Berry, G., and M. Carter. 1992. "Assessing Crime Prevention Initiatives: The First Steps." Crime Prevention Unit Paper 31. London: Home Office.

Brantingham, P. J., and F. L. Faust. 1976. "A Conceptual Model of Crime Prevention." *Crime and Delinquency* 22:284–96.

Brody, S. 1976. "The Effectiveness of Sentencing." Home Office Research Study no. 35. London: H.M. Stationery Office.

Burrows, J. 1991. "Making Crime Prevention Initiatives Pay: Initiatives from Business." Crime Prevention Unit Paper 27. London: Home Office.

Burrows, J., and K. Heal. 1979. "Police Car Security Campaigns." In *Crime Prevention and the Police*, edited by J. Burrows, P. Ekblom, and K. Heal. Home Office Research Study no. 55. London: H.M. Stationery Office.

Clarke, R. V. 1983. "Situational Crime Prevention: Its Theoretical Basis and Practical Scope." In *Crime and Justice: A Review of Research*, vol. 4, edited by M. Tonry and N. Morris. Chicago: University of Chicago Press.

———. 1992. "Introduction." In *Situational Crime Prevention: Successful Case Studies*, edited by R. V. Clarke. New York: Harrow & Heston.

———. In this volume. "Situational Crime Prevention."

Clarke, R. V., and P. M. Harris. 1992. "Auto Theft and Its Prevention." In *Crime and Justice: A Review of Research*, vol. 16, edited by M. Tonry. Chicago: University of Chicago Press.

Clarke, R. V., and P. Mayhew. 1980. *Designing out Crime*. London: H.M. Stationery Office.

Clarke, R. V., and D. Weisburd. 1994. "Diffusion of Crime Control Benefits: Observations on the Reverse of Displacement." In *Crime Prevention Studies*, vol. 2, edited by R. V. Clarke. Monsey, N.Y.: Criminal Justice Press.

Cohen, L., and M. Felson. 1979. "Social Change and Crime Rate Trends: A Routine Activity Approach." *American Sociological Review* 44:588–608.

Coleman, A. 1985. *Utopia on Trial*. London: Hilary Shipman.

Cooper, Barrymore. 1989. "Preventing Break-Ins to Pre-payment Fuel Meters." Research Bulletin, Home Office Research and Planning Unit. London: Home Office.

Dowds, L., and P. Mayhew. 1994. "Participation in Neighbourhood Watch: Findings from the 1992 British Crime Survey." Home Office Research and Statistical Department, Research Findings no. 12. London: Home Office.

Ekblom, P. 1986a. "Community Policing: Obstacles and Issues." In *The Debate about Community: Papers from a Seminar on Community in Social Policy*, edited by Peter Wilmott. Policy Studies Institute (PSI) Discussion Paper 13. London: PSI.

———. 1986b. "The Prevention of Shop Theft: An Approach through Crime Analysis." Crime Prevention Unit Paper 5. London: Home Office.

———. 1992. "The Safer Cities Programme Impact Evaluation: Problems and Progress." *Studies on Crime and Crime Prevention* 1:35–51.

Ekblom, P., and K. Pease. In this volume. "Evaluating Crime Prevention."

Engstad, P., and J. L. Evans. 1980. "Responsibility, Competence and Police Effectiveness in Crime Control." In *The Effectiveness of Policing*, edited by R. V. Clarke and J. M. Hough. Farnborough, Hants: Gower.

Farrell, G. 1993. "Repeat Criminal Victimisation." Ph.D. dissertation submitted to the University of Manchester, October.

———. In this volume. "Preventing Repeat Victimization."

Farrell, G., and K. Pease. 1993. "Once Bitten, Twice Bitten: Repeat Victimisation and Its Implications for Crime Prevention." Crime Prevention Unit Paper 46. London: Home Office.

Felson, M. 1994. *Crime and Everyday Life*. Thousand Oaks, Calif.: Pine Forge Press.

Field, S. 1990. "Trends in Crime and Their Interpretation: A Study of Recorded Crime in Post War England and Wales." Home Office Research Study 119. London: H.M. Stationery Office.

———. 1993. "Crime Prevention and the Costs of Auto Theft: An Economic Analysis." In *Crime Prevention Studies*, vol. 1, edited by R. V. Clarke. Monsey, N.Y.: Criminal Justice Press.

Forrester, D., M. Chatterton, and K. Pease, with the assistance of Robin Brown. 1988. "The Kirkholt Burglary Prevention Project: Rochdale." Crime Prevention Unit Paper 13. London: Home Office.

Forrester, D., S. Frenz, M. O'Connell, and K. Pease. 1990. "The Kirkholt Burglary Prevention Project: Phase II." Crime Prevention Unit Paper 23. London: Home Office.

Foster, J., and T. Hope. 1993. "Housing, Community and Crime: The Impact of the Priority Estates Project." Home Office Research Study no. 131. London: H.M. Stationery Office.

Gladstone, F. 1980. "Co-ordinating Crime Prevention Efforts." Home Office Research Study no. 47. London: H.M. Stationery Office.

Goldstein, H. 1979. "Improving Policing: A Problem Oriented Approach." *Crime and Delinquency* 25:236–58.

———. 1990. *Problem-oriented Policing*. New York: McGraw-Hill.

Hill, N. 1986. "Prepayment Coin Meters: A Target for Burglary." Crime Prevention Unit Paper 6. London: Home Office.

Home Office. 1984. "Crime Prevention." Home Office Circular 8/84. London: Home Office.

———. 1989. *Report of the Working Group on the Fear of Crime*. London: Home Office.

———. 1990. "Crime Prevention: The Success of the Partnership Approach." Home Office Circular 44/90. London: Home Office.

———. 1992. "Reducing the Costs of Crime: Measures Taken by Government Departments." Unpublished report. London: Home Office.

———. 1993. *A Practical Guide to Crime Prevention for Local Partnerships*, prepared for the Home Office by Crime Concern. London: Home Office.

Hope, T. In this volume. "Community Crime Prevention."

Hope, T., and J. Foster. 1992. "Conflicting Forces: Changing the Dynamics of Crime and Community on a 'Problem' Estate." *British Journal of Criminology* 32:488–504.

Hope, T., and D. Murphy. 1983. "Problems of Implementing Crime Prevention: The Experience of a Demonstration Project." *Howard Journal of Criminal Justice* 22:38–50.

Hotson, B. 1969. "Thefts from Pre-payment Meters." Unpublished manuscript. Cambridge: Institute of Criminology.

Houghton, G. 1992. "Car Theft in England and Wales: The Home Office Car Theft Index." Crime Prevention Unit Paper 33. London: Home Office.

Husain, S. 1988. "Neighbourhood Watch in England and Wales: A Locational Analysis." Crime Prevention Unit Paper 12. London: Home Office.

Johnson, V., J. Shapland, and P. Wiles. 1993. "Developing Police Crime Prevention Management and Organisational Change." Crime Prevention Unit Paper 41. London: Home Office.

Laycock, G. 1986. "Property Marking as a Deterrent to Domestic Burglary." In *Situation Crime Prevention: From Theory with Practice*, edited by K. Heal and G. Laycock. London: H.M. Stationery Office.

———. 1992. "Operation Identification or the Power of Publicity?" In *Crime Prevention: Successful Case Studies*, edited by R. V. Clarke. New York: Harrow & Heston.

Levi, M., P. Bissell, and T. Richardson. 1991. "The Prevention of Cheque and Credit Card Fraud." Crime Prevention Unit Paper 26. London: Home Office.

Liddle, M., and A. Bottoms. 1991. "Implementing Circular 8/84: A Retrospective Assessment of the Five Towns Initiative." Unpublished report. London: Home Office.

Liddle, M., and L. Gelsthorpe. 1994a. "Interagency Crime Prevention: Organising Local Delivery." Crime Prevention Unit Paper 52. London: Home Office.

———. 1994b. "Crime Prevention and Interagency Co-operation." Crime Prevention Unit Paper 53. London: Home Office.

Lipton, D., R. Martinson, and J. Wilks. 1975. *The Effectiveness of Correctional Treatment: A Survey of Treatment Evaluation Studies*. New York: Praeger.

McConville, M., and D. Shepherd. 1992. *Watching Police, Watching Communities*. London: Routledge.

Marplan Limited. 1973. "Report on a Survey to Monitor the Relative Effectiveness of Three Methods of Communicating Crime Prevention Publicity." Unpublished report R 4325/4353. London: Home Office.

Mayhew, P. 1988. "Site Specific Crime Analysis: Some Recent British Research." Paper presented at a conference on Research Future in Environmental Criminology, Orillia, Ontario, October.

Mayhew, P., D. Elliott, and L. Dowds. 1989. "The 1988 British Crime Survey." Home Office Research Study no. 111. London: H.M. Stationery Office.

Mayhew, P., and M. Hough. 1983. "A Note on the British Crime Survey." *British Journal of Criminology* 23:394–95.

Ministerial Group on Crime Prevention. 1992. *Reducing the Costs of Crime: Measures Taken by Government Departments.* London: Home Office.

Morgan, J. 1991. *Safer Communities: The Local Delivery of Crime Prevention through the Partnership Approach.* London: Home Office.

National Opinion Polls, Market Research Limited. 1979. "Car Security Advertising: Pre and Post-stage Research." Unpublished report NOP/4100. London: Home Office.

Newman, O. 1972. *Defensible Space.* New York: Macmillan.

Pawson, R., and N. Tilley. 1994. "What Works in Evaluation Research?" *British Journal of Criminology* 34:291–306.

Pearson, G., H. Blagg, D. Smith, A. Sampson, and P. Stubbs. 1992. "Crime, Community and Conflict: The Multi-agency Approach." In *Unravelling Criminal Justice*, edited by D. Downes. London: Macmillan.

Pease, K. 1991. "The Kirkholt Project: Preventing Burglary on a British Public Housing Estate." *Security Journal* 2:73–77.

Peat Marwick. 1991. *Counting out Crime: The Nottingham Crime Audit.* Nottingham: Nottingham Safer Cities Project.

Pengelly, R. 1994. "All Bark and No Bark." *Police Review* 102(5260):28–29.

Poyner, B. 1983. *Design against Crime: Beyond Defensible Space.* London: Butterworths.

———. 1992. "Video Cameras and Bus Vandalism." In *Situational Crime Prevention: Successful Case Studies*, edited by R. V. Clarke. New York: Harrow & Heston.

Research Bureau Ltd. 1977. "Car Theft Evaluation, 1976–1977." Unpublished report, prepared for the Central Office of Information, job no. 94066–11352. London: Home Office.

Riley, D., and P. Mayhew. 1980. "Crime Prevention Publicity: An Assessment." Home Office Research Study no. 64. London: H.M. Stationery Office.

Rosenbaum, D. P., ed. 1986. *Community Crime Prevention: Does It Work?* Beverly Hills, Calif.: Sage.

Rosenbaum, D. P., D. A. Lewis, and J. A. Grant. 1986. "Neighbourhood-based Crime Prevention: Assessing the Efficacy of Community Organising in Chicago." In *Community Crime Prevention: Does It Work?* edited by D. Rosenbaum. Beverly Hills, Calif.: Sage.

Safe Neighbourhoods Unit. 1993. *Crime Prevention on Council Estates.* London: Department of the Environment.

Safer Cities. 1989–93. *Annual Progress Reports.* London: Home Office.

Spencer, E. 1993. "Car Crime and Young People on a Sunderland Housing Estate." Crime Prevention Unit Paper 40. London: Home Office.

Thornton, D. M. 1989. "Treatment Effects on Recidivism: A Reappraisal of the 'Nothing Works' Doctrine." In *Applying Psychology to Imprisonment*, edited by B. J. McGurk, D. M. Thornton, and M. Williams. London: H.M. Stationery Office.

Tilley, N. 1991. "Opportunity Knocks! Crime Prevention and the Safer Cities Story." Paper presented at the 1991 Social Policy Association national conference, published in summary as "Crime Prevention and the Safer Cities Story" in 1993 in *Howard Journal of Criminal Justice* 32:32–57.

————. 1992. "Safer Cities and Community Safety Strategies." Crime Prevention Unit Paper 38. London: Home Office.

————. 1993. "After Kirkholt: Theory, Methods and Results of Replication Evaluations." Crime Prevention Unit Paper 47. London: Home Office.

Tilley, N., and J. Webb. 1994. "Burglary Reduction: Findings from Safer Cities Schemes." Crime Prevention Unit Paper 51. London: Home Office.

Titus, R. M. 1984. "Residential Burglary and the Community Response." In *Coping with Burglary*, edited by R. Clarke and T. Hope. Boston: Kluwer-Nijhoff.

Webb, B., and G. Laycock. 1992. "Tackling Car Crime." Crime Prevention Unit Paper 32. London: Home Office.

Webb, B. A. 1994. "Steering Column Locks and Motor Vehicle Theft: Evaluations from Three Countries." In *Crime Prevention Studies*, vol. 2, edited by Ronald V. Clarke. New York: Criminal Justice Press.

Webb, J. 1993. *Neighbourhood Concern Groups: Daring to Care in the Inner City.* Nottingham: York House Publications.

Paul Ekblom and Ken Pease

Evaluating Crime Prevention

ABSTRACT

Most evaluations of crime prevention are carried out with little regard for methodological probity. Of work that aspires to methodological adequacy, the standard designs are the before-after comparison group and the interrupted time series. The critical questions are whether a program has an effect (and if not, whether because of theory failure, implementation failure, or measurement failure), the extent of any effect achieved, and the means by which it was achieved. The reduction of crime is a measure of outcomes, but others are often used. Clarity is necessary in the use of noncrime measures. Too often, evaluators settle for the "consolation prizes" of reductions in fear and incivilities. Distinct evaluative requirements attach to different types of prevention. Improvements in standard methodology and innovation by nonstandard approaches are needed. The "scientific realist" tradition eschews conventional one-shot quasi experimentation in favor of repeated manipulations leading to the cataloging of possible mechanisms and consistency of outcome pattern with presumed mechanisms. Different actors (practitioners, evaluators, administrators) have different objectives and interests; evaluators must take account of those differences.

Crime prevention research has been dominated by two evaluative designs and a great deal of self-serving unpublished and semipublished work that does not meet even the most elementary criteria of evaluative

Paul Ekblom, principal research officer in the Home Office Research and Planning Unit, has responsibility for evaluating the Safer Cities Programme and for the Unit's other work on crime prevention. Ken Pease is professor of criminology at Manchester University. The help of the following, by criticism and direction to overlooked evaluations and commentaries, is warmly acknowledged: Richard Davies, Graham Farrell, David Farrington, David Howes, Ho Law, Gloria Laycock, Pat Mayhew, Ray Pawson, Larry Sherman, Mike Sutton, Nick Tilley, Michael Tonry, and Dick Wiggins.

Published with the permission of the Controller of Her Britannic Majesty's Stationery Office.

585

probity. For those persuaded of the need for good evaluation, there are many textbooks on evaluation research in social science (see, e.g., Winer 1975; Weiss 1985; Freeman and Rossi 1989). Our aim is to describe the problems in evaluation that are particularly acute in the crime prevention context, suggest ways of thinking about them, and present some strategies and tactics that may help in resolving them, or in working round them.

Evaluation in crime prevention began in earnest in the late 1970s with the advent of demonstration projects that explored, tested, and proselytized situational approaches. Studies employed one of two designs. The first is known as a before-after comparison group design. To take an example, research suggested that some crime on London Underground stations could be prevented by the introduction of closed-circuit television (CCTV) cameras (Burrows 1980). The sector of the system where theft and robbery was most prevalent was identified. Four of the nineteen stations in this sector were equipped with CCTV equipment in November–December 1975. The study compared rates of crime before and after installation on the four CCTV-equipped stations, the change being contrasted with that in the fifteen other underground stations in the sector that were not equipped with CCTV and with crime in the other sectors of the system. It was found that *thefts* from users of the CCTV stations in the first twelve months of operation fell to around 27 percent of the level experienced in the twelve months before any special measures had been adopted. The other fifteen stations in the most vulnerable sector fell to 73 percent of their preproject level, and other stations on the network fell to 65 percent of the preproject level. *Robberies* on the four CCTV stations fell from nine to seven incidents over the same period but rose from thirteen to sixteen on the fifteen comparable stations, and from forty-three to ninety-three on the remainder of the system.

The CCTV study was typical in respects other than its basic design. The stations chosen were among the most victimized on the system. This means that reductions in crime may be attributable to treatment effects, to regression to the mean, or to both. Regression effects occur when a problem is as severe as it will ever get. At that point things will improve whether or not action is taken. Campbell (1969) describes the trapped administrator who, by acting only when things are at their worst, guarantees success.

Closed-circuit television was not the only change introduced. Changes in patrolling took place some eleven months before CCTV:

special uniformed and plainclothes police officers patrolled the "worst" stations at the times when most crimes had occurred. The extra patrols appear to have been discontinued at the point at which the CCTV equipment was activated. This means that effects could not be ascribed to a single simple change. Even solitary changes are never simple, since they change motives and practices. In this instance, the effect of CCTV in the project could be described as effects in the context of recent heightened police presence. Without that precursor, the effects may have been different. The "before" part of the comparison comprised the twelve months before the special policing had been deployed, not the twelve months before CCTV. It is a tricky question as to what the right "before" period in this study would have been.

Displacement was only partially measured. Stations close to those protected by CCTV exhibited a smaller decrease in crime than those elsewhere, suggesting that at least some crime was so displaced. Furthermore "some geographical displacement of offenses could not be ruled out. . . . There was little possibility of knowing whether any incidents were displaced outside, as such offenses were likely to be 'lost' in the greater volume of street offenses" (Burrows 1980, p. 81). The contrasting trends of theft and robbery also leave open the possibility of limited tactical displacement, with some offenders taking to robbery elsewhere on the Tube network.

Designs of the kind employed in the Tube study were and remain common. They are exemplified in Poyner's (1988, 1991) study of bus vandalism, in which some buses were equipped with CCTV surveillance and the level of vandalism in these buses was compared with that in the remainder of the fleet. Laycock's (1985) study of burglaries from chemists' shops compared rates of crime against shops after target hardening with crime against other shops. The same type of design is featured in many of the studies collected in Rosenbaum (1986) and elsewhere. The basic design, and criticisms of it, is the modal evaluative battleground in situational crime prevention.

Where an innovation extends across an entire country, the comparison group design is not feasible, and here a simple interrupted time-series design is typical. Thus the introduction of car steering column locks in West Germany (see Webb 1994) was evaluated by comparison of rates of car theft before and after the date of the relevant statute—with all the complications to which such a design is prone (see Campbell 1969; Lurigio and Rosenbaum 1986). It may be a testament to the power of simple opportunity reduction measures that the size of effects achieved is so great that most readers will find them persuasive on the basis of contiguity alone despite the weakness of the design. For instance, Knutsson and Kuhlhorn (1981, 1991) addressed the problem of check fraud in Sweden by the requirement to incorporate a cardholder's photograph on check guarantee cards. National losses by check fraud fell to some 10 percent of their prephotograph levels within a year of the change.

Although the standard designs seem pleasingly simple, the label "evaluation" embraces an extremely wide range of activities. Figures 1a and b present a framework of different types of evaluation, showing the key series of linked questions that can be asked. The major distinction is between the implementation of preventive action and its impact or effectiveness.

Considering implementation, there is the limited managerial exercise of monitoring (Was the preventive action targeted on the right people or properties? Did the scheme deliver appropriate activity to the targets?) and the more qualitative study of process (How was implementation achieved, and what were the practical difficulties?). As for impact, the key questions concern whether there was a real fall in crime as opposed to random fluctuation or background trends. If there was, How much of the fall could be attributed to the preventive action? Were there unintended effects of the action (e.g., exacerbation of fear, displacement of crime to or from surrounding localities, stigmatization of areas or potential offenders)? How cost-effective was the action? Could effects be reproduced elsewhere?

Impact evaluation is the primary focus of this essay, but it also covers aspects of implementation vital for interpreting and exploiting the findings of impact studies. We span the range of activities that come under the rubric "crime prevention" but concentrate on evaluations of schemes and programs targeted on local areas rather than on individuals (or at least, on individuals taken out of their area context). Although some attempts have been made to evaluate prevention efforts in terms of cost-effectiveness (see, e.g., Forrester et al. 1990), these have been limited and hampered by an inadequate body of information on the costs of crime and the costs of preventive action. Accordingly, this type of approach is not examined.

Beneath the apparently simple questions posed by evaluation lie uncertainty and risk, due to limitations of the evaluation methods themselves, shortcomings in implementing preventive action, and

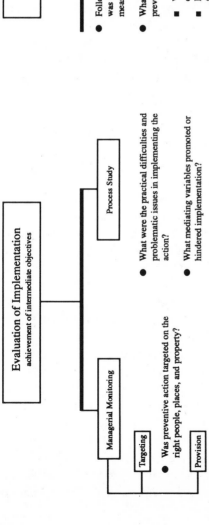

Evaluation of Implementation
achievement of intermediate objectives

Managerial Monitoring

Targeting

- Was preventive action targeted on the right people, places, and property?

Provision

- Was the appropriate preventive action delivered to the target people, places, and property?

Process Study

- What were the practical difficulties and problematic issues in implementing the action?

- What mediating variables promoted or hindered implementation?

- How did the implementors assign action—on what basis did they choose particular targets, particular preventive methods, and particular resource input levels?

- Can these answers be generalized to other circumstances? What contextual factors influenced implementation?

Most of the above implementation questions are also relevant to impact evaluation.

a

Evaluation of Impact
achievement of ultimate objectives

- Following the implementation of the preventive action, was there a real change in crime or other outcome measures?

- What proportion of that change can be attributed to the preventive action?

  - Were there coincidental background changes and confounding events?
  - How did the preventive action actually achieve any fall in crime—by what mechanisms?
  - What mediating variables may have accounted for or suppressed the measurable expected effects of the action?

- What were the side effects of the action (or effects on other objectives)—e.g., increased fear, displacement to more vulnerable victims?

- How cost-effective was the action?

- Can these answers be generalized to other circumstances? What contextual factors influenced impact?

b

Fig. 1.—Types of crime prevention evaluation: key questions. *a*, Evaluation of implementation. *b*, Evaluation of impact.

poorly defined theory justifying the action. These limits to evaluation are discussed in Section I, together with ways of coping with them.

Section II addresses the performance or outcome criteria of impact evaluations. The most suitable candidate is that of net reductions in the occurrence of crimes, but others are considered. To provide a framework for this discussion (in Sec. III), a classification of preventive action is briefly set out that focuses on preventive methods and how they work—that is, the cause-effect relations that are at the heart of evaluation.

Section IV identifies some ways of improving evaluation, ranging from the conventional to the innovative. In particular, two new approaches to evaluation are described. The first—designed to cope with the extreme difficulties of evaluating the Safer Cities Programme, a major English initiative involving over three thousand diverse schemes in twenty cities—is a kind of "prospective metaevaluation," in which new methods have been developed to link measures of action to measures of outcome at the small-area level, considering the effects of large numbers of schemes simultaneously. Identifying which schemes may have the potential to influence which outcome measures and where ("scoping") and how much preventive input is exerting itself at each site ("scoring") promises wider applicability. The second new approach to evaluation is a radical attempt to rework the philosophical basis on which cause and effect are considered in evaluation, using "scientific realist" notions of cause—in particular emphasizing "mechanism" and "context" in a way that is critical of conventional "quasi-experimental" or "random-assignment" approaches alike. This approach has the potential to deliver better evaluation. The concepts of mechanism and context are useful in illuminating the contents of the "black box" of how interventions are supposed to have their effect.

Section V moves beyond methodology to consider the changing context of evaluation—failure to address which will render even the finest designs unusable. Problems and issues are discussed regarding the various stakeholders in evaluation: practitioners, who may be suspicious of and uninterested in evaluation; administrators, who often entertain unrealistic expectations of what evaluation can achieve, with what resources; and evaluators themselves—particularly evaluators with academic backgrounds who may carry baggage of inappropriate assumptions and traditions. For example, the proper balance between avoidance of mistakenly inferring success and avoidance of mistakenly inferring failure is likely to differ in academic and applied evaluation research. Some solutions to these problems are suggested (many of which will be familiar to experienced evaluators) that depend on a clear understanding by all parties involved of the function or functions the evaluation is to serve, a wider sensitivity to the implementation context, and an appreciation of user needs. Willingness to undertake replications, and the need for all parties to anticipate and exploit failures, are deemed central. The possibility of "giving away" evaluation skills to nonprofessionals is considered, but an open verdict is returned.

I. Simple Questions, Uncertain Answers

Two key questions lie at the heart of all evaluations of the impact of crime preventive action: Following the implementation of the action, was there a real fall in crime or other indicators? What proportion of any change observed can be attributed to the preventive action, as opposed to the many other influences likely to have been operating at the same time? The aims of all impact evaluation techniques are to rule out plausible alternative explanations for the observed data, or at least to render them so unlikely that they can safely be discounted, and to arrive at quantitative estimates of impact in order to feed into administrative decision making (or increasingly quantitative theory).

The main problem in detecting change and estimating its size is fluctuation.[1] In crime statistics, aggregation over large areas and periods may give the appearance of a deluge of offending. But in the short term and at the local level—where most current approaches to crime prevention exist—crime is typically rare. When numbers are small, fluctuation is great. The modest effects of a successful intervention will be hard to distinguish from expected variation. The issue was brought home to one of us on his very first ride in a police patrol car, in a place in the North-East of England called, appropriately enough, Pity Me. The police beat was supposed to be high in crime, but as the hours of darkness crawled by and nothing happened, the accompanying police officer kept shaking his head and saying, "You should have been here last week!" Since then, we have met the YSHBHLW

---

[1] We are tempted to say "random fluctuation," but it is more appropriate to say "residual determined fluctuation." The distinction between a "random" fluctuation due to unknown, often multiple, causes and the operation of known confounding events or influences is arbitrary and largely a function of the level of detail the evaluator is willing or able to pursue. The two key questions—detecting "real" change and attributing cause—are two aspects of a whole. This fusion becomes even closer with designs that measure impact in terms of change differentially associated with preventive action, usually in some kind of statistical interaction.

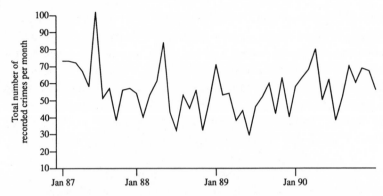

FIG. 2.—Fluctuation in crime at the small-area level. Total recorded crimes, one police beat, West Midlands. Source: Data provided by the West Midlands Police.

phenomenon on many occasions. Another example of random fluctuation, from a police beat in the English West Midlands, is seen in figure 2.

One way to filter out such fluctuations (together with seasonal changes and background trends) is to use the statistical technique of time-series analysis. Unfortunately, it is often difficult to obtain a series long enough (perhaps sixty months' worth of figures). The police sometimes destroy data after two years, beat boundaries are changed, and so on. In the U.K. police service at least, the culture of data collection for analysis has been slow to arrive. Even where data exist, trends may show exponential growth or decline and thus make estimation difficult (for an example in which there was a sudden rapid growth of Post Office robberies following the "discovery" by offenders that the anti-bandit screens were weak, see Ekblom 1987).

On the second key question—How much of a change can be attributed to a program?—keeping track of cause and effect is notoriously difficult. There may be many other influences on the level of crime in the experimental area—police patrolling, the local economy, the weather, the incarceration of its normally most active offenders. All conspire to confound even the most sophisticated design. The evaluator often has to explore the data retrospectively and judge the plausibility of different explanations for an observed fall in crime. Often it is desirable to aid this process by developing theoretical models of the processes that are supposed to be happening and measure intervening variables and intermediate outcomes (Skogan 1985). Most evaluations conducted beyond the social psychologist's laboratory are quasi-experimental (Campbell and Stanley 1963)—that is, they do not involve the random assignment of the preventive "treatment" to one set of people rather than another or to one area rather than another; rather, assignment is the subject of "real-world" administrative decisions. Such designs are weaker in teasing out cause and effect. This is principally because unmeasured causes cannot be eliminated, although they can be reduced by careful matching of treatment and control areas.

Quasi experimentation has to be supplemented by studies of implementation. In particular, it requires an understanding of the assignment process (Judd and Kenny 1981; Skogan 1985)—of the ways in which implementers have decided to establish preventive action at the chosen times and places. Are they seeking to site preventive action where other initiatives, such as public housing management schemes, have already been located, in order to benefit from "prepared ground" (which will tend to overestimate the preventive effect)? Are they by contrast trying to find "green field sites" for the preventive schemes to stand alone (which will underestimate the preventive effect if the areas chosen for comparison have a greater probability of experiencing other confounding interventions)? Are they—like Campbell's trapped administrator—targeting action on the basis of neighborhoods where last year's crime statistics were highest? Given the strong "random" component of crime statistics, such figures are likely to fall, mimicking the pattern of impact. Are they relying on longer-term indicators of crime distribution that will be more stable but by the same token will iron out recent increases in the crime baseline that are "real" and, with the benefit of hindsight, permanent?

Given all these problems, it is rarely possible for the evaluator to draw a "watertight" conclusion about the impact of preventive action. There is always a degree of uncertainty, which can be very large and impossible to quantify.[2] There is also an element of risk in conducting any evaluation—it is rare for things to work out as originally planned. Well-chosen comparison areas can show unexplained falls in crime (e.g., Bennett 1990); control over significant confounding events can break down—the police can suddenly increase patrols in the experimental area (e.g., Webb and Laycock 1992). Police in comparison areas can become determined that they will outperform the selected experi-

---

[2] A fuller treatment of the issue of uncertainty in crime prevention evaluation is in Ekblom (1990).

mental areas. Taken together, uncertainty and risk may yield "measurement failure" (Rosenbaum 1986). This is the failure of an impact evaluation to detect the real effect of a successful crime prevention scheme.[3]

Measurement failure, significant though it is, is not the whole story. Rosenbaum (1986) identifies two other important kinds of failure in accounting for negative or inconclusive results of an impact evaluation: "theory failure" (the basic idea or mechanism of prevention was unsound) and "implementation (or program) failure" (the idea was sound, but it was not properly put into effect). Implementation failure is perhaps the most common reason for an impact evaluation to fail to put the "theory" to a fair test (see Hope and Murphy 1983; Hope 1985; Bennett 1990), although sometimes it provides an "alibi" for what would otherwise have been measurement failure.

Reducing the margin of uncertainty and the likelihood of measurement failure can be done—at a price. Uncertainty and risk can be minimized by better control over events, allowing more time for preventive activity to take effect and to be reliably measured, boosting the strength of the intervention to increase "effect size" (Weisburd 1993), using more experimental and control areas, collecting more diverse data, applying more sophisticated designs and analytical techniques, and finding an appropriate balance between false positive and false negative errors (a point to be taken up later). Basic research into the nature, magnitude, and variation of "random" or residually determined fluctuation of crime rates at the local level (Ekblom 1990) could help set parameters such as the appropriate sample size of a survey to obtain maximally affordable statistical power to detect change (for a discussion of power in the evaluation context, see Weisburd 1993). Random assignment (Weisburd and Garner 1992) offers a step improvement in reducing cause-effect uncertainty, and increasingly evaluators are overcoming administrative obstacles and resolving ethical issues to the application of appropriate designs. However, the practical obstacles and ethical issues are such as to ensure that the bulk of crime prevention evaluations will remain quasi-experimental. Random assignment of cases to treatment conditions requires a minimum number of cases to distribute irrelevant but confounding influences evenly. Such numbers may be achievable for relatively modest cost with evalu-

[3] In the terms of inferential statistics, this is a "type II," or "false negative" error. "Type I," or "false positive" errors—mistakenly inferring success—and the balance to be struck between the two are discussed at various points below.

ations of treatment of individual offenders or victims much more readily than with evaluations of treatment of areas—although random assignment of patrolling at the area level has been achieved with the Minnesota study of high-crime "hot spots" (Sherman, Gartin, and Buerger 1989).

There will always be a trade-off between resources put into an evaluation, the quality and certainty of the results of the evaluation, and the timeliness of results becoming available. Bluntly put, evaluators and their customers have to live with this. To anticipate Section V, circumstances and the function of the evaluation will determine the most appropriate balance to be struck. In one context, for example, the local police will want to know whether a scheme to prevent parking lot crime has worked at one location. Other, more senior police managers may want to know whether the experimental scheme is worth reproducing elsewhere. Policymakers in central government may want to know if the scheme is worth reproducing nationwide and whether preventing crime in parking lots is likely to have a significant effect on car crime as a whole. As focus shifts from the local to the national, it may make sense to change the character of the evaluation: to reduce its uncertainty and risk by investing in more resources and greater sophistication of design and by taking a longer time. Of course, such coolness may sit ill with pressing national crime problems. For those deciding on the cheapest evaluation of a scheme of potential general applicability, the adage "Buy cheap, buy twice" should be borne in mind. It is as true in the choice of evaluation as in most other contexts.

Protecting against theory failure requires evaluators to be careful where they invest their effort (although they may not have the luxury of a choice). Beyond this, they have to do all they can to ensure that the theory and mechanism of the preventive scheme in question are well specified and plausible (Skogan 1985). From a different angle, however, evaluators have to be sanguine about theory failure—after all, to find that the theory was wrong and failed to prevent crime is an acceptable, albeit disappointing, conclusion consistent with the purpose of evaluation. Protecting against implementation failure likewise requires evaluators to ensure that the plausible mechanisms can be implemented in principle and that monitoring systems are in place to facilitate implementation in practice.

Although theory failure is particularly frustrating to implementers and implementation failure particularly frustrating to impact evaluators, both are informative. If the worst happens, good evaluators will have placed themselves in a position to salvage much that is of use from the study beyond the bleak conclusion that the theory was wrong or the implementation was weak. Lessons learned about implementation and insights into theory can be accumulated from even the most negative or unclear results (although this has not yet happened much with crime prevention evaluation—one happy exception being the Priority Estates Project Study [Hope and Foster 1992; Foster and Hope 1993]). A close a priori linkage with theory, and the collection of diagnostic information on implementation and the processes hypothesized to have been influenced by the intervention, serve as an insurance policy against the hazard of negative findings. They also serve to cross-check, interpret, and assess the generality of positive ones.

All types of failure risk cannot be minimized simultaneously. Reducing one type of risk will usually increase another.[4] In particular, there may be a trade-off between measurement failure and implementation failure. Preventive schemes that cover a smaller territory, which often means they are better-targeted and easier to implement, may have more impact on crime than larger ones covering, for example, more streets or more households; but establishing this may be harder because of greater interference from "random" fluctuation. Bennett, in his (1990) evaluation of two London neighborhood watch schemes aimed at reducing burglary, explicitly chose large schemes in order to reduce the chance of measurement failure through insufficient statistical power, but the very size of the schemes made for implementation failure. Weisburd (1993), in a review of the issue of statistical power, showed that, contrary to the theoretical outworking of the power formula, the empirically observed power of designs to detect impact actually decreases as the number of cases sampled grows. The value of a collective of small schemes, known as "cocoon" neighborhood watch and each involving a burglarized household and its immediate neighbors, was suggested in the Kirkholt Study (Forrester, Chatterton, and Pease 1988; Forrester et al. 1990). It seems that small is not only beautiful, but evaluable too. This strategy has been adopted by Painter (1988, 1989a, 1989b, 1991) in a series of studies of the effects of lighting on crime that are individually very small but in the aggregate substantial.

---

[4] This is similar to the antagonistic relationships between the various "validities" as described, e.g., in Judd and Kenny (1981)—such as internal validity (did the intervention cause the outcome?) versus external validity (can the conclusions be generalized to the real world?). The degree of experimental control required to boost the former often reduces the latter.

II. Connecting to the Bottom Line

Section I distinguishes various kinds of failure and the links among them. However, the question "Failure to do what?" has not been addressed. The reader may take it as self-evident that the bottom line of crime prevention programs is crime prevention. Indeed, the most suitable candidate for the ultimate bottom line of crime prevention evaluations—that which practitioners and policymakers as "consumers" of evaluations are supremely interested in—is the achievement of reductions in the occurrence of crimes. As is elaborated later, the pattern of crime change should be that which can be linked to the substance of a crime prevention effort. For instance, Graham Farrell's essay (in this volume) describes attempts at the prevention of *repeat* victimizations. In this case, the number of crimes suffered by those previously victimized is crucial, preferably without any increase in the prevalence of victimization. Crime prevention is central, but the reduction of crime must be measured in a way that reflects the scope for change and the mechanisms by which it is to be achieved. However, crime reduction is by no means the only criterion in current use. The reduction in fear of crime is often cited as an objective. Paracrimes, like incivilities and disputes short of criminal offending, may be regarded as worthy of change; these have the methodological advantage of being more frequent events, to enable more reliable patterns to be established faster.[5] It is important to be clear about the role of such measures. They can be regarded as precursors or facilitators of crime or as objects of change in their own right and irrespective of their relationship to crime. Taking fear reduction as an example, do we wish people to become less fearful because crime reduction will come in the train of fear reduction; or do we wish to reduce fear because it will improve the quality of life of those who become less afraid? This choice is crucial and must be made clearly. If fear reduction is an end in its own right, evaluation becomes more straightforward, requiring attitude and belief measurement before and after the fear reduction treatment. The moral terrain, however, becomes more treacherous. The finding that fear levels vary inversely with victimization risk is well nigh universal. However, the contention that fear is adaptive among those for whom the trauma or consequences of victimization would be greatest must be taken seriously. Proponents of fear reduction programs must be satisfied that

[5] Aircraft near misses offer an analogy. Near misses are thought valuable because their provenance is thought to be the same as that of crashes. Preventing near misses—which are more frequent and of which the crew live to tell the tale—will prevent crashes.

they are not increasing victimization risks among those least able to cope with the consequences. Why is this moral point made in an essay about evaluation? It is that in the world of unpublished and semi-published crime prevention exercises, fear reduction is often seen as a consolation prize when crime has not been reduced, a second-best achievement to show to funders and others.

Three "bottom-line" positions are defensible. The first is that the aim is crime reduction, and no evaluation that does not reflect this can be regarded as adequate. The second is that quality-of-life measures are defensible and can thus be measured as outcome variables in their own right. The third is that quality-of-life or paracrime measures are useful as short-term proxies for a longer-term measurement of crime reduction. In this case, the relationships between the chosen proxy measures and the crime changes they augur should be well established, and a means of checking on the anticipated longer-term crime changes should be incorporated into the evaluation design.

Unless the second route outlined above is taken (which effectively takes an evaluation outside the sphere of crime relevance), the "reduction in crime" criterion remains central. Following its logic through forces a confrontation with some important divides within prevention itself, and consequently within its evaluation. Of course, defensibility of an evaluative stance on the evaluator's part is far from representing the end of the story, particularly where a program was favored, argued for, and implemented by committed citizens or policymakers. Here, citizens whose area feels better, or where rewarding contacts have been achieved, or where the crime problem is placed in a new perspective by community action, are liable to lynch an evaluator whose skeptical stance appears inflexible and indifferent to their sense of achievement.[6] Perhaps there should be an escape clause in an evaluator's contract to allow customers or concerned citizens to say that they are no longer primarily concerned about crime problems. At that stage the evaluator should either go away or reconstitute herself as an evaluator of community change.

III. Coping with the Diversity of Crime Prevention

An immense diversity of activities sail under the flag of crime prevention. Such diversity often has the characteristics of a cultural divide—

---

[6] We have seen practitioners and evaluators nearly come to blows in report-back sessions in several countries.

favored methods of implementation, endorsed examples of a successful paradigm, and typical evaluation strategies. These are underpinned by different values and assumptions concerning individuals and society. This section begins by offering a classification developed by one of the authors for an evaluative context and then discusses evaluation problems peculiar to the different types of prevention.

A. Classification

Over the years, attempts have been made to map out the divides by classification. It is not the intention to review existing classifications (some of which are drawn on elsewhere in this volume); they concentrate on targeting, that is, who or what receives the action (e.g., Brantingham and Faust's [1976] primary, secondary, and tertiary prevention).[7] They focus insufficiently on causal mechanism—the nature of the action in a given preventive scheme and how it is intended to work (see Ekblom 1994a for an expansion of this discussion, and Sec. IVB below).[8] After all, questions about cause are at the heart of evaluation. One approach that does explicitly strive to get close to cause is described in Ekblom (1994a) which defines crime prevention very broadly as intervention in mechanisms that cause criminal events. That approach is adopted here. To paraphrase the theoretical model behind Ekblom's classification, there are a number of key causal components (termed "proximal circumstances") common to all criminal events. These include, at their most basic, a potential offender and the situation. The potential offender brings to the situation a set of dispositions ranging from motives, emotions, skills, knowledge, ways of perceiving, and decisions. Every disposition has two subcomponents: the potential to respond in particular ways in particular situations, such as an inherited capacity for violence or a developmentally acquired attitude of disregard for others' rightful ownership of property; and the current state, which results from the influence of recent circumstances in activating and directing the potential—for example, entering the situation

---

[7] According to the Brantingham and Faust (1976) classification, *primary prevention* addresses the reduction of crime opportunities without reference to criminals or potential criminals. *Secondary prevention* addresses the change of people, typically those at high risk of embarking on a criminal career, so that they remain law-abiding. *Tertiary prevention* is focused on the truncation of the criminal career, in length, seriousness, or frequency of offending, i.e., it deals with the "treatment" of known offenders.

[8] Van Dijk and de Waard's (1991) extension of the "primary-secondary-tertiary" schema to include a second dimension of "targeting on victims, offenders and situations" is a clear improvement but in our opinion does not go far enough.

of a criminal event in a state of hunger or anger. The situation in turn can be divided into several subcomponents—the target of criminal behavior (usually an object or a person), modulators (roles who intervene before, during, or after the criminal event to make its occurrence or recurrence more or less likely), and, as background, the physical and social environment itself. (There are further subdivisions, but for the present purpose we need go no further.)

Causal mechanisms of prevention operate, by definition, by intervening in the causal mechanisms of criminal events and ultimately through influencing the dispositional and situational components just described. Every preventive scheme can be classified in terms of which of these components it seeks to operate through, however remotely.[9] The key divide is between reducing crime by changing the immediate situation in which offenses may occur, and changing potential offenders generally in terms of the dispositions, motives, knowledge, and skills they bring to situations. These two main branches are each further divided. The divisions on the situational side are well described by Ron Clarke's essay in this volume and reflect a focus on the target of crime (e.g., strengthening doors), on modulators (e.g., "lock it or lose it" campaigns or surveillance), and on the environment (e.g., clearing shrubs to reduce hiding places and introducing antispeeding bumps otherwise known as "sleeping policemen"). On the offender-oriented side, it is possible to distinguish between two types of activity. There are attempts to influence people's early lives in order to bring about changes in the trajectories of development and "programming-in" of motivations, emotions, learning, and life chances (as are discussed in Richard Tremblay and Wendy Craig's essay in this volume)—what could be called "criminality prevention."[10] However, there are at-

[9] All preventive activity, whatever its nature, and however causally remote its starting point, has ultimately to operate through these components of the proximal circumstances of criminal events. Even approaches that target an entire locality have their effect mediated through individual changes in behavior, perception, and motivation. A successful Neighbourhood Watch scheme may work because potential offenders may come to see a locale as protected or its residents may come to act in ways that protect it. There is no way in which it can operate other than through such individual-level processes, albeit reflecting important emergent properties of social-level patterns. It may be convenient for purposes of description to refer to a project as a social or community project, but the mechanism must lead through individual perceptions and actions; there is no "action at a distance." The same is true of physical measures. The physical location of liquor outlets, for instance, will determine the perceptions and behavior that together determine the extent and type of occupancy of such areas.

[10] This is a fairly loose term with no standard definition. An attempt to agree to a range of definitions and stick to them would seem to be a prerequisite if crime prevention is to become a proper discipline (Ekblom 1994a).

tempts to influence the current life circumstances of individuals or groups that may be (perhaps temporarily) setting their current state of motivation or otherwise directing them to offend, such as debt, bad housing, or offending peer groups. (The greatest problem in such an enterprise is to separate motivational accounts of offending from real motives for offending.) The classification is illustrated in figure 3.

This classification omits the terms "community" or "social" crime prevention (although there are other dimensions to Ekblom's framework that enable social/community aspects to be represented). The terms "social" or "community" are unsatisfactorily loose and difficult to pin down (see Ekblom 1986; Willmott 1986): the description of a crime prevention project as social or communal often flags a set of values as much as a set of methods and causal mechanisms. It can also confuse action for the community (as in community safety, aspiring to a broad collective benefit) with action through the community (using community-level processes to intervene in the causation of criminal events but which might only be intended to have an impact on specific potential offenders and situations) and action with the community (involving explicit participatory processes). In practice, these approaches can always be conceived as a composite of situational and offender-oriented approaches, but operating through role relationships, networks, and common interests (Ekblom 1994a) rather than dealing with individual situations or (potential) offenders in isolation; they are typically implemented at the level of a locality. Unless pinned down as operating through these specific processes and structures, the terms "community" and "social crime prevention" remain confusing and elusive for evaluative purposes. This said, it is important to note that we are not decrying the actions implemented under the rubric "community/social crime prevention"; we are criticizing the labels and the (lack of) conceptual framework much more than any vagueness of mechanism. But given that the labels remain in virtually exclusive currency to denote broad areas of prevention, we regretfully have to continue to use them (as sparingly as possible) in the following pages.

B. Problems in Evaluating the Different Approaches to Prevention

The aim here is to discuss particular problems of situational, offender-oriented, and, with the regret just expressed, community-oriented prevention. Evaluations of situational and offender-oriented prevention encounter distinctive problems in estimating impact according to the "net reductions in crimes" criterion; all that can be

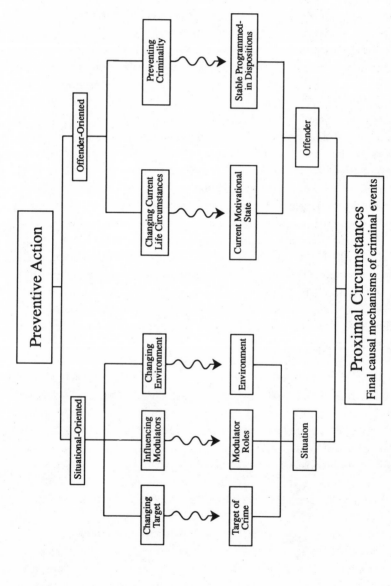

Fig. 3.—A classification of crime prevention based on final causal mechanisms of criminal events. For further details, see Ekblom (1994*a*).

measured are gross changes, leaving an unsatisfying residuum of uncertainty. For situational approaches the problem concerns displacement of offending; for offender-oriented approaches, replacement of offenders.

1. *Situational Prevention.* Situational crime prevention methods may thwart an offender at one time and place, but the purposive nature of much criminal behavior raises the possibility of displacement to other times, places, targets, or types of crime. This phenomenon is crucial, because any boundaries drawn around a prevention program are always going to exclude some possibly "deflected" crime (see Barr and Pease 1990). Displacement/deflection is an issue of substantive interest in any evaluation—threatening to undermine or redistribute preventive gains.[11] There is also a potential methodological problem, in that displacement from the *action* area to any nearby *control* area may lead to double counting and an exaggeration of impact. Paradoxically, any "diffusion of benefits" from the action to the control area (occasioned, e.g., by cautious offenders giving the action area a wider berth than strictly necessary) may lead to an underestimate of impact (Clarke and Weisburd 1994). In effect, the more successful a program is in spreading benefits beyond its boundaries, the less success may be attributed to it.

Another problem for evaluating situational crime prevention stems from the probability that a scheme will have a limited life span of effectiveness (see Gloria Laycock and Nick Tilley's essay in this volume; Berry and Carter 1992). The trajectory of effectiveness has crime fluctuations superimposed. Identification of the trajectory (typically early in its course) poses particular difficulties for cost-benefit analyses of preventive action: what is the money buying? It may buy no more than a "breathing space" before offenders return with a new method of circumventing the latest car security device or simply discover that a particular neighborhood watch scheme was "all bark and no bite." However, it should be noted that the problem is not unique. For instance, it affects the introduction of new antibiotics: germs mutate all the time and develop resistance to once-potent drugs.

Perhaps we should evaluate not only the performance of one-off

---

[11] In the Barr and Pease (1990) usage, "displacement" connotes pessimism in failing to prevent a crime, whereas "deflection" connotes success in moving a crime from its intended target. The preference in their discussion for the more upbeat term reflects the process of choosing a crime profile by means that are likely to include the deliberate and undisguised use of deflection.

preventive *schemes* but also the performance of the *preventive process* (Ekblom 1988)—the problem-oriented approach that endeavors to keep track of changes in crime patterns and devise, implement, and evaluate preventive action. This is akin to containing crime, which poses its own evaluative problems. The longer any successful containment proceeds, the harder it may be to evaluate except at the margins, as with the question of assessing the effectiveness of "the police" or of "the existence of prisons." Strategies of total removal (as with assessing the effects of police strikes or breakdown of government power as in Somalia) may then be the only possible evaluative ploy, although their validity is jeopardized by their association with unusual circumstances. One apparently successful micro-level example of removal has however occurred in the crime prevention area. Poyner and Woodall (1987) collaborated with a major department store on London's Oxford Street in installing physical security systems designed to prevent shoplifting. The recorded theft rate duly went down; on subsequent removal of the systems, the theft rate quickly increased again.

2. *Offender-oriented Prevention.* Evaluation of offender-oriented action, particularly criminality prevention, has its own traditions and has connections with the evaluation of "correctional" treatment for offenders in prison or on probation. Although this is a somewhat arbitrary and undesirable separation, reviewing relevant material in full is beyond the compass of this essay: only selected aspects of the evaluation of offender-oriented prevention are covered. Its brief discussion underscores how different measurement of successful criminality prevention is from the measurements appropriate for crime prevention.

Offender-oriented prevention schemes, because they aim to change motivation or remove current causes of criminal motivation, are unlikely to suffer from displacement. However, especially if they operate at the level of individuals rather than whole communities, they are likely to be affected by replacement or recruitment. Their effect will be offset, partially or completely, if other people are recruited into crime or those who remain criminally active offend more often.[12] Some analogies and examples may make the argument more plausible. In the

---

[12] Some readers will note echoes of the literature on criminal careers here. The criminal career can be specified in terms of the following variables: *participation*—how many people embark on such a career; *duration*—the elapsed time from first to last offense; *frequency*—how often during the active career crimes are committed; and *seriousness*—how heinous the committed crimes are. The discussion in the text could be amplified to incorporate these parameters of the career (see Blumstein et al. 1986).

world of business, there are limited opportunities. These are taken up by the best business people. If a plague suddenly wiped out all such entrepreneurs, the business opportunities they left behind would not thereafter be neglected. They would be taken up by other entrepreneurs being recruited into the market. This happens in the illicit drug trade, where the amount of money to be made is such that there is no shortage of willing recruits to become couriers or dealers. Locking up or otherwise incapacitating or demotivating drug couriers and dealers, however frequently they offend, would have only a brief effect in disrupting drug traffic, so lucrative is it for new recruits.[13] The arrest (and remotely possible conviction) of a Mafia *capo di tutti capi* only temporarily disrupts the organization, if at all. What is dramatically true for the drug trade and the Mafia may well be true, to varying extents, for other offenses.

The issue of recruitment into crime as a career is a key area in which research is urgently needed, despite the attention paid to it in many sociological theories of criminality.[14] The message for evaluation is that changes in rates of criminality may differ from changes in rates of crime, in magnitude or even direction. Measured reductions in crime do not necessarily imply commensurate (or even any) reduction in individual criminality. Criminality prevention does not necessarily imply reductions in crime. It is of vital interest to continue to conduct research and evaluation that tries to measure the link between criminality and crime, in order to connect back to the bottom line of crime prevention evaluation. It would be insufficient to cast this in terms of relatively narrow statistical analyses in the criminal careers tradition— rather, what would be required would be something far more ecological, looking at available "niches" for "predators" of a certain "ferocity" (rate of offending) in particular communities. In the meantime, it is crucial to devise intermediate measures of impact both to explore the crime-criminality link and to enable the continued development, evaluation, and refinement of offender-oriented schemes. To take an exam-

---

[13] This is equally true for the rate of offending of known offenders. The take-up of criminal opportunities is likely to be a function of *both* recruitment into crime and rate of offending of known offenders. Insofar as it is the first, it will influence the prevalence of criminality. Insofar as it is the second, it will not.

[14] One issue that has been remarkably neglected in criminology is that of co-offending (Reiss 1988). There is a clear minority of experienced offenders who commit crimes with criminal neophytes (see Reiss and Farrington 1991). These "recruiters" are disproportionately important in determining rates of criminality. Understanding patterns of co-offending is crucial for policies of criminality prevention.

ple, the appropriate measure of prevention by attention to known offenders lies in the reconviction rates of those offenders and in the proportion of those found guilty or admitting guilt who have prior records. Both of these measures should decline after a successful prevention program. If the first but not the second declines, the suggestion is that other established offenders replace those desisting from crime. If the second declines but not the first, the inference would be that the crime was attractive enough to recruit the emerging criminal.

As for preventing offenders without criminal records from entering crime, the appropriate measures are again twofold: the prevalence of criminality in the cohort studied, and the proportion of crime that can be attributed to known offenders. Prevalence in the sense used here refers to the proportion of an available population that falls into the condition of interest. In this case, we are interested in those within an age cohort who are officially processed as criminal. This is the uniquely appropriate intermediate measure for assessing the success of predelinquent programs. The supplementary measure mentioned above is, of course, the number of offenses per known offender, which should increase to the extent that more active criminals increase their frequency of offending to take up the criminal opportunities that remain unexploited by the increasing proportion of their peers who now refrain from crime.

Hirschi (1986) explicitly argues for a division of responsibility in which some theories focus on variations in rates of criminality, while others focus on the determinants of crime events. A similar distinction, with a similar conclusion, was offered by Bennett (1986). In the short and middle terms, the division makes good sense. Nonetheless, links between the traditions (e.g., in individual differences in the perception of situations as offering opportunities for crime, and in the distinction between offenders who are opportunity makers and those who are opportunity takers [see Clarke and Harris 1992]) mean that in due course a rapprochement between the approaches should be attempted.

Another basic problem attending the evaluation of offender-oriented techniques, especially those involving criminality prevention with the very young (as with preschool programs), is that they need time to "work through," so that the time at which criminality should decline can be so far into the future that other changes will obscure the determination of success or failure. It is this feature of criminality prevention that is so frustrating for those who wish effective programs to be recognized as such—namely, that evaluation can so often be indefinitely postponed.[15]

3. *"Community Crime Prevention."* Some attention must be given to efforts described in these terms because the use of the term is widespread, and the phrase "community safety" is often now used in place of "crime prevention." We earlier criticized the terminology of community/social crime prevention as loosely referring to a mix of particular targeting strategies, preventive methods, and participative style. One possible defining characteristic of community crime prevention is that community residents rather than authorities define the outcomes to be sought, and the interventions are delivered at least in part through community organizations. Community stakeholding involves a proprietary interest in its success in whatever terms hindsight will allow. Owing perhaps to community differences in perceptions of the causes of crime, what is actually implemented may be a compromise or a diffuse set of measures with no theoretical core (see Rosenbaum 1986). In other terms, they lack construct validity; that is, they are characterized by the absence of an adequate theoretical basis or adequate effectuation of theoretical constructs (Yin 1977, 1979).

Community crime prevention, because of its focus on negotiation by citizens, tends to be less specific and more compromised about its presumed mechanisms of change and cannot stray far from vernacular understanding. Therefore, when some change does occur (for whatever reason, connected or unconnected with a project), the "preventer" is in a good position retrospectively to posit a mechanism of change that precisely fits the facts of change. The spurious benefits that hindsight confers are well documented in cognitive psychology (see Fischoff 1983). Situational and some offender-oriented techniques, while reliant on a specification of the mechanism of how prevention should work, involve a simplicity in that mechanism that is not reflected in initiatives involving community (or police) change more generally. They are, for better or for worse, easier to impose without participation, and their technical nature can set them apart from vernacular understanding of cause and effect, sometimes at the cost of implementation failure or problems of credibility of findings.

Another difficulty with evaluating community crime prevention,

[15] This is not to deny the importance of the work of criminality prevention or to fail to acknowledge good evaluative work in this area (see Gendreau and Ross 1987; Kazdin 1987; Graham 1990).

which connects with the "assignment" issue discussed in Section I, is the company it keeps. When an agent of change encounters an area with multiple problems, her perspective naturally tends to favor multiple changes. It seems unlikely to succeed, even offensive, to put Band-Aid solutions on those suffering from multiple deprivations. Community crime prevention, given its holistic flavor, is a more tempting approach in such circumstances. Yet the preventive scheme is unlikely to be the only initiative implemented in that area. Since high-crime areas may suffer from a range of other problems, any evaluation is likely to have to contend with the probability that it will have to disentangle the effects of crime prevention from those of housing schemes, environmental improvement, poverty alleviation, or whatever.

This section has carried a somewhat damning account of community crime prevention efforts. The reader should be clear that this is because the focus of the chapter is evaluation. It may very well be contended that the virtues of community action, even if unevaluable, are worth having, and community action may well have real crime prevention effects. Accounts (not to be confused with evaluations) of community action may have an important role in enlarging the repertoire of evaluable crime preventive activities.

There have been various efforts to compare the effects of situational versus "social" or "community" crime prevention schemes in meta-analyses or reviews of evaluations (e.g., Polder 1992; Poyner 1993). These have reached conclusions that favor situational approaches. While probably sound as a basis for immediate action, these overviews have paid insufficient attention to evaluative problems peculiar to each preventive approach, on balance to the disadvantage of offender-oriented and "community" approaches. Measuring offender-oriented schemes in terms of crime rate changes is as indirect as measuring offender-oriented schemes in terms of changes in the prevalence of criminality.

IV. New Approaches to Evaluating Crime Prevention

The previous sections identified respects in which improvements in evaluation methods may be possible by continued refinement of orthodox techniques. However, more radical shifts in perspective and paradigm may be needed if real progress is to be achieved. Possibilities discussed begin with the conventional and technical and end with the unconventional and contextual. For the most part, the focus is on crime prevention rather than criminality prevention.

A. Perfecting Conventional Approaches

The type of data collected for evaluation purposes varies according to funding and project emphasis. Police records or self-report offending surveys could in principle be used, depending on whether the focus is on where offenses are committed or where offenders live. Victimization surveys are an expensive but desirable adjunct to ambitious crime prevention initiatives. Since a single data set has validity problems, more than one relevant data set offers considerable advantages.

Perfecting a pretest/posttest comparison group design might involve steps like the following. Pre- and postintervention data collection should be carried out in both target and comparison areas to establish whether any change is an artifact of changes in rates of crime reporting. Where victimization or self-report measures are considered, a posttest-only comparison group design should be contemplated because of the possibility of the pretest sensitizing people to the effects of a campaign. Ideally, there should be multiple target areas and multiple comparison areas (Skogan 1985) to overcome area-specific confounding influences and to protect against the risk of "unkind history" destroying the comparability of a single comparison area by, for example, the closure of a major employer. Otherwise, if there must be just one comparison area, the evaluation should seek to get an alternative measure of coincidental background changes in crime by obtaining recorded crime figures for the whole city (or large district) in which the preventive action took place.

If a panel design is used, a Solomon four-group design would be desirable to test for pretest × treatment interaction effects (see Campbell and Stanley 1963). In this design, two of the four groups experience the "treatment," and two are comparison groups. One of the treatment groups and one of the comparison groups has measurement taken only after the period in question, thereby measuring interaction between pretest and treatment effects. By comparisons of all four groups, such interaction can be taken into account.

Victimization surveys should extend over enough crimes, areas, and time so that measurement of displacement and diffusion of benefits should capture at least a high proportion of events displaced or benefits diffused.

Ideally, interviews with citizens and offenders and other empirical data should be collected to be confident that the mechanism of any change was as it was supposed to be. For instance, domestic burglary prevention by installation of security hardware should be accompanied by offender reports of deterrence and by an initial increase in the ratio of attempts to completions of the offense.

We know of no experiment in crime prevention that remotely approximates to these standards. Even in those studies in which random allocation has been possible, agencies have typically retained the right to identify cases that should not be regarded as available for random allocation, although in North America the problem of agency approval of random allocation designs has in recent years become much less confining. Most random allocation designs have concerned criminality prevention (see Cornish and Clarke 1972; Farrington 1983). There are probably grounds for supposing that the scale and cost of a perfected evaluation for a single project puts it beyond the realms of the practicable in most if not all circumstances. Even the most "perfect" evaluation is neither free from uncertainty nor immune from risk of implementation or measurement failure.

If crime prevention progress were to depend on end-to-end perfected evaluations, it would be even slower than it now is. While improvements in the general competence of typical designs are to be applauded, the perfection of such designs is not a realistic general way of advancing—although this is not to say that improvements in technique should not be attempted and that sophisticated and large-scale studies should never take place.

B. Linking Micro to Macro: The Safer Cities Programme Impact Evaluation

The Safer Cities Programme (SCP) was set up by the Home Office in 1988, as part of Action for Cities—the United Kingdom government's wider program of coordinated action aimed at dealing with the multiple social, physical, and economic problems of some of our larger urban areas. The SCP's objectives are to reduce crime, lessen the fear of crime, and create safer cities within which economic enterprise and community life can flourish.

The SCP is locally based (see App. A). Projects have been established in each of twenty English cities or large urban boroughs (and at the time of writing, these are closing as planned, in many cases being handed over to local management while a new wave of forty projects is being implemented). In each area, the project is guided by a steering committee representing local government, police, probation, voluntary bodies, and commerce, which sets priorities for the project and oversees the implementation of measures against crime. Each project is directed by a local coordinator with an assistant and a secretary whose salaries and running expenses are paid by the Home Office, which has also provided £250,000 per year per project for funding local organizations to implement preventive action. The kind of preventive action funded covers the entire range of methods—from physical improvements of blocks of flats to educational schemes for young people; from the installation of a single streetlight outside a retirement home to improvement of security on a large residential housing estate; from a purely geographical focus on a local neighborhood to the targeting of vulnerable groups such as ethnic minorities, women, or the elderly; from a city-center safety strategy to a citywide publicity scheme. The flavor of SCP action can be gleaned from the progress reports published annually (e.g., Home Office 1993).

The Research and Statistics Department of the United Kingdom Home Office is evaluating the *impact* of the program as a whole on its objectives, although it has to draw on basic information about aspects of the monitoring of implementation (what schemes have been implemented, where, targeted on which crime problems and which victims) and the implementation process (how the coordinators are assigning preventive action to one neighborhood rather than another). The evaluation is ongoing and due to deliver results from mid-1994. Methodological issues are described more fully in Ekblom (1992). In Campbell and Stanley's (1963) terms, the strategy started out as a nonequivalent control group design and has since moved some way toward a correlational design. The strategy of the evaluation is worth discussing in some depth, both to introduce some new perspectives it offers on evaluation in general and to describe the new methods it required to be developed. For the technically minded, key features of these methods are described in greater depth in Appendix B.

Principal sources of data include action data from SCP's Management Information System, showing for each of nearly three thousand schemes progress on implementation, the crime problems targeted, nature of preventive action, timing and financial input; action location data showing the site of each scheme, from interviews with the coordinators; outcome data including police-recorded crime statistics for selected offenses by month and police beat in eleven SCP cities and city-level statistics in nine comparison cities; and covariate data from the 1991 Census Small Area Statistics and other sources.[16]

[16] Geographic data on offender residence were also considered for inclusion but had to be omitted for reasons of poor quality and incompleteness.

In addition, survey data are available from eleven SCP project cities and eight comparison cities, covering victimization by crime, nuisance and racial harassment, fear, community satisfaction, and measures of social and economic activity. About four thousand adult residents were interviewed in 1990—before the bulk of Safer Cities action—and the same again in 1992, after much action had been implemented.[17] The survey is of the "embedded panel" kind (Skogan 1985)—a bit less than half of the respondents participating in both waves.

The basic design involves looking for associations between the action data and the outcome data, by asking whether crime or fear decrease where the SCP schemes are located. The evaluation has to take account of confounding influences such as other Action for Cities work proceeding at about the same times and places as that of SCP, which might distort the findings. Before-after changes in the action areas are to be compared with before-after changes in comparison areas where there has been no SCP action. This filters out background changes common to all areas (and England saw some very large countrywide increases in recorded crime over recent years). Two types of comparison are to be used, both drawing on police crime data and survey data. Internal comparison will be based on areas within SCP project cities which are the subject of varying amounts of SCP action; external comparison will be based on an aggregation of otherwise similar cities outside SCP.

The conventional evaluation of crime-preventive action involves assessment of a single scheme, carefully selected and located in advance and subject to reasonably tight control. But despite these ideal conditions, as Section III made clear, even the best-designed evaluations rarely provide results that are beyond dispute. The SCP impact evalua-

---

[17] Establishing a suitable sample size to give a reasonable probability of detecting the weak effect size expected was not straightforward (Ekblom 1991). The burglary rate was selected as the basis for these estimates as it is a common crime and was likely to be a popular target for preventive action. Estimates of the parameters for the calculation (including baseline prevalence of burglary, expected common trend in burglary rate from before to after, and estimated differential changes in burglary rate between action and comparison areas) were derived from several sources and several considerations and produced an eightfold range of N. The top of the range was 100,000 respondents, and even this had a worrying probability of making a false negative error. In the end, it was decided to opt for an N at the lower end of the range and to reduce aspirations from detecting differential changes in victimization (which are dependent on the occurrence of rare events) to detecting differential changes in fear and going-out behavior, on which all respondents can immediately report without waiting for victimization. These "feel-good, use the amenities" measures were a more fundamental bottom line for the evaluation than crime rates themselves, given that SCP's objectives were ultimately to improve community life.

tion faces difficult conditions that center on having to detect the effects of a set of preventive schemes that are very diverse in size and nature (some being extremely modest), that may or may not be successfully implemented, that started at different times, that possibly overlap (if not directly, then sometimes in terms of their potential "displacement zones"), and whose locations are not merely scattered but unknown in advance (a kind of "blindfold" evaluation). The effects have to be detected against a background of non-SCP preventive activity in the SCP areas themselves and in the country as a whole and against a range of other Action for Cities programs that together dwarf the SCP in funding terms.

These harsh conditions reflect the real world of program evaluation and make for a significant risk of measurement failure. The basic design was developed to face up to this risk and to cope with it economically. The strategy was to be extremely flexible, to adapt to the evolving nature of the SCP, to the unpredictable occurrence of confounds, and to emergent problems with individual data sources. The results will inevitably be surrounded by a considerable margin of uncertainty.

The most serious design problem centers on the scattered and unpredictable location and timing of the preventive action and its relatively modest scale.[18] The consequences of this conjunction of adverse features are threefold. First, the effect of a given scheme is likely to be lost when buried among "random" fluctuations and background changes in crime over whole cities; schemes with action subject to share-out over a wide area or a large number of people or properties are particularly hard to detect in comparison with schemes of an equivalent amount of input, but concentrated in a smaller zone. Second, with a partial overlap between where and when the action is located, and where and when we measure, the effects of the action on our outcome measures will suffer from dilution. With the survey, for example, at a given sampling point we may be interviewing a set of respondents, some of whom have had the preventive action but others of whom may not have, because they lived a little further down the same road. Third, not knowing in advance where the action would be located meant that, at the time of planning the location of the sampling points for the before survey, we had no guarantee of hitting any action at all.

For these reasons, we cannot have much hope of finding change in the outcome measures if we look for it "top-downward" at the city

---

[18] Other problems are described in Ekblom (1992).

level (£250,000 per year is not much to be spending in a large city); but there are similar limitations in conducting the evaluation by working "bottom-upward" from the assessment of individual schemes. While the impact of individual schemes could well be detected where they are large, concentrated geographically, and well implemented, it was methodologically and logistically difficult to envisage any way of evaluating the individual impact of many of the smaller or more diffuse schemes—and not to include these would seriously distort the picture. Besides this, there was an issue of principle—the evaluation was after all aimed at the program as a whole and its overall performance in reducing crime and fear (although individual schemes are obviously of interest from a "what works in crime prevention" perspective).

1. *The Principle of Adjusted Expectation.* The evaluation aim was to conduct a "fair test" of the program, seeking a balance between false positive and false negative errors. To cope with problems of the modest scale of preventive action, share-out of influence, and dilution of measurement, a fundamental principle of the evaluation was evolved: to look for impact only where and when it might reasonably be expected to be observed, and impact of a magnitude which it might reasonably be expected to attain. This might be called the principle of adjusted expectation.

There are several elements to the approach chosen to realize this principle, acting at both the data collection stage and analysis. They include retrospective concentration, simultaneous consideration of the impact of many schemes, a quantitative approach through statistical modeling, and a dose-response analysis. These are covered in turn.

a) Retrospective Concentration. Retrospective concentration is an approach midway between the classic alternatives of top-down and bottom-up evaluation. It involves prospectively collecting outcome data broken down into small areas that together cover a sufficiently large proportion of the territory of project cities to be sure of having a reasonable chance of hitting action; and retrospectively, during analysis, contrasting those small areas where action has turned out to have been successfully implemented with areas of no action. These no-action areas therefore support internal comparison; the small areas measured in the non-SCP cities support external comparison.

b) Simultaneous Consideration of Schemes. Considering the schemes (and the small areas in which they are sited) simultaneously greatly improves the capacity to detect impact when there are weak signals from individual schemes and plenty of background noise. This is a way of circumventing the measurement paradox that smaller schemes may be better implemented, but taken individually their impact is harder to detect.

c) Quantification and Statistical Modeling. The design also seeks to quantify the impact of the preventive action on the outcome measures, because quantitative estimates of impact are much more useful to administrators and managers. Further, with the scale and variety of preventive action implemented, a quantitative approach may offer the only real hope of demonstrating the action-outcome link. Statistical modeling is the only kind of approach to analysis capable of linking outcome to action and covariates on such a large scale and of providing quantitative estimates of impact.

d) Dose-Response Analysis. Considering the simultaneous impact of large numbers of varied schemes presents a problem. Simply to include within a statistical model a term representing "presence or absence of scheme" in a given small area would make finding a relationship difficult, because there would be immense variation in the amount of action implemented between one scheme and the next; the probability that quite a few of the small areas measured will have more than one scheme sited there further confuses the relationship. It was necessary, therefore, to modify the "present-absent" internal comparison originally envisaged in retrospective concentration by adopting an approach that enabled consideration of the effects of many schemes in their respective small areas simultaneously and that enabled the contrast of small areas with differing amounts of scheme action. A way of meeting these requirements is to conduct a dose-response analysis, often used in medical experiments. In this case, though, rather than studying the effect of increasing amounts of a drug, what is of interest is the effect of increasing amounts of preventive action falling within the small areas studied. The finding expected is that the more the action in a given small area, the greater the fall in crime and related outcome measures (or at least, given the large background increases in crime in the United Kingdom over the last few years, the smaller the rise). The dose-response perspective should provide a quantified measure of impact that is easy, moreover, to communicate to nonprofessional users of the evaluation.

2. *Realizing the Principle of Adjusted Expectation.* Putting the principle of adjusted expectation into practice involved prospective data col-

lection and retrospective analysis. Survey and crime data are handled differently; most emphasis is given to the survey, although it helps to begin by contrasting with the crime data.

a) Data Collection. The crime data in theory provide more or less total coverage of the SCP cities and thus can be guaranteed to "hit" most of the preventive action. On cost grounds this was obviously not possible for the survey—there was a trade-off between interviews that were "spread too thinly on the ground" to be useful versus those that were sufficiently concentrated but which risked being in the wrong place. Because the survey locations had to be planned in advance of the implementation of the schemes, a dual strategy was devised to maximize the chances of locating sufficient concentrations of interviews in areas where preventive action would subsequently occur. In each case, Census Enumeration Districts (EDs—about 150 households each) comprised both the small areas for the analysis and the sampling points for the survey.

Within each SCP city, interviews were conducted in a sample of fifteen EDs identified as "high-crime" through ACORN—a Census-based area classification system that had been calibrated against the British Crime Survey (Mayhew, Elliott, and Dowds 1989, app. G)—and hence of a kind to which SCP coordinators would consider as-signing preventive action.[19] Interviews were conducted on a similar basis in the external comparison cities.

In addition, to hedge bets, in the SCP cities only, sixteen "targeted action areas" in total were identified where coordinators did know in advance that there would be plenty of preventive action. These were "neighborhood-sized" territories, and interviews were conducted in up to nine EDs within each. The survey sampling strategy worked: 470 schemes, costing about £3 million, received "direct hits," including 157 burglary schemes, costing over £1.5 million.

b) Data Analysis. Modeling the effects of action on the outcome measures required development of a way of scoring the dosage of action in each small area where those outcome measures were collected. Before this could be done, it was necessary to solve another major problem in linking action to outcome. In traditional evaluation it is implicit that the survey conducted, and the crime figures collected, will be in the right place and at the right time to detect the expected change in

[19] Using ACORN had the additional advantage of independence from the other source of outcome measures, the police-recorded crime statistics.

outcome measures and will be oriented toward the particular crime problem targeted by the scheme and any population groups targeted such as ethnic minorities. In the Safer Cities evaluation none of this could be taken for granted. The action involved nearly 3,000 schemes that are scattered in space and time, targeted on a wide range of crime problems and a range of population groups. Before- and after-interviews were conducted in several hundred EDs grouped in eleven SCP cities, posing questions on a range of problems and covering a range of locations (e.g., household, neighborhood, city center) and time periods (e.g., last week, the last year, the last two years). These ecological factors intervene between knowledge of the amount of preventive action injected into an area and measurement of outcome, and it was necessary to develop ways of taking them into account in order to make the link between action and outcome as clear as possible.

The task was thus retrospectively to link knowledge of the location and timing of the action and on whom and on what crime problems it was targeted with knowledge of the location, spatial scope, and time period of outcome measures and the kinds of problems and people to which they related. All this had to be done in a context in which both action and outcome measures were extremely wide-ranging.

Practically, for logistical and methodological reasons it was inappropriate to operate on a "craft-oriented" basis with measurement and analysis fitted uniquely to each individual scheme in the traditional way; rather, an "industrial" scale had to be adopted.[20] To make matters even more difficult, action and outcome could only be linked at the analysis stage, because only then were the sites of implementation known.

The solution to the linkage problem and to the requirement to represent and estimate the dosage of action falling within each small area measured was to develop a dual-aspect process called *scoping* and *scoring*. For each statistical model constructed during the course of analysis, the starting point involved choosing a particular outcome measure (an item, or a scale, from the survey—e.g., fear of burglary—or a particu-

[20] Within the SCP itself, efforts to conduct reviews of individual evaluations focused on particular *themes* (e.g., car park crime prevention schemes [Tilley 1993*b*]) have been possible but have been considerably constrained by the usable base of individual scheme evaluations. Further afield, an attempt to link action and outcome in a recent assessment by the Dutch of their crime prevention program (Polder 1992; Junger-Tas 1993) relied on a metaanalysis of what eventually became quite a small set of individual evaluations because of successive attrition from implementation failures and measurement failures; results were unfortunately rather limited.

lar category of recorded crime from the crime data—e.g., auto crime). *Scoping* refers to the mainly qualitative process of determining whether any specific scheme of preventive action has the potential to influence this outcome measure at a particular measurement point. If a scheme is "in scope" of a particular measurement point, *scoring* is the quantitative process of representing the dose of in-scope action present.

It is worth briefly describing the basic principles developed for scoping, scoring, and modeling in the SCP evaluation, as they offer new perspectives that may be applicable in other large, multisite crime prevention evaluations and elsewhere. They may also open up new angles on single-scheme evaluations. Further details are in Appendix B.

3. *Scoping.* There are four dimensions to characterize the way in which a given preventive scheme can be said to be in scope of a given outcome measure—that is, to have the potential to influence it. First, space—is a given scheme located close enough to a point of measurement for the outcome measure to be potentially influenced? Second, time frame—is the timing of the action such that it could exert an influence on the outcome measure? Third, problem—time and space apart, is there a plausible cause-effect relationship between the nature of the action in a given scheme and the crime or fear problem measured by the outcome measure in question? Fourth, subgroups—is the outcome measure directed toward a particular population subgroup—for example, women? Is a given scheme directed toward the same subgroup?

To implement scoping, each outcome measure (that is, a particular survey question or a particular police-recorded crime category) is specified in terms of zones of detection having these four dimensions, and each scheme in terms of a zone of influence with the same dimensions. A scheme whose zone of influence overlaps a zone of detection of a given outcome measure is considered to be "in scope" and to have the potential to influence the outcome measure at the relevant point of measurement. It is only these "in-scope" schemes that contribute to action scores and are thus included in the modeling.

4. *Scoring.* Having now constructed a way of linking particular schemes to particular outcome measures taken at particular sampling points, we can return to the issue of the action dosage. There are two considerations: the nature of the dosage concept and estimation of the dosage. These are discussed more fully in Appendix B, but in brief, it was decided to define dosage quantity in terms of financial input rather than output of action. However, to reflect the likely different

performance of different types of action, it was further decided to generate separate action scores *based* on financial inputs, *but* defined in terms of "output types": for example, "£ input of situational schemes," "£ input of offender-oriented schemes," and so forth. The output types are to be identified using a classification of preventive action developed for the evaluation (Ekblom 1994*a*), one dimension of which was employed in abbreviated form in Section III of this essay.

The survey outcome measures concern (for example) the risk of being burglarized over a particular time period, averaged over a group of respondents sampled in a particular ED. The risk is averaged per household in the ED, for burglary, say, or per individual in the ED, for assault. Generalizing, this is the risk per unit at risk of victimization. To link this outcome figure to dosage in a conceptually tight way suitable for statistical modeling with quantitatively meaningful results, it was necessary to arrive at a score representing the dose of input of preventive action received for the same units—that is, the input per unit at risk of victimization.

Since it is not possible to know exactly which households or individuals among those within a given scheme's zone of influence received output from a given scheme, the approach has to work with averages.[21] These averages operate both over the populations and households contained within territories and over the time periods of measurement. The financial input to a scheme is adjusted by factors representing geographic share-out of action and dilution of measurement, and temporal share-out and dilution. The geographic adjustments are based mainly on household or resident populations in the spatial zones of influence, overlap, and detection; the temporal adjustments on the number of months over which a scheme overlaps with the time period in a survey question, divided by the total number of months which the survey question covers (more details are in App. B). If more than one scheme of the same output type overlaps with the zone of detection at a particular measurement point, the adjusted inputs from each scheme are summed. The end result is an action score for a particular output type which represents the £ input per unit at risk of victimization in the measured area, averaged over the relevant unit population in the area and over the period of measurement.

5. *Modeling Outcome on Action: The Dose-Response Analysis.* Scoping

---

[21] Respondents were asked about awareness of action, but this was extremely limited, although it may be taken into account in the modeling.

and scoring is followed by construction and exploration of statistical models. For the dependent variables there is a choice of outcome measures; explanatory variables include the relevant action dosage scores and a range of covariates. Models have to represent change in risk of victimization (or other outcome measure) between the before- and after-survey, as experienced by respondents in a given ED sampling point. In particular, do sampling points receiving more action show a greater fall in risk of victimization? And what is the rate of change of fall with input—the dose-response slope itself?

A concrete example of the clearest kind of result sought could be along these lines: "For every £100-worth of antiburglary action received on average per household in the areas measured, and fully active over the year prior to the after-survey, the probability of burglary per household over the year in question was 0.06 less than the level expected. This expected level was based on taking account of levels of risk before the action had been implemented, background changes common to areas with greater and lesser amounts of action, and demographic covariation."[22]

The survey design produced hierarchical data pairs of panel interviews (for some of the respondents), individual respondents grouped within EDs, grouped in turn within cities.[23] The best way of handling such data is through multilevel modeling (MLM) (Goldstein 1987), also known as hierarchical linear modeling (Bryk and Raudenbush 1992). Multilevel modeling is based on regression. It is a relatively new technique originating in educational studies seeking to separate out influences on pupils' progress stemming from individual pupil factors (such as ability), classroom factors (such as teacher style), and school-level factors (such as size). In criminology it offers the prospect of linking individual to area causes of crime (see Osborn et al. 1992; Raudenbush 1993) and in general of surmounting the notorious "ecological fallacy"

[22] Such a statement would apply most closely to those SCP schemes where preventive interventions were directly funded. In cases where the scheme funds were used less directly, e.g., to employ a worker to identify and deal with problems of local young people or to establish a local residents' association in order to give the neighborhood the capacity for collective action against crime—some more cautious generalization would have to be applied. To the extent that the SCP funds served to leverage additional resources from other donors, as they sometimes did, the dose of SCP funds has to be treated as something like an "investment in prevention" rather than an accurate indicator of how much preventive action took place on the ground. Given that the primary aim is to evaluate the effect of the SCP as a whole, this presents no problems. However, it does mean that the results of the evaluation have to be disentangled carefully before any conclusions can be drawn about the effectiveness of different types of preventive method.

[23] The recorded crime data are also hierarchical: monthly crime totals within beats within cities.

in which area characteristics are misleadingly attributed to individual residents. Further details of MLM are to be found in Appendix B.

Exploration of the data begins here, accompanied by interpretation based (among other things) on a consideration of key process issues such as the ways in which the SCP coordinators assigned action to particular places within their cities and the nature of the chain of implementation which may involve several steps, several agencies, and additional resource inputs.[24]

6. *Scoping, Scoring, and Modeling: Wider Considerations.* At the time of writing, the scoping, scoring, and modeling process had only just begun. In the short term, there is only time to apply the approach in its simplest form and based on elementary working assumptions to deliver answers to decision makers considering the future of the Safer Cities Programme. Looking to the longer term, there are many unknowns that can only be resolved through exploration of variants of the approach. (Unknowns are discussed in App. B, and some of the possible variants are further discussed in Ekblom 1994*b*.) In this we are fortunate to have what should prove a substantial database of details of action and measures of outcome (and covariates) in the SCP.

Looking beyond the unknowns, it will be important to highlight connections between the assumptions made in the scoping and scoring process with theory—criminological, geographical, or other assumptions.[25] In some cases the scoping and scoring process can be used not only to draw on and incorporate theory (as assumptions in the model)

[24] As discussed in Sec. I above, the assignment process is critical to interpreting the results of quasi-experimental designs. Mark (1983) in particular noted that evaluations based on dosage levels are themselves subject to misinterpretation through assignment processes. To take some examples from Skogan (1993), e.g., do implementers follow the apparent success of a scheme by pumping in more money, thus exaggerating any dose-response coefficient; or are there those who are so keen to succeed that they pertinaciously "bang their heads against the wall" with a failing scheme by sending good money after bad, thus causing understatement of the dose-response coefficient? Interviews with SCP coordinators have revealed great complexity in the assignment process; this picture will be supplemented by a geographical analysis of scheme location.

[25] Given the extreme diversity of the preventive methods employed by the SCP schemes, any overall "macro" theory of "the" mechanism of Programme impact was impossible to consider. Rather, scoping and scoring seek to represent collections of micro mechanisms, albeit fairly crudely at first, operating in small areas repeated on the macro scale. Context can similarly be represented, again crudely, through small area-level data such as derive from the Census or from mean fear scores of respondents surveyed in the area. Macro theories of implementation could be another matter and will receive attention in the analysis of the process of assignment of the preventive action and the subsequent sequence of implementation (relating, e.g., to such explicit but difficult-to-operationalize themes as "partnership"). In this connection, Tilley (1992) endeavored to characterize a common macro process through which SCP coordinators sought to establish community safety structures and policies in the local government of their area, coming in as "moneyed strangers."

but to test and put quantitative estimates on influences—for example, to look for evidence of diffusion of benefit and how this shades into displacement.[26] Theory will be far better served if the collection of quantitative action data in some future evaluation can be extended beyond monetary input, to include reliable and comprehensive measures of output and data on offender residence. It will also benefit from taking account of the influence of contextual factors (e.g., the demographic composition of small areas) on any dose-response relationships identified.

A major limitation of the "performance indicators" approach to management is that local changes in the performance indicators—outcome criteria—are rarely linked to changes in the local input of resources or output of action. The "design" of evaluations of preventive action which rely on little more than observing changes in performance indicators alone, qualified by some post hoc interpretation, is extremely weak. *Provided* that one day the police are able to implement a crime database that is incident-based and georeferenced (a facility that already exists in some U.S. forces), and *provided* that there is some ongoing management information system recording the amount, type, and location of preventive action implemented, the scoping and scoring approach is capable of linking action and outcome in real time to feed into management assessments of routine preventive activity rather than (as at present) into a more one-off evaluation exercise of specific schemes or programs. There is no reason scoping and scoring could not be extended to cover the preventive functions of conventional policing.

In evaluation itself, scoping and scoring could act rather like an extension of the "power of the test" approach to assessing whether a particular evaluation design, for a particular scheme or program, is worth conducting—that is, has a reasonable chance of detecting impact. It can contribute to the estimation of "effect size" (e.g., Weisburd 1993). In a practitioner context it has connections with Berry and Carter's (1992) concept of "preevaluation"—estimating in advance of implementation whether the scheme in question has much chance of making a real difference to crime levels. It is fair to say that even the best-designed evaluations of individual preventive schemes are inescapably affected by issues of scoping and scoring—share-out of action in

---

[26] In this case there is some convergence with physical sciences where today's theory is tomorrow's measuring instrument or the following day's mass-produced consumer device.

its zone of influence, overlap with the zone of detection, and dilution of measurement within the zone of detection—but seem, so far, largely to have been blind to them. Attempts to derive a body of quantitative ("what works, to what degree for what cost?") knowledge within crime prevention are unlikely to deliver any findings with meaningful numbers attached to them unless scoping and scoring are incorporated. The same applies even more to metaevaluations or reviews of prevention schemes.[27]

Altogether, the scoping, scoring, and dose-response approach described here has many possibilities to set alongside its many uncertainties—in methodology, theory, practice, and evaluation. It may even, in the longer term, help connect the strategic planning and evaluation of crime prevention with econometrics and quantitative ecology.

C. Causation Reconsidered: The Scientific Realist Approach

A very different approach to improvement, stemming from philosophical considerations of the concept of causation, is to change the nature of evaluation more fundamentally. A persuasive explanation of how this may be put into place is provided by Pawson and Tilley (1992) in an article that applies to the evaluation of situational, offender-oriented, and "community" crime prevention alike. In brief, they oppose "method-driven evaluation, and in particular the view of causation implied in most quasi-experimental thinking in evaluation research. What is proposed is *theory-driven* or *explanatory evaluation*" (p. 1). They quote Rosenbaum (1988, p. 382) who contends that "[there is] a compelling need to open up the 'black box' of community crime prevention and test the many presumed causal links in our theoretical models. We are past the point of wanting to report that crime prevention does or does not work, and now are interested in specifying the conditions under which particular outcomes are observed." Pawson and Tilley refer to their approach as "scientific realist."[28]

Scientific realism is a well-established approach in the philosophy of science (Bhaskar 1978; Harre 1986), distinguished by its view of causa-

[27] The Dutch metaevaluation mentioned earlier (Polder 1992; Junger-Tas 1993) identified a factor related to share-out, the "intensity" of a scheme, as a predictor of its success. From the scoping and scoring perspective, this may relate to measurement issues, and the power of the evaluation, as much as it comprises a substantive finding about scheme effectiveness.

[28] As a result of comments on an earlier draft of this essay, it seems worth pointing out that scientific realism has nothing in common with the U.K. criminological school of "left realism," other than the use of the word "realism."

tion as "generative" rather than "successionist" (Harre 1972). It is difficult to encapsulate this difference in a nutshell (further elaboration is in Pawson and Tilley [1994] and Harre [1972]), but "generative" implies theorizing about interactive causal mechanisms (e.g., the causes of gunpowder exploding involve not just a spark, but the propensity of the gunpowder to be ignited by the spark in dry conditions) while "successionist" implies emphasis on individual causes taken in isolation (e.g., talking just of the spark being "the cause" of the explosion). Generative causation is seen as being fundamentally "real," whereas for the successionist, statements about causation are considered merely as inferences from the juxtaposition of events. The causes and effects remain as detached observations plugged loosely into a black box. Conventional experiments involve plugging treatment in at one end of the box and looking for statistically linked effects emerging at the other.

The purpose behind the scientific realist approach is the establishment and test of the mechanisms presumed to underpin regularities in causal relationships. While many of the standard features of quasi-experimental or experimental evaluation would remain in place in a scientific realist approach—careful measurement, before-after comparison, and so forth—the function of such devices is changed from that of "experimental control" to one of "mechanism hunting." The matching necessary to choose a comparison group "is conceived under the one-dimensional constant conjunction notion of causality in which variables can only 'act upon' other variables and have no other explanatory function. The ontological depth afforded by the notions of 'mechanism' and 'context' is missing. Matching thus seeks to cancel out what needs to be counted in if the proper scope of experimental understanding is to be realized" (Pawson and Tilley 1992, pp. 9–10). With the scientific realist approach, "the three core ideas of programme efficacy—mechanism, context, regularity—play the guiding hand in enquiry" (p. 12). The ideal design would involve obtaining a strong, reliable/replicable effect and manipulating it to see the contexts under which it works and to throw further light on theory and mechanism.

The most effective criticism of traditional approaches by Pawson and Tilley is their (1994) dissection of Bennett's (1991) evaluation of police contact patrols, which were intended to reduce fear and enhance communication by establishing routine contacts between police and residents. Acknowledging Bennett's study as representing the pinnacle of traditional quasi-experimental design, they nevertheless point out that the evaluation has at its center a large and rather empty black box.

First, exactly what is meant by "contact" and how it is supposed to work (its mechanisms) are completely glossed over; contact is treated like some amorphous ingredient spooned into the action areas. Second, the design irons out interesting and little-remarked-on differences between the two action areas, which could have been used to identify key contextual factors necessary to the success of the intervention.

Elements of the scientific realist approach have of course featured in earlier evaluations. Research in the community crime prevention literature that most closely approximates the approach was undertaken by Hope and Foster (1992), who described the context of (inter alia) resident confidence, physical vulnerability, and housing mix to account for changes in crime and criminality.[29] The Kirkholt burglary-reduction project (Forrester, Chatterton, and Pease 1988; Forrester et al. 1990) was also mentioned as linking the mechanism of change to what was achieved. Pawson and Tilley could also have devoted space to the work of Bottoms, Wiles, and their colleagues on the changing patterns of crime and criminality on Sheffield housing estates (Bottoms, Mawby, and Xanthos 1989; Bottoms and Wiles 1991, 1992).

The Kirkholt experience illustrates the centrality of change mechanisms. While repeat domestic burglaries had fallen virtually to zero, and first-time burglaries had fallen substantially, there remained a stubborn hump in September. Further analysis revealed that the problem lay in a two-week period of September and that victims were disproportionately elderly. It became clear that the September hump was a function of the distinctive holiday habits of the elderly, retained from a period in which the mills were closed for a week or fortnight for maintenance and holidays for the workforce. This recognition made the refinement of preventive action possible.

Another way in which the Pawson and Tilley formulation is attractive concerns the study of repeat victimization, dealt with in detail by Farrell in his essay in this volume. In one area, the creation of a domestic violence unit within one division of a city force produced a total number of calls to the police that was the same as that of the year before it was established. However, dividing calls into those that were repeats and those which were first time from an address showed an interesting pattern. The prevalence of victims calling the police in-

[29] The scientific realist approach of Pawson and Tilley is one in which good quasi-experimental or randomized designs are retained where the causal sequence is less than simple. The Hope and Foster study of which Pawson and Tilley approve is a quasi-experimental (nonequivalent control group) design—albeit a "good" one.

creased, but the number of calls per victim decreased in the division. This is consistent with an explanation as follows: establishing and publicizing a service for the victims of domestic violence may reduce the threshold at which a victim makes contact. However, insofar as the service provided reduces the problem, there will be fewer repeat calls. These two effects offset each other to produce an impression of no effect. Whether this is a reasonable account of how domestic violence units are likely to work or whether it is just a post hoc rationalization, only replication will tell.[30] The point is that the importance of analysis of the data along the lines of the mechanisms of change cannot be overemphasized. This approach also has the advantage of offering an understanding of displacement/deflection mechanisms that transforms that phenomenon from the bogeyman brought forward by extreme-case pessimists in crime prevention to an effect which may be malign or benign and offers measurement opportunities (see Barr and Pease 1990, 1992). The scientific realist approach has as its natural aim the understanding of how to shape crime as much as how to eliminate it.

The scientific realist approach gives replication a key role in teasing out mechanism and context. However, as Tilley (1993a) himself notes, defining precisely what counts as a replication and what does not is conceptually problematic. He illustrates the problem with an examination of a number of Safer Cities schemes attempting to replicate, more or less closely, the Kirkholt antiburglary project. For example, he identifies ten distinct mechanism-based attributes of the project that may or may not feature in a replication and assesses the extent to which the "candidate replicates" share these attributes. He distinguishes three positions on replication: the "strict," the "relativist," and the "scientific realist." The first by definition almost writes itself out of the realms of practical possibility, for obvious reasons. The second accepts that strict replication is not possible, holding instead that what constitutes a replication has to be based on consensus within the scientific community. The scientific realist position is that this is too vague for practical or academic use. The scientific realist concepts of mechanism and context can, however, fit the requirement quite nicely: they can articulate just exactly what lay at the heart of a scheme to be replicated and how both mechanism and context can be systematically altered to achieve the progression of deliberately slightly different variations that are re-

---

[30] Victims who have made calls and then stopped should also be interviewed to ensure that they stopped calling because the problem was resolved rather than because they felt no real help was available.

quired for understanding how the scheme works, in which contexts, and how to develop the best practical combinations of ingredients. Understanding the mechanisms of changes is crucial for their generalization to other contexts, as discussing the reasons for failure to change (both theory/mechanism failure and implementation failure) are crucial for revising plans.

With all its apparent advantages, there are some drawbacks to the scientific realist approach, particularly if it does not incorporate some element of prediction. There is a danger that the realist strategy, unhindered by the obligation to predict, would generate a vocabulary of explanation that owes more to theoretical fashion than to cause. Merseyside police area during the late 1980s, for example, showed substantial reductions in rates of recorded crime against the national trend. The area is also a national center of the Natural Law Party. That party contends that a key number of its adherents practicing transcendental meditation in the area is the cause of that reduction.[31]

To some extent the threat from post hoc specification of mechanism may be minimized if appropriate measures of intermediate impact have been taken. In a study of the effectiveness of experimental police truancy patrols (Ekblom 1979), an apparent success story (in terms of reductions in numbers of children at large in school hours) was shown to be suspect by virtue of the finding that the patrols stopped hardly any children. However, other problems in identifying mechanism remain. Many preventive methods (as Sec. III argued and as the CCTV example below illustrates) may operate by multiple mechanisms, leading to complexity of inference. And preventive action is often deliberately introduced in the form of a package of measures using different preventive methods and mechanisms, in order, for example, to remove obvious "Achilles' heels"—easy routes to displacement of method of offending (such as failure to target harden door frames and windows at the same time as improving locks—see Forrester, Chatterton, and Pease 1988) or to provide for complementary focusing on situational, offender-oriented, and community crime prevention in the hope of achieving synergy. These issues do not reduce the value of the scientific

---

[31] Demonstrating that this is not a plausible interpretation of what happened is perhaps an instance of scientific realism in practice. If a simple miasma produced by meditation were the change agent, changes should occur across crime types and be no smaller in the division of the Merseyside Police close to the building where meditation was practiced. However, change was limited to some crime types, and crime rose in parts of Merseyside where the meditation took place.

realist approach. They simply note that the web of cause and consequence it rightly seeks to get to grips with is large and complex.

Practicality also competes with the full realization of any thoroughgoing approach, including scientific realism. We have difficulty enough in establishing an effect in the first place, and when practical, political, resource, or time scale constraints impose themselves, what then? Is it feasible to do enough such replications to take account of the combined effects of extraneously varying factors (which may or may not be measured)? On many occasions the answer again is probably not—which is why we are forced into random-assignment experimental designs, or quasi-experimental ones with matched comparisons to neutralize those factors. It is unlikely, to take an extreme example, that replication of the Safer Cities Programme and its evaluation could ever be achieved, and it is difficult to discern a clear and unitary impact mechanism running through what is essentially a vehicle for implementing a deliberately eclectic assemblage of schemes. Under certain circumstances, however, the replication/manipulation approach can be effected. Poyner and Woodall's (1987) study of shop theft in a major department store on London's Oxford Street was able to observe crime-reducing effects of the implementation of particular security measures, followed by an increase in crime again once the measures were removed. This enlightening process (akin to medical research where the effects of a hormone, say, are investigated by adding and then removing it) was observable because the rate of offending was sufficiently high (a steady flow of incidents rather than a trickle of individual rare events) for changes to be tracked rather fast, because the intervention was easy to manipulate, and because the experimental environment, being in a single private institution, was subject to a high level of control.

Pawson and Tilley began as critics of existing evaluation methods. By the time this volume is published, several retrospective evaluations using the scientific realist approach—or at least part of it—will have been published. In the first such evaluation, Tilley looked at the effects of CCTV on parking lot crime in those Safer Cities schemes which implemented this measure. The distinctive feature of Tilley's approach was the careful listing of the possible mechanisms through which an effect would be obtained. These were as follows:

a) CCTV reduces car crime by making it more likely that present offenders will be caught, stopped, removed, punished and deterred;

b) CCTV reduces car crime by deterring potential offenders who will not wish to risk apprehension and conviction by the evidence captured on videotape or observed by an operator on a screen on which their behavior is shown;

c) The presence of CCTV leads to increased use of car parks, because drivers feel less at risk of victimization. Increased use enhances natural surveillance which deters potential offenders, who feel they are at increased risk of apprehension in the course of criminal behavior;

d) CCTV allows for the effective deployment of security staff or police officers towards areas where suspicious behavior is occurring. They then act as a visible presence deterring potential offenders. They may also apprehend actual offenders red-handed and disable their criminal behavior;

e) The publicity given to CCTV and to its usage in catching offenders is received by potential offenders who avoid the increased risk they believe to be associated with committing car crimes in car parks. The perceived risks of offending exceed the perceived benefits, and offending either ceases or is displaced by place or offense;

f) CCTV, and signs that it is in operation, symbolize efforts to take crime seriously and to reduce it. The potential offender perceives crime to be more difficult or risky and is deterred;

g) Those car crimes that can be completed in a very short space of time will be less reduced than those that take more time, as the offender calculates the time taken for police or security officers to come, or the probability that the panning cameras will focus in on him or her;

h) CCTV, and notices that it is in operation, remind drivers that their cars are vulnerable, and they take greater care to lock them, to operate any security devices, and to remove easily stolen items from view;

i) Cautious drivers, who are sensitive to the possibility that their cars may be vulnerable and are habitual users of various security devices, use and fill those car parks with CCTV and thereby drive out those who are more careless, whose vulnerable cars are stolen from elsewhere. [Tilley 1993*b*, pp. 3–4]

These possibilities, although exhausting, are not exhaustive, but they do imply different patterns of crime following CCTV installation, and in principle a settled view of mechanism could be approximated to. Because Tilley's analysis was retrospective, some of the data necessary to distinguish between his alternatives were not collected. The reader is referred to the original monograph for the complexities of Tilley's conclusions. To give their flavor, his analysis makes it clear that theft of cars is reduced more by CCTV than theft from cars. It also makes it clear that the number of arrests is extremely small. The "active ingredient(s)" seem therefore to be linked to offender perceptions rather than to an elevated risk of detection, and one that has more effects on car thieves than on thieves from cars. One would have expected it to be the other way around, since thieves from cars will be captured by CCTV as they leave cars while heavily laden (not the typical pattern of the shopper, for example). One possibility is that thieves of cars are more often opportunity takers than thieves from cars. Another is that CCTV "brings into play" perceptions of risks at vehicle exits through barriers, which do not exist when one leaves as a pedestrian.

The scientific realist approach is interesting and provocative and in our view is likely to prove an immensely valuable contribution to the literature.[32] For evaluations of individual methods of intervention, it has a lot to commend it as the exclusive one to adopt. It may however be less suitable for the evaluation of large and amorphous preventive programs. But it should be possible to supplement the latter type of evaluation by scientific-realist-driven analyses, and the car park CCTV evaluation just described is just such a theme-based supplement to the basic Safer Cities Programme evaluation.

While some would claim that scientific realism is just a fancy name for a well-understood development in evaluation over the last two decades, this would be to overlook its major thrust and explicit philosophical foundations. And while others have made it clear that the analysis of mechanism and context is crucial to progress (and we have cited Skogan and Rosenbaum to this effect), the state of the art at the time of writing suggests that many evaluators do not behave as though this were true.

The scientific realist approach clearly and elegantly communicates these issues and, as an instance of the practical nature of philosophy, offers a way of articulating them in the service of implementing and evaluating preventive schemes. One of the many virtues of the ap-

[32] Indeed, it should be noted that the use of the term "mechanism" in this essay stems from a reading of scientific realist works.

proach is that it requires intending preventers of crime to clarify their methods, how they will know they have succeeded, what are the incidental or incompatible effects of success, and so on. It will generate better considered crime prevention, at least.

The tendency of those given responsibility for crime prevention to rediscover the wheel, however, is substantial. If the literature remains unread, how optimistic can we be that the discipline of prospective specification of mechanism will be observed? The key practical ingredient in implementing a scientific realist approach to evaluation is whether it will prove possible to convince practitioners, collaborators, or administrators, as commissioners of research, of the value of repeated trials, evaluations, and adjustments focusing on a particular method and mechanism, instead of pursuing an unconsolidated conquest of virgin territory through a series of unrelated one-shot studies. To end on a positive note, in England the approach has begun to engage the interest of both practitioners and crime prevention administrators.

V. The Context of Evaluation

Theory, techniques, and logistics are not the only determinants of successful evaluation. No amount of methodological sophistication can help if evaluations are difficult to commission, burdensome to gain agreement for, and exhausting to make users trust enough to apply their results. "Credibility failure" ought perhaps to be added to Rosenbaum's (1986) other three failures.

In all this, it is the context of evaluation that is important. In the United Kingdom at least, the situation has fairly recently changed following a government drive on "value-for-money" known as the Financial Management Initiative, from one in which evaluators were able to "parachute in" and conduct an evaluation on their own terms to one where they are increasingly "shackled together" with administrators and practitioners and are jointly responsible for arriving at an answer.[33] However, there are still many problems and issues to resolve, and in several respects this greater closeness makes them all the more significant. In setting out these issues, and proposing solutions, it is useful to recall who has an interest in an evaluation, as commissioners, collaborators, and consumers of results. Academics (who may have had vary-

---

[33] North America got there first; e.g., the Canadian government produced sophisticated guidelines on evaluation over a decade ago.

ing degrees of experience with evaluation), consultants, local and national administrators and policymakers, commercial companies, and practitioners like the police and local crime prevention teams may all have a stake. Their understanding of evaluation, its various functions, its constraints and possibilities, will differ. As might be expected, many of the differences of opinion that arise center on the issue of uncertainty and how to handle it. So, too, will the stakeholders' interest in the results differ—sometimes quite dramatically.

A. The Practitioner: Never Mind the Quality, Feel the Width

At the practitioner level, the biggest problem with the evaluation of crime prevention is still its absence rather than its flaws when present.[34] Even where there is some kind of evaluation, most accounts of crime prevention purpose and performance deal with implementation or output rather than impact or outcome.

Conversations with police and probation officers reveal a profound cynicism about the use of well-founded evaluation techniques in improving the service they offer. There is no professional culture of self-evaluation in the criminal justice agencies. Part of this may be because of the gulf between formal and informal goals.

There is a lack of evaluative expertise. This may sound strange in a land overflowing with social science graduates, but the typical grounding in methodological knowledge is not strong.

There has been a relationship between the measurement of success and professional status. High-status professions measure success as output. The number of kidneys competently transplanted is taken as a measure of success. The number of competently handled transactions is not an acceptable measure of the success of a shopkeeper. The profit shown is. The number of files opened is the Ministry of Circumlocution's success in Charles Dickens's *Little Dorrit* (1880). Dickens would prefer a measure of outcome. Given that police status remains high (or at least that the need for policing, like medicine, is completely unquestioned), measures like the numbers of Homewatch schemes started have been an acceptable substitute for a measure of outcome in terms of crime prevented or criminals detected. An encouraging trend is that outcome-based performance measures have begun to appear in the United Kingdom, at least for routine police activity.

---

[34] Strictly speaking, "absence" is not quite the right description—rather, it is a case of evaluation by anecdote, glossy publications, and press briefings as a substitute for formal and rigorous assessment.

Goldstein (1979), in an influential article, was among the first to argue that policing was obsessed with process and output at the expense of outcome. How do we get from the present position of indifference to or skepticism about evaluation to a position of defensible evaluation without going through the forest of flawed designs, behind each of whose trees lies a skeptic, academic, or practitioner, all too willing to scoff and destroy? The answer, advanced below, depends on what is perceived to be defensible evaluation.

B. The Administrator Problem: Bring Me Solutions Yesterday!

Administrators and policy makers are now beginning to come to grips with evaluation. They want answers that are reliable, valid, fast, cheap, and risk-free. Difficulties often emerge when evaluators tell them that they cannot have speed, certainty, and economy all at the same time. In some cases, it is all too easy for administrators to maintain unrealistic expectations about what evaluation can achieve—and to try to leave the resolution of such trade-off questions to the professional evaluators alone. There is also a particular problem about the handling of failure. Failure of some preventive action to have an impact can be highly instructive if it was anticipated in conceptualizing the intervention in terms of mechanism and in planning the collection of diagnostic data on what might go wrong and if the knowledge gained is fed into a cycle of repeated corrections, trials, and improvements.[35] For this to work would seem to require a major reorientation of administrators' understanding of evaluation, down to and including the basis of organizational reward for practitioners.

C. Evaluators: If You're Not Part of the Solution, You're Part of the Problem

So much for practitioners and administrators; but part of the problem may stem from evaluators themselves. Coming, as most of them do, from a background in social research, they may fail to realize that they have changed the context in which they are operating and consequently fail to realize that the function of the evaluations that they are conducting may also have changed. "Academic" evaluations and academic research require, of course, exceptionally rigorous quality

---

[35] Of course, this is not to imply that the discovery of a prima facie success story should not also be accompanied by thorough cross-checking and diagnosis in the context of a good design and thorough analysis, although we suspect that such successes are often given an "easier ride."

control, in order to ensure that only the most reliable and valid findings are admitted to the body of cumulative academic knowledge. In particular, the risk of mistakenly inferring a successful impact on crime (the "false positive" error) is considered more important to avoid than the risk of failure to detect an effect (the "false negative" error). This is embodied in the usual tests of statistical significance. This orientation can be entirely inappropriate (Ekblom 1990; Weisburd 1993) when rigidly applied to evaluation in its prospective function of guiding decisions in the real world and was a significant element in the "nothing works" era in which the climate of pessimism was pervasive (see Lipton, Martinson, and Wilks 1975; Brody 1976).[36]

Practitioners and administrators cannot take "don't know" for an answer merely because p has just exceeded .05, a value that was set by convention for reasons of quality control (Oakes 1986; Ekblom 1990). Nor may they always give greater importance to the avoidance of "false positive" errors than the avoidance of "false negatives." It depends on the consequences, to the users, of making one or other type of error regarding the decision in question. What the reasonable user does want is the clearest answer possible for the resources and time available—and increasingly, she wants a quantified answer. To what extent does the scheme work, at what cost? Research and evaluation is undoubtedly becoming more quantified, but the form the quantification takes may not be at all "user-friendly" for the nonprofessional: how many administrators or practitioners are able to make sense of a regression coefficient (especially a logistic one)?[37] The associated danger if academic evaluators cannot adapt their methods, or convince administrators to adapt their requirements, is that administrators will enlist the private sector in evaluation. Whatever the competence of management consultants and private-sector evaluators, there will always be a commercial pressure to define the problem and its solution unquestioningly in the form in which the client offers.

D. Some Partial Solutions

Evaluators must sell evaluation to the other interested parties, in terms of obtaining their agreement to sponsor, commission, or participate in the evaluation; their commitment to continue supporting the

---

[36] This was despite the availability of more sophisticated texts that explicitly addressed notions of trade-offs between statistical error types in social interventions (see Crane 1983).

[37] The same question might be asked of evaluators.

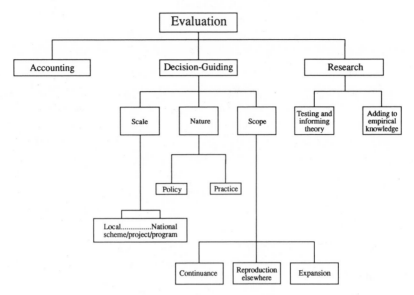

F<small>IG</small>. 4.—Some functions of evaluation

evaluation by supplying adequate data and minimizing breakdowns of control, pulling out of sponsorship, or drastically changing the questions to be addressed; and their readiness to take the results seriously. But these others, too, have responsibilities to assume. A first step is for all parties to recognize that evaluation is not one simple homogeneous activity. Evaluation has a number of different aspects (focus on impact, focus on implementation, etc.). Evaluation also has a divergence of functions that it can serve. Figure 4 shows the range of functions (although it does not pretend to be exhaustive). Accounting evaluations are limited, backward-looking exercises essentially checking whether money (devoted to a given crime prevention scheme, for example) has been properly spent and value obtained. Decision-guiding evaluations serve to inform (if not always to determine) policy or practice in the real world. (There is, of course, the purely theory-testing evaluation, but in the nature of social science funding, theory testing is much more likely to be done as a by-product—albeit an important one—of decision-guiding evaluation.) The scale of these decisions can vary from local to national or, along related lines, from scheme to program evaluation, and their scope can vary from continuance (should we keep funding this scheme or this program?) to reproduction elsewhere (should we set up more schemes like this one?). Evaluations can be conducted in different ways, depending on the function they are intended to serve and how important it is to the user to avoid getting an answer that could be wrong, inconclusive, or too late to be useful. In particular, evaluations can be carried out at different levels of technical sophistication, with more or less resources and over a longer or shorter time scale—for example, simple, cheap, and quick with a wide margin of uncertainty and risk of measurement failure versus sophisticated, costly, and slow but more certain and more sure. This involves trade-offs between conflicting constraints—it is of course rarely possible to have an evaluation that is simultaneously simple, quick, cheap, and reasonably sure. What is to be aspired to is a move away from standard, off-the-shelf, and often inadequate designs toward approaches informed by the emphasis on mechanism and encouragement of the wit to understand the package of consequences that would be derived from a particular mechanism and how that might be assessed as a package. All involved in the evaluation enterprise should move toward the willingness to fail and the readiness to learn from failure.

1. *Professional Evaluators: Uncompromising Rigor Is Rigor Mortis.* Social researchers, when they become professional evaluators contributing information for the guidance of decisions in policy and practice, often have to reorient themselves—learning to apply their methods to altered circumstances. What follows may be familiar to professional evaluators who have "made the change," but since we have seen sufficient cases of those who have not, it is worth outlining the nature of the change, for the benefit of novice evaluators and novice users of their services alike.

The methods do not greatly change from basic research to evaluation—rather, the change comes in the way they are applied and attuned to give the best possible answers to questions posed in a range of contexts—from "blue skies—funds no problem" to the far more likely real-world circumstances of financial constraint, short time scales, deficient data, and imperfect experimental control. This should not be misunderstood: we are not remotely advocating a relaxation of professional discipline. Rather, we are suggesting that professional evaluators are required to meet more exacting requirements than those in academic research. Instead of working within comfortably fixed parameters such as "$p = .05$," they have to work from first principles. In some cases, the .05 criterion has to be relaxed; but in others, it might actually have to be tightened (Skogan 1985) to .01 or better. In some circumstances, where the measure is cheap or free, the criterion should not be based on the risk of mistaking a false difference for a real one, but of mistaking a real difference for a false one. Crane (1983) calculates (for other contexts) the number of true differences missed by applying the conventional criteria, and this is crucial information, particularly when an intervention is cheap and easy.

The "ideal" study from a traditional perspective is one in which a design is set up with almost every last detail elaborated in advance and then launched on a ballistic path to completion; neither the evaluation measures nor the activity being evaluated is adjusted in mid-trajectory for fear of contamination. Such aspired-to purity renders the evaluation totally hostage to fortune: the only evaluation certainty is that the unexpected will happen. There is little point in remaining pure, if the evaluation suffers from avoidable measurement failure or if the decision not to provide feedback to correct practical shortcomings that emerge leads straight to implementation failure, leaving little worthwhile to evaluate (Skogan 1985). Under most circumstances, then, evaluators should be ready to adopt the approach of "formative" evaluation (see Weiss 1985), in which they feed back on progress and problems to the implementers. In this, they must accept that the results of their evaluations may only generalize to initiatives where there is an evalua-tor involved (or at least a "monitor," briefed by earlier professional evaluations), capable of supplying such feedback. But with complex and expensive preventive activity, this should surely be part of the implementation management process anyway.

Evaluators should be prepared to move (and to take administrators and practitioners along with them) from a "one-shot" view of evaluation to one in which there is built-in scope for learning from failure, adjust-ment, and repetition. In so doing, this should contribute to the shift from the "nothing works" perspective to "what works, in what con-text?" (Rosenbaum 1988; Ekblom 1990; Pawson and Tilley 1992).

More generally, professional evaluators are required to be versatile in the use of statistical techniques (and aware of their individual limita-tions); clever and imaginative at creating research designs and able to identify weaknesses imposed by external constraints and to find the next-best remedies; accustomed to collecting and using diagnostic in-formation, much of which may be qualitative; and able to strike sensi-ble balances between different sources of uncertainty—for example, it is little use deciding to devote a great deal of resources to reducing statistical uncertainty, if you can drive a coach and horses through the broader cause-effect uncertainty. Evaluators must be able to adjust the parameters of the study, its resources, and timing according to the context in which it is to be used. In some circumstances an expensive, very high-quality evaluation will be appropriate; in others, a simple, cheap, rough-and-ready one.[38] But in all cases, to be able to decide which is needed, the evaluator requires a sophisticated grasp of first principles and an awareness of the functional framework mentioned above. (This is not unlike the modern health-care situation, where professionals and administrators have to choose which patient gets the expensive and sophisticated treatment and which gets the low-cost version.) This has particular implications for the conduct of evaluators at the start and the finish of evaluations.

At the start, the evaluator has to raise the issue of uncertainty with the user of the evaluation, pointing out in particular the trade-off between false positive and false negative errors. Rather than allowing administrators to delegate the task to the evaluators, evaluators must stand their ground and make a joint responsibility of the setting of cost, time, uncertainty, and risk parameters, together with criteria for defining a program as successful (Skogan 1985)—for example, will a 5 percent reduction in crime, or a 10 percent reduction, mean success? But the trade-off is not infinitely elastic: there will be times when the evaluator should be prepared to tell the user that within the constraints of resources and timing that have been set, the uncertainty is likely to be so great that an evaluation would be worthless.

At the end of an evaluation, the analysis of data will have to be exploratory—it is really only at this stage that some of the problems of data or of inference emerge. Such exploration is usually open-ended, in that there is no single point at which the evaluator can say "eureka!": there are always other possible explanations to consider, even in the best randomly assigned or scientific realist study. The point of completion is a matter for the evaluator's professional judgment, that the balance of plausibility of the alternative explanations for the findings has tipped sufficiently far toward the side of the conclusion drawn.[39]

[38] To state a contrary principle, it can be argued that there is a kind of "tithe" to be paid in generating a collective benefit to practitioners, theorists, and policymakers alike from investing in a better class of evaluation than the immediate context dictates. And a cynic might say that if the fate of evaluations is often to be ignored by those who commission them, then the evaluator might as well look to a wider audience, whether in terms of theorists or practitioners, in ensuring that the effort and the findings are put to some good use.

[39] This is not to say that such judgment is infallible or that further debate is unlikely: the results of the Kansas City preventive patrolling experiment (Kelling et al. 1974) are

Once quoted, numbers have a tendency to forget their uncertain origins. Having finally produced some results, the evaluator cannot simply hand over an unqualified answer and run the risk that it will be taken at face value by the user. Fortunately, the competent manager or administrator is accustomed to decision making under conditions of uncertainty, so the solution is to provide the user with an assessment that contains the evaluative judgment together with the associated range of uncertainty. On the quantitative side, this can be done by providing an estimate of the size or strength of a preventive effect together with confidence limits.[40] (These confidence limits need not be completely based on statistical tests, which only cover some of the sources of uncertainty—one might give a range of values for the preventive effect based on a comparison of estimates derived from different measures or based on different assumptions. For example, much of Farrell's work cited in his essay in this volume incorporates calculations of this kind.) When victimization surveys are used to estimate levels of crime and its reduction, some respondents say that they have been repeatedly victimized but that they do not know how many times or that there were too many times to remember. How many this is taken to mean can be very influential in determining rates of victimization and the size of preventive effects, and a range of assumptions should be made. Similar problems faced Forrester, Chatterton, and Pease (1988) in their attempt to estimate how many thefts from prepayment coin meters could be attributed to the householder and how many to burglars. Ekblom's (1987) evaluation of an initiative to combat post office robberies in London by improving the security screen was faced with estimating how much of the fall in robberies that followed implementation was attributable to the security initiative versus how much to common background falls in robbery, for which there was also some evidence. Three different assumptions were made: that the entire face value fall could be attributed to the initiative, that the rate

---

still the subject of dispute. One way of protecting against such disputes in advance might be to conduct simulation studies, a further development of the power analyses described by Weisburd (1993) in which the evaluation design is, or is not, shown to have a decent chance of detecting a properly implemented, theoretically sound effect of a reasonable size. This is like passing test signals of known amplitude through a radio detector and seeing whether they are picked up.

[40] Effect size must of course be distinguished from the effect's degree of statistical significance (Oakes 1986): large samples can confer significance on substantively trivial effects.

of all other robberies of business premises in London could indicate the background fall (which could then be indexed out), and that one of the methods of robbery in the post offices not directly affected by the security measure (attacks on staff or customers outside the secure area) could itself be used to indicate the background fall. Each of these estimates was judged to be biased in a particular direction, and a decision was made (a kind of "intelligent averaging") as to the weight to place on each. With an acknowledged wide margin of error, it was estimated that the initiative had reduced the rate of successful robberies in London by about forty-five per year. It may be possible to apply techniques of sensitivity analysis in circumstances similar to that of the post office robberies study—varying the values of some of the parameters in the calculations to see how robust the estimate of impact is, in the face of errors of measurement and of alternative assumptions.

A wider range of user-friendly and easily communicable outcome measures can be developed to convey quantitative effects in a meaningful way. The Safer Cities evaluation, for example, focuses on a "dose-response" analysis, as previously described. It is perhaps a truism that all evaluations of the impact of crime prevention, being assessments of "nonevents," have to compare observed crime levels with levels expected had the intervention not taken place. Ekblom's (1987) evaluation of an antirobbery initiative in post offices, just described, used a variant of the observed-expected technique known as "shift-share" in econometrics, to generate expected robbery levels for comparison with actual levels. Each of the alternative estimates of the background fall in robberies were used to generate estimates of the proportional fall expected in the outcome measure of post office robberies involving attacks on the security screen over the same period. These were converted to absolute falls and subtracted from the observed fall to yield the net figures.[41] Atkins, Husain, and Storey (1991), in their evaluation of the impact of street lighting improvements on crime, used an index of "relative percentage change"—how much the observed change from before to after differed from the change expected on the basis of the

[41] Davidson (e.g., Davidson and Locke 1992) has developed this "shift-share" approach to compare the crime rate in local areas with that in wider territories (district, regional, and national) in order to index out these contextual factors and leave behind an estimate of the local difference or deviation from the background. He has also developed a spreadsheet software package that carries out both these static comparisons and comparisons of change over time—in the latter case subtracting district, regional, and national changes in crime rates to produce an estimate of the purely local component of change, for use in evaluation.

performance of their comparison data over the same period. They followed a sequence of zone-by-zone lighting improvements in the London borough of Wandsworth and used the daytime crime rate in each zone as the comparison for the nighttime crime rate (involving some interesting discussion about possible night-to-day displacement). The expected fall was calculated using the shift-share approach as just described. Relative percentage change was calculated as (observed fall − expected fall/expected fall × 100). The result was negative—no impact on crime.

The previous two illustrations were based on outcome measures in "before versus after" × "action versus comparison" conditions analyzed in simple contingency tables. Multivariate analysis represents a challenge to the communicator, but the approach known as "sample enumeration" (which has nothing to do with survey design) can be used to generate, from a multiple regression model, expected values in the "after/treatment" condition while holding the effects of covariates constant (Davies 1992a, 1992b). Essentially, this involves applying the calibrated model to each case in the sample and summing the results. The "expected" model is one in which the term measuring impact (usually an interaction term representing differential change in crime in the action area relative to crime in the comparison area) is omitted; the "observed" model is one in which the interaction term is included. This technique amounts to bringing together the simplicity of a 2 × 2 contingency table with the power of multivariate analysis.[42]

To step back from technical considerations to take the broadest view, there is a need for a sustained period of mutual education and accommodation between administrators and evaluators, much like that which has successfully happened in Britain over the last fifteen years regarding administrators and social researchers. Such a process could be accelerated by the adoption of a practice of drawing up explicit contracts between the two parties, which set the broad parameters for each individual evaluation. There are risks, however. Closer contact means greater threat to the independence of evaluators and evaluations—this must be safeguarded by institutional means as well as those depending on personal integrity.

2. *Do All Evaluators Have to Be Professional Evaluators?*   As the new

[42] For the statistically minded, sample enumeration avoids a shortcoming of the more conventional odds ratios, which change as a function of incorporating or excluding covariates in the model, even when these are uncorrelated with the explanatory variable (Davies 1992b).

approaches to crime prevention move from experimental activity to routine, there is a desperate need for reasonably well evaluated information on "what preventive methods work, in what circumstances," in order to guide practitioners in their choice of preventive strategies. Unfortunately, there is so far only a relatively limited body of this knowledge. One way to reduce this "knowledge gap" is to increase the number of professionally trained evaluators. This is obviously good for employment prospects, but there are limits. A cheaper approach might be to try to teach some of the skills of evaluation to practitioners in crime prevention; in particular, to give them cheap and simple evaluation techniques that will serve them adequately for most of the time. This sounds efficient and pleasantly egalitarian, and various attempts are being made to carry the idea forward (Hibberd 1990; Berry and Carter 1992). Care has to be taken when proceeding in this direction. The possibilities for making the wrong inferences in an evaluation are enormous—and the more limited the data and the design of the evaluation, the greater the scope for making such mistakes. We may not be talking about making a conclusion "80 percent as good as that provided by a professional evaluator, for 20 percent of the cost": errors in evaluation tend not merely to gradually degrade the quality of the result—they can lead to completely the wrong answer. Saving money or time on the design and data collection aspects of an evaluation means that greater sophistication is often required to extract a reliable and valid conclusion. To follow Skogan (1985), the stronger the design, the easier the analysis.

There is also the crude question of keeping your job. We have all experienced organizational self-evaluations that endorse the success of programs in the absence of comparison groups or base expectancy rates. It is naive to suppose that personal and organizational self-interest does not inform these conclusions.

Professional judgment is most needed at the start and finish of an evaluation: first, in deciding whether the decision-making context and the preventive activity to be evaluated necessitate a simple or a sophisticated design; and second, when the design is under way, in extracting and interpreting the pattern of results. Knowledge of techniques may be less important than the possession of a clear conceptual framework covering the key questions evaluation asks, plus a list of commonly occurring alternative explanations for findings (Campbell and Stanley's [1963] "threats to internal validity") which must be tested and eliminated. The development of a computerized expert knowledge base founded on these questions might be a practical, user-friendly way to guide practitioners. Our personal experience suggests that they are far more receptive to plain-language questions than to dusty textbooks that are usually the size of a telephone directory and often written in academic jargon. However, it may be that a combination approach is best, with crime prevention practitioners given elementary guidance and training in evaluation, together with access to a professional advisory and support team able to help them at critical moments of designing, conducting, and analyzing the results of an evaluation (see Berry and Carter 1992). But even the most technically adept in-house researchers and evaluators may be unable to exercise their critical independence if they are isolated and lacking sufficient "clout" within the organization and moral support from outside. Ultimately, the answer to this important speculation may be to try it and see—to set up a range of evaluation exercises and pit professionals against lay evaluators acting alone or with some guidance.

VI. Conclusion

Crime prevention advances only by the determination of how much, if at all, interventions reduce crime or some other chosen variable. Background fluctuation in the variables of interest, uncertainties in the interpretation of cause and effect, and vagaries in how programs are implemented are among the recurring problems. No design will safeguard the evaluation totally, but some tactics will serve to reduce the likelihood of catastrophic error. One such tactic is the incorporation of theory into the evaluation enterprise. This essay has accordingly emphasized the case for putting theory in the service of evaluating, understanding, and being able to replicate good practice. But it should not be forgotten that practical interventions in their turn offer extremely rich material for informing and testing theory. It is often only when change is introduced that the resultant perturbations reveal processes that are normally hidden—as, for example, occurred in the Priority Estates Project evaluation (Hope and Foster 1992; Foster and Hope 1993). Aside from the role of theory, a case can be made for small and precisely focused studies that are likely, in the aggregate, to be more informative than a smaller number of large studies.

Banal as it sounds, evaluators and practitioners must specify and agree on the effects to be taken as the bottom line of an enterprise, preferably in advance. This should incorporate considerations of both the type and the extent of anticipated effects. There is a particular obligation to justify outcome measures other than that of crime reduction.

The rubric "crime prevention" subsumes a wide variety of practices, including situational, offender-oriented, and so-called community crime prevention. This classification was devised so as to be attuned to considerations of cause that should lie at the heart of an evaluative strategy and to overcome the problems posed for the evaluator by the predominance of loose terminology.

Two responses to evaluation problems can be identified. The first involves the intelligent refinement of traditional approaches. The second involves clearer departure from past practice. This article describes a complex evaluative enterprise current in the United Kingdom (the Safer Cities Programme), which is original in offering a synergistic design to allow the simultaneous consideration of a variety of scheme elements and in quantifying action for linkage to outcome. If large-scale crime prevention programs are politically inevitable, their evaluation by complex and sophisticated designs like the one described has much to commend it and will provide much information at the policy and program level.

However, they will probably have least impact for small individual schemes. The route forward for evaluation of small schemes is the development of evaluative techniques that set out and test the data in terms of the effects which the presumed mechanisms of change should have. For instance, lighting effects should be evident in changes in night/day ratios of offending and should be linked to changes in use or occupancy of newly lit dwellings. If lit streets are more heavily used at night by residents, entry points in night burglaries should change from front to back (and possibly increase, because of reduced occupancy). Detection rates for offenses in lit areas should increase for nighttime offenses only. The pattern of predicted changes should in principle be absolutely specific to the presumed mechanism of change, and this approach allows the use of data limited only by imagination and availability.

It is a mistake to regard the search for technical perfection as the sole route forward. Rather, the context of evaluation—its commissioning, support, and use—is crucial. The plethora of studies of crime risk in contrast with the extreme paucity of their application in preventive programs is a testament to the neglect of research in the everyday tasks of crime prevention. The greatest challenge in evaluating crime prevention is the development of curiosity and open-mindedness among practitioners in wishing to evaluate appropriately. When that challenge is met, the resulting challenge is to satisfy it within the constraints of evaluators' methodological rigor and communication skills.

Evaluation is evolving under the pressure of several influences—the technology of data collection and data handling, changes in managerial practices, methodology, philosophy of causal inference. These are not always easy to reconcile. It is important, therefore, that as the influences work their way through the practice of evaluation, evaluators continue to talk to one another and to other stakeholders—above all to practitioners subjected to evaluation and users of the results of evaluations.

APPENDIX A

The Safer Cities Programme in England

Objectives of program:

Reduction of crime

Reduction of fear of crime

Creation of safer cities within which economic enterprise and community life can flourish

Structure of program (first phase):

Budget of £7 million per year

Central administrative team

Twenty local projects (starting up from late 1988 and winding up by 1995):

Each covering a city scoring high on an index of urban deprivation

Each with:

Local steering committee

Coordinator, assistant, secretary

Computerized management information system

Each funding an average of 150 separate local schemes, drawing on £250,000 per year grant money

Up to sixteen projects evaluated using surveys and/or recorded crime statistics

Nature of schemes:

Over three thousand implemented

Individually targeted on a wide range of crime types, victims, and potential offenders

Focused on whole city, city center, neighborhood, or vulnerable social groups

Ranging from small (under £500) to large (£100,000)

Employing a wide range of preventive methods

Realizing the Principle of Adjusted Expectation in the Safer Cities
Evaluation—Further Details

A. Introduction

The principle of adjusted expectation aimed to look for impact only where
and when it might reasonably be expected to be observed, and impact of a
magnitude which it might reasonably be expected to attain. Putting the principle into practice involved a particular prospective data collection strategy and
several aspects of analysis, described in the main text: retrospective concentration, simultaneous consideration of schemes, quantification and statistical modeling, and dose-response analysis.

This appendix describes the analysis stage in more detail (there is some
repetition of the main text, to make this account self-contained). Modeling the
effects of action on the outcome measures required development of a way of
scoring the dose of action in each small area where those outcome measures
were collected. But before this could be done, it was necessary to solve another
major problem in linking action with outcome. In a traditional evaluation of a
single scheme, it is implicit that the survey conducted, and the crime figures
collected, will be in the right place and at the right time to detect the expected
change in outcome measures and oriented toward the particular crime problem
targeted by the scheme and any population groups targeted. In the Safer Cities
evaluation, none of this could be taken for granted. The action involved nearly
three thousand schemes scattered in space and time and targeted on a wide
range of crime problems and population groups. Regarding the outcome measures, before- and after-interviews were conducted in several hundred Enumeration Districts (EDs) grouped in eleven Safer Cities Programme (SCP) cities,
posing questions on a range of problems and covering a range of locations
(e.g., household, neighborhood, city center) and time periods (e.g., last week,
the last year, the last two years). These ecological factors intervene between
knowledge of the amount of preventive action injected into an area and measurement of outcome, and it was necessary to develop ways of taking them
into account in order to clarify the link between action and outcome.

The task was thus retrospectively to link knowledge of the location and
timing of the *action* and on whom and on what crime problem it was targeted
with what was known about the location, spatial scope, and time period of
outcome measures and the kinds of problems and people to which they related.
All this had to be done in a context in which both action and outcome measures
were wide-ranging and general purpose, rather than neatly dovetailing around
a single scheme.

For logistical and methodological reasons, it was inappropriate to operate on
a "craft-oriented" basis with measurement and analysis fitted uniquely to each
individual scheme in the traditional way. An "industrial" scale had to be adopted.
To make matters more difficult, action and outcome could only be linked at the
analysis stage, because only then were the sites of implementation known. In this
context the solution to the linkage problem, and to the requirement to represent
and estimate the dosage of action falling within each small area measured, was
to develop a dual-aspect process called "scoping and scoring."

For each statistical model constructed during the course of analysis, the starting point is choosing a particular outcome measure (an item, or a scale, from the survey—e.g., fear of burglary—or a particular category of recorded crime from the crime data—e.g., auto crime). *Scoping* refers to the mainly qualitative process of determining whether any specific scheme of preventive action has the potential to influence this outcome measure at a particular measurement point. If a scheme is in scope of a particular measurement point, *scoring* is the quantitative process of representing the *dose* of in-scope action present. The survey rather than the recorded crime side is illustrated.

B. Basic Principles of Scoping

There are four dimensions to characterize the way in which a given preventive scheme can be said to be in scope of a given outcome measure—that is, to have the potential to causally influence it. First, *space*—is a given scheme located close enough to a point of measurement for the outcome measure to be potentially influenced? Second, *time frame*—is the timing of the action such that it could exert an influence on the outcome measure? Third, *problem*—time and space apart, is there a plausible cause-effect relationship between the nature of the action in a given scheme and the crime or fear problem measured by the outcome measure in question? Fourth, *subgroups*—is the outcome measure directed toward a particular population subgroup—for example, women? Is a given scheme directed toward the same subgroup?

To implement scoping, each outcome measure (in this case, a particular survey question) is specified in terms of a zone of detection, each scheme in terms of a zone of influence, and overlaps are sought.

1. *The Zone of Detection of an Outcome Measure.* A given outcome measure will have certain scoping characteristics. It will have particular *spatial* implications (the interviews are located at particular sampling points and from these "lookout positions" respondents answer questions about, e.g., "burglary in this household," "burglary in this area," or "disorder in the city center"), it will have particular *time frame* implications (e.g., "in the last year?" vs. "in the last week?"), it will relate to a particular *crime or fear problem*, and it may have *subgroup* implications (e.g., "women only"). These four dimensions determine the zone of detection that fans out around the outcome measure and each of its sampling points.

2. *The Zone of Influence of a Scheme.* Around each individual preventive scheme, the zone of influence stretches out in terms of space, time, problem, and subgroups. In the Safer Cities case, the spatial dimension was identified by presenting each coordinator with an ED map of their city and getting them to specify which EDs were likely to be affected by a given scheme. Information on the other dimensions came from the action data in the Management Information System.

3. *The Zone of Overlap.* If in modeling a particular outcome measure, a given scheme's zone of influence happens to overlap on all four dimensions with a specific zone of detection of the outcome measure, then by definition that scheme has the potential to influence the value of the outcome measure for the survey respondents at that particular sampling point. The scheme in question is then said to be in scope, and its action score can be included in

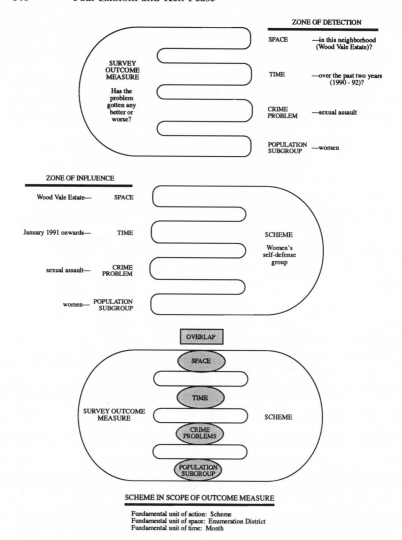

FIG. B1.—Safer Cities Programme Evaluation: an example of scoping

the modeling exercise, paired up with the scores on the outcome measure of the relevant zone of detection and the relevant covariates. For a larger or a longer scheme, only part of the scheme may be in the scope of a given outcome measure's zone of detection.

Scoping is illustrated in figure B1. Units chosen to define zone of detection, influence, and overlap were the 1991 Census ED and the month. The minimum overlap between a zone of detection and a zone of influence is therefore one ED for one month. In some respects, smaller spatial units still (such as postal codes) would have given a finer-grained picture, but the numbers of interviews per spatial unit would have had to be too small for modeling; besides, limitations of the data restricted choice.

C. Basic Principles of Scoring

Having now constructed a way of linking particular schemes to particular outcome measures taken at particular sampling points, we can return to the issue of the action dosage. There are two considerations: the nature of the dosage concept and estimation of the dosage quantity.

1. *The Dosage Concept: Input or Output?* When the broad idea of dosage was first considered, it was not clear exactly what this meant. In particular, was it to represent input of resources—usually money—into funding preventive schemes; or output of preventive action from those schemes, in terms of houses protected, offenders diverted, and so forth? In principle, output would be better, because it is causally much closer to outcome. But for the purposes of this evaluation, outputs were considered too diverse qualitatively to use in a generic approach—"houses target-hardened, youth club set up, crime prevention bus driven round city"; and even within types, they are hard to compare quantitatively—how do you even compare the impact of identical new locks on two different types of door frame (in different schemes), let alone crude counts of houses target-hardened, when the target hardening has been done to some unknown and variable degree in each scheme? Or even worse, how do you compare the value of the youth club experience received by each unit of output (i.e., each "reformed" club member) attending different clubs? To add to these problems, Management Information data on output were far less reliable and complete than data on input, which were both inherently simpler and were entered on a mandatory basis as part of the SCP financial accounting system.

It was thus decided to estimate dosage in terms of input. However, the absolute input into a scheme, in financial terms, was not fully adequate as a measure. Qualitatively, lumping the input of all kinds of preventive action together is likely severely to obscure relationships in modeling and miss useful detail. Therefore it was decided to generate separate action scores *based* on financial inputs, *but* defined in terms of "output types": for example, "£ input of situational schemes," "£ input of offender-oriented schemes," and so forth. The output types are to be identified using a classification of preventive action developed for the evaluation (Ekblom 1994*a*), one dimension of which was employed in abbreviated form in Section III of this essay.

2. *Dosage Estimation.* The survey outcome measures concern (for example) the risk of being burgled over a particular time period, averaged over a group of respondents sampled in a particular ED. The risk is averaged per household in the ED, for burglary, say, or per individual in the ED, for assault. Generalizing, this is the risk per unit at risk of victimization. To link this outcome figure to dosage in a way suitable for statistical modeling with meaningful results, it was necessary to arrive at a score representing the dose of input of preventive action received for the same units—that is, the input per unit at risk of victimization.[43]

[43] Given the discussion in Sec. II above on alternative bottom lines for evaluation, instead of "risk of victimization per unit at risk of victimization," an alternative repeat-

Since it is not possible to know exactly which households or individuals among those within a given scheme's zone of influence received output from a given scheme, the approach has to work with averages, as will be seen. These averages operate over both the populations and households contained within spatial territories and over the time periods of measurement.

On the spatial/geographic side, a particular scheme's zone of influence may be much bigger than the zone of detection with which it overlaps. The zone of detection will then receive only a proportion of the total input. Therefore, the input score must be adjusted to reflect the share-out of the input over the wider area. Likewise, only part of the zone of detection may be affected by the scheme, if the zone of detection is something relatively large like the neighborhood in which the surveyed ED is located. In this case the input has to be diluted further to reflect the reduced probability that any particular respondent received the action. Both geographical share-out and dilution are calculated using population data from Census ED statistics relating to the zones of influence, overlap, and detection. If a scheme is directed at women, then the adult female population is used as the base; if directed at households (e.g., targeted on residential burglary), then households are the base.

On the temporal side, adjustments are again to be made for share-out and dilution. Share-out adjustments vary with the type of scheme. For a capital scheme such as target hardening, temporal share-out depends on whether the scheme is operational or not in any given month. Many capital schemes "latch on"—that is, they keep exerting their effect after the expenditure is complete.[44] An example would be a strengthened front door. Others "latch off"—cease to reduce risk the minute they are stopped—such as a temporary window shutter being removed. This requires thought about how particular types of action work on potential offenders—physical blocking of the offense, surveillance, heightening perceived risk, or some combination. "Revenue" or running-cost schemes such as funding youth club staff may have to be scored on the basis of their monthly input rather than their total input; again they can latch on (as with changing young people's fundamental motives and behavior) or latch off (as with diverting them from crime merely while the club existed).

On dilution of measurement over time, a survey item may ask whether a household was burgled in the past year, that is, September 1991–October 1992, and the average risk of victimization for this period at a given ED sampling point is calculated from the proportion of respondents who reported being then victimized. But a scheme may not have started, say, until January 1992—that is, halfway through the period over which the risk of victimization was measured. Respondents in the ED therefore only received the preventive input for half this time, so their average input received over the whole period has to be halved.

Altogether, the financial input to a scheme is adjusted by factors representing geographic share-out of action and dilution of measurement and temporal

---

victimization outcome criterion could be "number of victimizations per victim." There might, however, be practical and conceptual difficulties in estimating the units at risk.

[44] This concept relates to that of Sherman's (1990) "residual deterrence."

KEY:
ZD = Zone of detection of outcome measure
ZI = Zone of influence of scheme
ZO = Zone of overlap

1. Geographic shareout of action input

Unit at risk of victimization ..... Household
Total input of scheme .... £20,000 in whole ZI
Shareout base .... 1,000 households in whole ZI
Shareout per unit at risk
    of victimization £20

2. Geographic overlap between action and measurement

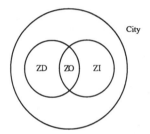

Number of units at risk
    in zone of overlap .... 100 households
Share of total scheme input
    in zone of overlap .... 100 x £20 = £2,000

3. Geographic dilution of measurement

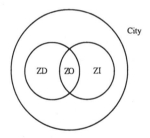

Number of units at risk
    in zone of detection .... 500 households
Total input in zone
    of detection .... = share of total
                                                        scheme input in
                                                        zone of overlap
                                                        = £2,000

Action score .... = £2,000 / 500
(Average input per
unit at risk in ZD) .... = £4

Fig. B2.—Safer Cities Programme Evaluation: an example of geographical scoring

share-out and dilution. If more than one scheme of the same output type overlaps with the zone of detection at a particular measurement point, the adjusted inputs from each scheme are summed. The end result is an action score for a particular output type that represents the £ input per unit at risk of victimization in the measured area, averaged over the relevant unit population in the area and over the period of measurement. An illustration of geographic scoring calculations is in figure B2.

Several action dosage scores, calculated on input from different types of scheme, and possibly incorporating different assumptions about share-out, latch on/off, and so forth, may go forward for simultaneous inclusion in the modeling—for example, a situational prevention dose and an offender-oriented prevention dose. This process will be constrained by data quality and the number of schemes falling within any specific category. But it may enable (very cautious) comparison of the relative effectiveness of different types of preventive method—for example, which has the steeper dose-response relationship? For the purpose of taking displacement into account, the intention is to estimate a dosage of adjacent action—for example, how much action is in the area immediately surrounding the zone of detection?

D. The Technology of Analysis

Readers could be forgiven for wondering long before this point just how it was intended to carry out these scoping and scoring operations without an army of clerks poring over maps. The scoping and scoring exercise is only conceivable because of the availability of the Geographic Information System (GIS)—a special kind of (relational) database combined with a graphical processor which together can handle points, lines, territorial boundaries, and topological relationships and link this spatial information to "attribute" information (e.g., linking a particular surveyed ED to the Census attribute "population" in such a way that the population could be used in scoring; or identifying the "neighborhood" zone of detection surrounding each surveyed ED by flagging up the EDs that surround it). There is a large range of possible choices in every session of scoping and scoring—defining zone of detection to fit the outcome measure currently in use, selecting which cities to include, which types of scheme, and which variants of score calculation—so a menu-based system has been developed which guides the user through the choices and provides interlocks to block delivery of any nonsensical combinations requested. This system is intended to reduce error, reduce user training time, and speed up exploratory analysis (the logistical difficulties of the analysis stage of large-scale studies are a neglected topic, and this menu-based approach may be of wider application). It may also facilitate secondary analysis. The GIS and menu system are described in more detail in Ekblom, Howes, and Law (1994), and an example menu screen is shown in figures B3a and B3b.

E. Modeling Outcome on Action: The Dose-Response Analysis

Scoping and scoring is followed by construction and exploration of statistical models. For the dependent variables there is a choice of outcome measures; explanatory variables include the relevant action dosage scores and a range of covariates. Models have to represent change in risk of victimization (or other outcome measure) between the before- and after-survey, as experienced by respondents in a given ED sampling point.[45] In particular, do sampling points receiving more action show a greater fall in risk of victimization? And what is the rate of change of fall with input--the dose-response slope itself?

[45] In most of the models the outcome variable is dichotomous—victim/nonvictim. This therefore requires logistic regression, explaining respondents' risk of being victimized.

A concrete example of the clearest kind of result sought could be along these lines: "For every £100-worth of antiburglary action received on average per household in the areas measured, and fully active over the year prior to the after-survey, the probability of burglary per household over the year in question was 0.06 less than the level expected. This expected level was based on taking account of levels of risk before the action had been implemented, background changes common to areas with greater and lesser amounts of action, and demographic covariation."

The survey design produced hierarchical data pairs of panel interviews (for some of the respondents), individual respondents grouped within EDs, grouped within cities. The best way of handling such data is through multilevel modeling (MLM). To give a basic description of MLM in the context of the SCP evaluation, the simplest models are those which apply cross-sectional analysis to the survey data. Here, before- and after-interviews are pooled and distinguished by a dummy variable "WAVE" ("before" is coded as 0, "after," 1). Level 1 of the model is the individual interview. The dependent variable is the outcome measure (e.g., burglary victimization), and the level 1 explanatory variables are WAVE and the individual-level demographics taken from the survey (e.g., age, gender, tenure) known to affect risk of burglary. In traditional ordinary least squares regression, the procedure estimates an intercept or constant and coefficients for each explanatory variable representing the size of the "effect" that variable has on the dependent variable.[46] MLM does the same, with the principal difference that it produces the estimates of intercept and coefficients separately for each level 2 group: in the SCP case, these are individual interviews grouped within EDs (around twenty to thirty interviews in each of over three hundred EDs). It then goes on to test whether the level 1 intercept varies significantly across the level 2 groups (indicating that the overall burglary risk differs across EDs); and likewise for the coefficients of the level 1 explanatory variables (indicating, e.g., that the rate of change of victimization with age varies across EDs). The next stage is to explain this random variation in intercept or coefficient across EDs, in terms of ED level (i.e., level 2) variables themselves, such as area unemployment rate. Does area unemployment (from the Census) explain the variation in burglary risk across EDs? Does it explain the variation in the "effect" of age on risk (e.g., are young respondents more at risk of burglary in high-unemployment areas, while the age difference flattens out in low-unemployment areas)? These examples are concerned with explaining the burglary risk. The evaluation comes into the model in a particular way. The level 1 explanatory variable of interest is a dummy, WAVE. First of all, does WAVE explain any of the variation in crime risk (e.g., has burglary grown worse from before to after?)? Second, does this WAVE effect vary across EDs? Now comes the critical link. The level 2 variable of interest is the dosage of SCP action received by the inhabitants of each ED. Third, is the between-ED variation in size of the "WAVE effect" significantly explained by the differing action dosage each ED receives? Computationally, this sequence of questions is represented by a cross-level

---

[46] "Effect" is in quotes because the SCP design is only quasi-experimental.

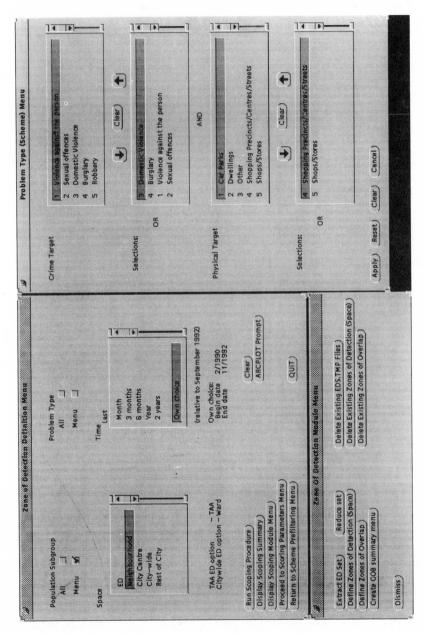

Fig. B3a.—Zone of detection definition menu

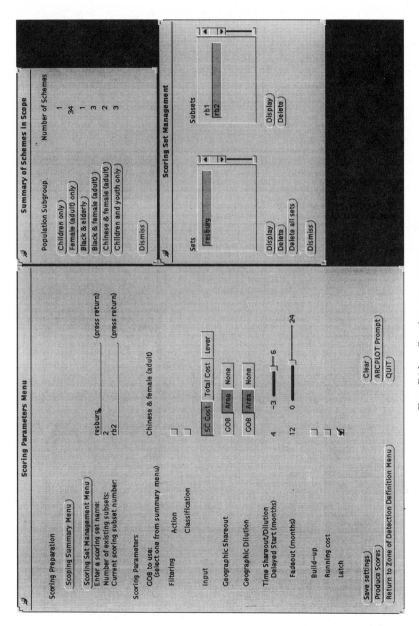

Fig. B3*b*.—Scoring parameters menu

"WAVE × dosage" interaction, equivalent to the more conventional "WAVE × treatment" interaction described, for example, by Skogan (1985). If the coefficient of this term is significant, there is a prima facie "Safer Cities effect." The coefficient is, quantitatively speaking, the change in burglary risk per unit at risk of victimization, associated with a unit increase in dosage: in other words, the dose-response relationship.

F. Scoping, Scoring, and Modeling: Unknowns

There are many unknowns in the scoping, scoring, and modeling process that can only be resolved through exploration of variants of the approach. (Some of the possible variants are discussed in Ekblom 1994b.) In this we are fortunate to have what should prove a substantial database of details of action and measures of outcome (and covariates) in the SCP.

The unknowns in question relate to the linkages between input of action and measurement of outcome and between error and uncertainty. *Linkages* have rarely been considered quantitatively before, let alone studied—what, for example, is the distance-decay function of the influence of a youth club on potential offenders, in terms of its form and magnitude? How long does it take for a change in the level of disorder in the city center to be perceived and then to alter people's decisions to visit the center? Qualitatively, which type of scheme can be characterized as latch on or latch off in its effects over time? How far is it necessary to differentiate between methods of prevention to isolate regularities of relationships in time and spaces? What progress can be made using just the basic distinction between situational and offender-oriented? Answering questions like these can only be done empirically, with repeated explorations of the database and trying out models with different qualitative and quantitative parameters—almost akin to tuning a radio receiver until the strongest signal comes through (and finding, moreover, that there are stations transmitting on many different frequencies). The linkages explored and specified through scoping, scoring, and modeling come closest, in this evaluation, to the focus on theory and causal mechanisms envisaged in the scientific realist approach described in the main text.

Error and uncertainty enter the process of scoping and scoring, and modeling dose response, at every stage, and in the spirit of Section V, it is worth declaring them. Apart from the usual errors and biases in data collection, and the equally familiar limitations of quasi-experimental designs (Judd and Kenny 1981), the scoping and scoring approach has a number of facets of error all of its own, stemming from the use of geographical methods of linking data (e.g., deriving the population bases in the beats from the Census EDs, when boundaries do not fully match); measurement on an industrial scale, which is not specifically attuned to the idiosyncrasies of individual schemes; and the role of stochastic processes in deciding which people, or properties, get how much action within the zone of influence and how survey sampling processes interact with these. This said, it should not be forgotten that the main reason for embarking on this whole approach was to reduce error in the first place—error introduced by the vicissitudes of incomplete coverage of measurement and incomplete knowledge of which individual household or individual received action. The expectation is that much more is gained through a clear qualitative and quantitative link between input of action and outcome than is lost through the uncertainty introduced (or merely made more visible) by the scoping and scoring.

REFERENCES

Atkins, S., S. Husain, and A. Storey. 1991. "The Influence of Street Lighting on Crime." Crime Prevention Unit Paper 28. London: Home Office.

Barr, R., and K. Pease. 1990. "Crime Placement, Displacement, and Deflection." In *Crime and Justice: A Review of Research*, vol. 12, edited by M. Tonry and N. Morris. Chicago: University of Chicago Press.

———. 1992. "A Place for Every Crime and Every Crime in Its Place." In *Crime, Policing and Place: Essays in Environmental Criminology*, edited by D. J. Evans, N. R. Fyfe, and D. T. Herbert. London: Routledge.

Bennett, T. 1986. "Situational Crime Prevention from the Offender's Perspective." In *Situational Crime Prevention: From Theory into Practice*, edited by K. Heal and G. K. Laycock. London: H.M. Stationery Office.

———. 1990. *Evaluating Neighbourhood Watch*. Aldershot: Gower.

———. 1991. "The Effectiveness of a Police-initiated Fear-reducing Strategy." *British Journal of Criminology* 31:1–14.

Berry, G., and M. Carter. 1992. "Assessing Crime Prevention Initiatives: The First Steps." Crime Prevention Unit Paper 31. London: Home Office.

Bhaskar, R. 1978. *A Realist Theory of Science*. Brighton: Harvester.

Blumstein A., J. Cohen, J. A. Roth, and C. A. Visher, eds. 1986. *Criminal Careers and "Career Criminals."* Washington, D.C.: National AcademyPress.

Bottoms, A. E., R. I. Mawby, and P. Xanthos. 1989. "A Tale of Two Estates." In *Crime and the City*, edited by D. Downes. London: Macmillan.

Bottoms, A. E., and P. Wiles. 1991. "Housing Markets and Residential Community Crime Careers." In *Crime, Policing and Place: Essays in Environmental Criminology*, edited by D. J. Evans, N. R. Fyfe, and D. T. Herbert. London: Routledge.

———. 1992. "Explanations of Crime and Place." In *Crime, Policing and Place: Essays in Environmental Criminology*, edited by D. J. Evans, N. R. Fyfe, and D. T. Herbert. London: Routledge.

Brantingham, P. J., and F. L. Faust. 1976. "A Conceptual Model of Crime Prevention." *Crime and Delinquency* 22:130–46.

Brody, S. R. 1976. "The Effectiveness of Sentencing." Home Office Research Study no. 35. London: H.M. Stationery Office.

Bryk, A., and S. Raudenbush. 1992. *Hierarchical Linear Models: Applications and Data Analysis Methods*. Newbury Park: Sage.

Burrows, J. N. 1980. "Closed Circuit Television and Crime on the London Underground." In *Designing Out Crime*, edited by R. V. Clarke and P. Mayhew. London: H.M. Stationery Office.

Campbell, D. T. 1969. "Reforms as Experiments." *American Psychologist* 24: 409–29.

Campbell, D. T., and J. C. Stanley. 1963. *Experimental and Quasi-experimental Designs in Social Research*. Chicago: Rand McNally.

Clarke, R. V. In this volume. "Situational Crime Prevention."

Clarke R. V., and P. M. Harris. 1992. "Auto Theft and Its Prevention." In *Crime and Justice: A Review of Research*, vol. 16, edited by M. Tonry. Chicago: University of Chicago Press.

Clarke, R. V., and D. Weisburd. 1994. "Diffusion of Crime Control Benefits: Observations on the Reverse of Displacement." In *Crime Prevention Studies*, vol. 2, edited by R. V. Clarke. Monsey, N.Y.: Criminal Justice-Press.

Cornish, D., and R. V. Clarke. 1972. "The Controlled Trial in Institutional Research." Home Office Research Study no. 15. London: H.M. Stationery Office.

Crane, D. 1983. *The Evaluation of Social Policies*. Lancaster: Kluwer-Nijhoff.

Davidson, N., and T. Locke. 1992. "Local Area Profiles of Crime: Neighbourhood Crime Patterns in Context." In *Crime, Policing and Place: Essays in Environmental Criminology*, edited by D. Evans, N. Fyfe, and D. Herbert. London: Routledge.

Davies, R. 1992*a*. "Sample Enumeration Methods for Model Interpretation." In *Statistical Modelling*, edited by P. van der Heijden, W. Jansen, B. Francis, and G. Seeber. Amsterdam: Elsevier.

———. 1992*b*. "The State of the Art in Survey Analysis." In *Survey and Statistical Computing*, edited by A. Westlake, R. Banks, C. Payne, and T. Orchard. New York: North-Holland.

Dickens, C. 1880. *Little Dorrit*. London: J. M. Dent.

Ekblom, P. 1979. "Police Truancy Patrols." In *Crime Prevention and the Police*, edited by J. Burrows, P. Ekblom, and K. Heal. Home Office Research Study no. 55. London: H.M. Stationery Office.

———. 1986. "Community Policing: Obstacles and Issues." In *The Debate about Community: Papers from a Seminar on Community in Social Policy*, edited by P. Willmott. Policy Studies Institute (PSI) Discussion Paper 13. London: Policy Studies Institute.

———. 1987. "Preventing Robberies at Sub-Post Offices: An Evaluation of a Security Initiative." Home Office Crime Prevention Unit Paper 9. London: Home Office.

———. 1988. "Getting the Best out of Crime Analysis." Home Office Crime Prevention Unit Paper 10. London: Home Office.

———. 1990. "Evaluating Crime Prevention: The Management of Uncertainty." In *Current Issues in Criminological Research*, edited by C. Kemp. Bristol: Bristol Centre for Criminal Justice.

———. 1991. "High Crime Areas, Crime Surveys and Evaluation: The Safer Cities Programme." Paper presented at the Third British Criminology Conference, York, July. Available from author.

———. 1992. "The Safer Cities Programme Impact Evaluation: Problems and Progress." *Studies on Crime and Crime Prevention* 1:35–51.

———. 1994*a*. "Proximal Circumstances: A Mechanism-based Classification of Crime Prevention." *Crime Prevention Studies* 2:185–232.

————. 1994*b*. "Scoping and Scoring: Linking Measures of Action to Measures of Outcome in a Multi-scheme, Multi-site Crime Prevention Programme." In proceedings of the Second International Seminar on Environmental Criminology and Crime Analysis, Miami University, May 1993.

Ekblom, P., D. Howes, and H. Law. 1994. "Scoping, Scoring and Modelling: Linking Measures of Crime Preventive Action to Measures of Outcome in a Large, Multi-site Evaluation Using a GIS and Multilevel Modelling." Paper presented at GIS Research United Kingdom 1994, Leicester University, April 12 (due to appear in conference proceedings).

Farrell, Graham. In this volume. "Preventing Repeat Victimization."

Farrington, D. P. 1983. "Randomized Experiments on Crime and Justice." In *Crime and Justice: An Annual Review of Research*, vol. 4, edited by M. Tonry and N. Morris. Chicago: University of Chicago Press.

Fischoff, B. 1983. "For Those Condemned to Study the Past: Heuristics and Biases in Hindsight." In *Judgment under Uncertainty: Heuristics and Biases*, edited by D. Kahneman, P. Slovic, and A. Tversky. Cambridge: Cambridge University Press.

Forrester, D. P., M. R. Chatterton, and K. Pease. 1988. "The Kirkholt Burglary Prevention Demonstration Project." Crime Prevention Unit Paper 13. London: Home Office.

Forrester, D. P., S. Frenz, M. O'Connell, and K. Pease. 1990. "The Kirkholt Burglary Prevention Project: Phase 2." Crime Prevention Unit Paper 23. London: Home Office.

Foster, J., and T. Hope. 1993. "Housing, Community and Crime: The Impact of the Priority Estates Project." Home Office Research Study no. 131. London: H.M. Stationery Office.

Freeman, P. H., and H. E. Rossi. 1989. *Evaluation: A Systematic Approach*. Newbury Park: Sage.

Goldstein, Harvey. 1987. *Multilevel Models in Educational and Social Research*. London: Griffin; New York: Oxford University Press.

Goldstein, Hermann. 1979. "Improving Policing: A Problem-oriented Approach." *Crime and Delinquency* 25:236–60.

Harre, R. 1972. *The Philosophies of Science*. Oxford: Oxford University Press.

————. 1986. *Varieties of Realism*. Oxford: Blackwell.

Hibberd, M. 1990. *Research and Evaluation: A Manual for Police Officers*. London: (U.K.) Police Foundation.

Hirschi, T. 1986. "On the Compatibility of Rational Choice and Social Control Theories of Crime." In *The Reasoning Criminal: Rational Choice Perspectives on Offending*, edited by D. B. Cornish and R. V. Clarke. New York: Springer-Verlag.

Home Office. 1993. *Safer Cities Progress Report, 1991–1992*. London: Home Office.

Hope, T. 1985. "Implementing Crime Prevention Measures." Home Office Research Study no. 86. London: H.M. Stationery Office.

Hope, T., and J. Foster. 1992. "Conflicting Forces: Changing the Dynamics of Crime and Community on a 'Problem' Estate." *British Journal of Criminology* 32:488–504.

Hope, T., and D. Murphy. 1983. "Problems of Implementing Crime Prevention: The Experience of a Demonstration Project." *Howard Journal of Criminal Justice* 22:38–50.

Judd, C. M., and D. A. Kenny. 1981. *Estimating the Effects of Social Interventions.* New York: Cambridge University Press.

Junger-Tas, J. 1993. "Policy Evaluation Research in Criminal Justice." *Studies on Crime and Crime Prevention* 2:7–20. Stockholm: National Council for Crime Prevention.

Kelling, G., T. Pate, D. Dieckman, and C. Brown. 1974. *The Kansas City Preventive Patrolling Experiment.* Washington, D.C.: Police Foundation.

Knutsson, J., and E. Kuhlhorn. 1981. *Macro-Measures against Crime: The Example of Check Forgeries.* Information Bulletin no. 1. Stockholm: Swedish National Council for Crime Prevention.

———. 1991. "Macro-Measures against Crime: The Example of Check Forgeries." In *Situational Crime Prevention: Successful Case Studies,* edited by R. V. Clarke. New York: Harrow & Heston.

Laycock, G. K. 1985. "Reducing Burglary: A Study of Chemists' Shops." Crime Prevention Unit Paper 1. London: Home Office.

Laycock, Gloria, and Nick Tilley. In this volume. "Implementing Crime Prevention."

Lipton, J., R. Martinson, and J. Wilks. 1975. *The Effectiveness of Correctional Treatment.* New York: Praeger.

Lurigio, A. J., and D. P. Rosenbaum. 1986. "Evaluation Research in Community Crime Prevention." In *Community Crime Prevention: Does It Work?* edited by D. P. Rosenbaum. London: Sage.

Mark, M. 1983. "Treatment Implementation, Statistical Power and Internal Validity." *Evaluation Review* 7:543–49.

Mayhew, P., D. Elliott, and L. Dowds. 1989. "The 1988 British Crime Survey." Home Office Research Study no. 111. London: H.M. Stationery Office.

Oakes, M. 1986. *Statistical Inference: A Commentary for the Social and Behavioral Sciences.* New York: Wiley.

Osborn, D. R., A. Trickett, and R. Elder. 1992. "Area Characteristics and Regional Variates as Determinants of Area Property Crime Rates." *Journal of Quantitative Criminology* 8:265–85.

Painter, K. 1988. *Lighting and Crime Prevention: The Edmonton Project.* London: Middlesex Polytechnic Centre for Criminology.

———. 1989a. *Crime Prevention and Public Lighting with Special Focus on Women and Elderly People.* London: Middlesex Polytechnic Centre for Criminology.

———. 1989b. *Lighting and Crime Prevention for Community Safety: The Tower Hamlets Study.* London: Middlesex Polytechnic Centre for Criminology.

———. 1991. *An Evaluation of Public Lighting as a Crime Prevention Strategy with Special Focus on Women and Elderly People.* Manchester: Faculty of Economics.

Pawson, R., and N. Tilley. 1992. "Re-evaluation: Rethinking Research on Corrections and Crime." *Yearbook of Correctional Education* 1992:19–49. Vancouver: Simon Fraser University.

————. 1994. "What Works in Evaluation Research." *British Journal of Criminology* 34:291–306.

Polder, W. 1992. "Crime Prevention in the Netherlands: Pilot Projects Evaluated." *Dutch Penal Law and Policy* 7. The Hague, Netherlands: Research and Documentation Centre.

Poyner, B. 1988. "Video Cameras and Bus Vandalism." *Security Administration* 11:44–51.

————. 1991. "Video Cameras and Bus Vandalism." In *Situational Crime Prevention: Successful Case Studies*, edited by R. V. Clarke. New York: Harrow & Heston.

————. 1993. "What Works in Crime Prevention: An Overview of Evaluations." *Crime Prevention Studies* 1:7–34.

Poyner, B., and R. Woodall. 1987. *Preventing Shoplifting: A Study in Oxford Street*. London: (U.K.) Police Foundation.

Raudenbush, S. 1993. "Modelling Individual and Community Effects on Deviance over Time: Multi-level Statistical Models." In *Integrating Individual and Ecological Aspects of Crime*, edited by D. Farrington, R. Sampson, and P.-O. Wikstrom. Stockholm: National Council for Crime Prevention.

Reiss, Albert J., Jr. 1988. "Co-offending and Criminal Careers." In *Crime and Justice: A Review of Research*, vol. 10, edited by Michael Tonry and Norval Morris. Chicago: University of Chicago Press.

Reiss, A. J., Jr., and D. Farrington. 1991. "Advancing Knowledge about Co-offending: Results from a Prospective Longitudinal Survey of London Males." *Journal of Criminal Law and Criminology* 82:360–95.

Rosenbaum, D. P., ed. 1986. *Community Crime Prevention: Does It Work?* London: Sage.

————. 1988. "Community and Crime Prevention: A Review and Synthesis of the Literature." *Justice Quarterly* 5:323–95.

Sherman, L. 1990. "Police Crackdowns: Initial and Residual Deterrence." In *Crime and Justice: A Review of Research*, vol. 12, edited by M. Tonry and N. Morris. Chicago: University of Chicago Press.

Sherman L., P. Gartin, and M. Buerger. 1989. "Hot Spots of Predatory Crime: Routine Activities and the Criminology of Place." *Criminology* 27:27–55.

Skogan, W. 1985. *Evaluating Neighborhood Crime Prevention Programs*. The Hague, Netherlands: Ministry of Justice, Research and Documentation Centre.

————. 1993. Personal communication with author, March 8. Northwestern University, Evanston, Ill., Center for Urban Affairs and Policy Research.

Tilley, N. 1992. "Safer Cities and Community Safety Strategies." Crime Prevention Unit Paper 38. London: Home Office.

————. 1993*a*. "After Kirkholt: Theory, Method and Results of Replication Evaluations." Home Office Crime Prevention Unit Paper 47. London: Home Office.

————. 1993*b*. "Understanding Car Parks, Crime and CCTV: Evaluation Lessons from Safer Cities." Home Office Crime Prevention Unit Paper 42. London: Home Office.

Tremblay, R. E., and W. Craig. In this volume. "Developmental Crime Prevention."

van Dijk, J. J. M., and J. de Waard. 1991. "A Two-dimensional Typology of Crime Prevention Projects: With a Bibliography." *Criminal Justice Abstracts* 23:483–503.

Webb, B. 1994. "Steering Column Locks and Motor Vehicle Theft: Evaluations from Three Countries." *Crime Prevention Studies* 2:71–89.

Webb, B., and G. Laycock. 1992. "Reducing Crime on the London Underground: An Evaluation of Three Pilot Projects." Home Office Crime Prevention Unit Paper 30. London: Home Office.

Weisburd, D., with A. Petrosino, and G. Mason. 1993. "Design Sensitivity in Criminal Justice Experiments." In *Crime and Justice: A Review of Research*, vol. 17, edited by M. Tonry. Chicago: University of Chicago Press.

Weisburd, D., and J. Garner. 1992. "Experimentation in Criminal Justice: Editors' Introduction." *Journal of Research in Crime and Delinquency* 29:3–6.

Weiss, C. H. 1985. *Evaluation Research: Methods for Assessing Programme Effectiveness*. Englewood Cliffs, N.J.: Prentice-Hall.

Willmott, P., ed. 1986. "The Debate about Community: Papers from a Seminar on Community in Social Policy." PSI Discussion Paper 13. London: Policy Studies Institute.

Winer, B. J. 1975. *Statistical Principles in Experimental Design*. 2d ed. New York: McGraw-Hill.

Yin, R. 1977. *Evaluating Citizen Crime Prevention Programs*. Santa Monica, Calif.: RAND.

———. 1979. "What Is Citizen Crime Prevention?" In *Review of Criminal Justice Evaluation 1978*, edited by the National Institute of Law Enforcement and Criminal Justice. Washington, D.C.: Law Enforcement Assistance Administration.

Author Index

Subject Index

Absence of guardianship in routine activity theory, 65, 100, 440, 499–500

Access control, 109–11

Action research methodology, 93, 282–83

Activity-sensitive offender monitoring units, 521–23

Adolescent Alcohol Prevention Trial, 401

Adolescent Transitions Program, 209–10, 214–15

Adopted children, criminal behavior studies of, 152

After-school clubs to reduce crime and prevent delinquency, 572–74

Airline hijackings: possibly responsible for increases in other terrorism, 123; reduced by baggage and passenger screening, 113

Alcohol: advertisements for, 386; banned in open places, 119; casual versus daily use of, 390; connection of public disorder, drugs, and, 449–51; as a crime facilitator, 112; classroom curricula with effect of preventing or delaying use of, 359; crimes more common at shops selling, 297; deaths related to, 353; effectiveness of laws for reducing consumption of, 344–45; effects of parents' use of, 382–83; effects of prohibition on use of,

386; general policies for reducing consumption of, 451–52; guardianship of people using, 452–53; initiation of use of, 385–86; as most widely used and accepted drug in the United States and Great Britain, 346–49, 352–53; preventing disorders related to, 454–55; regulation of availability and price of, 360–61; risk for commission and victimization of homicide increased by heavy use of, 352; use versus abuse of, 354

Alcoholism, 370, 380, 381, 397

American Psychiatric Association definition of substance abuse, 354–55

American Psychological Association, issues involved in honesty/integrity tests assessed by, 324

Anger control training programs for children, 162

Antibandit screens in British post offices: deterrence effect of, 131; evaluating the program for, 639–40

Antisocial behavior, development of, 152–53, 159–61

Arrests, deterrent effects of, 6

Arson, costs of retail, 302

Assaults: as impulsive, 7; as situational conflicts, 456–57; social control situations for, 457–58; on store staff, 280, 305–6, 329

681